Foundations of Business Accounting

Second Edition

Roy Dodge

INTERNATIONAL THOMSON BUSINESS PRESS
I ⓣ P® An International Thomson Publishing Company

London • Bonn • Boston • Johannesburg • Madrid • Melbourne • Mexico City • New York • Paris
Singapore • Tokyo • Toronto • Albany, NY • Belmont, CA • Cincinnati, OH • Detroit, MI

Foundations of Business Accounting second edition

Copyright ©1997 Roy Dodge

I(T)P® A division of International Thomson Publishing Inc.
The ITP logo is a trademark under licence

British Library Cataloguing-in-Publication Data
A catalogue record for this book is available from the British Library

First edition 1993 published by Chapman & Hall
This edition 1997 published by International Thomson Business Press

Typeset by R & D Graphics
Printed in the UK by the Alden Press, Osney Mead, Oxford

ISBN 186 152 1537

International Thomson Business Press
Berkshire House
168–173 High Holborn
London WC1V 7AA
UK

International Thomson Business Press
20 Park Plaza
13th Floor
Boston MA 02116
USA

http://www.itbp.com

Contents

Preface to the second edition

There is a common misconception among those who have never studied financial accounting that its principles, rules and practices are set in tablets of stone. If that were true someone could write a text book on accounting that would last for 100 years, save for the occasional tinkering with format and style of presentation.

I wrote the first edition of this book in 1992 and it was published in 1993. It was intended as a text book that would lead students through the technical aspects of double-entry accounting and financial reporting at what can be loosely described as a foundation level. I used the syllabuses of various examining bodies, such as A level and the professional associations, to guide me over its technical boundaries. Writers of books on the more advanced aspects of financial reporting have become accustomed to the rules changing before the printer's ink is dry. But surely nothing changes dramatically at a foundation level – or does it?

Well, I was probably just as surprised as the publishers to realize how much of the first edition had to be changed in the light of developments over the past four years. To take but one example: at the time of the first edition, the 'cash flow statement' had only just become established as one of the primary statements that companies were required to publish in their annual report. At that time we were going through a transitional period where a predecessor of the cash flow statement was still being published by some companies. Since then, not only has the cash flow statement become established as an international standard (even forming part of accounting practice in countries that were previously part of the former Soviet Union) but the original UK regulation was changed in 1996.

The 1996 changes to UK cash flow statements are an interesting signpost to how accounting practices are likely to evolve over the next ten years or so. An unsophisticated review of these changes might suggest that they are little more than cosmetic – some might say they are nothing more than a change in the way that the figures are presented. But I believe something much more fundamental is taking place. The accounting profession is starting to recognize that investors need information that will enable them to evaluate the economic worth of their investment in a company. This has not been the traditional role of financial accounting.

The role of financial accounting has been to provide investors with an annual account of how directors have used the funds entrusted to them by investors. This approach is called stewardship accounting. The directors are seen as stewards of the investors' funds, and so they should provide a periodic account of how those funds have been used. The practice of stewardship accounting has evolved over thousands of years, but how relevant is it to the needs of investors in a world where the competition for their capital is increasing? Investors are more concerned about what is likely to happen in the future than what happened in the past.

In order to solve this problem it will be necessary to bring together some of the principles and ideas that are currently studied as three separate disciplines: financial accounting, management accounting and investor accounting. Financial accounting was developed to satisfy the demands of stewardship by providing an account of what has happened (in financial terms) over the past year. Management accounting was developed to provide managers with the information needed for making decisions and controlling the business entity.

Investor accounting is a recent phenomenon. Until quite recently, some of the principles on which it is based would have been studied as part of management accounting and some as part of a subject which is usually called corporate finance (or financial management). One of the underlying philosophies of investor accounting is to determine the value of the business based on the 'free cash flows' which that business is expected to generate in the future. The original cash flow statement did not allow users to identify free cash flow for the past year very easily; the revised version does. So here we see the first signs of financial accounting rules providing data that can be built into a forward-looking model for a shareholder value approach.

It is a small start, but there is likely to be an increasing convergence of principles that were previously separated by the three disciplines. There is a growing awareness that much of the information included in financial accounts is not used by management. Those who are calling for change argue that, if the management does not need the information for managing the business, then it is of limited use to users of the financial statements. An ability to see an entity through the eyes of management enhances a user's ability to predict the actions of management that will affect the entity's prospects of future cash flows.

However, these are all interesting developments to which our current generation of accounting students will be able to contribute as they progress through their chosen profession. In the meantime we have to learn how to use the existing system. The stewardship role of financial accounting has stood the test of time and forms the basis of legal accounts in all the major economies of the world.

The first seven chapters deal with the basic principles of double-entry accounting and financial reporting. There are some accounting regulations that affect this particular level of study but, on the whole, these regulations are little more than a codification of practices which have been established for very many years.

One troublesome aspect for teachers and learners is that these basic recording principles have to be explained in the context of handwritten records. Yet we know that such records hardly exist in real life. The use of computers for double-entry accounting is no longer an expensive luxury. Even the smallest of businesses can make use of computer technology if it intends to keep its records on double-entry principles. Handwritten books are likely to be used only where transactions are recorded on a cash basis. Chapter 5 includes some material that attempts to reconcile this conflict but it is something that needs to be addressed by examiners since they continue to set questions as if double-entry recording is done in handwritten books. It must be quite puzzling for students operating computer systems to be asked to solve problems that were the bane of earlier generations.

The range of subjects covered in the entire book is more than adequate for the financial accounting segment in the A Level examinations and for Foundation Paper 1 of the Association of Chartered Certified Accountants (ACCA). There are many other courses, such as those for the HNC and HND in business studies, where the book can be used for the financial accounting module, and many professional courses such as those for the Chartered Institute of Bankers (CIB), the Association of Accounting Technicians (AAT) and the Chartered Institute of Management Accountants (CIMA), where the book can be used selectively to suit the syllabus in question. The first edition has been used quite extensively in various undergraduate courses, including first year accounting degree courses, and I trust that the second edition will continue to gain acceptance in this important area of academic study.

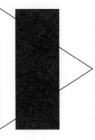

Sources and acknowledgements

It is no longer possible to write a text book on accounting, even at a foundation level, without making references to the accounting standards and documents of a similar standing published by the Accounting Standards Board (ASB). These documents are the copyright property of the ASB and, apart from making references to them, I have included the occasional extract where I thought it would aid the learning process.

In view of the size and complexity of some of the latest standards I have resorted to other sources for guidance and interpretation in some cases. My most constant companion for this task has been *UK GAPP* (fourth edition, Ernst & Young, 1994, Macmillan Press Ltd).

Some of the new material in this edition has been influenced by the writings of Terry Smith in the second edition of his book *Accounting for Growth*. There is a full reference to this book at the end of Chapter 20.

I am grateful to the following examination boards for permission to reproduce questions from their examination papers:

- Association of Chartered Certified Accountants (ACCA)
- Chartered Institute of Management Accountants (CIMA)
- Association of Accounting Technicians (AAT)
- Associated Examining Board, for GCE A Level (AEB)
- University of London School Examination Board, for GCE A Level (ULSEB)
- Chartered Institute of Bankers (CIB)

None of the answers (nor any hints on answers) within this book have been provided by any examination board; they are entirely my own responsibility.

Using this book

Using the sequence of topics

Most teachers of accounting have their own ideas as to what constitutes the best sequence of topics. This suggests that teachers would prefer their students to use a text book that is flexible regarding the order in which chapters are studied. The main danger of such a book is that it is likely to pigeonhole each topic, one of the things that this book aims to avoid. Students need to develop their skills within a wide perception of the subject as they proceed through the various stages of learning. Examination questions are not usually subject specific.

In order to encourage students to broaden their view of accounting, the way in which subjects are dealt with in this book is quite different to many existing books. Perhaps the most noticeable difference is the way that methodology is integrated with the conceptual, the regulatory and the qualitative aspects of the subject, at each stage of the learning process. This integrated approach provides learners with a rewarding sense of achievement as they proceed through the book.

The alternative is to present methodology in an intellectual vacuum, and then deal with the more erudite aspects in a subsequent chapter. But separating the subject in this way usually involves students in having to re-learn topics covered earlier. The integrated approach might appear to slow down progress in some of the early stages but it does eventually prove to be an efficient way of using the time available for learning.

There is also some interplay between various chapters, particularly in the earlier stages of the book. Quite often the concepts and information developed from learning activities in one chapter are used in a subsequent chapter. This is sometimes done deliberately to discourage the idea that accounting techniques are divided into watertight compartments. Consequently, it might be difficult to pick and choose topics from the earlier chapters. This is particularly so with Chapters 1 to 7, which really need to be studied as a complete module in the order presented by the book. The way in which trading stocks are dealt with (and ideas such as retained profits for a sole trader) might not work unless this pattern is followed.

This is not to suggest that the book is entirely inflexible on sequence. If teachers wish to alter the order of learning in some of the later stages of the book, there are several possibilities. For example, although a link has been made between sectional activity (departments and branches) in Chapter 17 and organizations not trading for profit in Chapter 16, it is not a particularly strong link. There is no reason why the subject of Chapter 16 should not be dealt with earlier in the course, such as after Chapter 9 on incomplete records.

In other cases, using a sequence that differs from that provided by the book might create difficulties. For example, the study of accounting problems relating to partnerships is presented after those relating to companies. This enables the accounting problem associated with converting a partnership into a limited company to be studied as part of a central problem on changes of ownership. Converting a partnership into a limited company does not have to be studied as a separate topic; it is simply a variation of a fundamental problem that arises when a continuing business changes its legal form of ownership.

When planning the book, it was recognized that the students who use it might have some previous knowledge of accounting, or they might be complete beginners. The level of material chosen for Chapters 1 to 7 is intended to work for both types of learner. For example, many of the topics introduced in Chapter 1 will be of interest (if not a complete surprise) to students who have studied accounting at a previous level. Students who are new to the subject can rest assured that they are well informed from the start.

Some of the topics dealt with in Chapter 1 are often not discussed until later chapters (if at all) in some books. In any event, some of the material in Chapter 1 relates to changes in professional practice that have taken place since 1990. Students who have some prior knowledge of accounting cannot afford to skip over Chapters 1 to 7, although their previous experience will undoubtedly help them to assimilate the subject quite quickly. Students who are new to accounting will find that the measured pace of the text in these chapters will enable them to get to grips with all the basic principles involved.

Beginners who are using the book without tutorial guidance are strongly advised to work through it in the order provided by the sequence of chapters.

Using activity based learning

The term 'activity based learning' seems to mean different things to different people. It is generally agreed that reading a book or listening to a lecture is not active learning; the learner is passively trying to absorb what someone else is saying. Passive learning provides no opportunity for exercising the mind other than in trying to remember what someone has said or demonstrated. Working through an exercise at the end of the session is an activity, but during the reading or listening stage the student has not been actively involved in the learning process.

Activity based learning requires some kind of interaction between the learner and the learning medium. This is easily achieved in a classroom, where the tutor encourages students to get involved by posing questions as the subject is gradually explored. Some questions are open-ended (they have no unique answer) and these are designed to stimulate thought and discussion. Others are closed questions (usually based on a simple model for the area concerned), whereby it should be possible to develop a specific answer.

These questions are not framed as a test of memory. Being able to remember something is a part of the learning process, but remembering is not thinking, nor is it using your mind to solve a problem. You will not be able to cope with the subject of accounting very well if you think of it as something that can be learned by rote.

The same kind of approach as is used for a live tutorial has been used in this text book. The tutor's words and questions have been turned into text and learning activities. It attempts to mimic (as closely as is possible in print) a live tutorial. In some ways this method of learning is better than a live tutorial because, as the tutor's words are permanently in print, you do not have the problem of trying to remember what was said. This enables the book to be used either for unsupervised study, or as a learning resource in the classroom. Tutors using it as a learning resource will find this duality works quite well on courses with large numbers of students; guidance can be directed according to individual needs.

The best way of finding out how the book works is to start using it. Some of the activities are intended to be thought provoking; others require you to perform calculations, prepare reports, or solve problems. You will notice that each activity is given a reference number, and from this you will be able to find the equivalent of tutorial feedback by referring to the Key at the end of each chapter. If you can, try to avoid glancing at the answers in the Key until after you have made your own attempt at producing an answer; otherwise the learning concept on which the book is based is likely to be ineffective.

You may not get everything right (or the same) according to the answer in the Key but the most important part of the process is to make an attempt. We all learn by making mistakes, not least those of us who try to teach the subject. Making mistakes might not do much for your self-esteem, but it works wonders on your inherent ability to learn. In any event, you might not necessarily be wrong simply because your answer differs from that in the Key. Quite often there is no unique answer and you will have to use your own judgement to assess whether your answer is satisfactory.

Some activity boxes provide blank spaces for you to write down an answer, others require you to use specified working sheets or to complete an outline format provided below the box. The basic idea is that you will be generating illustrative examples which in a more traditional text book are supplied by the author. In some cases you are asked to work activities on your own paper. In these cases, the illustration developed by working the activity is not an essential link to the text which follows, and can be filed in your own set of notes.

If you feel apprehensive about writing down your answers in the book, you could use a pencil for your first attempt. You can always tidy up your answer (should that be necessary) after referring to the Key. The alternative is to rough out an answer on scrap paper before writing in the book. But you should finish up with an answer in the book where this is required, otherwise it will be difficult to review the subject at a later date. In cases where activities require written answers, you should try to develop the idea of writing down **key words** and **phrases** rather than complete sentences. Some ideas on this are given in the Key for the earlier chapters.

Using each chapter as a complete learning kit

The learning activities tend to concentrate on exploring the basic principles. You will need to practise applying these principles to situations that are more comprehensive than those used during the learning stage. For this purpose there is an ample supply of assignment material at the end of each chapter. Most of this is based on past examination questions set by various examining bodies.

Approximately one-half of the questions are provided on a self-assessment basis – suggested answers and tutorial feedback are set out at the end of the book. Questions without answers are included in order to provide tutors with an additional resource should they wish to use it – answers are published separately in the *Teacher's Manual*. Quite often the answers to both types of question provide additional tutorial guidance.

As you progress through the book you will find that questions become more comprehensive and less subject specific. You will be applying principles covered by earlier chapters, as well as those in the current chapter. Care has been taken (particularly in the earlier chapters) to ensure that the questions do not require the application of principles that have not been covered previously. This made it necessary to amend or modify some of the earlier examination questions. You can see where this has been done from the note acknowledging the source of each question.

In some questions you might have to use a little imagination or lateral thinking. This is deliberate because you must not expect your skills to be examined in situations that form an exact replica of those used when learning. Business activity is not stereotyped; there is no unique set of circumstances in which a principle or technique is used. The ability to apply principles in solving a myriad of business problems is an important 'soft skill' that accountants have to develop.

Using a pronoun

A troublesome decision for authors of interactive texts is whether to use 'I' or 'we'. Without either the text sounds remote. The problem with 'I' is that it tends to impose the author on the reader. The problem with 'we' is ambiguity; who are *we*? It could mean the human race, a section of society such as the accounting profession, the company who published the book, or the author and reader exploring the subject together. (There are several other connotations, but they are not likely to spring to mind when reading this book.)

In this book *we* usually signifies a mutual exploration of the subject by author and reader, in much the same way as tutors use 'we' during a live tutorial. On rare occasions it does mean the accounting profession (as in 'the way *we* dealt with this before the rules were changed was to …'). Its meaning should be clear from the context.

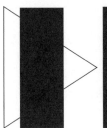

Abbreviations

The normal convention on technical abbreviations has been adopted: a full description is given when the name is first introduced, followed by the abbreviation in brackets. Thereafter, the abbreviation is used on the assumption that readers know what it means. In cases of doubt you should refer to the following:

ACCA	Association of Chartered Certified Accountants
ACT	Advance corporation tax
ASB	Accounting Standards Board
ASC	Accounting Standards Committee
CCAB	Consultative Committee of Accountancy Bodies
DOG	Degree of operating gearing
EPS	Earnings per share
FII	Franked investment income
FRC	Financial Reporting Council
FRRP	Financial Reporting Review Panel
FRS	Financial Reporting Standard
HCA	Historical cost accounting
IIMR	Institute of Investment Management and Research
MCT	Mainstream corporation tax
P/E ratio	Price/earnings ratio
ROCE	Return on capital employed
SSAP	Statement of standard accounting practice
UITF	Urgent Issues Task Force
VAT	Value added tax

Abbreviations used to identify the sources of past examination questions are given in the 'Sources and acknowledgements' section.

Occasional use is made of 'the Act' when referring to the Companies Act. It will be clear from the context whether this refers to the main 1985 Companies Act or to the subsequent 1989 Companies Act.

1 ▷ The accounting environment

Objectives

After you have completed this chapter, you should be able to:
- recognize the different forms of business ownership and various types of economic activity, and assess their influence on accounting practices
- differentiate between the types of accounting information needed to satisfy the needs of the main groups of users
- distinguish between the role of book-keeping and the role of accountancy, and explain why computers have not reduced the demand for accountants
- discuss intelligently some of the controversies and common misconceptions that exist regarding information contained in financial statements
- undertake your study of accounting with an enquiring mind that concentrates on the purposes and limitations of accounting information rather than the passive role of recording it in the books

Introduction

What sort of answers do you think you would get if you asked the first five people you met in the street today: what is accountancy? Or, more to the point, what is an accountant? Probably something fairly meaningless – vague notions such as: someone who is good at figures, someone who helps you to fiddle the tax, someone who adds up money – or you may even get a blank face and a shrug of the shoulders.

Reactions like these should not be surprising; accountancy, unlike law or medicine, does not capture the imagination of the general public. Most people can manage their own financial affairs without the specialist skills of an accountant. Sometimes accountancy makes headline news when a large corporation suddenly fails and investors lose their money. When this happens, the financial reporting system comes under attack for failure to give warning signals of the impending disaster. But apart from these occasions, the role of accountancy in our society is rarely discussed by the general public.

Having chosen accountancy as a subject for study, presumably you know more about it than the general public. Even so, you must not underestimate the scope and importance of this first chapter. If you have studied accounting before, you will be familiar with many of the topics but there are some that are likely to be new to you. Some of the theoretical aspects dealt with in this chapter, and some of the facts, tend to be covered by later chapters (or not dealt with at all) in many introductory text books on accounting.

The word 'profits' has been used in this chapter without any explanation of its technical meaning. It was assumed that most readers would have some idea (however vague) of what is meant by profit. There is no need at this stage to be bothered over its precise meaning; you will soon find out how the word is used in accounting. You will even discover that accountants are not entirely sure what they mean by profits.

1.1 Economic influences on accounting practice

Accounting provides financial information about a business enterprise to various interested parties. But business enterprises differ materially from one another, as do the requirements of the various people who use accounting information.

These two aspects (business type, and users' needs) have a significant impact on the accountant's work and on the study of accountancy.

Business type

Accounting is affected by two main factors: the class of activity in which the business is involved, and the type of ownership.

Class of activity

Some businesses buy the goods they sell; others have to make them, build them, grow them, or extract them from the earth, before they can be sold. Some sell services instead of goods, or they may sell both.

One retailer may sell goods from a single shop, whereas others have a number of branches operating throughout the country. Some businesses operate entirely within the home market; others trade overseas or may set up a section of their own business in a foreign country. Some goods are traded on cash or monthly credit terms; others are sold through hire-purchase agreements.

Ownership

Some businesses are owned by one person; others by a few people operating together in some way. Most of the larger businesses, whose names have become household words, are not owned by individual people but by a separate legal entity known as a company. Ownership of the company may be shared among thousands of people who have nothing at all to do with the day-to-day running of the business.

Users' needs

The users of accounting information can be classified under two broad headings: external users and internal users. The accounting system is designed to provide information for both groups. The type of information provided is different for the reasons given below.

External users

Some people simply invest money in a business and do not take part in its day-to-day management. Financial accounting has evolved as a means of providing this group with periodic information concerning the business in which they have invested. Financial accounting forms a bedrock for all accounting studies; it attracts most of the attention in terms of academic research, accounting legislation, and professional regulations. Apart from investors, other external users include banks, employees and taxing authorities.

There is a further discussion on the information needs of external users in section 1.5. Accounting information for external users is communicated to them in documents that are generally identified by the term 'financial statements'. If you are new to accounting and are not sure what these are, you will find out by the time you reach the end of this chapter.

Internal users

People who manage the business require detailed accounting information for making decisions, planning and controlling the day-to-day operations. Most of this information is derived from the same data as those used for financial accounting but, except for small businesses, the kind of accounting reports dealt with in this book will not enable management to run the business effectively.

Management accounting has evolved as a separate discipline, and includes making use of forward looking data such as budgets. The techniques were developed much more recently than financial accounting. They are not subject to any regulations other than those dictated by the needs of the business.

1.2 Forms of business ownership

This book will cover four main types: sole traders; partnerships; companies; and non-trading organizations.

Sole traders

Where there is a sole trader, ownership of the business vests in one person, although there could be several employees. In strict legal terms, the law does not recognize any distinction between the business entity and any private assets owned by the proprietor.

Activity 1

If a business owned by a sole trader should fail, there might not be enough assets left in the business to pay the debts of those who have supplied it with goods and services. What is the likely consequence of this as far as the proprietor is concerned?

It is this exposure to the loss of private assets, together with the limitations in the amount of money that can be put into the business by a single owner, that tends to restrict the size of a sole trader's business.

For accounting purposes, the business is treated as a separate entity. This idea is sometimes described as the entity concept. The financial statements of sole traders are not governed by any regulations, the type of information produced has mainly developed from professional practice and the requirements of taxing authorities.

Partnerships

A partnership exists where two or more people own the business and run it with a view to sharing the profits on some agreed basis. There are some statutory regulations in the Partnership Act 1890 that can affect the accounts of partnerships, but they only apply where the partners have failed to make a private agreement between themselves.

The law in England, Wales and Northern Ireland does not treat the partnership as a separate legal entity (Scottish law does). The partners are said to be jointly and severally liable for the firm's debts. This means that anyone owed money by a partnership could claim payment from an individual partner, or against all the partners jointly. The assets available for satisfaction of business debts are not limited to those owned by the partnership; each partner is liable to the full extent of his or her own private estate.

Activity 2

Compare ownership of a business by a partnership with that of a sole trader. Make a note of some advantages and disadvantages that might exist if the business is owned by a partnership.

Advantages	Disadvantages

Commercial undertakings may be owned by partnerships, but you will find this form of ownership is much more common among entities that provide professional services.

Activity 3

Make a note of some of the sorts of professional services that you think are likely to be run as partnerships.

Partnerships evolved from commercial practices in the eighteenth century. They were seen as a logical way of extending the operations of a sole trader. The development of partnerships may have given an impetus to the modern art of double-entry book-keeping. The need to determine each partner's share of the profits at regular intervals required a reliable system for recording the firm's transactions.

But by the middle of the nineteenth century it became legal to register limited liability companies. These offered entrepreneurs a type of organization more suited to large-scale operations and so the formation of partnerships became less common.

Companies (or corporations)

A company has a separate legal identity of its own, quite distinct from the human persons who formed, manage, or own it. It is sometimes described as a separate legal person, or separate legal entity. A company enters into transactions in its own name. Those who deal with the company can look only to the company for satisfaction of their debts.

The most common way of forming a company is by registration under the Companies Act 1985. These companies will have either the word 'Limited' (usually abbreviated to 'Ltd') at the end of their name, or the letters 'PLC'. These name terminations indicate the type of company. Some companies are registered as **private companies** – they must use the word 'Limited' (or Ltd) at the end of their name. Other companies are registered as **public limited companies** and must either include the words 'public limited company' at the end of their name or, as is more common, use the letters PLC (or plc) as an abbreviation.

Although the company owns the business, ownership of the company (whether public or private) is shared among a body of people known as the shareholders. They become shareholders either by acquiring 'shares' from the company when they were first issued, or by buying existing shares from another shareholder through the various capital markets that exist for buying and selling shares.

Shares issued by companies are in units that have a 'nominal' value, such as £1.00 per share. The nominal value is a way of naming the share, it is not a value in an economic sense. It represents the **minimum** amount that the company must receive when the shares are issued. When a company invites people to subscribe for shares, the asking price might be higher than the nominal value. Providing the issue price has been fully paid, any person owning the share cannot be asked to pay any of the company's debts (hence the origin of the word limited).

A shareholder cannot withdraw money paid to a company for a share, but the share itself can be sold to another person. In general terms, the main difference between a private company and a public company is that the shares of a private company cannot be traded freely among the general public. Consequently, private companies tend to be small organizations with shares being owned by various members of a family.

On the other hand, a shareholder owning shares in a public company can sell them to anyone prepared to buy them, and various 'markets' such as the Stock Exchange exist to facilitate this process. The price at which shares are traded will depend on the market for that share; share prices are influenced by supply and demand in much the same way as the price of anything.

Activity 4

Many factors will affect the demand for a particular company's share. Make a note of some of the factors that you think might affect this demand.

A portion of the company's profits is paid out to the shareholders from time to time, usually half-yearly. This payment is called a 'dividend' (profits are divided in the sense that each shareholder is paid an amount according to the number of shares owned). Shareholders see these dividends as investment income, in much the same way as interest earned on money deposited at a bank represents investment income.

But dividends differ from interest because the rate is not fixed in advance (some exceptions to this are discussed in Chapter 10). In most cases, the amount of dividend paid will depend on the company's profits. If the company has had a good year it might pay a higher dividend than in the previous year. When this happens, there is likely to be an increase in the demand for the company's shares and their market price will rise.

Activity 5

The tremendous growth in commercial activity since the industrial revolution can be linked to the establishment of limited liability companies. Most large businesses are owned by companies that have existed for many years. The largest are usually public companies with thousands of individual shareholders. Make a note of reasons that might explain why the limited company has become such a successful form of enterprise.

The expression 'limited liability' is a reference to the limitation of the shareholders' liability, not to the company's. The liability of shareholders is limited to the amount they agreed to pay to the company for the shares when they were issued. The company is fully liable for the whole of its debts. If the company's assets are not sufficient to meet these debts, no action can be taken against shareholders providing they have paid the amounts due on their shares.

The financial statements sent to shareholders each year are highly regulated by both legislation and professional standards. In addition, companies whose shares are listed for trading on the Stock Exchange must comply with further regulations imposed by the Stock Exchange itself.

The statutory regulations are included in the Companies Act 1985. This Act contains various accounting regulations, including those relating to:

- the publication of financial statements
- the accounting principles to be used
- the format of published financial statements
- the information that must be disclosed in these statements

The Act also requires the directors of the company to have the accounting records examined by an independent qualified accountant called the 'auditor' (or the 'auditors' when the work is done by a firm). These auditors must give a report to the shareholders stating their opinion on whether the financial statements show a true and fair view of the company's affairs.

A copy of the audited financial statements of all limited companies must also be filed with the 'Registrar of Companies' (a statutory office) and is available for inspection by any member of the public on payment of a small fee.

Activity 6

Over the last century there has been a succession of Companies Acts, which has gradually increased the amount of legislation affecting the preparation and audit of a company's annual financial accounts. There is virtually no legislation affecting the accounts of sole traders or partnerships, nor any statutory requirement that the accounting records of these two types should be examined by an auditor. Why do you think there has been so much legislation regarding financial accounts of companies?

The practice of requiring directors to give an account of the company's operations to those who have provided the finance is sometimes called 'stewardship accounting'. This description is quite interesting because the ancient entrepreneurial activities from which it originates have had some influence on how financial statements are prepared today.

The practice of entrusting money to someone else in the hope that they will make it grow through trade is clearly a very old one. Many stories on this have survived from earlier times, including the parable of the talents in the New Testament. Servants entrusted with their masters' money (or other property) were required to give an account of their dealings at the end of a certain time, and were often rewarded according to the gains made.

Those who managed their master's possessions (especially on estates and farms) were known as stewards. They were entrusted to deal with the assets in any way that would increase the wealth of their master. Ancient records show that accounting has always been concerned with keeping a record of stewardship. The modern equivalent is that directors are responsible for giving an account to the shareholders, showing the results of trading for the past year and a statement of the company's financial position at the end of that year.

Non-trading organizations

The motive for forming many associations is not primarily to make a profit. Their aim might be to provide facilities (such as sport, entertainment, religion, culture, etc.) for the benefit of members. It has become more fashionable to call them **not-for-profit organizations**, a term which is probably derived from a reference in the Companies Act 1985 to an 'undertaking not trading for profit'.

Entities under this heading can range from very small sports and social clubs, to organizations such as trade unions, charities and universities. In some cases, there may be legislation that affects the financial reports of such associations (e.g. if registered under the Companies Act, or Acts relating to friendly societies) but, in many cases, they are informal associations with their own set of rules.

Activity 7

The financial statements prepared for clubs tend to be similar to those prepared for commercial undertakings; the differences are little more than a matter of description. Make a note of why you think there is this similarity.

That concludes your initial study of the different types of ownership and their effect on financial accounting. Perhaps now that you have considered ownership as having some importance for trading and accounting matters, you could take a different view of the businesses operating in (say) your own local high street. As you walk along see if you can spot whether the business is likely to be owned by a sole trader, a partnership, a private company, or a public company.

It will not be easy; so many businesses like to use trading names that have nothing at all to do with ownership. But you can sometimes spot the name of the owner somewhere on the shop front. The business must be owned by someone (either a human or legal 'person') falling under one of the types mentioned; there is no such person as 'Next' or 'The Body Shop'.

Activity 8

In order to get you interested in this idea, we have drawn a typical commercial street below. See if you can work out the type of ownership, and make any other observations that you think may have an effect on their financial accounts. Your notes can be written in the table given.

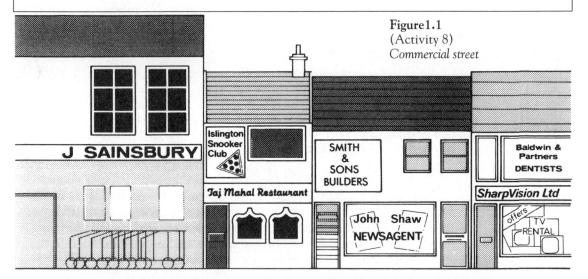

Figure1.1
(Activity 8)
Commercial street

Name	Ownership	Observations
John Shaw		
J. Sainsbury		
Smith and Sons		
Baldwin and Partners		
Sharpvision Ltd		
Islington Snooker Club		
Taj Mahal Restaurant		

In the case of small businesses, such as John Shaw, the accounting records are not likely to be kept on the 'double-entry' principles dealt with in Chapters 3 to 5. What usually happens is that the trader takes whatever accounting records have been kept to a practising accountant once a year. These records are usually not much more than a cash book giving an analysis of cash received and cash paid. The accountant then prepares annual financial statements from these records, mainly for purposes of agreeing the trader's annual tax liability. You will learn the techniques for preparing accounts from these records in Chapter 9.

Large public companies (such as J. Sainsbury plc) are usually quite happy to send copies of their annual report to organizations which request them. You might be able to find copies at your local library, or a library attached to a college that provides accounting courses. You can also obtain copies of the annual reports of companies listed on the London Stock Exchange through the *Financial Times* annual report service. If you look on the last page of the share listings in the *Financial Times* you will find details of this service in the bottom right corner. The service extends to any company in the listings that is annotated with a ♣ symbol. You can obtain an annual report by telephoning the number given, although you will have to buy a copy of the *Financial Times* to find the telephone number and a code number which you will be asked to quote when you call them.

1.3 The accounting profession

The title 'accountant' is not legally protected in the same way as, for example, the word 'solicitor'. There is nothing to stop anyone from setting up practice as an accountant, although there might be limits to the type of work that such a person is legally permitted to do. For example, an accountant who does not possess the requisite qualifications will not be allowed to carry out the audit of a limited company.

The accountancy profession is organized through a number of professional associations or institutes; collectively they are known as the 'accountancy bodies'. A 'qualified' accountant is a member of one of these bodies. Membership is achieved by passing examinations set by the body, and satisfying certain conditions regarding practical experience and training.

These professional bodies influence the technical standards of their members through the examination and training requirements. They also set standards of ethical conduct, which are enforced through the procedures of Disciplinary Committees. There are basically three types of 'qualified' accountant: chartered accountants, certified accountants, and management accountants. There is a fourth type, the accountant employed by a public corporation such as a local authority. Until quite recently, the accounting reports produced by these organizations were significantly different from those of commercial organizations. This is changing and the financial statements produced by public authorities are starting to replicate commercial practices.

Chartered accountants dominate the professional services provided by practising accountants. These services include: auditing, accounting (for entities that do not employ accountants), taxation, management consultancy, company rescue and insolvency work. Certified accountants obtain their practical experience either in a professional practice, in industry, or in the public sector. Those with practising certificates are qualified to provide the same professional services as chartered accountants. Management accountants train and work in industry, although some set up practice as management consultants.

Activity 9

The type of accounting information produced by the accountant in public practice tends to differ from that produced by the accountant employed in industry. From what you have learned so far, set out a comparison between the two types of information.

Public practice	Industry

But this distinction between the two types of work is not as clear cut as suggested by the activity. The accountant working in industry does have the responsibility of ensuring that the accounting system provides the information needed for the annual financial statements, and is also responsible for preparing these statements. Quite often, the practising accountant (while acting as auditor) provides advice and support to help the company meet its regulatory obligations, and also assists in the design of accounting systems.

The names and addresses of the major professional bodies are listed in Appendix 1 to this chapter. If you have not already done so, you could write to these bodies for details of how to become a student member, and for a copy of their examination regulations and syllabus. Even if you do not intend to seek a professional qualification, the information you receive should help to broaden your view of accountancy as a subject.

1.4 Professional accounting standards

The accountancy bodies have played an important role in the research and codification of accounting practices. During your initial studies of the mechanics of accounting you can easily be misled into thinking that accounting is an exact science. But this is not the case. With certain types of transaction there are a number of different accounting practices that could be used, each one producing different figures for the financial statements. When there is a choice of practices, the one chosen by the business is known as its 'accounting policy' for the type of transaction concerned. Reported results can depend on the policy chosen.

In 1970 the major accountancy bodies set up a joint committee called the Accounting Standards Committee (ASC) to deal with this problem. The ASC established a procedure which enabled the accountancy bodies to issue definitive statements to their members. These statements are called 'Statements of Standard Accounting Practice' and are usually referred to by the acronym SSAPs (pronounced saps). Each SSAP deals with a particular area of accounting practice and prescribes the 'accounting standard' for that particular area.

This initial self-regulation process tended to be criticized by the general public, particularly over the way SSAPs were issued and enforced. As a result, the process of making and issuing accounting standards was transferred to an autonomous body known as the Accounting Standards Board (ASB) in 1990. At its first meeting (August 1990) the ASB agreed to adopt the 22 SSAPs that had already been issued by the ASC, and has since issued accounting standards of its own making.

The ASB includes members from outside the accounting profession. It receives strong government support by way of funding and supporting legislation, but it is not government controlled. It continues to operate as part of the private sector process of self-regulation, but with much greater autonomy than the ASC, and with strong legal backing for the enforcement of accounting standards.

Full details of this standard setting process are dealt with in Chapter 20. For the time being, you should approach your studies with an awareness that the main objective of accounting standards is to reduce the number of acceptable practices for measuring and reporting the results of particular transactions. Your first encounter with a SSAP is in Chapter 4.

1.5 Information for external users: Qualitative characteristics

Although this section relates to financial statements prepared by companies, the topics covered are of sufficient general interest to apply to financial accounting generally.

In 1975, the ASC published a document for public discussion called 'The Corporate Report'. Its purpose was to chart a route for future developments in the publication of accounting information. Some of the recommendations have subsequently been incorporated into law, some into accounting standards, and in some cases companies provided the information suggested on a voluntary basis.

Since September 1991 the ASB has been busily working on a conceptual document which it has called *Statement of Principles for Financial Reporting*. This document has gone through various draft stages and the latest version was published in 1996. Some of the accounting regulations introduced by the ASB have been based on the principles which it contains. It is an extremely long document and has seven chapters dealing with various aspects of financial accounting which we will be considering throughout this book.

Chapter 1 of this document deals with the objectives of financial accounting and a portion of the exposure draft for that chapter is reproduced in Appendix 2 (page 26). You are required to read this extract now and then deal with the activity which follows.

Activity 10

The draft document identifies seven external user groups. Make a note of the seven groups here.

Information needs of each group

Not all the information needs of these groups can be met by financial statements, but there are needs that are common to all users. In particular, they all have some interest in the financial position of the company, and in its operating performance for a past period.

Activity 11

The ASB's draft _Statement of Principles_ (Appendix 2) recognizes that the information needs of each user group are different but implies that these information needs can be satisfied by a single set of financial statements. Make a note here of how the ASB considers this conflict can be resolved.

The qualitative characteristics of financial statements

The approach taken by the ASB is to link various characteristics to the objective of making the information 'useful' to users. Two primary characteristics that make information useful are 'relevance' and 'reliability'. Information is relevant when it helps users to make decisions, and reliable when it is free from material error and bias.

The analysis then goes on to consider two secondary characteristics which, if lacking, would limit the usefulness of information. These secondary characteristics are 'comparability' and 'understandability'.

Comparability is necessary for analysing results. This analysis often involves comparing the results of the current year with those of previous years, and comparing the results of one company with another in the same line of business. You will be practising these analytical skills in Chapter 13. Comparability is improved by limiting the choice of accounting policies through accounting standards, and through the disclosure of information that explains the accounting policy adopted in those cases where there is a choice.

Understandability is bound to be related to the user's ability. But information has not been communicated unless it can be understood by those who receive it. The way information is presented and described can have a significant impact on understandability.

You should note that it is impossible to refer to financial statements as being correct. You will see shortly that many figures in financial statements are subjective in the sense that someone has to make a judgement on what the amount should be. But this does not negate their usefulness, providing that the judgement is exercised faithfully, and the limitations in this respect are understood.

1.6 Accounting studies, book-keeping and the computer

It is important for students of accounting to consider the wide horizons of the accounting function. In the past, the recording or double-entry book-keeping aspect was over-emphasized in accounting literature and examination syllabuses.

Quite a number of current text books on accounting describe book-keeping procedures that bear no relationship to what happens in the real world. It is still necessary for accountancy students to understand double-entry principles, but the study of detailed book-keeping has declined in importance in recent years.

This may be related to the increased use of computers as a tool for recording, and the fact that it is impossible to design a single recording system that will suit all the different types of organization. It is also futile to learn a set of rules for recording without any regard to the purposes for which the information is required. If accounting were simply a matter of processing data it could be left to the computer.

Your ideas of what accounting involves are likely to change as you proceed through the various stages of learning. A study of the following diagram will help to put some of the practical (rather than the theoretical) aspects of accounting into perspective.

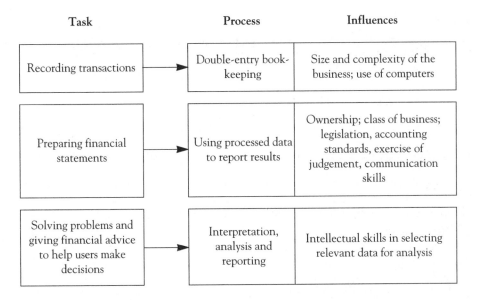

Task	Process	Influences
Recording transactions	Double-entry book-keeping	Size and complexity of the business; use of computers
Preparing financial statements	Using processed data to report results	Ownership; class of business; legislation, accounting standards, exercise of judgement, communication skills
Solving problems and giving financial advice to help users make decisions	Interpretation, analysis and reporting	Intellectual skills in selecting relevant data for analysis

Even at the level of recording, it is necessary for the accountant to understand the basic principles in order to manage the system that processes the data.

Computers faithfully process the data they are given, and most computer programs incorporate controls to reduce the likelihood of incorrect data being processed. But these controls are not foolproof. The accountant cannot blindly accept information produced by the computer, without comparing it to the information that was expected from the data supplied. Accountants cannot know what information to expect from the computer unless they are well versed in the basic principles of recording transaction data.

The exercise of judgement, and the selection of data for analysis and decision making, is not possible without the intervention of human intellect. In these cases, the computer is merely a powerful tool for processing data once it has been selected.

1.7 Problems with the unit of measurement

In order to communicate information about an enterprise, accountants use the unit of currency for the country in which the business operates. Most transactions ultimately result in an exchange of money, and accounting is possible only because these transactions can be measured in terms of money. If we used something other than money, like so many packets of cigarettes in John Shaw's shop, so many unsold magazines, and so on, the details would become a meaningless jumble of information.

But the problem with money is that it does not represent a stable unit of measurement. Consider the following problem:

> Business A acquired its property many years ago at a cost of £20,000. This is one of the figures that will appear as an asset in the statement of assets and liabilities of the business. Business B acquired a similar kind of property last week at a price of £100,000. This figure will also be shown as an asset in the financial reports produced by Business B.

Activity 12

An observer comparing the financial statements of Business A to those of Business B could easily be misled by the information given. Make a note of why the information is misleading.

It is quite easy to see how inflation causes a misleading picture of what a company owns, but it is less easy to see (at this stage of your studies) how it creates difficulties over how profits should be measured. You can get some idea from the following example.

Example

A company buys 12 kilos of a product for £10, which it sells to a customer for £15. The accountant reports that a profit of £5 (£15 – £10) has been made. In order to stay in business the company decides to buy another 12 kilos of the same product but, due to inflation, the purchase cost has increased to £12. Should the accountant still report a profit of £5 in these circumstances?

Commentary

There is no short answer to this; it all depends on what is meant by profit. One of the reasons for calculating profit is to see how much money can be paid to the owners. In a continuing business the maximum amount that should be paid to the owners is the profit made on trading. Imagine what would happen if this company decides to pay the profit of £5 to the shareholders before the new stock is purchased. There would be £10 left over from the sale proceeds and it would have to buy 10 kilos instead of the 12 kilos that it owned before the original transaction. The size of the business will start to shrink.

This situation is no different to the one that many of us have experienced at a personal level. If we purchase a house for £80,000, and some years later sell it for £100,000, we might feel inclined to say we have made a profit of £20,000. But if it then costs £100,000 to buy another house to live in, how can we say we have made a profit of £20,000? Looking at the physical units of wealth (instead of the monetary units) we started with a house and finished up with a house. If we had used this (so-called) profit of £20,000 for private consumption, we would have had to buy a smaller house.

The problem of measuring profits when prices are affected by inflation is a subject that accountants have not really solved, and one that academics continue to research. The process of deducting the original cost of items sold in order to determine profit is known as 'historical cost accounting'. Alternatives to historical cost accounting have been devised but they have never been very popular. The additional cost of collecting data to make adjustments for inflation tended to outweigh the benefits. Consequently, historical cost accounting continues to be the basic convention used for preparing financial statements.

1.8 Facts and judgement

Many of the figures appearing in financial statements are the result of certain facts, e.g. an item of stock did actually cost £120, or there is actually £350 in the bank, and so on. Yet there are also a number of figures that result from the exercise of judgement.

Take, for example, an asset that has a limited life, such as a delivery van. Two businesses, A and B, both buy exactly the same type of van at a cost of £10,000. At this stage there is no difficulty; both businesses will record the cost of the van as £10,000.

But the purchase cost of a delivery van is as much an expense of running the business as is (say) the cost of employees' wages. The only difference is that the original cost of the van will have to be spread over the number of years the van is used, whereas the cost of wages relates to one specific year. In order to spread the cost of the van it is necessary to estimate the number of years it is likely to be used in the business.

Assume that the accountant for Business A considers the van will be used for 4 years and then scrapped; the accountant for Business B thinks it will be used for 10 years and then scrapped. A fairly common practice in these circumstances would be to spread the original cost evenly over the years during which the asset is used. There are other ways of dealing with this (and other factors to consider) but you will learn about these in Chapter 6.

 Activity 13

Both businesses decide to spread the original cost of their van evenly over the number of years that they estimate the van will be used. Calculate the amount that will be treated as an annual expense by each business.

Business A:

Business B:

Unless we are very careful, these differences in judgement can impair the usefulness of the information provided in the financial statements of these businesses. The original cost of the van is a matter of fact, but the number of years over which this cost will be treated as an expense in calculating profit is a matter of judgement.

Activity 14

Refer back to section 1.5, which dealt with the qualitative characteristics of accounting information, and answer the following:

1. The annual expenses reported by Business A and Business B might violate one of the primary qualitative characteristics. State which characteristic this is, and explain why.

2. How can the comparability between these two businesses be improved?

1.9 The format of financial statements

The most striking aspect of financial accounting is that despite all the different forms of ownership, and the complexity of different types of business activity, there is one single format for the financial statements of all types of business. The specific details and descriptions may differ, but the basic format remains the same.

You will get some idea of what information these statements contain by studying the following simplified versions of each one. The financial statements shown here are for a sole trader. Although these are not subject to any accounting regulations, the regulations applicable to companies have had some influence over accounting practices for sole traders.

Profit and loss account for year ending 31 December 1996		
Sales		100,000
Cost of goods sold		40,000
Gross profit		60,000
Expenses:		
Salaries and wages	22,000	
Rent and business rates	4,000	
Motor running expenses	10,000	
Depreciation of delivery van	4,000	
		40,000
Net profit		20,000
Statement of retained profits:		
Retained profits at 1 January 1996		5,200
Net profit for the year		20,000
		25,200
Owner's drawings		4,200
Retained profits at 31 December 1996		21,000

Balance sheet

31.12.95		31.12.96
	Fixed assets:	
20,000	Delivery vans at cost	40,000
8,000	Accumulated depreciation	12,000
12,000	Net book value	28,000
	Current assets:	
1,000	Stock	2,000
2,000	Debtors	2,500
1,000	Cash	1,500
4,000		6,000
	Creditors due wthin one year:	
800	Trade creditors	1,000
3,200	**Net current assets**	5,000
£15,200		£33,000
	Capital and reserves:	
10,000	Contributed capital	12,000
5,200	Accumulated retained profits	21,000
£15,200		£33,000

Cash flow statement for year ending 31 December 1996

	£
Operating activities	
Cash received from customers	99,500
Cash paid to suppliers	(40,800)
Cash paid to employees	(22,000)
Other cash payments	(14,000)
Net cash inflow from operating activities	22,700
Capital expenditure:	
Payments to acquire fixed assets	(20,000)
Distribution of profits:	
Cash withdrawn by proprietor	(4,200)
Net cash outflow before financing	(1,500)
Financing:	
Additional cash introduced by proprietor	2,000
Increase in cash	500

Unless you have studied accounting previously, it will be quite difficult for you to read these financial statements. Do not worry about this; you can learn a number of important things just by looking through them.

Notice how the profit and loss account is used to calculate income (net profit) from trading operations for the past year. The balance sheet shows the financial position at the year end in terms of assets and liabilities (figures for the end of the previous year are given for comparison). If some of the terms are new to you don't worry, you will soon get used to them. You probably know that **debtors** are people who owe money to the business, and **creditors** are people who are owed money by the business.

Notice how the balance sheet shows two totals: (1) the net assets of £33,000, and (2) the sources from which these net assets were funded (£12,000 from cash introduced by the proprietor and £21,000 from profits that have been retained in the business since it began).

Notice how the assets are classified as either fixed assets or current assets. **Fixed assets** are those that the business intends to keep for a number of years. **Current assets** consist of cash and assets that will soon be turned into cash such as trading stocks and debtors. The business can never be sure whether all of its debtors will pay and so the amount in the balance sheet is often calculated by excluding those thought to be doubtful. Accountants refer to this process as being 'prudent' and it is another example of where estimates have to be made.

The firm's liabilities have to be classified under two headings: amounts payable within one year and amounts payable after one year. The first will include trade creditors, the second (none in the example) will include any medium-term or long-term loans.

The cash flow statement in the example is based on the first accounting standard (FRS 1) introduced by the ASB in 1991. This accounting standard was revised in 1996 and you will learn about it in Chapter 11. The standard applies to companies but some of the ideas on which it is based can be used to help a sole trader understand the financial effect of all the business transactions undertaken during the past year.

One of the problems with the two primary statements (profit and loss account, and balance sheet) is that it is difficult to see the link between them. If you compare the opening balance sheet (at 31.12.95) with the closing balance sheet, you will see that the total net assets of the business have increased over the year by £17,800. But this increase is not wholly explained by the fact that the business made a profit of £20,000 for the year.

It would be reasonable for someone not trained in accounting to assume that if a business makes a surplus of £20,000, the total wealth of the business should increase by £20,000 – yet the net assets have increased by £17,800. Someone completely illiterate in accounting might think that a profit of £20,000 will result in an increase in the cash balance of £20,000. Notice in the example that the cash balance has increased by a mere £500 over the year.

The idea of the cash flow statement is to help explain changes in financial position in a way that users can understand, and to provide information that can be used in assessing the entity's operations. The new (1996) format might eventually result in a shift of focus from profit to 'free cash flow'. This is discussed in Chapter 11.

One of the difficulties for companies is that the statutory regulations require a lot of detailed information to be disclosed in the financial statements. In order to communicate clearly, the normal practice is to include key figures in the primary financial statements and to give most of the detailed information in supporting notes.

Summary

In this chapter you have mainly been considering the influences on accounting. It is possible to identify several factors that influence present-day practices:

- the demands of management
- the demands of ownership, particularly in relation to stewardship
- the demands of law
- the varied nature of business activity
- the influence of professional bodies
- the influence of other regulating bodies such as the Stock Exchange
- the influence of economic conditions such as inflation
- the development of accounting as an academic discipline

The text in this chapter included a number of technical terms, some of which may have been new to you. These terms will be used in the following chapters on the assumption that you know what they mean. Before proceeding, you should make sure that you understand the following (listed in the same sequence as they appeared in the relevant text):

External users	Stewardship accounting
Financial accounting	Accounting policies
Internal users	SSAPs
Management accounting	Accounting Standards Board
Sole trader	Financial statements
Partnership	Profit and loss account
Non-trading organization	Balance sheet
Entity concept	Cash flow statement
Limited company	Net profit
Private limited company	Fixed assets
Public limited company	Current assets
Shareholder	Net assets
Nominal value of a share	Debtors
Audit	Creditors

Activity 1

The **debts** may have to be **satisfied** out of any **private assets** owned by the proprietor.

Activity 2

Advantages could include: combination of different skills; more funds available for investment in the business; sharing responsibilities. Disadvantages could include: disagreements between the partners; liability for actions taken by other partners; difficulties when a partner dies or wants to leave the firm.

Activity 3

Your list might have included: accountants, solicitors, doctors, dentists, surveyors and estate agents.

Activity 4

There are several, including: profit announcements by the company (e.g. if profits have fallen, the demand will fall); rumours of a take-over bid; public announcement by the company of a new profitable contract with government.

Activity 5

You could have included: perpetual succession (a company cannot die, even if all the shareholders should die); an active capital market from which to raise funds; investors can spread their savings over many companies and thus reduce their risk; the owner of 'fully paid' shares cannot be called upon to pay any of the company's debts.

Activity 6

Key phrase: **protection to outsiders**.

Several points may have occurred to you. They are mainly to do with the protection that should be given to those who invest in the company, or trade with it in some way. (1) A company uses shareholder's money to finance the business and therefore the directors have an obligation to inform shareholders on how that money has been used; (2) the directors are in a position to manipulate the figures if they were so minded, therefore an independent examination by an auditor provides added protection to the shareholders; (3) those who trade with the company, or lend it money, are taking a risk because they can look only to the company for payment of their debts; (4) companies dominate the economy; it is important for governments to have access to information regarding their operations.

Activity 7

There is the same **stewardship role**. Club officials are using the members' money, provided by way of subscriptions and other means.

Activity 8

Name	Ownership	Observations
John Shaw	Sole trader	A simple retailing organization.
J. Sainsbury	Public limited company: J Sainsbury plc	Vast retailing organization with many branches. Thousands of shareholders to whom the annual audited accounts must be sent.
Smith and Sons	Could be a partnership, but the name might have survived from a previous ownership of the business	There may be a problem of accounting for building contracts that have not been completed by the end of the year. You will learn about this in a later chapter.
Baldwin and Partners	Partnership	There might be a partnership agreement stating how profits are to be shared.
Sharpvision Ltd	Private limited company	There might be hire-purchase transactions. The accounts must be audited, and a copy of the audited accounts filed with the Registrar of Companies.
Islington Snooker Club	Non-trading organization	There might be club rules concerning the accounts.
Taj Mahal Restaurant	Probably a sole trader or a partnership	There might be problems of accounting for tips.

Other points, equally valid to those shown in the table above, may have occurred to you.

Activity 9

Public practice: concerned with **stewardship accounting**, i.e. letting the owners know what has happened during the last year.

Accountant in industry: providing detailed accounting **information to help management** to plan and control the business. This will include the use of forward looking information such as budgets, and individual financial reports to assist management with decision problems.

Activity 10

Investors and their advisers, employees, lenders, suppliers and other trade creditors, customers, governments and their agencies, and the public.

Activity 11

Investors provide the risk capital and information designed to meet their needs is likely to meet most needs of other users. Statements prepared for investors can be used as a frame of reference by other users when evaulating specific information obtained through dealing with the company.

Activity 12

Business B appears to be much more wealthy than business A (A has an asset shown at £20,000, whereas B has an asset shown at £100,000) and yet in terms of physical items they both own more or less the same thing.

Activity 13

Business A's annual expense will be £2,500 for the next 4 years.
Business B's annual expense will be £1,000 for the next 10 years.

Activity 14

1. The characteristic of reliability. The period over which the van will be treated as an expense might be influenced by human bias (e.g. Business B might have deliberately overestimated the number of years in order to show a lower annual expense).
2. By disclosure (in supplementary notes) of the number of years over which each business has decided to treat the original cost of the van as an annual expense.

Questions for self-assessment

Answers to self-assessment questions are given at the end of the book.

1.1 Financial statements convey monetary information relating to the operating activities and financial position of an enterprise. Some of the amounts included in these statements are related to matters of fact. Others are related to matters of judgement.

Describe the difference between matters of fact and matters of judgement in the context of financial statements, and give examples. State how comparability can be improved when information is based on matters of judgement.

1.2 The following fictitious audit report has been contrived so as to include three deliberate mistakes. Even if you have never seen an audit report before, the mistakes should be apparent from your reading of this chapter. The mistakes are related to accounting matters.

Report of the auditors to the directors of XYZ Ltd.

We have audited the financial statements on pages 10 to 18 of this annual report in accordance with auditing standards. We certify that the accounts are correct and have been properly prepared in accordance with the Companies Act 1985

Identify the three deliberate mistakes in this audit report.

1.3 State three different regulatory influences on the preparation of the published accounts for companies whose shares are quoted on the Stock Exchange, and briefly explain the role of each one.

(ACCA 1.1, Dec 89, adapted)

1.4 Describe the main limitations of preparing balance sheets and profit and loss accounts on an historic cost basis in times of inflation.

(CIMA 1, Nov 87)

Questions without answers

Answers to these questions are published separately in the *Teacher's Manual*.

1.5 *Petrol retailers raised petrol pump prices from midnight after increases in the Rotterdam spot market for oil prices. An energy spokesperson said the petrol pump increases were unjustified because petrol now being sold to motorists had been bought before oil prices rose.*

Comment on the above report.

(ACCA 2.8, Jun 92)

1.6 State three classes of people, other than managers and owners, who are likely to need to use financial accounting information. Discuss whether you think their requirements are compatible.

(ACCA 1.1, Dec 87)

1.7 *Financial accounting is non-dynamic, backward looking, conservative, as objective as possible and subject to statutory and other regulation. Management accounting is future oriented, dynamic, produces forward looking figures, should not be too concerned with objectivity, and is not generally subject to external regulation.*
Professor Michael Bromwich, June, 1988

Comment on this statement.

(ULSEB A Level, Jun 90, adapted)

1.8 In financial reporting it is essential to ensure that information is communicated in a manner that can be understood by the recipients of the report. In addition, it is of the utmost importance that company statutory reports do not become over-burdened with unnecessary detail and that the costs of collecting and publishing the information are kept within reasonable bounds.

What is the reasoning behind this statement and what are the implications?

(ACCA 2.8, Jun 91)

1.9 It has been suggested that published accounting statements should attempt to be relevant, understandable, reliable, complete, objective, timely and comparable.

Required:
(a) Explain briefly, in your own words, the meaning of these terms as applied to accounting.
(b) Are there any difficulties in applying all of them at the same time.

(ACCA 1.1, Jun 90)

1.10 The following letter has been received from a client: 'I gave my bank manager those audited accounts you prepared for me last year. But he says he needs more information before he will agree to increase my overdraft. What could he possibly want to know that he can't get from those accounts? If they are not good enough why bother to prepare them?'

Required:
Outline the major points which should be included in a reply to this letter.

(ACCA 1.1, Jun 91)

Appendix 1

Useful addresses and telephone numbers

Some of the major accountancy bodies in the UK:

The Institute of Chartered Accountants in England and Wales
Student Recruitment Section
Chartered Accountants Hall
Moorgate Place
London EC2P 2BJ
Tel.: 0171 628 7060

The Chartered Association of Certified Accountants
29 Lincoln's Inn Fields
London WC2A 3EE
Tel.: 0171 242 6855

The Institute of Chartered Accountants in Ireland
87–89 Pembroke Road
Dublin 4
Tel.: 00 353 1 680400

The Institute of Chartered Accountants of Scotland
27 Queen Street
Edinburgh EH2
Tel.: 0131 225 5673

The Chartered Institute of Management Accountants
63 Portland Place
London W1N 4AB
Tel.: 0171 637 2311

The Association of Accounting Technicians
154 Clerkenwell Road
London EC1R 5AD
Tel.: 0171 837 8600

Extracts from an Exposure Draft issued by the Accounting Standards Board – *Statement of Principles for Financial Reporting*

Chapter 1: The Objective of Financial Statements

Objective

1.1 The objective of financial statements is to provide information about the financial position, performance and financial adaptability of an enterprise that is useful to a wide range of users for assessing the stewardship of management and for making economic decisions.

1.2 Stewardship in this context is the accountability of management for the resources entrusted to it. Those users who wish to assess the stewardship of management do so in order to make economic decisions; for example, whether to hold or sell their investment in the enterprise or whether to reappoint or replace the management.

1.3 Financial statements prepared for the purpose set out in paragraph 1.1 meet the common needs of most users. However, financial statements do not provide all the information that users may need to make economic decisions, since they largely portray the financial effects of past events and do not necessarily provide non-financial information.

1.4 The information presented in financial statements is subject to various further limitations. It is subject to uncertainty because it incorporates estimates and because the effects of transactions are allocated to discrete reporting periods. Information that cannot be expressed in monetary terms cannot be reflected in the primary financial statements. Moreover the information in financial statements is largely historical, in that it relates to the position at a point in time and performance for a prior period.

Users and their information needs

1.5 Investors, as the providers of risk capital to the enterprise (and their advisers), are interested in information that helps them to assess the performance of management. They are also concerned with the risk inherent in, and return provided by, their investments, and need information that helps them to assess the ability of the enterprise to pay dividends, and to determine whether they should buy, hold or sell their investments.

1.6 While not all the information needs of all users can be met by financial statements, there are needs that are common to all users; in particular, they all have some interest in the financial position, performance and financial adaptability of the enterprise as a whole. Financial statements that meet the needs of providers of risk capital to the enterprise will also meet most of the needs of other users that financial statements can satisfy. This does not imply that other users are to be ignored: the information prepared for investors is useful as a frame of reference for other users, against which they can evaluate more specific information they may obtain in their dealings with the enterprise.

1.7 Users of financial statements other than investors include employees, lenders, suppliers and other trade creditors, customers, governments and their agencies and the public. They use financial statements to satisfy some of their different needs for information. These needs include the following:

(a) **Employees.** Employees and their representative groups are interested in information about the stability and profitability of their employers. They are also interested in information that enables them to assess the ability of the enterprise to provide remuneration, employment opportunities and retirement benefits.

(b) Lenders. Lenders are interested in information that enables them to determine whether their loans will be repaid, and the interest attaching to them paid, when due.

(c) Suppliers and other creditors. Suppliers and other creditors are interested in information that enables them to decide whether to sell to the enterprise and to assess the likelihood that amounts owing to them will be paid when due. Trade creditors are likely to be interested in an enterprise over a shorter period than lenders unless they are dependent upon the continuation of the enterprise as a major customer.

(d) Customers. Customers have an interest in information about the continuance of an enterprise, especially when they have a long-term involvement with, or are dependent on, the enterprise.

(e) Governments and their agencies. Governments and their agencies are interested in the allocation of resources and, therefore, the activities of enterprises. They also require information in order to regulate the activities of enterprises, assess taxation and provide a basis for national statistics.

(f) The public. Enterprises affect members of the public in a variety of ways. For example, enterprises may make a substantial contribution to a local economy by providing employment and using local suppliers. Financial statements may assist the public by providing information about the trends and recent developments in the prosperity of the enterprise and the range of its activities.

1.8   The management of an enterprise (in the case of a company, the board of directors) carries the responsibility for the preparation and presentation of the financial statements of the enterprise. Management is concerned with the form and content of financial statements because these are the prime means of communicating financial information on the enterprise to external parties. Management has access to additional information that helps it carry out its planning, decision making and control responsibilities, and has the ability to determine the form and content of such additional information to meet its own needs. The reporting of such information is beyond the scope of this Statement of Principles. Nevertheless, the information given by the published financial statements should be consistent with that used by management in assessing the financial position, performance and financial adaptability of the enterprise.

2 ▷ The basis of financial statements

Objectives

After you have completed this chapter, you should be able to:
- use the accountant's basic working terminology
- differentiate between revenue and capital transactions and show their effect on the financial position of an entity
- discuss the 'matching' convention, and the concepts of 'materiality' and 'going concern'
- manipulate figures in financial statements to show the twofold aspect of each transaction
- prepare simple financial statements from specified data

Introduction

In this chapter you will be manipulating simple figures in a balance sheet in order to discover the underlying principles on which financial statements are based.

The text and activities have been shaped in a way that should appeal both to beginners and to those who have some prior knowledge of accounting. Care has been taken to ensure that any technical expressions used have been introduced earlier in the text. Consequently, you may have some difficulty in working through this chapter if you tended to skip over Chapter 1. One of the aims of Chapter 1 was to increase your technical vocabulary, and you may find it worthwhile to review the terms listed in the Summary to see if you are likely to have any problems in this respect.

Further technical expressions are introduced at the start of this chapter. You must not think of these as words that you might be asked to define. Recognition of their meaning is important but many of them are used to convey a particular working convention. The activities have been designed to help you to use the terms rather than to define them.

The accountant's working language is a little mysterious at times; some of the words do not mean quite the same thing as in their ordinary English usage, some are specific to accounting, and some seem to have more than one meaning even within the realms of accounting.

Words with restricted meanings

You need to understand how the words 'sales', 'purchases' and 'expenses' are used, and also understand an accounting convention known as 'matching'.

Sales (turnover)

If you look back to the profit and loss account in Chapter 1, you will notice that the first figure is described as 'sales'. Sometimes the word 'turnover' is used instead. The word 'turnover' will always be used in the accounts of a limited company because it is a description specified in the prescribed formats for company accounts. Turnover is a generic term and covers all income earned, whether from the sale of goods or from the provision of services.

The word 'sales' sounds as if it is referring to the total sum of money earned over a period of time for everything that was sold during that period. But in accounting, the word 'sales' refers to the sale of trading goods. In particular, it does not refer to the sale of a fixed asset such as a delivery van. Any profit, or loss, on the sale of a fixed asset has to be accounted for separately and so the money received must not be included in 'sales'.

Activity 1

There is one situation where the sale of a delivery van would be treated as 'sales' in a profit and loss account. See if you can think what this is and make a note of it here. This sounds like a trick question but if you read the second sentence in the previous paragraph again, you will probably be able to see the answer.

A business might also receive money from sources other than for the sale of goods or the sale of fixed assets.

Activity 2

Can you think of any other money that a business might receive that would not be classified under either 'sales' or the sale of fixed assets? Aim at finding three but be satisfied with two. There was one example in the cash flow statement in Chapter 1.

The Companies Act 1985 defines 'turnover' in the following way:

> ... the amounts derived from the provision of goods and services falling within the company's ordinary activities, after deduction of –
> (i)   trade discounts
> (ii)   value added tax ...

There is no need to memorize this definition, it has been included here to help to explain what accountants mean when they use the word 'sales'. Value added tax (VAT) has very little impact on the financial statements; it is mainly a matter of book-keeping. Any VAT added to the sales price of goods sold is not sales income of the business. The VAT collected from customers has to be paid over to Customs and Excise. The book-keeping for VAT is covered in Chapter 7. Until then, VAT will be ignored in the explanation of book-keeping.

Purchases

This has a restricted meaning in much the same way as 'sales'. It does not refer to everything purchased, but only to the purchase of trading stock that the business intends to sell in the course of trade. In particular, it does not refer to the purchase of fixed assets.

If you look back to the profit and loss account in Chapter 1 again, you will notice that there is no figure in that statement described as 'purchases'. But there is a figure described as 'cost of goods sold' — the second item in the statement. This includes the cost of purchases. The reason why it is called cost of goods sold (usually written as 'cost of sales') instead of purchases is because some of the trading stock purchased had not been sold by the end of the accounting period. The adjustment for unsold stock is a good example of a process called 'matching'.

Matching

When calculating business profits for a period, the sales income for that period and the costs of earning that income must be matched with one another in the profit and loss account. In the case of purchases, if some of the goods purchased have not been sold by the end of the period, the matching convention requires the cost of unsold stock to be deducted from purchases when calculating profit. The adjusted figure for purchases is then called 'cost of sales'. It is the cost of the goods that were sold, rather than the cost of the goods that were purchased, that must be matched with sales.

Activity 3

Imagine that you have purchased 10 watches that you intend to sell for a profit. They cost you £2 each and so you have spent £20 on purchases. During the next month you sell 6 of them for £5 each, giving you total sales of £30. Use the matching convention and set out a calculation of your profit for the month.

Notice that although you are showing a profit of £18, your cash balance has increased by only £10 (£30 received less £20 spent). The difference of £8 is represented by your stock of watches (4 at £2 each), which are just as much an asset as cash. You will be hoping to be able to sell them next month. If you do, you will be able to treat their cost as the cost of sales in that month. An accountant would say that your profit of £18 for the last month is represented by an increase in cash of £10 and an increase in stocks of £8.

You might consider that your stock of watches is worth more than £8 because you can sell them for £5 each. But accounting will not recognize this gain until the watches are actually sold. You will be studying the accounting for stock in much more detail in Chapter 4.

Expenditure, expenses and costs

These words are sometimes used rather carelessly. The word 'expenditure' relates to any money spent and so it does not convey anything very useful in accounting unless it is qualified by an adjective. You will see in a moment how accountants use expressions such as 'capital expenditure' and 'revenue expenditure' in order to explain one of the most important conventions used in financial accounting.

There seems to be very little difference between the words 'costs' and 'expenses'. But it is helpful to try to make a distinction because not all of the costs incurred by a business are treated as expenses. You might recall from Chapter 1 that the 'cost' of a fixed asset was treated as an 'expense' for each year that the asset was used.

This idea is related to the 'matching' process. Some costs represent money expended on acquiring benefits (such as use of a delivery van) that generate income over a number of years. These costs can be thought of as long-term expenses that are gradually matched with sales income as each year passes.

All the other day-to-day running costs of a business are usually called 'expenses'. In a simple profit and loss account, the various types of running cost are classified according to their nature, such as wages, motor running expenses, stationery, etc. If you look at the profit and loss account in Chapter 1 again, you will see the word 'expenses' has been used as a heading for this group of costs. The item called 'depreciation' is explained later in this chapter.

As stated earlier, the word 'expenditure' relates to any type of cost incurred for which a benefit of some kind is received. This expenditure can be classified either as capital expenditure or as revenue expenditure.

Capital expenditure and revenue expenditure

Some expenditure may provide the business with long-term benefits, such as when it buys a delivery van that will be used in the business for several years. This type of expenditure is referred to as capital expenditure.

Other forms of expenditure result in benefits that are used up immediately, such as the payment of wages for the services of an employee. This type of expenditure is referred to as revenue expenditure.

The costs of all benefits consumed in earning sales income for a period are treated as expenses and are matched with the sales income when calculating profit.

 ## *Activity 4*

By now you should have noticed that the calculation of profit is not simply a matter of adding up all the money received in a period and deducting all the money paid out in that period. Refer back to the first month of your imaginary trading in watches (in Activity 3) and assume that the total transactions for that month were as follows:

Borrowed £10 from a friend to help with the cost of purchasing the watches
Purchased 10 watches at £2 each, £20 in total
Sold 6 watches at £5 each, £30 in total
Paid out £2 in postage for sending watches to customers
Bought a new pair of shoes for £6
Paid back £5 to your friend from whom you had borrowed the money

On your own paper, set out a calculation of your profit for trading in watches and then check your figures with the Key.

Words with specific meanings in accountancy

Here are two easy ones to start with: **gross profit** and **net profit**. You can easily sort these out yourself (if you do not know them already) by looking at the profit and loss account in Chapter 1 and using Activity 4 as a reference.

Activity 5

Describe gross profit and net profit, and state the amounts of gross profit and net profit for your imaginary sales of watches in Activity 4.

Description	Amount
Gross profit	
Net profit	

Now here are two words that must be used with care: **capital** and **revenue**. You have already seen how they are used to qualify the word 'expenditure' in order to make a distinction between capital expenditure and revenue expenditure. This is their most important usage and it stems from the way we use the word 'capital' as a name for all the things we own.

If you own your own house you would think of that as part of your capital. Consequently, if you spent £5,000 on an extension to your house you would think of that as capital expenditure because the money you have paid out has been replaced by something else (the house improvement) that will provide benefits long into the future. The cost would probably increase the value of the property, and therefore the money you have spent remains as a part of your capital (you have simply converted money into buildings).

On the other hand, if you spent £200 on electricity to run your house you would think of this as revenue expenditure because the benefit has been consumed. The money has gone out and left nothing of value in its place.

When accountants use the word capital as the name of something they could be talking about either of two things:

- the net assets of a business, i.e. an aggregate of all the assets less all the liabilities. Used in this context, the net assets are referred to as the capital of the business; or
- the amount invested in the business by the proprietor. Used in this context, the word 'capital' refers to the capital of the proprietor. Note that this is not the total capital of the proprietor. The proprietor will own other assets outside of the business, but the entity concept excludes these from the business accounts.

In monetary terms, these two things (the net assets, and the amount invested in the business by the proprietor) have the same value, and form the basis of the two sets of figures in a balance sheet. When using labels for the various groups of figures in a balance sheet, the word 'capital' is used only to describe the proprietor's capital.

Capital and revenue transactions: Why the distinction is important

For convenience, we can use the word 'transaction' (or item) to refer to either a receipt or a payment. The reason why it is important to distinguish between capital and revenue transactions is because revenue items are dealt with in the profit and loss account, whereas capital items are dealt with in the balance sheet.

You have probably noticed already how the profit and loss account brings all the revenue transactions together in one statement. Income from the sale of goods is matched with the costs of earning that income, such as the cost of sales and the day-to-day running expenses.

Capital transactions are dealt with in the balance sheet because their effect is to alter the make-up of the business capital (the net assets) rather than to increase or decrease the total.

If a business spends £100,000 on buying a factory, notice what happens:

- one of the assets (cash) is reduced by £100,000, but
- another asset (buildings) has increased by £100,000, and so
- the total capital has remained the same.

Even if the business borrows money from someone there is no change in the business capital at the time the money is received; cash has increased and liabilities have increased by the same amount.

Being able to distinguish between capital and revenue items is one of the most important skills you will use when it comes to preparing financial statements.

Activity 6

See if you can identify whether the following would be treated as capital or revenue transactions:

Payments	Delete as appropriate
1. Purchase of a delivery van by a vegetable retailer	Capital/Revenue
2. Payment of wages to employees	Capital/Revenue
3. Repayment of a loan	Capital/Revenue
4. Payment for electricity	Capital/Revenue
5. Purchase of goods for resale	Capital/Revenue

Receipts	
1. Sale of trade goods	Capital/Revenue
2. Loan received	Capital/Revenue
3. Sale of a fixed asset	Capital/Revenue
4. Rent received on sub-letting part of the business premises	Capital/Revenue
5. Further cash introduced into the business by the proprietor	Capital/Revenue

Note that the cash introduced by the proprietor increases the net assets of the business, and also increases the proprietor's capital. It does not alter the proprietor's own personal stock of capital; a reduction of the proprietor's private cash is cancelled by an increase in the amount invested in the business.

Drawings

The accounting term 'drawings' relates to any money paid to (or for) the proprietor by the business. Its usage is specific to businesses owned by sole traders or partnerships. It is not applicable to businesses owned by limited companies. An explanation of drawings has to be seen in the light of the entity concept. Where businesses are owned by sole traders or partnerships, the net assets of the business are artificially separated from the proprietors' private estates for accounting purposes. In the case of a company, this separation is a reality because a company is a separate legal entity.

If Ratna Patel sets up business as a sole trader and pays £10,000 into a separate business bank account in order to start trading, this does not create any income of the business; nor does it create an expense for Ratna Patel. All she has done is transfer money from one part of her estate to another. The same concept applies when she draws money out of the business and pays it into her own private account. This is not an expense of the business and is not income of Ratna Patel; it is merely another transfer of money between two parts of her estate.

Ratna might consider that if she works for the business she is entitled to be paid a wage, and also entitled to interest on the money she has invested in the business. But the business belongs to her and so her real income is represented by the business profits. She can either leave these profits in the business or withdraw them. If she withdraws them by paying herself money from the business, the payments are classified as 'drawings'. If personal expenses of the proprietor are paid out of the business account (as with the shoes in Activity 4) these payments are also classified as drawings.

Since drawings cannot be treated as a business expense, they have to be dealt with as transfer of profits between the business and the owner.

Activity 7

Refer to the profit and loss account in Chapter 1 and note how drawings have been treated. Then delete the appropriate part of the following statement:

Drawings have been treated as: a business expense/a reduction of retained profits.

There is nothing to stop a sole trader from withdrawing amounts in excess of retained profits but, in these cases, the excess has to be treated as a withdrawal of the contributed capital.

Depreciation

You will not be learning how to account for 'depreciation' in this chapter, but you should have some idea how the word is used. Accounting academics have argued for years over the precise meaning of depreciation and it even caused problems for the Accounting Standards Committee. They issued a Statement of Standard Accounting Practice in 1977 that included a definition of depreciation and then, ten years later, changed their minds and revised the definition.

At this stage of your studies, it is more important to understand how the word is used rather than worry about definitions. By thinking about depreciation now, you will be able to appreciate some of the basic concepts used in accounting.

One of the problems with accounting is that although the business continues to operate year after year, we have to divide it into slices called the accounting period. This division into accounting periods is purely artificial: a business does not start on 1 January and end on 31 December; it goes on year after year.

A fixed asset generates sales income over all the years that it is used. Consequently, the cost of a fixed asset has to be 'matched' with the sales income for those years. As you know, this is done by treating a portion of the original cost as an expense each year. This expense is called 'depreciation'.

Activity 8

Look back at Activity 13 in Chapter 1 and make a note here of the annual depreciation charge for each business.

Business A:

Business B:

The amount of original cost that has not been treated as an expense is called the 'net book value' of the asset, and is included under fixed assets in the balance sheet.

Activity 9

For each business in Activity 8, calculate the net book values of the van at the end of the first year, and at the end of the second year

Net book values at end of:
first year   **second year**

Business A:

Business B:

This process makes no attempt to measure the market value of fixed assets. It is simply a way of dividing capital expenditure into annual slices of revenue expenditure. The presentation of fixed assets at their 'net book value' is justified on the grounds of a concept known as the **going concern** concept. In a continuing business, the fixed assets will be held for several years and, since they are not likely to be sold in the near future, their market value is unlikely to be useful information. If the business is on the verge of liquidation, it can no longer be thought of as a 'going concern' and so fixed assets should be shown at their market value.

There are other costs that provide benefits over a number of years where the amounts involved are so insignificant that they do not warrant being treated as capital expenditure. For example, a pocket calculator costing £10 might last 5 years, but there would be little point in classing this as a fixed asset to be treated as an expense at the rate of £2 a year. The cost of £10 will be treated as an expense for the year in which it was paid.

This is an example of a concept known as **materiality**. A balance sheet is not meant to be a financial inventory of everything that a business owns; its intention is to provide information that will enable users to make informed assessments of the business. Knowledge that the business owns a pocket calculator is not likely to influence the user in making this assessment. An item is regarded as material if knowledge of it is likely to influence a user.

In the ASB's Statement of Principles, materiality is discussed in the following way:

> Materiality is a threshold quality. If any information is not material, it does not need to be considered further. Information is material if it could influence users' decisions taken on the basis of the financial statements. If that information is misstated or if certain information is omitted the materiality of the misstatement or omission depends

on the size and nature of the item in question judged in the particular circumstances of the case.

(Chapter 2: The qualitative characteristics of financial information)

2.2 The effect of the double-entry principle

You will be able to see the effect of double-entry by working through a series of transactions and finding out how each one alters the figures in a balance sheet. After that, it will be easier to make sense of some of the technical jargon used in Chapter 3 to explain the mechanics of double-entry in the book-keeping.

Double-entry simply recognizes that every transaction has a twofold aspect. You have already seen some examples of this when trying to make sense of capital and revenue expenditure. For example, on buying a building, the two aspects of the transaction were:

1. the cash balance was reduced, and
2. the fixed assets (buildings) were increased.

Every transaction has this twofold aspect.

In the following series of activities, you are going to prepare a balance sheet after each transaction for a fictional business. In practice, there are literally thousands of transactions during any one period and it would be pointless to produce a balance sheet after each one. One of the reasons why the business needs an accounting system is to classify, collate and record all the transactions for a period. This enables a single balance sheet to be produced at the end of that period to express the result of all transactions during the period.

As you know from Chapter 1, the balance sheet contains two groups of figures. One group represents the net assets of the business, the other represents the owner's interest in that business. The formats for balance sheets can vary, particularly between practices in the UK and those on mainland Europe. In the UK (and the USA) we prefer the format illustrated in Chapter 1, where one group of figures (assets and liabilities) are set out above the owner's interest. The assets and liabilities are set out in a particular way and in certain parts of the statement liabilities are deducted from assets. In mainland Europe a two-sided format is used and there is no set-off between assets and liabilities.

In our series of exercises we will be using the format that is popular in the UK. The two-sided format as used in mainland Europe does not communicate information to the user very well. Before starting work on the activities we will review an outline of the format. The figures in the following example (see next page) are not connected with the series of activities that you will be working shortly. They are included to show where the figures are normally placed.

You can learn quite a lot by studying this simple balance sheet. First notice the two groups of items. In this case, the total is £10,000. One group represents total net assets (the total of all the assets less all of the liabilities) and is relatively easy to comprehend. The other group is the one that causes most confusion to beginners because of its abstract nature. It does not describe actual resources, it describes the source of funding for the various resources employed in the business. We will make more sense of this later but for now we will concentrate on the group of figures which are less abstract.

We have not yet stated how the terms 'assets' and 'liabilities' are used in accounting, and for the time being you can think of them as having their everyday

Balance sheet of (name of proprietor) at 1 January 1996

	£	£
Fixed assets		
Delivery van		11,000
Current assets:		
Stock	2,000	
Debtors	1,000	
Cash at bank	3,000	
	6,000	
Creditors falling due within one year		
Trade creditors	2,000	
Net current assets		4,000
Total assets less current liabilities		15,000
Creditors falling due after one year		
Bank loan		5,000
Total net assets		10,000
Capital and reserves		
Contributed capital		8,000
Retained profits		2,000
Total ownership interest		10,000

meaning of things owned and money owing. This is not how the ASB has defined assets and liabilities but we need not be concerned with this until Chapter 19.

- **Fixed assets:** the first item in the net asset section of the balance sheet is 'Fixed assets'. These are assets which the firm has acquired and intends to keep for a number of years in order to run the business. In other words, these assets were not purchased with the intention of selling them in the course of trade. (UK Company law defines them as: *assets that are intended for use on a continuing basis in the company's activities.*)

- **Current assets:** the next heading in the balance sheet is 'Current assets'. This refers to assets such as cash, or assets which will soon be turned into cash such as trading stocks. Current assets also include amounts owing to the firm for goods sold on credit terms which have not been paid at the balance sheet date. The total amount owing to a firm by its customers is called debtors (the persons who owe the money are also called debtors). The equivalent term in US terminology is accounts receivable.

- **Creditors falling due within one year:** the next main heading is 'Creditors falling due within one year'. There was a time when this group of items was called 'current liabilities' in UK practice. However, the new description is more precise. The most common items under this heading are trade creditors (amounts owing by the firm for goods and services acquired on credit terms). It will also include the balance on a bank overdraft because banks usually have a legal right to require the firm to repay the overdraft immediately if the conditions under which it was granted are dishonoured in some way.

- **Sub-totals:** working further down the balance sheet you will see two items ('Net current assets' and 'Total assets less current liabilities') which are simply descriptions of two successive sub-totals. Net current assets is a sub-total of current assets less creditors due within one year. When this net amount is added to the total of fixed assets (the top item) there is a further sub-total which represents the total of all assets (fixed and current) less the current liabilities.

- **Creditors due after one year:** the final heading in our simple balance sheet is 'Creditors falling due after one year'. This is where we will see any medium-term or long-term loans. When the total of these loans is deducted from the sub-total called total assets less current liabilities we have a final net figure representing the total of all assets less all liabilities.

- **Total net assets:** the final figure for this section of the balance sheet (which we have called 'Total net assets') is a net amount representing the total of all assets less all liabilities. The term 'net assets' is used in some of the provisions in the Companies Act 1985 (although not in relation to accounting law) and it is defined as *the aggregate of the company's assets, less the aggregate of its liabilities*.

- **Capital and reserves:** you will understand the bottom group of items better after we have worked a few activities. We have given the total a name based on the ASB's Statement of Principles. The term 'ownership interest' is used constantly throughout Chapter 3 (The elements of financial statements) of that document and is defined in the following way:

> **3.39 Ownership interest is defined as follows:**
> Ownership interest is the residual amount found by deducting all of the entity's liabilities from all of the entity's assets.

The word 'residual' indicates a final claim on the firm's assets. If the business in our example were to be liquidated, and the assets realized the amounts shown in the balance sheet, there would be a residual amount of £10,000 after paying off all liabilities. This residual amount belongs to the owner.

Notice that the total amount invested in the business by the proprietor (£10,000) arises from two sources, namely:

1. cash paid into the business (usually when the business is started), and
2. profits earned by the business that have not been withdrawn by the proprietor.

The figure for retained profits is an accumulated amount; it represents all the profits that have been earned and not withdrawn by the proprietor since the business began.

Activities

Below (in Activities 10–19) you will find blank outline balance sheets in which you can enter the descriptions and figures after each transaction. Some of the group headings will not necessarily be applicable to your answers, in which case you should leave them blank. They are included to help you to become familiar with the format of the balance sheet, and to make sure that you enter items in the appropriate place. Check your balance sheet after each activity with the relevant answer in the Key before proceeding to the next activity.

Activity 10

Mr Chileshe has set up business as a trader in computers. His first transaction is to put £10,000 of his own private savings into a separate business bank account. Set out the balance sheet of his business (in the form provided) following this first transaction.

Balance sheet of Mr Chileshe after completing Transaction 1		
	£	£
Fixed assets		
Current assets:		
Creditors falling due within one year		
	———	
Net current assets		
Total assets less current liabilities		———
Creditors falling due after one year		
Total net assets		———
		═══
Capital and reserves		
Contributed capital		
Retained profits		
Total ownership interest		———
		═══

Note: Don't forget to check with the Key before going on to the next transaction. Take notice of the niceties of format, such as the position of the figures, setting out the totals and sub-totals on each section of the balance sheet. By taking care over small things like this you will start to develop a methodical approach to all your accounting activities.

Activity 11

The second transaction was to purchase a delivery van, for use in the business, at a cost of £3,000. Before setting out the new balance sheet, answer the following question: will Mr Chileshe's ownership interest alter as a result of this transaction?

Answer:

Activity 12

Now prepare the balance sheet following Transaction 2.

Balance sheet of Mr Chileshe after completing Transaction 2

	£	£
Fixed assets		
Current assets:		
Creditors falling due within one year	———	
Net current assets		———
Total assets less current liabilities		
Creditors falling due after one year		
		———
Total net assets		═══
Capital and reserves		
Contributed capital		
Retained profits		———
Total ownership interest		═══

Activity 13

Mr Chileshe realized that the money he had invested in the business himself would not be enough and so his third transaction was to get his friend, Mrs Kateka, to lend £1,000 to the business. Mrs Kateka agreed that the loan could be interest free and repaid at any time during the next 5 years. Show the new balance sheet after Transaction 3. (Make sure you present the loan in the right place.)

Balance sheet of Mr Chileshe after completing Transaction 3

	£	£
Fixed assets		
Current assets:		
Creditors falling due within one year	———	
Net current assets		———
Total assets less current liabilities		———
Creditors falling due after one year		
Total net assets		———
		═══
Capital and reserves		
Contributed capital		
Retained profits		———
Total ownership interest		═══

The fourth transaction was to buy two computers (intended for resale) at a cost of £3,500 each. Mr Chileshe paid for them by a cheque drawn on the business bank account. Set out the new balance sheet.

Balance sheet of Mr Chileshe after completing Transaction 4

	£	£
Fixed assets		
Current assets:		
Creditors falling due within one year		
	___	
Net current assets		___
Total assets less current liabilities		
Creditors falling due after one year		
		___
Total net assets		═══
Capital and reserves		
Contributed capital		
Retained profits		
		___
Total ownership interest		═══

You will notice that Transactions 2 to 4 have not affected the total of Mr Chileshe's total ownership interest; all that has happened is that the composition of the net assets has changed. It is worthwhile pausing at this stage to think about this a little further.

Activity 15

See if you can think of three types of transaction that will cause the proprietor's Interest in the business to alter in total. They have been mentioned earlier, but you may have forgotten them. List them in the space provided below, and indicate whether the transaction will increase or decrease the proprietor's capital.

Transaction	Effect on owner's interest
1.	Increase/Decrease
2.	Increase/Decrease
3.	Increase/Decrease

Activity 16

Mr Chileshe's fifth transaction was to sell the two computers for £5,000 each (£10,000 in total). The customers paid for them in cash, which Mr Chileshe put into the business bank account. Work out the amount of gross profit Mr Chileshe has made. Make a note of the amount here and state where it will be shown in the balance sheet.

Amount of gross profit made:

Presented in the balance sheet as:

Check your answer with the Key before working on the next balance sheet.

Activity 17

Set out Mr Chileshe's balance sheet after completing this fifth transaction.

Balance sheet of Mr Chileshe after completing Transaction 5	£	£
Fixed assets		
Current assets:		
Creditors falling due within one year		
	———	
Net current assets		———
Total assets less current liabilities		
Creditors falling due after one year		
		———
Total net assets		═══
Capital and reserves		
Contributed capital		
Retained profits		
		———
Total ownership interest		═══

Notice how the net assets of the business have increased by £3,000 because you have replaced an asset that was previously in the balance sheet at £7,000 (the stock) with another asset worth £10,000 (the cash banked). Mr Chileshe has not yet withdrawn any of the profit and so the amount of £3,000 can be referred to as retained profits.

Activity 18

Mr Chileshe now carries out the following additional transactions:

1. Pays his assistant £200 for wages
2. Withdraws £500 for himself
3. Pays back £200 to Mrs Kateka as a part repayment of the loan

One of these transactions will not affect Mr Chileshe's total interest in the firm. Make a note here of which transaction this is, and explain why.

Activity 19

Show what the balance sheet would look like after the transactions in Activity 18 have been completed. You should deal with the £500 withdrawn by Mr Chileshe as a withdrawal of profit by reducing the amount shown as retained profits.

Balance sheet of Mr Chileshe after completing the transactions in Activity 18

	£	£
Fixed assets		
Current assets:		
Creditors falling due within one year		
	———	
Net current assets		———
Total assets less current liabilities		
Creditors falling due after one year		
		———
Total net assets		═══
Capital and reserves		
Contributed capital		
Retained profits		
		———
Total ownership interest		═══

That is as far as we will take this series of transactions. Throughout the exercise you have been showing the balance of retained profit as a single figure in the balance sheet. It was easy enough to do that because the transactions were few and simple.

In practice, a single figure for retained profit is not very informative; the proprietor will want to know how the profit for the period has been calculated. As you know, we set out the details in a separate statement called the profit and loss account. When a profit and loss account is prepared for a sole trader the bottom line is called 'net profit'. (This term is not appropriate when preparing the financial statements of companies.) Drawings are not deducted when calculating net profit; they are dealt with in a separate statement. We will ignore drawings for the moment and concentrate on the profit and loss account itself.

Activity 20

Draw up a profit and loss account for Mr Chileshe's first period of trading. You had some practice on this in Activity 4, and you can use the example in Chapter 1 as a model. Make sure that you end your statement with 'net profit' (ignore the 'statement of retained profits'). The amount of net profit will not agree with the final figure in the above balance sheet because drawings are being ignored for the time being. Set out the descriptions and figures in the form of a statement, using the space provided below.

Profit and loss account for the first accounting period

There are several ways of presenting the figure for drawings in the financial statements. One is to show it as a separate deduction from profit in the balance sheet. It becomes a little cumbersome to do this after the first year because the figure for retained profit will have to be shown as a balance derived from three components, namely:

1. profits retained at the end of last year, plus
2. net profit for the current year, less
3. drawings during the current year.

A modern approach is to include an additional statement at the foot of the profit and loss account. This statement is sometimes called an 'appropriation account' and sometimes a 'statement of retained profits' (as in the example set out in Chapter 1). In the case of Mr Chileshe, this statement could be set out as follows:

Retained profits brought forward from previous period	nil
Add: Net profit for the period	2,800
	2,800
Less: Drawings	500
Retained profits at the end of the period	2,300

Some text books do not refer to this idea of keeping the figure for retained profits separate from contributed capital. Instead, they deal with cash introduced, profits and drawings all as part of one global figure for capital. (Unfortunately, some exam questions do the same.) In these cases, there is a single figure for capital, which is brought forward from the previous year, to which profits are added and drawings deducted. Any additional cash introduced during the year is also added to the amount brought forward. The details are usually presented on the **face of the balance sheet** in the following way:

Capital account:

Balance brought forward	X
Add: Cash introduced during year	X
Net profit for the year	X
	X
Less: Drawings	(X)
Balance carried forward	X

Apart from being untidy, it is impossible to distinguish between contributed capital and retained profits. Further, if you use the approach adopted in this book you will find that there is not so much 're-learning' to do when it comes to dealing with company accounts.

In the balance sheet of a company, the amount of cash paid to the company by shareholders when the shares are first issued must be shown separately from the retained profits. There are enough similarities between the amount invested by shareholders on a share issue and the amount of cash introduced to a business by a single proprietor for the same approach to be adopted in both cases.

Notice how this explanation refers to 'the amount' of cash invested (or introduced), not the cash itself. As you now know, the actual cash is put into a bank account and after it has been spent loses its separate identity. The next time you look at a balance sheet and see the words 'cash introduced' you will know that it refers to the source of the cash, not to the cash itself.

Summary

In this chapter you have mainly been working with the underlying principles on which financial statements are based. It is possible to identify six important rules:

- business transactions can be divided between revenue items and capital items
- revenue items affect the calculation of profit; capital items alter the composition of net assets
- accountants sometimes have to make judgements on the materiality of an item when deciding whether it should be classed as capital or revenue
- each transaction has a twofold aspect
- balance sheets show the sources of funds (e.g. amounts introduced and retained profits), and where those funds are invested in the business in terms of its net assets
- the proprietor's investment in the business will be equal to the investment by the business in its net assets (proprietor's capital equals net assets)

Activity 1

When a delivery van forms part of the trading stock of a business, e.g. a motor dealer. Notice how the trading stock of one business can become the fixed asset of another.

Activity 2

Your answer could include: money paid into the business by the proprietor; money borrowed from someone for business purposes; any other income of the business, such as rents received from sub-letting part of the premises.

Activity 3

Your figures may have looked something like this:

Sales	30
Less cost of sales	12
Profit for the month	18

Activity 4

Your answer could be as follows:

Sales	30
Less cost of sales	12
	18
Expenses:	
Postage	2
Profit	16

Note the following:

- the purchase of a pair of shoes is said to be 'private expenditure' (it has nothing to do with running the business entity)
- the receipt of borrowed money is not sales (see Activity 2); consequently, its repayment cannot be treated as an expense.

Later on, you will see how all these items are dealt with in the financial statements.

Activity 5

Gross profit: Sales less cost of sales. Amount £18
Net profit: Gross profit less expenses. Amount £16

Activity 6

Payments:
1. Capital; 2. Revenue; 3. Capital; 4. Revenue; 5. This is a little awkward. If you have put revenue, you can consider your answer correct. But, strictly speaking, it depends on whether or not the goods have been sold. It is only the cost of those sold that will be treated as a revenue item – as cost of sales. (Write the words 'if sold' in your answer to make it clear.)

Receipts:
1. Revenue; 2. Capital; 3. Capital (later on you will have to learn how the profit on this sale is dealt with as a revenue item); 4. Revenue; 5. Capital.

Activity 7

Dealt with as a reduction of retained profits (in the 'statement of retained profits').

Activity 8

Business A = £2,500; Business B = £1,000.

Activity 9

Business A: end of first year £7,500; end of second year £5,000.

Business B: end of first year £9,000; end of second year £8,000.

Activity 10

	£	£
Balance sheet of Mr Chileshe after completing Transaction 1		
Fixed assets		
Current assets:		
Cash at bank	10,000	
Creditors falling due within one year		
	———	
Net current assets		10,000
Total assets less current liabilities		10,000
Creditors falling due after one year		
		———
Total net assets		10,000
Capital and reserves		
Contributed capital		10,000
Retained profits		
		———
Total ownership interest		10,000

Activity 11

No, not in total, but the composition of business assets will change. Some of the cash has been converted into a van.

Activity 12

Balance sheet of Mr Chileshe after completing Transaction 2

	£	£
Fixed assets		
Delivery van		3,000
Current assets:		
Cash at bank	7,000	
Creditors falling due within one year		
	———	
Net current assets		7,000
		———
Total assets less current liabilities		10,000
Creditors falling due after one year		
		———
Total net assets		10,000
		=====
Capital and reserves		
Contributed capital		10,000
Retained profits		
		———
Total ownership interest		10,000
		=====

Activity 13

Balance sheet of Mr Chileshe after completing Transaction 3

	£	£
Fixed assets		
Delivery van		3,000
Current assets:		
Cash at bank	8,000	
Creditors falling due within one year		
	———	
Net current assets		8,000
		———
Total assets less current liabilities		11,000
Creditors falling due after one year		
Loan – Mrs Kateka		1,000
		———
Total net assets		10,000
		=====
Capital and reserves		
Contributed capital		10,000
Retained profits		
		———
Total ownership interest		10,000
		=====

Activity 14

Balance sheet of Mr Chileshe after completing Transaction 4

	£	£
Fixed assets		
Delivery van		3,000
Current assets:		
Stock	7,000	
Cash at bank	1,000	
	8,000	
Creditors falling due within one year		
Net current assets		8,000
Total assets less current liabilities		11,000
Creditors falling due after one year		
Loan – Mrs Kateka		1,000
Total net assets		10,000
Capital and reserves		
Contributed capital		10,000
Retained profits		
Total ownership interest		10,000

Activity 15

1. Introducing more cash into the business; capital increase. 2. Making a profit; capital increase. 3. Drawings; capital decrease.

Activity 16

Gross profit £3,000 (sales £10,000 less cost of sales £7,000). The profit will be shown as an item under Capital and reserves and called 'retained profits'. This will be added to the cash introduced in order to arrive at the proprietor's total capital.

Activity 17

Balance sheet of Mr Chileshe after completing Transaction 5

	£	£
Fixed assets		
Delivery van		3,000
Current assets:		
Stock	nil	
Cash at bank	11,000	
	11,000	
Creditors falling due within one year		
Net current assets		11,000
Total assets less current liabilities		14,000
Creditors falling due after one year		
Loan – Mrs Kateka		1,000
Total net assets		13,000
Capital and reserves		
Contributed capital		10,000
Retained profits		3,000
Total ownership interest		13,000

Activity 18

Transaction 3. The decrease in an asset (cash) is compensated by a decrease in a liability (Mrs Kateka's loan) and so the net assets of the business will stay the same in total.

Activity 19

Balance sheet of Mr Chileshe after completing the transactions in Activity 18

	£	£
Fixed assets		
Delivery van		3,000
Current assets:		
Stock	nil	
Cash at bank	10,100	
	10,100	
Creditors falling due within one year		
Net current assets		10,100
Total assets less current liabilities		13,100
Creditors falling due after one year		
Loan – Mrs Kateka		800
Total net assets		12,300
Capital and reserves		
Contributed capital		10,000
Retained profits		2,300
Total ownership interest		12,300

Workings: Retained profits: 3,000 – 200 – 500. Bank: 11,000 – 200 – 500 – 200.

Activity 20

Profit and loss account for the first accounting period

Sales	10,000
Cost of sales	7,000
Gross profit	3,000
Expenses:	
Wages	200
Net profit	2,800

Questions for self-assessment

Answers to self-assessment questions are given at the end of the book.

2.1 Each of the following transactions are unrelated. Explain the effect in monetary terms on the total amount of net assets in a business, at the time of each transaction:

(a) The proprietor spends £50 of the business cash on private household expenses.
(b) The business borrows £2,000 from a finance company.
(c) A delivery van which had a net book value in the balance sheet of £4,000 was sold for £3,500.
(d) Paid £600 as commission to the sales staff.
(e) Lent £100 of the business cash to an employee.
(f) Trading stock which had cost £5,000 was sold for £4,800.
(g) Paid £400 as a part repayment of a loan.
(h) A customer who owed the business £100 (a debtor) paid the full amount due.
(i) Purchased a warehouse for £65,000. This transaction caused the bank account to go into an overdraft (agreed by the bank) of £5,000.
(j) The proprietor withdraws cash of £1,000 in anticipation of profits.

2.2 The following table shows a series of balance sheets for a business. Each balance sheet in the series was prepared after a particular transaction (or combination of related transactions). You are required to identify and explain each transaction that took place. Use the transaction number as a reference for your answer.

Transaction number		1	2	3
Assets:				
Freehold property	100,000	100,000	100,000	100,000
Plant and machinery	60,000	60,000	60,000	80,000
Stocks	10,000	15,000	8,000	8,000
Debtors	20,000	20,000	20,000	20,000
Bank	2,000	2,000	12,000	2,000
	192,000	197,000	200,000	210,000
Liabilities:				
Trade creditors	12,000	17,000	17,000	17,000
Loan	50,000	50,000	50,000	60,000
Capital and reserves				
Cash introduced	80,000	80,000	80,000	80,000
Retained profits	50,000	50,000	53,000	53,000
	192,000	197,000	200,000	210,000

Note: In order to economize on space, the assets are shown on the top, the liabilities and proprietor's capital are shown on the bottom. This is a rearrangement of the two-sided format. Apart from the two main headings (assets and liabilities) items are not grouped according to their sub-classification (fixed assets, current assets, etc.).

2.3　From the following information, prepare the balance sheet of Mrs Thakrar, a trader in television sets, at 1 January 1996. There is one item of information which has been deliberately not given, but it can be derived as a balancing figure. You must not get irritated by this kind of thing: accounting examiners do not always give you all the information needed, and expect you to use your knowledge of accounting to find missing figures.

(a)　Fixed assets of the business are a delivery van that cost £4,000 and some office equipment that cost £1,000.
(b)　There was £2,000 in the bank.
(c)　Customers owed the business £100 for televisions purchased.
(d)　The stock of televisions on hand had cost £600.
(e)　Mrs Thakrar owed her suppliers of television sets £500.
(f)　There was £800 outstanding on some money that Mrs Thakrar had borrowed from Miss Laxmi (on a long-term basis) to help finance the business.
(g)　Mrs Thakrar had introduced £5,000 when setting up the business, but had not introduced any further cash since it had started trading.

2.4　During the first week of January, Mrs Thakrar (in Question 2.3) carried out the following transactions:

(a)　Sold one of the television sets on hand for £300. This television had cost £200 to buy. The customer paid cash and the money was banked.
(b)　Paid (by cheque) £10 for some repairs on the delivery van.
(c)　Purchased a television set for £100, but did not pay any money because the supplier had agreed that it could be paid for at the end of the month.
(d)　Sent a cheque of £100 to Miss Laxmi as part repayment of the loan.
(e)　Paid herself £50 by cheque.

Note: The purchase of a television set in transaction (c) must be accounted for as a transaction even though no money has been paid.

Draw up a profit and loss account for the week ending 7 January, a statement of retained profits, and Mrs Thakrar's new balance sheet at the end of the week.

Questions without answers

Answers to these questions are published separately in the *Teacher's Manual*.

2.5　Mary Rogers is the owner of a small retailing business in Barnstock. She has reached the end of her first year's trading and makes the following statements to you concerning her accounts.

(a)　"I have been anxious to keep my drawings down to achieve as high a profit figure as possible."
(b)　"I really cannot see the point of producing a profit and loss account. As far as I am concerned, if the combined cash and bank balance is going up then the business must be making a profit and if it is going down then the business must be making a loss."
(c)　"The business is registered for VAT and I think that I have correctly recorded the purchases and sales. For example, if I sell goods for £200 and add on £35 (17.5%) for VAT, I have included £235 as sales."

Required:
Comment from an accounting point of view on each of the numbered statements made by Mary Rogers.

Author's note: When answering Statement (b), try to give examples of cash transactions that will not affect profit.

(AAT Certificate, Dec 91, adapted)

2.6 The following table shows the cumulative effects of a succession of separate transactions on the assets and liabilities of a business.

Required:
Identify clearly and as fully as you can what transaction has taken place in each case. Do not copy out the table but use the reference letter for each transaction.

Transaction		A	B	C	D	E	F
Assets:	£000	£000	£000	£000	£000	£000	£000
Buildings	80	80	80	80	80	80	80
Equipment	78	78	88	88	88	88	88
Stocks	33	38	38	36	36	36	36
Debtors	42	42	42	42	42	31	31
Bank	14	14	11	14	10	21	18
	247	252	259	260	256	256	253
Capital	126	126	126	127	127	127	124
Loan	75	75	82	82	82	82	82
Trade creditors	46	51	51	51	47	47	47
	247	252	259	260	256	256	253

Author's notes:
1. Notice that 'capital' is dealt with as a single balance (any profits or drawings will affect this balance).
2. There are two possible answers to transaction 'F'; try to identify both.

(*AAT Prelim., Jun 88, adapted*)

2.7 In the context of period profit measurement, consistent classification is required of both income and expenditure between capital and revenue items.

Required:
(a) Distinguish between capital and revenue items, illustrating your answer with examples.
(b) Explain the importance of the consistency concept in relation to this distinction.

(*CIMA, May 88*)

3 ▷ The basic double-entry system

Objectives

After you have completed this chapter, you should be able to:
- enter transactions in the ledger by double-entry
- extract a trial balance
- identify the effect of certain types of book-keeping error
- prepare simple financial statements from a trial balance
- balance off the ledger at the end of the period
- use concepts and principles to solve problems that you have not previously experienced

Introduction

In this chapter you will be using the transactions from the activities in Chapter 2 to find out how the double-entry is recorded in the books and how information in the books is used to prepare financial statements.

3.1 Double-entry and the book-keeping

The books

As was mentioned in Chapter 2, there would be no point in producing a balance sheet after every transaction. All transactions for a period are entered in the books as they occur, and only one set of financial statements (i.e. a profit and loss account, and a balance sheet) is produced at the end of the period.

When recording the transactions in the books, the twofold aspect of each one must be recognized. The procedure is called double-entry book-keeping, simply because both aspects of each transaction are recorded. In book-keeping jargon, the two aspects of each transaction are referred to as **debits** and **credits**, and a great deal of the study of double-entry book-keeping centres around trying to make sense of these two terms.

Before looking at debits and credits, however, we must first be a little more specific over what is meant by 'the books'. It is becoming increasingly difficult for present-day students to visualize something called 'the books' (even for those who work in accounting) because so much book-keeping is actually done by computers. But there is no fundamental difference between book-keeping done on the computer and book-keeping done in the traditional sense of writing figures into a book.

In both cases there is a basic process of capturing the data, classifying it, and then, finally, recording the double-entry. You will learn how this is done in Chapter 5. For the time being, the point you need to understand is that although there are several stages in the recording process, the book in which the double-entry is finally entered is known as the **ledger**. This book is often called the **general ledger** (you will see why when you reach Chapter 5).

The transactions used for the balance sheet activities in Chapter 2 were so simple and few in number that we can enter the double-entry directly into the ledger without any initial processing. You therefore need to have some idea about how the ledger works in a manual book-keeping system.

The ledger and the ledger accounts

Try to imagine the ledger as a book with lots of pages, where each page represents a single **ledger account**. The financial statements will be prepared from details on each one of these ledger accounts. In order to make sense of double-entry book-keeping, you need to understand how these ledger accounts are used.

Each individual ledger account is used to collect figures relating to one particular item in the financial statements. Some of these accounts provide figures for items appearing in the profit and loss account; for example, there will be separate ledger accounts for sales, cost of sales, wages, electricity, and any other class of expense. These accounts enable the total amount for the period to be calculated in respect of each type of transaction.

The remaining ledger accounts record details to enable the final balance for each class of asset and liability to be determined. As you know, it is these balances that are set out in the balance sheet and so there will be accounts to show the balances at the end of the period for items such as cash at bank, stock, debtors, creditors, loans, individual types of fixed asset (such as vehicles, buildings, etc.), and the proprietor's capital.

Each ledger account is divided into two halves by a line down the middle of the page, and we talk about the account as having two sides, the left-hand side and the right-hand side. Authors and teachers often refer to ledger accounts as 'T' accounts because the form of a ledger account can be simulated by setting out an enlarged version of the letter 'T'. For example, a ledger account for transactions with the bank can be simulated as follows:

Bank account

Why do we need two sides for each ledger account? Well, there are often two types of transaction to record in a ledger account, one type being opposite to the other. The ledger account for the bank is a good example. The business will keep a record of all its transactions with the bank in a ledger account similar to the one shown above. There are two basic types of transaction: money is paid into the bank, and money is paid out. By recording all the money paid in on one side, and all the money paid out on the other, we can easily find the bank balance at any one time by simply deducting the total on one side from the total on the other.

Debit and credit

These two terms are used to describe the two aspects of a double-entry. Although we might talk about debiting an account and crediting an account, there is no easy way of describing how these terms are used. Their usage tends to be mechanical, such as debits are entered on the left of the account and credits on the right, or every debit must have its corresponding credit. The mechanical aspects of double-entry book-keeping evolved over many centuries from a series of innovations without any conscious design or serious formulation of principles.

It is possible for beginners to make some progress in understanding debits and credits by thinking about the origin of the terms, but there are limitations in trying to learn this way. With sufficient practice at debiting and crediting, you will find yourself using the terms without having to think what they mean.

The words debit and credit as used in book-keeping are English translations of the Italian words *dare* and *avere*. The present-day art of double-entry book-keeping stems from practices developed by Italian merchants in the thirteenth century, and the first book to be published on the subject was written in Italian. When the Italian usage of these two words was rendered into English, the words became debit, meaning 'to give', and credit, meaning 'to receive'. It is easier to see how these original meanings apply by considering transactions between the business and a person (or organization) outside the business.

If I give (in the sense of transferring the asset, not in making a gift) some of my business assets to someone outside the firm, I debit them; if I receive assets from someone outside the firm, I credit them. It only requires a slight twist of the way we normally think to use this explanation to understand transactions with the bank. If I receive money from Miss Kateka and pay it into the bank, I have received money from Miss Kateka and given it to the bank. (I could also say: I have been 'given' money by Miss Kateka, but this will not allow me to complete the statement. What did I do with the money after I received it?) If I pay a cheque to Mr Patel, I have received money from the bank and given it to Mr Patel.

Activity 1

Using the above explanation of debits and credits, state whether money paid into the bank will be debited or credited to the bank account, and whether money paid out will be debited or credited to the bank account, in the trader's ledger.

1. Money paid into the bank account is

2. Money paid out from the bank account is

Unfortunately, most beginners find this explanation to be at odds with information given on their own bank statements. The confusion arises because banks will talk about your account being 'in credit' when you have money in the bank. But the bank is a business entity with its own double-entry records, and the bank statement is a record of your ledger account in their books. If they receive money from you, they credit you. If you tell them to pay some of this money to someone (by writing a cheque) they have given you some of your money back, and so they debit you. The bank statement is simply a mirror image of the bank account in your own ledger.

It is quite easy to sort out debits and credits once you have understood how they work on the bank account in the ledger. Most transactions ultimately result in money being paid into or out of the bank.

The debits to an account are entered in the left-hand side of that account, and the credits are entered on the right. Thinking back to the bank account, the various amounts paid into the bank will be entered on (debited to) the left-hand side of the bank account in the ledger, and the cheque payments are entered on (credited to) the right-hand side of that account. This is merely a long-standing convention in manual book-keeping, we could just as easily have done it the other way round. Computers can easily process numbers that have opposite signs (positive and negative) and so they don't need to use opposite sides of a ledger account.

In double-entry book-keeping, every debit has a corresponding credit. In other words, when a transaction results in one account being debited, there must be another account that is credited with the same amount. For example, if a debtor pays the amount due and the money is banked, the two sides of the transaction are:

- the business has received money from the debtor, and so the debtor's account is credited
- the money has been given to the bank, and so the bank account is debited.

This idea of giving money to the bank, and receiving money from the bank, requires a little licence when trying to see the double-entry for some types of transaction such as the purchase of fixed assets and the payment of expenses. But providing you can remember that money paid out of the bank is credited to the bank account (and money paid in is debited to the bank account) the other side of the double-entry will fall into place without much thought being needed. Most students manage to come to terms with double-entry by using the bank account (in the ledger) as a focal point.

If you were to add up all the items on the debit side of an account, and then add up all the items on the credit side of the same account, you would find that either the total of the debits exceeds the credits, or vice versa. If total debits exceed total credits we refer to the balance on that account as a **debit balance**; where credits exceed the debits we refer to the balance as a **credit balance**.

This leads to another idea that can be used to try to make sense of debit and credit. The balance on an individual ledger account is the amount that will be shown for that item in the financial statements. This item will appear in either the profit and loss account or the balance sheet. When we look at the whole set of ledger accounts in the ledger, we find that each individual account falls under one of four main headings, as follows:

- those to be included in the profit and loss account will be either **income** or **expenses**, and
- those to be included in the balance sheet will be either **assets** or **liabilities**.

These four groups can be related to debit and credit as follows:

- the **debit balances** will represent either **expenses** or **assets**, and
- the **credit balances** will represent either **income** or **liabilities**.

It should be clear from the name of the account which debit balances are expenses and which are assets, and also whether a credit balance represents an item of income or a liability.

Activity 2

The following are the balances on some of the ledger accounts in an imaginary ledger. Classify each one in terms of: asset, expense, liability, or income. Take care over items 4, 5 and 6: it is easy to jump to the wrong conclusion unless you read the details carefully.

Classification

1. Sales account: £40,000 credit balance

2. Land and buildings account: £100,000 debit balance

3. Wages account: £2,000 debit balance

4. Rent account: £500 credit balance

5. Loan account: £2,000 debit balance

6. Bank account: £1,000 credit balance

7. Cost of sales account: £20,000 debit balance

We can now practise debiting and crediting by working on the transactions from the activities in Chapter 2. The first activity is to try to identify the double-entry on each transaction by naming the account to be debited, and the account to be credited.

Activity 3

A brief description of the transactions in Chapter 2 for Mr Chileshe's business is reproduced below. All money received by the business was banked and all payments were by cheque. State which account will be debited, and which account will be credited, for each transaction. You should select a short name that you consider to be a suitable description of each account.

Account debited   **Account credited**

1. Mr Chileshe introduced £10,000

2. Purchased a delivery van for £3,000

3. Borrowed £1,000 from Mrs Kateka

4. Bought trading stock for £7,000

5. Sold entire stock for £10,000
   Note that two double-entries are needed:
   (a) for the sale proceeds
   (b) for cost of goods sold

6. Paid £200 for wages

7. Withdrew £500 for himself

8. Repaid Mrs Kateka £200

Posting

Now we can mimic entering these transactions in the ledger itself. The next activity is to enter each double-entry in its respective ledger account. In book-keeping jargon this is known as 'posting'.

When posting an entry to a ledger account, it is usual to include a short description of the item as well as the amount. The usual procedure is to write the name of the account to which the opposite entry has been posted. For example, when entering the receipt of £10,000 for the sale of goods, the debit entry in the bank account will include the description 'sales'; the credit entry in the sales account will state 'bank'. This helps to identify the source and destination of each entry.

In practice, more detail will be entered in the ledger account than we are able to do in this exercise; for example, the date of the transaction would be shown.

Activity 4

The ledger accounts to be used in this activity are on page 66, following the summary to this chapter. You could write these out on your own paper if you prefer to practise before writing in this book. The last two ledger accounts on the same page will not be used until you reach Activity 8.

Post the double-entries identified in Activity 3 to their respective ledger accounts. Post the transactions in chronological sequence and make sure that you post both debit and credit as you work through the list. Check your answer with the Key after completing the posting. You will be using these ledger accounts again in a later activity.

Trial balance

The next stage in the process is to set out what is known as a **trial balance**. This is simply a list of all the balances in the ledger set out on a piece of paper. This list consists of the name of each ledger account and two cash columns, one for listing the debit balances and one for the credit balances. One of the reasons for doing this listing is to check the double-entry posting. If the total of the debit balances in the list equals the total of credit balances, we know that all double-entries have been completed.

In practice, the ledger accounts are formally 'balanced off' before setting out the trial balance but we will ignore this for the time being. In Activity 8, you will be learning how this formal 'balancing off' process works at the end of Mr Chileshe's first accounting period.

In any case, most of the ledger accounts for Mr Chileshe have only one entry in them and it is quite easy to see the balance. In cases where there is more than one entry, work out the balance (in the space given in Activity 5) and make a note of it in pencil close to the relative account. Make sure that you can identify whether each balance represents a debit balance or a credit balance.

In accounting exercises, you are often asked to prepare the financial statements from the details in a trial balance. If you look at the trial balance that you have prepared for Mr Chileshe in Activity 5, you can probably imagine how the information could be used to prepare a profit and loss account for the period, and a balance sheet at the end of the period. Some of the questions at the end of this chapter require you to use this approach.

Set out the trial balance for Mr Chileshe using the outline format given below. Add both columns and write in the totals. Make sure that the two totals agree with each other before checking with the Key.

Name of account	Debit balances	Credit balances
Bank		
Capital – cash introduced		
Motor vehicles		
Loan payable		
Stock		
Sales		
Wages		
Drawings		
Cost of sales		
Totals		

In manual book-keeping systems, the trial balance is an internal accounting control that keeps a check on the double-entry posting. But even when the list of debit balances agrees with the list of credit balances, it does not mean that no mistakes have been made in the books. Some mistakes, such as entering items in the wrong account, are not revealed by the trial balance procedure.

Assume that the errors listed below had been made when posting transactions into Mr Chileshe's ledger. Consider whether each error will cause the trial balance totals to agree or not agree. Indicate your answer by ticking the appropriate column.

Error	Totals will still agree	Totals will not agree
1. The £200 repaid to Mrs Kateka was debited to wages and credited to bank.		
2. The £200 paid for wages was credited to motor vehicles and credited to bank.		
3. The £500 drawings was credited to bank but no debit entry was made.		

Book-keeping errors have been given names according to the nature of the error, although I am not entirely sure why this was thought to be necessary. It may have been an attempt by the earlier writers of accounting to bring an air of academic respectability to a subject (the mechanics of double-entry) which has very few principles capable of definition. The utility of error classification is that it helps to identify the various things that can go wrong (and provides fodder for the examiners) and so the time spent in learning about it will not be wasted.

Unfortunately, the classical distinction between different types of error is not very precise. The earlier writers on book-keeping were not always consistent with their own definitions, let alone consistent with the definitions given by other authors. The following is an indication of how errors have been classified:

- **Errors of principle**: in the context of the rules of double-entry, this can mean that a rule has not been observed, e.g. an account has been debited instead of credited. In a more general context, it often means that the wrong class of account is debited or credited. For example, the proprietor's drawings are debited to wages.
- **Errors of omission**: these occur when a transaction is completely omitted from the books and neither side of the double-entry is recorded.
- **Errors of commission**: sometimes these are simply defined as incorrect postings (e.g. an item for £200 is entered in an account at £2,000). More frequently, they relate to errors where the correct amount is debited or credited to the wrong account in the same class. For example, a payment to a creditor J. Smith was debited to another creditor's account in the name of J.R. Smythe. In this context, errors of commission can be distinguished from errors of principle.
- **Transposition errors**: these occur when the digits in the amount for one side of the entry are transposed, e.g. an item for £970 is posted as £790. When this type of mistake occurs in both sides of the entry, it probably stems from an error of original entry (see below).
- **Compensating errors**: these occur where two separate (unrelated) mistakes are made, but because one mistake cancels the effect of other, the two totals in the trial balance will still agree with each other.

Another class of error is known as an **error of original entry**, but you will need to complete the study of Chapter 5 before you can appreciate what this means. Many of the errors that occur in manual book-keeping systems cannot occur with computerized recording.

Balancing off the ledger at the end of the period

If your trial balance in Activity 5 agrees with the Key, we can carry out the final book-keeping procedure. We need to do something with the balance in each ledger account. What we do with it will depend on whether the account is for a 'revenue' item to be dealt with in the profit and loss account, or a 'capital' item to be summarized in the balance sheet.

If the balance is for an item dealt with in the profit and loss account (e.g. sales, cost of sales, wages, etc.) the balance is transferred to an account called 'profit and loss account'. Note that the profit and loss account (unlike the balance sheet) is one of the accounts in the ledger. We may present the figures to the user in the form of a statement, but in the books there is actually a 'profit and loss account', with debits on the left and credits on the right.

If a ledger balance represents an asset or a liability, the balance is carried forward on the individual ledger account itself. In other words, the closing balance at the end of one period becomes the opening balance at the start of the next period. It is these balances that are summarized on a piece of paper called the balance sheet.

The transfer from individual revenue accounts to the profit and loss account is done by double-entry; for example, the double-entry for the balance on the sales account is:

Debit: Sales account
Credit: Profit and loss account

The balance on the profit and loss account (being the net profit) is then transferred to an account called 'Capital – retained profits'. This is also done by double-entry, as follows:

Debit: Profit and loss account
Credit: Capital – retained profits account

Activity 7

The balance on Mr Chileshe's drawings account will also have to be transferred to another account. See if you can sort out what this transfer will be and set it out in the form of a double-entry.
Debit:

Credit:

The balance on retained profits is one of the figures shown in the balance sheet, and so the balance on the retained profits account is carried forward into the new period in the same way as other balance sheet items. It is a little difficult for beginners to learn how to balance off ledger accounts without someone demonstrating how it is done. Here are three examples, based on Mr Chileshe's ledger. From these, it should be possible to work out how the others would be dealt with.

Loan payable – Mrs Kateka			
Bank	200	Bank	1,000
Balance c/d	800		
	1,000		1,000
		Balance b/d	800

Sales account			
Profit and loss a/c	10,000	Bank	10,000
	10,000		10,000

Profit and loss account	
Sales	10,000

Note the following points:

1. After you have transferred a balance to the profit and loss account, or carried the closing balance forward, each side of the ledger account is totalled, the total on one side agreeing with the total on the other. These totals are not used for any purpose other than as a part of the balancing-off exercise.
2. The abbreviation 'c/d' is used for 'carried down', and 'b/d' for 'brought down'. Sometimes 'P & L a/c' is used as an abbreviation for profit and loss account.
3. You can even think of the carrying down, and bringing down, of a balance as a kind of double-entry, e.g. in the loan account for Mrs Kateka, the double-entry (in effect) was:

   Debit   the old period with £800;
   Credit   the new period with £800.

4. The profit and loss ledger account has not been completed; the one entry has been made for illustration purposes. You will have to transfer all the individual expense items to this account before it can be balanced off.

Activity 8

Balance off the ledger accounts for Mr Chileshe by transferring balances to the profit and loss account, or by carrying the balances down, as appropriate. There are blank ledger accounts for profit and loss, and retained profits, at the foot of the Worksheet on page 66.

Transfer the balance on the profit and loss account, and the balance on drawings account to the retained profits account and carry the balance of retained profits down into the next period. Check your ledger accounts with the Key after completing the activity.

After completing Activity 8 (and checking with the Key) look back through all the ledger accounts and notice the following:

1. All ledger accounts for revenue items have been 'emptied' in the sense that there are no cumulative figures carried forward into the next period. We need to start the next period with a clean sheet because items in the profit and loss account relate to events that occur during the period covered by that account, not those that occurred in an earlier period.
2. The only accounts with balances are those that show the amount of an asset or a liability at the end of the period. You can even think of retained profits as an amount due to the proprietor – as explained in Chapter 2.

We therefore talk about the profit and loss account as being **for** a particular period, and the balance sheet as being **at** a particular date. It could be that the balance sheet got its name from the fact that it is a sheet of paper on which the balances carried forward at the end of the period are summarized. But most people think of it as a balance sheet simply because the total of one set of figures is the same as the total of the other – it balances in the sense that the total for each set of figures is the same.

If you look back to the balance sheet that you did for Activity 19 in Chapter 2, you will find that it is a summary of the ledger balances carried forward in Activity 8 of this chapter. The questions at the end of this chapter require you to prepare financial statements from information in a trial balance.

Summary

The important learning points in this chapter can be identified as follows:
- although there are several stages in the processing of accounting data, the double-entry is completed within the general ledger
- each account in the ledger is given a suitable name to identify the nature of transactions recorded within it
- the twofold aspect of each transaction is posted to ledger accounts in the form of debits and credits; each debit must have a corresponding credit
- debits are entered on the left of the account, credits on the right
- money paid into the bank is debited to the bank account; money paid out of the bank account is credited to the bank account
- most double-entries can be identified by thinking how the transaction would be recorded in the bank account
- the balance on each account at the end of any period will be either a debit balance or a credit balance
- debit balances will be either assets or expenses; credit balances will be either income or liabilities

- these balances are listed in a trial balance to check if the total of the debit balances agrees with the total of the credit balances
- some errors affect the agreement of trial balance totals, others do not
- financial statements are often prepared from information in a trial balance
- the ledger accounts are balanced off at the end of the period; some balances are transferred to the profit and loss account, and some are carried forward into the next period as assets or liabilities
- the balance on the profit and loss account, and the balance on the drawings account, are transferred to the proprietor's capital account and identified as retained profits

Ledger accounts in the ledger of Mr Chileshe
In a real ledger, each of these accounts would be on a separate page.

Bank account		Capital – cash introduced	

Motor vehicles		Loan payable – Mrs Kateka	

Stock		Sales	

Wages		Drawings	

Cost of sales	

Two additional ledger accounts needed for **Activity 8**

Profit and loss account		Capital – retained profits	

Key to activities

Activity 1
Money paid in is debited (the business has given money to the bank). Money paid out is credited (the business has received money from the bank).

Activity 2
1. Income. 2. Asset. 3. Expense. 4. Income (it must be rents received). 5. Asset (a loan receivable). 6. Liability (an overdraft). 7. Expense.

Activity 3

No.		Account debited	Account credited
1.		Bank	Capital (cash introduced)
2.		Motor vehicles	Bank
3.		Bank	Loan payable – Mrs Kateka
4.		Stock	Bank
5.	(a)	Bank	Sales
	(b)	Cost of sales	Stock
6.		Wages	Bank
7.		Drawings	Bank
8.		Loan payable	Bank

Activity 4
Ledger accounts in the ledger of Mr Chileshe after completing Activity 4

Bank account					Capital – cash introduced		
Capital	10,000	Motor vehicles	3,000			Bank	10,000
Loan	1,000	Stock	7,000				
Sales	10,000	Wages	200				
		Drawings	500				
		Loan	200				

Motor vehicles				Loan payable – Mrs Kateka			
Bank	3,000			Bank	200	Bank	1,000

Stock				Sales			
Bank	7,000	Cost of sales	7,000			Bank	10,000

Wages				Drawings			
Bank	200			Bank	500		

Cost of sales			
Stock	7,000		

Activity 5

	Debit balances	Credit balances
Bank	10,100	
Capital – cash introduced		10,000
Motor vehicles	3,000	
Loan payable		800
Stock	nil	
Sales		10,000
Wages	200	
Drawings	500	
Cost of sales	7,000	
	20,800	20,800

Activity 6

Error 1. Trial balance will agree; there was a debit and a credit even though the debit was to the wrong account.

Error 2. Trial balance will not agree; there were two credit entries instead of a debit and a credit.

Error 3. Trial balance will not agree; the double-entry has not been completed.

Activity 7

It will be transferred to 'Capital – retained profits account'. As a double-entry it is:

    Debit: Capital – retained profits account with £500
    Credit: Drawings account with £500

Activity 8

Ledger accounts in the ledger of Mr Chileshe after completing Activity 8

Bank account

Capital	10,000	Motor vehicles	3,000
Loan	1,000	Stock	7,000
Sales	10,000	Wages	200
		Drawings	500
		Loan	200
		Balance c/d	10,100
	21,000		21,000
Balance b/d	10,100		

Capital – cash introduced

Balance c/d	10,000	Bank	10,000
	10,000		10,000
		Balance b/d	10,000

Motor vehicles

Bank	3,000	Balance c/d	3,000
	3,000		3,000
Balance b/d	3,000		

Loan payable – Mrs Kateka

Bank	200	Bank	1,000
Balance c/d	800		
	1,000		1,000
		Balance b/d	800

Stock

Bank	7,000	Cost of sales	7,000
	7,000		7,000

Sales

P & L a/c	10,000	Bank	10,000
	10,000		10,000

Wages

Bank	200	P & L a/c	200
	200		200

Drawings

Bank	500	Capital – retained profits	500
	500		500

Cost of sales

Stock	7,000	P & L a/c	7,000
	7,000		7,000

Profit and loss account

Cost of sales	7,000	Sales	10,000
Wages	200		
Capital a/c –			
retained profits	2,800		
	10,000		10,000

Capital – retained profits

Drawings	500	P & L a/c	2,800
Balance c/d	2,300		
	2,800		2,800
		Balance b/d	2,300

Questions for self-assessment

Answers to self-assessment questions are given at the end of the book.

3.1 Using the information provided below for Mrs Thakrar, you are required to:
(a) open up her ledger accounts at 8 January 1996 (see note below)
(b) post her transactions for week ending 14 January 1996
(c) extract a trial balance from the ledger at 14 January 1996
(d) prepare financial statements from the trial balance

You are not required to balance off the ledger accounts except for where it is necessary to do this for requirement (c).

Note: When we talk about opening up ledger accounts for an existing business, we simply mean that the closing balances on each ledger account at the end of the previous period (the various assets and liabilities, and proprietor's capital accounts) are brought down as the opening balances for the new period. The information for these opening balances is often given in the form of a balance sheet at the end of the previous period.

Information:
1. The opening balances are to be taken from Mrs Thakrar's balance sheet at 7 January 1996 as given in the answer to Question 2.4, Chapter 2.
2. Mrs Thakrar's transactions during week ending 14 January 1996 were as follows:
   8 January: received £50 from one of the debtors
   9 January: paid £400 to the trade creditors
   10 January: sold some of the existing stock of televisions £700. Customers paid for them in cash. The televisions had cost Mrs Thakrar £400 when they were originally purchased
   10 January: purchased some more office equipment for £100
   14 January: paid a shop assistant £80 wages for the week
   14 January: withdrew £100 in anticipation of profits
3. All payments were by cheque; cash received is banked on the day received.

(You should adopt the method of accounting for stock as used for Activity 4 in this chapter, i.e. cost of stock purchased is debited to the stock account, and the cost of stock sold is credited to the stock account. The balance on the stock account will then represent cost of stock to be included in the balance sheet. You will learn a different way of dealing with this in the next chapter.)

3.2 The following balances have been extracted from the ledger of T. Zatopec, an insurance broker, after posting transactions for the year. As you see, the list does not identify whether each amount is a debit balance or a credit balance. You are required to set out the list in the form of a trial balance showing debit balances separate from credit balances.

Although the list includes a few items that you have not encountered in this book, you should be able to use your knowledge of general principles to identify the nature of these items.

List of balances:

Drawings	13,600
Commission earned	34,384
Staff salaries	14,430
Rent and business rates	2,800
Telephone, postage and stationery	1,200
Travelling and entertaining expenses	800
Loan payable	1,000
Office equipment	5,000
Debtors	6,000

Creditors	4,000
Cash at bank (i.e. not overdrawn)	5,000
Investments	3,000
Interest received on investments	200
Interest paid	100
Capital account:	
cash introduced	10,000
retained profits brought forward to be derived	

3.3 The following book-keeping errors occurred when posting transactions into the ledger of Miss L. Gifford. You are required to give a type name to each error, and to describe the effect that each error will have on agreement of the trial balance totals.

1. A payment of £600 to a creditor was completely left out of the books of account.
2. A payment of £2 for a stapling machine has been debited to office equipment.
3. A receipt of £690 for the sale of stock was correctly recorded in the bank account but was credited to sales as £960.
4. A payment of £100 for rent has been credited to rents received.
5. A receipt of £40 for the sale of stock has been debited to the bank account as £40 and credited to the sales account as £400.
6. A receipt of £100 for the sale of stock has been correctly entered in the bank account, but credited to sales as £110. Independently, a payment of £980 for wages has been correctly entered in the bank account, but debited to wages as £990.
7. A payment of £10,000 for a new delivery van has been debited to land and buildings.

Questions without answers

Answers to these questions are published separately in the *Teacher's Manual*.

3.4 Mrs C. Glassbrook owns a small shop, retailing in jewellery. All the hard work of posting in the ledger for year ending 31 December 1996 has been completed, and a trial balance of the ledger accounts at this date was as follows:

Land and buildings	80,000	
Fixtures and equipment	10,000	
Drawings	16,000	
Sales		150,000
Cost of sales	100,000	
Assistants' wages	20,000	
Rent, rates and insurance	2,000	
Stationery and telephone	1,000	
Debtors	8,000	
Trade creditors		6,000
Bank account		2,000
Stock	20,000	
Capital account – cash introduced		70,000
Capital account – retained profits		29,000
	257,000	257,000

You have checked some of the postings and discovered the following:

(a) A cheque of £200 made out to Mrs C. Glassbrook for drawings has been debited to the wages account.

(b) One of the payments for insurance includes an amount of £100 for Mrs Glassbrook's own private residence (this residence is not used for business purposes).

(c) Overdraft interest of £100 has been charged by the bank, but this has not been entered in Mrs Glassbrook's ledger.

Required:
Prepare financial statements for Mrs Glassbrook based on the information given.

3.5 This question is based on one set by the AAT for their Certificate in Accounting. One of the items has been removed since the subject has not yet been covered by the book.

Sam Dors and Mike Ford are employed by Octagon Ltd and had been asked to prepare some draft accounts for the year end. Before starting, however, Sam wanted to discuss a number of issues which had been concerning him, including the accuracy of the accounting records which they would use. Mike, on the other hand, was confident that all was well and wanted to start work as soon as possible. Sam insisted on discussing the following:

1. Sam started talking about depreciation. Although they had already considered buildings and equipment, which had been depreciated in previous years, he was now worried about small items such as office staplers. He said, 'I know they only cost about £2.50 each but they do last for about 5 years. Shouldn't we treat them as an expense at the rate of 50p per year?'

2. Sam then moved on to the subject of errors that a new book-keeper, Geoff Reid, had been making. 'The other day I found out by chance that he had entered £100 sales in both the sales account and the bank account as £1,000.' 'Well that is why we extract a trial balance,' said Mike. 'If he debited the bank account with £1,000 instead of £100, the bank balance would be too large and so the trial balance would not balance.'

3. Next Sam wanted to discuss the figure for equipment in the balance sheet which was to be shown at net book value. 'I know it's very unlikely,' he said to Mike, 'but if the business came to a sudden end, perhaps because it could not pay its debts, and the equipment had to be sold off quickly, then we would not get as much for it as the net book value in the balance sheet. Do you think we should re-work all the balances so that the assets are shown in the balance sheet at the prices they would fetch if they were sold off quickly?'

4. Sam had one final point concerning the work of Geoff Reid. 'I suspect that when the building redecoration and repairs were carried out, some of the payments were debited to the buildings account and some to the repairs and maintenance account.' 'I do not think it matters,' said Mike. 'It certainly should not make any difference to the profit and loss account or to the balance sheet.'

Required:
Comment fully on the points of discussion made between Sam Dors and Mike Ford.

(AAT Certificate, Dec 90)

4 ▷ Stock and credit

Objectives

After you have completed this chapter, you should be able to:
- record entries for stock and purchases in the books, and calculate cost of sales from the information recorded
- identify trading account data in trial balances that are based on different book-keeping systems
- prepare financial statements that include opening and closing stock, and credit transactions
- use and discuss some of the concepts and regulations included in SSAP 2 and SSAP 9
- demonstrate the effect on profit measurement of the various methods used for the valuation of closing stock
- identify the point at which revenues and costs should be recognized in the financial statements

Introduction

In this chapter, you will be working on the top section of the profit and loss account, where the gross profit is calculated. This section is sometimes called the trading account. You will learn more about some of the concepts used in accounting, and also use regulations contained in two accounting standards.

The lesson on trading stock occupies the largest part of the chapter. This is because there are various practical book-keeping problems to consider, as well as quite a number of concepts and accounting regulations that affect the way stock is dealt with in the financial statements.

4.1 Trading stock: The book-keeping problems

Up to now, you have dealt with the account for trading stock in much the same way as the account for cash at bank. Stock received (purchased) during the period has been debited to the stock account; the cost of stock sold during that period has been credited to the stock account and debited to cost of sales. The difference between the cost of stock received and the cost of stock sold gave the cost of stock on hand at the end of the period (in the same way as a bank balance is found from the difference between cash received and cash paid).

This approach looks sound in theory, but we have conveniently disregarded some of the practical difficulties associated with trying to keep an accounting record for trading stock in this way.

Small businesses

The next time that you buy something from a small local shop, try to imagine what accounting records might have been kept as a result of your purchase (a sale of stock by the shop). Forget about double-entry for the time being, simply think about the way accounting data might have been accumulated by the system to enable the double-entry to be posted later. There might be a series of events something like the following:

> You take the items (magazine, bar of chocolate, etc.) from the shelf and offer cash to the assistant. The assistant uses the cash till to add up the total price of the goods you are buying, takes your money, and gives you your change and a till receipt. There is probably a register in the till to keep a running total of all sales throughout the day so that the cash in the till can be checked with this total from time to time.

The trader in the above story is likely to have kept a record of the amount paid for purchases during the year, and sales can be determined from the cash takings.

Activity 1

Think about previous activities where stock purchased was debited to the stock account, and the cost of stock sold was credited. It is unlikely that you will be able to do this in the case of a small business because certain data regarding the movement of stock has not been recorded by the accounting system. Make a note here of the data concerned.

It is simply not practical for a small trader to make a note of the cost price of every item in the shop, let alone record these costs at the time of sale. The goods often have a label on them to show the sales price to the customer, but not the cost price to the trader.

At this point, you may be wondering about some of the larger supermarkets where you see computerized cash tills and bar codes being used. In some of these cases, it is quite likely that an amount is recorded for both sales and the cost of sales at the same time. But even here there are practical difficulties in using the cost of sales information produced by the system to keep a reliable account for stock in the same way as we do for cash at bank.

You will appreciate how these problems are resolved if you concentrate on the small trader who makes no attempt to keep a continuous record of the cost of sales. As you know, one of the steps in calculating profit is to match the sales revenue for a period with the cost of the goods sold in that period. You also know that the cost of stock at the end of the period is one of the items included under current assets in the balance sheet. Accountants tend to talk about the stock at the end of the period as being the 'closing stock'.

Activity 2

Think about the cost of closing stock. If, as suggested by the above notes, there is no practical way in which we can use the accounting system to produce a reliable figure for the cost of closing stock, how could it be determined?

This procedure is often called the 'annual stocktaking'. You can imagine that with some businesses it can take quite some time to complete. Sometimes you see notices on the front of a shop saying 'closed for annual stocktaking', although it is more usual to do it over a weekend in order to avoid too much disruption of trade.

Any trader, no matter how small, will keep an accounting record of the cost of goods purchased during the period. From the annual stock count we can calculate the cost of the closing stock. It is not too difficult to put these two things together in your mind to see how cost of sales can be determined. Since sales are recorded, and the cost of sales can be calculated, we can also determine the gross profit.

Activity 3

Consider the first year of a new business, i.e. one with no stock at the beginning of the year. During the year, cost of purchases amounts to £50,000. Total sales for the year are £60,000. The closing stock is counted and valued as follows:

at cost price £10,000; at sales price £15,000

Calculate:

1. Cost of sales

2. Gross profit

Notice how the sales price of the closing stock (£15,000) is not used in any of the calculations. It was included in the information mainly to force you to think about the relevant figure. We can also use it to bring out a further principle in the next activity.

If we had used the selling price of closing stock in our calculations, the cost of sales would have been £35,000 (i.e. £50,000 less £15,000) and, therefore, the gross profit would have been calculated as £25,000.

Activity 4

The trader in this example will eventually make a gross profit of £25,000 on the goods purchased. The goods cost £50,000 to buy, some have already been sold for £60,000, and those still on hand can be sold for £15,000. Try to describe what you think is wrong with recognizing a gross profit of £25,000 (instead of £20,000) in the accounting period being considered. The point was mentioned briefly in Chapter 2.

This principle is sometimes called the 'realization' principle because profits must only be recognized in the accounting period during which such profits are realized. For the time being, you can think of profits as being realized in the period during which the sales price is received in cash. When dealing with credit transactions later in this chapter, you will see that profits are considered to be realized if the ultimate receipt of the sales price becomes reasonably certain. This allows goods sold on credit to be treated as sales at the time of sale, even though the cash will be received at a later time.

In the case of unsold stock, there is no certainty that the ultimate sales value will be received and so the unrealized profit (£5,000 in Activity 3) must be ignored until the stock is sold. This is conveniently achieved by valuing the closing stock at cost when determining the figure for cost of sales. By deducting the cost of closing stock from the cost of stock purchased, the balance represents the cost of stock sold in the period. This can then be matched with the sales income for the period to determine the gross profit realized.

Ledger accounting for stock

In order to translate the book-keeping method used in previous chapters into one that can be used for a small business, it is best to work through a series of small steps. We will do this by using the details from Activity 3 above.

The first step enables a comparison to be made with the double-entry for stock used in Chapter 3 by assuming that the trader has kept a primary record of cost of sales. A primary record is one where accounting data are accumulated prior to posting in the ledger.

Activity 5

Assume that the trader in Activity 3 keeps a primary record of the cost of goods sold, purchases are paid by cheque on the day of purchase, and all sales are for cash, which is banked immediately.

1. Make a note of the double-entry for the relevant transactions using the method adopted in Chapter 3

	Account debited	Account credited
Purchase of stock £50,000		
Sales £60,000		
Cost of sales £40,000		

2. State how the balance on the stock account (£10,000 debit) would have been dealt with at the end of the period. You can answer in the form of a double-entry if you wish.

The relevant ledger accounts (prior to the transfers to profit and loss account) would be as follows:

Stock					Sales			
Bank (purchases)	50,000	Cost of sales	40,000				Bank	60,000
		Stock c/d	10,000					
	50,000		50,000					
Stock b/d	10,000							

Cost of sales				Bank			
Stock	40,000			Sales	60,000	Stock	50,000

In this case, the figure for cost of sales was recorded in the primary records and then posted in the ledger by double-entry so that the stock account itself revealed the cost of stock on hand at the end of the period.

The next step is to assume that no primary record is kept for cost of sales (which is usually the case for a small trader) and the annual stock count reveals stock on hand of £10,000 at cost price. We now need to write the cost of closing stock into the books because it is not a balance revealed by entries in the stock account itself.

Activity 6

Assuming that purchases have been debited to the stock account (there are other methods, as you will see in a moment), can you think of a way of writing the cost of closing stock into the stock account by means of double-entry? It will help if you recall that closing balances are, in effect, written into the ledger by way of double-entry. If you can think of an answer, make a note of it here.

At this stage the ledger accounts will look a bit odd – something like the following:

Stock					Sales			
Bank (purchases)	50,000	Stock c/d	10,000				Bank	60,000
Stock b/d	10,000							

Cost of sales				Bank			
				Sales	60,000	Stock	50,000

You will often have to use this idea of carrying down a balance on ledger accounts in order to calculate a figure needed for the profit and loss account. In this case we are using the idea to determine cost of sales. If you look at the stock account you will see that it has a debit balance of £40,000 (£50,000 debit less £10,000 credit), which represents the cost of sales. You can now post the double-entry for cost of sales in order to balance off the stock account.

Activity 7

Go back to the above ledger accounts, post in the double-entry for cost of sales and balance off the stock account. Then compare the ledger accounts resulting from this activity with those following Activity 5. Make a note of what you notice.

All we have done is alter the sequence of entries in the stock account. By posting the cost of sales first (assuming we had a record of the amount), the balance represents the cost of closing stock; by entering the cost of closing stock first, the balancing figure represents cost of sales.

Opening stock

In the steps so far, we have been looking at the first year of a new business. There were no balances in the books at the beginning of the year and, in particular, no stock at the beginning of the year. The closing balances (for assets and liabilities) at the end of one year will become the opening balances at the start of the next year. In the case of stock, the closing stock at the end of Year 1 will become what is known as the 'opening stock' at the start of Year 2.

Activity 8

Think about the stock account for the second year of the above trader. There will be two types of entry on the debit side of the account. See if you can think what they are and make a note of them here.

At the end of the second year, the trader will count the stock again, calculate the cost of this stock, and then write it into the books in the same way as was done at the end of the first year.

Activity 9

During the second year, our trader (Activities 3–7) purchased stock at a cost of £70,000. Sales amounted to £102,000. The stock at the end of the second year was counted and valued at the cost price of £12,000.

Calculate:

1. Cost of sales for the second year.

2. Gross profit for the second year.

Notice how the calculation for cost of sales is set out in the answer to Activity 9. In the case of sole traders, this calculation is often set out on the face of the profit and loss account.

Different book-keeping systems for purchases and stock

The last step is to consider how the book-keeping might differ depending upon what tools are used for recording the original transaction data. Accountancy students are usually required to deal with accounting information beyond the trial balance stage. In other words, you would not be expected to write up the primary books or post double-entries in a ledger. But you must understand the various recording processes in order to make sense of the information given in a trial balance.

Unfortunately there is no one single method of recording for purchases and stock. There is a basic pattern, and you will have to rely on your ability to visualize this when interpreting information given by examiners.

In all previous activities, you have been dealing with all the stock entries (opening stock, purchases, cost of sales, closing stock) in one single account called 'stock'. Whether or not it would be done this way in practice will depend upon the recording system being used.

With the increasing use of computers to record accounting information, there is a growing tendency for even a small business to keep an account for stock in the sense that both the stock movements inwards (purchases) and the stock movements outwards (cost of sales) are recorded in the stock account as they occur – in much the same way as cash movements in and out are recorded in a bank account.

One of the reasons for keeping such an account is to provide an accounting control over stocks. The account will tell the trader what the cost of stock on hand should be at any one time. This can then be checked against a valuation of the actual physical quantities to see if there are any losses and, if there are, have them investigated.

Activity 10

A book-keeping system that keeps a record of all movements of stock (in and out) on a stock account will produce a figure for the cost of stock on hand at any one time. But this balance would not be sufficiently reliable for the annual financial statements and it will still be necessary for the trader to carry out an annual stock count in order to determine the cost of stock on hand at the end of the period. See if you can think of a reason why this is so, and make a note of it here.

Because of the varied nature of stock, and the fact that it is often on open display, it is much more difficult to exercise control over stocks than it is for cash at bank. If stock has been 'lost', the cost of these losses forms part of the cost of sales for the year, even though the stock has not actually been sold. This is achieved by deducting the cost of actual stock on hand when calculating cost of sales. You can see how this works by completing a simple activity.

Activity 11

A trader buys four items of stock at a cost of £10 each, two are sold but only one is left in stock at the end of the period (one was stolen). Calculate the cost of sales.

Note that the cost of the goods actually sold is £20 (2 × £10) but the loss of one item of stock is also a cost of earning sales income and so 'cost of sales' is measured at £30.

Book-keeping systems that give a running balance for cost of stock on hand are usually part of a cost accounting system. You will learn about these when studying cost accounting. In simple financial accounting, the cost of sales is not recorded and has to be calculated from the formula previously used, namely:

opening stock, plus purchases, less closing stock.

Furthermore, in simple financial book-keeping the purchases of stock are usually debited to a separate account called 'purchases' and not to the account called stock. The cost of purchases is transferred to the profit and loss account at the end of the year by the double-entry:

debit profit and loss account; credit purchases.

Consequently, the only figure on the stock account throughout the year will be the value of stock brought down from the close of the previous year and forming the opening stock for the current year. It will stay on that account until it is transferred to the profit and loss account at the end of the current year by the double-entry:

debit profit and loss account; credit stock.

Notice how at this point, the profit and loss account has been debited with the cost of opening stock, and the cost of purchases. These are the first two items in the formula for calculating cost of sales. In order to complete the procedure, we need to bring the closing stock (at the end of the current year) into the accounts. This is also done by a double-entry, as follows:

debit stock; credit profit and loss account.

The profit and loss account will now include two debits (the opening stock and the purchases) and one credit (the closing stock). These three items equate to the formula for calculating cost of sales, namely: opening stock, plus purchases, less closing stock. The ledger account called 'cost of sales' does not usually exist in simple financial book-keeping (although it does exist in systems that incorporate cost accounting). Instead, the components for cost of sales are represented by the debits and credits entered in the profit and loss account.

The balance on the stock account is a debit for the cost of closing stock at the end of the current year (opening stock having been transferred to the profit and loss account). When balancing off the ledger at the end of the year, this balance is simply carried down (credit old period; debit new) to become the opening stock for the following year.

The credit balance on the account for sales is transferred to the profit and loss account (debit sales; credit profit and loss) in the normal way, and so the balance on the profit and loss account at this stage will represent the gross profit.

Activity 12

Using the transactions for the second year of the trader in Activity 9, write up the following ledger accounts using the revised system of book-keeping referred to in the above notes. There is no need to balance off the bank account (in any case, we do not know all the entries), but you must deal with all other accounts (stock, purchases, sales, profit and loss) as if balancing off the ledger at the end of the year. Carry down the gross profit on the profit and loss account.

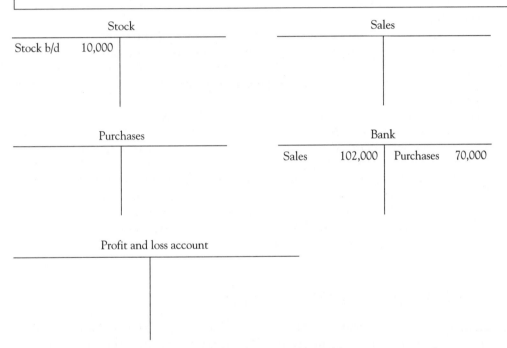

Stock

| Stock b/d | 10,000 | |

Sales

Purchases

Bank

| Sales | 102,000 | Purchases | 70,000 |

Profit and loss account

Many years ago, accountants presented the profit and loss account to the user in a form that was nothing more than a facsimile of the profit and loss account in the ledger. The top part of this account would have looked like the profit and loss account above. You can probably imagine that after bringing down the gross profit on the credit side, the account would have continued with a list of expenses on the debit side of the account.

Figures presented in this format were almost meaningless except for users who had been trained in double-entry book-keeping. Notice, for example, that they do not reveal an amount for cost of sales. A small evolutionary step was to put all the figures for cost of sales on the debit side and present this as an inset calculation, but the profit and loss account was still set out in the form of a two-sided ledger account.

As you know, the profit and loss account today is presented in the form of a narrative statement so that the key figures can be identified by the user. But it is worthwhile thinking about the older format because it acts as a reminder that the profit and loss account (unlike the balance sheet) is an account in the ledger, even though the figures are presented as a narrative statement.

Activity 13

Devise a way of presenting the profit and loss account written up for Activity 12 as a narrative statement. You have done something similar before, but with less detail.

The Key sets out two formats that are in popular use. You might have chosen the first (abbreviated) format because this was used in earlier activities. This form of presentation is prescribed by one of the official formats for limited companies, although it has started to become popular for the accounts of sole traders and partnerships.

However, at this stage of your studies, you should adopt the second format, that is, the one with full details of how cost of sales has been calculated. Most examination questions on the accounts of sole traders set out the profit and loss account in this form, and it seems to be expected that students will present their own answers in a similar way.

This top section of the profit and loss account is sometimes called the 'trading account' because it is where the gross profit on trading is calculated. The next section of the statement, where various operating expenses are deducted from the gross profit, is then called the profit and loss account. You may still find some examiners referring to the complete statement as a 'trading and profit and loss account', but it has become more common to drop the word 'trading' and simply call the whole thing a profit and loss account. Although it now sounds 'old-fashioned' to use the term 'trading and profit and loss account' you had best be guided by the language of the examiner.

Trial balance information

Examiners are not always consistent in the way trial balance information is presented in examination questions. This is partly because they need to test whether students have understood the underlying principles, or whether they have simply learned techniques by rote. Students who have relied on rote learning are likely to get into difficulties when examination information is given in a form that differs from the way information was given when they were learning. The relationship between stock, purchases and cost of sales is a good example of where information can be presented in many different ways.

We will use the second year of our trader in the previous activities to illustrate the point. Interpretation of information in the trial balance will depend on what stage the book-keeping has reached at the time of preparing the trial balance. The trial balance is normally prepared before the closing stock has been entered in the books. In this case the trial balance will include the following figures:

	Debits	Credits
Stock	10,000	
Purchases	70,000	
Sales		102,000

The closing stock (£12,000) is then given as one of the notes to the question and you will have to bring it in to the financial statements as you prepare them. This would simply involve treating it as a credit in the profit and loss account (by deducting it in the cost of sales calculation) and as an asset in the balance sheet.

Apart from tradition, there is no reason why the trial balance has to be given to you in this form.

Activity 14

Suppose the trial balance, in this example, included a debit item of £68,000 that was described as: 'cost of sales'. Which of the following items would you also expect to find in the trial balance?

(a) Stock £10,000 debit.

(b) Stock £12,000 debit.

(c) Neither of these.

Sometimes the trial balance includes a figure for 'gross profit' (which might be called 'trading profit') and sometimes a figure for net profit. These trial balances are simply an expression of the balances in the ledger at particular stages in the balancing-off process. For example, if the trial balance includes a figure described as 'net profit', it simply means that all the revenue items (sales, purchases, stocks, expenses) have been transferred to the profit and loss account in the ledger. Consequently, these individual revenue items will not be shown separately in the trial balance.

If you have worked through the questions at the end of Chapter 3, you will also know that a trial balance is sometimes given as one long list of figures without any distinction between debits and credits. You will have to use your knowledge of book-keeping to identify which is which.

4.2 Trading stock: The conceptual problems

You have been considering the problems of trading stock in so far as they affect the double-entry book-keeping, and the interpretation of accounting information in a trial balance. There are other problems for which practical solutions have to be found based on the accounting concepts involved.

Prudence

Prudence is a fundamental concept in accounting. It was mentioned (briefly) towards the end of Chapter 1. Prudence involves a consideration of two aspects in the calculation of profit:

1. Profits are not anticipated, and are only recognized in the period during which they are received, or their ultimate receipt is reasonably certain. Where profits are recognized in advance of their receipt, a conservative view should be taken of the amount to be received.
2. All losses are recognized as soon as they are known to exist, whether they have been realized or not.

As was mentioned in Chapter 2, one of the problems in accounting is that we have to divide something that is really continuous (the business operating year after year) into artificial slices called the accounting period. In the long term all profits and all losses will be realized, but when calculating profit for any one particular period we need to take a conservative view. Remember that the figure for profit produced by the accountant is often used to determine how much can be distributed to (or withdrawn by) the proprietors. If profits are overstated, and too much is distributed, it could lead to financial problems in subsequent years.

You must now think about unrealized losses in relation to stock. Suppose a trader had purchased an item of stock at a cost price of £10. He had intended to sell it for £15 but it has become damaged (or maybe the demand for this item has dropped) and it can only be sold for £8, which is £2 less than the cost price.

If it is eventually sold for £8 the trader will make a loss of £2, but supposing by the end of the accounting period it has not been sold and forms part of the stock on the shelf – the prudence concept still wants us to recognize the anticipated loss in the current period even though it has not been realized.

Activity 15

See if you can think of a practical way that would ensure that the anticipated loss of £2 is recognized in the profit and loss account for the current period.

You can see how this works by assuming that the purchase of this item was the only transaction in the period. If closing stock had been valued at £10 (its cost price), the trading account would have been as follows:

Sales		nil
Less cost of sales:		
Purchases	£10	
Less closing stock	10	
		nil
Gross profit		nil

Neither a profit nor a loss would have been recognized. If the stock is valued at £8 (its realizable value), the trading account would be as follows:

Sales		nil
Less cost of sales:		
Purchases	£10	
Less closing stock	8	
		2
Gross loss		2

From this simple example, you can see that profits will vary according to the principles used for the valuation of closing stock. Because of this, the Accounting Standards Committee (ASC) issued an accounting standard on stock (known as SSAP 9) several years ago. Strictly speaking, SSAPs are only applicable to the financial statements of companies, but since they represent the codification of best practices they are usually applied universally.

You will learn quite a lot about SSAP 9 as you progress through this book, but for now, we will concentrate on a basic requirement of this standard, which is that closing stock must be valued at the lower of cost or net realizable value. In the above example, cost was £10, net realizable value was £8, the lower of these being £8.

The wording of SSAP 9 had to be a little more precise than this in order to prevent it from being misinterpreted (deliberately or otherwise). In effect, the wording states that stock must be valued on the basis of:

> the total of the lower of cost and net realizable value of the separate items of stock.

Activity 16

See if you can interpret the wording by working on this example. A trader has three items in stock, valued as follows:

	Cost	Net realizable value
Item A	100	200
Item B	200	50
Item C	300	600
Total	600	850

Calculate the value of the stock to be included in the financial statements, using the principles in SSAP 9.

SSAP 9 defines cost as being:

> all expenditure in the normal course of business in bringing stock to its present location and condition.

Some aspects of this definition have more significance in the case of a manufacturing business, which you will be studying in a later chapter. But notice how the definition allows delivery costs incurred (when acquiring the stock) to be included as part of the cost.

Net realizable value is defined as the estimated selling price less the costs of completion and the costs of selling and distribution. Selling and distribution costs relate to things like sales commission and delivery costs; these must be deducted from the estimated selling price when calculating 'net' realizable value.

In the profit and loss account, such costs are not treated as part of the cost of sales in arriving at gross profit – they are usually classified as an expense item called selling and distribution costs, and will be deducted from gross profit along with any other running expenses. The calculation of net realizable value for stock valuation purposes is said to be a 'memorandum' exercise, that is, it is calculated to enable a figure to be written into the ledger; it is not a figure generated by the double-entry book-keeping itself.

It may seem a bit odd to talk about the cost of completion in the definition, but remember that some businesses manufacture or construct their trading stock rather than purchase it from someone else. At any particular accounting date these firms may have stock that is still in the process of being made. Such stock is called 'work-in-progress' and it has to be valued at the lower of cost or net realizable value in the same way as any other stock.

This aspect of the definition for net realizable value can also be applied to a trader who simply buys things for resale. Consider the following example:

> A trader had purchased an item of stock for £100. It could normally be sold for £150 but it has become damaged in the shop and as it stands it could only be sold for £50. However, the trader can get it repaired at a

cost of £20 and if this repair is carried out it is estimated that the item could eventually be sold for £110. The accounting date occurs prior to the repair being carried out.

Activity 17

Try using the definitions and principles from SSAP 9 to calculate the value that would be placed on this item of stock in the accounts.

The estimated loss that will be realized when this item is eventually sold is £10, based on the estimated sales price of £110, less the original cost of £100, and the cost of repairing it at £20. By bringing this item of closing stock into the accounts at a value of £90, the estimated eventual loss of £10 is recognized during the current period. You can prove this for yourself in the next activity.

Activity 18

Assume that the purchase of this stock item was the only transaction in the period. It is valued at £90 for closing stock. On your own paper, set out the trading account for the current period. You have already seen a demonstration of this idea following Activity 14. Your figures should prove that the estimated loss of £10 will be recognized during the current period.

The calculation of net realizable value is a further example of how estimates have to be used in accounting; you have already seen how depreciation has to be estimated.

Costs and unstable prices

It is all too easy to talk about using the cost of an item when valuing stock, and to imagine that this cost is an objective figure. But suppose (as is usually the case) cost prices have been changing throughout the period as a result of inflation – which of all these costs should we use in the calculation? Consider the following example.

A trader deals in one particular type of stock. Throughout the period, 20 items were purchased. Their cost prices in chronological sequence were as follows:

	Total cost (£)
4 items cost £10 each	40
6 items cost £12 each	72
5 items cost £14 each	70
5 items cost £16 each	80
Total 20	262

During the same period, 14 items had been sold for a total amount of £252, and so there were 6 items left in at stock the end of the period.

Out of the 20 items purchased, do we really know which 6 are left on the shelf? When we come to count them we will not find a little label on each one to show how much it had cost. You might be tempted to say: surely the 6 on the shelf would be the 5 that cost £16 each, and 1 out of the 5 that had cost £14 each. You may be right, but we do not know this as a fact. What you have done is make an assumption that the first items to come in would have been the first items to go out.

The situation we have come across here is one where the business will have to adopt what is known as an 'accounting policy'. This involves making an assumption, as you may have done when looking at the example.

It is usually quite realistic to assume that the movement of stock would be on a 'first in, first out' basis. This basis is often used by businesses in determining their accounting policy for stock valuation – it is usually known by the acronym FIFO (pronounced as spelt). But it is not the only policy that could be adopted. There may be cases where the trader considers that a 'last in, first out' basis (known as LIFO) should be used, or even average cost (AVCO).

Apart from being realistic, the FIFO basis also avoids the need for a small business to keep a continuous record of all stock movements. Purchase prices for the units of closing stock can be found by simply working backwards from the accounting date until the number of units purchased equals the number in the closing stock. In the case of LIFO and AVCO, a certain amount of guesswork is needed unless a continuous record of all stock movements is kept.

Accounting systems that keep a perpetual account of stock (i.e. that records stock received and stock sold as each transaction occurs) are normally part of a cost accounting system. The stock account (sometimes called a 'perpetual inventory') will give the cost of stock on hand at any one time, based on the policy adopted for pricing the cost of goods sold.

It is possible to value closing stock under LIFO or AVCO based on details of purchase prices but, unless you are given full details of all stock movements, you will have to use what is known as a 'periodic' basis (as distinct from a 'perpetual' basis). This involves making assumptions. For example, if you were asked to value the 6 items of stock (in the previous example) using a LIFO basis, you would have to assume that the stock consisted of the first 4 items costing £10 each, plus 2 out of the 6 that cost £12 each. A valuation produced by this 'periodic' basis can differ from that produced by a 'perpetual' basis. For example, if you had been given the dates of stock movements, you might have found that the first four items had been sold before the next six arrived.

If a perpetual inventory is kept, and the prices of goods sold are based on AVCO, a new average price is calculated each time stock is purchased. Without details of stock movements, a stock valuation at the end of the period using AVCO has to be based on the average prices for the whole period (£13.10 in the example being discussed). Apart from valuing stock at fictitious prices, the periodic AVCO basis can be criticized on the grounds that the cost of closing stock is influenced by the prices of goods that have long since been sold.

In financial accounting it is usually sufficient to be aware of the different policies that could be adopted for determining the cost of stock, and to understand how reported profits will vary according to the accounting policy chosen.

Activity 19

Do two calculations of gross profit for the above trader. In one calculation use the FIFO basis for valuing closing stock, and use LIFO for the other. You can assume that this is the first year of business, and also assume that the cost of the 6 items on a LIFO basis would be 4 at £10 and 2 at £12. In all cases, net realizable value is in excess of cost and can be ignored.

	FIFO basis	LIFO basis
Sales		
Less cost of sales		
Purchases		
Less closing stock		
Gross profit		

Notice how the effect of FIFO is to charge an amount for cost of sales based on the earliest prices in the period; LIFO charges the latest prices. Consequently, in times of rising prices, FIFO will produce higher profits than LIFO. Which of the two is correct? There is no sensible answer to this question. We cannot really talk about the figures being correct; we can only say they are in accordance with the accounting policy chosen.

You might think that in view of the significant difference in reported profits between the two policies, there would be some rule in SSAP 9 to state which one should be used. There is no rule in SSAP 9, although there are some guidelines.

The SSAP recognizes that the problem of identifying costs when they have been changing throughout the period is a practical problem, not a matter of principle. Consequently, it requires management to choose a method that gives the fairest practicable approximation to actual expenditure on the stock. It then goes on to suggest that LIFO will not normally do this. So the use of LIFO is not specifically banned by the standard, we are simply discouraged from using it.

Other guidance notes in the SSAP state that it would not normally be appropriate to use the latest price for all units in stock since this might involve recognizing an unrealized profit. Look back to our example and you should be able to see that if the 6 units in stock had been valued at £16 each, we would be recognizing a profit of £2 that had not been realized – the trader never purchased 6 items at £16, only 5.

One method that is acceptable under SSAP 9 for a small business is to value stock at selling price and then deduct what is known as the gross profit 'margin'. In practice, this method will give only an approximation to actual cost. The gross profit margin is usually expressed as a percentage of the selling price. For example, if a trader buys an item for £10 and sells it for £15, we would say the gross margin is (5/15), which equals 33.33% (or one-third).

Notice that the £5 added to the cost price is actually 50% of the cost. In order to avoid confusion over this when discussing the percentage of gross profit, the amount added to cost (50%) is called the 'mark up'; the proportion of the selling price which represents gross profit (33.33%) is called the 'margin'. If you look at the trading account in Activity 19 where FIFO was used, you should be able to calculate that the gross profit margin (84/252) is one-third (or say 33.33%) and the mark up is 84/168 or 50%.

4.3 Credit trading

The final part of this chapter deals mainly with the concepts involved when accounting for the purchase and sale of goods on credit terms. You will be learning the general mechanics of the book-keeping in this chapter; the detailed book-keeping is dealt with in Chapter 5.

Revenue recognition: Accruals concept

The concepts involved are related to the realization principle referred to earlier in this chapter. We need only extend the idea a little further to see how it is related to credit transactions. Consider the following sequence of events:

On Monday, a motor parts dealer receives a telephone call from a regular customer asking for a clutch slave cylinder for an old Rover 2000. The dealer does not have one in stock but can order it from a supplier, to arrive on Tuesday. The customer agrees to this arrangement.

On Tuesday, the part arrives at the dealer's premises. On Wednesday the dealer telephones the customer to say it has arrived and the customer asks for it to be delivered. On Thursday the dealer delivers the part, and hands the customer a delivery note but does not collect any cash.

On Friday the dealer sends the customer an invoice. The customer pays the invoice two weeks later. The dealer pays the supplier one month later.

If the whole of this trading cycle had occurred within one accounting period we would not be bothered about anything as far as accounting is concerned – there would have been a purchase and a sale within the period, no matter what principles had been applied. But accounting periods have a habit of ending during the course of hundreds of similar cycles, and so we need to apply rules that will determine the point at which profit should be recognized.

In this example, we need to determine the point at which it would be reasonable to conclude that a sale had been made by the dealer. Between Monday and Wednesday there is very little certainty in the transaction; all kinds of things could have gone wrong that would have allowed either party to back out of the deal. It is quite likely that a lawyer would argue that the sale had actually been made on the Wednesday, because it was at this point the customer had agreed to accept the article (at whatever price was quoted) and the dealer had put it to one side (appropriated it) for the customer.

For practical accounting purposes, it would be more realistic to conclude that the sale had occurred on the Thursday (when delivered) because at this point there was no doubt that the article had been accepted by the customer. It is quite likely that the invoice made out on the Friday was actually dated for Thursday; this is quite normal in practice.

If you accept that the sale was made on the Thursday, it follows that the purchase must have been made on the Tuesday when it was accepted from the supplier. So for Tuesday and Wednesday this article simply becomes a purchase, and an item of stock, as far as the dealer's accounts are concerned.

You will notice that in both cases (sale and purchase) the date at which the cash was exchanged is irrelevant. This is another fundamental concept in accounting. It is called the 'accruals concept'. The accruals concept results in revenues (e.g. sales) and costs being recognized when they are earned or incurred, which is not necessarily the same as when the exchange of cash takes place.

Mechanics of the book-keeping

From the work you have done in earlier chapters, you should be able to sort out the basic double-entry for credit transactions by working on a few simple activities.

Activity 20

During the first year of a new business, a trader sells goods on credit amounting to £50,000. Cash sales amount to £10,000. During this same year, the credit customers pay the trader £45,000 in settlement of their debts. All receipts are paid into the bank immediately. Describe the double-entries that will be made for the following:

1. Sale of the goods on credit.

2. Cash sales.

3. Receipt of cash from the debtors.

Debtors will amount to £5,000 (50,000 − 45,000) at the end of the year. In the books, this balance is carried down into the next year. Several examples of balance sheets that included debtors under current assets have been given in earlier chapters.

Activity 21

At the beginning of the year, a trader owes his suppliers £20,000. During the year, stock amounting to £40,000 is purchased on credit. Cash purchases amount to £5,000, and an amount of £55,000 is paid to the credit suppliers. All payments are made by cheque.

(a) Describe the double-entries that will be made for the following:

1. Credit purchases

2. Cash purchases

3. Payment to creditors

(b) Calculate how much is owing to creditors at the end of the year, and describe where this balance will appear in the financial statements.

The balance owing to creditors could have been found by setting out a ledger account, as follows:

Creditors

Bank	55,000	Balance b/d	20,000
Balance c/d	5,000	Purchases	40,000
	60,000		60,000
		Balance b/d	5,000

An important point to notice in these examples is that cash received from debtors is not treated as a credit to sales; and cash paid to creditors is not treated as a debit to purchases. Receipts from debtors are credited to debtors, payments to creditors are debited to creditors. The actual sales and purchases were entered in the ledger at the time they occurred – to enter them again when the cash comes in or goes out would be double counting.

You should also notice that the book-keeping in these two activities is sufficient to enable the financial statements to be prepared, but it would not be sufficient to enable the trader to run his business. The trader will need to keep a record of the amounts owed by individual customers, and the amounts owing to individual creditors. You will see how this is achieved as part of the book-keeping system when working on Chapter 5.

That concludes your work on credit transactions for the time being. The remainder of this chapter deals with one of the basic accounting standards that all accountancy students should understand and be able to apply, even if it is not specifically mentioned in your syllabus.

4.4 SSAP 2: Disclosure of accounting policies

You have now done sufficient work to appreciate the full impact of one of the basic accounting standards – SSAP 2. This standard does two things:

1. it identifies (and defines) four fundamental accounting concepts
2. it requires companies to disclose (in a note to the financial statements) the accounting policies used in those cases where they have a choice.

The fundamental accounting concepts

Some accounting concepts are observed as a result of long-standing convention. These concepts are so fundamental to the preparation of financial statements that a user can always presume they have been observed unless there is a note to the effect that a different concept has been applied.

The four fundamental concepts identified and defined in SSAP 2 are as follows:

- Going concern
- Accruals
- Consistency
- Prudence

You have come across examples of the accruals concept, and the prudence concept, in this chapter.

Activity 22

Make a note of the situations where you have used the accruals and prudence concepts.

Accruals:

Prudence:

The **accruals concept** is closely related to the 'matching' process mentioned in Chapters 2 and 3, but SSAP 2 does not use the word 'matching' to identify a concept. It does, however, mention (in a discussion of the accruals concept) that revenues should be 'matched' with costs within the same period where their relationship can be reasonably established. A good example of applying the matching (or accruals) convention is when the cost of unsold stock is carried forward at the end of the period – this ensures that the cost of such stock is not matched with the sales for that period.

The **consistency concept** is really concerned with ensuring that accounting policies are not changed from one period to the next. For example, if a business uses FIFO for determining the cost of closing stock in one period, it should not change this to AVCO at the end of the next. If it did so, this would be what is known as a 'change of accounting policy'.

It is permissible to change accounting policies but only where the new policy gives a fairer view. In these cases there must be a note in the financial statements to explain that the accounting policy has been changed, and an indication of the effect this has had on the reported results for the year. This note is required because the fundamental concept of consistency has not been observed.

Activity 23

Why do you think it is important to discourage firms from changing their accounting policy?

The **going concern concept** is mainly concerned with the basis used for determining the amounts shown for assets in the balance sheet. This was mentioned (briefly) in Chapter 2. Balance sheet items are measured and presented on the basis that the business will continue to operate into the foreseeable future, and not on the basis that the business is about to be sold or liquidated.

Activity 24

You came across an example of the going concern concept when learning the meaning of the term depreciation in Chapter 2. Try to describe the example. Think about figures in the balance sheet, not the profit and loss account.

Disclosure of accounting policies

SSAP 2 uses the term 'accounting bases' to describe the methods developed for applying the fundamental concepts. Where there is a choice of accounting bases for particular items, the firm must adopt one of them. Once adopted, this base becomes the firm's accounting policy. This policy must be applied consistently, and disclosed as a note to the financial statements. Consider the following example of an accounting policy note:

> Stock is valued at the lower of cost and net realizable value. Costs are determined on a first in first out basis.

A breakdown of this statement could be as follows:
1. The two fundamental concepts to be applied in the case of stock are accruals (or matching) and prudence. This is achieved by carrying forward closing stock at the lower of cost and net realizable value.
2. There is a choice of accounting bases for identifying cost; the firm could have used FIFO, LIFO, AVCO or one of several others. It has chosen FIFO and so this becomes its accounting policy.

Summary

You have covered a lot of ground in this chapter, but the main learning points can be identified as follows:
- in simple financial book-keeping there is no such thing as a stock account to record the continuous movements of stock received and stock sold

- the cost of stock received is debited to an account called purchases, the cost of stock sold is not recorded
- stock on hand at the end of the period has to be counted and valued at the lower of cost or net realizable value for each item of stock
- once counted and valued, this stock is written into the books by double-entry – debit stock; credit profit and loss account
- trial balances can be extracted at different stages of the book-keeping process; exam questions often expect students to identify the stage reached
- cost of sales is a calculation derived from the formula: opening stock, plus purchases, less closing stock
- the valuation of closing stock has a significant impact on the figure for cost of sales and, therefore, on the amount of profit reported
- because of this, there is an accounting standard (SSAP 9) which defines cost and net realizable value, and also sets out the principles to be used for stock valuation
- when costs have been changing throughout the period, the firm has a choice of accounting bases that could be used to identify particular costs
- the accounting base chosen (FIFO etc.) becomes the firm's accounting policy, which must be applied consistently from one period to the next
- profit is recognized on an accruals basis, e.g. sales are recognized as soon as they are earned, which may be in advance of the cash receipt in the case of a credit transaction
- the accruals concept is always tempered by prudence, e.g. sales are recognized only if their ultimate realization is reasonably certain, but all losses are recognized as soon as they are known to exist, even if unrealized
- SSAP 2 recognizes four fundamental concepts that are presumed to have been observed in the preparation of financial statements, namely: going concern, accruals, consistency, and prudence.

Activity 1
The cost of sales is unlikely to have been recorded.

Activity 2
By physically counting all the items in the shop, listing them on a piece of paper, and then calculating their cost from information on the purchase invoices.

Activity 3
The cost of goods sold in the period can be found by deducting the cost of closing stock from the cost of goods purchased during that period.
1. Cost of sales = £40,000, i.e. cost of purchases £50,000 less cost of closing stock £10,000.
2. Gross profit = £20,000, i.e. sales of £60,000 less cost of sales £40,000.

Activity 4
The additional £5,000 gross profit has not yet been earned. It will be earned only when the goods are eventually sold, presumably during the next accounting period.

Activity 5
1. Purchases £50,000: debit stock; credit bank.
   Sales £60,000: debit bank; credit sales.
   Cost of sales £40,000: debit cost of sales; credit stock.

2. The debit balance is carried down to the next period by crediting the old period with £10,000 and debiting the new period with £10,000.

Activity 6
By carrying down the £10,000 as closing balance on the stock account, i.e. credit the old period with £10,000 and debit the new.

Activity 7
They are exactly the same.

Activity 8
(1) The cost of opening stock (last year's closing stock brought down), and (2) the cost of purchases during the second year.

Activity 9
1. Cost of sales is £68,000, calculated as follows:

Cost of opening stock	10,000
Add cost of purchases	70,000
	80,000
Less cost of closing stock	12,000
Cost of sales	68,000

2. Gross profit is £34,000, i.e. sales of £102,000 less cost of sales £68,000.

Activity 10
The stock account only shows what the cost of stock on hand should be; this will not necessarily be the same as the actual quantities valued at cost. Stock may have been lost or pilfered, or book-keeping errors could have been made. The financial statements must show an amount for the actual stock, not an amount which it should be according to the books.

Activity 11

Cost of purchases (4 × £10)	40
Less cost of closing stock (1 × £10)	10
Cost of sales	30

Activity 12

Stock

Stock b/d	10,000	P & L a/c	10,000
P & L a/c	12,000	Stock c/d	12,000
	22,000		22,000
Stock b/d	12,000		

Sales

P & L a/c	102,000	Bank	102,000
	102,000		102,000

Purchases

Bank	70,000	P & L a/c	70,000
	70,000		70,000

Bank

Sales	102,000	Purchases	70,000

Profit and loss account

Opening stock	10,000	Sales	102,000
Purchases	70,000	Closing stock	12,000
Gross profit c/d	34,000		
	114,000		114,000
		Gross profit b/d	34,000

Activity 13

There are two popular formats:

1. The abbreviated format used in previous activities:

Profit and loss account for year 2

Sales	102,000
Cost of sales	68,000
Gross profit	34,000

This format is normally used in the annual financial statements presented to the shareholders of a company.

2. A detailed format, as follows:

Profit and loss account for year 2

Sales		102,000
Less cost of sales:		
Opening stock	10,000	
Purchases	70,000	
	80,000	
Less closing stock	12,000	
		68,000
Gross profit		34,000

Activity 14

The answer is (b). If cost of sales has been determined, the closing stock must already have been entered in the books and so it will appear as one of the debit items in the trial balance.

Activity 15

By including this item in closing stock at its realizable value of £8 instead of at its cost price of £10.

Activity 16

In total, the cost of £600 is lower, but SSAP 9 requires the lower of cost and net realizable value to be considered for each separate item. Consequently the values to use are: A £100, B £50, and C £300, i.e. a total of £450.

Activity 17

The answer is £90. Cost is £100; net realizable value (i.e. eventual selling price of £110, less cost of completion £20) is £90; the lower of these two is £90.

Activity 18

Sales		nil
Less cost of sales:		
Purchases	100	
Less closing stock	90	
		10
Gross loss		10

Activity 19

	FIFO		LIFO	
Sales	252		252	
Less cost of sales:				
Purchases	262		262	
Less closing stock	94		64	
		168		198
Gross profit		84		54

Activity 20

1. Debit debtors £50,000; credit sales £50,000.
2. Debit bank £10,000; credit sales £10,000.
3. Debit bank £45,000; credit debtors £45,000.

Activity 21

(a) 1. Debit purchases £40,000; credit creditors £40,000.
   2. Debit purchases £5,000; credit bank £5,000.
   3. Debit creditors £55,000; credit bank £55,000.
(b) Closing creditors will be: £5,000, i.e. 20,000 + 40,000 − 55,000. This will appear under creditors due within one year in the balance sheet.

Activity 22

Your answers could have been:
Accruals, when recognizing a sale at the time it occurred and not when the cash was received. Prudence, recognizing a loss as soon as it was known to exist, even if unrealized, e.g. by reducing the value of closing stock to net realizable value when this was less than cost.

Activity 23

It would be possible to manipulate the figures (e.g. profits) between periods by simply changing the policy used.

Activity 24

Fixed assets are shown at cost less the amount written off as depreciation. This is called 'net book value' and no attempt is made to determine the realizable value of fixed assets.

Questions for self-assessment

Answers to self-assessment questions are given at the end of the book.

4.1 From the following trial balance extracted from Ann Ford's books at 30 June 1993, and the additional notes, prepare her financial statements for the year.

	Debit	Credit
Sales		100,000
Stock	10,000	
Purchases	70,000	
Delivery expenses	2,000	
Salaries and wages	20,000	
Electricity	1,000	
Drawings	5,000	
Debtors	4,000	
Creditors		2,000
Bank	1,000	
Long-term loan		10,000
Freehold property	50,000	
Motor vehicles	10,000	
Capital – cash introduced		40,000
Capital – retained profits		21,000
	173,000	173,000

Notes: Stock at 30 June 1993 was counted and valued as follows: the total cost amounted to £13,050, but on closer inspection it was found that one of the items, which had cost £100, had a net realizable value of £50. Depreciation has been, and is to be, ignored.

4.2 Brian Fuzzy runs a small retail business, and his cousin Ima Medlar keeps the books. Ima had been on a course to learn double-entry book-keeping, and had done most of the entries correctly. Like a lot of students, Ima always found the book-keeping for closing stock a little confusing and tended to skip over the subject, hoping she would be able to sort it out with a little practical experience. After taking out a trial balance at 31 December 1993 she was very pleased to find that she could make it balance. The trial balance was as follows:

	Debit	Credit
Sales		130,690
Stock at 1 January 1993		10,700
Stock at 31 December 1993	7,800	
Purchases	92,150	
Selling and distribution expenses	6,000	
Administration expenses	10,600	
Drawings	9,000	
Debtors		5,000
Creditors	5,800	
Bank	7,100	
Long-term loan payable	6,000	
Freehold property	50,000	
Motor vehicles	10,000	
Capital – cash introduced		40,000
Capital – retained profits		18,060
	204,450	204,450

Ima shows you the trial balance and asks you to check it for any errors. You notice that there are a few mistakes. The amounts and descriptions were correct but it looks as if it balanced only because Ima was determined to make it do so by shuffling the balances around.

Following your examination of the trial balance, you are invited to check some of the transactions during the period. You find that the following matters need to be taken into account:

(i) the closing stock of £7,800 was valued at cost, but some of the items included at a cost of £600 had a net realizable value of £100;

(ii) cash of £300 received from one of the debtors has been credited to sales instead of to the debtors account;

(iii) some of the purchases supplied by a creditor had been returned to the supplier because they were damaged in transit. The supplier has accepted the goods back and promised to send Brian Fuzzy a credit note. The original purchase of £600 has been recorded in the books but because no credit note had been received by the end of the year, no adjustment for the return has been made.

Required:

(a) Set the original trial balance out correctly. You must ignore the adjustments resulting from notes (i), (ii) and (iii) when doing this.

(b) Use your corrected trial balance resulting from (a) together with the additional notes (i), (ii) and (iii), in order to prepare the financial statements for year ending 31 December 1993. Depreciation is to be ignored.

4.3 The following question appeared in the June 1990 ACCA Level 1 Accounting exam. At this stage of your studies, you may have difficulty in recognizing the significance of some of the information given. Because of this, some tutorial guidance notes are included at the end of the question, which obviously did not appear in the original. Also, some of the wording has been changed in order to make the information easier to recognize.

A firm produces a standard manufactured product. The stages of the production and sale of the product may be summarized as follows:

Production stage	A	B	C	D
Production activity	raw material purchased	WIP stage 1	WIP stage 2	finished product
Costs to date	£100	£120	£150	£170
Net realizable value	80	130	190	300

Trading stage	E	F	G	H
Trading activity	available for sale	sale agreed	delivered to customer	account paid
Costs to date	£170	£170	£180	£180
Net realizable value	300	300	300	300

Required:

(a) What general rule do accountants apply when deciding when to recognize revenue on any particular transaction?

(b) Apply this rule to the above situation. State and explain the stage at which you think revenue will be recognized by accountants.

(c) How much would the gross profit on a unit of this product be? Why?

(d) Suggest arguments in favour of delaying the recognition of revenue until stage H.

(e) Suggest arguments in favour of recognizing revenue in appropriate successive amounts at stages B, C and D.

Tutorial guidance notes:

1. Manufactured products may go through several distinct stages in the manufacturing process, e.g. cutting, assembly, finishing. At the end of each intermediate stage (e.g. cutting and assembly) the partly manufactured stock is called 'work-in-progress', often abbreviated to WIP as in the question. Costs on the product will accumulate as it progresses through the various stages. At the end of the final process (e.g. finishing) the item is available for sale and is usually called a finished product.

2. Both raw materials and WIP will have a net realizable value, which can be more or less than cost. You may be puzzled over why the raw materials in the question should have a net realizable value which is less than their cost immediately after they have been purchased. After all, if the business paid £100 for raw materials, surely they could be sold for £100. There could be several explanations, e.g. maybe there are disposal costs, or maybe the raw materials are specialized components that could only be sold for scrap if not incorporated into the finished product. You must simply accept the figures, and discuss accordingly.

Questions without answers

Answers to these questions are published separately in the *Teacher's Manual.*

4.4 Colin Meadows started a new business as a retailer on 1 January 1993. His first transaction was to introduce cash of £150,000 into the business. At the end of his first year of trading, he presents you with a list of the balances in his ledger and asks you to prepare the financial statements. The list was as follows:

Capital – cash introduced	150,000
Land and buildings	70,000
Fixtures and fittings	14,000
Stock	60,000
Cost of sales	240,000
Sales	300,000
Debtors	60,000
Creditors	40,000
Long-term loan payable	10,000
Interest	1,000
Rent	2,000
Wages	20,000
Rates and insurance	6,000
Sundry expenses	4,000
Drawings	18,000
Bank	9,000

As you can see, some of the information is not clear, particularly as balances are not identified as debits and credits. You can assume that the list is complete, that no book-keeping errors have been made, and that when the list is properly arranged the trial balance will balance.

Required:

(a) Set out the list in the form of a trial balance, so that you can ascertain the correct nature of (i) rent, (ii) interest, and (iii) bank.

(b) Prepare the financial statements, ensuring that the profit and loss account shows full details of how 'cost of sales' was derived.

4.5 Caroline Davey is a sole trader who started trading on 1 July 1993. In preparation for the opening of the business she had introduced her own cash into the business and also cash of £48,000, which she had borrowed from her father on an interest free business loan. The total amount of cash introduced was sufficient to purchase premises costing £70,000, fixtures and fittings costing £6,000, 40 items of stock at £120 each, and leave cash in the business bank of £2,200. The loan from her father was to be repaid over 12 years, the first repayment being due in 1 year's time.

Caroline deals in one particular product and during July 1993 the following stock movements (in addition to the purchase of opening stock) took place:

10 July	Purchased 30 items at £120 each
15 July	Sold 50 items for £200 each
20 July	Purchased 20 items at £130 each
25 July	Sold 10 items for £250 each

During July, Caroline paid operating expenses of £560 for the month. By 31 July, Caroline had paid for all the purchases apart from the stock purchased on 20 July. She had also been paid for all the sales apart from those made on 25 July. Caroline had not made any withdrawals of cash for herself, and the bank balance at 31 July was £8,040.

Required:
(a) Showing clearly all your workings, and using the FIFO method of stock valuation, prepare Caroline Davey's profit and loss account for the month of July 1993, and her balance sheet at 31 July 1993. Depreciation of fixed assets should be ignored.
(b) Calculate the closing stock value on a LIFO basis, using:
  (i) a perpetual basis for the valuation
  (ii) a periodic basis for the valuation.

(AAT Certificate, Dec 90, modified, part (b) added)

4.6 The annual final accounts of business are normally prepared on the assumption that the business is a going concern.

Required:
Explain and give a simple illustration of

(a) the effect of this convention on the figures that appear in those final accounts.
(b) the implications for the final accounts figures if this convention were deemed to be inoperative.

Note: Although the examiner has asked for only one illustration, try to give three separate examples.

(ACCA 1.1, Jun 86)

4.7 (a) A firm buys and sells two models, P and Q. The following units costs are available (all figures are in £s and all the costs are borne by the firm).

	P	Q
Purchase cost	100	200
Delivery costs from supplier	20	30
Delivery costs to customers	22	40
Coloured sales packaging costs	15	18
Selling price	150	300

Required:
Calculate the figure to be included in closing stock for a unit of each model, according to SSAP 9.

(b) A firm has the following transactions with its product R

Year 1
Opening stock: nil
Buys 10 units at £300 per unit
Buys 12 units at £250 per unit
Sells 8 units at £400 per unit
Buys 6 units at £200 per unit
Sells 12 units at £400 per unit

Year 2
Buys 10 units at £200 per unit
Sells 5 units at £400 per unit
Buys 12 units at £150 per unit
Sells 25 units at £400 per unit

Required:
Calculate on an item by item basis for both year 1 and year 2:

(i) the closing stock;
(ii) the sales;
(iii) the cost of sales;
(iv) the gross profit;

using, separately, the LIFO and the FIFO methods of stock valuation. Present all workings clearly.

(c) Paragraph 39 of SSAP 9 suggests that the LIFO stock figure at the end of year 1 in (b) above would be a 'misstatement of balance sheet amounts' and would potentially cause a 'distortion of current and future results'.

Required:
Comment on these suggestions, using the situation and calculations from part (b) above as an illustration. Your answer should indicate the extent to which you agree with the comment in paragraph 39 as regards the use of the LIFO method of stock valuation.

(ACCA 1, Jun 94)

5 ▷ The basic framework of the books

Objectives

After you have completed this chapter, you should be able to:
- design a basic double-entry book-keeping system
- write up books of original entry, and use them for posting to the ledger
- operate a book-keeping system where accounts for debtors and creditors are segregated from other accounts in the ledger
- locate book-keeping errors, identify their effect, and make corrections
- identify components in a computer book-keeping system

Introduction

This chapter completes the story on the basic process of double-entry recording. It puts the last piece of the puzzle in place, and is the last chapter in which you will be working on the book-keeping in any great detail.

The learning activities are designed to give you an opportunity of working with all the key elements in the book-keeping system, although examiners usually test your competence in this subject by setting problems on book-keeping errors. This is quite realistic; accountants in practice are not usually involved in writing up books but they must know how the system works in order to locate and correct any errors made. It is impossible to acquire the skills on this unless you first acquire the basic skills in processing the transactions.

Although value added tax (VAT) has its strongest impact at the book-keeping level covered by this chapter, it will again be ignored in all the activities. To do otherwise would slow down the learning process unnecessarily. You will find it quite easy to see how the basic system has to be modified to accommodate VAT when studying Chapter 7.

5.1 The need for a primary record of transactions

In the previous two chapters, you posted the double-entry for various transactions directly into the ledger accounts. You were able to do this either because there were only a few transactions, or the information needed (total sales, or total purchases, for the period) was provided as part of the data. We gave no thought as to how such data would have been collected by the system in the first place.

When you think of the thousands of transactions that are likely to take place during an accounting period, it is quite unrealistic to imagine that a double-entry for each one could be posted shortly after it occurs. The system will have to include some form of initial record for each transaction to enable the double-entry to be posted at a later stage. For recurrent transactions (such as sales and purchases) it will be necessary to accumulate periodic totals for posting rather than attempt to post a double-entry for each single transaction.

The accountant must therefore organize the recording process to capture accounting data at source (i.e. when the transaction occurs), and then to sort these data into various groups to enable the appropriate double-entries to be posted in the ledger.

All accounting records up to the stage where the double-entry is finally posted are called primary accounting records. If any 'books' are used in this process they are referred to as primary books, or books of original entry. They contain information for the double-entry posting; they are not books in which any aspect of the double-entry is posted.

Most businesses need to process large volumes of data and use computers to deal with many stages of this process, including the final double-entry. Consequently, only the smallest of entities use 'books' that are written up manually. However, the basis of recording is the same whether the process is carried out in handwritten records or on a computer. Since it is easier for learners to visualize books in which figures are entered manually, the book-keeping covered by this chapter is based on a manual system. The same principles are applied to electronic systems, and some insight into this is given at the end of the chapter.

When a transaction takes place, there is usually some kind of document (produced or received) that forms an initial record of the transaction, e.g. a business selling goods on credit will send a sales invoice to the customer and keep a copy of the invoice as a record of the transaction. Documents such as copies of sales invoices are often called 'source documents' since they are the source from which the first entries are made in the books.

The complete cycle of recording can be illustrated as follows:

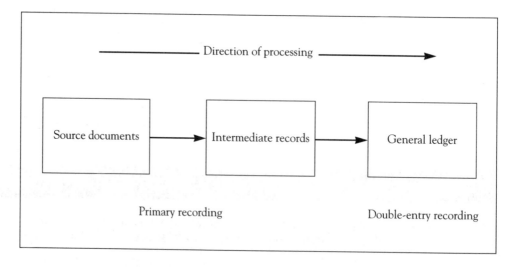

![Activity 1 icon]

Activity 1

Various documents are used as a source for primary recording. See if you can name documents that might be used to record the following transactions.

Transaction	Source document used for primary recording
1. Sale of goods on credit	
2. Purchase of goods on credit	
3. Cheque payment to a supplier	
4. Payment for a cash purchase	
5. Cash received through the post from credit customers	
6. Money paid into the bank	

5.2 The journal

It is easier to appreciate the modern structure of primary accounting records if we first look back a few hundred years to see how our ancestors might have entered transactions in a book of original entry.

In those days, transactions were relatively few in number. Each one could be entered in a book of original entry almost as soon as it occurred. The book used was called a 'journal' – meaning a daily record or diary. Initially, the journal simply contained a description of each transaction as it occurred, very much like an entry in a diary. For example:

> Jan 3 Purchased 50 kettles from Mr Black at a cost of £2 to be paid in one month's time.

The journal would then be taken up by the book-keeper from time to time and used to post the double-entry in the ledger.

Eventually, the journal evolved into a book where each transaction was described in double-entry format. Notes were added to explain the entry. The previous example might have been entered in the journal as follows:

		Debit	Credit
Jan 3	Purchases account	£2	
	Mr Black		£2

> Being the purchase of 50 kettles from Mr Black on one month's credit

You will have to try to imagine this entry being made on a page in a book that has two cash columns down the right-hand side, one headed 'Debit' and the other 'Credit' (sometimes the abbreviations **Dr.** (for debit) and **Cr.** (for credit) are used instead).

It would still have been necessary for someone to post the double-entry in the ledger. The only difference between this and the first example is that the name of the ledger accounts to be debited and credited have been set out in the journal entry, together with the amount to be posted to each account. In other words, the journal is being used partly as an initial record of the transaction, and partly as an instruction to the person writing up the ledger to debit and credit the specific accounts named in the journal.

The journal is still used this way in modern practice but (as you will discover in a moment) it is not used to record every single transaction. You will see why after you have worked through the following activity. Initially, you must think of this activity as an opportunity to practice your ability to recognize the double-entry aspect of individual transactions.

Activity 2

Following this activity box there is a list of transactions for the first month of a new business. You are required to set these out as entries in the journal. In other words, for each transaction you must identify the account to be debited by naming that account and putting the amount in the debit column; then set out the credit aspect in a similar way. You can omit the notes that normally follow each journal entry.

A sample set of working sheets is provided at the end of this chapter (pages 126-9). These are intended to be used for various stages in one particular exercise. If you feel apprehensive about making mistakes when writing in the text book, you could either use a pencil, or your own paper, for your first attempt. Working Sheet 1 represents a blank page from the journal and should be used for this first activity.

Details for the activity

P. Muhone has set up business trading in cement. All money received is banked immediately, all payments are made by cheque. The following are the first month's transactions:

Jan 1   Opened up a business bank account for the new business with £10,000 paid in from personal funds
Jan 2   Purchased delivery truck for £5,000
Jan 3   Purchased £5,000 worth of cement from Portsea Ltd on credit
        Purchased office stationery from Pronto Printers Ltd for £50 on credit
Jan 4   Sold cement to I. Chitalu on credit for £200
Jan 5   Sold cement to P. Chilumbu on credit for £350
Jan 6   Sold cement to A. Tembo on credit for £6,000
Jan 7   Cash sales of cement £300
Jan 8   Purchased another £500 worth of cement from J. Godfrey Ltd on credit
Jan 9   Sold cement to TAC Ltd on credit for £1,000
Jan 10 Received cheque of £150 from I. Chitalu
Jan 11 Received cheque of £350 from P. Chilumbu
Jan 12 Received cheque of £4,500 from A. Tembo
Jan 16 Withdrew £1,000 from the business bank account for personal use
Jan 17 Paid Portsea Ltd £1,000
Jan 18 Paid £500 to MPC Garages for motor running expenses
Jan 19 Paid J. Godfrey Ltd £400

Return to these notes after completing the journal entries, and after checking your work with the answer given in the Key.

You have made an initial record of each transaction in a journal but the double-entry must still be posted in the ledger. Imagine how laborious this would be, even with a simple contrived example like this one – it seems as if we are doing everything twice. Furthermore, some ledger accounts will have a large number of entries in them if each individual transaction is posted.

Activity 3

Look back through your journal entries and you will find there are certain types of transaction that seem to occur quite frequently. There are four types. See if you can identify them and write down an appropriate heading for each type.

1.
2.
3.
4.

In a business of any size, there would normally be separate staff (or departments) to deal with each of the four types of transaction. This makes it impracticable to have a single journal which is passed around from one department to the other. This separation of duties suggests that separate journals for each particular type of transaction are needed.

Separate journals are used for credit sales and credit purchases. The journal for credit sales is sometimes called the 'sales journal' although it is more usual to call it the sales day book. The same thing applies to credit purchases; the journal for these is sometimes called the 'purchases journal' but it is more common to use the name purchases day book. You might still come across instances where these books are referred to as journals, but in modern practice they are usually called 'day books' – they certainly do not look anything like the journal that you wrote up for Activity 2.

5.3 The design and function of the day books

In designing the layout of any accounting record, we have to keep in mind the way in which the information recorded might have to be used in the future. We will look at credit sales first.

Credit sales

In the case of credit sales, the day book will record details to help with various subsequent tasks, including details to help someone find a copy of the sales invoice when a customer complains about the amount charged. In the context of double-entry book-keeping, it is more important to realize that the information in the day book is used in a subsequent stage of the recording process, i.e. when posting the double-entry in the ledger.

> ### Activity 4
>
> With these points in mind, make a note of the kind of information that you think should be recorded in the sales day book.

Each page of the sales day book could therefore be ruled up as follows:

Date	Invoice no.	Name of customer	Amount

The above ruling would be sufficient for a business that does not intend to analyse sales according to product type. If such an analysis is required, it will be necessary to include analysis columns to the right of the amount column. These columns will be headed according to the desired classification of sales, for example food, confectionery, clothing, etc.

Activity 5

Working Sheet 2 at the end of this unit includes a blank page from the sales day book of P. Muhone. Enter the credit sales from Activity 2 into this day book.

Imagine you have got a copy of the sales invoice in front of you as you make each entry. Since the details given in the exercise did not include any invoice numbers, you can assume that the first invoice was pre-numbered 001, the next 002, and so on.

The mistake that beginners often make at this stage is to include cash sales in the day book. But the sales day book is used for recording credit sales; you will see how cash sales are dealt with when we look at bank transactions in a moment.

Activity 6

Before going on you should stand back for a moment and reflect on the entries in the sales day book that you have written up. You can probably imagine how each entry will be used to debit the accounts of individual customers, such as I. Chitalu, P. Chilumbu, etc., but think about the ledger account for sales. Do we really need to credit the sales account with each individual amount?

Activity 7

Go back to your sales day book and, if you have not already done so, add up the 'amount' column and write in the total at the foot of that column.

In effect, the details in the sales day book are a substitute for a composite journal entry which, if it had been set out in the actual journal, would have taken the following form:

	Debit	Credit
I. Chitalu	200	
P. Chilumbu	350	
A. Tembo	6,000	
TAC Ltd	1,000	
Sales		7,550

Being credit sales for the month of January

You will be posting the double-entry from the details in your sales day book in a later activity but, before doing that, you must write up the complete set of books of original entry.

Credit purchases

The purchases day book is similar to the sales day book in design and function, but there are likely to be credit transactions other than those for the purchase of goods for resale. For example, in the case of P. Muhone there was a credit purchase of stationery. In fact, most businesses will have credit suppliers for various items, such as garage services, packing materials, and so on.

The purchases day book for P. Muhone could be ruled up similar to the example given below. The exact number of analysis columns will depend on how many different types of credit transaction are likely to occur. The column headed 'etc.' has been included here to indicate that further columns might be needed in the future (but not for the present activity).

Date	Invoice ref.	Name of supplier	Total	Purchases	Stationery	etc.

The invoice reference column might be used in one of two ways:

1. to enter the supplier's invoice number – this would be useful when entering details in the supplier's account; or
2. the business may assign its own serial number for filing purposes – this would enable the invoice to be traced should there be a query later.

There is no universal system.

It might seem a little strange to have a 'total' column as well as the individual analysis columns, but there are various reasons for this. In the first place, a particular credit supplier may provide more than one type of supply, e.g. goods for resale and also stationery for use in the office. In this case it is the amount in the total column that will be entered in the supplier's account.

Later on you will see how the total column is used when the ledger itself is sub-divided, but there is no need to think about this for the time being.

Notice how the accuracy of the total column can be checked by adding the totals for the analysis columns. In manual book-keeping, this kind of check is called 'cross casting'.

As was the case with the sales day book, you can think of the purchases day book as representing a kind of composite journal entry. If the details for this entry had been set out in the actual journal, they would have been in the following form:

	Debit	Credit
Purchases	5,500	
Stationery	50	
Portsea Ltd		5,000
Pronto Printers Ltd		50
J. Godfrey Ltd		500
	5,550	5,550

Being credit purchases for the month of January

Now that you have seen how credit transactions are recorded in the primary records, we can turn our attention to the other group of transactions that recur frequently: money banked and money paid out of the bank.

5.4 Bank transactions

Up to now, you have always entered bank transactions directly into a ledger account called 'bank'. The sheer volume of bank transactions that occurs in a real business makes this process impracticable.

Cheque payments

As regards cheque payments, the initial record could be the details written out on the cheque stub. This should show the date of the cheque, the person to whom the cheque was paid, the reason for the payment, and the amount.

We could pass the cheque stubs to the book-keeper from time to time in order to post up the double-entry for each payment. This is not very sensible because apart from the volume of entries, there will be certain types of payment that are repetitive. This suggests that we need a system for accumulating periodic totals so that only one debit entry needs to be made in the ledger for each type of payment.

The book in which this collating process is carried out is usually called the 'cash book'. Sometimes the cash book is designed to record both receipts (bankings) and payments, although in a business of any size, the receipts and payments are dealt with in separate books. Apart from convenience, this division enables the work to be segregated between two employees, and segregation of duties is one way in which a business can reduce the risk of losses through fraud.

In this text book we will assume that receipts and payments are dealt with in separate books.

Activity 10

A number of analysis columns will be needed in the payments cash book in order to accumulate periodic totals for each class of payment. Look back to the transactions in Activity 2 and see if you can set out a list of the headings that will be needed. Take your time over this; it is not such a simple problem as it might at first appear.

You must be careful over how you interpret two of these headings, i.e. fixed assets and creditors.

Fixed assets (you may have written down motor vehicles) are not acquired very often and only one column is needed to cope with the various classes of fixed asset that might be purchased. It will be easy enough for the book-keeper to look back to an individual entry in the cash book to see the class of fixed asset (motor vehicles, premises, office equipment, etc.) that was purchased.

As regards creditors, beginners often make mistakes over this. You may have been tempted to write down the heading as purchases. But payments to credit suppliers such as Portsea Ltd are not payments for purchases, they are payments to creditors.

Activity 11

If we had headed the column 'purchases' (and included the payments to Portsea Ltd and to J. Godfrey Ltd under this column), the total of the column would be debited to purchases at the end of the period. Describe why this would be wrong in this particular case.

Activity 12

It might be necessary to have a column in the payments cash book for purchases (but not in our example). See if you can think when this would be, and make a note of it here.

There are usually more payments to creditors than any other class of payment, and so the first analysis column in the payments cash book is often used to record payments to creditors.

Activity 13

A blank payments cash book has been set out in Working Sheet 2. Enter the cheque payments from Activity 2 and total the columns.

If this book is now collected by the person who writes up the ledger, it can be used to post the double-entry for cheque payments.

Activity 14

Simulate the effect of this double-entry posting by setting out a composite journal entry, in the same form as those demonstrated earlier for the day books.

                              Debit   Credit

These composite journal entries are not actually written out anywhere in practice. We have been doing them merely to illustrate how the books of original entry are used to collate data for the periodic double-entry posting in the ledger.

Bank receipts

The receipts are dealt with in a similar fashion to payments. One difference you will find in practice is that there are fewer classifications of receipts than there are of payments, although this may not be very apparent from our simple example.

Activity 15

Read through the receipts in Activity 2 and identify the headings that will be needed for the receipts cash book.

The total column will show the total of daily bankings. As with creditors, you must be careful over how you think about cash received from debtors. The sale to debtors is recorded as a result of entries in the sales day book; we do not credit sales again when the cash is received, we credit the debtor.

Activity 16

A suitable cash receipts book has been set out in Working Sheet 2. Use this to enter the relevant transactions from Activity 2.

At this stage of your studies, you can probably use your imagination to see how the double-entry posting would be carried out from the information in this book.

You might be wondering about the total of receipts from debtors (£5,000) since we do not seem to be using this figure anywhere in the double-entry posting. Similarly, there seems to be no use made of the total payments to creditors recorded in the payments cash book. You will see the significance of these totals when we come to divide up the ledger during the later stages of this chapter.

5.5 The role of the journal

If you think about the work you have been doing in Activities 5 to 16, you will realize that all the transactions originally written into the journal have now been entered in four different books of original entry, namely:

- credit sales in the sales day book
- credit purchases in the purchases day book
- cheque payments in the cash paid book
- money banked in the cash received book.

In the case of P. Muhone, no entries have been left in the original journal. The journal is still used in modern book-keeping practice, but not for the day-to-day transactions. There will be unusual transactions (and a number of adjustments) which must be recorded in a book of original entry that do not fall under any of the four categories listed above. Consider the following example:

Instead of bringing cash into the business, the proprietor introduces another type of asset such as a motor car worth £5,000. This transaction must be entered in the books and it must be recorded in a book of original entry (double-entries are never written directly into ledger accounts). The only place where the transaction can be written down is in the journal.

Activity 17

The original capital introduced into a business by a sole trader includes a motor car valued at £5,000 which will be used to visit customers. Record this transaction (including the narrative) in the journal. Ignore the distinction between contributed capital and retained profits by assuming that a single capital account will be kept.

              Debit   Credi

The journal is also used to set out double-entries for the correction of errors, and for any adjustments at the end of the period such as depreciation and closing stock. You will be using the journal for correcting errors later in this chapter.

5.6 Practice exercise in posting from books of original entry

You have now set up four books of original entry which contain all the transactions from Activity 2. If your books agree with the Key, we can proceed with the next stage.

Activity 18

You must now post the double-entries in the ledger by using figures from your books of original entry. The ledger accounts are set out on the **two** pages for Working Sheet 3. Please take account of the four points listed below before proceeding.

1. The entries must be made from the books of original entry, not from the list of journal entries from Activity 2. For example, there should only be one entry on the debit side of the bank account, and only one entry on the credit side.
2. In order to save time, and in view of the restricted space on each ledger account, you should observe the following rules:
   (a) dates (and invoice numbers for debtors) may be omitted on all accounts;
   (b) the short description that normally names the account in which the opposite entry has been posted can be omitted. In its place you should name the book of original entry from where the figure was obtained. You may use the following abbreviations:

SDB = sales day book   PCB = payments cash book
PDB = purchases day book RCB = receipts cash book

3. Ignore the two accounts with no headings on them for the time being; you will be using these later. The accounts for individual debtors and creditors have been separated from other accounts in the ledger (see the second page of Working Sheet 3, but you should think of them as being part of the general ledger for this activity). You will see why they have been separated when working on Activity 21.

4. Do not balance off any of the ledger accounts at this stage, and check your work with the Key after completing the activity.

There are several variations to this basic system. For example, you may find that the cash book is not separated between receipts and payments, the balance on the bank account is carried down in the cash book itself, and there is no bank account in the actual ledger.

In these cases, the system is operated as if the ledger account for bank had been physically removed from the ledger, entries in the bank account being represented by entries in the cash book itself. Such a system uses the cash book as a ledger account and a book of original entry at the same time. You will only find this being done in small organizations.

5.7 Sub-dividing the ledger

If you look back at your ledger in the previous exercise you will notice there are quite a number of accounts for debtors. In a real business there could be many hundreds of debtors, and also a great many creditors. In book-keeping jargon the accounts for these debtors and creditors are referred to as 'personal accounts'.

The book-keeping can be operated more efficiently if these personal accounts are removed from the ledger and dealt with in separate sub-ledgers. Some of the reasons for doing this are as follows:

1. The detailed book-keeping for debtors and creditors can be carried out by separate departments, one department being responsible for the debtors and another for creditors. These two departments are usually referred to as the sales ledger department and purchase ledger department, respectively. Other labels are sometimes used.

2. If the personal accounts were left in the ledger, the trial balance would be long and unwieldy. You will see in a moment that when the personal accounts are removed from the ledger they are replaced by two single accounts, one giving the total amount owing by debtors and one giving the total amount owing to creditors. The balances on these single accounts are then included in the trial balance.

3. Some book-keeping errors result in the trial balance failing to agree. It can be quite difficult to locate these errors but the task is made much easier if the ledger has been divided into sections. It may be difficult for you to appreciate this point until after you have seen how the system works.

The accounts remaining in the ledger after removing the personal accounts are sometimes called 'nominal' accounts, and the ledger itself is usually called the **nominal ledger**. In most businesses there will, therefore, be three ledgers, i.e.

- the nominal ledger
- the sales ledger (with an account for each debtor)
- the purchase ledger (with an account for each creditor).

This sub-division is achieved by removing the personal accounts from the main ledger and replacing them with two single accounts called **control accounts**. One of these accounts is called the **sales ledger control account** and the other is called the **purchase ledger control account**. These control accounts are kept in the nominal ledger and the double-entry system is designed so that the sales ledger control account gives the total amount owing by debtors, and the purchase ledger control account the total amount owing to creditors.

The trial balance is actually extracted from the nominal ledger, and this will include the balances on the two control accounts. The two subsidiary ledgers (for debtors and creditors) provide a detailed breakdown of these control accounts by showing how much is owing by individual debtors, and how much is owing to individual creditors.

5.8 Control accounts

The control accounts in the nominal ledger serve several functions, one being to ensure that the nominal ledger is self-balancing. The trial balance extracted from the nominal ledger will then contain all the information needed to prepare the financial statements, including total debtors and total creditors. You will see in a moment why the accounts in the nominal ledger are called 'control' accounts. For the time being, you should think of them as total accounts.

Debtors

The control account for debtors will be debited with the total sales for the period and credited with the total cash received from debtors during the period (in much the same way as the bank account was debited with total bankings and credited with total payments). The balance carried down on this account will then represent the total debtors at the end of the period (and total debtors for the start of the next).

Activity 19

Look back to the books of original entry used in Activity 18. See if you can find where the total amounts for posting to the control account are recorded. Make a note (including the amounts) in the following table:

Figures for sales ledger control account	Where recorded	Amount
1. Total sales to debtors		
2. Total cash received from debtors		

Creditors

The control account for creditors is dealt with in a similar way to that for debtors. The total of credit purchases will be credited to the control account, and the total payments to creditors will be debited. The balance represents the total amount due to creditors carried down into the next period.

Look back to the books of original entry used in Activity 18. See if you can find where the total amounts for posting to the control account are recorded. Make a note (including the amounts) in the following table:

Figures for purchase ledger control account	Where recorded	Amount
1. Total purchases on credit		
2. Total payments to creditors		

The next activity should be completed in stages. Try not to rush the activity; it provides a key to the whole basic process.

Do this in stages.

Stage 1
Go back to the ledger accounts that you wrote up for Activity 18 and head up the two blank ledger accounts. Name one of them 'Sales ledger control account' and the other 'Purchase ledger control account'.

Stage 2
Now imagine that the individual debtors and creditors accounts have been removed from the ledger and are replaced by these two control accounts (the page separation and the dotted lines might help you to form an image of separate ledgers). Post the relevant totals noted in Activities 19 and 20 to these two control accounts.

Stage 3
Balance off the two control accounts by carrying the balances down into the next period.

The double-entry when control accounts are used

The double-entry posting is actually completed in the nominal ledger. Entries in the sales ledger, and in the purchase ledger, are an additional sub-routine and do not form part of the double-entry posting. This sub-routine is obviously important because although the financial statements are prepared showing total debtors and creditors, the business entity will want to know how much is owed by each debtor and how much is owing to each creditor.

You can get an idea of the revised double-entry system by thinking about debtors. When the individual debtors were treated as separate accounts within the general ledger we saw that the double-entry was effectively as follows:

	Debit	Credit
I. Chitalu	200	
P. Chilumbu	350	
A. Tembo	6,000	
TAC Ltd	1,000	
Sales		7,550
	7,550	7,550

When the individual debtors are removed from the general ledger, they are replaced by a single control account. In this case, the double-entry becomes:

	Debit	Credit
Sales ledger control account	7,550	
Sales account		7,550

As an additional sub-routine, the individual debtors accounts are debited with their respective amounts, but you must not think of these debits as being a part of the double-entry. You must be clear over this because it affects the way you will deal with certain types of book-keeping error.

There ought not to be any doubt over the way the double-entry works when control accounts are kept in the nominal ledger. Unfortunately, some text books have created a slight ambiguity in the subject by suggesting that the double-entry is to the individual personal accounts and that the control account is an extra 'memorandum' record (i.e. not part of the double-entry). This is completely at odds with modern practice and makes a nonsense of the self-balancing nominal ledger. In order to remove any doubt, most examination questions on this topic make it clear that the control accounts are an integral part of the nominal ledger.

Using the control accounts

In our simple system, the books of original entry will have to be passed to the person who keeps the nominal ledger, and to those who keep the sub-ledgers for debtors and creditors. The person writing up the nominal ledger will post up the totals; those who write up the sub-ledgers will use the individual amounts in order to keep a detailed account for each debtor or creditor.

You can see the end result of this process by looking at the ledger accounts for P. Muhone. Admittedly you had already posted up the personal accounts during the first part of the exercise, but you can easily imagine that they would look as they do now if they had been posted up after entering the totals in the control accounts.

If the transactions for the period are posted in total to control accounts, and then posted individually to the personal accounts, the balance on the control account should equal the total of all the balances on the individual accounts. In this way the two control accounts in the nominal ledger act as a control over accuracy of processing in the sub-ledgers.

At regular intervals (usually at the end of each month) there is a routine reconciliation procedure to ensure that the balance on each control account agrees with the total of all the individual balances in the personal ledger. The sales ledger department will make a list of all the amounts owing by individual debtors and the total of this list should agree with the balance on the sales ledger control account. The same procedure is applied to creditors.

Activity 22

Balance off the personal accounts in P. Muhone's sales ledger and purchase ledger. Write out a list of the individual debtors and creditors in the space below. Total each list and check that the totals agree with your control account balances in the nominal ledger.

Debtors listing

I. Chitalu

P. Chilumbu

A. Tembo

TAC Ltd

Total _____

Creditors listing

Portsea Ltd

J. Godfrey Ltd

Pronto Printers Ltd

Total _____

It should now be possible for you to work out how control accounts help to locate book-keeping errors. Consider the following:

Suppose, when balancing off the accounts, you had calculated A. Tembo's balance as £500 instead of £1,500. If the personal accounts were part of the ledger (i.e. control accounts had not been used), the trial balance would not have agreed. In order to locate the error you would have to check through all the nominal accounts and all the personal accounts.

By using control accounts, the error in balancing A. Tembo's account will not affect the trial balance. But since the total of the list of debtors will not agree with the balance on the control account, we know that there must be an error either in the control account or in an individual debtor's account. The system has helped to isolate where the error has occurred.

5.9 Identifying the effect of errors and making corrections

The skills that you have been learning in this chapter are usually tested by accounting examiners in the form of questions on book-keeping errors. Quite often you are asked to correct these errors through the journal. The first stage in the learning process is to think about the effect of each error.

The effect of errors

The effect varies according to the nature of the error. The following activity is designed to see if you can identify the effect that different types of error will have on:

1. agreement of the trial balance totals, and
2. agreement of the control account balance with the total of the list of debtors.

Activity 23

Delete the words Yes or No, as appropriate, in the following table:

Description of six mutually exclusive errors	Will the trial balance totals agree?	Will the total of the debtors list agree with the control account?
1. A sale of £100 to J. Smith has been debited to the account of J. Smythe	Yes/No	Yes/No
2. A sales invoice of £390 for R. Brown has been entered in the day book as £930	Yes/No	Yes/No
3. The balance on J. Patel's account has been worked out at £450 whereas it should have been £45	Yes/No	Yes/No
4. The total sales in the day book was shown as £6,500, whereas it should have been £6,600	Yes/No	Yes/No
5. The total of £7,500 in the sales day book was correctly credited to sales, but debited to the sales ledger control account as £7,800	Yes/No	Yes/No
6. An item in the sales day book of £530 for G. Gloor was debited to his account as £350	Yes/No	Yes/No

The next stage is to identify which accounts are incorrect, and by how much. You can think about this in terms of accounts being overstated and understated. Some errors result in two (sometimes three) accounts being wrong, in others only one account will be wrong. You must try to think this through carefully because the way in which errors are corrected is simply a logical progression from understanding the effect of each error.

Activity 24

For each of the errors in Activity 23, identify, as appropriate, any account overstated or understated, and the amounts in each case. Set out your answers in the following table:

Error no.	Accounts overstated and the amount	Accounts understated and the amount
1		
2	Three accounts are overstated (i) (ii) (iii)	
3		
4		Two accounts are understated (i) (ii)
5		
6		

Correcting the errors

Where only one account has been affected, the error is usually corrected by a direct manual alteration of the incorrect figure. Where two accounts are incorrect by the same amount (one having the wrong debit and the other the wrong credit) the error can be corrected by setting out a double-entry in the journal.

The other point to keep in mind is that entries in individual debtor's accounts do not form part of a double-entry; they are memorandum entries. Consequently, if an incorrect amount is debited (or credited) to a single debtor, only one account will be affected and it cannot be corrected by setting out a double-entry in the journal.

In Chapter 7 you will see how something called a 'suspense account' is used to make the trial balance totals agree (or to make the total of the list of debtors agree with the control account) until the errors are found and corrected. In such cases it will be possible to correct all errors by a double-entry in the journal, but there is no need to think about this at the moment.

In the above exercise, errors 3, 5, and 6 will have to be corrected by alteration of the incorrect figures. In error 2, the account of R. Brown will also be corrected in this way. The remaining errors can be corrected by setting out a double-entry in the journal.

For example, in the case of error number 1, the debit is on J. Smythe's account instead of J. Smith's. This can be corrected by a journal entry set out as follows:

	Debit	Credit
J. Smith	£100	
J. Smythe		£100

*Being invoice number ... originally posted to
J. Smythe's account in error, now corrected*

Sometimes the sales ledger department will have its own journal for this kind of correction. A separate journal is then used for corrections in the nominal ledger.

Activity 25

Set out journal entries to correct errors in the nominal ledger resuling from error number 2 and error number 4.

	Debit	Credit
Error 2		
Error 4		

In a well-designed computer book-keeping system, none of the errors described in Activity 23 should arise. Errors 3, 4, 5 and 6 would be impossible (unless the program had been corrupted in some way), and errors 1 and 2 should be caught by controls built into the system.

Error 1 (debiting the wrong personal account) should be caught by what is known as a redundant data check, whereby data input consists of two identifiers, i.e. the customer's account number and the customer's name. If the two identifiers do not match, the input is rejected. Error 2 (which is an error of original entry) will be caught by a control procedure known as a 'batch total'. The batch of sales invoices being processed is manually totalled prior to processing on the computer. This total is then compared with a total generated by the computer after the batch of invoices has been processed. Any discrepancy between the two totals will indicate an error in data transcription.

However, examination questions continue to be set in this area as if all book-keeping is done on a manual basis.

5.10 Sales returns and purchase returns

There is one further small point to think about in order to conclude your studies in this chapter. It is quite easy to follow, and simply requires you to think about sales and purchases in reverse.

Sometimes, goods purchased on credit terms are returned to the supplier. This usually happens when the goods are found to have been damaged in transit, or when the wrong goods have been delivered.

When goods are despatched to a customer, a sales invoice is raised and entered in the sales day book. When goods are delivered by a supplier, an invoice will be received and entered in the purchases day book. What happens if the goods (in whole or in part) are later returned by the customer, or returned to the supplier?

Sales returns and credit notes

In order to cancel (or reduce) the original charge to the customer, a 'credit note' is raised. All credit notes are then entered in a 'sales returns day book' in much the same way as all invoices are entered in the sales day book. The individual entry in the sales returns day book will be credited to the debtor's personal account, thereby cancelling (or reducing) the original debit from the invoice in the sales day book.

In the nominal ledger, an account called 'sales returns' is usually kept. The balance on this account is debited to the profit and loss account at the end of the period. When the profit statement is prepared for the user, sales returns are deducted from sales – although it is more usual in practice simply to show one figure for the net sales (i.e. sales, less sales returns).

Activity 26

Describe the double-entry in the nominal ledger for the periodic total of all credit notes entered in the sales return day book.

Debit:

Credit:

Purchase returns and debit notes

The treatment of purchase returns is a mirror image of that for sales returns. Instead of waiting for a credit note to be received from the supplier, a debit note is raised and entered in the purchase returns day book. This will be debited to the supplier's personal account to cancel (or reduce) the original credit entry.

In the nominal ledger, a purchases returns account is kept. This is dealt with in a similar way to sales returns, i.e. the credit balance on the purchases returns account will be deducted (or set against) purchases in the profit statement.

Activity 27

Describe the double-entry in the nominal ledger for the periodic total of all debit notes entered in the purchase returns day book.

Debit:

Credit:

5.11 Computer systems

Electronic data processing (EDP) is really a separate subject but the work that you have been doing in this chapter will help you to recognize the elements in a computerized system. For example, if your role is to enter payments received from debtors, you will have to navigate your way through a series of menus on the computer screen. In some ways this is similar to the way that you withdraw cash from a cash dispenser at a bank where you first have to enter an identification (ID) number before you are allowed access to a series of subsequent menus. In computerized accounting systems the ID number is replaced with a password.

The way that you access the various accounting modules will depend on the application package being used. The following brief explanation is based on the TAS BOOKS system developed by ComoPharm Ltd trading as MEGATECH Software. This is a DOS based program which can be run through Windows 3.1 or Windows 95. In the explanation and graphics that follow, we have assumed that the system is being operated through Windows 95 and that your role is to enter payments received from debtors. After the password procedure you will be presented with a screen on which a number of menus are offered. The following graphic shows part of the screen.

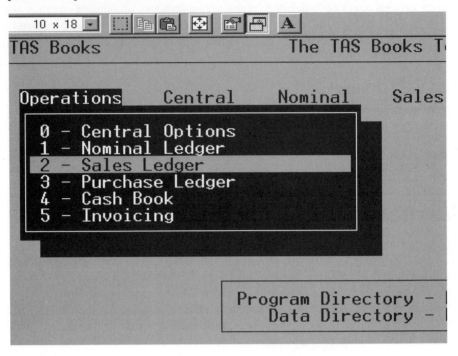

In this case we have highlighted Module 2, Sales Ledger. When you press the enter key (or type the number 2) the pop-up menu will switch to the sales ledger module and you will be presented with the following options.

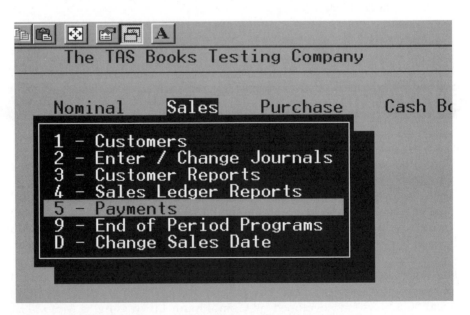

We have highlighted option 5 (Payments). When you press the enter key (or type 5) you will be presented with a sub-menu, as follows.

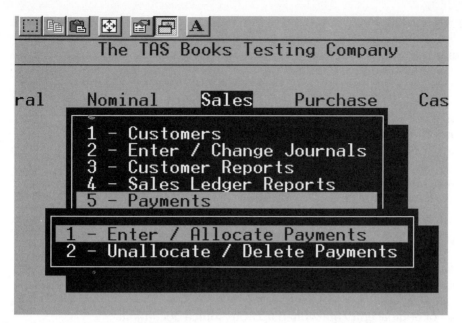

By selecting option 1 you will gain access to the program that allows you to enter a batch of receipts from customers.

In this particular system, all double-entry recording is done in real time. For example, entering receipts from customers will update both the sales ledger accounts and the bank account. You might have noticed that the first screen shot included a module for Invoicing (Module 5 in the opening screen). This particular module will debit the customer and credit the relevant nominal account at the time the invoice is prepared (it also provides a check on the credit status of the customer). The same real time processing occurs when posting invoices received from suppliers.

The impact of computers on double-entry book-keeping has presented accounting examiners with a difficult problem. In the first place, the examiners recognize that it is vital for those who operate a computerized system to have training in double-entry accounting. The computer has removed the task of writing down figures, casting and posting entries to a manual ledger, but the whole system is still based on the double-entry principles discussed in this and earlier chapters. It could be quite dangerous for anyone to operate a computerized system without knowledge of these principles. The producers of computer accounting packages recognize this: TAS Books, for example, include a short tutorial on double-entry accounting in their training manual.

But it seems that the only way of training and examining students on double-entry accounting is through the medium of manual book-keeping records which hardly exist any more. If a small business intends to rely on manual book-keeping, those records are not likely to be kept on double-entry principles. They will be kept on a cash basis as described in Chapter 9 (Incomplete records). If a small business does intend to keep double-entry records it will use a computer system since such systems are no longer an expensive luxury. We cannot claim that manual double-entry records have a place in the underdeveloped world – you do not have to visit too many of these countries to find that businesses there are using the latest computer technology.

There is nothing wrong in learning double-entry principles through the medium of handwritten records providing examiners would stop setting questions on book-keeping errors that cannot occur in a computerized system. As was stated in section 5.9, most of the book-keeping errors that students are asked to cope with in accounting exams are not likely to occur in a well-organized computer book-keeping system. The program itself will eliminate arithmetic errors in the processing of data. Many errors of data input can be detected either by controls that are built into the program or by controls that are operated manually in conjunction with the program.

We can still make errors – a wrong nominal ledger code will result in an incorrect posting – but many of the errors that were the hallmark of manual book-keeping questions simply do not exist any more. It must be quite difficult for trainees who are operating computer systems to come to terms with things that might have happened in a previous generation.

Summary

The key learning points in this chapter can be summarized as follows:

- transactions cannot be entered directly into ledger accounts; they must first be recorded in books of original entry
- books of original entry are written up from source documents
- there are four main books of original entry for credit transactions, namely: the sales day book; the purchases day book; the sales returns day book; and the purchase returns day book
- the cash book is used as a book of original entry for bank transactions
- in small entities, the cash book replaces the bank account in the ledger and contains a detailed record of individual receipts, individual payments and the balance at bank
- in larger organizations, the cash book is divided between the receipts cash book and the payments cash book. An account for bank is retained in the ledger for recording total receipts for the period, total payments for the period and the balance at bank
- all books of original entry are designed to enable periodic totals to be posted to accounts in the nominal ledger, and individual amounts to personal accounts
- personal accounts (debtors and creditors) are not carried in the nominal ledger; they are dealt with in subsidiary ledgers; they are represented in the nominal ledger by two single control accounts in which total transactions for the period are recorded
- transactions posted individually to personal accounts are also posted in total to control accounts
- at the end of a period, the balance on a control account should equal the total of all the balances in the subsidiary ledger
- the double-entry is carried out in the nominal ledger; entries in subsidiary ledgers are not part of the double-entry
- the journal is also a book of original entry but is mainly used for unusual transactions and for the correction of errors; entries in the journal state the names of the accounts to be debited and credited, together with the amounts
- electronic systems are based on the same book-keeping structure as manual systems; they eliminate the likelihood of arithmetic errors being made, and most errors of data input can be detected by appropriate controls

The following diagram summarizes the manual book-keeping structure dealt with in this chapter. For the sake of clarity, returns day books have been omitted.

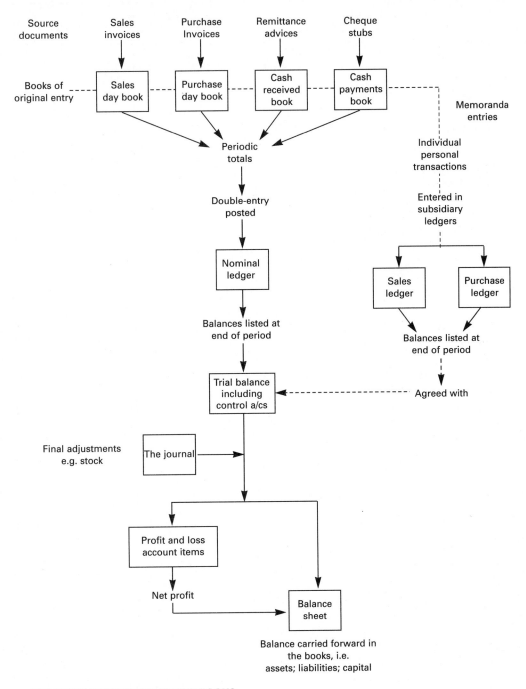

THE BASIC FRAMEWORK OF THE BOOKS

Journal of P. Muhone

	Debit	Credit

Working sheet 2

The four books of original entry for P. Muhone

Sales day book:

Date	Inv. no.	Name of customer	Amount

Purchases day book:

Date	Inv. no.	Name of supplier	Total	Purchases	Stationery	etc.

Payments cash book:

Date	Name	Amount	Creditors	Fixed assets	Drawings	Motor expenses

Receipts cash book:

Date	Details	Total	Debtors	Cash sales	Drawings

P. Muhone's ledger

Nominal accounts

Capital account

Motor vehicles

Purchase

Stationery

Sales

Motor expenses

Drawings

Bank

P. Muhone's ledger

Creditors

Portsea Ltd

Pronto Printers Ltd

J. Godfrey Ltd

Debtors

I. Chitalu

P. Chilumbu

A. Tembo

TAC Ltd

Activity 1

You might have stated the following:

1. A copy of the sales invoice
2. The purchase invoice received from the supplier
3. Perhaps the cheque counterfoil (cheque stub)
4. The invoice received from the supplier
5. A remittance advice of some kind (quite often the invoice, or monthly statement, returned by the debtor with the cheque)
6. Copy of the bank paying-in slip

Activity 2

		Debit	Credit
Jan 1	Bank	10,000	
	Capital a/c – cash introduced		10,000
Jan 2	Motor vehicles	5,000	
	Bank		5,000
Jan 3	Purchases	5,000	
	Portsea Ltd		5,000
Jan 3	Stationery	50	
	Pronto Printers Ltd		50
Jan 4	I. Chitalu	200	
	Sales		200
Jan 5	P. Chilumbu	350	
	Sales		350
Jan 6	A. Tembo	6,000	
	Sales		6,000
Jan 7	Bank	300	
	Sales		300
Jan 8	Purchases	500	
	J. Godfrey Ltd		500
Jan 9	TAC Ltd	1,000	
	Sales		1,000
Jan 10	Bank	150	
	I. Chitalu		150
Jan 11	Bank	350	
	P. Chilumbu		350
Jan 12	Bank	4,500	
	A. Tembo		4,500

Jan 16	Drawings	1,000	
	Bank		1,000
Jan 17	Portsea Ltd	1,000	
	Bank		1,000
Jan 18	Motor expenses	500	
	Bank		500
Jan 19	J. Godfrey Ltd	400	
	Bank		400

Activity 3

You might have spotted (though not necessarily in this order) the following:
1. Credit sales
2. Credit purchases (but not as frequent as credit sales)
3. Cheque payments
4. Cash bankings

Activity 4

You could have included: date of sale; customer's name; invoice number (in case we need to trace it later); amount charged to the customer.

Activity 5

You will find a complete set of books of original entry on page 134.

Activity 6

No, we could credit the sales account with total sales for the month.

Activity 7

Total sales are £7,550 (deliberately not included in the answer to Activity 5).

Activity 8

By using analysis columns, similar to those used by a business that analyses its sales according to product type.

Activity 9

You will find a complete set of books of original entry on page 134.

Activity 10

Apart from a total column, we will need the following four headings for the analysis columns: Fixed assets; Drawings; Creditors; Motor expenses.

Activity 11

Because the purchases from Portsea Ltd and J. Godfrey Ltd would have been debited to purchases as a result of the entry in the purchases day book. We should not debit purchases again when the payment is made – we must debit the creditor.

Activity 12

If some purchases are made on cash terms instead of credit.

Activity 13

You will find a complete set of books of original entry on page 134.

Activity 14

	Debit	Credit
Portsea Ltd	1,000	
J. Godfrey Ltd	400	
Motor vehicles	5,000	
Drawings	1,000	
Motor expenses	500	
Bank		7,900
	7,900	7,900

Activity 15

Columns will be needed for: Capital; Cash sales; Debtors; and the Total.

Activity 16

You will find a complete set of books of original entry on page 134.

Activity 17

	Debit	Credit
Motor vehicles	5,000	
Capital		5,000

Activity 18

The ledger accounts for this activity are set out on pages 135–6.

Activity 19

1. Sales day book, total of 'amount' column £7,550.
2. Cash received book, total of 'debtors' column £5,000.

Activity 20

1. Purchases day book, total of 'total' column £5,550.
2. Payments cash book, total of 'creditors' column £1,400.

Activity 21

Your control accounts should look like the following:

Sales ledger control account			
Jan 31 Sales	7,550	Jan 31 Bank	5,000
		Jan 31 Bal c/d	2,550
	7,550		7,550
Feb 1 Bal b/d	2,550		

Purchase ledger control account			
Jan 31 Bank	1,400	Jan 31 Purch.	5,550
Jan 31 Bal c/d	4,150		
	5,550		5,550
		Feb 1 Bal b/d	4,150

Activity 22

Debtors listing		Creditors listing	
I. Chitalu	50	Portsea Ltd	4,000
P. Chilumbu	0	J. Godfrey Ltd	100
A. Tembo	1,500	Pronto Printers Ltd	50
TAC Ltd	1,000		
	2,550		4,150

Activity 23

Error number	Trial balance agree?	List/control agree?	Tutorial comment
1	Yes	Yes	The debit is simply on the wrong debtor's account
2	Yes	Yes	The wrong amount has been recorded in sales and in the control account; and also in the debtor's account
3	Yes	No	The balance on J. Patel's account is not included in the trial balance (the trial balance includes the control account)
4	Yes	No	Totals are posted in the nominal ledger; the wrong total has been posted to both sales and the control account
5	No	No	Debits in nominal ledger are £300 more than the credits; an incorrect amount has been debited to the control account
6	Yes	No	Total of debtors list will be less than the balance on the control account

Activity 24

Error no.	Accounts overstated and the amount	Accounts understated and the amount
1	J. Smythe, by £100	J. Smith, by £100
2	(i) Sales, by £540 (ii) Sales ledger control, by £540 (iii) R. Brown by £540	None
3	J. Patel by £405	None
4	None	(i) Sales, by £100 (ii) Sales ledger control, by £100
5	Sales ledger control, by £300	None
6	None	G. Gloor, by £180

Activity 25

	Debit	Credit
Error number 2		
Sales	£540	
Sales ledger control		£540

Being invoice number … to R. Brown, incorrectly entered in the sales day book as £930 instead of £390

	Debit	Credit
Error number 4		
Sales ledger control	£100	
Sales		£100

Being correction of error resulting from the sales day book being undercast by £100

Activity 26

Debit sales returns account; credit sales ledger control account.

Activity 27

Debit purchase ledger control account; credit purchases returns account.

The complete set of books for P. Muhone are set out below.

Books of original entry for P. Muhone

After completing **Activity 5**, your sales day book should look like this:

Date	Invoice no.	Name of customer	Amount
Jan 4	001	I. Chitalu	200
Jan 5	002	P. Chilumbu	350
Jan 6	003	A. Tembo	6,000
Jan 9	004	TAC Ltd	1,000

After completing **Activity 9**, your purchases day book should look like this:

Date	Invoice no.	Name of supplier	Total	Purchases	Stationery	etc.
Jan 3		Portsea Ltd	5,000	5,000		
Jan 3		Pronto Printers Ltd	50		50	
Jan 8		J. Godfrey Ltd	500	500		
			5,550	5,500	50	

After completing **Activity 13**, your payments cash book should look like this:

Date	Name	Amount	Creditors	Fixed assets	Drawings	Motor expenses
Jan 2	Delivery truck	5,000		5,000		
Jan 16	Self-drawings	1,000			1,000	
Jan 17	Portsea Ltd	1,000	1,000			
Jan 18	MPC Garages	500				500
Jan 19	J. Godfrey Ltd	400	400			
		7,900	1,400	5,000	1,000	500

After completing **Activity 16**, your cash received book should look like this:

Date	Details	Total	Debtors	Cash sales	Capital
Jan 1	Capital introduced	10,000			10,000
Jan 7	Cash sales	300		300	
Jan 10	I. Chitalu	150	150		
Jan 11	P. Chilumbu	350	350		
Jan 12	A. Tembo	4,500	4,500		
		15,300	5,000	300	10,000

P. Muhone's ledger

Nominal accounts

Capital account

		RCB	10,000

Motor vehicles

PCB	5,000		

Purchases

PDB	5,500		

Stationery

PDB	50		

Sales

		SDB	7,550
		RCB	300

Motor expenses

PCB	500		

Drawings

PCB	1,000		

Bank

RCB	15,300	PCB	7,900

Creditors

Portsea Ltd

PCB	1,000	PDB	5,000

Pronto Printers Ltd

	PDB	50

J. Godfrey Ltd

PCB	400	PDB	500

Debtors

I. Chitalu

SDB	200	RCB	150

P. Chilumbu

SDB	350	RCB	350

A. Tembo

SDB	6,000	RCB	4,500

TAC Ltd

SDB	1,000	

Questions for self-assessment

Answers to self-assessment questions are given at the end of the book.

5.1 Extract a trial balance from P. Muhone's nominal ledger (this chapter, Working Sheet 3) and prepare his financial statements. The closing stock is valued at a cost price of £500. Depreciation is to be ignored.

5.2 The opening balances in Mary McGregor's books at 1 January included the following:

	£
Purchase ledger control account	15,892
Sales ledger control account	34,975

During the year to 31 December, the following transactions (among others) took place:

	£
Credit sales	418,930
Cash sales	86,450
Credit purchases	278,560
Cash purchases	10,398
Amounts received from credit customers	398,764
Amounts paid to suppliers	262,318
Returns to credit suppliers	1,456
Returns by credit customers	682

Write up the purchase ledger control account, and the sales ledger control account, for the year. Balance off the two accounts at the end of the year.

5.3 Sellabrick, a firm trading as builders' merchants, purchases stock on credit from a large number of suppliers. The company maintains a purchase ledger control account as an integral part of its double-entry book-keeping system and in addition maintains supplier accounts on a memoranda basis in a purchase ledger. At the end of the financial year ended 31 May 1987 the balance of £25,450 on the purchase ledger control account failed to agree with the total of balances from the purchase ledger. The following errors have subsequently been discovered.

1. Goods which cost £350 and which were purchased on credit from Green, a supplier, had been entered in the purchase day book at their retail price of £600
2. An amount of £1,500 paid to Hunt, a supplier, had been correctly entered in the cash book but had been entered in Jackson's account as £1,550
3. The return of goods purchased on credit and costing £800 had been completely omitted from the books
4. The purchases day book had been undercast by £2,220

Required:
(a) A purchase ledger control account showing clearly all of the amendments to the original balance.
(b) A calculation showing the total of the balances in the purchase ledger before the corrections were made.

Author's guidance note: For part (b) you have to assume that after correcting the errors discovered, the total of the list of balances will agree with the control account.

(AEB A Level, Jun 87)

5.4 On 1 January 1991 the accounting records of Wholesalers plc included the following balances (all figures are in £000):

Sales ledger control account   50

Individual sales ledger memorandum balances:

Customer			
A	debit	10
B	debit	20
C	debit	8
D	debit	9
E	debit	6
F	credit	2
G	credit	1

The following unaudited information is presented to you concerning the year 1991:

Sales day book			Receipts cash book	
Customer	Amount		Customer	Amount
A	30		A	37
B	35		B	30
D	18		C	5
E	9		D	20
F	8		E	12
G	7		F	6
			G	4
	117			114

Sales return book	
Customer	Amount
A	2
F	3
	5

Required:

(a) Prepare sales ledger control account, and memorandum sales ledger accounts for each customer, for the year 1991. Carry down year-end balances and prove that the sales ledger control balance reconciles with the memorandum balances. The ledger accounts may be presented in any summarized form you find convenient, provided all entries are clear.

(b) State **two** advantages of preparing both memorandum and control records.

Author's guidance notes:
1. Give some weight to the word 'unaudited'.
2. There are many reasons why debtors' accounts are sometimes credit balances. You will be thinking about this in Chapter 7; in the meantime simply accept it.

(*ACCA 1.1, Dec 91, modified*)

Questions without answers

Answers to these questions are published separately in the *Teacher's Manual*.

5.5 The accounts department of Winterperry plc is divided into various sections. The section in which you work is responsible for entering relevant transactions into the Journal, the Sales Journal, and the Returns Inwards Journal. The following list represents all the transactions that took place on Monday 10 December. Some of these require action by your section; others will be passed on to different sections:
1. An invoice for £327 is issued to B. Danbury for the sale of goods.
2. It is discovered that goods costing £322 and purchased from D. Gaunt on 20 November had been entered in the account of A. Gaunt.
3. Howson Supplies Ltd sell £686 of goods to Winterperry plc on credit.
4. Cash sales of £185 are made to H. Linton.

5. A credit note is issued to T. Goodwin for £43.
6. Repairs to machinery costing £123 are paid by cheque.
7. An invoice is received from A. Clarkson for goods costing £294.
8. New equipment is purchased from Stanton Supplies Ltd for £2,120. Payment is made by cheque.
9. It is discovered than an invoice for £73 (for goods purchased) received in October from Dennis & Co had been treated in the books as a credit note received.
10. Credit notes are received from J. Pearce for £61 and N. Nogan for £126.
11. An invoice for £420 is issued to P. Craft for the sale of goods.
12. It comes to light that during the previous month the total of the Purchases Journal, amounting to £9,420, had been debited to the sales account.
13. Goods totalling £46 are returned by J. Fortune, a credit customer, and the relevant documentation is issued.

Required:
Enter the transactions belonging to your section into a Journal, a Sales Journal and a Returns Inwards Journal, as appropriate. Narratives are not required.

Author's guidance note: You should assume that personal accounts are kept in the general ledger (this note was not in the original question).

(AAT Certificate, Dec 90, modified)

5.6 The trial balance of Happy Bookkeeper Ltd, as produced by its book-keeper, includes the following items:

Sales ledger control account   £110,172
Purchase ledger control account   £ 78,266

You have been given the following information:
(i) The sales ledger debit balances total £111,111 and the credit balances total £1,234.
(ii) The purchase ledger credit balances total £77,777 and the debit balances total £1,111.
(iii) Included in the credit balance on the sales ledger is a balance of £600 in the name of H. Smith. This arose because a sales invoice for £600 had earlier been posted in error from the sales day book to the debit of the account of M. Smith in the purchase ledger.
(iv) An allowance of £300 against some damaged goods had been omitted from the appropriate account in the sales ledger. This allowance had been included in the control account.
(v) An invoice for £456 had been entered in the purchase day book at £654.
(vi) A cash receipt from a credit customer for £345 had been entered in the cash book as £245.
(vii) The purchase day book had been overcast by £1,000.
(viii) After making corrections relating to the above, a trial balance was extracted from the nominal ledger. The total of the credit balances exceeded the total of the debit balances by £5.

Required:
Record corrections in the control accounts. Attempt to reconcile the sales ledger control account with the sales ledger balances, and the purchase ledger control account with the purchase ledger balances. What further action do you recommend?

(ACCA 1.1, Dec 87, extracts)

5.7 A new clerk takes over responsibility for some of the sales records on 1 January 19X2. The summary figures he receives from his predecessor are as follows (at 1 January 19X2).

	£
Sales ledger control account	10,000
Sales ledgers: total of debit balances	10,483
Sales ledgers: total of credit balances	497

At 31 December 19X2, after his first year of responsibility, the clerk arrives at the following summary figures.

	£
Sales ledger control account	16,600
Sales ledgers: total of debit balances	15,547
Sales ledgers: total of credit balances	£551

On investigation you find the following facts, all of which relate to between 1 January 19X2 and 31 December 19X2.

(i) The June sales total had been added as £9,876 when it should have been correctly added as £8,967.

(ii) A sales invoive which should have been charged to A's ledger account with an amount of £642 had actually been charged to B's ledger account with an amount of £426.

(iii) A credit note for customer D of £123 had been incorrectly treated as a sales invoice in her ledger account. (Customer D's account had a large debit balance at 31 December 19X2.)

(iv) Contra entries of £800, correctly entered in the separate ledger accounts, had been omitted from the control accounts.

(v) Cash discounts given of £74 have been completely ignored by the clerk.

Required:

(i) Calculate, with necessary workings, the adjusted figures at 31 December 19X2 for sales ledger control account, total of sales ledger debit balances and total sales ledger credit balances.

(ii) Produce a clear statement of the net amount of the remaining errors which the clerk appears to have made during the year 19X2 which have not yet been discovered. *(ACCA 1.1, part, Dec 93)*

5.8 The following sales ledger control account has been prepared by an inexperienced member of staff from the accounting records of HAC plc at 20 September 1994:

Sales ledger control

	£		£
Balance b/d	92,580.23	Returns outward	11,376.19
Sales	318,741.90	Debtors receipts	299,878.43
Discount allowed	12,702.18	Discount received	10,419.76
Decrease in provision for		Bad debts written off	5,318.23
doubtful debts	10,429.61	Balance c/d	160,387.70
Purchase ledger contras	49,516.27		
Returns inwards	3,410.12		
	487,380.31		487,380.31

The total of the individual balances in the sales ledger (net of credit balances) has been calculated to be £86,476.15 on 30 September 1994.

An investigation revealed the following:

1. A credit balance of £4,381.22 on an individual account within the sales ledger was included in the calculation of the total of the individual balances as though it were a debit balance.

2. One of the pages of the sales day book has been incorrectly totalled. The total calculated was £2,291.18 more than the correct sum of the individual entries.
3. A credit note issued to a customer for £742.37 had been entered in the returns inwards day book as £472.37.
4. No entries had been made in the individual accounts to record:
   (i)   the purchase ledger contras; or
   (ii) the decrease in the provision for doubtful debts.
5. A bad debt of £421.33 written off in 1992 was recovered in September 1994; the correct entries have been made in the individual customer account.

Required:
(a) Make entries that you consider necessary in the sales ledger control account, commencing with the closing balance given, and to reconcile the listing of the individual debtor balances to the closing balance shown on the control account (as amended).
(b) Explain why control accounts are used.

(CIMA, Nov 94)

6 End of period adjustments

Objectives

After you have completed this chapter, you should be able to:
- explain the basic concept of depreciation
- calculate depreciation and incorporate the figures in accounting records
- account for the sale of fixed assets
- make adjustments for bad and doubtful debts
- calculate accruals and prepayments, and record them in accounting records

Introduction

The book-keeping described in previous chapters was concerned with recording the day-to-day transactions. The end product of this recording process was a trial balance from which the financial statements were prepared. In most cases, however, adjustments have to be made to the trial balance figures before they are incorporated into the financial statements. These adjustments are usually dealt with at the end of the accounting period.

In exams, the information needed to make these adjustments is given in the form of supplementary notes to the trial balance. In practice, the double-entry for each one is recorded in the journal prior to posting in the ledger.

There are various ways in which an examiner can test the subject matter covered by this chapter, other than by asking for the preparation of financial statements that incorporate end-of-year adjustments. The activities and self-assessment questions have been designed to help you develop the necessary skills to deal with any kind of problem.

6.1 Depreciation

The general nature of depreciation

Most fixed assets have a finite life. It is unlikely that any asset created by mankind will last for ever. Some of them, such as buildings, may last for a very long time;

others, such as motor vehicles, have a relatively short life. Depreciation is concerned with assets that have a finite life.

Activity 1

There is one type of asset (owned by many businesses) that can be assumed to have an infinite life. It is a natural asset – not one created by mankind. See if you can think what this asset is and make a note of it here.

Although depreciation is concerned with assets that have a finite life, the calculations are not based on the total expected life of the asset – they are based on the length of time that the business intends to use the asset.

In previous chapters, we have simply treated the cost of a fixed asset as capital expenditure and carried the total cost forward in the balance sheet. The amount paid for fixed assets did not, therefore, feature among any of the expenses that were deducted from sales income in the profit and loss account.

But, as was mentioned in Chapter 2, the cost of a fixed asset is just as much a cost of earning sales revenue as is the cost of wages, rent, electricity, and so on. The only difference is that the benefits derived from buying fixed assets are consumed over several accounting periods, whereas the benefits derived from paying wages, rent, etc. are consumed in the specific accounting period during which the costs are incurred.

The matching convention requires a proportion of the cost of fixed assets to be treated as an expense in the profit and loss account for each of the years that the asset is used. This expense is called depreciation. At any particular accounting date, the proportion of original cost that has not been treated as an expense is carried forward in the balance sheet, and is usually described as the 'net book value' of the asset.

Depreciation defined

For many years, it was a favourite pastime among accounting academics to hold intellectual arguments over the exact nature of depreciation. To some extent this still goes on, but for all practical purposes the matter has been settled by a definition promulgated by the Accounting Standards Committee (ASC) (and now adopted by the Accounting Standards Board) in SSAP 12.

Interestingly enough, even the ASC has had two attempts at defining depreciation. The definition in its original SSAP 12 was revised in 1987. Part of the problem is the word 'depreciation' itself; it seems to imply a measurement of the loss in value – in fact the definition used in the original SSAP 12 referred to depreciation in terms of a loss in value. The revised version refers to a reduction of economic life.

The current definition in SSAP 12 can be paraphrased as follows:

> The measure of wearing out, consumption, or other reduction in useful economic life of a fixed asset; whether through use, passage of time, or obsolescence.

Notice the word 'value' is not used anywhere; the key phrase is a **reduction in useful economic life**. Useful economic life is defined in SSAP 12 as the period over which the present owner will derive economic benefits from using the asset.

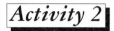

Activity 2

Read the definitions again and then answer the following question. Do you think it will be necessary to calculate depreciation for an asset that is gaining in value, such as a building? Give reasons for your answer.

Activity 3

The expression 'net book value' refers to the proportion of expenditure on a fixed asset that has not been transferred to the profit and loss account as an expense at the accounting date. Why do you think the term 'net book value' is used?

Depreciation measurements

SSAP 12 requires depreciation to be provided on all assets which have a finite useful economic life by:

allocating the cost less estimated residual value fairly to the accounting periods expected to benefit from use of the asset.

In practice, several methods are used in order to do this. SSAP 12 does not insist on any particular method; it simply states that the method chosen should be the most appropriate for the type of asset and its use.

The two most popular methods used in practice are:
1. The straight line method
2. The reducing balance method.

You will learn about other methods in Chapter 19.

The straight line method

The straight line method, as the name suggests, calculates depreciation as an equal amount for each year. The annual amount is found by dividing the cost of the asset (less its estimated residual value) by the estimated number of years that the business intends to use the asset.

Activity 4

A businessman buys a van for £8,000 at the beginning of his first year of trading. He intends to use it in the business for 4 years and estimates that the van can be sold for £2,000 at the end of the fourth year. Calculate the annual depreciation expense using the straight line method.

Activity 5

Calculate the 'net book value' of the van (in Activity 4) at the end of the businessman's second year of trading.

In some examination questions, the rate for calculating straight line depreciation is simply given as a fixed percentage of the cost. For example, if you are told that depreciation is to be calculated at 20% of original cost, this is another way of saying that the original cost is to be written off on a straight line basis over five years.

The reducing balance method

The reducing balance method calculates depreciation for each year as a fixed percentage of the net book value at the beginning of the year. The expression 'reducing balance' refers to the net book value, which is reduced each year by the amount treated as depreciation. Since depreciation is based on a fixed percentage of the net book value, the depreciation charge for each successive year will also decrease.

Activity 6

The trader in Activity 4 decides to use the reducing balance method for calculating depreciation. Calculate depreciation for years 1 to 4 using a rate of 30%. You can do this by completing the figures in the following outline computation (work to the nearest £1 in year 4):

Cost at start of year 1	8,000
Depreciation for year 1 (30% of 8,000)	_____
Net book value at start of year 2	
Depreciation for year 2	_____
Net book value at start of year 3	
Depreciation for year 3	_____
Net book value at start of year 4	
Depreciation for year 4	_____
Net book value at end of year 4	

Notice that the net book value at the end of year 4 is not equal to the estimated residual value of £2,000 mentioned in the details for Activity 4. If the trader had intended to reduce the net book value to £2,000 by the end of year 4, the rate of 30% was set a little too high.

In exams, the percentage to be used for depreciation calculations with the reducing balance method is always given. You do not have to worry over how the rate may have been determined in the first place. If you are interested in how the annual rate is calculated, there is a formula. It very rarely produces a whole number and so the rate used in practice will only be approximate. The formula can be stated as:

1 less the nth root of the fraction: $\dfrac{\text{estimated residual value}}{\text{original cost}}$

The root (n) is the number of years over which the asset is to be written down to its estimated residual value (4 in our example). Set out in mathematical symbols, the formula for our example is:

$$1 - \left[\sqrt[4]{\frac{2000}{8000}} \right]$$

If you care to do the calculations you will find the percentage is roughly 29.29%.

Time-apportioned charges

Depreciation rates are normally expressed in terms of an annual rate. But since the depreciation expense is concerned with the passage of time, the amount treated as depreciation should be related to the length of time the asset was used during the period.

In the example you have been working, the asset was acquired at the beginning of the first year and it was appropriate to calculate depreciation for the whole of that year. If it had been purchased half way through the year, the depreciation in the first year should be based on one-half of the amount for the whole year.

Although this idea of time-apportionment is faithful to the theory of depreciation, it is quite often ignored in practice, and depreciation for a full year is provided in the year of purchase. Most examination questions clarify this point by stating the accounting policy to be used. If the question does not state any accounting policy for the year of purchase you should always relate the charge to the length of time the asset was owned in that year.

Balance sheet presentation

You will get a much better idea of how the book-keeping is normally done if we think about the balance sheet first.

The amount carried forward in the balance sheet at the end of each year is the net book value, but it is more informative to present the figures so that the user can see how this net book value has been determined. This is easily achieved by presenting three figures for each class of fixed asset, namely:

1. the cost of fixed assets
2. the accumulated depreciation
3. the net book value (cost less accumulated depreciation).

For each fixed asset, the accumulated depreciation at the end of any year represents the total amount of original cost that has been treated as an expense for all the years since the asset was acquired. In accounting jargon, the accumulated depreciation is referred to as a 'provision for depreciation'. Since the word 'provision' is not something that a layman would readily understand, it is usually described as accumulated depreciation in the balance sheet (although the ledger account on which it is recorded is usually called 'provision for depreciation').

The three figures are normally set out in the form of a grid, and you will get some idea of how this works by carrying out the following two activities.

Activity 7

Complete the following grid for the van in Activity 4, where depreciation was calculated on a straight line basis. This grid is designed to show the relevant figures for balance sheets at the end of years 1, 2, 3 and 4. The first two years have been completed in order to get you started. Assume that the van was still owned at the end of year 4.

	Cost	Accumulated depreciation	Net book value
At end of year 1: Motor vehicles	8,000	1,500	6,500
At end of year 2: Motor vehicles	8,000	3,000	5,000
At end of year 3: Motor vehicles			
At end of year 4: Motor vehicles			

Activity 8

Now do the same thing again but this time use the depreciation amounts calculated under the reducing balance method for Activity 6.

	Cost	Accumulated depreciation	Net book value
At end of year 1: Motor vehicles	8,000		
At end of year 2: Motor vehicles	8,000		
At end of year 3: Motor vehicles	8,000		
At end of year 4: Motor vehicles	8,000		

In most businesses there will be several classes of fixed asset, e.g. motor vehicles, freehold premises, office equipment, etc. Each class is shown on a separate line of the grid. For example, if the trader in Activity 8 had also purchased office equipment during year 1 for £6,000, and £1,000 of this cost had been charged to the profit and loss account as depreciation for that year, the fixed asset section of the balance sheet would be as follows:

Balance sheet at end of year 1	Cost	Accumulated depreciation	Net book value
Fixed assets:			
Motor vehicles	8,000	2,400	5,600
Office equipment	6,000	1,000	5,000
	14,000	3,400	10,600

Notice how this explanation refers to 'classes' of fixed asset. This involves grouping similar types of asset under one heading – it would be too unwieldy to show each individual asset in the balance sheet.

The book-keeping

The book-keeping is quite simple. There will be one ledger account to record the cost for each class of fixed asset, and another ledger account to record the accumulated depreciation for each class of fixed asset.

The ledger account for cost is debited (bank credited) as the assets are purchased. These costs are accumulated and the balance carried forward from year to year.

The ledger account for accumulated depreciation is called 'provision for depreciation' and this account is credited each year with the annual depreciation figure. The amounts are accumulated and carried forward from year to year.

These two balances (cost and depreciation provision) are set out in the balance sheet in order to derive net book value, as demonstrated in Activities 7 and 8.

The amount credited to the provision for depreciation in any particular year will represent the expense for that year and so the double-entry is completed by debiting the profit and loss account. The expense is simply described as 'depreciation'.

In strict book-keeping terms, it is bad form to debit any expense directly to the profit and loss account. You will recall that expenses such as wages, rent, etc. are initially accumulated on separate ledger accounts before being transferred to the profit and loss account at the end of the year. We should deal with depreciation in much the same way, and so we need an account called 'depreciation expense'. This account is debited with the depreciation charges for the various classes of asset and the total is transferred to the profit and loss account.

Activity 9

A trader started business on 1 January 1995 and intends to prepare accounts to 31 December each year. During year ended 31 December 1995 the following fixed assets were purchased:

1 January	Office equipment	£4,000
1 April	Delivery van 1	£6,000
1 July	Delivery van 2	£8,000

During year ended 31 December 1996 the only transaction on fixed assets was as follows:

1 January   Purchased a computer for office use at a cost of £2,000

Depreciation on the office equipment is to be calculated at a rate of 25% per annum on the reducing balance. Depreciation on the delivery vans is to be calculated on a straight line basis. The trader intends to use the delivery vans for 5 years and at the end of this time the residual values are estimated to be as follows:

Delivery van 1   £1,000
Delivery van 2   £2,000

You are required to write up the relevant ledger accounts (which are set out below) for the first two years of trading. Be careful with the depreciation calculations in 1995 (some will have to be time-apportioned). Balance off the accounts at the end of each year. Assume all assets were paid for by cheque.

Office equipment – cost

Provision for depreciation – office equipment

Motor vehicles – cost		Provision for depreciation – motor vehicles

Depreciation expense	

The sale of fixed assets

This is the last topic in this chapter relating to depreciation of fixed assets. It is a popular topic among examiners and is often used in various types of question to test whether students have understood the basic book-keeping principles relating to fixed asset accounting.

When a fixed asset is sold there are two things to deal with in the books:

1. accounting for the sale proceeds
2. eliminating the cost, and the depreciation provision, for the asset sold.

It is unlikely that any of the estimates used in calculating the total depreciation of an asset will turn out to be correct. The asset may be sold well before the end of its useful economic life. Even if it were kept for exactly the same length of time as was originally thought, the amount received on disposal is likely to be different to the residual value that was estimated at the time of purchase.

Consequently, there will usually be a difference between the sale proceeds and the net book value at the time of disposal. This difference is usually described as a profit or loss on disposal, although strictly speaking it relates to depreciation under- or over-provided in the previous accounts.

It is easy enough to see the end result when figures for the particular asset are known, for example:

if the cost of the asset was	£8,000
and	
the accumulated depreciation on this asset was	£3,000
then	
the net book value will be	£5,000
and	
assuming it is sold for	£6,000
there is	
a difference, described as 'profit on sale', of	£1,000

The total depreciation of a fixed asset is originally estimated by deducting the estimated residual value from the original cost. This total is then allocated to the accounting periods expected to benefit from use of the asset. But we will never know the true total depreciation until the asset is sold.

In the above example, the true total depreciation is £2,000 (i.e. original cost of £8,000 less sale proceeds of £6,000) and yet £3,000 has been treated as an expense in all the accounting periods up to the time of sale. We have charged £1,000 too much for depreciation in those previous periods.

This has arisen simply because the original accounting estimates have turned out to be incorrect. But we cannot go back and revise all the accounts for previous periods, and so an adjustment is made in the year when the asset is actually sold (and the true figures are known). In the above example, this would be done by including a credit of £1,000 in the profit and loss account, which is described as profit on sale.

Activity 10

It could be a bit confusing to the user of accounts to see this £1,000 credit being described as a profit on sale. See if you can describe why this might be so.

Some accountants might describe the adjustment of £1,000 as an over-provision of depreciation in previous years – still confusing for the layman, but marginally better than describing it as a profit. Sometimes the amount is simply amalgamated with the depreciation expense and is not disclosed separately. However, you will have to describe these adjustments as profits or losses on sale since that is the normal convention in exams.

Before we look at the book-keeping, we should consider depreciation in the year of sale. This can sometimes create doubts in a situation which, in all other respects, is unambiguous.

When you were learning depreciation calculations, you saw that annual depreciation is usually time-apportioned in the year of purchase in order to relate the expense to the length of time the asset was used in that period. This might suggest that we should do the same thing in the year of sale.

In practice, depreciation is not usually calculated for the year in which the asset is sold. There would be no point; calculating a figure based on estimates that are now known to be wrong does not make any sense. In any event, if a depreciation expense is charged in the profit and loss account for the year of sale, it will only be 'clawed back' through an increased profit on sale, or 'topped up' by an increased loss on sale. You can discover this for yourself by working through Activity 11.

Activity 11

A delivery van, which had cost £8,000, is being depreciated at the rate of £1,000 per annum. At the end of the previous period, the accumulated depreciation was £3,000. It was sold half way through the current period for £6,000. Time-apportioned depreciation for the current period (if charged) would therefore be £500.

On your own paper, calculate the charges and credits that would appear in the profit and loss account for the current year if:

1. depreciation is charged in the year of sale
2. depreciation in the year of sale is ignored.

When you have done this, compare the two methods and note what effect they will have on the amount of net profit for the year.

In examination questions, the examiner may state whether or not depreciation is to be provided in the year of sale. If the question is silent on this, you can assume that depreciation should not be calculated for the year of sale. On the other hand, you should always assume that depreciation in the year of purchase is time-apportioned unless there is an instruction to do otherwise.

Book-keeping on sale of fixed assets

The objective of the book-keeping is to:

1. remove the cost of the asset from the books,
2. remove the accumulated depreciation (on that asset) from the books,
3. account for the cash received and the profit or loss on sale.

This is quite easily achieved by bringing all the figures together on one ledger account called 'sale of fixed assets'. The cost of the asset sold is transferred to the debit side of this account, the accumulated depreciation transferred to the credit side, and the cash proceeds are credited. The balance will then be the profit or loss on sale which is transferred to the profit and loss account.

Activity 12

Write down the double-entries for the example in Activity 11, based on the second scenario, i.e. where no depreciation was calculated for the year of sale.

		Name of account	Amount
1. Cost of van sold	Debit:		
	Credit:		
2. Accumulated depreciation	Debit:		
	Credit:		
3. Cash received	Debit:		
	Credit:		
4. Profit on sale	Debit:		
	Credit:		

Activity 13

Summarize the effect of all this by writing up the 'sale of fixed assets account' in the blank ledger account below.

Sale of fixed assets account

The delivery van in the above example may have been the only vehicle owned, or it may have been one of several that were included in the balance on the motor vehicles account. In either case, the cost and its related accumulated depreciation have now been removed from the books. If it were one of several, the balance remaining on the account for motor vehicles at cost, and on the account for accumulated depreciation, will relate to vehicles still owned.

Fixed asset register and movements in fixed asset accounts

Since there is only one ledger account for each class of fixed asset (motor vehicles, office equipment, etc.), it would be quite difficult to find the relevant details for any single asset within each group – particularly if there are a large number of assets in that group and several years have passed since the asset was purchased.

To cope with this problem, a subsidiary (memorandum) record is often kept for certain types of fixed asset. This record is called a fixed asset register and it will contain details (date of purchase, cost, identification number, depreciation, etc.) for each individual asset. In a well-organized system, the fixed asset register will show how the balance on the ledger account for cost, and for accumulated depreciation, is made up in terms of individual assets. In practice, these subsidiary records are usually part of a computerized system.

In exams you do not have the luxury of details from fixed asset registers, and you are normally expected to work out how much depreciation would have been provided on any particular asset sold.

Activity 14

A trader makes up accounts to 31 December. The balances in the books for office equipment at 31 December 1995 were as follows:

Cost	£40,000
Accumulated depreciation	18,000

During year ended 31 December 1996, a computer, which had cost £4,000 on 1 July 1993, was sold for £1,000. Depreciation on office equipment is based on the reducing balance method, using a rate of 25% per annum. In the year of purchase, the annual charge is scaled down according to the length of time the asset was owned.

There were no other transactions for office equipment during 1996. On your own paper, calculate the figures for cost and accumulated depreciation that will appear in the balance sheet at 31 December 1996 (worked to the nearest £1).

Fixed asset accounting: Some conceptual problems

The study of fixed asset accounting is not restricted to the mechanical book-keeping aspects dealt with in the foregoing text. Accountancy students are usually expected to be able to discuss some of the conceptual issues that surround the subject. The main areas to consider at this stage of your studies relate to:

- the purpose of depreciation
- measuring the amount of expenditure to be capitalized.

Purpose of depreciation

Depreciation principles are mainly related to the accruals (or matching) concept. Expenditure on fixed assets relates to the acquisition of benefits that will be consumed (used up) over a number of years. Depreciation is a process of attempting to match the consumption of this expenditure with the sales revenue generated through use of the asset. This underlying concept is now fairly well established, but it does call into question whether the choice between the straight line and reducing balance methods can be related to the basic concept in some way.

As you know, straight line depreciation writes off the expenditure at an even amount per year, whereas the annual amounts under the reducing balance method decline as the net book value reduces. This suggests that firms should base their choice of method on the rate at which the benefit of capital expenditure is assumed to be depleted. For example, if the productive capacity of a fixed asset is likely to decline as each year passes, the reducing balance method would seem to be the most appropriate method.

In reality, there is no objective way of identifying the rate at which the benefit of capital expenditure is likely to be consumed, and so the choice between straight line and reducing balance tends to be an arbitrary decision.

Another conceptual issue that students are often required to discuss is concerned with the extent to which depreciation provides a fund for the replacement of assets. This idea has survived from some of the earlier text books on accounting, when writers attempted to justify the depreciation charge on grounds other than the matching concept. In order to bring some kind of theoretical respectability to the idea, examples were produced to show how depreciation did leave enough cash in the business to replace the asset at the end of its life. These examples were highly contrived since they involved:

- all transactions on a cash basis
- no capital transactions other than the original purchase of the fixed asset
- all profits (after charging depreciation) withdrawn by (or distributed to) the owners.

It was a curious way of trying to explain the purpose of depreciation. It would be equally feasible to produce examples to show that by charging the cost of stock sold against sales income, the charge for cost of sales provided a fund for the replacement of the stock. Yet we would never think of the charge for cost of sales in that way.

If you are ever asked whether depreciation 'provides' a fund for replacement your answer should be quite categoric – it does not. If you think about the double-entry for depreciation you can see that no cash is involved. If it were possible to create 'funds' by debiting depreciation expense and crediting a provision for depreciation, we would all be doing it, thereby becoming millionaires simply by writing double-entries in the books. The provision of actual funds for the replacement of fixed assets is a matter of financial management, not a function of depreciation.

The most than can be said for depreciation in this context is that it reduces the profits available for distribution to the owners. This will encourage retention of funds within the business (since distributions should not exceed the profits) but such funds could be represented by many different kinds of asset other than cash.

Capitalized expenditure

In the majority of cases the amount to be capitalized on purchase of an asset is known with certainty; it will be the purchase cost. In this context, the accounting rules in the Companies Act 1985 refer to 'purchase price or production cost'.

This Companies Act rule does highlight one area where there could be uncertainties – the amount to be capitalized when the firm constructs the asset itself. But there are other problems such as delivery costs, installation costs, enhancement expenditure, significant repairs and replacements, and interest payments. There are virtually no codified rules in respect of the items and so it is necessary to rely on generally accepted accounting principles.

A general rule for the amount to be capitalized could be stated as: **all expenditure incurred in bringing the fixed asset into use**. Such a rule would allow delivery and installation costs to be included as part of the capital expenditure, but would exclude all the costs of actually using the asset, such as repairs, replacement parts, and running costs. Any costs incurred in improving the asset (enhancement costs) are likely to increase the productive capacity of the asset and should also be treated as capital expenditure.

In the case of assets constructed by the firm itself, the production cost will include the cost of all raw materials used and the cost of labour employed on the project. There is also some justification for including a proportion of the firm's overheads (electricity, etc.) as a part of the capital cost of the asset.

With regard to interest payments, most accountants take the view that interest is a cost of borrowing money rather than a part of the cost of acquiring an asset with the borrowed money. Interest payments should, therefore, be matched with revenue over the life of the loan, and not over the life of any asset acquired with the borrowed money. Some companies in the construction industry consider that money borrowed for the specific purpose of constructing an asset is a part of the cost of that asset. Capitalizing these interest payments is a highly dubious practice, but at the moment there are no regulations to prevent it.

The sale proceeds of an asset are usually known with certainty. In those cases where there are disposal costs (such as delivery costs or sales commissions) the sale proceeds should be based on the net amount after deducting disposal costs.

There are further aspects to study in relation to fixed asset accounting, notably the revaluation of fixed assets, and the revision of an asset's life. The accounting regulations and accounting practices for these topics are covered in Chapter 19. Some aspects regarding the revaluation of fixed assets are included in Chapter 10.

6.2 Bad and doubtful debts

Bad debts written off

If an asset turns out to be worthless, it will have to be 'written off'. This means that the debit balance which represents the book value of the asset is transferred to the profit and loss account and treated as an expense.

This frequently happens with trading debts. If all efforts to recover the amount owing have failed, and the debt is considered to be irrecoverable, the debit balance on the debtor's account is transferred to the profit and loss account and described as 'bad debts written off'.

As mentioned earlier, it is bad form to write items directly into the profit and loss account, and an expense account called 'bad debts' is normally written up first. This account may include many bad debts written off during the period; the total at the end of the period is then transferred to the profit and loss account.

Activity 15

A trader keeps a debtors control account as part of the double-entry in the ledger. The balance on debtors control account is £18,765 at 31 December 1996. One of the debtors, Mr Sloe, has failed to pay a debt of £450 and the amount is now considered to be irrecoverable. Describe the double-entry that will have to be made in relation to this item.

Debit:

Credit:

The account for Mr Sloe will also have to be written off in the memorandum account kept in the sales ledger, but this is not a part of the double-entry. The balance on the bad debts account is transferred to the profit and loss account at the end of the period.

What happens if Mr Sloe suddenly has a twinge of conscience and actually pays the amount due in a subsequent accounting year? The best way of dealing with this is to treat the cash received as a 'windfall' profit. It will then be credited to the profit and loss account and described as 'bad debts recovered'.

There are various practices regarding the ledger account to be used for recording bad debts recovered prior to transferring the amount to the profit and loss account. In some cases, a separate 'bad debts recovered' account is used; in others, the bad debts recovered are credited to the 'bad debts' account. If all entries are dealt with in a single bad debts account, the net amount transferred to the profit and loss account at the end of the year represents bad debts written off, less bad debts recovered. Even when a separate account for bad debts recovered is kept, it is still normal practice to present a single net figure in the profit and loss account.

Provision for doubtful debts

A business can never be absolutely certain which debtors are likely to pay and which are likely to turn out to be bad. But experience might suggest that there will certainly be some bad debts. The prudence concept (Chapter 4) will therefore require the recognition of possible losses through bad debts, even though these losses may not be certain at the accounting date.

This situation is dealt with in the ledger by setting up an account called 'provision for doubtful debts'. The amount provided will be estimated. This estimate might be made by considering the circumstances of specific debtors, or by taking a percentage of all outstanding debts. If the provision relates to particular debtors, it is called a 'specific provision'; if it is based on a percentage of debtors, it is called a 'general provision'. This distinction has some relevance to the calculation of taxable profits (general provisions are not tax deductible) but does not affect the book-keeping.

In terms of double-entry, the first provision is set up by debiting the profit and loss account and crediting the account called 'provision for doubtful debts'. Since this is a single end-of-year adjustment, the debit is often made directly to the profit and loss account. The debit to the profit and loss account is treated as an expense (usually called 'provision for bad debts') and the credit balance on the 'provision for doubtful debts account' is carried forward in the books. In the balance sheet, this provision is deducted from the debtors.

After setting up the initial provision, it will probably have to be adjusted at the end of each successive year in order to recognize the changing circumstances. It may have to be reduced, or it may have to be increased. This is normally done by carrying down the revised closing provision on the doubtful debts account at the end of the year. Any difference between the provision brought forward from the previous year and the closing provision carried forward at the end of the current year is transferred to the profit and loss account.

This difference represents an increase, or a decrease, in the provision for doubtful debts and is described as such in the profit and loss account. See if you can sort out this explanation by working on the following activity.

Activity 16

A trader commenced business on 1 January 1995. At 31 December 1995, debtors amount to £40,000. At 31 December 1996, the debtors are £52,000. It is a normal practice in this business to recognize that 2% of debtors will never pay, and a provision for these doubtful debts is made at the end of each year. Demonstrate how this would be done by writing up the 'provision for doubtful debts' in the account below. Make sure that your entries give the name of any account to which the opposite entry is posted.

Provision for doubtful debts

Notice that the individual debtors' accounts are not affected; they are still shown as outstanding debts in the books. But the figure shown for debtors in the balance sheet at the end of each year is reduced by the provision for doubtful debts. In the above example, the figures in the two balance sheets would be as follows:

31 December 1995 (40,000 – 800)	£39,200	
31 December 1996 (52,000 – 1,040)	£50,960	

It is good book-keeping form to keep the bad debts account and the provision for doubtful debts as two separate accounts. Unfortunately, some examiners like to mix them up and have one account – often called 'bad and doubtful debts'.

This single account will contain a concoction of entries. There will be the debits for bad debts written off, credits for bad debts recovered, and the provision for doubtful debts brought forward and carried forward. In these cases, the final transfer to the profit and loss account is a mixture of bad debts written off, bad debts recovered, and the adjustment to the provision.

You might also find other variations. Sometimes the provision for doubtful debts that was made in a previous period includes an amount for a debtor which the business has now decided to write off. In this case the debit will be to the provision for doubtful debts account (credit the debtor) and not to the bad debts account. Sometimes the provision for doubtful debts is called a provision for bad debts. All of these variations are easy enough to sort out once you have understood the basic principles involved.

6.3 Accruals and prepayments

Many expenses, such as electricity, rent, insurance, etc. are recorded in the books as they are paid. As you know, the amounts to be treated as expenses in the profit and loss account for any particular year should be the expenditure incurred for that year, and in many cases the expenditure incurred is different to the amount paid during the year. Some expenses, such as electricity, are paid in arrears; others, such as insurance, are usually paid in advance.

Accruals and prepayments are simply ways of making adjustments to the amounts paid so that the profit and loss account is charged with the expenditure incurred. They represent further examples of applying the accruals concept in accounting. (Note that although the word 'accruals' is used as a label for one of these adjustments, the 'accruals concept' has much wider implications than the accruals adjustment dealt with in this chapter.)

Accruals are a way of recognizing any expenses owing at the end of the year; the amounts are often estimated. Prepayments recognize that some payments have been made in advance of the period to which they relate; the amounts are usually calculated on a time-apportionment basis. The total of all accruals will be included with creditors in the balance sheet; total prepayments are included with debtors.

The easiest way of coping with the double-entry for accruals and prepayments is to carry them down on the ledger account for the expense concerned. As mentioned on many previous occasions, a double-entry is being made when balances are carried down on a ledger account. For example, when carrying down a credit balance, the double-entry is effectively: debit the old period, credit the new.

In the context of accruals and prepayments, the effect of the double-entry is as follows:

Accruals: a debit to the current period, and a credit to the next period
Prepayments: a credit to the current period, and a debit to the next period.

Try to sort this out for yourself by working on the following Activity.

Activity 17

Write up the expense accounts for electricity and insurance for year ending 31 December 1996 based on the following data.

A trader set up business on 1 January 1996. During the year to 31 December 1996, the amount paid for electricity was £820. An invoice for electricity was received in February 1997 (before the accounts for 1996 were finalized) for £300 and it was estimated that two-thirds of this related to 1996. On 1 April 1996, the trader paid £1,200 for insurance, which related to the year from 1 April 1996 to 31 March 1997. Use the blank ledger accounts set out below.

Electricity

The balances are simply left on these accounts and, in effect, provide an automatic adjustment for expenses relating to the earlier stages of the next period. For example, when the electricity bill of £300 is eventually paid it will be debited to the electricity account. Setting this debit against the credit of £200 brought forward from 1996 leaves a net debit of £100 which relates to the expense for the first part of 1997 (one-third of £300). Similarly, the debit of £300 brought down on the insurance account relates to the expense for the period 1 January 1997 to 31 March 1997, which will not be paid during 1997 (it was paid in 1996).

It will be necessary to repeat the procedure at the end of 1997. Consequently, the expense incurred for any particular year will be based on either:

1. the amount paid, less accruals brought down, plus accruals carried down, *or*
2. the amount paid, plus prepayments brought down, less prepayments carried down.

In preparing yourself for exams (as opposed to writing up the books) it is preferable to try to develop the habit of calculating figures for the financial statements rather than sorting them out through the medium of 'T' accounts. You should try this with the following activity but if you find it difficult to do as a calculation, set out the relevant 'T' accounts on your own paper.

Activity 18

Calculate the expenses that will be charged to the profit and loss account for the year ending 31 December 1996 in the following two cases:

1. The accrual for electricity at 31 December 1995 was £400. Payments for electricity during 1996 were £1,800. The accrual for electricity at 31 December 1996 was £600.

2. Insurance is paid one year in advance on 1 April each year. The premium paid in 1995 was £1,200. The premium paid in 1996 was £1,800.

As stated earlier, it is normal practice for the amounts carried down as accruals to be included with the figure for creditors in the balance sheet; the amounts carried down as prepayments are included with debtors. If they are amalgamated in this way, the descriptions in the balance sheet should be changed to:

1. Debtors and prepayments; and
2. Creditors and accruals.

But at this stage of your studies you should show accruals as a separate item in the balance sheet following the creditors. The figure is simply described as accruals. Similarly, prepayments should be shown as a separate item following the debtors.

6.4 Extended trial balance

All end of period adjustments have to be written into the books before the ledger accounts can finally be balanced off at the end of the year. The preparation of financial statements could be delayed until these adjustments are written into the books but, in practice, it is more usual to make use of a working paper known as an 'extended trial balance'.

This is a tabulated document which uses the trial balance prior to adjustments as a starting point. Columns to the right of the trial balance are designed to allow adjustments for items such as closing stock, accruals, prepayments and depreciation. The adjusted trial balance figures are then extended into two sets of columns; one of these sets is for the profit and loss account and the other is for the balance sheet. The whole process is simply a practical way of ensuring that the full double-entry effect is given to each adjustment, without waiting for the adjustments to be written into the ledger. You will see how the extended trial balance works by considering the following example.

Example

The following table includes the initial trial balance together with the adjustments:

	Trial balance		Adjustments		Profit and loss		Balance sheet	
	Debit	Credit	Debit	Credit	Debit	Credit	Debit	Credit
Sales		80,000						
Opening stock	10,000							
Purchases	60,000							
Wages	10,000							
Rent	1,800		200					
Insurance	1,100			100				
Sundry expenses	1,000							
Office equipment:								
Cost	8,000							
Office equipment:								
Prov. for depn.		2,400		800				
Debtors	3,000							
Bank	2,000							
Creditors		2,600						
Capital account		17,900						
Drawings	6,000							
	102,900	102,900						
Closing stock:								
Profit and loss a/c				12,000				
Balance sheet			12,000					
Accruals				200				
Prepayments			100					
Depreciation exp.			800					
Net profit								
			13,100	13,100				

The adjustments relate to the following:
- Closing stock is valued at £12,000
- Rent accrued is £200
- Insurance prepaid is £100
- Depreciation of office equipment is based on 10% of original cost.

The extension into the final columns has not yet been completed.
The totals for each pair of columns (debit and credit) should agree with each other.

Activity 19

See if you can sort out how the extended trial balance works by extending figures into the appropriate columns to the right of the table. Net profit is a figure that will make the debits equal the credits in the profit and loss account columns. By including the net profit figure in the credit column for the balance sheet, the debits should equal the credits in the balance sheet columns.

This kind of working paper is often set up on a computer spreadsheet. Through a system of formulae, the figures are automatically extended into the appropriate final column.

Summary

The important learning points in this chapter are as follows:
- expenditure on fixed assets is a long-term expense and should be charged against sales revenue over all periods that benefit from using the asset
- this is done by first calculating the estimated total depreciation of each asset, i.e. its cost less estimated residual value
- this total depreciation is then allocated as an expense over the estimated number of years it will be used in the business (useful economic life)
- there are two popular methods of allocation: straight line and reducing balance
- the cost of assets are recorded in a separate account for each class; the accumulated depreciation for each class of asset is recorded in a separate account
- balance sheet figures are presented by deducting accumulated depreciation from accumulated cost for each class of asset; the difference is described as net book value
- when fixed assets are sold, the cost of the asset together with its related accumulated depreciation must be removed from the books
- the cost and accumulated depreciation for the asset sold are transferred to an account called sale of fixed assets
- this account is also credited with the cash received; the resulting balance represents a profit or loss on sale which is transferred to the profit and loss account
- the amount of expenditure capitalized should be based on all costs of bringing the asset into use, excluding the costs of using the asset and excluding the costs of borrowing money to acquire the asset
- all trading debts considered to be bad must be written off to the profit and loss account as an expense
- provisions for doubtful debts are set up by debiting the profit and loss

account and carrying the provision forward as a credit balance; after setting up the initial provision, it is only necessary to charge or credit profit and loss with the amounts needed to increase or decrease the provision

- accruals and prepayments relate to expenses that are accounted for on a cash paid basis; they ensure that expenses charged to profit and loss relate to the expense incurred for the period, as distinct from the amount paid
- an extended trial balance is a working paper that uses the trial balance figures prior to final adjustments as a means of preparing figures for the financial statements

Activity 1

Land. This does cause a slight practical problem because the price paid for freehold business premises will relate partly to the land and partly to the buildings that are standing on the land. The proportion of the purchase price relating to land is not subject to depreciation.

Activity 2

According to SSAP 12, the answer is yes. Buildings have a finite economic life, and the periodic depreciation measurements will be based on the reduction in useful economic life resulting from the passage of time during the accounting period.

Activity 3

There are several acceptable answers. Probably the most pertinent is to try to prevent users of accounts from thinking that the figure carried forward in the balance sheet represents the market value of the asset. Despite common misconceptions, balance sheets make no attempt to measure the economic value of the assets.

Activity 4

£1,500, i.e. (£8,000 – £2,000) ÷ 4

Activity 5

£5,000. The amount transferred to the profit and loss account as depreciation over the two years would be £3,000 (i.e. 2 × £1,500), leaving £5,000 (i.e. £8,000 less £3,000) to be carried forward as the net book value.

Activity 6

Cost at start of year 1	8,000
Depreciation for year 1 (30% of 8,000)	2,400
Net book value at start of year 2	5,600
Depreciation for year 2 (30% of 5,600)	1,680
Net book value at start of year 3	3,920
Depreciation for year 3 (30% of 3,920)	1,176
Net book value at start of year 4	2,744
Depreciation for year 4 (30% of 2,744)	823
Net book value at end of year 4	1,921

Activity 7

	Cost	Accumulated depreciation	Net book value
At end of year 3:			
Motor vehicles	8,000	4,500	3,500
At end of year 4:			
Motor vehicles	8,000	6,000	2,000

Activity 8

	Cost	Accumulated depreciation	Net book value
At end of year 1:			
Motor vehicles	8,000	2,400	5,600
At end of year 2:			
Motor vehicles	8,000	4,080	3,920
At end of year 3:			
Motor vehicles	8,000	5,256	2,744
At end of year 4:			
Motor vehicles	8,000	6,079	1,921

Activity 9

Office equipment – cost

1 Jan 95 Bank	4,000	31 Dec 95 Balance c/d	4,000
	4,000		4,000
1 Jan 96 Balance b/d	4,000	31 Dec 96 Balance c/d	6,000
1 Jan 96 Bank	2,000		
	6,000		6,000

Provision for depreciation – office equipment

31 Dec 95 Balance c/d	1,000	31 Dec 95 Depreciation expense	1,000
	1,000		1,000
31 Dec 96 Balance c/d	2,250	1 Jan 96 Balance b/d	1,000
		31 Dec 96 Depreciation expense	1,250
	2,250		2,250
		1 Jan 97 Balance b/d	2,250

Motor vehicles – cost

1 Apr 95 Bank	6,000	31 Dec 95 Balance c/d	14,000
1 Jul 95 Bank	8,000		
	14,000		14,000
1 Jan 96 Balance b/d	14,000	31 Dec 96 Balance c/d	14,000
	14,000		14,000
1 Jan 97 Balance b/d	14,000		

Provision for depreciation – motor vehicles

31 Dec 95 Balance c/d	1,350	31 Dec 95 Depreciation expense	1,350
	1,350		1,350
31 Dec 96 Balance c/d	3,550	1 Jan 96 Balance b/d	1,350
		31 Dec 96 Depreciation expense	2,200
	3,550		3,550
		1 Jan 97 Balance b/d	3,550

Depreciation expense

31 Dec 95	Prov for dep MV	1,350	31 Dec 95 Profit & loss account	2,350
	Prov for dep OE	1,000		
		2,350		2,350
31 Dec 96	Prov for dep MV	2,200	31 Dec 96 Profit & loss account	3,450
	Prov for dep OE	1,250		
		3,450		3,450

Calculations:

Year ending 31 December 1995

Office equipment: 25% of 4,000 = 1,000
Motor vehicles:

Van 1 (6,000 – 1,000)/5 × (9/12) =	750
Van 2 (8,000 – 2,000)/5 × (6/12) =	600
Total	1,350

Year ending 31 December 1996

Office equipment 25% of (3,000 + 2,000) =	1,250
Motor vehicles 1,000 + 1,200 =	2,200

Activity 10
It might be a bit difficult for a layman to understand. After all, selling an asset for £6,000 which had originally cost £8,000 suggests a loss on sale of £2,000.

Activity 11
Both methods result in a credit to profit and loss account of £1,000, as follows:

1. Depreciation expense	500
Profit on sale (£6,000 – £4,500)	1,500
Net credit	1,000
2. Depreciation expense	nil
Profit on sale (£6,000 – £5,000)	1,000

Activity 12
1. Debit 'sale of fixed assets' £8,000; Credit 'motor vehicles – cost' £8,000.
2. Debit 'provision for depreciation – motor vehicles' £3,000; Credit 'sale of fixed assets' £3,000.
3. Debit bank £6,000; Credit 'sale of fixed assets' £6,000.
4. Debit 'sale of fixed assets' £1,000; Credit profit and loss account £1,000.

Activity 13

Sale of fixed assets account

Motor vehicles – cost	8,000	Provision for depreciation	3,000
Profit and loss account	1,000	Bank	6,000
(profit on sale)			
	9,000		9,000

Activity 14
Cost = £36,000 (i.e. £40,000 less £4,000).
Accumulated depreciation £20,977 found as follows:

Accumulated depreciation at 1 January 1996	18,000
Less: accumulated depreciation on asset sold (working 1)	2,031
	15,969
Add: depreciation for the current year (working 2)	5,008
Accumulated depreciation at 31 December 1996	20,977

Working 1. Depreciation charged in previous accounting periods:

		Total
1 July 1993 Cost	4,000	
Depreciation 1993	500	500
	3,500	
Depreciation 1994	875	875
	2,625	
Depreciation 1995	656	656
		2,031

Working 2. Depreciation for current year:

Cost of assets owned at end of year	36,000
Accumulated depreciation on these assets at beginning of year (18,000 − 2,031)	15,969
Net book value at beginning of year for assets owned at the end of the year	20,031
Depreciation charge for the year: 25% of £20,031 =	5,008

Activity 15

Debit bad debts account £450; credit debtors control account £450.

Activity 16

Provision for doubtful debts

31 Dec 95 Balance c/d	800	31 Dec 95 Profit and loss account	800
	800		800
31 Dec 96 Balance c/d	1,040	1 Jan 96 Balance b/d	800
		31 Dec 96 Profit and loss account (increase in provision)	240
	1,040		1,040

Activity 17

Electricity

31 Dec 96 Bank	820	31 Dec 96 Profit and loss account	1,020
31 Dec 96 Accrual c/d	200		
	1,020		1,020
		1 Jan 97 Accrual b/d	200

Insurance

1 Apr 96 Bank	1,200	31 Dec 96 Prepayment c/d	300
		31 Dec 96 Profit and loss account	900
	1,200		1,200
1 Jan 97 Prepayment b/d	300		

Activity 18

1. Electricity £2,000 (1,800 − 400 + 600).
2. Insurance £1,650 (1,800 + 300 − 450).

Activity 19

The extended trial balance (extended figures in italics) as follows:

	Trial balance		Adjustments		Profit and loss		Balance sheet	
	Debit	Credit	Debit	Credit	Debit	Credit	Debit	Credit
Sales		80,000				*80,000*		
Opening stock	10,000				*10,000*			
Purchases	60,000				*60,000*			
Wages	10,000				*10,000*			
Rent	1,800		200		*2,000*			
Insurance	1,100			100	*1,000*			
Sundry expenses	1,000				*1,000*			
Office equipment:								
Cost	8,000						*8,000*	
Office equipment:								
Prov. for depn.		2,400		800				*3,200*
Debtors	3,000						*3,000*	
Bank	2,000						*2,000*	
Creditors		2,600						*2,600*
Capital account		17,900						*17,900*
Drawings	6,000						*6,000*	
	102,900	102,900						
Closing stock:								
Profit and loss a/c				*12,000*		*12,000*		
Balance sheet			*12,000*				*12,000*	
Accruals				*200*				*200*
Prepayments			*100*				*100*	
Depreciation exp.			*800*		*800*			
Net profit					*7,200*			*7,200*
			13,100	*13,100*	*92,000*	*92,000*	*31,100*	*31,100*

Questions for self-assessment

Answers to self-assessment questions are given at the end of the book.

6.1 In the year to 31 December 19X9, Amy bought a new fixed asset and made the following payments in relation to it:

Cost as per suppliers list	12,000
Less: agreed discount	1,000
	11,000
Delivery charge	100
Erection charge	200
Maintenance charge	300
Additional component to increase capacity	400
Replacements parts	250

Required:
(a) State and justify the cost figure which should be used as the basis for depreciation.
(b) What does depreciation do, and why is it necessary?
(c) Briefly explain, without numerical illustration, how the straight line and reducing balance methods of depreciation work. What different assumptions does each method make?
(d) Explain the term 'objectivity' as used by accountants. To what extent is depreciation objective?
(e) It is common practice in published accounts in Germany to use the reducing balance method for a fixed asset in the early years of its life, and then to change to the straight line method as soon as this would give a higher annual charge. What do you think of this practice? Refer to relevant accounting conventions in your answer.

(ACCA 1.1)

6.2 The following balances appeared in the ledger of Vale & Co. at 1 March 1996:

Vans – cost	13,050
Office equipment – cost	8,100
Provision for depreciation – vans	8,975
Provision for depreciation – office equipment	6,240

The policy of the company is to provide a full year's depreciation in the year of purchase and none in the year of sale. Vans are depreciated at 40% per annum on the reducing balance method, and office equipment at 10% per annum on cost.

A new van was purchased on 1 December 1996 at a cost of £6,800 less 10% trade discount. A van that had originally been purchased in June 1994 for £6,000 was part exchanged for the new van – the trade-in price was £1,650.

Required:
Write up the accounts for: vans – cost; provision for depreciation – vans; and sale of fixed assets; for year ending 28 February 1997.

6.3 At 31 March 1997, the trial balance of Tipsy Turvey Traders included the following balances:

	Debits	Credits
Sales ledger control account	12,360	
Provision for doubtful debts		410
Bad debts recovered (received from G. Davies)		970

Further information:
1. The account for G. Davies had been written off in year ended 31 March 1996.
2. The following debts were considered to be irrecoverable and are to be written off:

I. T. Pink	210
N. O. Money	50

3. The provision for doubtful debts account is not used for actual bad debts written off, or for bad debts recovered.
4. The company's policy is to maintain a provision for doubtful debts of 2% of outstanding debtors at the end of each year.

Required:
(a) Write up the provision for doubtful debts account for the year ended 31 March 1997.
(b) Show what expenses (or credits) will be included in the profit and loss account for year ended 31 March 1997.
(c) Show how the figure for debtors will appear in the balance sheet of Tipsy Turvey Traders at 31 March 1997.

Questions without answers

Answers to these questions are published separately in the *Teacher's Manual.*

6.4 The trial balance of Mr Toby at 31 December 1996 is as follows:

	Debits	Credits
Capital account – cash introduced		10,000
Capital account – retained profits		19,000
Sales and purchases	61,000	100,000
Sales returns and purchase returns	2,000	4,000
Debtors and creditors control		
accounts	20,000	7,000
Land and buildings at cost	40,000	
Plant (cost and depreciation		
provision at 1 Jan 1996)	50,000	22,000
Long-term loan		30,000
Stock at 1 January 1996	15,000	
Administration expenses	12,000	
Distribution expenses	10,000	
Bank account		8,000
Sundry account (see 2 below)		10,000
	210,000	210,000

Notes:
1. Closing stock is £18,000 at cost.
2. The book-keeper was not quite sure how to complete the double-entry for two cash receipts and has temporarily credited them to a 'sundry account'. The two amounts received were as follows:

Further capital introduced	8,000
Cash received on sale of plant	2,000

3. The plant sold had cost £4,000 in 1994. Plant is depreciated on a straight line basis over 10 years (residual values are considered to be nil). Depreciation for the whole year is provided in the year of purchase. Land and buildings are not depreciated.
4. The long-term loan was received on 1 October 1996. Interest payable on this loan is at the rate of 12% per annum, payable at half-yearly intervals in arrears. The first interest payment is due on 31 March 1997.
5. Administration expenses include a payment of £1,200 for insurance in respect of year ended 28 February 1997.

6. By mistake, Mr Toby's drawings of £5,000 for the year have been charged to administration expenses.

Required:
Prepare Mr Toby's profit and loss account for the year to 31 December 1996 and his balance sheet at that date.

6.5 Larchmont Ltd was established on 1 January 19X3 to manufacture a single product using a machine which cost £400,000. The machine is expected to last four years and then have a scrap value of £52,000. The machine will produce a similar number of goods each year and annual profits before depreciation are expected to be in the region of £200,000. The financial controller has suggested that the machine should be depreciated using either the straight line method or the reducing balance method. If the latter method is used, it has been estimated that an annual depreciation rate of 40% would be appropriate.

Required:
(a) Calculations of the annual depreciation charges and the net book values of the fixed asset at the end of 19X3, 19X4, 19X5, and 19X6, using:
   (i) the straight line method;
   (ii) the reducing balance method.
(b) A discussion of the differing implications of these two methods for the financial information published by Larchmont Ltd for the years 19X3 to 19X6 inclusive. You should also advise management which method you consider more appropriate bearing in mind expected profit levels.

(CIB Diploma)

6.6 The machinery register of Ethelred Engineering plc on 1 January 19X1 contained the following items:

Machine	Cost £	Year of Purchase
A	10,000	1980
B	12,000	1984
C	15,000	1986
D	16,000	1989
E	20,000	1990

Depreciation policies are as follows:

Machines A and B on straight line basis assuming zero scrap value, over 10 years.

Machine C on reducing balance basis at 20% p.a. assuming scrap value of £1,000.

Machines D and E on straight line basis assuming a scrap value equal to 10% of the original cost, over 5 years.

All machines receive a full year's depreciation in the year of purchase.

Relevant transactions during the year to 31 December 19X1 are as follows:

(i) Machine B is taken in part exchange by the supplier of machine F. The invoice for machine F reads as follows:

	£	£
New machine – list price	25,000	
trade discount	1,000	24,000
Allowance on your old machine		2,000
		22,000
Delivery of new machine	1,500	
Collection of old machine	1,000	2,500
Total due		24,500

(ii) The motor in machine E is discovered to be inadequate. By agreement it is replaced with a more powerful motor. The new motor costs £6,000 as compared with £4,000 for the original motor. The old inadequate motor is taken back by the supplier and full credit of the original £4,000 is given against the £6,000 cost of the new motor. This change is not expected to increase the life of the machine and it is agreed to treat this as a correction of the original cost.

The depreciation policy for the new machine F is the same as for machines D and E.

Required:
(a) Prepare a table showing for each machine: cost, depreciation to date, and net balance sheet figure, and the profit and loss account entries for the year 19X1.

A loan of £20,000, at 15% interest, has been taken out especially to help finance the purchase of machine F. The managing director of Ethelred Engineering suggests that the interest payable on this loan in 19X1 should be regarded as part of the cost of the machine.

Required:
(b) Comment briefly on the managing director's proposal, supporting your opinion by reference to accounting conventions.

(ACCA 1.1, Jun 91)

6.7 GBA is a sole trader, supplying building materials to local builders. He prepares his accounts to 30 June each year. At 30 June 1995, his trial balance was as follows:

	Debits £	Credits £
Capital at 1 July 1994		55,550
Purchases and sales	324,500	625,000
Returns	2,300	1,700
Discounts	1,500	2,500
Stock of building materials at 1 July 1994	98,200	
Packing materials purchased	12,900	
Distribution costs	17,000	
Rent, rates and insurance	5,100	
Telephone	3,200	
Car expenses	2,400	
Wages	71,700	
Provision for doubtful debts at 1 July 1994		1,000
Heat and light	1,850	
Sundry expenses	6,700	
Delivery vehicles – cost	112,500	
Delivery vehicles – depreciation at 1 July 1994		35,000
Equipment – cost	15,000	
Equipment – depreciation at 1 July 1994		5,000
Debtors and creditors	95,000	82,000
Loan		10,000
Loan repayments	6,400	
Bank deposit account	15,000	
Bank currrent account	26,500	
	817,750	817,750

The following additional information at 30 June 1995 is available:

(i) Closing stocks of building materials £75,300
   Closing stocks of packing materials £700

There was also an unpaid invoice of £200 for packing materials received and consumed during the year.

(ii) Prepayments:
     rent, rates and insurance   £450

(iii) Accrued expenses:
     heat and light   £400
     telephone   £500

(iv) Wages includes £23,800 cash withdrawn by GBA.

(v) Debtors have been analysed as follows:
     Current month   £60,000
     30 to 60 days   £20,000
     60 to 90 days   £12,000
     over 90 days   £3,000

and provision is to be made for doubtful debts as follows:
     30 to 60 days   1%
     60 to 90 days   2.5%
     over 90 days   5% (after writing off £600)

(vi) Sundry expenses includes £3,500 for GBA's personal tax bill.

(vii) The loan was taken out some years ago, and is due for repayment on 31 March 1996. The figure shown in the trial balance for 'loan repayments' includes interest of £800 for the year.

(viii) The Bank deposit account was opened on 1 January 1995 as a short-term investment; interest is credited at 31 December annually; the average rate of interest since opening the account has been 6% per annum.

(ix) At 1 July 1994, GBA decided to bring one of his family cars, valued at £8,000, into the business. No entries have been made in the business books for its introduction.

(x) Depreciation is to be provided as follows:
       at 20% on cost for delivery vehicles;
       at 25% on the reducing balance for the car;
       at 25% on the reducing balance for equipment.

Required:

(a) Prepare a trading and profit and loss account for the year ended 30 June 1995.

(b) Prepare a balance sheet at 30 June 1995.

(c) Explain to GBA why *four* of the transactions which have occurred in his business during the year have affected his bank balance but have not affected the calculation of his profit for the year.

(CIMA, Nov 95)

7 ▷ Sundry book-keeping procedures

Objectives

After you have completed this chapter, you should be able to:
- reconcile the balance on the bank account in the ledger with the balance shown on the bank statement
- account for sundry transactions such as cash discounts and carriage charges
- account for value added tax
- discuss aspects of financial management as far as debtors are concerned
- demonstrate how petty cash transactions are dealt with in a double-entry system
- correct book-keeping errors where a suspense account has been written up in order to make the trial balance agree

Introduction

There are a few minor book-keeping topics that were omitted from previous chapters in order to accelerate the learning process. They are dealt with in this chapter and are as follows:
1. Bank reconciliations
2. Accounting for cash discounts
3. Accounting for value added tax
3. Accounting for carriage charges (for goods received and goods delivered)
4. Petty cash transactions
5. Suspense accounts (a temporary 'pigeon-hole' for book-keeping errors)
6. Contra balances.

Some of these (e.g. suspense accounts and carriage charges) tend to be relics from the past. Suspense accounts are used as a technique for dealing with book-keeping errors in a manual system; such errors should not arise in a properly controlled computerized recording system.

Despite their antiquity, carriage charges and suspense accounts must be studied since they still feature in accountancy exams. In any event, topics such as suspense accounts will reinforce your mental perception of the concepts of double-entry book-keeping and accounting. The study of cash discounts provides an opportunity to make a preliminary study of some aspects of financial management.

The subject of value added tax (VAT) is often ignored in many accounting exams. This is quite reasonable since VAT is more of a book-keeping topic than an issue that has any serious impact on financial reporting.

7.1 Bank reconciliation statements

Most of us (even if we are not in business) try to keep track of how much money we have in the bank. We might do this by keeping a running balance on our cheque book stubs. When the bank statement arrives, we usually check to see if the balance in our cheque book agrees with that on the bank statement. We either have a nasty shock or a pleasant surprise – the balance on the statement is rarely the same as what we thought it should be.

When we check our figures with those on the bank statement, we will find several reasons why the two balances do not agree. For example, there may be bank charges that we did not know about until we received the statement, or cheques that were written prior to the balancing date but have not yet gone through the account.

If we sorted out all the reasons that explain the difference, and then wrote them down on a piece of paper, we would be doing a form of bank reconciliation.

Most businesses arrange to receive a bank statement at the end of every month and so a monthly bank reconciliation is a regular and formal procedure. The objective is to ensure that entries in the books for bank transactions are accurate and complete (and also to make sure that the bank has not made any mistakes).

Activity 1

As stated above, there are a number of reasons why the balance on the statement does not agree with the balance on the bank account in the books at any particular date. See if you can think of six reasons and list them below:

1.

2.

3.

4.

5.

6.

The bank reconciliation procedure is roughly as follows:

1. Enter items in the cash book that have not previously been entered, such as:

   • bank charges
   • direct debits and credits
   • items omitted in error.

2. Correct the cash book in respect of any errors made, e.g. cheques entered for the wrong amount.
3. Determine the revised balance in the books following these corrections.
4. Compare entries in the cash book with those on the bank statement (particularly for the few days prior to the balancing date) in order to ascertain details of any unpresented cheques and any uncleared lodgements.
5. On a piece of paper, write down the balance according to the statement, and then:

- deduct any unpresented cheques, and
- add on any uncleared lodgements.

The resulting figure should agree with the revised balance in the cash book.

Activity 2

The procedure set out in 5 above will vary according to whether the statement shows a balance of cash at bank, or an overdrawn balance. Write down an answer to the following two questions:

1. What assumption has been made in the explanation (i.e. that the statement showed there was cash at bank, or that it was overdrawn)?

2. How would the procedure vary if the opposite state existed?

The exact way in which omissions and corrections are dealt with in the ledger will depend on the structure of the books. If (as is normal) a bank control account is maintained in the nominal ledger, the effect of omissions and corrections will be written into the ledger by means of a journal entry, e.g. to deal with bank charges there will be a journal entry to debit bank charges and credit bank account.

But preparation of the reconciliation statement itself is simply a clerical exercise to provide a numerical explanation of the difference between the bank balance in the books (as corrected) and the balance on the bank statement. The following simple example demonstrates the basic process.

Example

At 31 March the books of R. Copeland show a balance at bank of £2,894. The bank statement at this date shows a balance of £2,956. On checking the entries in the statement with those in the books the following points are discovered:

Two cheques dated 28 March have not yet been passed through the bank account. One cheque is for £62 and one is for £138. Bank charges amounting to £48 have not been entered in the books. A banking has been entered in the books as £870 but appears on the bank statement as £780 – the bank statement was found to be correct.

The bank reconciliation procedure is as follows:

Corrected bank balance in the books:

Original balance		2,894
Less: Bank charges	48	
Banking overstated	90	
		138
		2,756

Reconciliation statement:

Balance per statement		2,956
Less: unpresented cheques	62	
	138	
		200
Balance per books		2,756

Notice the distinction between items that need to be entered (or corrected) in the books, and items that are dealt with in the reconciliation statement. There are several ways of setting out two sets of figures whereby the total of one set agrees with the other, but your answer will not be correct unless you have sorted the items into their two categories, as indicated above. Generally speaking, the actual reconciliation statement will deal with unpresented cheques, uncleared lodgements and (sometimes) the correction of any errors made by the bank. All other items will relate to corrections in the cash book.

The following activity attempts to mimic a real situation. It is quite important for you to practice carrying out the bank reconciliation procedure; it tends to be quite a popular topic in first year accounting exams. These problems do not pose any great strain on the intellect but they do require a methodical approach, which is a skill that needs to be applied to many different kinds of accounting problem.

Activity 3

The details on Mr Laker's bank statement for the month of April, and his cash book for the corresponding month, are set out below. On your own paper:

1. Prepare a bank reconciliation.
2. Explain (briefly) which items appear to require further investigation. You may make any assumptions that you consider appropriate.

Mr Laker's bank statement for April

Date	Particulars	Payments	Receipts	Balance
1 April	Balance			1,053.29
2 April	236127	210.70		842.59
3 April	Bank Giro Credit		192.35	1,034.94
6 April	236126	15.21		1,019.73
6 April	Bank charges	12.80		1,006.93
9 April	236129	43.82		963.11
10 April	427519	19.47		943.64
12 April	236128	111.70		831.94
17 April	Standing order	32.52		799.42
20 April	Sundry credit		249.50	1,048.92
23 April	236130	77.87		971.05
23 April	236132	59.09		911.96
25 April	Bank Giro Credit		21.47	933.43
27 April	Sundry credit		304.20	1,237.63
30 April	236133	71.18		1,166.45

Mr Laker runs a small business and keeps a single cash book for bank transactions in which he records the bankings, cheque payments and balance. His cash book for the month of April was as follows:

Receipts			Payments			
Date	Detail	£	Date	Detail	Cheque no.	£
1 April	Balance	827.38	5 April	Purchases	128	111.70
2 April	Sales	192.35	10 April	Electricity	129	43.82
18 April	Sales	249.50	16 April	Purchases	130	87.77
24 April	Sales	304.20	18 April	Rent	131	30.00
30 April	Sales	192.80	20 April	Purchases	132	59.09
			25 April	Purchases	133	71.18
			30 April	Wages	134	52.27
			30 April	Balance		1,310.40
		1,766.23				1,766.23

Check your solution with the Key before leaving this subject. There is a tendency for examiners to set bank reconciliation questions that cannot be completely resolved due to lack of information. The idea behind this is to prevent students from shuffling figures around until the two totals agree with each other, and to see if you can suggest appropriate lines of enquiry in order to resolve the problem.

7.2 Cash discounts

The book-keeping problem

Cash discounts are deductions allowed for early settlement of accounts. Consider the following fictitious sales invoice, on which VAT has been ignored for the time being:

	Pronto Printers Ltd 347 Nowhere St Oxbridge
Ashford Traders 743 High Street Favingbourne	1 January 1997

INVOICE

To supplying 20 reams of headed notepaper	£200.00
Less trade discount (10%)	20.00
	£180.00

Credit terms: 1 month. 1% cash discount for payment within 14 days

You will notice that there are two types of discount: a trade discount of 10% and a discount for early settlement of 1%.

The trade discount does not create any specific accounting problem. In the books of Pronto Printers Ltd, there will be a credit to sales of £180 and a debit to debtors of £180. The fact that the sale would have been £200 if it had been to a non-trade customer is of no significance – the sale was for £180 and that is an end to it as far as the book-keeping is concerned.

However, the discount for early settlement does create an accounting problem.

Activity 4

Assume that Ashford Traders do pay the account within 14 days and that they deduct £1.80 (i.e. 1% of £180.00) from the amount of the invoice. What accounting problem does this create in the books of Pronto Printers Ltd?

Continuing to look at this problem from Pronto Printers' point of view, the remaining debit balance of £1.80 on the account for Ashford Traders will have to be written off and treated as an expense. This expense is called 'discounts allowed'.

Activity 5

Assuming that Pronto Printers maintain a sales ledger control account as part of their double-entry system, describe the double-entry to be made in the nominal ledger as far as this £1.80 is concerned.

Debit:

Credit:

The account for Ashford Traders in the sales ledger will have to be credited with £1.80, but this is a memorandum entry. The balance on the 'discounts allowed' account in the nominal ledger will be transferred to the profit and loss account at the end of the period as an expense.

If we now look at this transaction from Ashford Traders' point of view we will see a mirror image of the same problem. Ashford Traders will initially debit an expense account (probably stationery) with £180 and credit creditors with £180. But only £178.20 is paid and so only £178.20 will be debited to creditors.

The credit balance of £1.80 that remains on the creditors account is not actually owing and so this is also written off, this time as an income item called 'discounts received'.

Activity 6

Assuming that Ashford Traders maintain a purchase ledger control account as part of their double-entry system, describe the double-entry to be made in the nominal ledger as far as this £1.80 is concerned.

Debit:

Credit:

The personal account for Pronto Printers Ltd will also have to be debited with the £1.80 as a memorandum entry. The total on the 'discounts received' account will be transferred to the profit and loss account at the end of the period, and treated as an income item.

You will recall from previous studies that double-entry postings in the nominal ledger are not made for individual transactions. Totals for the period are accumulated in the primary books and double-entry postings are made for the total. The same system applies for discounts allowed and discounts received. But the question is: where do we write down the individual amounts so that the totals for the period can be determined?

It will not be known whether a cash discount has been taken by a debtor until the cash is received. Similarly, the point at which the payer knows that a cash discount deduction has been taken is when the account is paid. The individual cash receipt will be recorded in the cash received book; the individual payment will be recorded in the cash payments book. By including an additional column in each cash book (or on each side of a single column cash book) cash discounts can be recorded as each amount is received or paid.

It is important to understand that although these additional columns are included in the cash books, they are not bank transactions. Similarly, you must keep in mind that no aspect of the double-entry is being recorded by entering discounts (received and allowed) in the cash book. Discount entries in the cash book are memoranda entries; the cash book is simply being used as a convenient place to write down each amount as it occurs. In effect, we are using the cash book as a journal in order to accumulate data for subsequent double-entry posting.

See if you have understood the general principle by dealing with the following activity.

Activity 7

A trader maintains a payments cash book and a receipts cash book. The nominal ledger includes control accounts for both debtors and creditors as part of the double-entry system. The trader allows cash discounts to his customers, and also takes cash discounts (when available) on payment to his suppliers.

1. Describe the double-entry that will be made for the total discounts recorded in the payments cash book.

Debit:

Credit:

2. Describe the double-entry that will be made for the total discounts recorded in receipts cash book.

Debit:

Credit:

As far as the personal accounts are concerned, the individual discounts allowed or received can be posted at the same time as posting the cash transactions.

Presentation in the profit and loss account

The total discounts allowed and/or received will be transferred to the profit and loss account at the end of the period. As far as presentation is concerned, a lot depends upon the circumstances. Discounts received can be treated as a separate income item and added to gross profit. Discounts allowed should be treated as an expense. If there are both discounts received and discounts allowed, the two figures are usually 'netted off' and either added to gross profit, or treated as an expense, according to whether the net figure is a credit or a debit. For example:

Sales		100,000
Less cost of sales		60,000
Gross profit		40,000
Discounts received	500	
Less discounts allowed	120	
		380
		40,380
Expenses:		
Wages etc.		

Note that cash discounts do not appear in the trading account.

Financial management of debtors

Offering cash discounts is a way of trying to reduce the amount of money invested in debtors and improve the cash flow of the business.

The amount being carried in the books for debtors is just as much an investment of business funds as is, for example, the purchase of a fixed asset. A business does not receive any of its funds free of charge. For example, if the money is borrowed from the bank there will be interest charges to pay. Even if the entire funding of the business has been provided by the proprietor, there is an opportunity cost – the proprietor has lost the opportunity of being able to invest those funds elsewhere and earn a return in the form of interest.

It might not be possible to reduce the amount of money invested in fixed assets without seriously curtailing the volume of business activity. In fact, if more money were invested in fixed assets the volume of business is likely to increase. But debtors are a different matter; reducing the amount of money invested in debtors is not likely to affect the volume of business, and the funds released by reducing debtors can be invested elsewhere. This investment could be within the business (expansion) or outside the business (external investment).

Unfortunately, reducing debtors by offering cash discounts is not always a good idea. In order to make the scheme attractive to debtors, the discount rates offered will usually have to be in excess of bank interest rates. (Don't forget, the debtors are also likely to be in business and by paying early will be using up their own source of funds.) Consequently, it may be cheaper to obtain funds from the bank rather than by getting debtors to pay early.

Furthermore, there is a practical problem with cash discounts. Some debtors will deduct the discount even if they are not entitled to it (because they paid late). Legally, the amounts not paid are recoverable debts, but the amounts involved are usually so small that it is not worth all the effort and cost of trying to collect them.

For these reasons, cash discounts are not a very popular arrangement.

Activity 8

It is good financial management to keep the amount of funds invested in debtors to the absolute minimum. See if you can think of any strategy open to management in this respect, other than by offering cash discounts. Write down your ideas here.

Most businesses prefer to handle this problem by operating strict credit control procedures.

7.3 Value added tax

How the tax works

The subject of VAT was mentioned briefly in Chapter 2, but has been ignored in all the subsequent explanations of double-entry book-keeping. It also tends to be ignored in most accounting exams. VAT might cause a number of practical problems for the businessman but it has very little impact on the financial statements.

In general terms, VAT is intended to be a tax on the final consumer; it is not a tax on the business community. Unfortunately, the business community is burdened with the task of collecting the tax and paying it over to the Inland Revenue. All businesses must be registered with the Customs and Excise, except where the taxable turnover of the business does not exceed a certain limit. This limit has gradually been increased since the tax was first introduced; from November 1996 it is set at £48,000. As you can see, all but the smallest of businesses must register for VAT.

The effect of registration is that the business must keep a record of all the VAT charged to customers, and of all the VAT it has been charged by its suppliers. The difference between the two amounts must be paid over to the Customs and Excise (on a quarterly basis). The term 'value added' relates to the successive amounts of profit added to a product as it proceeds down the distribution chain from original supplier to final consumer.

But businesses do not have to work out the value added, they simply charge VAT on the goods sold. The tax added to sales less the tax charged on goods and services received is paid to the Customs and Excise and is, in effect, a tax on the value added. There are currently three rates of VAT: a standard rate of 17.5%, a rate of 8% for domestic fuel (to be reduced to 5% from September 1997) and a zero rate. The zero rate is charged on certain supplies such as food, text books, exports, and children's clothing. You can get some idea of the concept of value added by considering the following contrived example.

Example

A trader is registered for VAT and all goods dealt with are subject to VAT at the standard rate of 17.5%. During the year ended 31 December 1996, total sales (exclusive of VAT) were £800,000 and purchases (exclusive of VAT) were £600,000. There were no opening or closing stocks. All transactions are on a cash basis.

In the following commentary, you will see how the total amount of VAT due to Customs and Excise for 1996 is calculated, and how this can be related to the concept of value added.

Commentary

The VAT added to sales and collected from customers is known as the 'output' tax. For 1996 the output tax amounts to $(800,000 \times 0.175)$ £140,000.

The tax charged on goods purchased and paid to suppliers is known as the 'input' tax. For 1996 the input tax amounts to $(600,000 \times 0.175)$ £105,000.

The total VAT which this trader will have to pay to Customs and Excise for 1996 is the excess of output tax over the input tax, i.e. £140,000 less £105,000 = £35,000.

This trader will record sales at £800,000 and purchases at £600,000, i.e. value added of £200,000. The VAT of £35,000 paid over to Customs and Excise represents 17.5% of the £200,000 value added.

This example was highly contrived in order to demonstrate the basic principles of the tax and show how it is related to the concept of value added.

In reality the idea of value added becomes somewhat hazy because the trader will be charged VAT on many different kinds of inputs, such as motor expenses, telephone, stationery and so on. The VAT charged on these inputs will also be offset against the output tax when calculating the amount due to Customs and Excise. Furthermore, goods purchased in any particular period might not be sold in that period (they will go to increase the stock) yet the input tax on unsold goods is still deductible from the output tax for that period.

The most important principle of VAT in terms of its impact on the book-keeping is known as the 'tax point'. This is the date at which the taxable supply is considered to have been made, or received. In general terms, the tax point on outputs is the same as when the revenue is recognized in the books and in most cases this will be the date of the sales invoice. Consequently, a trader might have to account for VAT on outputs before the tax is actually received from the customer. This cash flow problem is ameliorated by being allowed to offset the input tax when the goods are purchased, and this could be in advance of when the supplier's account is actually paid.

The VAT regulations are quite extensive, and provide the small trader with a number of different schemes for operating the tax. One of these allows VAT to be accounted for on a cash basis (as opposed to an accruals basis) if the trader's turnover falls below a certain limit. It is not necessary in the study of financial accounting to learn all these different rules; it is sufficient to be aware of the general impact of VAT on the recording system.

The double-entry records

The double-entry for the VAT element of each transaction is quite simple. The trader will open a ledger account with the Customs and Excise. Although this is a personal account (in the sense that it is used to record transactions with a 'person' outside the business) it is normally kept in the nominal ledger.

The VAT charged on outputs (the amount added to the sales price) is credited to Customs and Excise. The VAT charged on inputs (the amount added to the purchase price of supplies received) is debited to Customs and Excise. The balance on the account with Customs and Excise shows the net amount due, and when this is paid the account is debited.

The complete double-entry for output and input tax depends on whether the transactions are on a cash or credit basis. For example, the VAT charged on cash sales will be debited to bank and credited to Customs and Excise; whereas VAT charged on credit sales will be debited to debtors and credited to Customs and Excise. A similar situation applies to the VAT on inputs. For example, the VAT on cash purchases will be debited to Customs and Excise and credited to bank; whereas VAT on credit purchases will be debited to Customs and Excise and credited to creditors.

Customs and Excise

Activity 9

A trader maintains the normal sales ledger control account and purchases ledger control account in his nominal ledger. All cash received is banked immediately. Transactions for year ended 31 December 1996 included the following:

		VAT added	Total
Cash sales	100,000	17,500	117,500
Credit sales	400,000	70,000	470,000
Credit purchases	300,000	52,500	352,500
Admin expenses (all paid by cheque)	40,000	2,000	42,000

Amount paid to Customs and Excise: £25,000.

Write up the account for Customs and Excise set out above (on p.182). Each entry in this account should identify the account to which the opposite entry is posted.

Notice that the normal trading items, such as sales, purchases and admin expenses, will be recorded as amounts that exclude the VAT element. For example, although the trader has charged £587,500 to its customers, £87,500 of this has been credited to Customs and Excise, leaving £500,000 to be credited to sales.

Recording VAT in the primary books

In order to accumulate the periodic totals for output and input tax, it will be necessary to include an additional column in each of the books of original entry (i.e. sales day book, purchases day book, cash received book, and cash payments book). These columns are used to record the VAT element of each transaction.

In order to see how these additional columns are used, we will look at the invoice from Pronto Printers Ltd again, but this time include the VAT charge. Here is the same invoice with the VAT charge added:

	Pronto Printers Ltd 347 Nowhere St Oxbridge
Ashford Traders 743 High Street Favingbourne	1 January 1997

INVOICE

To supplying 20 reams of headed notepaper	£200.00
Less trade discount (10%)	20.00
	£180.00
VAT 17.5% × (£180.00 − £1.80)	31.18
	£211.18

Credit terms: 1 month. 1% cash discount on the invoiced price of £180.00 for payment within 14 days

Notice that the invoice price for the supply is £180.00 but because Pronto Printers Ltd is offering a cash discount of £1.80, VAT is charged on the discounted amount irrespective of whether the cash discount is eventually taken. Notice also that the cash discount being offered is based on the VAT exclusive amount (another complication that makes cash discounts an unpopular device).

Looking at the transaction in the books of Ashford Traders, this is a credit purchase of stationery and will originally be recorded in the purchases day book. The entry in this book will be as follows:

Purchases day book

Date	Name	Total	VAT	Purchases	Stationery	etc.
1 Jan	Pronto Printers	211.18	31.18		180.00	

The VAT of £31.18 will be included in the total input VAT on credit purchases to be debited to Customs and Excise. The account for Pronto Printers Ltd will be credited with £211.18. If Ashford Traders pay the account within 14 days, and take the £1.80 cash discount offered, the entry in the cash payments book will be as follows:

Payments cash book

Date	Name	Disc.	Payment	VAT	Creditors	Purchases		
14 Jan	Pronto Printers	1.80	209.38		209.38			

Notice that the VAT is not entered again (neither is the cost of stationery) because this payment is for the settlement of a creditor (and VAT would have been recorded at the time of purchase). The VAT column in the payments cash book is used to record any input VAT paid on cash transactions, such as the payment of motor expenses or cash purchases. The entries in the primary books of Pronto Printers will be a mirror image of those shown above.

It should be fairly clear by now that the items appearing in the profit and loss account for income and expenses are exclusive of VAT. For this reason, VAT is usually ignored when explaining the principles on which financial statements are based.

You might be presented with a trial balance which includes an item described as 'VAT' but this will be the balance on the account for Customs and Excise. It will either be a creditor or a debtor and should be presented as such in the balance sheet. A debit balance on this account will arise when the input tax exceeds the output tax. This can happen in several situations, for example where a trader's outputs include a high proportion of exports which are chargeable to VAT at the zero rate. The debit balance represents an amount which will be refunded to the trader by Customs and Excise and so it should be treated as a debtor in the balance sheet in the normal way.

7.4 Carriage charges

It might seem a bit odd to single out a particular expense, such as carriage, for specific study. After all, we would not expect to spend time studying expenses such as electricity charges. This odd state of affairs stems from the history of business activity – even the word 'carriage' itself seems to conjure up an image of goods being delivered by horse and cart.

In the past, a purchase of goods would often result in two charges – the cost of the goods purchased and the cost of having them delivered to the business premises. Looked at from the purchaser's point of view, the delivery charge would be referred to as 'carriage inwards'. If the purchaser then sold the goods to another customer, and incurred further delivery charges, this cost is referred to as 'carriage outwards'.

Nowadays, the price quoted for goods being purchased will usually be inclusive of any delivery charge, and so a separate charge for carriage inwards (or outwards) is not very common. In cases where separate carriage inwards charges are incurred, the cost should be added on to the cost of purchases in the trading account. You can probably recall the definition of the cost of stock in SSAP 9 – all costs of bringing stock to its existing state and location. Consequently, a proportion of carriage inwards charges should be added to the purchase cost when determining the cost of closing stock.

Any carriage outwards charges should be treated as an expense in the profit and loss account, not the trading account. They are usually included in an item called 'selling and distribution costs'. Accounting for carriage charges is, therefore, nothing more than treating carriage inwards as a component of cost of sales in the trading account, and treating carriage outwards as an expense in the profit and loss account.

7.5 Petty cash transactions

It would be inconvenient for a business to pay all its expenses by cheque. There will be some payments that are best dealt with on a cash basis, such as the cleaner's fee, odd items of stationery from the shop across the road, travelling expenses, and so on.

Activity 10

The business will have to obtain the cash from somewhere in order to pay for these expenses. Make a note of where you think the cash will come from (this is obviously important if we are to make the correct book-keeping entries). There are two likely sources; try to identify both.

In a small business such as a retail shop, the owner often pays for expenses (and purchases) out of the cash takings in the till. You may even see this taking place if you happen to be in the shop at the time. But these businesses do not normally have a properly controlled system of double-entry book-keeping. You will be learning how to deal with their accounting system in Chapter 9, 'Incomplete records'.

A business of any size should not pay cash expenses out of takings. If the business is owned by a company, the auditors will undoubtedly advise management to establish a system that ensures all takings are banked intact on a daily basis. This system provides an element of internal control over cash takings (something you will learn if you study auditing).

In these cases, cash required for petty cash disbursements must be obtained from the bank by writing a cheque. The member of staff who looks after the petty cash will keep it in a safe place and also keep a record of disbursements. From time to time the petty cash float will be replenished by writing a further cheque.

In a well-controlled organization, the petty cash will be kept on what is known as an **imprest system**. This means that management will decide on the maximum amount that the petty cashier needs to hold in order to meet normal expenses – this amount is known as the 'imprest' amount. Petty cash vouchers are then kept as a record of each payment, and at any one time the cash on hand plus the total of the vouchers should equal the imprest amount.

At regular intervals, the petty cashier will summarize the petty cash vouchers and obtain a reimbursement of the cash spent. At this point the amount of cash on hand will equal the original imprest amount.

The summary of petty cash vouchers will show a total for each type of expense (travelling, stationery, etc.) and this summary is used as a medium for posting the double-entries in the ledger. In some cases the payments are entered in a book (a petty cash book) which is kept on much the same lines as the main cash book.

Activity 11

Describe the double-entries that will be made in the ledger for the following:

1. £200 cash withdrawn from the bank in order to set up a petty cash imprest.

Debit:

Credit:

2. Petty cash expenditure for the month: stationery £56, travelling expenses £102.

Debit:

Credit:

7.6 Suspense accounts

Some book-keeping errors (but not all of them) result in the trial balance failing to agree. You have already worked on this situation in Chapter 5. In practice, the errors will be traced and the trial balance agreed before the financial statements are prepared. Some errors can be corrected by a double-entry (through the journal), whereas others (such as an error in balancing off an account) will require alteration of a single figure.

Many years ago, someone must have suggested that where the trial balance does not agree, a fictitious balance (called a 'suspense account') should be inserted into the trial balance in order to make it agree. The inference seems to have been that this procedure would reduce delays in preparing the financial statements.

If the errors had not been found by the time the financial statements were prepared the treatment of the suspense account depended on whether or not it was a credit or a debit. To be on the safe side, a credit balance would be treated as a liability, whereas a debit balance would be treated as an expense. But such an approach is dangerous; the suspense account could be hiding very many errors. In view of this, the technique is very rarely used in practice.

It does, however, have one interesting side effect; it enables all book-keeping errors to be corrected by double-entry. This has ensured survival of the suspense account as a book-keeping procedure because it provides examiners with a model for testing a student's double-entry skills. Questions involving the correction of errors often include a situation where a suspense account has been set up as a result of the trial balance failing to agree.

It is only errors that cause the trial balance to disagree that will be corrected by a double-entry involving the suspense account. In some cases a serious error can be made and the trial balance will still agree. Take, for example, a business that maintains a sales ledger control account as part of the double-entry system. If the sales day book has been overcast by £1,000, both sales and debtors will be overstated by £1,000 and so the trial balance will agree.

Activity 12

Describe the double-entry that will be made in order to correct the error mentioned in the previous paragraph.

Activity 13

The error dealt with in Activity 12 would most likely have been found as a result of a difference arising in another balancing procedure at the end of the period. See if you can recall what this procedure is and describe the effect this error would have had.

Where the error causes the trial balance to disagree, and a suspense account is inserted in the trial balance in order to make it agree, the error will be corrected by a double-entry that includes the suspense account.

Activity 14

A business maintains a sales ledger control account as part of the double-entry in the ledger. The total of the sales day book for April was £45,000. This was posted to the debit of the sales ledger control account but was completely omitted from the sales account. This was the only error made in the books.

1. If a suspense account is inserted in the trial balance in order to make it agree, will it be a debit balance of £45,000 or a credit balance of £45,000?

2. Describe the double-entry that will be made in order to correct this error.

Debit:

Credit:

The same approach can be used in order to deal with errors in the subsidiary ledgers for debtors and creditors. In this case the suspense account is included in the list of debtors or creditors in order to make the total of the list agree with the balance on the respective control account. All errors made in the personal accounts can then be corrected by double-entry. Any balance remaining on the suspense account after correcting errors in the personal ledger will relate to errors on the control account. As soon as the control account has been corrected, the suspense account is deleted from the list.

Suspense account in computerized systems

Posting errors requiring the imposition of a suspense account to force a trial balance to agree do not occur in computerized systems (see section 5.9 in Chapter 5).

In a computerized system, suspense accounts are used only to receive the posting of entries where the correct account is not known at the time of the posting run. Examples would include the bank giro credit and standing order mentioned in Activity 3 (bank reconciliation).

An item is posted to the debit or credit of the suspense account as a temporary expendiency until the correct account is identified. After making enquiries to discover the account to which it should have been posted, the item will be transferred from the suspense account to the correct account by a journal entry.

7.7 Contra balances

This short heading has been used to cover two separate topics. One of them involves a simple book-keeping adjustment; the other is concerned with presentation in the balance sheet.

Debts payable to, and receivable from, the same person

Sometimes a business will buy goods from a supplier, and also sell goods (or services) to that same person. Consequently, there could be a creditor in the creditors ledger, and a debtor in the debtors ledger, for the same person.

Each party could settle their separate debts in the normal way, or (since there is likely to be an equitable right of set-off) the two balances could be combined and only the difference paid or claimed. If the right of set-off is applied, the procedure is known as a settlement by contra. This involves a simple double-entry to transfer the smaller amount from one ledger to the other. Where control accounts are kept, the double-entry will be between the two control accounts, with corresponding entries in the relevant person accounts.

Creditors in the debtors ledger, and vice versa

Most balances in the sales ledger will be debit balances but sometimes a debtor's account will be a credit balance.

Activity 15

Make a note of any reasons that occur to you as to why a debtor's account may be a credit balance.

The same situation could occur in the purchases ledger, i.e. the accounts for some suppliers could be debit balances – for various similar reasons.

There are no book-keeping adjustments to make in respect of these items, but they should be presented correctly in the balance sheet. For example, any creditors in the sales ledger should be included with creditors. Failure to do this would mean that the figure shown for debtors in the balance sheet is a net figure of debtors less any creditors in the sales ledger. In the same way, any debtors in the purchases ledger should be included with debtors in the balance sheet and not be allowed to reduce the figure shown for creditors. If these presentation rules are not applied, the financial statements could be misleading (and will contravene the Companies Act in the case of limited companies).

In the relevant control account, the amount carried down at the end of the period could be a net balance or two separate balances. For example, the balance carried down on the sales ledger control account could be the net balance of debtors less creditors, or as two balances, one balance for total debtors and the other for total creditors. The list of balances extracted from the sales ledger will usually show the debtors separately from the creditors.

Summary

The important learning points in this chapter are as follows:
- monthly bank reconciliations provide an opportunity to ensure that the bank account in the ledger is complete and correct
- a distinction must be made between items that require entry (or correction) in the cash book and those that appear in the reconciliation statement
- discounts received are a form of income and discounts allowed are a type of expense
- because cash discounts originate at the time of payment or receipt of cash, they are recorded in a memorandum column of the cash book
- relics from the past, such as three column cash books, are difficult to remove from the study of modern book-keeping
- VAT is a tax on the final consumer which has to be administered by the business community
- businesses charge VAT on their outputs and pay VAT on their inputs; the excess of VAT on outputs over VAT on inputs must be paid to Customs and Excise
- the VAT element in each transaction is recorded in the primary books and the procedure is such that items in the profit and loss account are exclusive of VAT
- carriage inwards forms part of the cost of sales; it should also be taken into account in calculating the cost of closing stock
- carriage outwards is a distribution expense dealt with in the profit and loss account
- petty cash transactions are normally dealt with on an imprest system
- suspense accounts are used to make a trial balance agree; all errors traced can then be corrected by a double-entry
- suspense accounts are also a relic from the past but they enable examiners to test a student's book-keeping skills
- personal accounts (debtors and creditors) are sometimes settled by contra
- any creditors in the sales ledger should be included with creditors in the balance sheet, and debtors in the purchases ledger should be included with debtors

The questions at the end of this chapter include a number of exam questions involving book-keeping errors, suspense accounts and control accounts. These provide a good opportunity to revise some previous studies, particularly those in Chapter 5. These questions could not be set at the end of Chapter 5 because they included items that you would not have recognized until you had completed this present chapter.

Activity 1

You could have included any of the following:

1. Bank charges (not previously entered in the payments cash book).
2. Cheques written prior to the statement date which have not passed through the account (these are usually called 'unpresented cheques').
3. Direct debits (such as standing orders) not entered in the payments cash book.
4. Direct credits (e.g. customers paying by direct debit) not entered in the receipts cash book.
5. Bankings made shortly before the statement date which have not been credited on the bank statement (this can happen when a lodgement is made at a branch other than the one where the account is kept – they are usually called 'uncleared lodgements').
6. Mistakes in the books.
7. Mistakes by the bank.

Activity 2

1. It was assumed that the statement showed a balance of cash at the bank.
2. If the account had been overdrawn, the uncleared lodgements would be deducted from the balance on the statement, the unpresented cheques would be added.

Activity 3

The problem includes two transactions for which assumptions have to be made.

1. A cheque numbered 427519 appears on the bank statement but the number does not correspond to the series of numbers currently being used according to the cash book. There are two likely explanations: (a) the bank has made a mistake and charged Mr Laker's account in error, or (b) Mr Laker uses two cheque books and this particular cheque has not been entered in the cash book. In the following solution it has been assumed that the bank has made a mistake (the alternative assumption is equally valid).
2. A cheque entered in the cash book as £87.77 (cheque number 236130) appears on the bank statement as £77.87. Either the bank or Mr Laker's book-keeper has made a mistake. It is assumed that the bank statement is correct and that the mistake is in Mr Laker's books.

Both items should be included with those requiring investigation.

Corrected cash book balance:

Balance per cash book			1,310.40
Less:	Bank charges	12.80	
	Standing order	32.52	
			45.32
			1,265.08
Add:	Bank Giro Credit		21.47
			1,286.55
Add:	overstatement of cheque 236130		9.90
			1,296.45

Reconciliation statement:

Balance per bank statement			1,166.45
Add: cheque 427519 charged in error			19.47
			1,185.92
Less: unpresented cheques	131	30.00	
	134	52.27	
			82.27
			1,103.65
Add: uncleared lodgement			192.80
			1,296.45

The following points require further investigation:

1. Cheque 427519 – is it Mr Laker's or is it a mistake by the bank?
2. Cheque 236130 – is it for £87.77 or £77.87?
3. Bank giro credit of £21.47 – who is it from and what is it for?
4. Standing order of £32.52 – who is it paid to and what is it for?

Activity 4

Pronto Printers Ltd have a debt outstanding of £180 and they receive cash of only £178.20 (i.e. £180.00 – £1.80). When the cash of £178.20 is credited to the debtors account there will still be a balance outstanding of £1.80 and yet nothing is legally owing since Ashford Traders were told they could deduct £1.80 if they paid within 14 days.

Activity 5

Debit discounts allowed £1.80; credit sales ledger control account £1.80.

Activity 6

Debit purchase ledger control account with £1.80; credit discounts received account £1.80.

Activity 7

1. Debit purchases ledger control account; credit discounts received account.
2. Debit discounts allowed account; credit sales ledger control account.

Activity 8

You may have thought of:

1. Operating a regime of strict credit control (e.g. obtaining credit references for new debtors, setting credit limits, sending statements and follow up letters on time, taking legal action where appropriate).
2. Charging interest on overdue accounts.

Activity 9

Customs and Excise

31 Dec 96 Purchases ledger control a/c	52,500	31 Dec 96 Bank (output VAT)		17,500
31 Dec 96 Bank (input VAT)	2,000	31 Dec 96 Sales ledger control a/c		70,000
31 Dec 96 Bank	25,000			
31 Dec 96 Balance c/d	8,000			
	87,500			87,500
		1 Jan 97 Balance b/d		8,000

Activity 10

(1) out of cash takings, and (2) withdrawing cash from the bank.

Activity 11

1. Debit	Petty cash account	£200	
	Credit Bank account		£200
2. Debit	Stationery	£56	
	Travelling expenses	£102	
	Credit Petty cash account		£158

The ledger account for petty cash will show a balance of cash on hand amounting to £42. This is simply carried forward as an asset.

Activity 12

Debit sales £1,000; credit sales ledger control account £1,000.

Activity 13

Agreeing the total of the list of debtors with the balance on the control account. If no other errors have been made, the list of debtors will be £1,000 less than the balance on the control account.

Activity 14

1. The suspense account will be a credit balance of £45,000.
2. Debit suspense account £45,000; credit sales £45,000.

Activity 15

There could be several reasons, e.g. the debtor paid more than was due; a credit note was sent to the customer after the account had been paid in full; or the debtor paid the account twice.

Questions for self-assessment

Answers to self-assessment questions are given at the end of the book.

The following is an AEB A Level question. You will find that it is necessary to do a bank reconciliation at the beginning of the month in order to determine the opening balance in the cash book. For some reason or other the examiner presented the bank statement in a most unrealistic manner, but this should not prevent you from compiling an adequate answer.

7.1   Leslie, a sole trader, has had his cash book stolen. Fortunately both his cheque book and paying in book are still available, as is his bank statement. His bank statement for the month of May is as follows:

	Dr £	Cr £	Balance £	
Opening balance			85	
J. Green	150		65	OD
R. Black	220		285	OD
Cash		210	75	OD
Johnson		45	30	OD
Cash		350	320	
C. Lord	142		178	
Smith	324		146	OD
Interest	24		170	OD
Cash		410	240	
Pryce	81		159	
Jackson		76	235	
Credit transfer – Mills		25	260	
Standing order – insurance	10		250	

The cheque for C. Lord was drawn on 28 April and entered in the cash book on that date. In addition the following lists have been extracted from Leslie's cheque book and paying in book for May:

Cheque book	£	*Paying in book*	£
J. Green	150	Cash	210
R. Black	220	Cash	350
F. Jones	415	Cash	410
G. Smith	324	Johnson	45
T. Pryce	81	Jackson	76
A. Wright	47	Lawton	186
		Arnold	210

Required:
Prepare the bank columns in the cash book of Leslie for the month of May and prepare a reconciliation of the closing balance with that given in the bank account.

The following question was set by the Chartered Association of Certified Accountants in the Level 1 Accounting exam. It is a little more involved than 7.1, but it is an excellent exercise and the time spent in trying to solve it will be well spent.

7.2   A young and inexperienced book-keeper is having great difficulty in producing a bank reconciliation statement at 31 December. He gives you his attempt to produce a summarized cash book and also the bank statement received for the month of December. These are shown below. You may assume that the bank statement is correct. You may also assume that the trial balance at 1 January did indeed show a bank overdraft of £7,000.12.

Cash book summary — draft

Jan 1 Overdraft b/d		7,000.12	Payments Jan–Nov	35,000.34
Jan–Nov receipts	39,500.54			
Add discounts	500.52			
		40,000.56	Balance 30 Nov	12,000.34
		47,000.68		47,000.68
Dec 1		12,000.34	Dec Payments	
			Cheque No.	
Dec Receipts	178.19		7654	37.14
	121.27		7655	192.79
	14.92		7656	5,000.00
	16.88		7657	123.45
		329.26	7658	678.90
Dec Receipts	3,100.00		7659	1.47
	171.23		7660	19.84
	1,198.17		7661	10.66
		4,469.40		
			Balance c/d	10,734.75
		16,799.00		16,799.00
Dec 31 Balance b/d		10,734.75		

Bank statement – 31 December	Withdrawals	Deposits	Balance
Dec 1			800.00
7650	300.00	178.19	
7653	191.91	121.27	
7654	37.14	14.92	
7651	1,111.11	16.88	
7656	5,000.00	3,100.00	
7655	129.79	171.23	
7658	678.90	1,198.17	
Standing order	50.00	117.98	
7659	1.47		
7661	10.66		
Bank charges	80.00		
Dec 1			3,472.34

Required:

Prepare:

(a) A corrected cash book summary and a reconciliation of the balance on this revised summary with the bank statement balance as at 31 December, as far as you are able.

(b) A brief note as to the likely cause of any remaining difference.

7.3 The following balances have been included in a sales ledger control account for the year ended 31 January 19X6:

Balance at 1 February 19X5	12,087
Sales (note 1)	117,635
Receipts from customers (note 2)	90,019
Discounts allowed (note 3)	3,000
Goods returned by customers	4,200
Bad debts written off (note 4)	1,550

Balances extracted from the sales ledger at 31 January 19X6 were:

Debit	35,588
Credit (note 5)	185

Notes:
1. It was discovered that a batch of sales invoices totalling £3,400 had been omitted from the accounting records.
2. Cash sales of £600 had been included in this total.
3. Discounts allowed of £350, included in this total, had been omitted from the personal ledger.
4. The personal ledger accounts of the 'bad debtors' had been debited with £1,550, whilst the correct entry had been made into the control account.
5. Credit balances in the sales ledger of £400 had been transferred during the year into the purchases ledger. No record of this transfer had been made in the control account, although the personal accounts had been correctly adjusted.

Required:
(a) Prepare the sales ledger control account for the year ended 31 January 19X6.
(b) Prepare a statement reconciling the sales ledger balances with the control account balance.
(c) Under which balance sheet heading should credit balances contained within a sales ledger be shown?

(ULSEB A Level)

Questions without answers

Answers to these questions are published separately in the *Teacher's Manual*.

7.4 After the extraction of the balances from the books of Bland, the totals of the trial balance failed to agree. In addition, the credit balance of £2,450 on the purchases ledger control account, included in the trial balance, did not agree with the total of balances extracted from the purchases ledger. The following items have subsequently been discovered:
1. The payment of £265 for office supplies has been entered correctly in the cash book but has been credited to the office expenses account in the nominal ledger as £256.
2. The payment of £290 for the maintenance of an item of machinery has been correctly entered in the cash book but has been debited to the machinery account.
3. The total of the discount received column in the cash book has been undercast by £27.
4. No entry has been made in the accounts relating to the return to a supplier of goods to the value of £175 which had been purchased on credit.
5. The purchase on credit of goods for £110 from Parks, who is a customer and a supplier, has been correctly entered in the accounts. It has now been decided to set off the amount owing against the balance on Parks' account in the sales ledger.

Required:
(a) A purchase ledger control account showing clearly the amendments to the original balance.
(b) A suspense account showing clearly the original discrepancy on the trial balance.

Author's guidance note: In order to answer the above question, you will have to assume that appropriate corrections clear the original discrepancies. This point has not been made clear in the question.

(AEB A Level)

7.5 A trial balance has an excess of debits over credits of £14,000 and a suspense account has been opened to make it balance. It is later discovered that:
1. The discounts allowed balance of £3,000 and the discounts received balance of £7,000 had both been entered on the wrong side of the trial balance.
2. The creditors control account balance of £233,786 had been included in the trial balance as £237,386.

3. An item of £500 had been omitted from the sales records (i.e. from the sales day book).
4. The balance on a current account with the owner's wife had been omitted from the trial balance. This item when corrected removes the suspense account altogether.

Required:
Open the suspense account and record the necessary corrections in it. Show, in the account, the double-entry for each item entered.

Author's guidance note: The current account referred to in item 4 is either a debtor or a creditor – but it has obviously been kept as a separate account in the nominal ledger and not in the debtors or creditors ledgers.

(ACCA 1.1, Jun 90)

The following A Level question is a good example of how students are expected to use accounting information in order to give practical business advice. Part (a) is a simple book-keeping problem, but parts (b) and (c) will require you to apply your general knowledge of accounting and business matters, some of which were dealt with in this chapter. You should be able to answer part (d) from earlier work.

This is the first time you have been asked to prepare financial information in a way that will help the business to make a decision. Such questions are a prominent feature in modern exams and the time spent trying to make sense of this one will be of considerable benefit to the way you approach your future studies.

7.6 Glover has been selling on a cash only basis for several years. However, faced with a decline in sales as a result of customers being able to obtain credit elsewhere, he decided in January 19X3 to sell on credit. Anticipating bad debts, he decided to create a provision for doubtful debts of 5% of debtors.

Glover's cash sales remained unchanged and his credit sales were £20,000 for the year ended 30 September 19X3 and £30,000 for the year ended 30 September 19X4. Normally a gross profit of 15% on selling price is earned and debtors were taking on average six months to settle their accounts. Debtors on 30 September 19X3 were £12,000 and on 30 September 19X4 were £15,000.

Actual bad debts incurred during the year ended 30 September 19X3 were £400 and during the year ended 30 September 19X4 were £1,300. In order to provide the necessary working capital for the change in policy Glover arranged a loan which incurred interest of £2,000 per annum.

Required:
(a) The bad debts account and provision for doubtful debts accounts for the years ended 30 September 19X3 and 19X4, respectively.
(b) A statement showing the effect on the revenue of the business during each of the two years of the decision to sell goods on credit.
(c) A critical examination of the matters which Glover would have to take into account in deciding whether he should continue to offer credit on his current terms.
(d) State and explain two accounting conventions involved in creating a provision for doubtful debts.

7.7 JC Ltd uses a computerized accounting system to record its transactions and produce a trial balance. The trial balance which was produced by the system at 31 March 19X0 showed that the bank balance was £12,879 overdrawn, but the bank statement which is reproduced below showed a balance on the same date of £5,467 credit. A bank account control report was printed by the accountants of JC Ltd so that the transactions could be compared.

JC Ltd
Computerized accounting system control report
Bank account Code 99 transactions from 01/03/X0 to 31/03/X0

Date		Dr £	Cr £	Balance £
01/03/X0	Balance			4,201
02/03/X0	J. Smith & Sons	1,405		
	White Brothers	697		6,303
04/03/X0	Brown & Co	234		6,537
07/03/X0	543987		279	
	543988		1,895	
	543989		11,987	(7,624)
10/03/X0	J. Lake	1,386		(6,238)
12/03/X0	543990		1,497	
	543991		547	
	543992		296	(8,578)
17/03/X0	Grey Enterprises	2,569		
	Hunt Lodges	34		
	B. Black	643		(5,332)
24/03/X0	543993		2,305	(7,637)
31/03/X0	543994		5,242	(12,879)

The bank statement for the same month was as follows:

Nattown Bank   Statement of account   31/03/X0

Date		Dr £	Cr £	Balance £
March				
1	Balance		3,529	
3	Counter credit		2,489	6,018
4	543986	237		5,781
6	Counter credit		2,102	7,883
7	Bank charges	195		
	543988	1,895		5,793
9	Counter credit		234	6,027
11	543985	68		5,959
13	Brown & Co cheque dishonoured	234		
	543989	1,197		4,528
14	Counter credit		1,486	6,014
17	543990	1,497		
	543992	296		4,221
23	Counter credit		5,332	9,553
25	Standing order: Rates	4,029		5,524
27	543991	57		5,467
31	Balance		5,467	

The balances on 1 March 19X0 were reconciled, the difference being partly due to the following cheques which were unpresented on that date:

Cheque	543984	£1,512
	543985	£68
	543986	£237

Required:

(a) Prepare a bank reconciliation statement at 31 March 19X0.

(b) List *three* reasons why bank reconciliation statements should be prepared reguarly.

(CIMA, May 90)

7.8 Polly Ltd has a year end of 31 December. At 30 November 19X3, the following balances exist in the ledger for the VAT, bank and debtors' accounts:

	£
VAT owing to Customs and Excise	3,250
Bank overdraft	6,250
Debtors	127,000

During December 19X3, the following transactions take place:

(i)   Sales of £85,000 plus VAT are made on credit.
(ii)   A motor car costing £8,000 plus VAT is bought and paid for by cheque.
(iii)   Materials are purchased on credit for £27,000 plus VAT.
(iv)   Materials costing £3,000 plus VAT are returned to the supplier and a refund given by cheque.
(v)   Administration expenses of £2,400 plus VAT are incurred and paid for by cheque.
(vi)   A VAT refund of £1,567 for the quarter ended 31 October 19X3 is received by cheque from Customs and Excise.
(vii)   Debtors pay the balance outstanding at 30 November 19X3 by cheque, deducting £2,000 cash discount.
(viii) Creditors are paid £42,000 by cheque.

VAT is 17.5% in all cases.

Required:
(a)   Prepare the VAT account for December 19X3, showing the closing balance.
(b)   Calculate the bank balance at 31 December 19X3.
(c)   Explain the purpose of the trial balance and describe *four* different types of error which could occur in the trial balance, which would prevent its agreement.

Illustrate your answer using simple examples.

(CIMA Specimen paper, 94)

The accounts of a manufacturer

Objectives

After you have completed this chapter, you should be able to:
- prepare the financial statements for a manufacturing entity
- identify some of the shortcomings of financial accounting when used as a management information system in a manufacturing entity
- outline the role of cost accounting in management information systems
- identify some of the additional accounting problems associated with divisional business activity

---

Introduction

Chapters 2 to 7 have dealt with the basic system for recording transactions and reporting the results of business activity in the form of financial statements. The concepts and mechanics of that system form a bedrock upon which financial accounting studies are based.

We can now move away from the actual books and start to apply the principles of financial accounting to the specific problems presented by the type of business entity. Some of these problems stem from the different forms of ownership, and some from the different forms of economic activity. In this chapter you will learn how the basic system is used to provide financial statements for a manufacturing business.

The type of financial statement dealt with in this chapter is another relic from the past. The techniques were developed long before cost accounting had become established. The result of this evolution in accounting practices is that we are left with a financial statement that is inadequate to enable management to run the business, and yet contains more detail than the owners need to enable them to assess the firm's performance. But the study of manufacturing accounts does provide an excellent bridge between the study of financial accounting and the study of cost accounting. It is also a popular subject in some financial accounting exams.

8.1 The accounting problem

In all previous chapters, business activity was confined to buying goods for resale. This made it relatively easy to determine the cost of sales for any particular period. The main difference between a retailer and a manufacturer as far as cost of sales is concerned is that a retailer simply incurs the cost of purchasing goods for resale whereas a manufacturer will incur the cost of making them. The additional accounting problem for a manufacturer is, therefore, to determine the cost of making the finished goods during the period.

Before studying that particular point, however, you will find it helpful to focus on the trading account. At the trading account level, there are broad similarities between the figures for a retailer and the figures for a manufacturer. The cost of manufacturing the finished goods will simply take the place of the cost of purchases when calculating cost of sales.

Activity 1

In the case of a retailer, cost of sales is determined from the basic equation:

opening stock + purchases − closing stock

Set out this basic equation as it would apply to a manufacturer. The principle is the same, but the descriptions will alter.

Notice that the stock being referred to here is the stock of finished (manufactured) goods. This description identifies an important point because a manufacturer will have various kinds of stock at any particular accounting date, but it is only the stock of finished goods (those ready for sale) that is used in this form of the cost of sales calculation. This finished goods stock is brought into the books at cost, although determining their cost is somewhat more of a problem than in the case of a retailer.

Activity 2

See if you can describe another class of closing stock that a manufacturer could be holding at the accounting date, other than finished goods.

There will often be another class of stock known as 'work-in-progress', i.e. goods that are in the process of manufacture but are not yet completed. This will happen where the manufacturing process is spread over a number of days, weeks or months, and the accounting date falls before the process is completed. Both the stock of raw materials and the stock of work-in-progress (if any) will be taken into account when determining the cost of finished goods manufactured during the period.

In financial accounting, the cost of making finished goods during the period is determined by preparing an additional statement known as a 'manufacturing account'. This statement precedes the trading account and so the full set of statements from which net profit is determined could be referred to as a manufacturing, trading, and profit and loss account.

8.2 Inadequacies of financial accounting for a manufacturer

Financial accounting has much earlier origins than cost accounting. The existence of manufacturing accounts in text books, and in examination syllabuses for financial accounting, probably owes more to the historical developments of accounting rather than contemporary usage. The manufacturing accounts that you learn about in this chapter are only likely to be found in the smallest of business entities. If you look at the published financial statements of some of the large manufacturers (such as ICI) you will not find a manufacturing account among their income statements – but there is a profit and loss account.

Financial accounting is concerned mainly with the periodic reporting of results, particularly to the owners, rather than with providing management with the information needed for decision making. A manufacturing account enables the total cost of all goods manufactured in the period to be determined. This may be adequate for determining profit but does not help a manager who wants to know the cost of individual products to exercise control over product costs.

In the early days of manufacturing, selling prices tended to be so much above total costs that there was no real need for detailed information on product costs. When competition became more intense, managers needed to look more closely at individual product costs. Cost accounting emerged as a means of satisfying this need (as well as satisfying the needs of government during the 1914–1918 war regarding the cost of armaments that were being purchased on a 'cost plus' basis).

Various systems of cost accounting were developed. In a manufacturing entity of any size today, there will be a 'sub-system' of cost accounting that is fully integrated with the financial accounts. Such a system actually generates a figure for cost of sales (for the profit and loss account) as well as providing management with all the detailed information needed on individual products. The cost accounting system has, therefore, taken the place of the manufacturing account in all but the smallest of businesses.

In view of this, the subject of manufacturing accounts has been removed from the accounting syllabus of some professional accounting examinations. It is still worthwhile studying the subject, even if it is excluded from your own particular syllabus. You will probably be studying cost accounting at some time (if not already) and some aspects of that subject can seem a little disjointed without the manufacturing account as a foundation.

8.3 Manufacturing costs

Given that the purpose of the manufacturing account is to determine the cost of all finished goods manufactured during the period, the first step in trying to make sense of this account is to think about the way in which such costs might be classified.

Activity 3

Think about an imaginary factory (or perhaps one that you know about) and make a list of some of the costs that are likely to be incurred in the manufacture of finished goods. Describe them in whatever manner seems appropriate.

The costs referred to in the key (and probably in your own answer) have been described by what is known as their natural classification, i.e. we have described them according to the nature (or type) of expense. This classification is sometimes referred to as a subjective classification.

It is more usual to group expenses under 'functional' headings (sometimes referred to as an objective classification). Each type of manufacturing cost can be included under one of three (sometimes four) main functional headings, namely:

- Direct materials
- Direct labour
- Manufacturing overheads.

Direct materials are those raw materials that can conveniently be identified and recorded as a constituent part of the cost of a finished product. You can get the idea by looking at some of the manufactured products in your own room. Think about a table or desk (perhaps the one you are sitting at while studying this chapter). There could be a wooden (or chipboard) top screwed to a steel frame and legs. It would be relatively easy to keep an accounting record of the timber and steel used to make the product, and these would be classified as direct materials.

But some of the raw materials used in its manufacture cannot easily be measured as forming a part of the direct cost and will have to be classified as overheads.

Activity 4

List some of the raw materials that might have been used in the manufacture of a product, such as a table or desk, which cannot easily be measured as forming a specific part of its direct cost.

Materials such as these are referred to as 'indirect materials' and form part of the total of manufacturing overheads.

The same consideration applies to labour costs. The expression 'direct labour' refers to the employees who are actually involved in putting the finished product together.

Activity 5

There will be many other employees in the factory, other than those who are directly involved in making the finished product. Make a list of some of these employees.

The cost of wages paid to these members of staff is referred to as 'indirect labour' and, as with indirect materials, the cost forms part of the total of manufacturing overheads. As you can imagine, there are many other manufacturing overheads apart from indirect materials and indirect labour, e.g. electricity, depreciation of manufacturing plant, and so on.

In cost accounting, the main difference between direct and indirect costs is that a basis has to be found for spreading indirect costs over all the products made in the accounting period, whereas direct costs are specifically allocated to particular products. A significant part of the foundation studies in cost accounting is directed towards learning how overheads are attributed to the cost of finished goods. As a subject it is usually called **overhead absorption**.

Manufacturing techniques have changed quite dramatically over the last 50 years or so. In the past, overheads formed a very small part of the total manufactured cost of a product and so it did not matter if the basis used for overhead absorption was somewhat arbitrary. But today, with the trend being towards automation, overheads are often the largest part of the cost of a product, and overhead absorption needs to be more scientific. This has resulted in the development of new cost accounting techniques, such as Activity Based Costing (ABC) for relating overheads to finished goods. In financial accounting, these problems can be ignored.

The total of direct material costs plus direct labour costs is called 'prime cost'. Sometimes there is an expense that can be classified as direct (other than direct materials and direct labour), which will form part of the prime cost. These costs are quite rare but a good example is production royalties, i.e. an amount that has to be paid to the inventor for each unit made.

The relationship between the different types of cost for a particular product can be set out as follows:

Direct materials	X
Direct labour	X
Direct expense (such as royalties)	X
Prime cost	X
Manufacturing overheads	X
Total factory cost	X

Prime cost is sometimes referred to as variable (or marginal) cost because the total amount expended in the period will vary according to the number of units made. By contrast, most manufacturing overheads can be treated as fixed costs because the total amount expended is not influenced by the number of units made.

The distinction between fixed and variable (marginal) costs is important when it comes to the calculation of the cost of finished goods stock for the trading account. The subject is dealt with in section 8.6.

In some cases, the details given to you in order to determine the total cost of all finished goods manufactured in the period are set out under headings similar to the following:

- Raw materials
- Manufacturing wages
- Manufacturing expense or overheads.

The manufacturing account can easily be built up from such a classification although when you come to study cost accounting in more detail you will need to appreciate that raw materials are not the same thing as direct materials, and that manufacturing wages are not the same thing as direct wages.

8.4 Raw materials

The raw material costs to be included as part of the cost of making finished goods for a particular period will be the cost of raw materials consumed (or used) during that period. This will not be the same figure as the cost of raw materials purchased since there will undoubtedly be some raw material stocks to take into account.

When calculating the cost of goods sold for a retailer we added the cost of opening stock to the cost of goods purchased, and deducted the cost of closing stock. The cost of raw materials consumed (used up) can be found by using the same approach.

Activity 6

The cost of raw materials in store at the start of an accounting period was £4,500. The cost of raw materials purchased from suppliers during the period was £102,800. The cost of raw materials in store at the end of the period was £5,300. Calculate the cost of raw materials consumed in the manufacture of finished goods during the period.

In a manufacturing business of any size there will be a control account for raw material stocks that forms part of the sub-system of cost accounting. This account records all movements (i.e. receipts from suppliers and issues to production) from which the balance of raw material stocks can be ascertained. In such a system, the cost of raw materials issued to production equates to the cost of raw materials consumed. The usual problem of changing prices arises, requiring the business to adopt a policy such as FIFO for pricing issues.

In financial accounting an assumption is made that raw material purchases are recorded in the 'raw material purchases' account and that raw materials consumed is derived by making adjustments to raw material purchases for opening and closing stock. In exams, the cost of raw material stocks on hand is usually provided as determined data.

8.5 Work-in-progress

Financial statements are prepared up to a particular date. If the manufacturing process is spread over several days, weeks or months, there are likely to be some goods that are only partly manufactured at the accounting date. Costs will have been incurred in getting these goods to their partly manufactured state, but such costs do not form part of the cost of manufacturing finished goods during the period.

Imagine a beer manufacturer, and assume that the brewing process takes 4 weeks. The accounting date falls during the middle of this 4-week process. At this point various costs have been incurred. The total manufacturing costs for the period will include costs that relate to this particular brew. Some of these costs will be included in raw materials consumed (grain, hops, malt, etc.) while others will be included under manufacturing wages and overheads.

The purpose of the manufacturing account is to determine the cost of finished goods manufactured during the period. If some of the costs recorded in this account relate to goods that are only partly manufactured, such costs will have to be deducted from the costs incurred in order to find the cost of finished goods manufactured.

Activity 7

During its first accounting year, a manufacturer incurred the following costs:

Raw materials consumed:	24,000
Direct wages:	68,000
Manufacturing overheads:	8,000

A measurement of work-in-progress at the end of the year showed that costs of £8,000 had been incurred in bringing this work-in-progress to its present state. Calculate the costs incurred in manufacturing finished goods during the period.

This is normally set out in the manufacturing account as follows:

Manufacturing costs:	
Raw materials consumed	24,000
Direct wages	68,000
	92,000
Manufacturing overheads	18,000
	110,000
Less cost of work-in-progress	8,000
Cost of finished goods manufactured	102,000

The cost of the work-in-progress will be carried forward into the next accounting period in the books and is treated as an asset in the balance sheet. Since this cost represents a form of stock, it is included under the heading of stocks in the balance sheet. Consequently, the current assets in the balance sheet of a manufacturer could include stocks under three sub-classifications, namely:

- Raw materials
- Work-in-progress
- Finished goods.

Activity 8

Think about the second year of the manufacturer in the previous example. Describe how the cost of opening work-in-progress will have to be treated in calculating the cost of manufacturing finished goods during the second year. The concept involved is similar to the way in which cost of sales (or cost of raw materials consumed) is determined.

By bringing the cost of work-in-progress forward from the previous year we are applying the matching concept. The costs were incurred in the previous year but they have been brought forward and form part of the cost of manufacturing finished goods during the current year.

A detailed manufacturing account can, therefore, be set out as follows:

Manufacturing costs during the period:

Raw materials consumed:		
Opening stock of raw materials	X	
Add: purchases of raw materials	X	
	X	
Less: closing stock of raw materials	(X)	
		X
Direct wages		X
Prime cost		X
Manufacturing overheads		X
		X
Add: cost of opening work-in-progress		X
Less: cost of closing work-in-progress		(X)
Cost of finished goods manufactured		X

In order to tidy up the presentation, some of the detail is often excluded. For example, raw materials consumed does not have to be calculated on the face of the manufacturing account. It can be calculated on a working paper and included in the manufacturing account as a single item called raw materials consumed.

Sometimes you will see manufacturing accounts where the details for opening and closing work-in-progress are not included; there will be a single figure described as an increase or decrease in work-in-progress. This increase or decrease relates to the difference between opening and closing work-in-progress.

Activity 9

Suppose you were given a figure which is described as a decrease in work-in-progress of £3,200. Would you add this to the manufacturing costs for the period, or deduct it, in order to determine cost of finished goods manufactured during the period?

If you find this idea difficult to grasp you may be able to sort it out in your mind by reasoning as follows:

If opening and closing work-in-progress had been the same figure, the cost of making finished goods during the period would be the same as the manufacturing costs incurred in that period. If opening work-in-progress is £3,200 greater than closing work-in-progress, the cost of making finished goods during the period will be £3,200 greater than the manufacturing costs incurred in that period.

Activity 10

From the following details, prepare a manufacturing account and a trading account. Use your creative skills to keep the amount of detail presented in the manufacturing account to a reasonable minimum.

Stocks:	Opening	Closing
Raw materials	£2,000	£2,800
Work-in-progress	4,600	5,100
Finished goods	14,800	15,500

Manufacturing costs for the period were:	
Raw materials purchased	87,000
Direct wages	92,000
Manufacturing overheads	73,000

Sales were £350,000

Use the space below for your answer.

8.6 Cost and net realizable value

All three categories of stock are subject to the valuation principles contained in SSAP 9 (see Chapter 4). This means that each item of stock, whether it be an item of raw material, work-in-progress or finished product, must be brought into the books at the lower of cost or net realizable value.

Cost

In exams, the cost of closing stocks of raw materials, work-in-progress and finished goods is often provided as given data in notes to the question. In practice, a cost accounting system is needed to determine the cost of work-in-progress and the cost of finished goods. It would be virtually impossible in a multi-product firm to determine these costs without a cost accounting system. As mentioned earlier, these cost accounting records are usually integrated with the financial accounting records, and this system makes it unnecessary to prepare a separate manufacturing account.

In the case of raw materials, it would be possible to determine their cost without a cost accounting system because the stock could be counted and purchase prices found from the purchase invoices.

In some examination questions, the cost of closing stock of finished goods is not given and has to be determined from quantitative data. These questions are highly contrived in the sense that they are usually based on an entity that manufactures one type of product. Determining the number of units in stock is relatively straightforward and usually assumes that no units were lost. In this case the calculation is based on opening quantity, plus quantity made, less quantity sold.

When it comes to calculating the cost of each unit for the closing stock valuation, there are two bases that could be used, namely:

1. marginal cost, or
2. absorbed cost.

Marginal cost per unit can be found by dividing total variable costs (direct materials, direct labour and any variable overheads) by the number of units made. In many questions, variable cost is often treated as being the same as prime cost (the total direct costs), although strictly speaking these are two separate concepts of cost.

Absorbed cost per unit is found by taking the marginal cost per unit and adding an amount for fixed production overheads per unit. According to SSAP 9 the amount of fixed production overhead per unit should be found by dividing the total fixed production overheads by the **normal** quantity that could be produced, not the actual quantity produced. However, in exams the normal production levels are not always given and actual production levels have to be used in the calculation.

Since the absorbed cost of finished goods stock is higher than marginal cost, reported profits will vary according to the basis used for valuing closing stock of finished goods. SSAP 9, which governs the valuation principle for limited companies, requires manufactured stock to be valued on the basis of absorbed cost.

In some accounting exams you could be asked to demonstrate how the two valuation principles affect reported profits. You can practise this in the next activity.

Activity 11

A sole trader has set up business to manufacture a single product. Manufacturing costs during the first period were as follows:

Raw materials consumed	42,000
Direct labour	38,000
Prime cost	80,000
Fixed production overheads	20,000
Total production costs	100,000

40,000 units were manufactured and there was no work-in-progress at the end of the period. 38,000 units were sold for a total sales value of £140,000. Prepare two trading accounts, using (a) marginal cost, and (b) absorbed cost, as the basis for valuing finished goods stock. You can answer this by completing the following two tables. Include your calculation of closing stock within the brackets.

(a) **Trading account**			(b) **Trading account**		
Stock at marginal cost			Stock at absorbed cost		
Sales		140,000	Sales		140,000
Cost of sales:			Cost of sales:		
Manufacturing costs	100,000		Manufacturing costs	100,000	
Less closing stock			Less closing stock		
( )		_____	( )		_____
Gross profit		_____	Gross profit		_____

Net realizable value

As regards net realizable value, there are no new aspects to consider except in the case of work-in-progress. In broad terms, net realizable value is defined as the ultimate selling price less the costs of completion and selling. This definition becomes quite useful in the case of work-in-progress.

Activity 12

At the accounting date of 31 December, a manufacturer had a partly manufactured item of stock on hand. The cost accounting records show that costs incurred on this item up to 31 December amount to £6,800. In its partly completed state it could be sold for scrap at a price of £2,000 but when it is finished it can be sold for £9,000. Estimated costs to complete the item during the next period amount to £1,200. State the value at which this item of work-in-progress should be included in the accounts at 31 December.

8.7 Divisional activity and transfer prices

The total business entity in many large organizations is often divided into segments called divisions. The separation of manufacturing activity from trading activity is one example of this divisional arrangement.

In many cases, the transfer of goods from the manufacturing division to the trading division is recorded at a price in excess of cost. In other words the manufacturing division is treated as if it had sold the goods to the trading division. Conversely, the trading division is treated as if it had bought the goods from the manufacturing division.

Each division then becomes what is known as a 'profit centre'. There will be a profit in the manufacturing division equal to the difference between the total transfer price of all the goods manufactured, and the cost of manufacturing those goods. This is sometimes called a manufacturing profit. Gross profit in the trading division is calculated in the usual way except that cost of sales is based on the price at which goods were transferred from the manufacturing division.

A moment's thought will tell you that this arrangement simply splits the total gross profit between the two divisions.

The reasons for structuring a business entity in this way are related to motivation. Line managers in the manufacturing division are likely to be more careful over cost control if their performance is to be judged by the profit made in their division. Similarly, the performance of the trading division is judged by a gross profit that bears some resemblance to what could be made if the goods had been purchased from an outside source. You will learn about the motivational aspects of transfer pricing and divisional activity if you ever have to study for an advanced course in management accounting. It is a complex issue.

In practice, this kind of divisional activity is often achieved by forming separate companies for each division. Each company is then a self-accounting entity, forming part of a total group for which supplementary group accounts are prepared. In exams, an artificial situation is often created whereby the manufacturing and trading divisions form part of a single accounting entity.

Up to a point, this situation does not cause any difficulty. The total transfer price of all goods manufactured is brought into the manufacturing account and compared to the cost of manufacturing finished goods. The difference between the two figures is described as manufacturing profit. The figures for cost of sales in the trading account are based on transfer prices, and gross profit (now reduced) is determined in the normal way. The manufacturing profit is then added to gross trading profit in the profit and loss account.

There is, however, a slight complication over the closing stock of finished goods because these stocks will contain an element of profit (the manufacturing profit) that has not been realized. Such profit will not be realized until the stock is sold, presumably in the following period. You will discover the impact of this problem by working through the next activity.

Activity 13

Prepare a new manufacturing account and trading account for the business dealt with in Activity 10, on the following basis:

The finished goods are transferred by the manufacturing division to the trading division at cost plus 10%. The transfer price of finished goods manufactured will therefore be (250,700 + 25,070) £275,770. This can be shown on an additional line in the manufacturing account following the cost of manufacturing finished goods. The manufacturing account then closes with a figure for manufacturing profit.

The stocks of finished goods for the trading account will be as follows:

Opening stock (14,800 + 1,480)	£16,280
Closing stock (15,500 + 1,550)	£17,050

You can carry out this activity by completing the two tables set out below. Some of the original figures have been included to save time. Don't forget to add the manufacturing profit to the revised trading profit in order to determine total gross profit. At this stage of the activity you will find that total gross profit is different to the figure in Activity 10. We will sort that out later.

Manufacturing account		Trading account	
Manufacturing costs:		Sales	350,000
Raw materials consumed	86,200	Cost of sales:	
Direct wages	92,000	Opening stock	
Manufacturing overheads	73,000	Manufactured price	
	251,200	of finished goods	_____
Less increase in work-in-progress	500		
Cost of finished goods	250,700	Closing stock	_____
Transfer price	_____		
Manufacturing profit	_____	Trading profit	
	=======	Manufacturing profit	_____
		Gross profit	

Notice that the total gross profit at the moment is £70 greater than it was in Activity 10. This cannot be allowed to stand because it is nonsense to think that profit of the combined entity can be increased simply by altering the prices at which internal transfers are made between the two divisions. This extra profit has arisen due to the value of finished goods stock being at a price in excess of cost. These stocks include the manufacturing profit which has not been realized by the firm as a whole.

The effect is different as between opening and closing stocks. Looked at from the point of view of the combined entity, the profit element in opening stock has artificially increased cost of sales, whereas the profit element in closing stock has artificially decreased cost of sales. It is easier to see how this is adjusted by concentrating on the balance sheet figures.

The stocks for the balance sheet must be shown at cost. The way in which this is dealt with in the books is to create a provision for unrealized profit. The double-entry made in order to set up this provision is similar to the one that you learned when setting up a provision for doubtful debts. In the case of unrealized profit the double-entry is:

> Debit: profit and loss account
> Credit: provision for unrealized profit

After setting up the first provision, it is only necessary to make an adjustment each year in order to increase (or decrease) the provision to the amount needed in respect of the closing stock. This closing provision is deducted from the transfer price of closing stock in the balance sheet so that stocks can be shown at their true cost to the entity.

In our example, the books at the beginning of the year will include a provision for unrealized profit on stock of £1,480. Stocks would have been shown in the previous balance sheet at (16,280 – 1,480) £14,800, which was their true cost to the entity.

Activity 14

1. Describe the double-entry that will be needed at the end of the year in order to make an adjustment to the provision for unrealized profit.

   Debit:

   Credit:

2. State the amount at which the stock of finished goods will be shown in the closing balance sheet.

Notice how the gross profit will now be £100,000 (100,070 – 70), which is the same as it was when the finished goods manufactured were transferred at cost price. This adjustment to the provision can be presented in the profit and loss account as a deduction from the total of manufacturing and trading profit (or as an addition when the provision is reduced).

Summary

The main learning points in this chapter can be summarized as follows:
  • the trading account of a manufacturer is similar to that of a retailer except that cost of sales is based on the manufactured cost of finished goods instead of on the purchase cost
  • the manufactured cost of finished goods stock could be based on marginal cost or absorbed cost (marginal cost plus a proportion of fixed production overheads)

- SSAP 9 requires the cost of finished goods stock to be based on absorbed cost – with overheads per unit determined on the basis of normal levels of production
- a manufacturing entity of any size will have a sub-system of cost accounting in order to determine cost of sales for the financial accounts
- in financial accounting, it is assumed that the old practice of preparing something called a manufacturing account is used in order to determine cost of all finished goods manufactured during the period
- the manufacturing account collects all manufacturing costs under appropriate headings, and such costs are adjusted for the effect of any costs included in work-in-progress
- manufacturing costs include raw materials consumed, which is found by taking the cost of raw materials purchased and making adjustments for opening and closing stocks of raw materials
- the balance sheet of a manufacturer usually includes three categories of stock: raw materials, work-in-progress, and finished goods
- sometimes the total entity is divided into operational segments and manufactured stocks are transferred to the trading division at a price in excess of cost
- where transfer prices exceed manufacturing cost, the total gross profit is divided between manufacturing profit and trading profit
- if finished goods stock is at a price in excess of manufactured cost, a provision for unrealized profit must be made in order to reduce stocks to their true cost to the entity
- after setting up the first provision, it is adjusted each year in order to change it to the amount of unrealized profit on the closing stock

Activity 1
Opening stock of finished goods + manufacturing costs − closing stock of finished goods.

Activity 2
You might have thought of raw materials or bought-in components.

Activity 3
There are literally dozens of different types of cost. You may have included things like raw materials; wages of those working in the factory; electricity, rent, rates and insurance of the factory; depreciation of any plant and machinery used in the factory; packing costs; running costs of fork-lift trucks; oil and lubricants.

Activity 4
You may have thought of things like screws, glue, varnish or paint. It would be much too inconvenient (if not impossible) to measure the quantities used on a specific product.

Activity 5
You may have included employees such as supervisors and foremen, security staff, cleaners, maintenance engineers, fork-lift drivers, store keepers, and so on.

Activity 6
£4,500 + £102,800 − £5,300 = £102,000.

Activity 7
The total manufacturing costs incurred during the period amount to £110,000 but £8,000 of this relates to the work-in-progress. Consequently, the cost of making those that were finished must have been (110,000 − 8,000) £102,000.

Activity 8
It will have to be added to the manufacturing costs incurred during the second year.

Activity 9
It should be added.

Activity 10
Manufacturing account:

Manufacturing costs:		
Raw materials consumed	86,200	
Direct wages	92,000	
Manufacturing overheads	73,000	
	251,200	
Less: increase in work-in-progress	500	
Cost of finished goods manufactured	250,700	
Trading account:		
Sales		350,000
Less cost of sales:		
Opening stock of finished goods	14,800	
Cost of goods manufactured	250,700	
	265,500	
Closing stock of finished goods	15,500	
		250,000
Gross profit		100,000

Activity 11

(a) **Trading account**			(b) **Trading account**		
Stock at marginal cost			Stock at absorbed cost		
Sales		140,000	Sales		140,000
Cost of sales:			Cost of sales:		
Manufacturing costs	100,000		Manufacturing costs	100,000	
Less closing stock			Less closing stock		
(2,000 × £2)	4,000		(2,000 × £2.50)	5,000	
		96,000			95,000
Gross profit		44,000			45,000

Activity 12

At cost of £6,800. Note that net realizable value is not the scrap value of £2,000. Net realizable value is the ultimate selling price of £9,000 less the costs of completion of £1,200. This amounts to £7,800 and is greater than cost.

Activity 13

Manufacturing account			Trading account		
Manufacturing costs:			Sales		350,000
Raw materials consumed		86,200	Cost of sales:		
Direct wages		92,000	Opening stock	16,280	
Manufacturing overheads		73,000	Manufactured price		
		251,200	of finished goods	275,770	
Less increase in work-in-progress		500		292,050	
Cost of finished goods		250,700	Closing stock	17,050	
Transfer price		275,770			275,000
Manufacturing profit		25,070	Trading profit		75,000
			Manufacturing profit		25,070
			Gross profit		100,070

Activity 14

1. Debit profit and loss account with £70; credit provision for unrealized profit on stock with £70.
2. Stock will be shown in the balance sheet at £15,500 (i.e. 17,050 – 1,550), which represents its true cost price to the entity.

Question for self-assessment

The answer to this self-assessment question is given at the end of the book.

8.1 Carter, a sole trader, commenced business on 1 September 19X6 as a manufacturer of three types of products. The following balances were extracted from his trial balance at 31 August 19X7.

	Dr. £	Cr. £
Purchases of raw materials	280,000	
Returns	1,000	4,000
Carriage in	2,000	
Selling and distribution costs	20,000	
Rent	15,000	
Royalties	12,000	
Indirect factory labour	24,000	
Direct labour	125,000	
Administrative costs	35,000	
Sales		540,000
General factory expenses	15,000	
Plant and machinery at cost	140,000	
Delivery vans at cost	10,000	

The following information is also available.

1. Rent was paid until the end of November 19X7 and was to be apportioned between the factory and general administration on the basis of 2:1.
2. Selling and distribution costs of £8,000 were accrued on 31 August 19X7.
3. Plant and machinery are depreciated by 20% per annum on cost and delivery vans are to be depreciated by 30% per annum on cost.
4. The stock of raw materials at 31 August 19X7 was valued at £40,000.
5. Although there was no work-in-progress at the end of the year there was a stock of finished goods of 3,000 units. Carter is uncertain as to how to value the goods, which at present are selling for an average price of £30 per unit. During the year, 25,000 units have been produced.

Required:
(a) The manufacturing account for the year ended 31 August 19X7.
(b) Using two accepted methods of valuing the closing stock of finished goods, complete trading and profit and loss accounts for the year ended 31 August 19X7.
(c) Explain to Carter the difficulties involved in calculating a separate cost of sales figure for each of the three products produced.

Note: You will have to assume that royalties are based on production. It is necessary to make an assumption on this because royalties are sometimes based on sales rather than production. Royalties payable on production are obviously a direct (variable) production expense, whereas royalties payable on sales are part of the cost of sales.

(AEB A Level)

Question without answer

The answer to this question is published separately in the *Teacher's Manual*.

8.2 The following balances as at 31 December 1990 have been extracted from the books of William Speed, a small manufacturer.

		£
Stocks at 1 January 1990:	Raw materials	7,000
	Work-in-progress	5,000
	Finished goods	6,900
Purchase of raw materials		38,000
Direct labour		28,000
Factory overheads:	Variable	16,000
	Fixed	9,000
Administrative expenses:	Rent and rates	19,000
	Heat and light	6,000
	Stationery and postage	2,000
	Staff salaries	19,380
Sales		192,000
Plant and machinery:	At cost	30,000
	Provision for depreciation	12,000
Delivery vehicles:	At cost	16,000
	Provision for depreciation	4,000
Creditors		5,500
Debtors		28,000
Drawings		11,500
Balance at bank		16,600
Capital at 1 January 1990 (see guidance note)		48,000
Provision for unrealized profit at 1 January 1990		1,380
Motor vehicle running costs		4,500

Additional information:

1. Stocks at 31 December 1990 were as follows:

	£
Raw materials	9,000
Work-in-progress	8,000
Finished goods	10,350

2. The factory output is transferred to the trading account at factory cost plus 25% for factory profit. The finished goods stock is valued on the basis of amounts transferred to the debit of the trading account.
3. Depreciation is provided annually at the following percentages of the original cost of fixed assets held at the end of each financial year:

Plant and machinery	10%
Motor vehicles	25%

4. Amounts accrued due at 31 December 1990 for direct labour amounted to £3,000 and rent and rates prepaid at 31 December 1990 amounted to £2,000.

Required:
Prepare a manufacturing, trading and profit and loss account for the year ended 31 December 1990 and a balance sheet as at that date. The prime cost and total factory cost should be clearly shown.

Author's guidance note: Since contributed capital has not been separated from retained profits, it will be necessary to add retained profit for the year to the capital brought forward.

(AAT Intermediate)

Further questions involving manufacturing companies are set at the end of Chapters 10 and 17.

9 ▷ **Incomplete records**

Objectives

After you have completed this chapter, you should be able to:
- prepare financial statements for a business whose accounting records are not kept on double-entry principles
- make use of the techniques to find missing figures in many different types of accounting problem

Introduction

The techniques covered by this chapter were originally developed to cope with the preparation of financial statements for traders who do not keep double-entry accounting records. You will learn the process in the context of such a business but you must appreciate that the same approach can be applied to any problem where accounting figures have to be derived from incomplete information.

Businesses owned by sole traders tend to be small with few (if any) employees. There is hardly likely to be a trained book-keeper on the staff and the accounting records will most probably be kept by the proprietor. The books are often little more than an analysis of receipts and payments. These accounting records are said to be incomplete because there is no double-entry posting to a nominal ledger. Your task is to learn how financial statements are prepared from such records.

It is a favourite topic among examiners; questions on incomplete records appear in very nearly every exam. Some of them are highly contrived and bear little relationship to real-life situations. The popularity of questions on incomplete records is probably due to the fact that they form an excellent basis for testing a student's skills in applying the principles of double-entry. If you have managed to make sense of the basic principles, you will have no problems at all in dealing with incomplete records.

9.1 The omitted records

Many small businesses (such as a retail shop) conduct a great deal of their business on a cash basis. The daily cash takings are often used to pay various expenses and the proprietor's drawings prior to banking the balance from time to time. Additional payments are made by cheque, particularly to settle the monthly accounts of credit suppliers.

These businesses usually arrange for a professional accountant to prepare their annual financial statements (mainly as a prelude to agreeing the proprietor's income tax liability). Most professional accountants advise the proprietor to keep two analysed cash books – one to provide an analysis of cash receipts and payments, the other to provide an analysis of bank receipts and payments. The analysis columns are designed to accumulate annual totals for different types of payment such as purchases, rent and rates, wages, drawings, etc.

Financial statements can then be prepared from these cash books providing there is some memorandum record of outstanding debtors and creditors at the accounting date.

As regards credit transactions, the trader will use various clerical procedures for keeping tabs on the amounts owed to creditors and the amounts owing by debtors. These procedures usually rely on some kind of filing system whereby the paid and unpaid invoices can be separately identified at any particular time.

Activity 1

Compare the accounting records outlined in the foregoing description with those of a business whose records are kept on a double-entry system. Make a list of the main books that are usually omitted in an 'incomplete record' system.

9.2 Finding the missing figures

In order to prepare financial statements from incomplete records, we simply apply our knowledge of accounting in order to calculate the figures needed.

Opening position

As a starting point, think about the opening balance sheet of an existing business. Assume that we were able to determine that the opening assets and liabilities of a business were as follows:

Delivery van – at net book value		6,000
Stock at cost	6,000	
Debtors	4,000	
Cash on hand	200	
Cash at bank	2,800	
	13,000	
Trade creditors	3,000	
Accruals	300	
	3,300	
		9,700
		15,700
Long-term loan		5,000
		10,700

Activity 2

From the above details it is possible to determine another item needed to complete the opening balance sheet. We are so accustomed to seeing it on a balance sheet that it might take you a little while to realize that it is missing. Describe the item and state the amount. This is quite important because you are required to determine this figure in most examination questions on incomplete records.

In examination questions you are usually expected to determine the opening capital from the various items of information on the opening position (often given in a disorderly fashion). In practice, the figure would be known from the balance sheet prepared at the end of the previous year.

The amount for capital in this example was simply derived as a balancing figure. This approach of finding a balancing figure lies behind most of the workings on incomplete record problems.

Transactions during the year

At this stage of your studies you will be well aware that the figures for income and expenses in the profit and loss account are not always the same as the corresponding amounts of cash received and cash paid. Profit and loss items are determined on an accruals basis, not on a cash basis. In other words, income relates to the amount earned in the period, and expenditure relates to the amount incurred in that period.

In a double-entry system the accruals concept is automatically applied, e.g. when a purchase invoice is received, purchases will be debited (through the purchases day book) and a creditor will be credited. In an incomplete record system, the first book-keeping entry will be made when the creditor's account is paid. But it is quite easy to build up the 'accrued' figure from the amount paid providing records are kept of the amounts owing at the end of the year.

Activity 3

If you were told that the amount paid for purchases during the first year of a new business amounted to £126,000, and that there was £4,800 owing for purchases at the end of the first year, what amount would be shown as purchases in the trading account for that year?

You probably found this quite easy and are starting to become suspicious that something more complicated is involved. Rest assured that the whole process is not much more complicated than this.

You will have to be a little more careful when dealing with the figures of a business that was trading in the previous year. Some of the amounts recorded as payments for purchases during the current year would have been to pay off the creditors at the end of the previous year. These payments relate to the previous year's purchases, not to those of the current year.

Think about this in relation to the trader referred to in Activity 2, where the opening position regarding assets and liabilities was given.

Activity 4

You ascertain that the trader in Activity 2 has recorded the following payments for purchases during the current year:

Purchases paid for by cash   6,200
Purchases paid for by cheque   56,300

You also ascertain that the amount owing for purchases at the end of the current year is £4,000. The amount of £3,000 shown in the opening balance sheet as trade creditors relates entirely to purchases.

Calculate the purchases figure for the current year.

This figure was found by a logical calculation. You could have determined the amount as a balancing figure on a 'control account' for purchases. These so-called control accounts are really 'total accounts' and are contrived simply to find missing figures. If we were to write up a control account for purchases in this example we would first write in all the known detail, as follows:

Purchase control account

Payments:	cash	6,200	Creditors b/d	3,000
	cheque	56,300		
Creditors c/d		4,000		
		66,500		

The balancing figure on this account represents purchases for the year. The completed account would be as follows:

Purchase control account

Payments:	cash	6,200	Creditors b/d	3,000
	cheque	56,300	Purchases (balance)	63,500
Creditors c/d		4,000		
		66,500		66,500

There is no need to worry over the fact that some of the payments would have been for cash purchases rather than credit purchases. We are only constructing the account in order to determine a total for purchases – the distinction between cash and credit purchases is of no significance.

You will notice some similarities between the above approach and the way in which you dealt with the opening and closing accruals for an expense item in cases where the books were kept by double-entry.

It is up to you to develop your own method of working. If the figures are relatively straightforward, as in the above example, the calculation approach could save time. Some students feel more secure when using 'T' accounts for all their workings but they do take longer to prepare. With sufficient practice you might eventually be able to see some of the figures very quickly. For example, in Activity 4 you could have reasoned that since the creditors have increased by £1,000, the figure for purchases will be £1,000 more than the amount paid.

Now see if you can sort out how the figure for sales would be calculated by working on the following activity. The approach is exactly the same as for purchases.

Activity 5

The trader in Activity 2 has recorded cash takings for the current period as £77,000 (see note below). If you look back at the opening balance sheet, you will notice that debtors at the start of the period were £4,000. You ascertain that debtors at the end of the current period are £4,500. Calculate the amount for sales to be included in the trading account for the current period.

Note: The expression 'cash takings' has been used to denote the total amount of money taken from all customers; some of this money will be for cash sales, and some will be the cash received from credit customers.

9.3 Putting it all together

You should now be able to prepare a set of financial statements by using the thought processes developed through completing the previous activities.

In the next activity, full details of the cash account have been given. This is a bit of a luxury because it implies that the trader has kept a properly balanced record of all cash transactions. In some examination problems (and nearly always in practice) some of the details for the cash account itself are missing. We will sort that out after completing the following problem.

Details for Activity 6

The trader in Activity 2 maintains an analysis book for cash transactions, and another one for bank transactions. The following is a summary of his cash and bank transactions for the year following the date of the balance sheet in Activity 2:

Cash account		Bank account	
Balance brought forward	200	Balance brought forward	2,800
Receipts:		Cash banked	58,700
Cash takings	77,000		61,500
	77,200	Cheque payments:	
Payments:		Purchases	56,300
Purchases	6,200	Electricity	900
Staff wages	8,000	Rent and rates	1,500
Drawings	4,000	Motor expenses	500
Cash banked	58,700	Loan interest	300
Balance carried forward	300	Private expenses	500
	77,200	Part repayment of loan	500
		Balance carried forward	1,000
			61,500

Depreciation of the delivery van is to be based on 20% of the reducing balance. The accrual of £300 in the opening balances sheet relates to electricity; the accrual for electricity at the end of the year is £400. There are no other accruals or prepayments. Closing stock at cost amounts to £7,500.

Activity 6

From previous activities you have already determined the figures for opening capital, purchases and sales. You should now prepare the financial statements for this trader on your own paper.

9.4 Incomplete cash information

You will notice how these incomplete record problems require you to think in terms of two different accounts for cash, namely:

1. the actual cash (bank notes and coins), and
2. the cash at the bank.

The bank account does not usually present any problem since the data can be checked with the bank statement. As with bank reconciliations, it might be necessary to make adjustments for errors, and also for unrecorded items such as bank charges.

But the cash account is slightly different. The information presented by the trader (in practice and in exams) might be complete or incomplete. If you are presented with a neatly balanced cash account, as in Activity 6, there is no additional problem. Where the cash information is incomplete you will have to build up a cash account to determine missing information.

In order to cope with problems where the cash information is incomplete, you need to have a fairly clear image of the cash account itself. In the following outline cash account, the key items are shown (the numbers are for identification purposes). One of the items has deliberately not been described.

Cash account

1. Balance b/d	X	3. Cash payments	X
2. Cash takings	X	4. (see Activity 7)	X
		5. Balance c/d	X
	X̲		X̲

Activity 7

Review the above outline cash account and describe what item 4 is likely to be.

The cash banked will appear as a receipt in the bank account (in effect there is a double-entry: debit bank and credit cash). If you have to build up a cash account from sketchy information, it is quite likely that the figure for cash banked will be given in the details for the bank account.

You will have to be careful if the total cash banked includes something other than the balance of cash takings. For example, the cash banked might include an amount for capital introduced by the proprietor. One way of dealing with this is to show the amount as a separate receipt on the debit side of the cash account – you can then include the total cash banked on the credit side. In other words treat all receipts as if they passed through the cash account, even though some might have been paid directly into the bank. The credit entry for all cash coming into the business can be posted from the cash account.

The first stage in any problem where cash information is incomplete (or incorrect) is to build up a cash account as far as you can from all the known details. If an item has been omitted completely, it can be found as a balancing figure. For example (referring to the outline cash account used for Activity 7), if you were given details of items 1, 3, 4 and 5 you could derive item 2 (the cash takings) as a balancing figure. Similarly, if you were given details of items 1, 2, 3 and 4 you could calculate item 5 (the closing balance).

Where a cash item has been incorrectly recorded, the cash account will not balance and reasonable assumptions will have to be made as to the nature of the item needed to make it balance. There are two situations that can arise in this context, and they will result in either the debits exceeding the credits, or vice versa.

Debits exceed the credits

Imagine that from the data presented to you, it has been possible to build up a cash account as far as the following:

Cash account

Balance b/d	100	Purchases	20,000
Cash takings	160,000	Office expenses	9,000
		Cash banked	120,800
		Balance c/d	200

You will notice that the debit side is £160,100 whereas the credit side adds up to only £150,000. Quite clearly there must be another item to enter on the credit side but it has not been given in the details for the problem.

Activity 8

Consider the above situation. Assume that there is nothing wrong with the amounts recorded for purchases, office expenses or cash banked. What item would you assume has been missed on the credit side of this account? Think about the proprietor and the fact that the business provides the proprietor with a source of income.

If you come across this kind of situation in an examination question, it is quite likely that you will be invited to make this assumption by being given information such as: 'drawings have not been recorded'.

Credits exceed debits

In practice (but not necessarily in exams) it is more likely that after writing up the cash account from information given by the trader, the credit side will be greater than the debit side. Consider the following example of a cash account written up from information provided:

Cash account

Balance b/d	100	Purchases	20,000
Cash takings	160,000	Office expenses	9,000
		Cash banked	120,800
		Drawings	11,100
		Balance c/d	200

You will notice that the debits total £160,100, whereas the credits total £161,100.

Activity 9

If there is nothing to throw doubt on any of the figures on the credit side, what do you think would account for the difference?

When this situation occurs in practice, it will be necessary to ask the client if there is any explanation for the fact that cash outgoings are £1,000 greater than the recorded incomings. The client may respond with something like: 'oh yes, I remember, I sold the car for £1,000 and paid the cheque into the bank'. But more often than not, the difference relates to unrecorded takings.

The fact is that business people are quite happy to record all their payments, but they tend to avoid recording all their receipts – overlooking the fact that if the money has been paid out, it must have been received.

In exams, the way in which cash account differences should be treated is likely to be clear from the wording of the question. If the question is silent on this, you should treat unrecorded payments as drawings and unrecorded receipts as takings.

Activity 10

A trader has not kept a full record of cash transactions. Build up a cash account from the following information: Cash in hand was £500 at the start of the period, and £600 at the end. Takings determined from till rolls amounts to £101,000 for the year. Invoices paid by cash have been analysed, and £32,000 was paid for purchases and £4,000 for motor expenses. The trader informs you that drawings are at the rate of £200 per week. No other payments are made by cash. The banking slips show that a total of £56,000 was banked, including a cheque for £2,000 relating to a legacy received from the estate of a deceased relative. Use the blank outline account provided below for your answer.

Cash account

Note that the capital introduced could be omitted from this account, providing the cash banked on the credit side is stated at £54,000. The bank account would then include two classes of transaction on the debit side, i.e. cash banked £54,000 and capital introduced £2,000. Either way the balancing figure on the cash account is £500, which should be treated as drawings unless there is something to suggest otherwise. Keep in mind that the main object of the exercise is to determine missing information, rather than to produce theoretically correct ledger accounts.

In some questions you might have to determine the amount of cash takings banked by building up a bank account; in these cases it is preferable to include items such as cash introduced in the debit side of the bank account.

9.5 Information missing from both sides of the cash account

In previous activities you discovered how unrecorded takings, or unrecorded drawings, could be calculated as a balancing figure. This was possible because there was enough detail on receipts and payments to make a reasonable assumption about any difference on the cash account derived from such information.

A more highly contrived situation is one where information is missing from both sides of the cash account. These problems are usually based on a situation where both takings and drawings have not been recorded. If both items are missing, neither one of them can be found as a simple balancing figure on the cash account.

In order to solve these problems it is necessary to use a link between the cash account and the trading account by making use of the gross profit margin (or gross profit mark-up), which is usually expressed as a percentage.

You did consider gross profit margins and mark-ups in Chapter 4 but in case you have forgotten about them let us look at the idea again, using figures from the accounts you prepared for Activity 6.

The gross profit margin is the amount of gross profit expressed as a percentage of sales. For the trader in Activity 6 this would be calculated as follows:

$$\frac{\text{Gross profit}}{\text{Sales}} \times \frac{100}{1} \quad \text{i.e.} \quad \frac{15,500}{77,500} \times \frac{100}{1} = 20\%$$

The gross profit mark-up is the amount of gross profit expressed as a percentage of the cost of sales. For the trader in Activity 6 this would be as follows:

$$\frac{\text{Gross profit}}{\text{Cost of sales}} \times \frac{100}{1} \quad \text{i.e.} \quad \frac{15,500}{62,500} \times \frac{100}{1} = 25\%$$

You must be careful over how you interpret information on gross profit percentages. If the percentage is referred to as a mark-up, then it is a percentage of the cost of sales; if it is referred to as a margin, then it is a percentage of sales. It is quite easy to convert one expression to the other. If 25% is added to cost to find the sales, then the amount added must be the same as 25/125 (20%) of the sales. If gross profit margin is 20% of sales then it must be 20/80 (25%) of the cost of sales.

We now have to think about how this gross profit percentage might be used. If we are dealing with a situation where both takings and drawings have not been recorded, then perhaps we can find one of them by using some of the other information available. If we can find one, the other can be derived as a balancing figure on the cash account.

The most fruitful approach will be to estimate cash takings by making use of the gross profit mark-up. It is quite likely that a figure for purchases can be determined from details of payments. Cheque payments for purchases can be ascertained from the bank account and cash purchases can be identified from the purchase invoices. From the figure for purchases it is possible to determine cost of sales, providing details of opening and closing stocks are available.

If we know the average gross profit percentage for the type of business concerned, then sales can be estimated from the cost of sales. From sales we can determine cash takings, providing details of opening and closing debtors are known.

Activity 11

Set out a formula for determining cash takings from figures for sales, and the opening and closing debtors.

The following activity provides an opportunity for you to practise the whole approach without having to prepare a complete set of financial statements. The details given are sufficient to enable you to prepare a balanced cash account, a crucial starting point in the preparation of financial statements for the type of situation described.

Activity 12

B. Dark, the owner of a small retail shop, has failed to keep any record of cash transactions. An analysis of his bank account includes the following details:

Cash banked	£82,500
Payments:	
Purchases	£68,000

From an examination of purchase invoices, the following cash payments are determined:

Purchases	£6,300
Motor expenses	800

Creditors for purchases at the start of the year were £6,000 and at the end of the year were £6,700. Opening stock at cost was £4,000 and closing stock was £5,500. Opening debtors were £2,000 and closing debtors £2,800. The balance of cash on hand at the end of each day is £100. The gross profit margin earned by B. Dark's type of business is 30%. Prepare a balanced cash account, using the blank account below. Use your own paper for the workings.

Cash account

9.6 Other types of missing information

Some of the thought processes used to solve the problem in Activity 12 may have to be used to determine other types of unknown information. A fairly common example is to estimate the cost of stock at any particular date. This might be necessary for the annual financial statements (where stock was not counted) or where stock has been destroyed by fire and a claim has to be made on the insurance company. See if you can solve the following activity:

Activity 13

The opening stock of a business was £22,000. During the accounting period there was a fire that destroyed most of the trading stock except for some that had cost £2,000. The purchases during the period up to the date of the fire amounted to £139,000. Sales during this period were £172,500. The normal gross profit margin for this type of business is 20%. Estimate the cost of closing stock lost in the fire.

9.7 Trading goods withdrawn by the proprietor

Most of these incomplete record problems relate to a small business owned by a sole trader. It is quite normal to find that the proprietor in such a business has used some of the trading stock for personal purposes. For example, the proprietor of a grocery shop may withdraw some of the trading stock for private use without paying for it.

There is hardly likely to be any accounting record of such transfers (no cash is involved) but an adjustment must be made in the financial statements for any estimated amounts. The value of these withdrawals must be debited to drawings but the credit side of the double-entry will depend on whether the figure given has been calculated at selling price or at cost price.

If the withdrawal is measured at cost price, the credit should be to purchases; if it is at selling price the credit should be to sales. As you can see, there will be a slight difference in reported profits depending on whether the adjustment is made at cost or selling price.

Activity 14

A proprietor withdraws stock during the year that has a cost price of £800 and a selling price of £1,000. Describe the double-entry that should be made to reflect this withdrawal in the financial statements if it is recorded at:

(a) Cost price

(b) Selling price

When calculating profits for income tax purposes there is a legal case requiring the adjustment to be made at selling price. In other words, the withdrawal has to be dealt with as if the goods had been sold by the business to the proprietor at the usual selling price. On the other hand, when treating the withdrawal as an output for VAT purposes, the withdrawal is valued at cost price. In accountancy exams, these tax implications are ignored and you have to make an appropriate adjustment based on whether the value given is at cost price or at selling price.

9.8 Complete absence of accounting records

In rare circumstances, there may be virtually no accounting records from which a conventional set of financial statements could be prepared. This may happen, for example, where all records had been lost in a fire.

In these circumstances it should still be possible to estimate a single figure of profit for the year. The calculation relies on the balance sheet equation. It should be possible to piece together enough information to calculate net assets at the beginning of the period and net assets at the end. Profit can then be related to the increase in net assets. It will be necessary to take other factors into account because, as you know, the net assets of a business will change through causes other than the earning of profit.

Activity 15

Identify two types of transaction that will cause the net assets of a business to change other than the earning of a net profit. One will cause the net assets to decrease, the other will cause them to increase. If you find this difficult to answer, concentrate on the proprietor's capital account (which equates to net assets) and think about transactions that cause this to change.

Type of transaction

1. Net assets will decrease as a result of:

2. Net assets will increase as a result of:

You need to think backwards in order to turn the equation into one that can be used to determine net profit. The calculation proceeds as follows:

Closing net assets	X
Less opening net assets	X
Increase in net assets	X
Add drawings	X
	X
Deduct cash introduced	(X)
Estimated net profit	X

Clearly, the figure for profit is only an estimate and its reliability is very much related to the reliability of the estimate for drawings.

Activity 16

A small trader has lost all accounting records in a fire. A statement of assets and liabilities at the date of the fire reveals net assets of £92,000. A copy of the balance sheet at the end of the previous accounting period show the net assets at that date to be £85,000. Between these two dates, the trader had inherited £5,000 and introduced this into the bank account of the business. An estimate of his drawings during this period (including goods withdrawn) was calculated at £4,000. Estimate profit for the period.

Summary

The main learning points in this chapter are as follows:

- proprietors of small businesses do not usually keep their accounting records on double-entry principles
- in many cases the proprietor will keep an analysed cash book for both cash and bank transactions
- the preparation of financial statements from cash and bank transactions is simply an application of the accruals concept
- cash amounts can easily be turned into accrued amounts by recognizing the effect of the opening and closing creditors and debtors
- where cash transactions are not fully recorded it is necessary to build up a cash account and determine the nature of any balancing figure
- if the recording of both cash receipts and cash payments has been neglected, it is necessary to determine cash takings through use of the gross profit percentage
- the usual approach is to determine sales from cost of sales and then determine cash takings by making adjustments for opening and closing debtors
- goods withdrawn by the proprietor should be debited to drawings; the credit depends on whether the amount is stated at cost or selling price
- if the value of goods withdrawn is stated at cost price, purchases should be credited; if stated at selling price, sales should be credited
- in cases where no reliable accounting records are available, a single figure of estimated profit for the period can be related to the increase in net assets, plus drawings, less cash introduced

Important note: The learning stages in this chapter have tended to concentrate on the basic principles and thought processes involved. It is imperative that you attempt some of the questions that follow, otherwise you will not have had sufficient practice in using these principles.

Professional accounting exams often test this subject in the context of a partnership or small private company. These aspects have not yet been covered.

Activity 1

Sales day book, purchases day book, creditors ledger, debtors ledger, and the nominal ledger.

Activity 2

Capital account of £10,700. We cannot differentiate between contributed capital and retained profits, but at least we know the total.

Activity 3

£130,800, i.e. the amount paid plus the amount owing.

Activity 4

£63,500. You might have thought this through as follows:

Amount paid during the current year (6,200 + 56,300)	62,500
Less payment of opening creditors	3,000
Paid during the current year for current year's purchases	59,500
Add closing creditors for purchases	4,000
	63,500

Activity 5

77,000 − 4,000 + 4,500 = £77,500 (or cash takings £77,000 plus increase in debtors of £500 equals £77,500).

Activity 6

Trading and profit and loss account:

Sales		77,500
Less cost of sales:		
Opening stock	6,000	
Purchases	63,500	
	69,500	
Closing stock	7,500	
		62,000
Gross profit		15,500
Expenses:		
Staff wages	8,000	
Electricity (900 + 400 − 300)	1,000	
Rent and rates	1,500	
Motor expenses	500	
Loan interest	300	
Depreciation	1,200	
		12,500
Net profit		3,000

Balance sheet:

Fixed assets:
Delivery van – at net book value (6,000 – 1,200)   4,800

Current assets:

Stock	7,500	
Debtors	4,500	
Bank	1,000	
Cash	300	
	13,300	

Creditors due within one year:

Creditors	4,000		
Accruals	400		
		4,400	
			8,900
			13,700

Creditors due after one year:

Long-term loan (5,000 – 500)	4,500
	9,200

Capital account – brought forward	10,700
Add net profit	3,000
	13,700
Less drawings (4,000 + 500)	4,500
	9,200

Activity 7
Cash banked. It is quite easy to overlook this item when building up a cash account in order to determine missing cash information.

Activity 8
The missing item (£10,100) is most likely to be 'drawings'.

Activity 9
It probably relates to unrecorded takings.

Activity 10

Cash account

Balance b/d	500	Purchases	32,000
Cash takings	101,000	Motor expenses	4,000
Capital introduced	2,000	Drawings (as given)	10,400
		Drawings (balancing figure)	500
		Amount banked	56,000
		Balance c/d	600
	103,500		103,500

Activity 11
Sales less closing debtors plus opening debtors (notice how this is the reverse of finding sales from cash information).

Activity 12

Workings:

Cost of sales:

Opening stock	4,000
Purchases (68,000 + 6,300 − 6,000 + 6,700)	75,000
	79,000
Closing stock	5,500
	73,500

Sales:

Cost of sales	73,500
Add mark-up (30/70 × 73,500)	31,500
	105,000

Cash takings: 105,000 − 2,800 + 2,000 = £104,200

Cash account

Balance b/d	100	Purchases	6,300
Cash takings	104,200	Motor expenses	800
		Cash banked	82,500
		Drawings (balancing figure)	14,600
		Balance c/d	100
	104,300		104,300

Activity 13

Opening stock	22,000
Purchases	139,000
	161,000
Less cost of sales (80% × 172,500)	138,000
The total closing stock was therefore	23,000
Deduct stock salvaged	2,000
Amount claimed as lost	21,000

Activity 14

(a) Debit drawings £800; credit purchases £800.
(b) Debit drawings £1,000; credit sales £1,000.

Activity 15

1. Drawings.
2. Cash introduced by proprietor.

Activity 16

92,000 − 85,000 − 5,000 + 4,000 = £6,000.

Questions for self-assessment

Answers to self-assessment questions are given at the end of the book.

9.1 The following summary for the year ended 31 October 1990 has been prepared from the cash book of Jean Black, a retailer.

1989	Receipts	Cash	Bank
Nov 1	Balances brought forward	142	2,830
	Cash sales	390	9,200
	Credit sales	110	37,500
	Cash from bank	748	
	Legacy from late aunt's estate		8,000
	Sale of motor vehicle		500
1990			
Oct 31	Balance carried forward		1,400
		1,390	59,430

	Payments	Cash	Bank
	Purchases of goods for resale		24,300
	Wages		7,400
	General expenses	240	6,510
	Cash from bank		748
	Drawings	900	10,600
	Purchase of motor vehicle		9,872
1990			
Oct 31	Balance carried forward	250	
		1,390	59,430

Unfortunately, Jean Black does not keep a full set of accounting records. However, the following additional information has been obtained for the accounting year ended 31 October 1990.

1. Jean Black's assets and liabilities, other than cash and bank balances, were:

As at	1 Nov 1989	31 Oct 1990
Motor vehicle valued at	300	7,404
Stock valued at	1,900	2,500
Trade debtors	3,100	3,900
General expenses: prepaid	390	–
accrued due	82	36
Wages accrued due	–	810
Trade creditors	2,100	5,400

2. During the year ended 31 October 1990, Jean Black withdrew goods costing £800 from the business for her own use.
3. The above cash book summary does not include bank charges of £40 debited to Jean Black's account by the bank on 31 October 1990.

Required:
(a) Prepare Jean Black's trading and profit and loss account for the year ended 31 October 1990.
(b) Prepare Jean Black's balance sheet as at 31 October 1990.

(AAT Intermediate)

9.2 Jim Hastings commenced in business on 1 May 19X7 trading as 'Orbit Records', a retail outlet dealing in records, cassettes and hi-fi accessories. When he commenced business he brought in £6,500 cash, which was banked immediately. He also brought in his car at the start of the business, which was valued at £4,100. On 1 August 19X7, the business borrowed £5,300 from a finance institution at an interest rate of 16% per annum. This loan was lodged in the business bank account on 1 August 19X7 and is repayable after eight years. Jim maintains the minimum of accounting records, but does keep details of all cash and bank transactions. Summary details of cash and bank transactions for the year ended 30 April 19X8 are listed below.

Transaction	Cash	Bank
Lease payments for premises		4,800
Wages to staff	3,200	7,050
Redecoration of premises		1,235
General operating expenses	320	1,375
Purchase of goods for resale		105,950
Lighting and heating	95	965
Fixtures and fittings		4,895
Interest payments on loan		425
Accountancy fees		355
Car expenses	155	1,050

Additional information:
1. The lease agreement, which was entered into at the start of the business, detailed the cost as £960 per quarter payable in advance.
2. Asset and liability balances at 30 April 19X8:

Cash	125
Cash at bank	8,150
Car	3,150
Fixtures and fittings	4,200
Stocks	14,500
Creditors for purchases	10,940

(There have been no sales of fixed assets during the year to 30 April 19X8.)
3. All sales were made on a cash basis and after meeting cash payments the net amount was banked daily.
4. Jim Hastings took £100 per week from the cash till for personal purposes and withdrew goods for personal use during the year valued at £335 in cost terms.
5. Included within general operating expenses was the payment of a personal life assurance premium which amounted to £215.
6. It has been estimated that one-fifth of the costs relating to the car are for private purposes.

Required:
(a) Prepare a cash account and a bank account for the year to 30 April 19X8.
(b) Prepare a trading and profit and loss account for the year ended 30 April 19X8 and a balance sheet as at that date.

Author's guidance note: You will notice that the amount for cash takings banked has not been given. This will have to be derived as a balancing figure on the bank account after preparing it as far as is possible from the information given.

(AEB A Level)

Questions without answers

Answers to these questions are published separately in the *Teacher's Manual*.

9.3 Although Janet Lambert has run a small business for many years, she has never kept adequate accounting records. However, a need to obtain a bank loan for the expansion of the business has necessitated the preparation of 'final' accounts for the year ended 31 August 1991. As a result, the following information has been obtained after much careful research:

1. Janet Lambert's business assets and liabilities are as follows:

As at	1 September 1990	31 August 1991
	£	£
Stock in trade	8,600	16,800
Debtors for sales	3,900	4,300
Creditors for purchases	7,400	8,900
Rent prepaid	300	420
Electricity accrued due	210	160
Balance at bank	2,300	1,650
Cash in hand	360	330

2. All takings have been banked after deducting the following payments:

Cash drawings – Janet Lambert has not kept a record of cash drawings, but suggests these will be in the region of	£8,000
Casual labour	£1,200
Purchase of goods for resale	£1,800

Note: Takings have been the source of all amounts banked.

3. Bank payments during the year ended 31 August 1991 have been summarized as follows:

	£
Purchases	101,500
Rent	1,390
Delivery costs (to customers)	3,000
Casual labour	6,620

4. It has been established that a gross profit of $33\frac{1}{3}$% on cost has been obtained on all goods sold.
5. Despite her apparent lack of precise accounting records, Janet Lambert is able to confirm that she has taken out of the business during the year under review goods for her own use costing £600.

Required:
(a) Prepare a computation of total purchases for the year ended 31 August 1991.
(b) Prepare a trading and profit and loss account for the year ended 31 August 1991 and a balance sheet as at that date, both in as much detail as possible.
(c) Explain why it is necessary to introduce accruals and prepayments into accounting.

(AAT Intermediate, Dec 91)

9.4 *Author's guidance note:* The following question is highly contrived. You should not have any difficulty with part (a), but part (b) presents a number of problems which might take some time to sort out. For example, total sales for 1991/92 will have to be determined from cost of sales by using the gross profit percentage. This is no problem because the cost of sales for 1991/92 is given, but the opening and closing stock figures are not. In order to determine the closing stock you need to know the opening stock. This will have to be determined as a balancing figure on the opening net assets.

Harold James, who commenced business on 1 April 1990 with a capital of £45,000, had a balance on his capital account of £50,000 a year later.

Unfortunately, during the year ended 31 March 1992, Harold James has not kept his accounting records up to date.

However, the following information is now available:

1. There have been no disposals of or additions to fixed assets since the commencement of the business, when the following were bought:

		£
Freehold buildings		20,000
Fixtures and fittings		12,000
Motor vehicles		10,000

Note: Depreciation is provided on fixed assets at the following annual rates on cost:

Freehold buildings	$2\frac{1}{2}$%
Fixtures and fittings	10%
Motor vehicles	25%

2. Current assets, in addition to stock, were as follows:

At	1 April 1991	31 March 1992
	£	£
Trade debtors	6,000	7,800
Amounts prepaid – insurances	300	500
Balance at bank	4,900	To be determined
Cash in hand	600	To be determined

3. The cost of goods sold during the year ended 31 March 1992 amounted to £180,000.
4. Current liabilities were as follows:

At	1 April 1991	31 March 1992
	£	£
Trade creditors	2,400	1,900
Amounts accrued due:		
Motor vehicle running costs	210	330
Heat and light	190	150

5. As in the previous financial year, Harold James withdrew £26,000 from the business during the year ended 31 March 1992 for his personal use; drawings are always by cash or cheque.
6. A uniform rate of gross profit of 40% on the cost of sales has always been achieved.
7. It is the practice to bank all receipts from cash sales after providing for cash drawings.
8. Summary of bank account transactions during the year ended 31 March 1992:

		£	£
Receipts:	Cash sales banked	10,040	
	Credit sale receipts	228,200	
			238,240
Payments:	Goods purchased	184,100	
	Wages	9,890	
	Heat and light	2,740	
	Motor vehicle		
	running costs	6,580	
	Insurances	1,500	
	Bank charges	410	
	Drawings	13,800	
			219,020

Required:

(a) Prepare a computation of Harold James' net profit for the year ended 31 March 1991.

(b) Prepare a trading and profit and loss account for the year ended 31 March 1992 and a balance sheet as at that date, both in as much detail as possible.

(c) Identify three factors which should be borne in mind when determining rates of depreciation.

(AAT Intermediate, Jun 92)

9.5 JB, a sole trader, does not maintain a set of ledgers to record his accounting transactions. Instead, he relied on details of cash receipts/payments, bank statements and files of invoices. He started business on 1 July 19X7 with private capital of £5,000 which comprised a second-hand van valued at £1,500 and £3,500 cash which he deposited in a business bank account on that date. He has not prepared any accounts since he commenced trading and you have agreed to prepare his first set of accounts for him in respect of the 18 months ended 31 December 19X8.

You have discovered:

1. A summary of his cash transactions from his cash book for the period was:

		£	£
Receipts:	Capital introduced	3,500	
	Cash sale receipts	21,250	
	Sale of motor van	850	
			25,600
Payments:	Cash paid to bank	21,350	
	Cash purchases	2,160	
	Postage and stationery	474	
	Motor expenses	919	
			24,903
Cash in hand at 31 December 19X8			697

2. A summary of his bank statement shows:

		£	£
Receipts:	Cash paid into bank	21,190	
	Bank loan	4,500	
	Credit sale receipts	1,955	
			27,645
Payments:	Purchase of goods	7,315	
	Office equipment	1,280	
	Motor van	4,000	
	Drawings	5,400	
	Rent and rates	1,850	
	Light and heat	923	
			20,768
Balance at 31 December 19X8			£6,877

3. The office equipment was purchased on 1 October 19X7.
4. The new motor van was purchased on 1 April 19X8 to replace the original second-hand van which was sold on the same date.
5. JB expects the office equipment to last 5 years but to have no value at the end of its life. The motor van bought on 1 April 19X8 is expected to be used for 3 years and to be sold for £700 at the end of that time.
6. The cost of goods unsold on 31 December 19X8 was £1,425. JB thought he would sell these for £2,560, with no item being sold for less than its original cost.
7. On 31 December 19X8 JB owed £749 for goods bought on credit and was owed £431 for goods sold on credit. Of these amounts £189 was due from/to XEN Ltd, which is both a customer and supplier of JB. A contra settlement arrangement has been agreed by both JB and XEN Ltd.

8. Rent and rates paid includes an invoice for £1,200 for the rates due for the year to 31 March 19X9.

9. No invoice was received for light and heat in respect of November and December 19X8 until 25 February 19X9, This showed that the amount due for the three months ended 31 January 19X9 was £114.

10. The bank loan was received on 1 January 19X8. Interest is charged at 10% per annum on the amount outstanding.

Required:

Prepare JB's trading and profit and loss account for the period ended 31 December 19X8 and his balance sheet at that date in vertical form.

(CIMA, May 89)

10 ▷ Limited companies: Capital and reserves

Objectives

After completing this chapter, you should be able to:
- write up ledger accounts on an issue of share capital and debentures
- explain common forms of funding available to limited companies
- interpret information regarding a company's capital and reserves
- discuss the implications of, and make the adjustments for, a rights issue and a bonus issue of shares
- prepare the financial statements of a limited company for internal use
- discuss some of the legal restrictions relating to statutory reserves

---

Introduction

Before starting work on this chapter, you will find it helpful to review the text and activities on limited companies in Chapter 1.

You have been learning accountancy in the context of a business owned by a sole trader. The majority of accounting principles and techniques learned up to now will apply equally to all enterprises, irrespective of the type of ownership. In this chapter you will discover how certain aspects differ when the business is owned by a limited company.

You will not be learning the detailed provisions of the Companies Act that regulate the form and content of financial statements for the annual report to shareholders. The regulations concerning these are quite extensive and are covered by Chapter 12. The type of financial statements dealt with in this present chapter are influenced by the annual reporting regulations but they would not be suitable for publication to shareholders. They are sometimes described as financial statements suitable for internal use.

A fairly high proportion of the subject matter covered by this chapter is knowledge based rather than skills based. The accountancy skills required to deal with any variations arising out of limited company status are relatively few and are quite easy to learn. Consequently, there is more explanatory text than normal but you should make some effort to deal with any thought provoking activities that have been posed. The knowledge gained will be useful in many situations outside the context of preparing financial statements.

10.1 The source of differences in financial statements

In the case of a sole trader, the separation of the business entity from all the external wealth of the proprietor is something that is done purely for accounting purposes. In some respects this separation is artificial because if debts of the business cannot be satisfied out of the business assets there is nothing to stop creditors from pursuing their claim against the private wealth of the proprietor.

The concept of separation in the case of a sole trader is achieved by keeping an account to record all transactions between the business and the proprietor. This account is called the capital account, and throughout this text book you have been advised to keep two capital accounts in order to separate contributed capital from accumulated retained profits. This practice is preferable although it is not strictly necessary. You have already seen many examples of exam questions where only one account for capital has been kept.

A limited company is a separate legal entity that can own assets and enter into obligations in its own name. Ownership of the company is shared among a number of individuals who are collectively known as the shareholders (or members). The business is owned by the company (not the shareholders) and therefore separation between the proprietors of the company and the business entity is a legal reality. In the normal course of events, creditors of the company can look only to the company's assets for satisfaction of their debts.

It is these two ownership perspectives (ownership of the business and ownership of the company) that form the basis of the two sections of a balance sheet. The net assets section expresses ownership of the business by the company – it outlines the company's assets and liabilities. The capital and reserves section expresses ownership of the company by the shareholders – it shows how their interest in the company has evolved in terms of contributed capital and retained profits.

Most of the basic differences between the financial statements of a limited company and those of a sole trader arise out of the legal separation of the company from its proprietorship. The two areas of accounting affected by this are:

1. the capital accounts, and
2. the appropriation of profit after it has been determined.

The following factors have an influence on the financial statements of a limited company, but they are all related to these two areas:

- a company obtains funds initially by issuing shares in the enterprise
- shareholders may sell their shares to other persons
- a company is a separate taxable person, paying corporation tax on its profits, whereas a sole trader pays tax on total income, including any income received from sources outside of the business
- a sole trader can decide how much profit to withdraw and how much to leave in the business, whereas shareholders of a company do not have this form of 'direct' access to the profits
- the decision as to whether any part of the profit (after providing for the tax thereon) should be paid to the shareholders is taken by the directors of the company
- when directors decide to distribute part of the profit to shareholders, the payment is known as a dividend (profits are 'divided' in the sense that each shareholder is paid an amount according to the number of shares owned)

- sole traders can withdraw part of their capital, whereas a company can only pay dividends out of realized profits (there are provisions that allow a company to purchase shares from shareholders but these are outside the scope of this chapter)

In the case of a sole trader, we have been keeping two single ledger accounts for capital to record all transactions between the business and the proprietor. On one of these accounts we kept a record of cash introduced and on the other we recorded the amount of retained profits. You will see in a moment that even in the case of a company, where proprietorship is shared by a number of persons, there will still be one ledger account to record the total cash paid into the company by shareholders, and one to record the total of retained profits.

Activity 1

Describe why you think it would be unworkable to have a separate capital account for each shareholder?

A company is required by law to keep a detailed record of its shareholders. This is done in a separate memorandum book known as the share register (or register of members), which will include the names and addresses of all shareholders and the number of shares each of them owns. In some respects this register is similar to the subsidiary ledgers that are used for debtors and creditors. The total number of shares owned by all individual shareholders will agree with the total on a single share capital account kept in the nominal ledger.

Activity 2

It is quite likely that many of the persons shown as owning shares according to the share register will never have paid any money to the company. How could this have occurred?

The fact that a person owns shares in a company is evidenced by an entry in the share register. Following entry in the share register, the company will send the shareholder a document called a share certificate. This shows the shareholder's name and the number of shares owned. It has to be sent back to the company when the shares (or some of them) are sold to another person.

10.2 Share capital: Introduction

The idea of a share, and the fact that shares can be sold or transferred to another person, might be a strange concept for beginners to grasp. It is easier to understand share capital if it is studied in the context of a newly formed company.

It is relatively easy to form a company. The main process requires the interested parties to file certain legal documents with the Registrar of Companies. When the Registrar is satisfied that the documents are in order, a certificate of incorporation is issued and the company comes into existence.

Among the documents filed are two known as 'the company's memorandum and articles of association'. Although these are two separate documents, they are usually bound into one combined set.

The memorandum of association is a short document, containing five clauses in the case of a private company and six in the case of a public company. These include the name of the company, its objects, and details of the share capital it is authorized to issue. A public company must include a clause stating that it is a public company; the absence of this clause results in the company being classed as a private company. There are several differences between a public company and a private company but these need not concern you at the moment.

It is sometimes said that a company's memorandum codifies the relationship between the company and the outside world, whereas the articles of association contain all the internal regulations of the company.

The clause in the memorandum that we need to consider is the one that sets out the amount of the company's authorized share capital. When deciding the amount to be included in this clause, the interested parties must consider how much money the company might wish to raise through an issue of shares.

Activity 3

When the memorandum is drafted, the clause which states the amount of authorized share capital is often set for an amount well in excess of what the company intends to raise from its first issue to shareholders. Can you think of any reason why this might be done?

All shares issued by the company must have a stated 'nominal' value. Sometimes this is called the face value, or par value, of the share and can be any denomination that the company chooses, such as 25p, 50p, or £1 per share. This is a value in 'name' only and will have very little bearing on the market value of the share.

This may seem a bit strange when you compare the transfer of shares to the way in which we use bank notes. The owner of a £5 bank note cannot exchange it for anything other than £5 (in goods, services, or other money) whereas the owner of a £1 share can sell it for any amount that the purchaser is prepared to pay.

Although both pieces of paper (bank note and share certificate) have a stated face value, they each give the owner different rights. A bank note allows the owner to exchange it for goods and services, whereas a share gives the owner a right to participate in the fortunes of the company. This right is something that can be traded in the market place and so the price at which shares are bought and sold is determined by the usual market factors of supply and demand.

When a company intends to issue shares it will invite various people to subscribe for them. These invitations might be made to a few specific individuals in the case of a private company, or to the general public in the case of a public company. The price payable to the company by those persons who take up the issue may be equal to, or greater than, the nominal value of the share. The difference between the nominal value of the shares issued and the issue price is known as the 'share premium'.

In the normal course of events, shares cannot be issued for an amount that is less than their nominal value. There are some provisions that allow companies to issue shares at a discount (i.e. at less than their nominal value) but the procedures involved require legal sanction and are rarely used in practice.

The amount received by the company for the nominal value of the shares issued must be credited to a 'share capital account'; any amount received by the company in excess of the nominal value of the shares issued must be credited to a 'share premium account'. There are provisions in the Companies Act that regulate how the credit balance on the share premium account can be applied; some of these are dealt with in section 10.8.

The following three activities relate to the essential learning points covered by the first two sections of this chapter.

Activity 4

A company is formed with an Authorized Share Capital of £500,000. State the number of shares it must issue if it intends to raise £400,000 and the following circumstances (all independent of each other) apply:

Number

1. The shares are denominated as £1 shares and are issued at par

2. The shares are denominated as 25p shares and are issued at par

3. The shares are denominated as 50p shares and are issued at 80p each

---

Activity 5

Assume that option 3 in Activity 4 is applied, and that 500,000 shares are issued by the company. Describe the double-entry for receipt of the money on this share issue:

Debit:

Credit:

Activity 6

Assume that option 3 in Activity 4 is applied, and that two months after the shares were issued the owner of 100 shares sells them to someone for £1 each. What entries will be made in the company's books?

10.3 Share capital: Different classes

So far we have been thinking of shares as if they were all portions in a single class of shares, with each one carrying the same rights as any other share in issue. This is not usually the case.

When raising money from an issue of shares, directors will be aware that potential investors have different attitudes towards risk. There are some people prepared to take high risks for a possible (but unguaranteed) high reward, whereas others are averse to risk and are quite content with a small return providing it is relatively certain and their investment is relatively safe.

In order to attract funds from these different types of investor, companies will usually have the power to issue different classes of share, some of which have special rights. These rights are usually set out in the articles of association.

Throughout the history of limited liability companies, many different classes of share have been devised. The two most important are known as (1) ordinary shares, and (2) preference shares. There are many variations to these two basic classes of shares but they are not relevant to your present studies of accounting.

Preference shares

Preference shares carry rights that give the owners certain priorities over ordinary shareholders. They are therefore seen as safer investments than ordinary shares.

Activity 7

There are two areas in which owners of preference shares usually have rights that are preferential by comparison to the rights of the ordinary shareholders. See if you can think what these two areas might be. One of them might occur to you quite quickly but the other could be a little more obscure since the situation concerned has not been discussed in any of the text.

1.

2.

Most preference shares have both of these rights, although they may only have one of them; usually the preferential right to a dividend. The actual rights attaching to particular preference shares will be set out in the company's articles.

In most cases the right to be paid a dividend in priority to ordinary shareholders is for a fixed amount. This is usually expressed as a percentage of the nominal value of the shares. For example, the company may denominate the shares as: 10% Preference Shares of £1 each. In this case the nominal value is £1 per share, and shareholders will receive an annual dividend which is fixed at 10p for each share owned.

Generally speaking, preference shareholders will not be paid a dividend in excess of the fixed amount, nor will they receive back an amount in excess of the nominal value of the shares in the event of the company being wound up. (There are some preference shares known as participating preference shares where additional amounts might be paid.)

Consequently, when the shares are issued in the first place, the company must set the fixed dividend at a rate which will be attractive to investors at that time. This rate is very much related to prevailing interest rates. The price at which these shares are later bought and sold on the market is also very much influenced by prevailing interest rates. The fortunes of the company, providing sufficient profits are being earned to pay the preference dividend, are not likely to have much influence on the demand for these shares.

Activity 8

A person owns 100 5% Preference Shares of £1 each which were acquired many years ago. The prevailing economic climate suggests that an investor in this type of share will require a return of 10% on the amount invested. Calculate how much the owner of these 100 shares is likely to receive if they could be sold to an interested buyer.

You should note that directors are not forced to pay the preference dividend, they are only required to pay it in priority to dividends paid to ordinary shareholders. If profits are poor (or losses have been made) the directors can withhold paying a preference dividend.

Preference shares carry less risk than ordinary shares because the amount of the dividend is known with reasonable certainty; the dividend paid to ordinary shareholders will depend on the level of profits and the prior claims of preference shareholders. (The term 'risk' has a technical meaning in the case of investments and is related to the degree of certainty of returns.) On the other hand, preference shares differ from (and carry more risk than) fixed interest loan capital, where interest must be paid irrespective of the state of profits.

Some preference shares are designated as 'cumulative preference shares', which means that if the preference dividend is not paid for any particular year, it is carried forward and added on to any preference dividend due for subsequent years. The amount carried forward in this way is referred to as 'arrears' of preference dividend.

Ordinary shares

Shares with no special rights to a dividend are known as 'ordinary shares'. Ordinary shareholders usually have all the voting rights (for passing resolutions in a general meeting of the company) and have an 'equitable' right to any surplus of the company, whether this arises through trading activities or on a winding up. This concept of an equitable interest in all surpluses, after satisfying the rights of those with a prior charge, has led to ordinary shareholders being referred to as those who own the 'equity' of the company. Ordinary shareholders are often referred to as the equity shareholders.

The idea of an equity interest is something that you may have come across in your personal life. If you (or your parents) own a house on which there is an outstanding mortgage, the difference between the value of the house and the mortgage is often referred to as the equity. It represents an amount you would receive if you sold (liquidated) your house and paid off those who had a prior charge on the property.

Activity 9

A company owns net assets that have a book value of £400,000. The capital and reserves side of the balance sheet is as follows:

Share capital:

500,000 Ordinary shares of 50P each	£250,000
100,000 10% Preference shares of £1 each	100,000
	350,000

Reserves:

Retained profits	50,000
	400,000

Assume the company goes into liquidation and that the net assets actually realize an amount of £400,000. Show (assuming the usual rights apply) how this £400,000 would be distributed between the two classes of shareholder:

Ordinary shareholders would receive a total of   £

Preference shareholders would received a total of   £

The ordinary shareholders are said to be the risk takers. They stand to gain handsomely if the profits are high, but will lose everything should the company become insolvent and unable to pay off all those persons who have a prior charge on the business assets.

Revised format – FRS 4

Although we will not be discussing accounting standards that affect presentation in this chapter, it is quite interesting to see how an accounting standard known as FRS 4 would have made it easier for you to answer the question in Activity 9. This standard includes a requirement that the balance sheet provides an analysis of the *equity* and *non-equity* interests. In Activity 9 the ordinary shareholders would be classed as equity and the preference shares as non-equity. Under this regulation the capital and reserves section could be presented as follows:

	£	£
Capital and reserves:		
Equity shareholders' interest:		
Ordinary share capital	250,000	
Retained profits	50,000	
		300,000
Non-equity shareholders' interests:		
Preference share capital		100,000
		400,000

Impact of taxation on fixed interest capital

Although you will find that many examination questions include preference shares as a part of the share capital, this form of funding has become less popular in recent years because of the present system of taxation on a company's profits.

Dividends, including preference dividends, are an appropriation of profit, they are not treated as an expense in arriving at taxable profit. When capital is raised by way of loans, the interest paid on such loans is treated as an expense for tax purposes. This difference in tax treatment can be related to the two types of obligation; interest must be paid under the terms of the loan agreement, whereas dividend payments (even preference dividends) are optional. The fact that companies obtain tax relief on interest paid has made loan capital a more popular form of funding than preference shares. Loan capital is dealt with in section 10.5.

10.4 Share capital in the ledger

Some of the text in this section will be easier to understand if you have previously studied the law of contract. It does not really matter if you have not done so; you should still be able to follow the general pattern of events, and understand how this is reflected in the books. The book-keeping for a share issue is simply a matter of reflecting the legal relationships created at different stages of the process.

Application and allotment

As mentioned in section 10.2, when a company intends to issue shares it first invites investors to apply for the shares. In most cases, the application for shares must be accompanied by a payment for part of the issue price. The directors will consider all the applications received and decide how many shares to 'allot' to each applicant. The elements of a contract in this process (in terms of offer and acceptance) are as follows.

The invitation to apply is simply an invitation (like an advertisement); it does not constitute any kind of offer by the company. The offer is made when those people who would like to become shareholders apply for the shares and send in the money due on application. The acceptance of this offer is made when the directors agree to 'allot' the shares to those who have applied. Allotment is simply a process whereby directors agree to issue the shares for which an applicant has applied.

The reason why this has been pointed out is that when the application money arrives in the company it cannot, at that point, be credited to a share capital account. There is no share capital as such until the directors agree to allot the shares to those who have applied. Up to the point of allotment, all application monies can be returned to the applicants. As soon as the directors allot the shares, the total amount due to be paid to the company at that point is classified as share capital.

In many cases, the terms of the issue are such that total amount to be paid for the shares is payable by two or more instalments. A fairly straightforward arrangement would be for a part of the issue price to be paid on application, with the balance to be paid on allotment. We will, therefore, need a ledger account to which we can credit the application monies received and also deal with the amounts due on allotment. The usual procedure is to have an account called 'application and allotment' account. The first entry in this account is to credit the total amount of application money received (bank being debited).

On page 266 there is a Working Sheet with the ledger accounts to be used in Activities 10 to 14. The entries in these ledger accounts will be built up in stages and so it is important to check your work with the Key after each activity.

Activity 10

A company is formed with an authorized share capital of £500,000. This is divided into 500,000 ordinary shares of £1 each. The company decides to issue 300,000 shares as its first issue. The issue price is set at £1.50 per share, which is payable by two instalments, i.e. 75p on application and 75p on allotment. Applications are received (together with application monies) for exactly 300,000 shares. Write up the relevant ledger accounts.

If we were to produce a balance sheet at this particular stage, the credit balance of £225,000 on the application and allotment account would simply be included as a creditor. Remember that at this point the directors have not accepted the offer and could (theoretically) return the application monies if they decided not to go ahead with the issue.

In this particular case, applications were received for exactly 300,000 shares. This would be unusual in an issue to the public – applications are likely to be for more, or for less, than the number that the company intends to issue. When this happens we would refer to the issue as being either over-subscribed or under-subscribed. You will see how this is dealt with later; for the time being we continue with our example where applications for exactly 300,000 shares were received.

Following receipt of the applications and application monies, the directors will allot the shares. In this particular issue, the directors would agree that all applicants should be issued with the exact number of shares for which they have applied. At this point there is a contract, and all applicants are contracted to become shareholders and to pay the balance due on their shares.

Although there is no monetary transaction at this point, we must recognize the legal position created by the allotment. The situation created is that share capital now exists, and there is a balance of money due to the company on the issue. This can be dealt with in the books by making a double-entry for the total amount due on both application and allotment, as follows:

Debit: Application and allotment account (with the total payable on application and allotment)

Credit: Ordinary share capital account with the nominal amount of the shares issued, and share premium account with the difference between the issue price and the nominal value.

A moment's thought will tell you that when this entry has been made there will be a debit balance on the application and allotment account. This is a debtor in the true sense of the word and represents the balance of money payable to the company by the applicants following allotment of their shares.

Activity 11

Go back to the working sheet and write in the double-entry for the allotment of these 300,000 shares.

Before dealing with the next stage in this issue, you will find it helpful to consider how the various balances arising so far would be described in the balance sheet. The descriptions used are regulated by provisions in the 1985 Companies Act.

Schedule 4 of the Companies Act 1985 prescribes the formats to be used for published financial statements. These formats were introduced into UK law in 1981; their objective is to harmonize accounting practices throughout the EU. They prescribe both layout (the order in which the various figures must be presented) and the descriptions to be used.

You are not studying published financial statements in this chapter but you will often be asked to present the figures for a company 'in good form'. You can satisfy this requirement by adopting practices based on the prescribed formats.

On the capital side of the balance sheet, five items are mentioned. From your studies up to now, you will be familiar with only three. They are described as follows:

Capital and reserves: (the prescribed heading for this group of figures)
Called up share capital
Share premium account
Profit and loss account

The item described as 'profit and loss account' is for accumulated retained profits, a concept that you should be familiar with from earlier studies. You will be studying how this figure is determined for a company later in this chapter.

The other two items, shown above the profit and loss account balance, are used to describe the balances you have created as a result of Activity 11. The expression 'called up' share capital is used because at any particular point (as in Activity 11) the amount due on shares may have been 'called up' by the directors but has not yet been received. In Activity 11, the amount due on allotment (£225,000) has been called up in the sense that, having allotted the shares, the directors are calling upon the applicants to pay the balance due.

The other side of the story in this case is that there is a total debtor of £225,000 for the balance due on the shares that have been issued. The prescribed formats require this item to be described as:

Called up share capital not paid

The formats permit this item to be presented in one of two places in the 'net asset' side of the balance sheet. It can either be shown as the very first item (i.e. above the fixed assets) or included under debtors – one of the items included under current assets. The usual practice is to include it under debtors. If we were to produce a balance sheet following Activity 11, it would look something like the following:

Current assets:	
Debtors:	
Called up share capital not paid	225,000
Bank	225,000
	450,000
Capital and reserves:	
Called up share capital:	
300,000 Ordinary shares of £1 each	300,000
Share premium account	150,000
	450,000

Notice how 'called up share capital' is a main description; full details of the called up share capital (300,000 Ordinary shares of £1 each) must be disclosed.

We can now continue with our example to see what happens when the money due from applicants is received. If everybody paid in full, the amounts received would simply be credited to the application and allotment account (bank debited) until the debit balance was cleared. In exams (it rarely happens in practice) a situation is contrived where some of the applicants do not pay. Up to the point where all efforts to collect the amount due have failed, there is no particular accounting problem – the balance due is simply left as a debtor on the application and allotment account.

Activity 12

In the example you are currently working, assume that all monies due on allotment are paid except that an applicant for 1,000 shares failed to pay the balance due. Write up the ledger accounts for the money received from the remaining applicants.

The reason why this situation has been contrived is so that the study can be extended to see what happens when the directors consider the amount due (£750) will never be collected from the original applicant. It would not make sense to continue showing the amount as a debtor in this situation. In order to cope with this, the company's articles will usually give the directors power to declare the shares as forfeited.

Forfeiture

When the directors declare any shares on which a call has not been paid as forfeited, the applicant loses all rights of ownership of the shares and also loses the money previously paid to the company. The legal situation created by this forfeiting process is that the shares are still considered to be in issue but they are now owned by the company.

There is nothing to prevent a company from purchasing shares in another company and holding them as an investment. In UK law, however, there is a general rule that prohibits a company from acquring its own shares. There are some exceptions and these include the acquisition of shares by forfeiture (section 143(d), Companies Act 1985).

The Companies Act formats for the balance sheet recognize the possibility that a company might find itself owning its own shares for a short period. These formats include a group of assets under a main heading for **Investments**. The different types of investment to be classified under this heading include investments in **own shares**. Shares acquired by forfeiture fall under this classification.

In our example, the applicant for 1,000 shares has not paid the balance of £750 due on allotment. If the directors now go through the formal process of declaring the shares forfeit, the 1,000 shares would be owned by the company. The owner of partly paid shares is liable for any outstanding calls and so, theoretically, the company is liable to pay the balance due on these 1,000 shares. If it did so, the £750 would be debited to an asset account called investment in own shares. The money would be paid to itself and when banked could be credited to the application and allotment account so as to clear the outstanding debt of £750.

But there is no need for the company to go through this process of paying money to itself. All that is necessary is for the debit balance of £750 on the application and allotment account to be transferred to the account called investment in own shares.

Activity 13

Return to the working sheet for the current series of activities. Assume that the 1,000 shares, on which the outstanding call of £750 has not been paid, are formally declared by the directors as forfeited. Make the necessary adjustments in the books.

A company that acquires shares by forfeiture must generally dispose of them within three years. This should not pose any problem; some money has already been received by the company and so they could easily be offered for sale at a price that is less than the price asked on the original issue. They cannot be sold at a price that would result in the company receiving in total (from original issue and a later sale) an amount that is less than their nominal value. Failure to observe this rule would be tantamount to issuing the shares at a discount, which is not normally permitted.

You should also keep in mind that following forfeiture of the shares, and making the adjustments in the books, all outstanding calls are deemed to have been paid. Any purchaser of the 1,000 shares in our example cannot be called upon to pay the outstanding £750.

The amount received by the company when the shares are sold will be credited to the investment account. The cash received is likely to be greater than the debit balance on this account; the resulting credit balance should be transferred to the share premium account.

The 1,000 shares owned by the company in our example are sold to a purchaser for £1.00 each. Write this transaction into the ledger and make any necessary adjustment resulting from the transaction.

After completing Activity 14, the company's balance sheet (assuming there were no transactions other than those relating to shares) will be as follows:

Current assets:	
Bank	450,250
	450,250
Capital and reserves:	
Called up share capital:	
300,000 Ordinary shares of £1 each	300,000
Share premium account	150,250
	450,250

The share premium account shows a balance of £150,250. This can be identified as relating to the difference between the total amount of money received and the total nominal amount of the shares issued, as follows:

299,000 shares at £1.50 per share	448,500
1,000 shares at (75p + £1.00) £1.75 per share	1,750
	450,250
Less nominal value	300,000
	150,250

Variations on the central theme

Activities 10 to 14 have covered the basic pattern of book-keeping for a series of events in a share issue, and also on a subsequent forfeiture of shares. The basic pattern of events can be varied but the book-keeping in these cases is quite easy to sort out, providing you have understood the basic principles involved.

There are two common variations: (1) the issue is under- or over-subscribed, and (2) the total amount due on the shares is payable over a number of instalments, some of which may be payable several months after the shares are allotted.

Most share issues by existing companies are 'rights issues'. This means that instead of the issue being made to the general public, existing shareholders have a right to apply for the shares on an agreed pro rata basis (such as 1 for 2). In these circumstances the issue cannot be over-subscribed. A general issue to the public can be over-subscribed but this does not cause any undue problems in the book-keeping. A company cannot issue more shares than it has advertised in any of the documents that precede a share issue, and so the directors will have to consider the applications received and decide how many shares to allot to each applicant.

In these cases there are various schemes for scaling down the number of shares that are allotted to each applicant. The rules to be applied in these cases must be set out in the original invitation to apply, otherwise the directors' action will be construed as a counter offer, which would have to be accepted by the applicants before it could become binding on both parties to the contract.

Excess application monies might be returned to the original applicants, or they might be retained as part payment towards the amount due on allotment. All book-keeping entries are dealt with through the application and allotment account, and are simply a logical expression of the agreed arrangements for dealing with the over-subscriptions.

Activity 15

Describe the double-entry that would be made if excess application monies are returned to applicants.

Debit:

Credit:

Where excess application monies are retained as a reduction of the amounts due on allotment, there are no entries in the ledger. The debit balance on the application and allotment account represents the revised total amount due on allotment.

If a share issue is under-subscribed, this is either bad fortune for the company or (as is usually the case) the issue will have been underwritten by a finance house and the shares have to be taken up by the underwriters. There is no book-keeping problem; the shares are simply issued to the underwriters. The underwriting will involve a cost, usually called 'underwriters commission', and if this is paid it can be debited to the share premium account.

In some share issues, the amounts payable on application and allotment will only be for a part of the issue price. The balance is payable later when 'called up' by the directors. In the interval between allotment and making the call, the shares are not fully paid. These shares can be traded in the market place as partly paid shares, although their price will reflect the fact that they are not fully paid. Any person acquiring partly paid shares will become liable to pay the call when it is made by the directors.

The book-keeping in this case is simply an extension of what you have learned up to now. At the time when the directors make the call, the application and allotment account will have long since been cleared. The additional amount due on the call must be credited to called up share capital and debited to an account – usually described as 'call account'. When the call monies arrive, the call account is credited.

In cases where the issue includes a share premium, the premium is usually paid either on application or on allotment. Section 101 of the Companies Act 1985 requires that a **public company** shall not allot a share 'except as paid up to one-quarter of its nominal value and the whole of any premium on it'. Consequently, at the time of allotment the total amount due to be paid must include the share premium. Since the share premium account will have been written up on allotment, it will not feature in the book-keeping for a later call.

Activity 16

A new issue of 100,000 Ordinary shares of £1 each is made at a price of £1.50 per share, payable on the following terms: 30p on application; 80p (including the premium) on allotment; and 40p on call by the directors. Following application and allotment, the share issue was fully subscribed and all amounts due at that time were paid. Three months later, the directors make their call for the final instalment. Describe the double-entry that will be made in respect of this call.

Debit:

Credit:

If a shareholder fails to pay the call, the shares could be forfeited. The procedures and book-keeping are similar to those for forfeiture following non-payment of money due on allotment.

10.5 Debentures and loan stock

A limited company has a much wider range of options for raising capital than a sole trader. For example, a sole trader can obtain loan capital only by borrowing money from another individual or from an institution such as a bank. A company can make a public issue of loan stock (or debentures), which can then be traded in the market place in the same way as shares.

A debenture is simply a written agreement setting out the terms of the loan such as the interest rate, date of repayment, any security for the loan, and the rights of the debenture holder should the company default in keeping to the agreement. In a public issue there is usually a trustee (often a financial institution) for the individual debenture holders who is empowered to act on their behalf should the occasion arise.

Most loan and debenture stocks carry a fixed rate of interest and are usually issued with terms that specify the date of redemption (repayment). Debenture holders are creditors of the company although they do not have to wait until the debentures are redeemed in order to receive a repayment – they can always sell their debentures to another person. Interest paid is an expense; it is not an appropriation of profit as with dividends. Directors have no choice over payment of interest; failure to pay would entitle the debenture holders to exercise their rights under the agreement and this could entail placing the company into liquidation.

Loan stocks are often issued in multiples of £100 nominal value. The interest rate is expressed as a percentage of the nominal value. Market prices are quoted in terms of a price for each £100 of nominal value. If you see a quotation listed as 5% loan stock at 50, this means that £50 will be paid to acquire stock with a nominal value of £100. A purchaser of such stock would receive an annual interest payment of £5 (5% of £100), which represents 10% on the amount paid of £50. In the case of fixed interest loan stocks, market forces affecting prices are dominated by changes in the interest rate – investors in loan stock expect to earn a return on their investment that reflects the current interest rates.

The book-keeping in a public issue of loan stock or debentures is similar to an issue of shares. But there are two important differences between debentures and shares that might have to be reflected in the book-keeping should the circumstances apply. These are: (1) a company is permitted to issue debentures at a discount (i.e. at less than their nominal value), and (2) a company is permitted to purchase its own debentures and hold them as an investment. Debentures might also be redeemable at a premium.

With regard to an issue at a discount, the money received is less than the par value that will eventually have to be repaid when the debentures are redeemed.

Activity 17

Make a note here of the accounting problem that arises when debentures are issued at a discount but are repayable at par. (Think about the double-entry on receipt of the cash.)

The total discount is a cost of borrowing and will have to be dealt with in accordance with an accounting standard known as FRS 4.

FRS 4: Capital instruments

Many of the provisions in this accounting standard are aimed at complex instruments issued by companies when raising capital funds. We will not be considering these complex issues, instead we will restrict our study to the provisions in FRS 4 on borrowing costs when debentures are issued at a discount and/or are redeemable at a premium.

The objective of the provisions on borrowing costs is that the difference between two figures should be accrued annually from the date that the instrument is issued. The computation of the total borrowing cost is as follows:

Amount to be paid on redemption of the loan	X	
Add interest paid over the period of the loan	X	
Total payments made		X
Less cash received when the loan was issued		(X)
Total borrowing cost to be accrued on an annual basis		X

In the case of a straightforward loan that is issued and redeemed at par, the borrowing cost is the same as the interest paid.

Activity 18

A company issues debentures with a nominal value of £100,000 at a discount of 15%. The debentures are repayable in three years' time at a premium of 15%. The rate of interest on the nominal value of the debentures is 6% per annum payable at the end of each year. Calculate the total borrowing costs for these debentures.

Implicit interest rate

In order to comply with the provisions of FRS 4 for the debentures issued in Activity 18, it is necessary to ascertain the interest rate implied by the cash flows. These cash flows were the receipt of £85,000 when the debentures were issued, three annual payments of £6,000 at the end of the following three years, and a payment of £115,000 at the end of the third year. It is virtually impossible to calculate the implied interest manually but it can be done quite easily on a computer spreadsheet. We will not explain how this is done, the objective here is to show the book-keeping entries. If you have to deal with this kind of problem in the exam, your examiner will give you the implied interest rate.

In the example used for Activity 18, the implicit interest rate is 17% (rounded). Now that we know the rate we can use it to see what book-keeping adjustments are necessary. Following the receipt of the proceeds of issue, the loan account will show a credit balance of £85,000. During the first year the company must charge (17% x £85,000) £14,475 to the profit and loss account as interest. However, the interest paid is only £6,000. The difference of (£14,475 – £6,000) £8,475 is charged to the profit and loss account by crediting the loan account. At the end of the first year the balance on the loan account will be increased to (£85,000 + £8,475) £93,475.

In the second year the charge to the profit and loss account will be 17% of £93,745. Any difference between this charge and the amount paid is credited to the loan account. This process continues so that by the time the redemption date arrives (after three years) the balance on the loan account will become £115,000. A summary of the amounts for each of the three years is as follows:

Year	Balance on loan account at start of year	Interest to be charged against profits (17%)	Interest actually paid	Amount to be credited to the loan account	Balance on loan account at end of year
1	£85,000	£14,475	£6,000	£8,475	£93,475
2	£93,475	£15,918	£6,000	£9,918	£103,393
3	£103,393	£17,607	£6,000	£11,607	£115,000
	Total	£48,000			

Notice that the total interest charged to the profit and loss account over the three years is equal to the amount that you calculated for Activity 18.

You should note that prior to the introduction of FRS 4 (in 1994) it was common practice to charge the discounts on issue and premiums on redemption to a share premium account if such an account existed. This practice is no longer permitted.

With regard to a company purchasing its own debentures and holding them as investments, this is usually part of a complex scheme associated with financing the redemption of the debentures. Such schemes are outside the scope of subjects dealt with in this text book, although the subject is mentioned briefly in Chapter 12.

10.6 Appropriation of profit

The basic pattern

The profit and loss account of a company (for internal use) will be the same as that for a sole trader, except for an additional section that follows on from the point where net profit is determined. As it happens, there is no item in a company's profit and loss account described as net profit. The equivalent of net profit in a company's profit and loss account is called 'profit before tax'. (Sometimes the term 'net profit' is used in exam questions for companies, particularly those that ignore taxation.)

The section of the profit and loss account that follows on from profit before tax is sometimes called the appropriation account. This is not an official description (it is not, for example, mentioned in the prescribed formats) although it is quite frequently used by examiners. The word 'appropriation' does, however, give an indication of what this section of the profit and loss account tries to convey to the users. It shows how the profit has been shared out (appropriated) to all those who have some claim on such profit, and how much has been retained by the company.

Activity 19

Describe items that you think will appear in the appropriation section of a company's profit and loss account.

In order to obtain a clearer picture of a company's profit and loss account, you should review the following example and then deal with the activities that follow. The form of presentation used is based on the most popular of the various formats permitted by the Companies Act.

Profit and loss account for year ending 31 December 1996

Turnover		600,000
Cost of sales		450,000
Gross profit		150,000
Distribution costs	30,000	
Administration expenses	40,000	
		70,000
Operating profit		80,000
Interest payable and similar charges		2,000
Profit before tax		78,000
Corporation tax on profits		18,000
Profit after tax		60,000
Dividends paid and proposed:		
7% Preference shares:		
interim dividend paid	3,500	
final dividend proposed	3,500	
	7,000	
Ordinary shares:		
interim dividend paid	6,000	
final dividend proposed	12,000	
	18,000	
		25,000
Profit for the year retained		35,000

Activity 20

Review the above statement from the first item down to the figure of £78,000 for profit before tax. Make a note of any instances where the manner of presentation appears to differ from the way you have become accustomed to setting out figures in a profit and loss account.

Although you are not really studying published profit and loss accounts in this chapter, there is no harm in using them (where this is possible) as a model for any accounts that you do prepare for a company. Unfortunately, this is not always possible in exams at this particular level of the subject. In particular, you may not be given sufficient information for grouping expenses under the appropriate headings and you will have to be content with listing them according to the type of expense (as you have been doing up to now).

There is no reason why you should not tidy your presentation of the figure for cost of sales. This is sometimes derived from a number of items such as stocks, purchases, carriage and returns. If these are all set out on the face of the profit and loss account, it becomes cluttered with detail. A neater way of dealing with this is to do the calculation as a working note and present a single figure in the statement.

You should note that the term 'operating profit' used in the above profit and loss account (i.e. the profit before interest) is not an official description from the Companies Act, but it has become semi-official through professional usage. It is used as a description in some accounting standards.

Taxation

The corporation tax of £18,000 shown in the profit and loss account will be due for payment nine months after the balance sheet date, that is on 1 October 1997. The nine-month time interval is the same for all companies. Consequently, the tax payable will not appear as an item in the trial balance and an adjustment (like an accrual) must be made at the end of the year. In exams, the amount of tax payable will be given to you in a note to the question. You simply have to treat it as a charge in the profit and loss account, and show it as owing in the balance sheet.

Activity 21

Make a note here of the main heading under which the unpaid tax will be presented in the balance sheet.

When you come to study Chapter 12, you will find the taxation aspects can be a little more involved than is outlined above. In particular, you will see that some of the corporation tax might have to be paid in advance of the normal due date. This happens whenever a dividend is paid. In these circumstances, the tax creditor will be based on the charge in the profit and loss account less the amount paid in advance. There is no need for you to be concerned with this at the moment.

Dividends

Look back at the profit and loss account and notice how the profits after tax are dealt with. In this particular case you will see that the only appropriations for this year relate to dividends. You will also see two types of dividend being detailed for each class of shareholder.

The two types are described as interim paid and final proposed. This is quite normal in practice. Directors will often decide to pay a dividend during the financial year as a part payment towards the total dividend for that year. In the case of preference shares, the dividend paid during the year is usually for half of the fixed amount. Dividends paid during the year are described as interim dividends. Dividends proposed are those that the company intends to pay for the year in question (1996 in the example) but which have not been paid by the end of that year.

Activity 22

Make a note of any reason that occurs to you as to why the directors did not pay the final dividends (£3,500 for the preference shareholders, and £12,000 for the ordinary shareholders) before the end of the year.

A resolution regarding the final dividend proposed by the directors does have to be passed by the shareholders at the annual general meeting (or the AGM, as it is often called). This meeting will take place several months after the end of the company's financial year. Various matters are dealt with at this meeting, including a consideration of the financial statements for the previous year. But shareholders have no direct power to increase the amount of final dividend proposed by the directors.

In accounting questions, information is often given to you in the form of a trial balance and as notes to the question. In the case of dividends, the trial balance will show the interim dividends paid; the notes will give details of any proposed dividends. Proposed dividends are dealt with in a similar way to accruals; the charge is made to the profit and loss account (appropriation section) and the amount owing is shown as a creditor. The creditor in the balance sheet is simply described as 'proposed dividends'. They are included under the heading for creditors due within one year.

Activity 23

If dividends had been proposed for the year prior to the current year, they would have been paid during the current year. But this payment will not be included in any of the debit balances shown in the trial balance at the end of the current year. Make a note of why this happens.

Other appropriations

Sometimes the directors decide to transfer some of the profit to a separate reserve. This may be done in some cases as a result of a legal requirement whereby it will be necessary to make the transfer in order to prevent the profits from being classed as distributable. The circumstances in which this might be necessary are not covered by this chapter.

The type of transfer that you may have to cope with at the current level of study is done partly for cosmetic (or psychological) purposes. Profits transferred to this reserve can still be used for payment of dividends. The most common type of transfer in this respect is a transfer of profits to a 'general reserve'.

Accounting profit is often misunderstood by the general public. High profits might result in various people (e.g. shareholders and trade unions) agitating to be paid more than what directors consider appropriate. The earning of profit does not necessarily result in an increase in liquid funds, and even if it does, the directors may have earmarked these funds to finance expansion of the business. By transferring some of the profit to a general reserve, the directors are showing their decision to treat part of the profit as not available for immediate distribution. In legal terms, these profits are still available for distribution and can be transferred back to the profit and loss account at a later date.

The book-keeping is quite logical. The amount transferred is shown as a deduction from profit in the appropriation section (usually before dividends) and described as a transfer to general reserve. The balance on the reserve at the end of the year (which might include amounts from previous years) is included under capital and reserves in the balance sheet and described as general reserve.

Accumulated retained profit

The concept of accumulated retained profit is something that you will be familiar with from the way you have been dealing with the accounts of a sole trader.

Activity 24

The balance of retained profit for the year (£35,000 in the earlier example) is not the amount that will appear in the capital and reserves side of the balance sheet. Make a note here to explain why this is the case.

In the case of companies, there are two ways in which figures for the accumulated total can be presented. In a straightforward case, retained profit brought forward from the previous year can simply be added on to the retained profit for the current year. The total will represent the revised balance of accumulated profit to be carried forward to next year. This balance is included in the 'capital and reserves' section of the balance sheet, and described as 'profit and loss account'.

This idea of adding on the retained profits brought forward to the retained profits for the current year should be used for the questions at the end of this chapter. In Chapter 12 you will have to cope with something known as a 'prior year adjustment' and in these cases it is preferable to set out a separate statement of retained profits.

Activity 25

Make a note of where the figure for retained profit brought forward from the previous year is likely to be given in an examination question.

In some cases (more often in exams than in real life) dividends paid and proposed for the current year are greater than the profits for the current year. This suggests that dividends for the current year are being paid partly out of profits earned and retained in previous years. There is nothing in the Companies Act to prevent this, although it might be seen by observers as a danger signal. In a healthy company, the current level of dividends will be well covered by the current level of profits.

The problem arising from this relates to presentation in the appropriation account. There are two ways of dealing with the problem, as follows:

1. The retained profits brought forward from previous years could be added to profits after tax in order to show the total available for distribution.

Dividends are then deducted to arrive at the accumulated retained profit carried forward. This tends to disguise the fact that dividends have been paid partly from profits earned and retained in previous years.

2. Deduct the dividends from the current year's profits and then describe the negative balance resulting from this as distribution from retained profits of earlier years. The retained profits brought forward can then be aggregated with this negative balance in the usual way.

10.7 Rights issues and bonus issues of shares

In section 10.4 you dealt with a cash issue of shares to the public. There are two other types of issue that you need to be aware of in order to conclude this study. In both cases the issues are made to a company's existing shareholders, and in both cases there is very little extra to learn regarding the book-keeping. The two types of issue are known as (1) a rights issue, and (2) a bonus issue.

When a company has become well established, it will raise any additional capital by making a rights issue to its existing shareholders. The terms of the issue are usually quite attractive and will be at a price that is less than the market value of existing shares. The term 'rights issue' is used because the right to apply for the new shares is given to existing shareholders, not to the general public.

The number of shares for which an existing shareholder may apply is related to the number of shares already owned by that shareholder. For example, if the rights issue is announced to be on a 2 for 5 basis, an existing shareholder can apply for 2 shares for every 5 currently owned. The issue price may be payable by instalments and the book-keeping will be the same as for a public issue.

Activity 26

A company's existing share capital is £200,000 (800,000 ordinary shares of 25p each). The existing shares are being traded at a price of £2.00 each. The directors decide to make a rights issue of 2 for 5 at a price of £1.50 each. Calculate how much money the company will receive if the issue is a success, and make a note of how this will be dealt with in the capital and reserves side of the balance sheet.

In a bonus issue (sometimes called a scrip or capitalization issue) shares are issued free to all existing shareholders. Technically speaking, the company uses part of its existing reserves (e.g. balance on profit and loss account, general reserve, or share premium account) to 'pay up' the nominal amount due on the shares. They are then issued free to the shareholders. The idea of using reserves to pay up amounts due on shares is a slippery concept to grasp; reserves are not money so how can they be used to pay for the shares?

The best way of looking at this is to imagine what would happen if the company made a cash distribution to shareholders and then asked them to send the money back in order to pay for the shares. We would debit the reserve (for the distribution) and credit share capital when the money came back. But there is no need for money to be exchanged; we can simply make a journal entry to debit reserves and credit share capital.

Theoretically, the shareholders receive nothing of value in a bonus issue. All that happens is that the total equity of the company is divided among a larger number of units. If the bonus issue was on a 1 for 1 basis, a shareholder who previously owned 100 shares will own 200 after the bonus issue. If these shares were trading at £2.00 per share prior to the bonus issue, then (in theory) the market price will drop to £1.00 per share following the bonus issue. The total value of the shareholding (£200) is the same both before and after the bonus issue. This raises the question as to why a company should make a bonus issue. There are several explanations.

In the first place, there might be a slight increase in the total market value of the shares. Evidence from empirical studies on this indicates that share values do not fall to their theoretical value following a bonus issue; there is always a slight gain. This might be explained by an increase in demand for the share when the price is reduced; or that there is likely to be more market activity with a larger number of low value shares than there is with a smaller number of high value shares.

Secondly, a company may have built up large reserves which it has no intention of ever distributing by way of dividends. A bonus issue from these reserves would bring the share capital more in line with what is being treated as permanent capital, hence the expression 'capitalization issue'.

The book-keeping on a bonus issue is simply to debit the nominated reserve, and to credit share capital, with the nominal value of the bonus shares issued.

10.8 Share premium account: Restrictive use

As was mentioned in section 10.2, the share premium account is subject to a number of legal restraints. These are designed to ensure that the share premium account is not reduced except in circumstances permitted by the Companies Act. For example, the share premium account cannot be treated as a realized profit from which dividends are paid. In other words, dividends cannot be debited to the share premium account.

There is no need for you to learn the complete set of rules on the share premium account at this stage of your studies. But while the subject is fairly fresh in your mind, you should deal with Activity 27. It will help you with some of your subsequent studies, and might help with your revision of some of the topics covered in this chapter.

Activity 27

At various points throughout this chapter, you have come across two instances where a company is permitted to reduce the balance on its share premium account. See if you can find these two situations and make a note of them here.

1.

2.

10.9 Revaluation of fixed assets

Another reserve that often appears in a company's balance sheet is called a revaluation reserve. This arises where some of the fixed assets, particularly assets such as land and buildings, have been revalued to an amount in excess of their net book value. The difference between net book value and the valuation must be credited to the revaluation reserve. The asset is then shown at valuation instead of cost, and subsequent depreciation charges must be based on the revalued figure.

There are a number of regulations, both statutory and professional, that affect this revaluation process, and these are discussed more fully in Chapter 19. The topic has been introduced here because a number of examinations based on the current level of study include asset revaluations in questions on company accounts. These questions merely require you to reflect the revaluation in the financial statements rather than discuss some of the controversies and rules that surround the subject.

The mechanics of the book-keeping on a revaluation are quite simple; it is even easier to make adjustments to a balance sheet to reflect a revaluation. The following is an abbreviated balance sheet for a company prior to a revaluation:

Fixed assets:		
Land and buildings at net book value		50,000
Current assets	20,000	
Creditors: amounts falling due within one year	10,000	
		10,000
		60,000
Capital and reserves:		
Called up share capital		40,000
Share premium account		5,000
Profit and loss account		15,000
		60,000

A professional valuation of the land and buildings reveals a value of £60,000 and the directors require this to be reflected in the balance sheet. The balance sheet after giving effect to the revaluation will be as follows:

Fixed assets:		
Land and buildings at valuation		60,000
Current assets	20,000	
Creditors: amounts falling due within one year	10,000	
		10,000
		70,000
Capital and reserves:		
Called up share capital		40,000
Share premium account		5,000
Revaluation reserve		10,000
Profit and loss account		15,000
		70,000

You will notice that the increase of £10,000 in the carrying value of the asset is simply counterbalanced by the revaluation reserve of £10,000 in the capital and reserves section of the balance sheet. This reserve represents an 'unrealized' profit (the asset has not been sold) and because of this it cannot be distributed to the shareholders in the form of dividends.

As regards the mechanics of the book-keeping, you need to keep in mind that net book value is derived from the balances on two ledger accounts; one for cost and one for the depreciation provision. Both of these balances should be transferred to an 'asset revaluation account'. In effect, this will debit the revaluation account with the net book value. This account is then credited, and the asset account debited, with the revalued amount. The credit balance on the asset revaluation account is then transferred to the revaluation reserve.

Summary

The main learning points in this chapter can be summarized as follows:

- most accounting principles and techniques apply equally to all entities irrespective of the type of ownership
- the two areas of accounting affected by limited company ownership are the capital accounts, and the appropriation of profit
- limited companies may issue different classes of share capital, some of which provide the holders with preferential rights over other classes
- ordinary shareholders are the risk takers, but they usually hold all voting rights and have an equitable claim to all surpluses after satisfying the claims of those with a prior charge
- the book-keeping for a share issue simply follows the legal relationships created at each stage of the process
- when shares are declared forfeit, they remain as part of the issued share capital and are treated as owned by the company until sold
- a company may raise loan capital by issuing debentures; debenture holders are creditors of the company
- debentures may be issued at a discount and are often redeemed at a premium
- the difference between cash received on issue and total payments (interest and redemption cost) must be treated as a borrowing cost to be spread over the period of the loan
- the profit of a company, after providing for corporation tax, is divided up according to decisions taken by the directors
- shareholders receive a dividend payment according to the number of shares owned; the accumulated balance of retained profit is carried forward to the following year
- rights issues are cash issues to existing shareholders at a preferential price; bonus shares are issued free to existing shareholders by capitalizing some of a company's reserves
- there are legal provisions that restrict the circumstances in which the share premium account may be reduced
- companies might revalue some of their fixed assets from time to time; this can be reflected in the balance sheet by increasing the carrying value of the asset to its revalued amount and crediting the increase to a revaluation reserve

At this stage of your studies, you will find that you can answer quite a large number of past examination questions. As with most types of question, those relating to companies will include topics from earlier studies such as fixed asset accounting, error correction and suspense accounts.

Working sheet

The following ledger accounts should be used for Activities 10 to 14. You will be building up the figures in stages and so it is important to check with the Key after each activity.

Bank		Application and allotment	

Called up share capital £1 Ordinary shares		Share premium account	

Investment in own shares	

Activity 1

There are likely to be too many; some public companies have thousands of shareholders. In the case of retained profit, the members have no direct claim to this profit and so the total amount must be kept separate from the capital subscribed.

Activity 2

They bought their shares from an existing shareholder, not from the company.

Activity 3

Companies may need to raise further capital several years after they were originally formed, and a company can raise capital only within the limits authorized by its memorandum. (A company can change the clauses in its memorandum but this involves a number of inconvenient legal formalities.)

Activity 4

1 = 400,000; 2 = 1,600,000; 3 = 500,000.

Activity 5

Debit bank £400,000; credit share capital account with £250,000 (500,000 × 50p) and credit share premium account with £150,000 (500,000 × 30p). The book-keeping is sometimes a little more involved than this – full details are in section 10.4.

Activity 6

The only entry will be in the share register, where the original owner will be shown as having sold the shares (and is no longer a shareholder) and the new owner recorded as having bought them. None of the money is paid to the company and so no entries are needed in the nominal ledger.

Activity 7

1. The right to a dividend before any is paid to the ordinary shareholders (you might have thought of that one).
2. In the event of the company being wound up, a right to a return of capital before any is paid to the ordinary shareholders.

Activity 8

The answer is £50. The dividend being paid on 100 shares is £5. If an investor is looking for a 10% return on the amount invested, the amount paid for an investment yielding £5 will be (£5 × 100/10) £50. Note that the dividend of £5 is then 10% of the amount paid for the investment.

Activity 9

Ordinary shareholders £300,000 and preference shareholders £100,000.

Activity 10

After completing this activity the relevant ledger accounts should be as follows:

Bank		Application and allotment	
Application & allotment a/c 225,000		Bank 225,000	

Activity 11

The accounts will now be as follows:

Bank

Application & allotment a/c	225,000		

Application and allotment

Share capital	300,000	Bank	225,000
Share premium	150,000	Balance c/d	225,000
	450,000		450,000
Balance b/d	225,000		

Ordinary share capital

		Application & allotment a/c	300,000

Share premium

		Application & allotment a/c	150,000

Activity 12

The accounts will be as follows:

Bank

Application & allotment a/c	225,000		
Application & allotment a/c	224,250		

Application and allotment

Share capital	300,000	Bank	225,000
Share premium	150,000	Balance c/d	225,000
	450,000		450,000
Balance b/d	225,000	Bank	224,250
		Balance c/d	750
	225,000		225,000
Balance b/d	750		

Ordinary share capital

		Application & allotment a/c	300,000

Share premium

		Application & allotment a/c	150,000

Activity 13

The two relevant ledger accounts will be as follows:

Application and allotment

Share capital	300,000	Bank	225,000
Share premium	150,000	Balance c/d	225,000
	450,000		450,000
Balance b/d	225,000	Bank	224,250
		Balance c/d	750
	225,000		225,000
Balance b/d	750	Investment in own shares	750
	750		750

Investment in own shares

Application & allotment a/c	750		

Activity 14

The two relevant ledger accounts will be as follows:

Investment in own shares					Share premium		
Application & allotment a/c	750	Bank	1,000		Application & allotment a/c		150,000
Share premium	250				Investment in own shares		250
	1,000		1,000				

There will also be a debit to the bank account for £1,000.

Activity 15

Debit application and allotment account; credit bank.

Activity 16

Debit call account £40,000; credit called up share capital (Ordinary shares) £40,000.

Activity 17

When the loan account is credited with the proceeds of the issue, it will show a liability for less than the amount which must eventually be repaid.

Activity 18

Redemption cost	£115,000
Interest paid	18,000
	133,000
Cash received on issue	85,000
Total borrowing cost	48,000

Activity 19

You could have written taxation, dividends, and profits retained. Note that although taxation is dealt with in this part of the profit and loss account, it can be argued that taxation is a charge against profit rather than an appropriation. Unlike dividends, the company has no option other than to pay the amount of tax demanded.

Activity 20

You may have spotted the following:
Sales is described as turnover. Cost of sales is a single figure instead of a detailed calculation involving adjustments to purchases for opening and closing stocks. All other costs (except for interest) have been aggregated under two functional headings (i.e. either under distribution costs, or under administration expenses) rather than being set out according to the type of expense, such as wages, electricity, depreciation, etc. The only item described according to the type of expense is interest.

Activity 21

Creditors: amounts falling due within 1 year.

Activity 22

The directors will wish to see the audited results for the year before deciding how much dividend to pay. This information will not be available until some time after the balance sheet date.

Activity 23

Because the payment will simply clear the creditor (for proposed dividends) set up at the end of the previous year.

Activity 24

Because there will be retained profits brought forward from previous years.

Activity 25

It will be one of the credit balances in the trial balance.

Activity 26

320,000 shares will be issued, total money received = £480,000. Share capital will be credited with (320,000 × 25p) £80,000, and share premium account will be credited with (320,000 × £1.25) £400,000.

Activity 27

1. Writing off share issue expenses (see underwriter's commission in section 10.4).
2. Issuing bonus shares (see section 10.7 on bonus issues).

Questions for self-assessment

Answers to self-assessment questions are given at the end of the book.

10.1 Queue plc. This question is based on one included in the ACCA Level 1 exams. A simple book-keeping adjustment on the bank account (included in the original question) has been removed, and point of principle (on stock valuation) has been incorporated in the version reproduced here. The question is relatively straightforward but it is a thorough 'work horse' and provides excellent practice in preparing a complete set of financial statements for a company. The revised question is as follows:

The trial balance of Queue plc at 31 December 19X9, before any of the items noted below, is as follows:

Issued share capital		
(£1 ordinary shares)		30,000
Freehold properties – at cost	40,000	
Motor vehicles:		
at cost	10,000	
depreciation to 31 December 19X8		4,000
Selling and distribution costs	2,000	
Administration expenses	9,000	
Stock at 31 December 19X8	12,000	
Purchases	70,000	
Sales		100,000
10% Debentures		15,000
Debenture interest	750	
Bank overdraft		1,000
Bank interest	250	
Debtors and creditors	25,000	15,000
Dividends paid	1,500	
Profit and loss account		
31 December 19X8		5,500
	170,500	170,500

The following notes are to be incorporated as appropriate:
1. Closing stock valued at cost is £10,200. An internal audit of the stock revealed that one item, which had been included at a cost price of £600, had been damaged and as it stood could only be sold for £200. However a customer has been found who would be prepared to buy the item for £500 providing it is repaired. It was estimated that the repair costs would be £100.
2. The debentures were issued on 1 April 19X9.
3. All the motor vehicles were purchased in 19X7. Depreciation has been, and is still to be, provided at the rate of 25% per year on cost. On 31 December 19X9 one vehicle, purchased on 1 January 19X7 for £4,500, was sold for £2,750. The sale was accepted in part settlement of the price of £4,000 for a new van. No entries have been made in the books with regard to these transactions, and no money has been paid or received. The company treats vehicle depreciation as a selling and distribution cost.
4. The corporation tax liability for the year to 31 December 19X9 is calculated to be £5,000.
5. A final dividend of 6p per share on the existing shares is proposed.
6. By agreement, 10,000 new £1 ordinary shares were issued on 31 December 19X9 at 125p per share, and the cash proceeds banked. The bank balance shown in the trial balance was struck prior to the banking. These shares will not rank for dividends in 19X9.

Required:
Prepare the financial statements for Queue plc in good order for internal use.

Author's note: Try to use the prescribed formats as far as possible.

(ACCA 1.1, *modified*)

10.2 Equity Ltd commenced business on 1 January 1992, with an authorized share capital of 300,000 ordinary shares of £1 each. During the twelve months to 31 December 1992, the following events occurred which related to share capital.

1. On 1 January 1992, the company issued 100,000 ordinary shares at a price of £1.90 each. Payment arrangements were as follows:

At date of issue	£1.00 per share
First call, 28 February 1992	£0.40 per share
Second and final call,	
31 March 1992	£0.50 per share

    All amounts due were paid on the stated dates.

2. On 30 June 1992, the company made a rights issue on a 'one for two' basis at £2.25 per share, payable in full on 10 July 1992. The issue was not underwritten, and only 80% of the issue was subscribed for by shareholders, with payment being made on the due date.
3. On 30 November 1992, the company decided to declare a bonus issue of shares by utilization of the full amount standing to the credit of the share premium account at that date.

Required:
(a) Show the ordinary share capital account and the share premium account of the company for the year ended 31 December 1992.
(b) Calculate the number of shares owned, and the total price paid for those shares, assuming that a shareholder had subscribed initially for 1,400 shares and had subsequently taken up the rights issue and then received the bonus issue.
(c) Explain the reasons why a company might wish to make a bonus issue of shares.

Author's note: If this issue had been by a public company, it would have contravened Section 101 of the Companies Act. The £1 payable on issue (allotment) will include the share premium of 90p. The remaining 10p is less than one-quarter of the nominal value.

(ULSEB A Level, *updated*)

10.3 Thingummy Ltd. The trial balance at Thingummy Limited at 1 January 19X9 is made up of the following balances:

	£000
Share capital (£1 ordinary shares)	200
Profit and loss account balance	80
Debtors	100
Bad debt provision	4
Creditors	90
Land and buildings	110
Plant and machinery: cost	140
depreciation	50
Prepayments for operating expenses	4
Accruals for operating expenses	10
Stock	100
Bank overdraft	20

At 31 December 19X9 you are given the following information relating to the year 19X9:

Sales	500
Cash receipts from debtors	440
Bad debts written off	20
Purchases	300
Payments to suppliers	310
Contra between debtors and creditors	5

Discounts allowed	15
Discounts received	10
Bad debts provision is to be 10% of debtors	
Shares issued (50,000 £1 ordinary shares)	75
Operating expenses paid	95
Payments for plant and machinery	60
Proceeds on disposal of plant and machinery (depreciated to half its original cost)	15
Profit on disposal of plant and machinery	6
Gain on revaluation of land and buildings	40

Required:

You are required to submit a trial balance as at 31 December 19X9 incorporating all the given information. You are not required to calculate the profits for the year, or to prepare a profit and loss account or balance sheet. Workings may be in any form you find convenient. All written workings should be clear and legible.

(ACCA 1.1, Dec 89)

Questions without answers

Answers to these questions are published separately in the *Teacher's Manual*.

10.4 Tecopac plc. The following financial information was available on Tecopac plc:

	Balance Sheets as at 31 December	
19X8 £m		19X9 £m
8.0	Fixed assets	11.0
5.4	Current assets	7.0
13.4		18.0
3.4	Less current liabilities	4.5
10.0		13.5
6.0	Called up capital £1 Ordinary shares full paid	6.0
2.0	Share premium	2.0
2.0	Retained earnings at 1 January 19X9	2.0
	Net profit for year ended 31 December 19X9	3.5
10.0		13.5

In respect of the financial year ended 31 December 19X9 the directors recommended the payment of a final ordinary dividend of 10p per share and the transfer of £3.0m to a general reserve. No interim dividend had been paid.

Hartington, an ordinary shareholder, purchased 30,000 shares at £1.50 per share on 1 January 19X9 (market value at 31 December 19X9 £1.80 per share). On receiving the company's annual statement he was disappointed to learn that he would receive a final dividend of only 10p a share, and he regarded the profit of £3.5m for 19X9 as unsatisfactory since the company employed a substantial amount of capital.

Hartington decided to write to the company's Chief Accountant with a number of suggestions which he hoped would increase the return to shareholders and improve the profitability of Tecopac plc. The suggestions were as follows:

1. The company should make a bonus issue of shares to keep the shareholders happy.
2. Use the share premium account to pay an increase in the dividend. This will also conserve cash resources.
3. Invest £3m of the company's retained earnings in 8% per annum fixed interest government securities.

Required:

(a) A profit and loss appropriation account for Tecopac plc for the year ended 31 December 19X9.

(b) As Chief Accountant of Tecopac write a reply to Hartington, commenting on each of the suggestions above.

(AEB A Level, Jun 90)

10.5 Fiddles plc. The following question requires correction of errors to a trial balance that has been prepared after striking a balance for operating profit. Take care with the adjustments for errors on stock – one of them affects the previous year's profits (requiring an adjustment to the profits brought forward) in addition to the current year.

The accountant of Fiddles plc has begun preparing final accounts but the work is not yet complete. At this stage the items included in the trial balance were as follows:

	£000
Land	100
Buildings	120
Plant and machinery	170
Depreciation provision	120
Share capital	100
Profit and loss balance brought forward	200
Debtors	200
Creditors	110
Stock	190
Operating profit	80
Debentures (16%)	180
Provision for doubtful debts	3
Bank balance (asset)	12
Suspense	1

Notes (i) to (vii) below are to be taken into account.

(i) The debtors control account figure, which is used in the trial balance, does not agree with the total of the debtors ledger. A contra of £5,000 has been entered correctly in the individual ledger accounts but has been entered on the wrong side of both control accounts.

A batch total of sales of £12,345 had been entered in the double-entry system as £13,345, although individual ledger account entries for these sales were correct. The balance of £4,000 on sales returns account has inadvertently been omitted from the trial balance, though correctly entered in the ledger records.

(ii) A standing order of receipt from a regular customer for £2,000, and bank charges of £1,000, have been completely omitted from the records.

(iii) A debtor for £1,000 is to be written off. The provision for doubtful debts balance is to be adjusted to 1% of debtors.

(iv) The opening stock figure had been overstated by £1,000 and the closing stock figure had been understated by £2,000.

(v) Any remaining balance on suspense account should be treated as purchases if a debit balance and as sales if a credit balance.

(vi) The debentures were issued three months before the year end. No entries have been made as regards interest.

(vii) A dividend of 10% of share capital is to be proposed.

Required:

(a) Prepare journal entries to cover items in notes (i) to (v) above. You are not to open any new accounts and may use only those accounts included in the trial balance as given.

(b) Prepare final accounts for internal use in good order within the limits of the available information. For presentation purposes all the items arising from notes (i) to (vii) above should be regarded as material.

(ACCA 1.1, Jun 91)

10.6 ABC Ltd has the following trial balance at 31 March 1992:

	Dr £	Cr £
Freehold land at cost	60,000	
Buildings at cost	50,000	
Plant and equipment at cost	120,000	
Motor vehicles at cost	32,000	
Provisions for depreciation:		
Buildings		20,000
Plant and equipment		74,000
Motor vehicles		16,800
Stock at 1 April 1991	74,000	
Debtors and creditors	122,500	99,800
Cash at bank	3,500	
Sales (all on credit)		249,760
Purchases (all on credit)	134,630	
Returns	12,900	4,875
Discounts allowed and received	3,200	1,850
Administration expenses	22,150	
Selling and distribution expenses	6,900	
Ordinary shares of £1 each, fully paid		100,000
Profit and loss reserve		69,695
Suspense		5,000
	£641,780	£641,780

Notes:
1. The balance on the suspense account represents the proceeds from the disposal of a motor van which had originally cost £14,000 and had a net book value of £6,000 on the date of disposal. The proceeds have been correctly entered in the bank account but no other entries have been made.
2. The closing stock of finished goods was valued at £124,875.
3. A review of the year-end ledger accounts shows that the following accruals and prepayments are required:

	Accruals £	Prepayments £
Administration expenses	4,500	12,000
Selling and distribution expenses	5,300	8,000

4. Depreciation is to be provided in full on all assets held at the end of the year using the following rates:

Buildings	4% per annum on cost
Plant and equipment	20% per annum on cost
Motor vehicles	25% per annum reducing balance

5. The directors propose a dividend of five pence per ordinary share.
6. The company's liability to corporation tax on the profit for the year is estimated to be £15,000.

Required:

Prepare, in vertical form:

(a) the company's trading and profit and loss and appropriation account for the year ended 31 March 1992;

(b) the company's balance sheet at 31 March 1992.

(CIMA, May 92)

10.7 Angora Ltd prepares its accounts to 31 October each year. Its trial balance at 31 October 19X3 was as follows:

	Dr £000	Cr £000
Premises – cost	600	
Manufacturing plant – cost	350	
Office equipment – cost	125	
Accumulated depreciation at 1 November 19X2:		
Premises		195
Manufacturing plant		140
Office equipment		35
Stocks at 1 November 19X2:		
Raw materials	27	
Work-in-progress	18	
Finished goods	255	
Sales of finished goods		2,350
Purchases of raw materials	826	
Returns inwards and outwards	38	18
Direct wages	575	
Heat, light and power	242	
Salaries	122	
Printing, postage and stationery	32	
Rent, rates and insurances	114	
Loan interest payable	12	
Loan		250
Trade debtors and creditors	287	75
Provision for doubtful debts		11
VAT account		26
Interim dividend paid	10	
Ordinary shares of £1 each		500
Share premium account		100
Profit and loss account balance		442
Bank balance	509	
	4,142	4,142

The following additional information at 31 October 19X3 is available:

(i) Closing stocks:

raw materials	£24,000
work-in-progress	£19,000
finished goods	£147,000

(ii) Prepayments:

rates	£17,000
insurances	£4,000

(iii) Accruals:

direct wages	£15,000
salaries	£8,000

(iv) Salaries are to be apportioned as follows:

manufacturing	20%
administration	80%

(v) Specific bad debts to be written off amount to £47,000, including VAT at $17\frac{1}{2}$%. The company maintains a separate bad debts account. The debts have all been outstanding for more than six months.

(vi) The provision for doubtful debts is to be amended to $2\frac{1}{2}$% of debtors, after adjusting for bad debts written off.

(vii) Depreciation of fixed assets is to be provided as follows:

premises	2% on cost
plant	10% on cost
office equipment	20% on reducing balance

25% of premises depreciation is to be apportioned to the manufacturing account.

(viii) The loan was taken out on 1 November 19X2, and the capital is to be paid as follows:

1 January 19X4	£100,000
1 January 19X5	£100,000
1 January 19X6	£50,000

Interest is to be charged on the outstanding capital at 20% per annum.

(ix) Other expenses are to be apportioned as follows:

heat, light and power	$\frac{1}{2}$ manufacuting
	$\frac{1}{2}$ selling and administration
rent, rates and insurances	$\frac{1}{3}$ manufacturing
	$\frac{2}{3}$ administration

(x) One line of finished goods stock, currently recorded at £8,000, has a net realizable value of £3,000.

(xi) A final dividend of 10p per share is to be proposed.

(xii) A provision for corporation tax of £35,000 is to be made on the profits for the year.

Required:
(a) Prepare a manufacturing account for the year ended 31 October 19X3.
(b) Prepare a trading and profit and loss account for the year ended 31 October 19X3.
(c) Prepare a balance sheet at 31 October 19X3.

The accounts are to be presented in vertical format, but not in a format for publication.

(CIMA Specimen paper, 94)

11 ▷ Cash flow statements

Introduction

Historically, the published financial statements of companies have placed much more emphasis on profit than on cash flow. It is only necessary to glance through the daily company news reports in the financial press to notice a constant reference to profits.

This preoccupation by the public with a single accounting measure called profit is considered by some commentators to be unwise and it is something which the ASB has been trying to remedy. Profit is a reporting concept devised by accountants, it is not a specific resource such as cash. The measurement of profit is highly subjective and the amount reported can be manipulated by creative accounting. The problem of creative accounting is discussed in Chapter 20, but you know enough from your earlier studies to realize how profit depends on the various estimates made and on the accounting policies adopted. Even at a simple level, profit can be changed by altering the estimate of fixed asset lives.

Cash flows are objective. The amount does not depend on the accounting practices of the country in which a company resides. In this respect cash flow can be thought of as an international language. By measuring cash flows we remove all the effects of different accounting practices and produce a measure that is truly comparable with other companies, either nationally or internationally. A requirement for companies to produce a cash flow statement now exists in all major market economies of the world, including countries in the Russian Federation. In some countries the requirement is codified in law, in others (such as the UK) the requirement is in an accounting standard (FRS 1) issued by the ASB.

11.1 Cash flows and profits

Financial accountants have the unenviable task of dividing up something that is continuous (a business operating year after year) into artificial time periods called 'the accounting year'. When attempting to explain why a company's financial position at the end of the year is different from what it was at the start of the year, financial accountants developed a measuring concept called 'profit'.

Difficulties with measuring profit

As you know, annual profit measurement requires sales income for a year to be matched with the costs of earning that income. This matching process can be highly subjective because it involves making judgements on incomplete transactions. For example, the purchase of a fixed asset (such as plant) will have occurred in one particular year but will remain in use over a number of years and then be sold. The difference between the original cost and sale proceeds represents a cost (called depreciation) that will have to be matched with sales income for each of the years when the asset was used.

In order to allocate this total cost to the accounting years concerned, the company has to make two estimates in the year when the asset was purchased:

1. an estimate of how many years the company is likely to use the asset, and
2. an estimate of what its disposal value is likely to be at the end of that time.

Quite often these estimates turn out to be wrong and adjustments have to be made when measuring profit for the year when the asset is sold (or scrapped). Estimating annual depreciation costs is only one of the problems in measuring profit. There are, as you know, many others.

Timing differences

Differences between profit and cash flows are simply a matter of timing. In the long run, total profits and total cash inflows from operating the business will be the same – they simply occur in different accounting periods.

In the fixed asset example mentioned above, the cash flows representing the net cost (purchase cost less sale proceeds) occurred at two points of time which were separated by several years. When calculating profit the same net cost was allocated to each of the accounting years between these two points in time. There was, therefore, a difference between the timing of actual cash flows and the years in which the net cost was recognized for measuring annual profit. This is said to be a long-term timing difference because it occurs over several years .

Some timing differences are short term in the sense that the expense or income is reported in the profit statement for one year and the cash outflows or inflows occur in the following year. This will arise from the use of accruals accounting where income and expenditure must be recognized at the time when the transactions occur, not when the cash is received or paid. Many business transactions are conducted on a credit basis. Theoretically, it is possible to make a profit in an accounting period without any cash being exchanged.

Assume, for example, that you purchase a stock item for £10.00 and the supplier allows you two month's credit. You then sell this item immediately for £15.00 and you tell your customer to pay for it after one month. If your accounting period ends on the following day, you would have to report a profit of £5.00 even though no cash had been paid or received.

The £15.00 that you are owed will be shown in your balance sheet as a current asset (a debtor) and the £10.00 that you owe will be shown as a current liability (a trade creditor). Your £5.00 profit is, therefore, represented in the balance sheet by net current assets of £5.00. Hopefully both amounts will be settled in the following accounting period and, if so, you will have reported a profit of £5.00 in one period and have a net cash inflow of £5.00 in the following period. Over the two periods, profits and cash flows are the same.

11.2 Cash flows apart from operating profit

An important item in a cash flow statement is the net inflow (or net outflow) of cash from operating activities. This is a measure of the net cash inflows (or net outflows) generated by transactions from which operating profit is determined. If you look back to the example of a company's profit and loss account in section 10.6 of Chapter 10, you will see that operating profit represents profit before interest and tax (in fact, some companies call it profit before interest and tax instead of operating profit).

One of the objectives of a cash flow statement is to explain changes in a company's cash resources over the year. It provides a summary, under specific headings, of all cash inflows and all cash outflows. The net total of all cash flows will represent the increase or decrease in the company's cash resources over that year. The net cash inflows (or outflows) from operating activities represents only one source of cash flow; there will be many others.

 Activity 1

List as many types of transaction as you can, other than those relating to operating profit, which will result in a cash inflow or cash outflow for a company.

Cash inflows   **Cash outflows**

If a company owns investments in another company it will receive dividends (or interest) from that company. This investment income is another cash inflow beyond the operating profit. It is presented in the same section of the profit and loss account as interest paid and is usually deducted from interest paid. The net result of this set off is then deducted from operating profit. In some cases the investment income exceeds the interest paid and, if this is so, the net amount is added to operating profit.

11.3 Historical developments

Funds flow

Between July 1975 and March 1992, it was standard accounting practice for companies to publish a statement known as a Statement of Sources and Application of Funds. This statement was being described in text books, and prepared on a voluntary basis, long before 1975. The funds flow statement was quite helpful in the case of small entities (such as sole traders) but it tended to complicate the facts rather than clarify them in the case of large organizations.

Looking back on it in the light of subsequent developments, it seems strange that we (the accounting profession) thought that this statement was providing useful information to users. All that it really did was to fuel an academic debate on the meaning of the word 'funds'. The main difficulty with the statement was that users (quite naturally) associated the word 'funds' with cash, but this was wrong. In most cases the word 'funds' was being used in the context of total working capital rather than cash. One of the first pronouncements by the new Accounting Standards Board (ASB) was to scrap the funds flow statement and replace it with a Cash Flow Statement according to specifications in FRS 1, issued in 1991.

Revision of FRS 1

The original requirements in FRS 1 were revised in 1996. The 1996 revision has changed the form of presentation and the treatment of cash resources. At this stage of your studies it will be quite safe for you to think of cash resources as being the bank and cash balances, and so we will start by concentrating on the differences in presentation. You should, however, keep in mind that some companies manage their surplus cash resources in a number of ways, such as by making short-term investments, and it is this aspect that prompted a change to the original standard as far as cash resources are concerned. In the original version the pure cash balances were aggregated with other cash equivalents (such as investments that were within three months of maturity) and this did not reflect clearly how the company was managing its cash resources.

Free cash flow: A new focus

Apart from the problem over the treatment of cash resources, the original (1991) format for the cash flow statement was reasonably adequate from a stewardship accounting perspective. It did not, however, make it easy to identify an amount known as 'free cash flow', which many investment analysts consider important. We will be discussing the concept of free cash flow in a moment. For the time being you should note that many commentators consider free cash flow to be far more important than the amount of profit available for distribution to equity shareholders.

It is conceivable that there will be a time in the not too distant future where the focus of attention for evaluating a company's performance will shift from profit to free cash flow. The concept of free cash flow has been used for many years in some of the more sophisticated methods for valuing a business (or a business strategy) and thereby obtaining a shareholder value based on projected cash flows rather than on projected profits. Unfortunately, there are several interpretations of the exact composition of free cash flows and in view of this the ASB's revision of FRS 1 fell short of requiring a figure for free cash flow to be disclosed. The new format will, however, make it easier for an analyst to identify the amount which is generally considered to represent free cash flow. An interesting aspect of this is how the role of financial accounting is starting to change from its traditional stewardship function to that of providing information previously seen as being in the domain of corporate financial management.

11.4 The formats

The cash flow statements in UK practice are required to be in a specific format with standard headings for various groups of items. As stated earlier, the original accounting regulation introduced by the ASB in September 1991 (effective from 1992) was revised in 1996. The revisions in 1996 do include some changes to the original 1991 format.

The 1991 format

In order to understand some of the reasons for the 1996 changes, it is necessary first to consider the format required by the original standard. The old format will also continue to form the basis of published figures for accounts ending on a date before 23 March 1997. It might also continue as the format required in examinations that allow a long time interval between the inception of a new standard and the exam diet in which it can first be examined. It is quite likely that students sitting professional exams will be required to apply the revised standard in examinations starting from the summer of 1997.

The following gives an overview of the standard headings used in the 1991 format. Some of these might seem a little mysterious at the moment, but you will soon be able to see how they are used. The outline format and standard headings are as follows:

1.	Net cash inflow (outflow) from operating activities	X
2.	Returns on investments and servicing of finance	(X)
3.	Taxation	(X)
4.	Investing activities	(X)
5.	Net cash inflow (outflow) before financing	X
6.	Financing	X
7.	Increase (decrease) in cash and cash equivalents	(X)

The numbers 1 to 7 are not part of the format; they have been included here so that we can refer to them in the text and activities.

Notice that item 5 is a sub-total of items 1 to 4. Also that item 7 is a final total showing the increase or decrease in cash for the year. Notice that some items are in brackets and some are not. The convention used is that cash inflows are shown without brackets and cash outflows are in brackets.

Headings 2, 4 and 6 in the above outline will often contain a number of individual items under that heading. Some of the individual items for each heading will be cash inflows and some will be cash outflows. For example:

- **Heading 2, Returns on investments and servicing of finance**. This might include cash inflows for dividends and interest received and cash outflows for dividends and interest paid.
- **Heading 4, Investing activities.** This might include cash inflows on the sale of fixed assets and cash outflows on the purchase of fixed assets.
- **Heading 6, Financing.** This might include cash received on a new issue of shares and cash paid out on the repayment of a loan.

The net amount for each of these headings might be a net inflow of cash or a net outflow depending on the circumstances.

Transition to the 1996 revision

As stated in 11.3, some of the 1996 revisions were concerned with the treatment of cash resources and some with a revised format that would allow external analysts to identify free cash flow. We will concentrate on the changes in presentation because this will enable us to see the underlying concept of free cash flow.

The concept of free cash flow was considered by the ASB when the original (1991) regulation was being drafted but, because of classification problems, the idea of identifying free cash flow in the cash flow statement was eventually rejected.

There were some companies, however, who considered the idea of free cash flow to be sufficiently important to publish details of the figure in their annual reports. If you look, for example, in the annual report of Guinness PLC for 1995 you will find the following comment on page 32 of its *Operating and financial review*:

Cash flow
Free cash flow before dividend payments was £484 million.

If you look at the actual cash flow statement, you will find that it has been presented in the format required by the original regulation but with an added comment stating that the free cash flow (before dividends) was £484 million. The notes to the cash flow statement give an explanation of how the free cash flow was calculated.

There is, as yet, no consensus on what is meant by free cash flow. The main problem area centres around what can loosely be called capital expenditure. You can get some idea of how the term free cash flow is used by considering the types of cash flows that are reported under the heading of 'Investing activities' in the original format (heading 4 in our description).

This particular heading will include:

- cash outflows on the purchase of fixed assets,
- cash inflows on the sale of fixed assets,
- cash outflows on the acquisition of another business and
- cash inflows on the disposal of business segments.

There can be many more types but these four will help you to understand the idea of free cash flow.

If you review the four types mentioned above you can imagine that some cash flows relate to maintaining the organic growth of existing activities and some to expanding the level of business operations through the acquisition of other businesses. Similarly, you could say that decisions to sell and replace fixed assets (or even to enhance an existing fixed asset base) are operational decisions, whereas decisions to acquire another business (or a new subsidiary) are strategic decisions.

Activity 2

Review the above list of four items that could be included under Investing activities in the 1991 format and make a note here of those cash flows which would arise from operational decisions and those which would arise from strategic decisions.

Cash flows arising from operational decisions

Cash flows arising from strategic decisions

The idea of free cash flow is that it should be measured before any cash flows that relate to strategic activities, such as the acquisition of another business. The following two paragraphs are taken from a draft document issued by the ASB when inviting public comment on proposed changes to the original regulation:

14 Several commentators requested that the format of the cash flow statement should be changed to highlight the free cash flows of an entity. There were several interpretations of the exact composition of 'free cash flows' but a key issue was to distinguish cash flows for investing to maintain the business from cash flows for investing to expand the business. Paragraph 81 of FRS 1 sets out the reasons why the Board did not include such a requirement when drafting FRS 1.

15 The Board believes that it is difficult to distinguish expenditure for expansion from expenditure for maintenance. However, after further consultation with representatives of users and preparers, the Board is consulting on the argument that it is useful to split the cash flows classified under investing activities by FRS 1 into those relating to capital expenditure and those relating to acquisitions and disposals. The [exposure draft] now proposes this split with the possibility of a subtotal after cash flows relating to 'capital expenditure'.

The words in square brackets are ours and are simply a substitute for the name of the exposure draft in which these matters were being discussed.

As it happened, the new regulation was a compromise. There is no definition of free cash flow and no sub-total as promised in paragraph 15 of the draft document. The new format will, however, make it possible to find the figure that most users think of as free cash flow. This required two revisions of the 1991 format to be made. One was concerned with investing activities and one with equity dividends paid.

Free cash flow and investing activities

The old heading of investing activities has been sub-divided into two new categories which are called:

- capital expenditure, and
- acquisitions and disposals.

The second of these two items is where companies will now report cash flows resulting from strategic decisions, such as the acquisition of a new business. All other cash flows for the purchase and sale of fixed assets will be reported under the first heading.

Free cash flow and equity dividends paid

Dividends paid to equity shareholders are known as equity dividends. The figure for free cash flow that is of interest to external analysts is free cash flow before equity dividends. It can be argued that this is something like the cash equivalent of profit available for equity shareholders. If you refer back to the note in the accounts for Guinness PLC you will see that it refers to free cash flow before dividends. To assist with the identification of this number it was necessary to change the position of cash outflows for equity dividends from what it was in the 1991 format.

Activity 3

See if you can recall the heading under which equity dividends paid were presented in the 1991 format and make a note of it here.

The new format for the cash flow statement requires equity dividends to be presented under a separate heading. This heading follows the new item called 'Acquisitions and disposals' mentioned above. The positioning of these dividends will now allow users to calculate free cash flow before equity dividends even though the new format does not require this amount to be specifically identified. The transition from the old format to the new as far as these changes are concerned can be illustrated by the following:

Headings in 1991 format		Revisions in 1996 format
Net cash inflow (outflow) from operating activities	X	
Returns on investments and servicing of finance	(X)	Equity dividends paid
Taxation	(X)	
Investing activities	(X)	Capital expenditure / Acquisitions/dispoals
Net cash inflow (outflow) before financing	X	
Financing	X	
Increase (decrease) in cash and cash equivalents	(X)	Liquid resources / Cash

A figure that corresponds to what most analysts consider to be free cash flow before equity dividends can now be found by striking a sub-total immediately after the new heading called 'capital expenditure'.

Cash resources

As stated earlier, the 1991 format was designed to show the increase or decrease in cash and cash equivalents as the last item in the cash flow statement. There were some practical difficulties over the definition of cash equivalents (which included short-term investments) that led to criticisms of this approach. The new standard now requires cash flows relating to assets that are akin to cash (such as short-term current asset investments) to be reported separately under a heading called 'management of liquid resources'. The final figure in the cash flow statement will, therefore, show the increase or decrease in amounts that can be thought of as pure cash such as cash and bank balances, bank deposits and overdrafts repayable on demand.

The 1996 format

Having explained the transition from the 1991 format you should find it relatively easy to make sense of the revised format. This requires that an entity should list its cash flows for the period classified under the following standard headings:

1. Operating activities
2. Returns on investments and servicing of finance
3. Taxation
4. Capital expenditure
5. Acquisitions and disposals
6. Equity dividends paid
7. Management of liquid resources
8. Financing.

The standard requires that the first six headings should be in the sequence set out above. There is no requirement (as there was in the 1991 version) for any specific sub-total, although the examples published with the new standard do include a sub-total in a position similar to that in the earlier format.

Activity 4

Refer to the eight headings set out above and identify the two headings between which a sub-total showing free cash flow before equity dividends could have been placed.

11.5 Preparing the cash flow statement

We can now concentrate on calculating cash flows and preparing the statement. We will be using the new format but there is an explanation at the end of this section to show how the figures would have been presented under the 1991 format. All of the figures needed for the cash flow statement can be calculated from the profit and loss account and the opening and closing balance sheets. We will be working on the following set of financial statements for a fictitious company called Expander Ltd.

Expander Ltd

Profit and loss account for year ended 31 December 1997

	£	£
Turnover		900,000
Cost of sales		720,000
Gross profit		180,000
Selling and distribution costs	24,000	
Administration expenses	60,000	
		84,000
Operating profit		96,000
Investment income	4,000	
Interest paid and similar charges	5,000	(1,000)
Profit before tax		95,000
Corporation tax on profits		20,000
Profit after tax		75,000
Dividends:		
Interim paid	20,000	
Final proposed	30,000	
		50,000
Profit for the year retained		25,000

Balance sheets at 31 December	1997	1996
	£	£
Fixed assets (including investments) at net book value	550,000	500,000
Current assets:		
Stock	110,000	40,000
Debtors	90,000	30,000
Current asset investment	1,000	–
Bank	11,000	10,000
	212,000	80,000
Creditors falling due within one year		
Trade creditors	10,000	20,000
Corporation tax	20,000	15,000
Proposed dividends	30,000	25,000
	60,000	60,000

Net current assets	152,000	20,000
Total assets less current liabilities	702,000	520,000
Creditors falling due after one year	45,000	50,000
10% Debentures		
	657,000	470,000
Capital and reserves		
Called up share capital	500,000	350,000
Share premium account	52,000	40,000
Profit and loss account	105,000	80,000
	657,000	470,000

Notes:
1. Total depreciation charged for the year was £20,000. Some of this cost is included in selling and distribution costs and some in administration expenses.
2. There were no sales of fixed assets and no changes in fixed asset investments during the year.
3. Debtors and creditors relate entirely to sales and purchases.
4. Current asset investments at 31 December 1997 are to be treated as liquid resources.

Cash from operating activities

We will start by working on Heading 1, 'Net cash inflow from operating activities'. In many respects this item is the most awkward to calculate. Most of the amounts for the other headings can be found fairly quickly but this one requires a little patience. The basic idea is to work out the net cash inflow (or outflow) resulting from the item in the profit and loss account called Operating profit (which some companies call profit before interest and taxation).

If you look at the profit and loss account of Expander Ltd for 1997 you will see that the operating profit is £96,000. This is a net figure resulting from many transactions such as the sale of goods, the purchase of goods and the payment of operating expenses. We have to work out whether the net result of all these transactions was a cash inflow or a cash outflow, and the amount of that net inflow or outflow.

There are several ways of doing the calculation. We could, for example, calculate three separate cash flow figures, as follows:

1. Cash received from customers
2. Cash paid to suppliers for goods purchased
3. Cash paid for the two types of operating cost.

The net result of these three figures will be the net cash inflow (or outflow) from operating activities. This kind of approach is called the direct method in FRS 1. (Strictly speaking, FRS 1 required the cash paid for operating costs to be split between cash paid to employees and other cash payments if the direct method was adopted.)

Unfortunately, if we use the direct method you will have difficulty in understanding one of the notes (a reconciliation note) included with published financial statements of most companies. The cash flow statement must be accompanied by a statement showing a reconciliation between operating profit and net cash inflow from operating activities. The revised standard states that this must be given either adjoining the cash flow statement or as a note. An example of this reconciliation statement is given in an appendix to the FRS in the following form:

Reconciliation of operating profit to net cash inflow from operating activities:

	£000
Operating profit	6,022
Depreciation charges	899
Increase in stocks	(194)
Increase in debtors	(72)
Increase in creditors	234
Net cash inflow from operating activities	6,889

In FRS 1, identifying net cash inflow from operating activities as a single figure based on this reconciliation note is called the indirect method. Since the majority of companies adopt this method you must understand how it works. It is quite possible that some readers will be able to see the underlying rationale for the various adjustments shown in the above example. We will, however, work through our own example in stages.

In order to understand the adjustments in the reconciliation note, you will find it helpful to look at one of the cash flows that would have been calculated had we been using the direct method. We will use cash received from customers to demonstrate the point.

Cash received from customers can be found by taking the figure for turnover in the profit and loss account and making adjustments for debtors. It is the reverse of how you found turnover from cash receipts and debtors when working on incomplete records in Chapter 9.

In order to calculate cash received from customers for 1997 in the case of Expander Ltd, the calculation could be as follows:

	£
Debtors at 1 January 1997	30,000
Add turnover for 1997	900,000
	930,000
Less debtors at 31 December 1997	90,000
Cash received from customers in 1997	840,000

There is, however, an alternative approach that we could have used and this forms the basis of adjustments in the reconciliation note mentioned earlier.

Activity 5

Refer to the above calculation to see if you can identify a shortcut for calculating the figure of £840,000.

In setting out the figures for cash received from customers we can simulate the approach adopted in a reconciliation note. On this basis the figures would be presented as follows:

	£
Turnover	900,000
(Increase)/decrease in debtors	(60,000)
Cash inflow from customers	840,000

Notice that the word 'increase' is in brackets, indicating that if the figure is in brackets it represents an increase in debtors and must be deducted from turnover. If it had been a decrease, the figure would have been without brackets and would have been added to turnover.

The purpose of the adjustments in the reconciliation note is to reconcile operating profit with the net cash inflows from operating activities. The cash inflow from customers is simply one item in this net figure. Since turnover is included in the calculation of operating profit, we can deduct the increase in debtors from operating profit as one of the adjustments for calculating net cash inflow from operating activities. We are now going to construct the reconciliation statement in stages. At this point we have the following for Expander Ltd:

	£
Operating profit	96,000
(Increase)/decrease in debtors	(60,000)

The next item in the profit and loss account after turnover is cost of sales. By using the opening and closing balance sheets of Expander Ltd we can see that the cost of sales for 1997 must have been calculated as follows:

	£
Cost of stock at 1 January 1997	40,000
Add cost of goods purchased in 1997 (see below)	790,000
	830,000
Less cost of stock at 31 December 1997	110,000
Cost of sales for 1997	720,000

The cost of goods purchased in 1997 is not given in the financial statements of Expander Ltd but it can be determined, either by including it in the above computation as a balancing item or through a logical analysis of the figure for cost of sales, as follows:

	£
Cost of sales for 1997	720,000
Less cost of opening stock (purchased in 1996)	40,000
	680,000
Add cost of closing stock (purchased in 1997)	110,000
Cost of goods purchased in 1997	790,000

Now notice that the cost of goods purchased could have been found by simply adding the increase in stocks to the figure for cost of sales. Since cost of sales is a negative figure in the calculation of operating profit (and can be linked to cash outflows) we will present the figures in brackets, as follows:

	£
Cost of sales for 1997	(720,000)
(Increase)/ decrease in stocks (£110,000 – £40,000)	(70,000)
Cost of goods purchased in 1997	(790,000)

If there had been a decrease in stocks, the amount would have been presented without brackets and would have been deducted from the cost of sales.

The amount of £720,000 for cost of sales has been deducted in arriving at operating profit for 1997 and yet we have now found that the amount for the cost of goods purchased in 1997 was £70,000 more than the cost of sales. We can now include the £70,000 as another adjustment in our reconciliation statement. At this stage the statement will be as follows:

	£
Operating profit	96,000
(Increase)/decrease in debtors	(60,000)
(Increase)/decrease in stocks	(70,000)

At this point we have made sure that our running calculation includes the cost of goods purchased during the year rather than the cost of sales. But, as you know, the cost of goods purchased is not the same as the amount of cash paid to suppliers when goods are purchased on credit terms. We now need to make an adjustment in the reconciliation statement to translate the cost of goods purchased to cash outflows for the purchase of goods. Expander Ltd is clearly purchasing some goods on credit terms since there are trade creditors in the opening and closing balance sheets.

Activity 6

Using the format provided below this box, calculate the cash paid to suppliers by Expander Ltd during 1997.

	£
Creditors at 1 January 1997	
Add cost of goods purchased during 1997	————
Less creditors at 31 December 1997	————
Cash paid to suppliers in 1997	————

Notice that the amount of £800,000 could have been calculated by adding the decrease in creditors of (£10,000 – £20,000) £10,000 to the cost of goods purchased. If we had done this our calculation would have been £790,000 + £10,000 = £800,000.

The adjustment made in the reconciliation statement for the increase in stocks was to translate cost of sales (in the profit and loss account) into the cost of goods purchased for the year. The cost of goods purchased is a negative item in the calculation of operating profit and so we can now simulate how the adjustment for creditors would translate this into a cash outflow, as follows:

	£
Cost of goods purchased	(790,000)
Increase/(decrease) in creditors	(10,000)
Cash outflow for payments to suppliers	(800,000)

We can, therefore, incorporate the adjustment for an increase in creditors into our running reconciliation statement as follows:

	£
Operating profit	96,000
(Increase)/decrease in debtors	(60,000)
(Increase)/decrease in stocks	(70,000)
Increase/(decrease) in creditors	(10,000)

Notice that the word 'increase' is, in the case of creditors, without brackets and 'decrease' is in brackets. This indicates that the figure of £10,000 is a decrease in creditors and, for the reasons discussed above, must be deducted from operating profit when determining net cash inflow from operating activities.

In the case of Expander Ltd, the three items in the profit and loss account which determine operating profit are: turnover, cost of sales, and two types of operating cost. We have dealt with the first two (turnover and cost of sales) in our discussions so far. This leaves operating costs, and in the case of Expander Ltd the two types of operating cost total £84,000. Yet you might be able to recall from the details that this total includes an expense item which did not involve a cash outflow.

Activity 7

The total operating costs shown in the profit and loss account for 1997 as £84,000 include an amount which was not a cash payment. Make a note of the item (and the amount) in the box. State whether this will be added to, or deducted from, operating profit in the reconciliation note.

1. The item and the amount

2. Add to or deduct from operating profit in the reconciliation note

The £20,000 is added to operating profit because it was deducted as an expense when calculating operating profit but did not involve a cash outflow. The reconciliation statement for Expander Ltd can now be completed as follows:

	£
Operating profit	96,000
(Increase)/decrease in debtors	(60,000)
(Increase)/decrease in stocks	(70,000)
Increase/(decrease) in creditors	(10,000)
Depreciation	20,000
Net cash (outflow) from operating activities	(24,000)

Notice that operating profit was £96,000 and yet the net cash outflow from operating activities was £24,000. You might have heard (or read) something about the failure of a company known as Polly Peck. Cash flow statements were not produced as part of UK accounting practice at the time of that company's collapse but an interesting study was done on its 1989 accounts. This showed that if a cash flow statement had been prepared, an operating profit of £139m would have translated into a net cash outflow from operating activities of £129m.

Whether this would have alerted investors to the impending failure of the company is pure speculation, but it is quite an interesting point.

Completing the statement

In an examination, preparing a reconciliation of net cash inflow (or outflow) from operating activities will be both a 'working' and a note that forms part of your answer. Most of the remaining figures can be calculated as you prepare the cash flow statement. In order to help with the learning process, we will calculate some of these figures before completing the statement. We will look at taxation, dividends paid, purchase of fixed assets and cash received on the new share issue.

1. **Taxation.** With regard to taxation you will recall from Chapter 10 that companies pay the corporation tax on their profits nine months after the end of the accounting period. If you look in the balance sheet of Expander Ltd at 31 December 1997 you will see that the corporation tax charged in the profit and loss account of £20,000 is shown as a creditor. This means that the cash outflow for taxation during 1997 would have been the tax owing at 31 December 1996.

2. **Equity dividends paid.** The normal practice is for companies to pay an interim dividend during the year and to propose a final dividend for that year. The final proposed dividend will be paid after the Annual General Meeting in which the financial statements are presented to the shareholders. The final proposed dividend will be shown as a creditor at the end of the year concerned. If you look at the balance sheet for Expander Ltd at 31 December 1997 you will see that the proposed dividend for 1997, shown in the profit and loss account as £30,000, is included with creditors. The equity dividends actually paid during 1997 must, therefore, be the proposed dividend for 1996 and the interim dividend for 1997.

3. **Purchase and sale of fixed assets.** In the case of Expander Ltd we are told that there were no sales of fixed assets during the year. The movement between the net book value of fixed assets at 1 January 1997 and 31 December 1997 must, therefore, relate solely to depreciation and the purchase of fixed assets. We are given the figure for depreciation.

4. **New share issue.** You will recall from Chapter 10 that when shares are issued, the nominal value received is credited to called up share capital and any premium is credited to the share premium account.

> ## *Activity 8*
>
> With the above points in mind, make a note here of the amounts that will be included in the cash flow statement for the following:
>
> 1. Taxation paid
>
> 2. Equity dividends paid
>
> 3. Cash paid to purchase fixed assets
>
> 4. Cash received on new share issue

Cash flows on investment income and interest paid will be equal to the amounts shown in the profit and loss account. There are other cash flows such as the reduction of debt and purchase of short-term investments but you will be prompted to find these as you complete the cash flow statement. The outline cash flow statement shown below the next activity includes a sub-total based on one of the examples published in the appendix to FRS 1. There is, however, no requirement in FRS 1 to include this sub-total.

Activity 9

Prepare the cash flow statement for Expander Ltd by completing the outline format shown below this box.

Expander Ltd
Cash flow statement for year ending 31 December 1997

Net cash outflow from operating activities (£)

Returns on investments and servicing of finance:
 Investment income   £
 Interest paid   (£)

                   (£)

Taxation
 Corporation tax paid   (£)

Capital expenditure
 Cash paid to purchase fixed assets   (£)

Equity dividends paid   (£)

Cash outflow before investment in liquid resources and
 cash flows relating to financing

Management of liquid resources
 Purchase of short-term investment   (£)

Financing:
 Cash received on share issue   £
 Reduction in debt   (£)
                   £

Increase in cash in the period

If you now refer to the balance sheets of Expander Ltd you will see that the bank balance at 31 December 1997 is £1,000 more than it was at 31 December 1996.

11.6 Using the 1991 format

For the benefit of students who might have to use the original (1991) format during a protracted transition period, the following shows how the figures for Expander Ltd would have been presented in that format:

	£	£
Net cash outflow from operating activities		(24,000)
Returns on investments and servicing of finance:		
Investment income	4,000	
Interest paid	(5,000)	
Dividends paid	(45,000)	
		(46,000)
Taxation		
Corporation tax paid		(15,000)
Investing activities		
Cash paid to purchase fixed assets		(70,000)
Net cash outflow before financing		(155,000)
Financing:		
Cash received on share issue	162,000	
Reduction of debt	(5,000)	
		157,000
Increase in cash and cash equivalents		2,000

Notice that the main differences in this particular example are that the dividends paid have been included under the 'servicing of finance' heading and that cash equivalents include the current asset investment. The only other difference is that the purchase of fixed assets has been included under a heading called 'Investing activities' rather than capital expenditure.

11.7 Using the cash flow statement

In this chapter we have been concerned with constructing the cash flow statement. In Chapter 13 you will be expected to use the cash flow statement as part of the information available when assessing the performance of an entity.

The example of Expander Ltd was perhaps extreme in the sense that there was a net cash outflow from operating activities. In most cases you are likely to find that operating profit generates a positive cash inflow. When reviewing the statement one of the things to consider is the extent to which expansion has been financed by internally generated cash and how much by raising additional finance. Normally we would expect long-term finance (such as a share issue) to be used for financing long-term investments such as the purchase of fixed assets. This is clearly not the case in Expander Ltd. The new capital has been used partly to finance increased investment in stocks.

The cash flow statement for Expander Ltd might raise the question: why was the share issue a success when the cash flow statement suggests that the company was having cash flow difficulties? The cash flow statement even seems to suggest that the payment of dividends was financed by the proceeds of the new share issue.

The problem with trying to make sense of these points is that we do not have enough information. We never do when using annual financial statements.

It could well be that the company had a positive cash flow from operating activities throughout most of the year. The new share issue, the purchase of fixed assets, and the build-up of stocks might have occurred during (say) the last month of the year. It might have been part of some planned expansion, the benefits of which (in terms of profit and cash flow) will not be felt until the following year. The annual cash flow statement is not necessarily representative of the cash position throughout the year.

11.8 Finding missing figures

Examiners often use cash flow statements as an opportunity of testing basic book-keeping skills. They do this by not giving all the information directly, you have to sort it out from related data. You can practise this aspect by working two activities.

Activity 10

The following figures are included in the opening and closing balance sheets:

Fixed assets:	Opening	Closing
	£	£
Cost	100,000	120,000
Aggregate depreciation	40,000	45,000

The profit and loss account includes the following details:

	£
Depreciation charged	9,000
Profit on sale of fixed assets	2,000

In the notes to the question you are told that the cost of additions to fixed assets was £30,000. Calculate (on a separate sheet of paper) how much cash was received for the sale of fixed assets during the period.

You should note that the profit on sale of fixed assets in Activity 10 will have to be deducted from operating profit in the reconciliation statement. It does not represent a cash flow, it is an accounting adjustment resulting from a cash flow.

Activity 11

You are given the following information regarding the opening and closing capital and reserves:

	Opening	Closing
	£	£
Share capital (£1 ordinary shares)	100,000	180,000
Share premium	20,000	30,000
Profit and loss account	300,000	340,000

You are also informed that a bonus issue of 20,000 shares had been made during the year, and that the share premium account was applied for this purpose. Calculate (on a separate sheet of paper) how much cash was received on any other shares issued during the period.

Most movements on reserves result from book-keeping entries rather than a flow of cash. A share premium received is one exception. Many companies revalue their fixed assets (particularly land and buildings) from time to time in order to increase them to current values. When they do, any revaluation surplus must be credited to a revaluation reserve. This does not result in any cash flowing into or out of the company, and will not feature in the cash flow statement. If the revaluation was done during the current year, you must be careful to recognize this when reconciling movements on the balance sheet figures in order to calculate fixed assets purchased.

Summary

The main learning points in this chapter can be summarized as follows:

- cash flow statements provide information on cash inflows and outflows for the period of the financial statements
- the cash inflows and outflows are identified under specific headings and in a prescribed format
- it is possible to determine cash flows by using information in the profit and loss account and the balance sheets – in general terms this process involves reversing the effects of accruals accounting in relation to debtors, creditors, stocks and depreciation
- cash flows express pure fact and are not influenced by accounting estimates or accounting policies
- the form of presentation for a cash flow statement was changed in 1996 – the former heading 'investing activities' has been sub-divided into two headings: capital expenditure and acquisitions and disposals
- the intention of this change is to distinguish between cash flows that relate to the maintenance of the existing asset base and those in respect of business acquisitions and disposals
- cash flows that result from strategic decisions to expand the business are usually excluded from a concept of cash flow known as free cash flow
- equity dividends paid are disclosed separately in the new format – this will enable users to identify free cash flow before dividends
- free cash flow before dividends is an important concept in the valuation of a business and in the calculation of shareholder value.

Activity 1

Cash inflows: Issue of shares. Issue of debentures (or receipt of a loan). Sale of fixed assets. Cash outflows: Payment of interest. Payment of taxation. Payment of dividends. Purchase of fixed assets. Repayment of loans.

These lists are not complete but they are sufficient for the time being. Make sure that your lists do not include any trading items, such as the payment of wages, because these are taken into account in arriving at the single figure called operating profit.

Activity 2

Cash flows from operational decisions: cash outflows on the purchase of fixed assets and cash inflows on the sale of fixed assets.

Cash flows from strategic decisions: cash outflows on the acquisition of another business and cash inflows on the disposal of business segments.

Activity 3

Returns on investments and servicing of finance (the second heading in the statement).

Activity 4

Between headings 4 and 5.

Activity 5

You might have noticed that you could have deducted the increase in debtors of £60,000 (£90,000 – £30,000) from the turnover of £900,000 for 1997.

Activity 6

	£
Creditors at 1 January 1997	20,000
Add cost of goods purchased during 1997	790,000
	810,000
Less creditors at 31 December 1997	10,000
Cash paid to suppliers in 1997	800,000

Activity 7

1. Depreciation amounting to £20,000 (see note at foot of balance sheet).
2. Add to operating profit.

Activity 8

1. Taxation paid £20,000.
2. Dividends paid (£25,000 + £20,000) £45,000.
3. Cash paid to purchase fixed assets (£550,000 + £20,000 – £500,000) £70,000.
4. Cash received on share issue (£500,000 + £52,000) – (£350,000 + £40,000) £162,000.

Activity 9

Expander Ltd

Cash flow statement for year ending 31 December 1997

	£	£
Net cash outflow from operating activities		(24,000)
Returns on investment and servicing of finance:		
Investment income	4,000	
Interest paid	(5,000)	
		(1,000)
Taxation		
Corporation tax paid		(15,000)
Capital expenditure		
Cash paid to purchase fixed assets		(70,000)
Equity dividends paid		(45,000)
Cash outflow before investment in liquid resources and cash flows relating to financing		(150,000)
Management of liquid resources		
Purchase of short-term investments		(1,000)
Financing:		
Cash received on share issues	162,000	
Reduction in debt	(5,000)	
		157,000
Increase in cash in the period		1,000

Activity 10

The answer is £8,000.

There are various ways in which you can solve this type of problem. The safety way is to set out all the given figures in 'T' accounts and derive the missing figures as a balance.

Activity 11

The answer is £90,000.

Nominal share capital has increased by £80,000 but £20,000 of this relates to the bonus issue and so the nominal amount received is £60,000.

The share premium account has increased by £10,000 but this account would have been reduced by £20,000 for the bonus issue and so the share premium received is £30,000.

Note that in this example the figure of £90,000 could have been found by simply comparing the opening and closing aggregates for share capital and share premium (£120,000 and £210,000). This would not have worked if the bonus issue had been made out of the profit and loss account.

Some of the questions included here originally required a statement of sources and application of funds. They have been modified in order to make them suitable for cash flow statements.

Questions for self-assessment

Answers to self-assessment questions are given at the end of the book.

11.1 The financial statements of a company are as follows:

Profit and loss account for the year:

Turnover	100,000
Cost of sales	60,000
Gross profit	40,000
Selling and admin costs	10,000
Profit before tax	30,000
Taxation	10,000
Profit after tax	20,000
Dividends paid and proposed	8,000
Profit for year retained	12,000

Balance sheets:	Opening	Closing
Fixed assets	200,000	240,000
Current assets		
Stock	40,000	50,000
Debtors	10,000	12,000
Bank	8,000	2,000
	58,000	64,000
Current liabilities		
Taxation	8,000	10,000
Proposed dividend	2,000	4,000
Trade creditors	20,000	25,000
	30,000	39,000
Net current assets	28,000	25,000
	228,000	265,000
Capital and reserves		
Share capital (Ordinary shares)	150,000	175,000
Profit and loss account	78,000	90,000
	228,000	265,000

Other information:
There were no sales of fixed assets during the year. Expenses in the profit and loss account include £20,000 for depreciation. Debtors and trade creditors relate to trading transactions.

Required:
Prepare a cash flow statement for the period, complying with FRS 1 (revised) as far as is possible from the information given.

11.2 The following question is based on one set in the ULSEB A level examination for June 1990. It requires a little more effort in terms of hunting for information. The terminology used in the profit and loss account is a little sloppy. You will have to convert some of the descriptions used in the question (such as 'net profit') into those that are used in practice.

The balance sheets of Ulseb Ltd as at 31 December 1988 and 1989 are as follows:

	31.12.88 £	31.12.89 £
Fixed assets (net book value)	190,000	337,000
Current assets:		
Stock	89,000	63,000
Debtors	10,000	13,000
Bank	—	12,900
Creditors due for payment within one year:		
Creditors	35,800	34,800
Taxation	14,000	13,000
Proposed dividends	16,000	12,000
Bank	54,600	—
	168,600	366,100
Creditors due for payment after one year:		
9% Debentures 1995–99		110,000
	168,600	256,100
Issued share capital:		
Ordinary shares of 50p each	16,000	20,000
Share premium account	20,000	23,000
Asset revaluation reserve		40,000
Retained earnings	132,600	173,100
	168,600	256,100

The summarized profit and loss accounts for the two years ended 31 December 1989 are as follows:

	1988 £	1989 £
Gross profit	170,500	194,300
Less expenses	103,700	130,300
	66,800	64,000
Profit on sale of fixed assets	700	4,500
Net profit	67,500	68,500
Less taxation	14,000	13,000
Net profit after tax	53,500	55,500
Dividends		
interim		3,000
final	16,000	12,000
	16,000	15,000
Retained earnings	37,500	40,500
Retained earnings b/f	95,100	132,600
Retained earnings c/f	132,600	173,100

Notes:

1. A summary of the company's fixed assets account in the general ledger for the year ended 31 December 1989 is shown below:

	£		£
1 Jan 1989 Cost b/f	270,000	31 Dec 1989 Disposal a/c	17,000
31 Dec 1989 Revaluations	40,000		
31 Dec 1989 Additions	172,000	31 Dec 1989 Cost c/f	465,000
	482,000		482,000

The assets which were disposed of realized £8,500. This was a profit on disposal of £4,500 when compared with their book value.

2. The expenses for 1989 include a payment of £5,000 for interest on the debentures.
3. Debtors and creditors relate entirely to trading items. There was no accrued interest.
4. There were no costs in connection with the new capital issues.

Required:
(a) Prepare a cash flow statement complying with FRS 1 (revised) as far as is possible from the information provided.
(b) Explain whether the directors could have paid a dividend out of the balance on the asset revaluation reserve at 31 December 1989.

(ULSEB A Level, Jun 90, amended)

Questions without answers

The answers to these questions are published separately in the *Teacher's Manual*.

11.3 The following question is based on one set by ACCA in December 1991 for Level 1. There is no profit and loss account and so you will have to use the two balance sheets to determine the profit figure. This is a common ploy used by examiners, but the relevant figures are easily found by working backwards from the bottom line of retained profit for the year. Note that taxation has been ignored.

You are given summarized balance sheets for Aida plc as shown below. All figures are in £000.

		31.12.90		31.12.91
Ordinary shares		20		25
Share premium		4		9
Property revaluation reserve		5		8
Profit and loss balance		16		16
Debentures (10%)		40		20
Debentures (15%)		0		40
		85		118
Property		25		45
Plant: cost	30		46	
Depreciation	15	15	24	22
Stock		46		44
Debtors		17		33
Bank		7		0
		110		144
Trade creditors	20		13	
Dividends	5		9	
Bank	0		4	
		25		26
		85		118

Notes:
1. Any issues and redemptions of shares or debentures occurred on 1 January 1991.
2. All debenture interest is paid within the accounting year in which it is charged.
3. Only one dividend is declared each year. Dividends are always paid early in the year following that to which they relate. No sales of fixed assets have occurred during the relevant period.
4. Debtors and creditors relate to trading items.

Required:
Prepare a cash flow statement based on the principles in FRS 1 (revised).

(ACCA 1.1, Dec 91, amended)

11.4 The balance sheet of CF plc for the year ended 31 December 1994, together with comparative figures for the previous year, is shown below (all figures £000).

	1994		1993	
Fixed assets		270		180
Less depreciation		(90)		(56)
		180		124
Current assets				
Stock	50		42	
Debtors	40		33	
Cash	–		11	
	90		86	
Current liabilities				
Trade and operating creditors	33		24	
Taxation	19		17	
Dividend	28		26	
Bank overdraft	10		–	
	(90)		(67)	
Net current assets		–		19
Net assets		180		143
Represented by				
Ordinary share capital £1 shares		25		20
Share premium		10		8
Profit and loss account		65		55
Shareholders funds		100		83
15% debentures, repayable 1998		80		60
Capital employed		180		143

You are informed that:
1. There are no sales of fixed assets during 1994.
2. The company does not pay interim dividends.
3. New debentures and shares issued in 1994 were issued on 1 January.

Required:
(a) Show your calculation of the operating profit of CF plc for the year ended 31 December 1994.
(b) Prepare a cash flow statement for the year, in accordance with FRS 1 (revised) *Cash Flow Statements*, including the reconciliation of operating profit to net cash inflow from operating activities and Note 1 as required by the standard, i.e. the 'gross cash flows'.
(c) Comment on the implications of the information given in the question plus the statements you have prepared, regarding the financial position of the company.
(d) FRS 1 supports the use of the indirect method of arriving at the next cash inflow from operating activities, which is the method you have used to prepare 'Note 1' required in part (b) of this question.
   What is the direct method of arriving at the net cash inflow from operations?
   State, with reasons, whether you agree with the FRS 1 acceptance of the indirect method.

(ACCA, June 95, amended)

12 Limited companies: Accounting regulations

Objectives

After you have completed this chapter, you should be able to:
- describe the type of information contained in published financial statements
- explain what is meant by ordinary activities, exceptional items, extraordinary items and prior year adjustment according to FRS 3
- apply some of the provisions in FRS 3 when preparing financial statements
- undertake some of the work involved in preparing published accounts, particularly at the level required for most foundation examinations
- discuss accounting law on share redemptions and distributable profit

Introduction

This chapter is mainly concerned with some of the legal and professional regulations that govern the annual financial statements sent to shareholders. These financial statements are often called the 'published accounts'.

The examination requirements on this subject vary from syllabus to syllabus. In some exams the subject area is specifically excluded; in others students are expected to have a general understanding of the topics concerned, while others require students to be able to prepare financial statements that take account of the relevant regulations.

It is difficult to acquire an understanding of anything in accounting without actively applying the principles involved. Unless the subject area covered by this chapter is specifically excluded from your syllabus, you will find it beneficial to work through the complete chapter, even though you might not be required to produce the relevant accounting statements. All topics are dealt with at a pre-professional level, and the areas covered are:

- regulations in the 1985 Companies Act regarding published financial statements
- ordinary activities, exceptional items, extraordinary items and prior year adjustments

- provisions in FRS 3
- regulations in the 1985 Companies Act regarding the redemption of shares
- regulations regarding distributable profit

12.1 Form and content

Apart from requiring a company to publish its annual financial statements, the Companies Act contains two important sets of regulations: (1) it requires the accounts to be set out in a particular format, and (2) it stipulates what information about the company's financial affairs should be included in the annual report.

In the past, a favourite question in professional accounting exams was to ask students to prepare a set of published financial statements from a mass of data. A fair proportion of the marks in these questions was allocated to points regarding the Companies Act requirements on disclosure of information. Fortunately, this type of question has become less popular in recent times – even in professional exams. There are two good reasons for this:

1. The questions were little more than a test of memory.
2. The regulations are now so vast that there is actually too much to remember.

It is impossible for the professional accountant to remember every regulation, let alone a student. In order to cope with the sheer volume of regulations that might apply to a particular company's accounts, the professional accountant uses something called a 'check list'. These check lists contain a series of questions; each question being designed to check whether a particular item of information has been properly disclosed. You might be interested to learn that a check list used by one of the larger professional firms runs to almost 60 pages and contains nearly 350 check questions.

Admittedly these lists are designed to cover every eventuality, and not all of the questions will be applicable to the accounts being checked. They are also designed to cover both legal and professional regulations. But the approach adopted by the professional accountant gives you some idea as to why it does not make sense for examiners to expect students to remember the full details of every legal requirement.

It is sufficient to learn the basic pattern of published accounts, and to have some idea of the type of information that they contain. Fortunately, you have already had some insight into the form of published accounts from your work in earlier chapters.

Published profit and loss account

If there are no discontinued activities during the year, the published profit and loss account will look like the example that we used for the cash flow statement (Expander Ltd) in Chapter 11. If there are discontinued activities during the year, the profit and loss account becomes a little more complex because FRS 3 requires the results of the discontinued activities to be separated from the results of continuing activities.

When preparing a published profit and loss account you should keep in mind that operating costs are presented according to their functional headings. There are three common types of operating costs, namely:

- cost of sales,
- selling and distribution costs,
- administration expenses.

Operating costs are not described according to their natural classifications such as wages, stationery, electricity, depreciation, and so on, as they might be in company accounts used for internal purposes.

The first section of the published profit and loss account results in a profit figure which is usually described as operating profit, although sometimes the description 'profit before interest and tax' is used instead. The sections in the profit and loss account following operating profit will disclose amounts for interest payments, investment income, taxation charges, and dividends. The profit and loss account ends with an amount described as 'retained profit for the financial year'. This kind of structure can be visualized in block form, as follows:

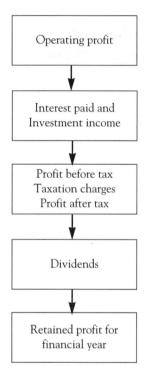

Published balance sheets

All of the balance sheets that you have been preparing up to now have been based on one of the formats (Format 1) in the Companies Act. But if you review the relevant section of the Companies Act 1985 in which the detail for these formats are given (Schedule 4) you will notice that they seem to be substantially different from the formats we have been using.

Appendix 1 to this chapter gives an outline of a set of published accounts that comply with the provisions of Format 1. Appendix 2 shows Format 1 as set out in the Companies Act. You are asked to review these two documents in the next activity. When doing this you should ignore the profit and loss account in Appendix 1 and simply concentrate on the layout of the balance sheet.

> **Activity 1**

Review the balance sheet in Appendix 1 (the usual form of publication) and then compare this with the balance sheet in Appendix 2, which gives details of Format 1 from the Companies Act on which the balance sheet in Appendix 1 is based. Make a note here of the most striking difference that occurs to you when you review the two documents.

This difference is explained by the fact that it is only necessary to include the headings preceded by a letter (A, B, etc.) on the balance sheet itself. Detailed information can be (and usually is) included in that part of the published accounts called 'notes to financial statements'. Even when presenting some of this detail in the 'notes', it is only necessary to adhere strictly to those headings that are preceded by a Roman number – items preceded by an Arabic number can be combined or adapted.

12.2 FRS 3: Reporting financial performance

This accounting standard was introduced in 1992 and amended in 1993. It contains a number of provisions that are not relevant to this stage of your studies. The following list gives an indication of the various provisions which it contains:

1. A new format for the profit and loss account.
2. Definitions and accounting treatment for exceptional items, extraordinary items, and prior year adjustments.
3. New measurement rules on Earnings Per Share
4. New measurement rules on profits or losses on the sale of fixed assets that had previously been revalued.
5. A new primary statement called a statement of total recognized gains and losses.
6. Two new notes to financial statements: one giving a reconciliation of movements in shareholders' funds and the other a calculation of historical cost profit.

In this chapter we will concentrate on items 1, 2 and 5. Items 3 and 4 will be dealt with in Chapter 19. It should be safe to ignore item 6 at a foundation level.

FRS 3 and the profit and loss account

The main provisions in FRS 3 that affect the published profit and loss account are concerned with the treatment of results from discontinued operations and the treatment of exceptional items. The structure of large organizations (usually groups of companies) is constantly changing. New entities are acquired and certain segments of the business are sold or closed down. If the operating results of these acquisitions and disposals are simply included in the total operating results for the year, it is impossible for an external user to assess what effect these changes in structure will have on future results.

FRS 3 requires that certain figures included in operating profit for the year should be analysed between continuing and discontinued operations. Continuing operations should also show the relevant figures for acquisitions during the year.

The FRS includes examples of how the analysis can be presented. The profit and loss account in Appendix 1 to this chapter is based on Example 2 in FRS 3. You should review this now and then deal with the following activity:

Activity 2

1. Has the company in Appendix 1 acquired any new businesses during the year?

2. Down to what level of profit is it necessary to analyse results between continuing and discontinued operations?

3. In what way do you think this form of presentation is helpful to the user?

Extraordinary and exceptional items

Extraordinary and exceptional items were previously regulated by SSAP 6 but this standard was superseded by FRS 3. If you look at Appendix 1 again you will see where extraordinary items should be presented. This positioning is the same as that previously required by SSAP 6 and it is consistent with requirements in the Companies Act. However, prior to FRS 3 there was a great deal of inconsistency, and some creative accounting, over the treatment of extraordinary items.

Prior to FRS 3 there was a tendency for companies to class unusual losses as extraordinary in order to exclude them from the all important figure of profit after tax on ordinary activities – a figure on which investors tend to place reliance when assessing a company's performance. This practice has been eliminated through a series of definitions in FRS 3, as follows:

> **Ordinary activities:** Any activities which are undertaken by a reporting entity as part of its business and such related activities in which the reporting entity engages in furtherance of, incidental to, or arising from these activities. Ordinary activities include the effects on the reporting entity of any event in the various environments in which it operates, including the political, regulatory, economic and geographical environments, irrespective of the frequency or unusual nature of the events.

> **Exceptional items:** Material items which derive from events or transactions that fall within the ordinary activities of the reporting entity and which individually or, if of a similar type, in aggregate, need to be disclosed by virtue of their size or incidence if the financial statements are to give a true and fair view.

> **Extraordinary items:** Material items possessing a high degree of abnormality which arise from events or transactions that fall outside the ordinary activities of the reporting entity and which are not expected to recur. They do not include exceptional items nor do they include prior period items

merely because they relate to a prior period. [An explanation of the definition of extraordinary items includes the following comment: *In view of the extreme rarity of such items no examples are provided*.]

In the former SSAP 6, examples of extraordinary items included the profits or losses on the sale or termination of a business segment. FRS 3 now includes this kind of item with exceptional items rather than extraordinary. As such it must be included in that section of the profit and loss account in which profits from ordinary activities are reported. FRS 3 has not completely outlawed extraordinary items but the provisions in FRS 3 make it clear that it is unlikely that any such items will ever be reported in the profit and loss account of a UK company.

FRS 3 requires that exceptional items should be included with the class of expense to which they relate (cost of sales, distribution costs, etc.), with the exception of the following:

- profits or losses on sale or termination of an operation,
- costs of a fundamental reorganization which have had a material effect on operations, and
- profits or losses on disposal of fixed assets (other than those that are merely marginal adjustments to depreciation previously charged).

These exceptions are required to be disclosed separately on the face of the profit and loss account between operating profit and profit on ordinary activities before interest.

Prior year adjustments

The definition of prior year adjustments in FRS 3 is in line with the former SSAP 6. They are defined as follows:

Material adjustments applicable to prior periods arising from changes in accounting policies or from the correction of fundamental errors. They do not include normal recurring adjustments or corrections of accounting estimates made in prior periods.

As you know, the preparation of financial statements requires estimates to be made based on the information available at the time of their preparation. These estimates often result in an adjustment being made in subsequent years. Examples are provisions for doubtful debts and provisions for taxation. Any corrections to these estimates in subsequent years cannot be treated as a prior year adjustment.

Activity 3

Review the financial statements and notes in Appendix 1 and then answer the following:

1. Describe an adjustment that was made during the current year to an accounting estimate made in the previous year but which has not been treated as a prior year adjustment.

2. Identify a prior year adjustment and state how it has been dealt with in the financial statements for the current year.

New primary statement

The term 'primary financial statement' has crept into the accountant's language without ever having been defined. It is clear what is meant by primary financial statements from various accounting standards issued by the ASB and from the ASB's draft Statement of Principles, published in 1996. The following is an extract from paragraph 8 of that document:

> Financial statements form part of the process of financial reporting. A complete set of financial statements at present contains a balance sheet, profit and loss account, statement of total recognised gains and losses, and cash flow statement ('the primary financial statements') together with those notes and other statements and explanatory material that are specified as an integral part of the financial statements.

This version of the draft statement was published following the publication of FRS 3. Prior to that there were three primary financial statements: profit and loss account, balance sheet and cash flow statement. FRS 3 introduced a new primary statement called a 'statement of total recognized gains and losses'. The key word is 'recognized'. This should not be confused with the word 'realized', which is important in the context of distributable profits.

The idea of the statement is to bring all gains and losses (of which profit is one) for the year into one statement. The items that are most likely to appear in this statement at this stage of your studies are:

- profit for the financial year (profit before dividends)
- unrealized surpluses/(deficits) on revaluation of properties
- prior year adjustments.

Activity 4

Review Appendix 1 and find the statement of total recognized gains and losses. Make a note here of a gain, other than profit, that has been included in the statement.

12.3 Taxation

At a foundation level, the full impact of company taxation is not tested by examiners. It is quite likely that the text in Chapter 10 on taxation will be sufficient for most examination questions. However, you will find it helpful to learn more about the subject of advance corporation tax (ACT). The accounting principle is quite easy to learn.

Perhaps you noticed from note 4 in Appendix 1 that there are several items included in the tax charge, but we are only interested in the item called 'corporation tax on profits for the year', i.e. the first item in the detailed note. This item is for the full amount of corporation tax payable on the profits for the year and is payable nine months after the end of the accounting year. But some of it may have to be paid in advance of this date. This happens when dividends are paid during the year.

When a company pays a dividend to the shareholders, it will also have to pay some tax to the Inland Revenue. The tax paid is called advance corporation tax (ACT for short) and is, in effect, an advance payment of the corporation tax for the year during which the dividend was paid. The amount of ACT is linked to the lower rate of income tax. If the lower rate of income tax is 20% then the amount of ACT is 20/80ths of the dividend paid.

In the study of accounting, there is little point in trying to make sense of how the fraction is derived; if ACT appears in your exam, the rate of ACT (or the amount) will be given. There is also no need to understand why it is related to dividends paid; you can simply accept that the formula (20/80ths of dividends paid) is used to calculate the advance payment.

The amount has to be paid to the Inland Revenue shortly after paying the dividend. The accounting treatment is quite simple. If some of the corporation tax for the year (as shown in the profit and loss account) has been paid in advance, only the remaining balance will be shown as a creditor in the balance sheet. This balance is called mainstream corporation tax (or MCT). It is easier to visualize the book-keeping by focusing on the two types of double-entry involved, namely:

1. The full amount of corporation tax for the year will be:
   Debit profit and loss account
   Credit Inland Revenue
2. The payment of ACT will be:
   Debit Inland Revenue
   Credit bank

Activity 5

The amount of corporation tax on profits for the year ended 31 December 1996 is estimated at £85,000. During the year ended 31 December 1996 the company paid dividends of £8,000 and also paid over the ACT resulting from this to the Inland Revenue. Assume that the rate of ACT is 20/80ths of the dividends paid.

Show the amounts that will be included in the published accounts for the following:

Corporation tax charge in the profit and loss account   £

Corporation tax creditor in the balance sheet   £

There are other topics to learn in relation to the treatment of tax in company accounts but they are outside the scope of any examination syllabus covered by this text book. These topics (which include tax credits on dividend income, ACT payable on proposed dividends, and the treatment of deferred tax) are studied and examined at a more advanced professional level.

12.4 Balance sheet and notes

The basic format of the published balance sheet is something that you are already familiar with from earlier chapters. In order to conclude this part of the lesson, you should now read through the balance sheet, and the full set of notes, in Appendix 1. As mentioned in the notes section, you are not expected to remember the detail. You are only being asked to read them so that you are aware of the kind of information included in published accounts.

All students should pay particular attention to Note 7 for fixed assets. This note sets out movements in fixed assets during the year, and also shows how the single figure in the balance sheet is made up in terms of the net book values for the different types of asset. Examiners sometimes ask for this schedule to be prepared, even in examinations that exclude published accounts, because it is a useful way of testing basic book-keeping skills.

12.5 Purchase and redemption of own shares

The redemption of share capital is another subject that is strictly regulated by a substantial amount of company law. At a foundation level it is only necessary to learn the basic principles. Most of the law is designed to maintain what is known as the 'permanent capital' of the company. You can get a fairly clear idea of what is meant by permanent capital if you think of it as being represented by the share capital and the share premium account.

You will recall from Chapter 10 that the Companies Act includes provisions which prevent the share premium account being paid to shareholders as a dividend. The share premium account represents part of the proceeds of a share issue and it would not make sense if the company were simply allowed to pay this back to shareholders as a dividend.

Similarly, a company cannot simply pay back the share capital after it has been received. If this were allowed, a company might deplete its funds to the detriment of its creditors. The law seeks to protect the interest of creditors in this respect. Consequently, the permanent capital (e.g. the share capital and share premium) is sometimes referred to as the 'creditor's buffer' and it cannot be reduced except in the circumstances prescribed by law.

A company can now (since 1980) buy back shares from existing shareholders, providing the redeemed capital is replaced by another form of permanent capital. This replacement capital can take one of several forms, namely:

1. A fresh issue of shares
2. The transfer of distributable profits to a non-distributable reserve known as 'capital redemption reserve'
3. A combination of 1 and 2

One of the main reasons why the current law was introduced was to benefit private companies. Shareholders in a private company do not have an active market in which they can sell their shares. If, for example, the management of a private company wanted to encourage worker participation by issuing shares to employees, those employees might consider they had received a worthless piece of paper unless the shares could be sold. By allowing the company to buy back its shares, the law is allowing the company to act as a substitute market place.

When the company does buy back its own shares, it is not allowed to hold them as an investment; they must be cancelled. The double-entry cannot, therefore, be: debit investment; credit bank. The debit must be to the share capital. This would reduce the permanent capital if it were not for the provisions regarding its replacement. We will see how it works in a moment.

Activity 6

When a company purchases its own shares, the debit side of the double-entry might be a little more involved than a simple debit to share capital. Can you think when this might be? The problem stems from the price paid, not from the law on redemptions.

The extra amount paid is called a premium on redemption. There are provisions to regulate where it may be debited. In order to cope with the book-keeping on a share redemption, there are three factors to take into account:

1. The proceeds (cash received) of any new issue of shares made for the purposes of financing the redemption
2. The nominal value of the shares being redeemed
3. The premium payable on redemption

We will look at 1 and 2 first. You will need to read the next paragraph fairly carefully, giving full weight to the words in bold. Don't worry if it does seem like a meaningless jumble of words, it will start to become clear when you do the activity. The relevant provisions in the Companies Act can be paraphrased as follows:

> Where the **nominal value** of the shares being redeemed exceeds the **proceeds** of the new issue, an amount equal to the excess must be transferred from **distributable profits** to a reserve known as the 'capital redemption reserve'.

See if you can interpret this regulation by solving the problem in the following activity.

Activity 7

A company has 1,000 ordinary shares of £1 each in issue. These were issued at a premium of 10p per share many years ago. The company is now about to purchase 500 of these from existing shareholders at a price of £1.20 each. The company will issue 200 shares (of a different class) at a price of £1.05 each in order to partly finance the redemption. Calculate how much must be transferred from distributable profits to capital redemption reserve.

The capital redemption reserve is considered to be part of the permanent capital. In the balance sheet it is usually presented as an item following the share premium account. The Companies Act severely restricts the way in which this reserve may be used by stating that it can only be applied for the purposes of making a bonus issue.

Activity 8

The transfer of distributable profits to capital redemption reserve does not, by itself, provide the company with any liquid funds. But it does do something to preserve the company's capital. See if you can think what this is and make a note of it here.

We can now look at the premium on redemption. In general terms, the Companies Act requires this to be debited to a distributable reserve (such as retained profits). In certain circumstances, the company may be allowed to debit the premium on redemption to an existing share premium account. There are two conditions which must first be satisfied before the company is allowed to do so, namely:

1. The shares being redeemed must have originally been issued at a premium.
2. The redemption scheme includes a fresh issue of shares (although it is not necessary for the new issue to completely replace the shares being redeemed).

Even where these two conditions are satisfied, there is a limit to the amount that can be debited to the share premium account. The amount is limited to the lower of two amounts, namely:

1. The premium originally received on the shares being redeemed.
2. The current balance on the share premium account, including the premium received on any new shares issued as part of the redemption scheme.

Activity 9

Make a note of any circumstances where the current balance on the share premium account might be lower than the premium originally received on the shares being redeemed.

Now see if you can interpret the rules regarding the premium on redemption by solving the problem in the following activity:

Activity 10

Assume the same details as in Activity 7 and also assume that the balance standing to the credit of the share premium account (prior to the fresh issue) was £100. Calculate how much of the premium on redemption can be debited to the share premium account.

The company is actually paying out a premium on redemption of (500 × 20p) £100 and so the remaining £50 must be debited to distributable profits.

In the case of a private company, there are some additional regulations that actually allow a reduction of permanent capital when shares are redeemed. These regulations are outside the scope of any examination syllabus covered by this text book.

12.6 Redeeming loans and debentures

There are no statutory provisions regarding the redemption of loans or debentures. Any arrangement for the repayment of loan capital is a matter of contract and the terms are usually set out in some form of loan agreement. The Companies Act does not seek to interfere in these private arrangements. The interests of trade creditors are not threatened by the repayment of loans and debentures, the company is simply paying off a liability. In many cases loans and debentures are 'secured' on the company's assets, and in the event of an insolvency the loan or debenture holder would be paid off in priority to the unsecured trade creditors in any case.

Although some companies (particularly in exams) might transfer distributable profits to a 'debenture redemption reserve' as part of a debenture redemption scheme, such transfers are not required by statute. In some schemes, the company transfers an annual amount of distributable profit to this reserve during the life of the debentures. The annual amount is calculated so as to build up a reserve equal to the redemption cost on maturity of the loan. Subject to any conditions in the loan agreement, a debenture redemption reserve represents distributable profits. In most schemes the debenture redemption reserve is released (usually by transferring the balance to a 'general reserve') as soon as the debentures are redeemed.

As you know, the transfer of distributable profits to a reserve does not provide the company with liquid funds for the redemption. The most that can be said for the practice is that it discourages the company from distributing these profits as dividends. Consequently, some schemes involve building up a separate pool of liquid funds in addition to the annual transfer of profits to reserve. These schemes are known as 'sinking funds' and the balance on the debenture redemption reserve is represented by an equal (or near equal) amount of liquid assets which are built up to a sufficient amount to fund the redemption on maturity.

There are many different arrangements for the actual redemption apart from a simple repayment on maturity. In some cases the company is empowered (e.g. through the loan agreement) to purchase its own debentures in the open market before the maturity date. If it does so, these debentures can either be held as an investment or they can be cancelled. Unlike shares, a company can hold its own debentures as an investment.

The classic book-keeping problem relating to debentures is concerned with the 'debenture sinking fund' mentioned earlier. The subject of sinking funds is outside the scope of any examination syllabus covered by this text book, and is not discussed further. At this level of study, it is sufficient for you to recognize the nature of a debenture redemption reserve, and to make any transfers to this reserve if instructed to do so in an examination question.

12.7 Distributable profits

The Companies Act only allows dividends to be paid out of distributable profits. This might sound like stating the obvious but the provision did not always exist. For most practical purposes, distributable profits are represented by the balance on the profit and loss account.

This is not strictly how the Companies Act defines distributable profits. In general terms, distributable profits are defined as accumulated realized profits less accumulated realized losses. The term realized is used in the sense that a profit (or loss) is realized if it is treated as such by generally accepted accounting principles. A sale to a debtor represents a realized gain even if the amount has not been settled in cash by the accounting date.

A full study of distributable profit is quite extensive but most of it is outside the scope of this text book.

During your study of company accounts (in this chapter and in Chapter 10) you have come across three reserves that cannot be applied for payment of dividends. Two of them are subject to specific restrictions, the third represents an unrealized reserve. See if you can recall the names of the three reserves and make a note of them here.

Another type of reserve that you might encounter is called an 'asset replacement reserve'. Some companies recognize that the total charge against profit for the depreciation of an asset could be less than the cost of replacing the asset at the end of its life. In recognition of this, a supplementary amount of distributable profit is transferred from the profit and loss account to the asset replacement reserve. SSAP 12 makes it clear that such a transfer should be treated as a movement on reserves, and not as an expense in arriving at profit. These transfers, as with all transfers of profit to reserve, are dealt with in the appropriation section of the profit and loss account.

As with depreciation itself, the mere transfer of profits to this reserve does not provide the company with the liquid funds needed for the replacement. It does, however, encourage the retention of funds within the business since it is a clear signal by the directors that they consider the amounts transferred are not available for distribution.

The provision of funds for replacement of assets is a matter of financial management. In the days when financial management was less sophisticated than it is today, it was often suggested that companies should provide for the replacement of assets by building up a sinking fund similar to that for the redemption of debentures. This would involve setting aside an amount of cash each year (equal to the annual depreciation charge plus any annual transfer to asset replacement reserve) and investing this cash in short-term securities. These schemes are not very popular with entrepreneurs since they consider that the returns on such investments will be considerably less than the returns that could be earned by allowing the funds to remain invested in the business.

A question sometimes arises as to whether an asset replacement reserve represents profits available for distribution. The reserve is built up from realized profits (the annual transfer from profit and loss account) and there are no statutory restrictions regarding its distribution. Most commentators consider that what the company is doing when it makes a transfer to the asset replacement reserve is to divide distributable profits between those that are available for immediate distribution and those that will become available for distribution at a later date. This argument maintains that as soon as the asset has been replaced, the function of the reserve (to encourage retention of profit) is finished and the accumulated amount can be released and treated as available for distribution.

This is not to suggest that the problem of higher replacement costs is entirely free of controversy. But any further discussion has to be conducted in the context of the impact of inflation on accounting, particularly as regards income theory, which falls outside the scope of subjects covered by this text book.

Summary

The main learning points in this chapter can be summarized as follows:
- it is preferable for accounting students to learn the basic framework of published financial statements, rather than the detailed regulations
- published accounts tend to include key figures on the face of the statements, the detailed information requiring disclosure is set out in a document called 'Notes to the financial statements'
- the results of discontinued activities down to operating profit must be shown separately in the published profit and loss account
- exceptional items are included with the expense classification to which they relate except where FRS 3 requires them to be shown separately on the face of the profit and loss account
- FRS 3 has defined extraordinary items in such a way as to prevent most items being treated as extraordinary
- prior year adjustments relate only to fundamental errors and the effect of changes in accounting policy – they do not relate to the correction of accounting estimates
- some of the company's corporation tax must be paid in advance of the normal due date if a dividend is paid; this payment is called ACT and it will reduce the outstanding creditor for taxation
- a company can purchase its own shares providing they are cancelled and the capital redeemed is replaced by a new issue of shares, or by transferring distributable profits to a capital redemption reserve
- the capital redemption reserve can only be applied for the purposes of making a bonus issue of shares
- any premium on redemption must be debited to distributable reserves unless the circumstances permit it to be debited to an existing share premium account
- arrangements for the redemption of loans and debentures are a matter of contract between the two parties, they are not subject to any statutory restrictions
- distributable profits are confined to accumulated realized profits less accumulated realized losses

Activity 1

You probably noticed that the official format includes much more detail than the balance sheet in Appendix 1.

Activity 2

1. No. If there had been, the results of continuing operations would have been analysed to show the amounts from acquisitions.
2. Profit on ordinary activities before interest.
3. It enables them to remove the effect of discontinued operations when assessing the profits earned by the net assets that remain in the balance sheet at the end of the year.

Activity 3

1. There is one in Note 6 – an over-provision of tax in the previous year.
2. See Note 14. Change of depreciation policy on freehold buildings. Depreciation relating to prior years has been deducted from the balance brought forward on the profit and loss account.

Activity 4

A surplus on the revaluation of property.

Activity 5

Corporation tax charge in the profit and loss account	£85,000
Corporation tax creditor (£85,000 – £2,000)	£83,000

Activity 6

The company might buy the shares at a price that exceeds their nominal value.

Activity 7

Using the description in the paragraph it works out as follows:

Proceeds of new issue	£210
Nominal value of shares redeemed	500
Transfer to capital redemption reserve	290

Activity 8

It prevents the profits from being distributed as a dividend.

Activity 9

Where the original share premium has been reduced in circumstances permitted by the Companies Act (share issue expenses, bonus issues, etc.).

Activity 10

The original premium received on the shares being redeemed was £50. The balance on the share premium account following the new issues is £110. The lowest of these is £50. Thus only £50 of the premium on redemption can be debited to the share premium account. The balance must be debited to distributable reserves.

Activity 11

1. Share premium account.
2. Capital redemption reserve.
3. Revaluation reserve.

Questions for self-assessment

Answers to self-assessment questions are given at the end of the book.

12.1 Greco Ltd. The following question was set by ULSEB in an A level examination. You will notice that formal 'notes' to the accounts are not required. For items where the normal practice is to disclose a single monetary amount in the actual statement (e.g. tangible fixed assets), you can indicate that details would be included in the notes by including a note reference number in your answer. In the original question, you were asked to treat the cost of closing the factory as an extraordinary item. This is not possible since the introduction of FRS 3 and the question has been modified to recognize this.

Greco Limited's trial balance at 31 May 19X9 was as follows:

	£	£
Audit fee	2,500	
Bad debts	8,584	
Bank interest	5,060	
Bank overdraft		64,450
Creditors		464,565
Delivery expenses	37,406	
Debtors	406,840	
Debenture interest	3,420	
Directors' salaries	46,700	
Fixtures and fittings (cost £55,000)	34,900	
Interim ordinary dividend	20,000	
Issued share capital:		
200,000 ordinary shares of £1 each		200,000
45,000 12% preference shares of £1 each		45,000
Leasehold premises (cost £580,000)	525,000	
Motor vehicles (cost £57,500)	24,550	
Profit and loss account		103,595
Purchases	378,474	
Rent	40,285	
Sales (exclusive of VAT)		657,462
Share premium account		45,550
Stock	50,580	
Cost of closing factory	8,578	
Wages and salaries	44,745	
12% debenture 199X/200X		57,000
	1,637,622	1,637,622

The following additional information is available:
1. Stock at 31 May 19X9 was valued at £94,400.
2. The delivery expenses and the depreciation on motor vehicles (see note 5) were the sole distribution costs during the year.
3. Authorized share capital:
   500,000 ordinary shares of £1 each
   50,000 12% preference shares of £1 each.
4. The outstanding debenture interest is to be accrued.
5. Depreciation is to be provided as follows:
   leasehold premises at 2% p.a. on cost
   motor vehicles at 25% p.a. on cost
   fixtures and fittings at 30% on reducing balance
6. The factory was closed on 3 June 19X8 and the operating results included in the trial balance do not include any amounts relating to this factory.

7. A final dividend of 6% is proposed on the ordinary shares, and the full year's preference dividend is to be provided for.
8. £4,500 is owing for wages and salaries, and £500 was prepaid for rent at 31 May 19X9.
9. £23,500 corporation tax for the year is to be provided for.
10. No fixed assets were bought or sold during the year.

Prepare Greco Limited's profit and loss account for the year ended 31 May 19X9 and a balance sheet as at that date, in a form suitable for publication and complying, in so far as the information permits, with the disclosure requirements of the Companies Act 1985 and FRS 3. While full working should be shown where necessary, formal notes to the accounts are not required.

12.2 Dennis plc. The following question was set by ULSEB in the A level examination for June 1990.

The directors of Dennis plc are to meet shortly to consider the amount of dividend which they should pay to the shareholders of the company. The draft audited balance shows the following reserves.

	£
Share premium account	60,000
Capital redemption reserve	100,000
Asset revaluation reserve	200,000
General reserve	50,000
Profit and loss account	100,000

The asset revaluation reserve arose during the year when a building was revalued from £300,000 to £500,000.
(a) State, with reasons, the extent to which each of the five reserves can be used for the payment of dividends.
(b) Calculate the maximum *percentage* dividend which could be paid, assuming that the issued share capital at the balance sheet date consisted of 2 million ordinary shares of 25p each.
(c) The company intends to replace its buildings in four years' time, at an anticipated cost of £1,500,000. It proposes to create an asset replacement reserve to ensure that sufficient cash is available to purchase the new buildings at the appropriate time. Comment on this proposal.

Questions without answers

Answers to these questions are published separately in the *Teacher's Manual*.

12.3 Lemon Ltd. The following question is based on one set by ULSEB in the A level examination for January 1990. One of the adjustments included in the original question has been excluded since the subject concerned (writing off goodwill) is dealt with in a later chapter of this text book.

	Dr £	Cr £
Ordinary share capital (£1 shares)		170,000
10% redeemable £1 preference shares		50,000
Debtors and creditors	96,800	65,302
Goodwill	20,000	
Fixed assets	187,600	
Stock	34,080	
Bank balance	94,200	
Profit and loss account		117,378
Share premium account		30,000
	432,680	432,680

The directors took the following decisions after the above trial balance was extracted. To:

1. convert the existing £1 ordinary shares into shares with a nominal value of 50p;
2. redeem the 10% redeemable £1 preference shares at a premium of 5% (the shares had been issued originally at a premium of 10%);
3. issue bonus shares by utilizing the value remaining in the share premium account after allowing for the premium payable on the redemption of the preference shares;
4. propose a dividend of 10p per share on all ordinary shares of 50p each, including those issued by way of bonus.

(a) Show the ordinary share capital account, the share premium account and the ordinary dividend account as they would appear after the above decisions were implemented.
(b) Prepare the (unpublished) balance sheet as at 31 May 1989, after the implementation of all the directors' decisions and assuming no other transactions.
(c) Give two reasons why a company might wish to issue bonus shares to its existing shareholders.

12.4 Blairgowrie plc. The following question was set in the AEB A level examination for November 1989. Part (c) relates to something dealt with in Chapter 6. Work to the nearest £000 in your fixed asset schedule; and use note 7 in Appendix 1 as a guide to presentation.

Blairgowrie plc produces its annual report and accounts for publication by 31 October. The company has a year end of 31 August and below are details relating to the tangible fixed assets of the company.

1. The tangible fixed assets of the company at 31 August 1988 were as follows:

	Cost	Aggregate depreciation	Net book value
	£000	£000	£000
Land	500		500
Buildings	725	145	580
Plant and machinery	490	201	289
Fixtures and fittings	91	33	58

2. The company had the land revalued by Mitchie and Partners, chartered surveyors, on 1 September 1988 at £750,000. The directors have decided to incorporate the revaluation in the accounts.
3. Plant and machinery with a cost of £35,000 and aggregate depreciation of £20,664 at 31 August 1988 was disposed of during the year.
4. Plant and machinery costing £53,000 was acquired on 28 February 1989 and fixtures and fittings costing £6,000 were acquired on 31 May 1989.
5. The methods and rates of depreciation applied to tangible fixed assets are as follows:

Asset	Method	Rate (per annum)
Land	not depreciated	
Buildings	straight line	$2\frac{1}{2}$%
Plant and machinery	reducing balance	20%
Fixtures and fittings	reducing balance	15%

6. No depreciation is charged in the year of disposal of an asset and depreciation is presumed to accrue evenly in the year of acquisition.

Required:
(a) What information regarding fixed assets is a public limited company required to disclose to shareholders?
(b) Prepare a detailed working note showing the figures relating to tangible fixed assets to be included in the annual accounts of Blairgowrie plc for the year ended 31 August 1989.

(c)   Explain why Blairgowrie plc has provided for depreciation of buildings, but not of land.

12.5 (a) **Curd Ltd** buys milk in bulk, and sells bottled milk, For many years they have manufactured their own glass bottles, but during the year ended 31 December 1994 the bottle-making plant was closed and the workers from the plant were made redundant. A trial balance for the company as at 31 December 1994 has been prepared, containing the following figures:

	£000
Ordinary shares of 50p nominal value	100
10% preference shares of 50p nominal value	50
16% debenture loan stock	100
Prepayments for operating expenses as at 1 January	25
Accruals for operating expenses at 1 January	30
Operating expenses paid	112
Sales	600
Sales returns	14
Cost of sales	290
Stock at 31.12.94	90
Trade debtors	150
Provision for doubtful debts as at 1.1.94	7
Bad debts expense	16
Fixed assets at cost	350
Depreciation as at 1 January	180
Profit and loss account balance (credit)	70
Trade creditors	80
Redundancy and closure costs	90
Bank deposits and cash floats	80

You are informed that:
(i)   depreciation should be provided at 10% per annum on cost.
(ii) the bad debts provision is required to be 2% of debtors.
(iii) corporate taxation for 1994 should be taken as £10,000.
(iv) accruals and prepayments for operating expenses as at 31 December 1994 are £33,000 and £29,000, respectively.
All calculations should be made to the nearest £000.

Required:
Produce a profit and loss account for 1994, highlighting the following items:
(i)   Gross profit
(ii) Net operating profit
(iii) Net profit
(iv) Profit for the year available for ordinary shareholders.
Submit all workings and calculations.

(b) A friend tells you that she thinks FRS 3, Reporting financial performance, is relevant to the preparation of a profit and loss account for Curd Ltd for publication purposes.

Required:
In what way is FRS 3 relevant, and what further information, beyond that already given in the question, would you need to know about the results of Curd Ltd for the year 1994 in order to apply FRS 3?

(ACCA, *Dec 95*)

Appendix 1

Below is an outline of published financial statements, based on Format 1 and Example 2 in FRS 3, for a company with no subsidiaries or associated companies.

In the financial statements which follow, each capital letter X represents a single monetary amount. The 'note' numbers are a cross-reference to a section of the published accounts called 'Notes to the financial statements'. These notes are set out following the balance sheet.

In practice, comparative figures for the previous year must be disclosed for each item in these financial statements. For the sake of clarity, comparative figures have not been included in the example provided here.

Profit and loss account for year ended ...	Note	Discontinued operations £000	Continuing operations £000	Total £000
Turnover		X	X	X
Cost of sales		(X)	(X)	(X)
		—	—	—
Gross profit		X	X	X
Selling and distribution costs		(X)	(X)	(X)
Administration expenses		(X)	(X)	(X)
		—	—	—
Operating profit	1	X	X	X
Loss on disposal of discontinued operations	2	(X)		(X)
		—	—	—
Profit on ordinary activities before interest		X	X	X
Interest payable and similar charges	3			(X)
				—
Profit on ordinary activities before tax				X
Tax on profit from ordinary activities	4			(X)
				—
Profit on ordinary activities after tax				X
Extraordinary items (included only to show positioning)				–
				—
Profit for financial year				X
Dividends	5			(X)
				—
Retained profit for the financial year				X
				═
Earnings per share				Xp

Balance sheet at ...

	Note	£000	£000
Fixed assets:			
Intangible assets			X
Tangible assets	7		X
Investments	8		X
			X
Current assets:	9		
Stock		X	
Debtors		X	
Cash at bank and in hand		X	
		X	
Creditors: due within one year	10	(X)	
Net current assets			X
Total assets less current liabilities			X
Creditors: due after one year	11		(X)
			X
Provision for liabilities and charges			
Deferred taxation	12		(X)
			X
Capital and reserves:			
Called up share capital	13		X
Share premium account	14		X
Revaluation reserve	14		X
Profit and loss account	14		X
			X

FRS 3 requires the following additional statement to be presented as a primary statement (in other words not as a note). It normally follows the cash flow statement.

Statement of total recognized gains and losses

	£000
Profit for the financial year	X
Unrealized surplus on revaluation of property	X
	X
Prior year adjustment (as explained in note 14)	(X)
Total gains recognized since last report	X

A further note is required by FRS 3 showing a reconciliation of movements in shareholders funds. If this is presented as a primary statement, it must follow the statement of total recognized gains and losses. Some companies are combining this with the statutory note that requires details of all movements in reserves to be disclosed. If the reconciliation is shown as a separate note, the example in FRS 3 is on the following lines:

Reconciliation of movements in shareholders' funds

Profit for the financial year	X
Dividends	(X)
	X
Other recognized gains/losses relating to the year (net)	X
New share capital subscribed	X
Goodwill written off	(X)
Net addition to shareholders funds	X
Opening shareholders funds (as restated but with a note to state what it was before any prior year adjustment)	X
Closing shareholders funds	X

Notes to financial statements

The following pages give an idea of the type of information that must be disclosed in the 'notes' in order to comply with the Companies Act. In some cases the note is presented as an example, in others there is a simple description of what must be disclosed. There is no need to try and remember the detail; be satisfied with a general idea. The only note that you are likely to be asked to prepare is the one on fixed assets.

1. Operating profit (an example of this note)

Operating profit has been determined after taking account of the following expenses:

	£000
Depreciation	X
Auditor's fee and expenses	X
Exceptional item (see below)	X
Directors' emoluments (see below)	X
Hire of plant and machinery	X

Exceptional item: obsolete stocks amounting to £.... have been written off.

Directors emoluments: the amount of £.... is made up as follows:

Directors' fees	X
Pension contributions	X
Pensions to former directors	X
Compensation for loss of office	X
Other emoluments	X
	X

The remuneration of the chairman was £.... The remuneration of the highest paid director was £.... Apart from these, the number of directors falling within various ranges of remuneration were as follows:

£ 0 to £ 5,000	1
£ 5,001 to £10,000	1
£15,001 to £20,000	2
£25,001 to £30,000	2

(Note that various items of information regarding employees other than directors must also be disclosed in some circumstances. Listed companies are required (under the Greenbury code) to give details of directors' bonus and share option schemes.)

2. Loss on disposal of discontinued operations

Further details must be provided.

3. Interest paid and similar charges

A certain amount of analysis is required for this item. In particular it is necessary to distinguish between interest payable on loans which are not wholly repayable within 5 years and interest on other forms of borrowing.

4. Taxation on ordinary activities (an example of this note)

Corporation tax on profits for the year	X
Over-provision of tax in the previous year	(X)
Tax credits on dividends received	X
Transfer to deferred tax account	X

5. Dividends

The Act is silent regarding detailed information, it merely requires the total of dividends (paid and proposed) to be disclosed. The normal practice is to show the split in this note between paid and proposed.

6. Not applicable to this example.

7. Tangible fixed assets

A full schedule is required showing movements on all major classes of asset, together with movements on the depreciation provision. These movements are shown in terms of brought forward figures, disposals, additions, revaluations, and carried forward figures. The following is an example of how this note is often presented:

	Land £000	Buildings £000	Plant £000	Total £000
Cost:				
Balance at beginning of year	X	X	X	X
Revaluation during the year	X			X
Disposals			(X)	(X)
Additions			X	X
Balance at end of year	X	X	X	X
Aggregate depreciation:				
Balance at beginning of year		X	X	X
Eliminated on disposals			(X)	(X)
Charge for the year		X	X	X
Balance at end of year		X	X	X
Net book value:				
At beginning of year	X	X	X	X
At end of year	X	X	X	X

8. Investments

Investments have to be analysed under several headings. There is no point in trying to learn these details at the moment. Some aspects of this will be covered when we deal with groups of companies.

9. Current assets

More information than that shown on the balance sheet has to be given. For example, debtors have to be split between those receivable within one year and those receivable thereafter. Stocks have to be split between the various components such as raw materials, work-in-progress, finished goods.

10. Creditors: due within one year

If this is grouped together as one item, the individual components must be set out in this note. Format 1 identifies several separate categories such as: trade creditors, accruals, taxation.

11. Creditors: due after one year

Full descriptions of all loans must be given. Where loans are being repaid by instalments, any instalment due during the next 12 months must be included in Note 10.

12. Deferred taxation

Movements on this account must be disclosed (deferred tax is not covered in this book).

13. Called up share capital

The kind of information that must be disclosed here is as follows:
- Full details of the 'Authorized' capital
- Full descriptions of the called up capital
- Movements on called up capital during the year

14. Movements on reserves (an example of this note)

	Share premium account	Revaluation reserve	Profit and loss account
Balances at beginning of year	X	X	X
Share premium received	X		
Revaluation of fixed assets		X	
Prior year adjustment (see below)			(X)
As restated			X
Retained profit for the year			X
Balances at end of the year	X	X	X

The prior year adjustment results from a change in the accounting policy for depreciation of land and buildings. With effect from the current year, your directors have decided that a provision for depreciation on freehold buildings should be made. The amount of £.... relates to the amount of depreciation that should have been provided in previous years on the basis of the current policy.

Sch. 4 – Form and Content of Company Accounts – Companies Act 1985

Balance Sheet Formats

Format 1

A. Called up share capital not paid (1)
B. Fixed assets

  I Intangible assets
    1. Development costs
    2. Concessions, patents, licences, trade marks and similar rights and assets (2)
    3. Goodwill (3)
    4. Payments on account

  II Tangible assets
    1. Land and buildings
    2. Plant and machinery
    3. Fixtures, fittings, tools and equipment
    4 Payments on account and assets in course of construction

  III Investments
    1 Shares in group undertakings
    2. Loans to group undertakings
    3. Participating interests
    4. Loans to undertakings in which the company has a participating interest
    5. Other investments than loans
    6. Other loans
    7. Own shares (4)

C. Current assets

  I Stocks
    1. Raw materials and consumables
    2. Work-in-progress
    3. Finished goods and goods for resale
    4. Payments on account

  II Debtors (5)
    1. Trade debtors
    2. Amounts owed by group undertakings
    3. Amounts owed by undertakings in which the company has a participating interest
    4. Other debtors
    5. Called up share capital not paid (1)
    6. Prepayments and accrued income (6)

  III Investments
    1. Shares in group undertakings
    2. Own shares (4)
    3. Other investments

  IV Cash at bank and in hand

D. Prepayments and accrued income (6)
E. Creditors: amounts falling due within one year
    1. Debenture loans (7)
    2. Bank loans and overdrafts
    3. Payments received on account (8)
    4. Trade creditors
    5. Bills of exchange payable
    6. Amounts owed to group undertakings
    7. Amounts owed to undertakings in which the company has a participating interest
    8. Other creditors including taxation and social security (9)

9. Accruals and deferred income (10)

F. Net current assets (liabilities) (11)

G. Total assets less current liabilities

H. Creditors: amounts falling due after more than one year
   1. Debenture loans (7)
   2. Bank loans and overdrafts
   3. Payments received on account
   4. Trade creditors
   5. Bills of exchange payable
   6. Amounts owed to group undertakings
   7. Amounts owed to undertakings in which the company has a participating interest
   8. Other creditors including taxation and social security (9)
   9. Accruals and deferred income (10)

I. Provisions for liabilities and charges
   1. Pensions and similar obligations
   2. Taxation, including deferred taxation
   3. Other provisions

J. Accruals and deferred income (10)

K. Capital and reserves
   I   Called up share capital (12)
   II   Share premium account
   III Revaluation reserve
   IV   Other reserves
        1. Capital redemption reserve
        2. Reserve for own shares
        3. Reserves provided for by the articles of association
        4. Other reserves
   V   Profit and loss account

Notes on the balance sheet formats

(1) *Called up share capital not paid* – (Formats 1 and 2, items A and C.II.5.)
This item may be shown in either of the two positions given in Formats 1 and 2.

(2) *Concessions, patents, licences, trade marks and similar rights and assets* – (Formats 1 and 2, item B.I.2.)
Amounts in respect of assets shall only be included in a company's balance sheet under this item if either:
(a) the assets were acquired for valuable consideration and are not required to be shown under goodwill; or
(b) the assets in question were created by the company itself.

(3) *Goodwill* – (Formats 1 and 2, item B.I.3.)
Amounts representing goodwill shall only be included to the extent that the goodwill was acquired for valuable consideration.

(4) *Own shares* – (Formats 1 and 2, items B.III.7 and C.III.2.)
The nominal value of the shares held shall be shown separately.

(5) *Debtors* – (Formats 1 and 2, items C.II.1 to 6.)
The amount falling due after more than one year shall be shown separately for each item included under debtors.

(6) *Prepayments and accrued income* – (Formats 1 and 2, items C.II.6 and D.) This item may be shown in either of the two positions given in Formats 1 and 2.

(7) *Debenture loans* – (Format 1, items E.1 and H.1, and Format 2, item C.1.)
The amount of any convertible loans shall be shown separately.

(8) *Payments received on account* – (Format 1, items E.3 and H.3, and Format 2, item C.3.)
Payments received on account of order shall be shown for each of these items in so far as they are not shown as deductions from stocks.

(9) *Other creditors including taxation and social security* – (Format 1, items E.8 and H.8, and format 2, item C.8.)

The amount for creditors in respect of taxation and social security shall be shown separately from the amount for other creditors.

(10) *Accruals and deferred income* – (Format 1, items E.9, H.9 and J, and Format 2, items C.9 and D.)

The two positions given for this item in Format 1 at E.9 and H.9 are an alternative to the position at J, but if the item is not shown in a position corresponding to that at J it may be shown in either or both of the other two positions (as the case may require).

The two positions given for this item in Format 2 are alternatives.

(11) *Net current assets (liabilities)* – (Format 1, item F.)

In determining the amount to be shown for this item any amounts shown under 'prepayments and accrued income' shall be taken into account wherever shown.

(12) *Called up share capital* – (Format 1, item K.1, and Format 2, item A.1.)

The amount of allotted share capital and the amount of called up share capital which has been paid up shall be shown separately.

(13) *Creditors* – (Format 2, items C.1 to 9.)

Amounts falling due within one year and after one year shall be shown separately for each of these items and their aggregate shall be shown separately for all of these items.

Profit and loss account formats
Format 1

1. Turnover
2. Cost of sales (14)
3. Gross profit or loss
4. Distribution costs (14)
5. Administration expenses (14)
6. Other operating income
7. Income from shares in group undertakings
8. Income from participating interests
9. Income from other fixed asset investments (15)
10. Other interest receivable and similar income (15)
11. Amounts written off investments
12. Interest payable and similar charges (16)
13. Tax on profit or loss on ordinary activities
14. Profit or loss on ordinary activities after taxation
15. Extraordinary income
16. Extraordinary charges
17. Extraordinary profit or loss
18. Tax on extraordinary profit or loss
19. Other taxes not shown under the above items
20. Profit or loss for the financial year

Notes on the profit and loss account formats

(14) *Cost of sales: distribution costs: administrative expenses* – (Format 1, items 2, 4 and 5, and Format 3, items A.1, 2 and 3.)

These items shall be stated after taking into account any necessary provisions for depreciation or diminution in value of assets.

(15) *Income from other fixed asset investments: other interest receivable and similar income* – (Format 1, items 9 and 10: Format 2, items 11 and 12: Format 3, items B.5 and 6: Format 4, items B.7 and 8.)

Income and interest derived from group undertakings shall be shown separately from income and interest derived from other sources.

(16) *Interest payable and similar charges* – (Format 1, item 12: Format 2, item 14: Format 3, item A.5: Format 4, item A.7.)

The amount payable to group undertakings shall be shown separately.

Financial statement analysis

Introduction

This is an interesting subject and involves the application of analytical skills in addition to performing calculations. You will be learning how the financial statements of an entity can be analysed so as to form opinions on its financial performance. Apart from the additional information which such an analysis provides, there is a secondary benefit for learners in that the techniques force you to critically examine a set of financial statements and gain a better understanding of their contents and limitations.

In order to carry out the analysis you will, for much of the time, be using a tool called 'ratio analysis'. But the tool itself is less important than the way it is used. Accounting ratios simply provide the analyst with extra information by expressing the relationship between two accounting items in a particular way. The analytical skills involved are not so much a matter of knowing how to calculate the ratios as of being able to form an opinion on the extra information which the ratio provides.

When forming these opinions you must not expect too much from the ratios themselves; they have their limitations in terms of what they can tell us about an entity's financial performance. We use them as a tool in our search for more information but they tend to raise questions rather than provide answers. It is almost impossible to draw any conclusions without answers to these questions.

Historically, this subject has tended to focus on the profit and loss account and balance sheet. Towards the end of this chapter you will be encouraged to extend your analysis to the cash flow statement. As suggested in Chapter 11, it is quite possible that in the future we will be paying far more attention to the cash flow statement than to the profit and loss account. We can already to see this trend in the writings of professional analysts such as Terry Smith (*Accounting for Growth: Stripping the Camouflage from Company Accounts*, 1996, Century Ltd).

13.1 The basis of ratio analysis

Think about the following: you invest £1,000 in a bank deposit account and one year later your account is credited with £50 interest. If you separate this from the rest of your financial affairs, you could produce a profit and loss account and a balance sheet to show the results of your investing activity. In doing so you would produce information that stated two separate things:

1. Profit and loss account: 'My income was £50 for the year.'
2. Balance sheet: 'My original capital of £1,000 has grown to £1,050 by the end of the year.'

These two statements say something about your investing activities but the two items (income and capital) have been separated, although one is dependent on the other. We can improve the usefulness of the two items of information by relating them to each other and expressing the relationship as a single measure.

Activity 1

In order to calculate a performance measure, we could express the income earned as a percentage of your investment. Calculate and show below the additional information (income as a percentage of capital invested) produced by this process.

Although this item of information has more significance than the two separate figures, it is still difficult to use without making a further comparison. Is 5% a good return or not? How can we judge this?

Activity 2

In order to assess your performance as an investor, we would have to compare the percentage rate of return you had achieved with something else. Make a note in this box of something that would form the basis of a useful comparison.

The concept of risk is quite important. You will appreciate this better when studying financial management. But even at an intuitive level you can probably appreciate that there must be some kind of correlation between risk and return.

High risk investments will offer a higher rate of return than low risk investments. History has many examples of people losing their savings because they were induced to part with their capital by the prospect of a high rate of return

Notice that this performance measure (income as a percentage of capital invested) gives no indication of the size of the capital invested. If you invested £100 and received interest of £10 you would say your rate of return was 10%. Yet the £10 in absolute terms is substantially less than the 5% return of £50 on the investment of £1,000. Accounting ratios are relative, as opposed to absolute, measures.

Imagine that at the start of the next year you inherit £100,000 and place this on bank deposit accounts. As a result of your investment you earn interest of £4,500 for the year. If you compare last year's interest (£50) with the current year's interest (£4,500), the amount for the current year is considerably higher. If these figures were profits earned by a company we would say there had been a substantial increase in profits during the second year.

But in relative terms your performance in the second year was less profitable than it was in the first year – the return on capital is 4.5% whereas it was 5% in the first year.

Despite the simplicity of Activities 1 and 2, the approach used forms a bedrock upon which all ratio analysis is based. Absolute figures are misleading. Ratios express two accounting measurements in relative terms, and allow meaningful comparisons to be made with similar activities involving similar risk (irrespective of size) and with performance in previous years.

Fundamentally, there is no difference between expressing interest as a percentage return on the cash invested, and expressing the profits of a business as a return on the amount of capital invested in that business. There are some practical differences and some problems in locating appropriate figures, but the basic idea is the same.

In case you are not familiar with the arithmetical notation used for calculating these percentages, we should point out that the figures from which the 5% for Activity 1 was calculated are usually set out (in long form) as follows:

$$\frac{\text{interest}}{\text{original investment}} \times \frac{100}{1} \quad \text{i.e.} \quad \frac{50}{1,000} \times \frac{100}{1} = 5\%$$

However, this is a cumbersome notation and it is unnecessary when using calculators with percentage keys. Even without the use of percentage keys we would normally shorten the form of notation to the following:

$$\frac{\text{interest}}{\text{original investment}} \quad \text{i.e.} \quad \frac{50}{1,000}$$

If you do this calculation on your calculator (£50 ÷ £1,000) the display will show 0.05.

When you become familiar with this (if you are not already) you will realize that there is no need to multiply the 0.05 by 100 (which is what the percentage key does) to find the 5. You can mentally move the decimal point two digits to the right. There is certainly no need to divide the result by one because any number divided by one will be the same as the original number.

With this short notation in mind, we can see the similarity between measuring the rate of return on the bank deposit and measuring the rate of return earned by a business on its assets, as follows:

$$\frac{\text{interest}}{\text{cash invested}} \qquad \text{simply becomes} \qquad \frac{\text{profit}}{\text{capital invested in the business}}$$

But there are many practical problems. First of all, a profit and loss account contains several profit figures; which one do we use? Second, what do we mean by capital? Unfortunately, there is no single answer to either of these questions and you will find that the ratio can be calculated in a number of different ways. Ratio analysis has many limitations; not least is the fact that comparisons are meaningless unless the ratios being compared have been calculated on the same basis.

Another difference between the bank deposit example and profits from a business investment is that we have no control over rates of interest being offered. Rates of interest can change frequently. However, the fact that interest rates have changed is an explanation for a variation in the ratio and this is how we use ratio analysis. It enables us to ask appropriate questions (why has something changed). It does not provide answers.

13.2 Ratio classification and structure

Any accounting number can be compared with another. Whether this comparison produces useful information is another matter. We can also calculate measures that show the relationship between financial and non-financial data, such as:

- sales per employee (turnover divided by the number of employees), or
- sales per square metre of shop space.

In this chapter we are concerned with analysing financial statements and will concentrate on traditional financial analysis.

There are various ways of classifying ratios; the following basis works quite well and provides a way of structuring the subject for study.

- **Business performance ratios.** These start with the primary ratio of return on capital invested in the business. This can then be sub-divided into secondary ratios that interlock with the primary ratio and help to explain its changes.
- **Working capital activity ratios.** Strictly speaking, these are a continuation of a hierarchy of ratios established under business performance ratios. But since they are concerned with the control of working capital they are usually treated as a separate group and measured in terms of a time period.
- **Solvency ratios.** These ratios consider the relationship between current assets and current liabilities. They are among the most difficult to interpret without further analysis and are frequently misunderstood by those who use them.
- **Investor ratios.** These can be divided into sub-groups, as follows:
  - **Financial capital (gearing) ratios.** These are concerned with the company's capital structure in terms of the proportion of loans to equity. They are important in the assessment of risk to equity investors.

- **Income based gearing ratios.** These ratios provide a measure to assess how two different levels of profit (operating profit and profit after tax) will respond to changes in sales levels.
- **Earnings ratios.** Ratios used by investment analysts, such as earnings per share (EPS), the price/earnings (P/E) ratio, dividend yield, and interest cover.

13.3 Expression of ratios

All ratios result from dividing one figure by another. The way that the result is expressed can vary. Sometimes we are dealing with a fraction which is expressed as a percentage, such as the percentage return on capital invested. In several cases we will be dividing a larger number by a smaller one. In these cases there are many different ways in which the result can be expressed. Think about the following:

$$\frac{£12,000}{£2,000}$$

Activity 3

The result of the above arithmetic can be expressed in at least three different ways. Make a note of them here.

1.

2.

3.

The idea of expressing the arithmetic in terms of the number of times the smaller figure goes into the larger one is often used where the larger figure is from the profit and loss account and the smaller is from the balance sheet. For example, if cost of sales for the year is £12,000 and stock is £2,000 we would say that stock 'is turned over six times a year'.

Some of the ratios in this category will be more readily understood by the user if they are converted into a time period. For example, another way of stating that stock is turned over six times a year is to say that stocks (on average) are held for two months before being sold.

Activity 4

By observation (not by calculation) see if you can find a useful relationship between the following two figures:

Sales for the year (all on credit)	£365,000
Debtors at the end of the year	£30,000

If you find it difficult to see anything, think about the fact that there are 365 days in a year.

The ratio in Activity 4 is called the debtors collection period and gives an indication of how long (on average) debtors are taking to pay their bills. If the figures had not been so obvious, the number of days could have been calculated by finding one day's sales (by dividing £365,000 by 365) and dividing this figure into £30,000. But this two-stage calculation can easily be resolved into a simple formula which is explained later.

13.4 Limitations of ratio analysis

The analytical skills involved in ratio analysis are not so much a matter of knowing how to calculate ratios (these are simple enough) as of being able to make judgements on the relevance of the information which they provide. In making this judgement, you must constantly be alert to the limitations of the technique.

It is not possible to make a judgement on an accounting ratio without some kind of yardstick for comparison. Two types of comparison are usually made:

1. Trend analysis: comparing the current year with the previous year (or years).
2. Inter-firm comparisons: comparing ratios with similar ratios in other firms that are operating in the same line of business.

It is possible for managers (and auditors) to compare actual and bud geted figures but this comparison is not available to an external analyst. We will concentrate on the above two. Both of them should be treated with caution.

Activity 5

Turnover during the current year is £104,000 compared with £100,000 in the previous year. This is an increase of 4%. State why it might be wrong to assume that the current year's results show an increase of 4% in the volume of trade.

The long-term effect of price increases can produce some severe distortions when measuring the primary ratio. The next activity is based on the financial statements of two companies. Review the following data before attempting Activity 6:

Company A's fixed assets were purchased ten years ago and are being written off over 15 years. Company B's fixed assets were purchased at the beginning of the current year and are also being written off over 15 years. Price increases for the type of fixed assets used by both companies have averaged 10% p.a. over the last ten years. A summary of each company's financial statements is as follows:

	Company A	Company B
Fixed assets at cost	30,000	75,000
Aggregate depreciation	20,000	5,000
Net book value	10,000	70,000
Net current assets	5,000	5,000
Net assets	15,000	75,000
Profit before depreciation	8,000	8,000
Depreciation	2,000	5,000
Profit before tax	6,000	3,000

Activity 6

Measure each company's Return on Capital Invested by comparing profit before tax with net assets and expressing this relationship as a percentage. After completing the calculations, make an observation which you think is relevant to the comparison.

	Company A	Company B
Percentage return		

Observation

The problem of comparing the ratios of one company with those of another company in the same line of business has many pitfalls unless you are aware of the limitations.

Activity 7

You are analysing the results of a company and calculate the Return on Capital Invested as 40%. This compares to an industry average of 30%. Make a note of three factors that might account for the difference apart from a better than average performance by the company being analysed.

1.

2.

3.

There are many other limitations in ratio analysis you will discover more as you work through the remaining parts of this chapter.

13.5 Business performance ratios

The primary ratio

The primary ratio has different names in different books. The name used depends on the author's preference. Here are the most popular names together with their usual abbreviations:

- Return on Capital Employed (ROCE)
- Return on Investment (ROI)
- Return on Net Assets (RONA).

These three names are all based on the same concept but none of them gives a clear indication of the figures to be used in the calculation.

One thing that will eventually become clear is why this ratio is called the primary ratio. It looks at profit in relation to the resources used to create that profit and forms the apex of a pyramid of secondary ratios. You will see what this means shortly.

The term 'Net Assets' (as in RONA) seems to suggest something that should have a definable meaning, but even this term is ambiguous. Where do we find a figure for Net Assets in the balance sheet? Is it the figure of total assets less current liabilities or total assets less all liabilities? You will know from your earlier studies that these two figures are different if the company has long-term loans.

The difference between Net Assets (as in RONA) and Capital Employed (as in ROCE) is, to some extent, a reflection of the two parts of the balance sheet used in UK practice. The top part of the balance sheet deals with net assets and the bottom part deals with capital.

There are, however, different viewpoints regarding the treatment of medium-term and long-term loans. Should they be treated as part of the capital, or should they be treated as liabilities to be deducted from net assets?

We will use the figures for Expander Ltd at 31 December 1997 (Chapter 11) to illustrate these two perspectives. Ignoring details in each part of the balance sheet, the relevant figures can be summarized as follows:

	£
Total assets less current liabilities	702,000
10% Debentures	45,000
Total net assets	657,000
Total capital and reserves	657,000

If we think of the debentures as being part of the capital (rather than a liability) then the total capital employed is (£657,000 + £45,000) £702,000. This is the same figure as total assets less current liabilities and is sometimes called 'Total Capital'. If we think of the loan as a liability (rather than a part of the capital) then we are thinking of capital as being owners' capital (total capital and reserves), which is the same figure as total net assets (total assets less total liabilities) in the top part of the balance sheet.

We can use either of these two bases providing we make sure that the capital base is related to the appropriate profit created by that capital. In both cases we normally use an appropriate pre-tax profit when measuring the rate of return.

If we think of total capital as being owners' capital plus loans, we should use profit before interest as representing the return created by that capital. This is usually called 'operating profit', although some companies call it profit before interest and tax.

If loans are treated as a liability, we are measuring the return on owners' capital and should use profits after interest (but before tax) as the return created by that capital. The two bases can be summarized as follows:

$$\text{Return on total capital} \quad = \quad \frac{\text{operating profit}}{\text{(profit before tax and interest)}} \Big/ \text{total assets less current liabilities}$$

$$\text{Return on owners' capital} \quad = \quad \frac{\text{profit before tax}}{\text{total assets less total liabilities}}$$

Notice that in setting out the formula for each of the above, we have described the denominator by using terms taken from the top part of the balance sheet. We could have used terms that describe the capital (such as owners' capital + loans for the first formula) but it is easier to see the connection between the primary ratio and the secondary ratios if we use terminology from the assets side of the balance sheet.

Neither basis has more merit than the other, they are simply two bases. Return on total capital (owners' capital plus loans) has an internal perspective since it indicates how effective management has been in the use of total capital funds. Return on owners' capital has an external perspective and is used to measure the return on the capital which shareholders have provided. If the share capital consists entirely of ordinary shares, the return on owners' capital is usually called the 'return on equity'.

There are two important things to keep in mind:

1. Return on total capital uses *profit before interest* whereas the return on owners' capital uses *profit after interest* (in both cases these are pre-tax profits).

2. Like must be compared with like. There is no point in comparing return on total capital in one company with return on owners' capital in another. It is also important to use the same capital base when sub-dividing the primary ratio into the secondary ratios.

There are also different ways of selecting a point of time to measure the appropriate capital. We could use any of the following:

- capital at the start of the period
- capital at the end of the period
- average capital for the period.

You might have noticed that when we used the bank deposit account to illustrate the concept (in section 13.1) the return was based on the opening capital. But this was for the sake of simplicity in the explanation. When dealing with business assets it is fairly common practice to use the capital at the end of the period.

Average capital is sometimes used. An external analyst will have to base this on an average of the opening capital at the start of the year and the closing capital at the end of the year. Managers could use a monthly average. Again, the key word when using ratio analysis is consistency rather than 'correctness'. There is no such thing as a correct basis – there are simply different bases.

Most of the remaining activities in this unit will be based on the financial statements of a fictitious company called Overload Ltd. These are set out in Appendix 1 at the end of this chapter.

The only comment we could make at the moment is that the rate of return has fallen by 5.5 percentage points. We will have to do a secondary analysis to see if we can find which aspects of the operating activities have contributed to this downturn.

Secondary ratios

Profit is derived from sales and these sales are generated by the net assets. The downturn in ROCE for Overload Ltd could be caused by any of the following:

- earning less profit on the sales
- generating fewer sales from the net assets
- a combination of both.

The purpose of secondary ratios is to isolate causes of the variation in ROCE by relating both profit and net assets to sales. In ratio analysis we tend to use the term 'sales' rather than 'turnover'. You will understand the formulae for the two secondary ratios after working Activity 9.

This reconciliation can be set out by including the multiplication and equals signs as follows:

$$\frac{\text{profit}}{\text{net assets}} = \frac{\text{profit}}{\text{sales}} \times \frac{\text{sales}}{\text{net assets}}$$

The ratio of profit to sales is usually called the 'profit margin' ratio and is measured as a percentage. The ratio of sales to net assets is usually called the 'asset turnover' (or asset utilization) ratio and is usually measured as a number of times (the number of times net assets divide into sales). There is a better way of expressing the asset turnover ratio, but we will look at that in a moment. In the meantime, carry out Activities 10 and 11.

Activity 10

Calculate the two secondary ratios for Overload Ltd. Make sure that you use the same profit figure and same capital (total assets less current liabilities) base as you used for the primary ratio.

	ROCE		Profit margin		Asset turnover	
	1995	1996	1995	1996	1995	1996
	29.5%	24%				

You can check the arithmetical accuracy of your calculations by working the next activity.

Activity 11

Check your calculations for the previous activity by seeing if the product of the two secondary ratios agrees with the primary ratio for each year.

1995	1996

Expressing the asset turnover ratio as so many times is traditional but the measure would be more meaningful if we called it pounds rather than so many times. If you look back at your calculation of the asset turnover ratio you might notice that what you have actually calculated is the amount of sales produced by each £1 of net assets. For example, in 1996 we could say that each £1 of net assets produced £4 of sales.

This allows us to explain the relationship between the secondary and primary ratios in a useful way. If we take 1996 as an example, the relationship can now be explained as follows:

- each £1 of net operating assets produced £4 in sales
- the operating profit on sales of £4 is (6% of £4) £0.24, and
- this operating profit is 24% of the £1 of net assets that produced those sales.

Each secondary ratio can now be broken down even further by using sales as a constant. For our analysis of the profit and loss account we can find the ratio of gross profit to sales, and expenses to sales. A statement that expresses all items in the profit and loss account as a percentage of sales is known as a 'common size statement'. For the balance sheet analysis we could relate the different classes of asset to sales.

This produces a pyramid of ratios as indicated by the following diagram. This simply shows the top part of the pyramid; each ratio at the base of this pyramid could be broken down even further. In this diagram the term 'net operating assets' has been used to signify total assets less current liabilities but, as stated earlier, a different basis for the primary ratio is sometimes used. The point to remember is that whatever basis is used for profit and capital in the primary ratio, the same basis should be used for the secondary ratios.

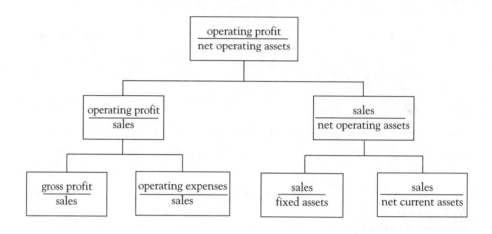

The profitability ratios (left-hand side of the pyramid) are expressed as percentages. Asset turnover ratios (right-hand side of the pyramid) are expressed as times or £s. Individual ratios can be reconciled to their parent ratio. For example, the percentage of gross profit to sales, less the percentage of expenses to sales, should equal the percentage of operating profit to sales.

In the case of Overload Ltd, the asset turnover ratio appears to be satisfactory by comparison to the previous year. We would, therefore, turn our attention to the profit and loss account.

Activity 12

Calculate the two additional profitability ratios for Overload Ltd and reconcile these to the percentage of operating profit to sales.

	1995	1996
Gross profit to sales (%)		
Operating expenses to sales (%)		
Operating profit to sales	8.25%	6%

The trend in both ratios indicates cause for concern although the change in gross profit percentage is more worrying than the expenses to sales ratio. Operating expenses will include some costs that are 'fixed' (meaning that they do not increase with increases in sales activity) and so we would normally expect to see this ratio fall with an increase in sales. However, without more information it is impossible to draw any conclusions.

As regards the fall in gross profit percentage, there are several factors that might have caused this.

Activity 13

Some of the following events will cause the gross profit percentage to fall, others will not. Consider each event and indicate (by answering yes or no) whether or not it will cause a fall in the gross profit percentage.

1. A fall in the level of turnover	Yes/No
2. Reduction in sales prices of products	Yes/No
3. Increase in administration costs	Yes/No
4. Increase in purchase prices of stocks purchased	Yes/No

In the case of Overload Ltd, you might have noticed that the fall in gross profit percentage for 1996 was accompanied by an increase in turnover for that year. This often suggests a deliberate marketing strategy – increasing sales volume by reducing prices.

We should now turn our attention to the right-hand side of the pyramid, the asset turnover ratios. You will find that the fixed asset turnover ratio works out at £5.80 for 1995 and £7.13 for 1996. The fixed assets have, therefore, been used much more efficiently in 1996.

If you do the same thing on net current assets you will find the variation does not appear very significant: £9.30 in 1995 and £9.10 in 1996. But it is the individual components of net current assets that should be analysed, not the net total. We will do this next but instead of expressing the ratios as £s (or times) we will use the time period measure, as discussed earlier.

Stocks, debtors and creditors

The time period ratios are calculated for stocks, debtors and creditors. They give an indication of how long stocks are being held, how long debtors are taking to pay, and how long the company is taking to pay its creditors. In each case the closing balance is related to the total of the appropriate class of transaction for the year, as follows:

Closing balance	**Appropriate transactions**
Stocks	Cost of sales
Debtors	Sales (turnover)
Creditors	Purchases (which can be derived from cost of sales)

We use a multiplier of 365 for an expression of the ratio in days, 52 for an expression in weeks, and 12 for an expression in months. Assuming an expression in days, the three formulae are as follows:

$$\text{Stock holding period} = \frac{\text{closing stock}}{\text{cost of sales}} \times 365$$

$$\text{Debtors collection period} = \frac{\text{debtors}}{\text{sales}} \times 365$$

$$\text{Creditors payment period} = \frac{\text{creditors}}{\text{purchases}} \times 365$$

Activity 14

Calculate these three ratios for Overload Ltd on a separate sheet of paper and make a note of your measurements here. Purchases can be calculated by making an adjustment to cost of sales for opening and closing stocks, as you did in Chapter 11. Opening stock for 1995 is given in the notes.

	1995	1996
Stock holding period		
Debtors collection period		
Creditors payment period		

The increase in Overload's stock holding period is quite significant (about 50%) and warrants further enquiry.

But we must be cautious before assuming that the increase indicates that stocks are taking longer to sell. A problem with balance sheets is that they are only snapshots showing the position at the end of a particular day. We have no way of telling from annual financial statements whether the closing stock is typical of the stock holding throughout the year. Overload Ltd could have had a large delivery of stocks on the last day of the year.

Activity 15

When an increase in turnover is accompanied by an increase in the debtors collection period (as with Overload Ltd) it sometimes indicates a deliberate marketing strategy. Make a ote of what this strategy might be.

We see many examples of this in our shops – publicity notices which say something like: 'Buy now: pay in three month's time.'

However, an increase in the debtors collection period is often something that calls for further investigation because it might be the result of poor credit control. But notice again that the ratio has simply enabled us to ask appropriate questions, such as why has the debtors collection period increased? It does not provide us with an answer.

Without a ratio, we might look at the debtors in the balance sheet and notice they have increased by £29,480 over what they were at the end of the previous year. But this information by itself is meaningless. If turnover increases (as it has in Overload Ltd) then we would expect the debtors to increase also. If a company maintains the same debtors to sales ratio, an increase of 10% in turnover would result in the amount for debtors increasing by 10%.

Solvency ratios

These ratios are quite easy to calculate but difficult to interpret without further analysis of the individual items that make up the total of current assets and current liabilities. They do, however, have a strong tradition in accounting literature and have been written about since the turn of the century. There are two common ratios: the current ratio and the liquidity ratio (or acid test).

The current ratio is simply the current assets divided by the current liabilities.

$$\frac{\text{current assets}}{\text{current liabilities}}$$

The result is then expressed as a value to 1.

Current liabilities are presented under the heading of creditors due within one year. If you calculate the current ratio for Overload Ltd you will find that is 2.67:1 at 31 December 1995 and 2.05:1 at 31 December 1996.

A traditional view of this is that there has been a deterioration in the ratio (by about 23%), which might be a cause for concern. But quite often a reduction in the current ratio is the result of careful planning. If you take the traditional view, presumably an increase in the ratio is a healthy sign – but is it? It could be the result of poor financial control, such as allowing the stock holding period and debtors collection period to increase.

There is no such thing as an ideal current ratio: it will vary according to the type of trade and the length of the net operating cycle. You can think of the net operating cycle as being the length of time between the date at which purchases are taken into stock and the date at which cash is received for the sale of that stock.

A manufacturer has a very long operating cycle because it purchases raw materials, retains these materials in stock for a while, converts them into finished goods, retains the finished goods in stock for a while and then sells them on credit terms. There is a substantial length of time between the receipt of the raw materials and the receipt of cash from customers for the finished goods produced from these materials. The current assets of a manufacturer are likely to be in the region of about twice the amount for current liabilities.

Retail supermarkets on the other hand, particularly those where a high proportion of turnover is food, purchase goods and sell them for cash in a much shorter time than the period of credit granted by their suppliers. In these cases the business can operate with a negative figure for net current assets. The current ratio will, therefore, be less than 1:1.

Activity 16

Appendices 2 and 3 are the balance sheets of Tesco PLC and Imperial Chemical Industries PLC (ICI). There is nothing on either balance sheet to state which one is for Tesco and which one is for ICI. Review these balance sheets in the light of the above discussion and state which one is which. In both cases, refer to figures for the 'group' not the 'company'.

Appendix 2 is the balance sheet of

Appendix 3 is the balance sheet of

The liquidity ratio (or acid test) is similar to the current ratio except that any current assets which will take a long time to turn into cash are excluded. It is normally calculated by excluding stocks from current assets, as follows:

$$\frac{\text{current assets less stock}}{\text{current liabilities}}$$

It suffers from similar defects to those for the current ratio. Quite often you will find that current liabilities (which we call 'creditors due within one year' on the balance sheet) include a bank overdraft. Although this can be recalled at short notice by the bank, many companies perceive it as a form of permanent finance rather than a short-term liability.

Why use solvency ratios?

Drawing conclusions from solvency ratios on their own is likely to be a pointless task. You can probably obtain a much better picture of a company's solvency position by considering the ratios alongside the mass of other information available in an annual report, such as the cash flow statement and the imminence of loan repayments (dates have to be published).

This raises the question of what use is made of solvency ratios. If we are using them to assess the creditworthiness of a company, it might be better to use one of the many proprietary sources that provide credit rating information on particular companies. The availability of this kind of information is mentioned later. If we are using solvency ratios to predict corporate failure, we need to be aware that a single ratio can easily be camouflaged by creative accounting. This is one of the reasons why the various proprietary systems used to predict corporate failure are based on weighting a number of ratios. (This process, known as multivariate analysis, is not covered in this book.)

13.6 Investor ratios

Capital based gearing ratios

Financial capital ratios are concerned with the way the entity is financed in terms of the relevant proportions of fixed interest capital (loans and preference shares) and equity capital. The ratios are often called capital 'gearing ratios', although the so-called 'gearing' effect is best seen by considering how different mixtures of financial capital will affect the rate of change in income available for equity shareholders. This is explained later.

Gearing is an extremely interesting subject, although you need to make a more detailed study of corporate finance before you can really understand its significance. From your work in this section you will gain some idea of why it is important.

The gearing ratio is expressed as a percentage. But there are two bases that can be used for calculating this percentage. Fixed interest capital can be expressed as a percentage of total capital, or as a percentage of equity capital, as follows:

$$\frac{\text{fixed interest capital}}{\text{total capital (loans + owners)}} \quad \text{or} \quad \frac{\text{fixed interest capital}}{\text{equity capital}}$$

The second basis is more correctly described as the debt to equity ratio. Fixed interest capital comprises loans and preference shares, where the rate of dividend is fixed at a specified rate and must be paid before any dividend is paid to equity shareholders.

Unfortunately, journalists often refer to gearing ratios without stating which calculation basis they are using. This also happens in the published annual reports, where companies disclose (voluntarily) gearing ratio percentages. If you think about the first basis (fixed interest capital to total capital) the percentage will always be less than 100%. The percentage for the second could be more than 100%.

Although we have stated above that fixed interest capital includes preference shares, there are differences of opinion on this. It can be argued that since preference shares do not represent a debt of the company they should be excluded. We will simplify our study of the subject by ignoring preference shares and basing it on the two basic types of capital – loan capital and equity capital.

We will not be calculating the gearing ratio for Overload Ltd because it is a small private company whose shares are not being traded on the stock market. The gearing ratio will not, therefore, be of interest to the equity investors. This is not to suggest that the gearing ratio is irrelevant in the case of private companies. If the ratio is very high it could be a danger signal and will be of concern to the providers of loan finance. In this session we are going to explore the effect of gearing ratios on the equity shareholders.

In the case of public listed companies, it is the way that equity shareholders see capital gearing as affecting the risk in their investment that is of interest. The term 'risk' has a technical meaning in investment analysis. All investments are risky but some carry more risk than others. It is possible to quantify risk but the methods used for this are not studied in this book. You can get some idea of how the term 'risk' is used by working the next activity.

Activity 17

You have an opportunity to make an investment and are considering a choice between Investment A and Investment B. Future returns have been assessed as follows:

Investment A. The return is expected to be between 10% and 12%.
Investment B. The return is expected to be between 1% and 40%.

Which of these two investments carries the greater risk?

Even if you reacted intuitively you noticed the estimated returns on Investment B seem to be less certain than those in Investment A. At a more scientific level you may have looked at the range of possible outcomes and noticed this is far greater in Investment B than it is in Investment A. It is the range of possible outcomes that forms the basis of all risk measurements.

We can now relate this to the way that equity investors view the effect of gearing levels on the range of returns available to them. Consider the next example. The financial structures of two companies operating in the same line of business are as follows:

	Company A	Company B
Ordinary shares of £1 each	5,000	1,000
Profit and loss account	5,000	1,000
	10,000	2,000
10% Loan Capital	–	8,000
	10,000	10,000

Notice that Company A is ungeared (gearing ratio is 0%) and that Company B has a gearing ratio of 80% (or 400% using the debt to equity ratio). The earnings before interest and tax for each company are the same. The tax rate is 35%. The results for two consecutive years are as follows:

	Company A		Company B	
	Year 1	Year 2	Year 1	Year 2
Operating profit	1,200	900	1,200	900
Interest	–	–	800	800
Profit before tax	1,200	900	400	100
Taxation (35%)	420	315	140	35
Profit available for equity	780	585	260	65

Notice that operating profit has fallen by 25% in both companies. We now need to consider what effect these results will have when viewed through the eyes of the equity shareholders. Even without making any measurements you will see that the profit available for equity has fallen at a much greater rate in Company B than it has in Company A.

There are various ways of measuring the rate of change in profit available to equity. We could simply measure the percentage fall. For example, the fall in profit available for equity in Company A is:

$$\frac{£780 - £585}{£780} \times 100 = 25\%$$

Notice that in this ungeared company, profit available for equity has fallen by the same rate as operating profit.

Activity 18

Carry out the same kind of calculation for Company B and make a note of your answer here.

Profit available for equity in Company B has fallen by:

Notice how the profit available for equity responds to changes in earnings. A fall of 25% in earnings causes the ungeared company's profits to fall by 25%. In Company B a fall in earnings of 25% causes these profits to fall by 75%, three times the rate of fall in operating profit.

It is this vulnerability to a wider range of possible outcomes that will cause Company B's shareholders to perceive a much greater risk in their shares by comparison with Company A. This particular risk is called 'financial risk' and it is one of several factors that comprise the total risk of an investment. It will have an impact on the share price as between the two companies. People will only invest in Company B if the rate of return on their investment is higher than it is for an investment in Company A.

The fact that Company B's fall in profit available to equity is three times the rate of fall in operating profit is the result of an income gearing effect which we will look at next.

Income based gearing ratios

There are two income based gearing ratios:

- the degree of operational gearing (DOG), and
- the degree of financial gearing (DFG).

Both of them measure a rate at which one 'level' of income will change in response to changes in a higher 'level' of income. The various levels at which income is reported in a profit and loss account can be summarised as:

1. Turnover (or sales)
2. Operating profit
3. Profit before tax
4. Profit after tax (profit available for equity).

The degree of operational gearing (DOG) measures the rate at which operating profit will change in response to changes in sales. In this case the gearing effect is between income at Level 1 and income at Level 2 (using the terminology adopted above).

The degree of financial gearing (DFG) indicates the rate at which profit after tax (profit available for equity) will change in response to changes in operating profit. In this case the gearing effect is between income at Level 2 and income at Level 4.

In order to understand these ratios we need to calculate them for one year and then use them to interpret changes to profit in the following year. In order to do this we will use the above accounts for Company B and extend them so as to include turnover and operating costs.

Example

This is an extension of the income statement for Company B that we used when explaining capital gearing. In this example, we will measure the income based gearing ratios for Year 1 and use them to interpret changes in profit for Year 2.

You will notice that the operating costs have been analysed between fixed and variable costs. This has been done so that we can calculate the DOG ratio. Although published financial statements do not disclose this kind of information, it is possible to use various techniques (such as regression analysis) to obtain approximate figures for the analysis. The purpose of the comments and arrows to the right of the figures will become apparent after we have calculated the ratios.

Company B

	Year 1	Year 2	
Sales	£8,000	£7,000	
Variable costs (70% of sales)	5,600	4,900	
Contribution	2,400	2,100	operational gearing
Fixed costs	1,200	1,200	
Operating profit	1,200	900	
Interest	800	800	
Profit before tax	400	100	financial gearing
Corporation tax (35%)	140	35	
Profit available for shareholders	260	65	

First we will calculate the DOG ratio for Year 1. The formula is quite simple and is as follows:

$$\frac{\text{sales less variable costs (usually called contribution)}}{\text{operating profit}}$$

The result is expressed as a number of times.

Activity 19

Calculate the DOG ratio for Year 1 and make a note of your calculation here.

An interpretation of this ratio rests on what it tells about the likely effect on results in the next year if there is a change in the level of sales for that year. For example, with a DOG ratio of 2 for Year 1 we can estimate that if sales in Year 2 were to fall by 10%, then operating profit will fall by (2 × 10%) 20% in that year.

Activity 20

Answer the following for Company B in order to demonstrate the validity of this argument.

Sales in Year 2 have fallen by £1,000 when compared with Year 1. Express the fall of £1,000 as a percentage of the sales in Year 1.

Using the DOG ratio of 2, state the percentage fall in operating profit that you would expect as a result of this percentage fall in sales.

Operating profit in Year 2 has fallen by £300 when compared with Year 1. Express the fall of £300 as a percentage of operating profit in Year 1.

If the DOG ratio had been 3 in Year 1, operating profit would have fallen by 30% in Year 2. This suggests that risk increases as the DOG ratio increases.

Now we will look at the degree of financial gearing (DFG) ratio. The formula is as follows:

$$\frac{\text{operating profit}}{\text{profit before tax}}$$

Activity 21

Measure the DFG ratio in Year 1 for Company B.

If you think back to the example when we were discussing capital based gearing ratios, you will recall that a fall of 25% in Company B's operating profit resulted in a fall of 75% in profit available for equity shareholders. You can now see that this is a result of the DFG for Year 1. With a DFG of 3 in Year 1, then with a fall of 25% in the operating profit for Year 2 we would expect to see profit available to equity to fall by ($3 \times 25\%$) 75% in that year.

In terms of risk, if a company takes on more loans and increases its capital gearing ratio, the equity shareholders will perceive a much greater risk in their shares. Equity shareholders will also view a company with a capital gearing of 60% (60% of its total capital is in the form of loans) as carrying a much higher risk than another company where the gearing ratio is only 10%. These perceptions of risk have an important bearing on the share price.

Income based investor ratios

Price/earnings ratio

The price/earnings (P/E) ratio is one of the most popular stock market indicators. The P/E ratios of companies listed on the London Stock Exchange are quoted in share price listings such as those published in the *Financial Times*. The ratio is simply the price per share divided by the earnings per share:

$$\frac{\text{price per share}}{\text{earnings per share}}$$

The ratio expresses the current share price as a multiple of earnings per share. For example, if the current price is £2.00 per share and the company reported earnings per share of 20 pence in it last accounts, the P/E ratio is stated as 10:1.

The price per share is based on the Stock Exchange share price listings. It can change every minute, although we are normally looking at changes on a day-to-day basis. Earnings per share (EPS) is a number that all UK listed companies must publish in their annual financial statements according to accounting regulations. They must also publish EPS in their half-yearly interim accounts as required by the Stock Exchange listing rules. The denominator of the fraction for the P/E ratio will, therefore, change twice a year.

How is the P/E ratio used? Share prices are influenced in the same way as prices generally, by supply and demand. The supply in the market will increase when someone sells their shares. The demand for a share might be influenced by a number of factors but one of them is bound to be the level of a company's earnings. If you listen to company news broadcasts, or read company news items in the financial press, you will often see references to how share prices have reacted to profit announcements.

The correlation between earnings and price is such that if EPS increases or falls, the price will increase or fall proportionately. If the change in price for a share is simply a response to a change in EPS, the P/E ratio for that company will remain fairly static.

Consequently, it is the changes in the P/E ratio of a company that attract attention. If the price of a share changes disproportionately to EPS, there must be some factor other than earnings that is affecting the price. This could be rumours of a take-over (and the likelihood of increased demand for the share) or the disposal of a large number of shares by a substantial shareholder (an increased supply to the market).

Activity 22

The shares of a company are currently trading at £3.50 each and the P/E ratio is 14:1. Interim results have just been produced and these show an EPS of 28 pence. What is likely to be the new price of these shares following publication of these results?

Price/earnings ratios are used in other contexts. For example, if you compare two companies who are operating in the same type of business and one has a P/E ratio of 10:1 and the other 15:1, there must be some reason worth investigating why the market is valuing the latter company at a much higher multiple of current earnings than the former.

For example, we might find that the two P/E ratios relate to pharmaceutical companies where one has announced some kind of breakthrough in scientific research which could lead, in the long term, to the marketing of a cure drug. The benefits of this discovery will not be visible in terms of increased earnings until some time in the future but the stock market has valued the prospective increase in earnings by way of an increase in the current price of the share.

Some text books suggest that P/E ratios can be used to value shares in an unquoted company. An unquoted company is one whose shares are not dealt with on a stock exchange and so there is no market mechanism to determine a price per share. In theory, it should be possible to use the P/E ratios of listed companies operating in a line of business similar to that of the unlisted company in order to value the shares of that unlisted company.

However, the valuation of shares through indicators such as the P/E ratio is fraught with danger, not least because EPS is based on accounting measurements for profit. Profit is a reporting concept that can easily be camouflaged. The serious players in the take-over game do not base their offers on prospective profits of the victim company; they base them on the present value of future cash flows which they consider can be obtained by investing in the victim company. This is why the concept of free cash flow (as discussed in Chapter 11) is important.

Dividend yield

The dividend yield ratio shows the rate of return being earned on an investment by relating the last dividend payment to the current price of the share. In basic terms, the formula is:

$$\frac{\text{dividend per share}}{\text{price per share}}$$

The fraction is expressed as a percentage. It gives an indication of the returns being demanded by equity. As with the P/E ratio, it often remains fairly static and prices simply respond to the dividend being paid.

The dividend yields quoted by the *Financial Times* in its share price listings are called 'gross' yields. This is because under UK tax law the dividend received by the shareholder is an after-tax amount. The gross yield is found by adding the tax deducted to the net dividend paid.

The dividend yield gives an indication of the rate of return expected by the providers of equity capital. By way of a simple example, if the last dividend paid by a company was 50 pence per share, and the current market price of the share is £5.00 each, we would say that the dividend yield is (50/500) 10%. In other words, equity investors in this type of company are expecting a return of 10% on their capital.

The shareholders' expected rate of return is signalled through the share price. If factors other than dividends are affecting the share price, the dividend yield will change. This might happen, for example, if a company suddenly increases its capital gearing ratio. The increased risk perceived by the shareholders will be reflected (as a result of market activity) by a fall in the share price. You can see how this affects the rate of return expected by working the following activity.

Activity 23

Consider the example mentioned above where a price of £5 per share was being quoted for a company that had just declared a dividend of 50 pence per share. At this stage we can assume that equity shareholders are content with a return of 10% on their investment. Now assume that the company takes on additional loans and increases its gearing ratio. The increased risk perceived by shareholders results in a flurry of share trading which is sufficient to cause the share price to drop to £4. Calculate the dividend yield at this new share price, assuming that future dividends will be 50 pence per share.

This higher return (12.5% compared to 10%) reflects the increased risk perceived by the shareholders as a result of the company increasing its gearing ratio. Shareholders do not telephone the company and say 'pay us a higher rate to compensate for our increased risk'; the higher rate required by shareholders is signalled through the share price as determined by the market mechanism.

Interest cover

This is an expression of how many 'times' profit before interest and tax (PBIT) covers the interest charge (PBIT ÷ interest charge). Since it gives an indication of the adequacy of profits to meet interest charges it will be of concern to both loan and equity investors.

You should note that PBIT might be a different figure to operating profit because PBIT can include investment income. Sometimes investment income is set against interest charges (or vice versa) and a net figure shown in the published profit and loss account. It might be necessary to separate these two items when calculating the interest cover ratio. The information that will enable you to do this can be found in the 'Notes to the financial statements'.

There is also a problem in calculating this ratio when the company concerned has treated interest paid as part of the cost of an asset rather than as an expense in the profit and loss account. This is known as the *capitalization of interest* and is discussed in the next section.

The interest cover ratio is useful when looking at trends over a period of time, or when considering the effect of any re-financing proposals. It is not possible to state any optimum ratio (or norm), nor is it always necessary to assume that a falling ratio is a cause for concern.

The interest cover ratio is simply one item of information and it needs to be used sensibly alongside other indicators such as the DFG, the capital based gearing ratios, and any other information regarding dates of repayment of loans. Even when the interest cover ratio falls to less than 1 (giving a loss before tax) it would be wrong to assume that the company's problems can be solved by reorganizing its financial structure. Such problems might result from poor operating profitability rather than from the level of debt finance.

13.7 Refining the analysis and writing reports

Some of the topics covered in this section are not likely to be relevant to students who simply have to use ratio analysis for answering examination questions. They are more appropriate to students who have to analyse the published accounts of a company as part of a course assignment. But all students are likely to benefit from studying the points covered, particularly the advice given on writing reports.

Year-on-year changes

In previous sections of this chapter we considered trend analysis purely from the viewpoint of observing changes in ratios over two years. It is also quite useful to analyse changes in absolute figures over a number of years, such as five years. Figures for the past five years are usually included in published annual reports on a voluntary basis. The auditors do not report on these figures and there is a tendency for companies to publish only those items which show favourable trends.

It is the percentage change (not the change in monetary value) from one period to the next that provides useful information. Some caution is needed in analysing the figures from this approach; for example:

- An increase in the level of working capital items (stocks, debtors, and creditors) should be consistent with the increase in sales activity. A 10% increase in debtors would be expected if there had been a 10% increase in the level of credit sales.
- The effect of inflation should not be ignored. A 10% increase in the monetary value of sales is not an indication that sales volume has increased by 10% because a part of the increase relates to price changes.

It is possible to remove the effect of inflation by using an appropriate index such as the retail price index (RPI).

If the year-on-year change analysis is produced for a sufficient number of years, and adjustments are made to remove the effect of inflation, it is possible to get some idea of trends in the company being analysed. This information can then be compared to similar information for competitors within the same industry.

Eliminating profit from discontinued activities

In the published financial statements of a UK company, profits from activities that were discontinued during the year are shown separately to profit from continuing activities. It has been mandatory for public companies to publish this kind of information since 1993.

Large public companies are constantly changing their organizational structure by closing down (or selling) some of their subsidiaries and acquiring new ones. The balance sheet at the end of the year shows the accounting value of net assets for continuing activities. This must be so because the net assets attributable to the discontinued activities will have been removed from the balance sheet at the date the business segment was sold.

If you are attempting to analyse the performance of a company that has closed down a part of its business during the year, it does not make sense to compare the total profit (at whatever level you choose) with the net assets in the final balance sheet. Some of the profit (or loss) for the year will have been created by net assets that are no longer in the balance sheet.

A sensible solution to this is to eliminate the profits (or losses) from discontinued activities from the total profit for the year and compare this adjusted figure to the year-end balance sheet. Failure to do this means that you are relating profits (or losses) to net assets that are no longer in the balance sheet.

Cash flow statements

Although the cash flow statement is a primary statement rather than a note, it is surprising how often it seems to be ignored when analysing a set of financial statements. The cash flow statement contains a lot of useful (and objective) information; it will be even more useful when companies start using the new format.

One relationship between the cash flow statement and the profit and loss account that is worth examining relates to operating activities. The first item in the cash flow statement is net cash inflow from operating activities. As you know from your study of Chapter 11, this item measures the net cash inflows generated by the transactions that determine operating profit in the profit and loss account. It is always worth looking at these two figures to see if cash flow is less than profit, or vice versa, or if there are any trends that call for further enquiries.

Here is an example. If you obtain a copy of the annual report of Dixons Group plc for 1995/96 you will find that the following comparisons can be made:

	1995/96 £m	1994/95 £m
Operating profit	128.1	99.8
Net cash inflow from operating activities	119.3	189.9

As you can see, there are some quite wide swings here. In 1994/95 cash flows from operating activities were far greater than operating profit. In 1995/96 these cash flows were less than operating profit. If we measure operating cash flows as a percentage of operating profit we have the following:

1994/95	190%
1995/96	93%

The ratio in 1995/96 has fallen to about a half of what it was in 1994/95. Why has it happened? If you refer to the reconciliation note (Note 25 in their report) you will find that the most striking factor is that the increases in stocks and debtors during 1995/96 are significantly greater than the increases in these items for 1994/95. We are not suggesting this is a worrying feature – it might be explained by all kinds of factors such as a change in strategy – but by examining the cash flow statement we now have more information about the company's financial affairs which we can include in our analysis.

We suggested in Chapter 11 that the concept of free cash flow before dividends bears some relationship to profit available for equity shareholders. When companies start to use the new (1996) format it might be worthwhile examining the relationship between these two items. We can do this now for companies that publish information on free cash flow. Here is an example.

The annual report of Guinness PLC for 1995 includes information on free cash flow. If we relate this to profit for the financial year (profit before dividends) we will find the following:

	1995 £m	1994 £m
Profit for the financial year	595	641
Free cash flow before dividends	484	460

As you can see, there is a fall in the level of profit (of about 7%) but an increase in free cash flow of about 5%. This might help to explain the increase in dividends for 1995 (increased from 13.8p per share in 1994 to 14.9p per share in 1995) even though the group profit for 1995 was less than that for the previous year.

Finding interest payments

A troublesome aspect of financial statements for some UK companies is the way that interest payments and similar financing costs have been treated. We have previously mentioned how interest reported in the profit and loss account is a net figure after deducting investment income. This needs to be unscrambled when calculating ratios such as interest cover.

This is a relatively minor problem. A more serious matter is the way that some UK companies capitalize interest payments by treating them as part of the cost of an asset. This is often done when assets are being constructed and loans are raised to finance the cost of the construction. The practice can be found in the financial statements of many different types of company, such as supermarkets (construction of new stores) and hotels (construction of new hotels).

If you obtain a copy of the financial statements of the Eurotunnel PLC group you will find that by 31 December 1994 the cost of their fixed assets (mainly the Channel Tunnel project) included total interest payments of £969,313,000. This represents almost 25% of the total cost of the tunnel project.

Interest is also capitalized in other situations, such as where trading stocks (like whisky and champagne) are left to mature over a number of years. When calculating ratios such as interest cover, it is important to review the notes to the accounts to find out if any interest has been capitalized. If it has you should include the amount with the interest reported in the profit and loss account when calculating interest cover.

Accounting policies

The above discussion on interest payments illustrates why it is important to examine the notes on accounting policies when analysing the financial statements of a UK company. There are several reasons for this.

If you are comparing the results of one company with those of another in the same type of business, you will need to establish the effect of any differences in accounting policy between the two companies. A review of the accounting policy note might also indicate where changes to accounting estimates have been made. The circumstances in which a company can change its accounting policy are restricted but there is nothing to prevent it from changing estimates on things such as asset lives. This matter is discussed more fully in Chapter 19 but even at this stage you will be able to appreciate that a change in assets' lives can have a substantial impact on the accounts being reviewed.

Information retrieval services

There are a number of proprietary information retrieval services that produce financial analysis data on public companies. Some include information on market sectors and credit ratings for individual companies. These services are usually available at university libraries. Some services are provided on line and some are provided on a CD-ROM.

When you access these services you will find that a lot of the financial information on each company is based on the ratios discussed in this chapter. You must, however, be careful over how you use these ratios. One of the popular services in UK universities is called FAME (Financial Analysis Made Easy). If you use this service, you will find that the basis used for some of the ratios is different from those in this chapter. You can obtain information on the bases used by FAME from its Help menu.

Constructing a report

Some words of warning are necessary here; for example:

- Do not draw any conclusions until you have calculated all ratios and trends that you consider appropriate.
- Set out the entire set of ratios in a schedule and include a schedule of industry averages, if this is available, for comparison purposes.
- Stand back and look at your schedule to see if there is any overall picture.
- Do not assume the worst. For example, an increase in the debtors collection period might have been a deliberate strategy to increase sales (budgeted information is useful here but is not always available).
- Do not talk about liquidity problems simply because current ratios are falling; have a look at the cash flow statement and things like loan repayment commitments.
- Remember that ratios are not prescriptive, they simply provide more information than is available by looking at figures in isolation.
- Give some thought to, and include some comment on, the limitations of ratio analysis when constructing the report. These limitations are just as important as the ratios themselves.
- Keep in mind the limitations of published financial reports, such as measurements being based on accounting estimates and accounting policies.
- Give the formulae for calculating your ratios. It is almost meaningless to state that the Return on Capital Employed is 20% without defining what you mean by return and what you mean by capital.
- Tailor your report to the perspective of the person for whom it is being prepared. You might, for example, be analysing the accounts for an investor or prospective investor, management, a lending institution, or a competitor. Each of these will require emphasis on the specific areas which are of interest to the person concerned.
- The normal rules on good report writing (such as an index, terms of reference,

summary or conclusions, and so on) should be applied. Reports on financial statement analysis are usually more effective if all calculations, graphs and tables are included in an appendix. But there is no hard and fast rule on this and it can be quite effective if the main body of the text is occasionally punctuated by a visual aid such as a graph.

Summary

The main learning points in this chapter can be summarized as follows:
- conclusions regarding an entity's performance cannot be made from a single accounting number isolated from the factors to which it is related
- individual accounting numbers are absolute; accounting ratios are relative
- accounting ratios are measurements that express a relationship between two accounting numbers; the relationship can be expressed in a variety of ways
- the additional information produced by an accounting ratio is useful only if it can be compared to something such as the same ratio in previous years or the same ratio in another firm carrying on a similar type of business
- caution is needed when interpreting accounting ratios; distortions can arise through various factors such as price changes, accounting policies, and the different bases used for calculating a particular ratio
- the primary ratio can be measured in several ways; they all attempt to relate profits earned to the capital employed, and express this relationship as a percentage
- a fairly common basis for the primary ratio is to relate operating profit to total assets less current liabilities (sometimes called total capital)
- the primary ratio can be sub-divided into secondary ratios, profitability ratios and asset turnover ratios
- the secondary ratios can be reconciled to the primary ratio and they provide more information to explain changes in the primary ratio
- asset turnover ratios for stocks, debtors and creditors are more meaningful if they are expressed as a time period
- ratios provide more information than the raw figures but they do not provide answers – they simply raise questions
- solvency ratios are difficult to interpret and it is often more informative to review the cash flow statement rather than draw conclusions from these ratios
- capital based gearing ratios express the relationship between debt and equity capital; the financial risk in an investment is related to the level of capital gearing
- the gearing effect is best seen by measuring income based gearing ratios such as the DOG and DFG
- risk is related to the range of possible outcomes
- equity investors pay particular attention to earnings based ratios such as EPS and the P/E ratios
- the dividend yield ratio gives an indication of the rate of return expected by shareholders on their investment
- the interest cover ratio indicates the ability of a company to meet interest payments out of its operating profit and investment income
- the profit (or loss) from discontinued activities should be removed from

the operating profit figure when measuring ROCE since the net assets that created that profit (or loss) are not included in the closing balance sheet

- useful information can be obtained by measuring the relationship between cash flow items and items in the profit and loss account
- it is important to examine the notes to published financial statements to ascertain various things such as interest capitalized and any changes to accounting policy or accounting estimates
- the accounting policies note is useful when comparing the results of two similar companies that have used different accounting policies
- there are a number of rules to follow when writing financial analysis reports

Activity 1
The rate of return on the original capital invested is 5%. In this case you can probably see the percentage without making any kind of calculation. If you are not familiar with the mathematics involved, there is an explanation later in the text.

Activity 2
The rate of return that could be obtained on investments of similar risk.

Activity 3
You could have written: (1) 6 times (the number of times the denominator goes into the numerator), (2) 6 : 1 (the ratio of £12,000 to £2,000), or (3) 600%.

Activity 4
You might have noticed that debtors represent 30 days' sales.

Activity 5
Part of the increase might be the result of price increases in the goods or services sold. If the rate of price increases affecting these products is 4% then there has probably been no increase in the volume of trade – the entire increase can be related to price increases.

Activity 6
You should have found that the rate of return for Company A is 40% and for Company B it is 4%. This suggests that Company A was much more profitable than Company B, yet the difference stems from nothing more than the different ages of each company's assets. In all other respects the two companies have identical operating results, as shown by profit before depreciation. (You should note that if the rate of price increases in fixed assets had been 10% for each year over the past 10 years, then an asset that cost £30,000 ten years ago would cost £77,812 at today's prices.)

Activity 7
There are several aspects that call for caution, such as:
1. Have you calculated the ratio on the same basis as those used for the industry average?
2. Is the comparison affected by the use of different accounting policies?
3. In what way does inflation affect the comparison?

Activity 8
1995: 33,000/112,000 = 29.5%.
1996: 34,835/145,000 = 24%.

Activity 9
You were expected to work out that the primary ratio is the product of the two secondary ratios. You can see this more clearly if you realize that sales in each of the secondary ratios can be cancelled against each other.

Activity 10
Profit margin:
1995: 33,000/400,000 = 8.25%.
1996: 34,835/580,000 = 6%.
Asset turnover:
1995: 400,000/112,000 = 3.57 times.
1996: 580,000/145,000 = 4 times.

Activity 11

1995: 8.25% × 3.57 = 29.5% (with rounding).
1996: 6% × 4 = 24%.

Activity 12

	1995	1996
Gross profit	25.00%	22%
Operating expenses to sales	16.75%	16%
Operating profit	8.25%	6%

Activity 13

1. No. The gross profit percentage is a relative measure.
2. Yes, assuming no corresponding reduction in purchase costs.
3. No. Administration costs are not included in the cost of sales.
4. Yes, assuming the increase is not passed on by increasing sales prices.

Activity 14

Stock holding period:
1995: 25,000/300,000 × 365 = 30.4 days.
1996: 56,550/452,400 × 365 = 45.6 days.
Debtors collection period:
1995: 37,260/400,000 × 365 = 34 days.
1996: 66,740/580,000 × 365 = 42 days.
Creditors payment period:
1995: 21,370/302,000 × 365 = 26 days.
1996: 55,775/483,950 × 365 = 42 days.
Note that purchases can be found by adding the stock increase to cost of sales, as discussed in Chapter 11 on the cash flow statement.

Activity 15

It could be (as with a reduction in sales prices) a strategy to increase trade by offering more generous credit terms.

Activity 16

Appendix 2 is ICI.
Appendix 3 is Tesco.

Activity 17

Investment B.

Activity 18

You should have found that profit available for equity has fallen by 75%.

Activity 19

£2,400/£1,200 = 2 times.

Activity 20

The fall is £1,000/£8,000 = 12.5%.
Operating profit would be expected to fall by 2 × 12.5% = 25%.
Operating profit has fallen by £300/£1,200 = 25%.

Activity 21

£1,200/£400 = 3 times.

Activity 22

14 × £0.28 = £3.92.

Activity 23

50/400 = 12.5%.

Case study for self-assessment

A suggested report for this case study is given at the end of the book.

Case study – Overload Ltd

The share capital of Overload Ltd is owned entirely by two brothers who are also the directors. You have been approached by a Mrs Firty who is interested in acquiring the company and intends to make an offer to the two brothers to acquire their shares.

You have no access to information on Overload Ltd other than the financial statements which Mrs Firty has obtained and given to you for the purposes of this case study (the financial statements are those used throughout the chapter). You may make any reasonable assumptions considered appropriate.

Mrs Firty has shown the financial statements to a friend, who has told her that the balance sheet shows the business is worth £145,000, according to the latest figures, but that Mrs Firty might be able to buy the company for less than this since it is running short of cash and therefore cannot have been very profitable during 1996.

Mrs Firty has given you a schedule of accounting ratios for firms operating as merchants in the same line of business as Overload Ltd. She had obtained this information from a cousin who works for the trade association; details are set out below.

Mrs Firty knows very little about accounting and does not really understand the significance of some of the ratios. You have had a short meeting with her during which you explained the key points in the financial statements and gave her a brief idea of how accounting ratios are used. She has now asked you to analyse the financial statements and give her a report on the company's financial affairs so that she can begin negotiations with the directors.

You are required to write the report. Your report must include a cash flow statement, and include references to this where appropriate.

Schedule of ratios obtained from the trade association:

Return on capital	32%
Asset turnover	4 times
Gross profit	24%
Net profit	8%
Stock turnover ratio	7.3 times
Debt collection period	36 days
Creditors payment period	30 days
Current ratio	2.8:1
Gearing	35%

The average rate of inflation for the industry's products during 1996 was 6%.

Question for self-assessment

The answer to this self-assessment question is given at the end of the book.

13.1 Jane Winters is currently considering which of two companies she should choose for the investment of a legacy from her late father's estate. The choice lies between purchasing all the share capital of A Limited and purchasing 40% of the share capital of B Limited. Whilst neither A Limited nor B Limited has paid any dividends in recent years, it is anticipated that the companies will resume dividends in the next year or two.

The summarized final accounts of the companies for their last completed financial year are as follows:

Trading and profit and loss accounts

	A Limited			B Limited	
£	£		£	£	
	160,000	Sales		240,000	
		Cost of sales:			
10,000		Opening stock	70,000		
140,000		Purchases	160,000		
150,000			230,000		
30,000		Closing stock	50,000		
	120,000			180,000	
	40,000	Gross profit		60,000	
		Less:			
10,000		Establishment expenses	14,000		
12,000		Administrative expenses	18,000		
6,000		Sales and distribution expenses	9,500		
3,000		Financial expenses	500		
	31,000			42,000	
	9,000	Net profit		18,000	

Balance sheets

	A Limited			B Limited	
£	£		£	£	
	80,000	Fixed assests:		180,000	
		Current assets			
30,000		Stock	50,000		
6,000		Debtors	20,000		
4,000		Balance at bank	10,000		
40,000			80,000		
		Creditors : Amounts falling			
		due within one year			
10,000		Trade creditors	20,000		
	30,000			60,000	
	110,000			240,000	
		Creditors: Amounts falling			
		due after more than one year			
	30,000	10% Loan Stock		5,000	
	80,000			235,000	
		Represented by:			
	60,000	Ordinary share capital		160,000	
	20,000	Retained earnings		75,000	
	80,000			235,000	

Required:
(a) Prepare a schedule of appropriate accounting ratios or financial ratios utilizing the information given on the two companies, A Limited and B Limited, to permit a comparison to be made between these companies in each of the following areas: Profitability, Effective use of resources, Short-term solvency, Long-term solvency. Answers should include 8 ratios or other statistics, each one of which should be stated at 2 decimal places. Taxation is to be ignored.
(b) Prepare a report to Jane Winters drawing attention to the comparative strengths and weaknesses of each of the companies A Limited and B Limited as revealed in the answer to (a) above and making reference to other significant matters which should

be borne in mind by Jane Winters when making her investment decision. Note: Assume that the report is from a financial adviser.

(AAT Intermediate, Jun 92)

Question without answer

The answers to these questions are published separately in the *Teacher's Manual*.

13.2 Thornville Ltd.

Guidance notes: Requests to make adjustments to existing figures (as required by part (i) of the question) are usually related to ensuring that the accounting policies for all years are on the same basis, and to give effect to any accounting errors. In the case of private companies (as in the question) you might also consider that some adjustment should be made for directors' remuneration in order to ensure that each year's results are on a comparable basis.

Thornville Ltd is a company, formed in 1979, which supplies computer software to businesses located in the west of England and south Wales. The company is run by Peter and John Sutton, who, together with members of their family, have owned the entire share capital, which amounts to £50,000 (100,000 shares with a nominal value of 50p each), since incorporation.

Peter and John visited your bank yesterday to request an increase in the overdraft facility, which currently stands at £90,000. They point to the substantial annual increase in both turnover and profit, in most years, as evidence of the continuing viability of their company. The following information is taken from the management accounts for the last five years:

Profit and Loss Account, year to 31 March £000

	1987	1988	1989	1990	1991
Turnover	2,460	2,706	2,977	3,274	3,601
Gross profit	775	852	893	949	1,008
Trading overheads:					
Directors remuneration	100	100	86	86	86
Wages and salaries	368	412	421	461	470
Depreciation	75	70	65	40	35
Interest charges	12	12	12	16	21
Other overheads	180	204	237	286	299
Operating profit	40	54	72	60	97
Corporation tax	10	13	18	20	29
Profit after tax	30	41	54	40	68

Figures for shareholders' equity, long-term liabilities (a 12% debenture repayable 1994), the bank balance (overdraft) and a price index constructed internally to measure the average price of goods sold are as follows:

31 March	Shareholders equity £000	12% Debenture £000	Bank balance (overdraft) £000	Price index for goods sold
1986	150	100	42	100
1987	180	100	45	104
1988	221	100	37	108
1989	275	100	44	115
1990	255	100	(30)	128
1991	323	100	(60)	144

The following additional information, relating to the figures stated in the above accounts, came to light during discussions with Peter and John Sutton:

(i) The directors explain that apparent performance suffered during 1989/90 due to the omission, from stock at 31 March 1990, of certain items, worth £21,000, located in the loading bay.

(ii) The depreciation charge includes £20,000 in respect of goodwill amortized for each of the years to 31 March 1989. In 1989/90 the company changed its accounting policy and instead wrote off the remaining balance of £60,000 against reserves.

Required:

A full appraisal of the financial information provided by the directors of Thornville Ltd. You should include in your appraisal:

(i) A clear indication of any adjustments necessary to enable valid comparisons to be made, year by year, between the figures for gross profit, net profit and shareholders' equity.

(ii) The following accounting ratios based on the figures you have revised under (i) above:

- gross profit percentage
- net profit percentage (pre-tax)
- return on year-end equity (pre-tax)
- interest cover
- total debt:equity ratio

(iii) Any other calculations you consider appropriate.

Notes:

(i) Ignore Advance Corporation Tax.

(ii) Assume none of the adjustments affects the corporation tax charge for the year.

(CIB Associateship, May 91)

13.3 You are considering the purchase of a small business, JK, and have managed to obtain a copy of its accounts for the last complete accounting year to 30 September 19X3. These appear as follows:

Trading and profit and loss account for the year to 30 September 19X3

	£	£
Sales		385,200
Less: Cost of goods sold:		
Opening stocks	93,250	
Purchases	174,340	
less Closing stocks	(84,630)	
		182,960
Gross profit		202,240
Less: Expenses:		
Selling and delivery costs	83,500	
Administration costs	51,420	
Depreciation	36,760	
		171,680
Net profit		30,560

Balance sheet at 30 September 19X3

	£	£
Fixed assets		
Assets at cost	235,070	
Less: Depreciation to date	(88,030)	
		147,040
Current assets		
Stocks	84,630	
Debtors and prepayments	36,825	
Bank and cash	9,120	
	130,575	
Less: Current liabilities		
Creditors and accurals	(62,385)	
		68,190
		215,230
Financed by		
Capital at 1 October 19X2		197,075
Net profit for the year		30,560
Proprietor's drawings		(12,405)
		215,230

You discover that JK has adopted the following treatment of certain items in the accounts:
1. In previous years, depreciation has been provided on the straight line basis over 10 years, but in the year shown above the reducing basis has been used, at a rate of 20% per annum, as there was sufficient profit to absorb a high charge this year.
2. The debtors figure includes several debts which have been outstanding for some time, despite repeated reminders to the customers concerned.
3. No allowance has been made in the account for expenses incurred for which invoices have not been received at the year end.

Required:
(a) Calculate the following accounting ratios from the accounts as presented above:
   (i) net profit percentage
   (ii) return on capital employed
   (iii) current ratio
   (iv) quick (acid test) ratio
(b) State the fundamental accounting concept which governs each of these three treatments:
   (i) depreciation of fixed assets
   (ii) outstanding debtors
   (iii) expenses incurred not yet invoiced
   and discuss the effects which each treatment will have on the ratios you have calculated.
(CIMA Specimen paper, 94)

13.4 You are given the following information about Firm X, a private company and a wholesaler:

	Firm X 1994	Firm X 1995	Industry Average 1995
Current ratio	1.7	1.5	1.3
Acid test ratio	0.9	0.9	0.9
ROCE (before taxation)	18%	18%	18%
ROOE (before taxation)	20%	22%	15%
Gearing (debt over equity)	50%	60%	30%
Debtors age	25 days	35 days	30 days
Creditors age	40 days	60 days	40 days
Stock age	70 days	65 days	70 days
Gross profit %	27%	25%	23%
Net profit %	11%	12%	10%

[ROCE = Return on capital employed]
[ROOE = Return on owner's equity]

Required:
Write a report to the shareholders of Firm X which highlights important points revealed or suggested by these figures relating to apparent management policies in the year 1995 and to possible future implications. You may assume that there has been no inflation over the relevant periods.

(ACCA, Jun 96)

Overload Ltd

Profit and loss accounts year ending	31 Dec 1995	31 Dec 1996
Turnover	400,000	580,000
Cost of sales	300,000	452,400
Gross profit	100,000	127,600
Operating costs	67,000	92,765
Operating profit	33,000	34,835
Interest paid and similar charges	5,000	5,835
Profit before tax	28,000	29,000
Taxation	4,200	4,350
Profit after tax	23,800	24,650
Dividends	nil	nil
Retained profit	23,800	24,650

Balance sheets at	31 Dec 1995	31 Dec 1996
Fixed assets	69,310	81,335
Current assets:		
Stock	25,000	56,550
Debtors	37,260	66,740
Bank	6,000	500
	68,260	123,790
Creditors due within one year		
Creditors	21,370	55,775
Taxation	4,200	4,350
	25,570	60,125
Net current assets	42,690	63,665
Total assets less current liabilities	112,000	145,000
Creditors falling due after one year		
10% Debenture 1999	50,000	58,350
	62,000	86,650
Capital and reserves		
Ordinary shares of £1 each	10,000	10,000
Profit and loss account	52,000	76,650
	62,000	86,650

Stock in the balance sheet at 31 December 1994 was £23,000. You will need this figure to calculate cost of purchases in 1995. Although the opening stock for the previous year is not normally disclosed as a specific item in published financial statements, the amount can usually be determined from the cash flow reconciliation statement. Depreciation charged during 1996 was £7,000 and there were no sales of fixed assets during that year.

Balance sheets at 31 December

	Notes	Group 1992 £m	Group 1991 £m	Company 1992 £m	Company 1991 £m
ASSETS EMPLOYED					
Fixed assets					
Tangible assets	12	**5,634**	5,128	**353**	1,079
Investments:					
Subsidiary undertakings	13			**5,800**	4,347
Participating interests	14	**455**	396	**255**	222
		6,089	5,524	**6,408**	5,648
Current assets					
Stocks	15	**2,273**	2,025	**417**	379
Debtors	16	**3,033**	2,716	**4,641**	815
Investments and short-term deposits	17	**507**	608	**–**	–
Cash	17	**220**	197	**12**	8
		6,033	5,546	**5,070**	1,202
Total assets		**12,122**	11,070	**11,478**	6,850
Creditors due within one year					
Short-term borrowings	18	**(671)**	(296)	**(17)**	(10)
Current instalments of loans	20	**(282)**	(220)	**(75)**	(156)
Other creditors	19	**(3,424)**	(2,894)	**(6,031)**	(1,281)
		(4,377)	(3,410)	**(6,123)**	(1,447)
Net current assets (liabilities)		**1,656**	2,136	**(1,053)**	(245)
Total assets less current liabilities		**7,745**	7,660	**5,355**	5,403
FINANCED BY					
Creditors due after more than one year					
Loans	20	**1,984**	1,763	**325**	400
Other creditors	19	**168**	159	**1,207**	1,053
		2,152	1,922	**1,532**	1,453
Provisions for liabilities and charges	21	**956**	606	**35**	14
Deferred income: Grants not yet credited to profit		**49**	52	**4**	5
Minority interests		**302**	288		
Capital and reserves attributable to parent company					
Called up share capital	22	**714**	711	**714**	711
Reserves					
Share premium account		**502**	469	**502**	469
Revaluation reserve		**63**	56	**–**	–
Other reserves		**546**	399	**541**	436
Profit and loss account		**2,428**	3,131	**2,027**	2,315
Associated undertakings' reserves		**33**	26		
Total reserves	23	**3,572**	4,081	**3,070**	3,220
Total capital and reserves attributable to parent company	24	**4,286**	4,792	**3,784**	3,931
		7,745	7,660	**5,355**	5,403

Appendix 3

Balance sheets at 27 February 1993

	Notes	Group 1993 £m	Group 1992 £m	Company 1993 £m	Company 1992 £m
Fixed assets					
Tangible assets	8	3,993.7	3,552.0	–	–
Investments:	9	5.5	–	20.4	15.0
		3,999.2	3,552.0	20.4	15.0
Debtors					
Amounts falling due after more than one year	10	2.5	3.8	2,050.0	800.0
Current assets					
Stocks (goods for resale)		240.0	221.7	–	–
Debtors	10	45.8	35.8	139.4	1,295.1
Money market investment and deposits	11	239.6	300.7	228.1	289.8
Cash at bank and in hand		–	38.3	–	–
		525.4	596.5	367.5	1,584.9
Creditors					
Amounts falling due within one year	12	1,055.7	1,003.5	371.7	381.5
Net current(liabilities)/assets		(530.3)	(407.0)	(4.2)	1,203.4
Total assets less current liabilities		3,471.4	3,148.8	2,066.2	2,018.4
Creditors					
Amounts falling due after more than one year	13	639.7	648.2	527.5	519.0
Provisions for liabilities and charges	16	78.8	53.6	3.6	1.2
		2,752.9	2,447.0	1,535.1	1,498.2
Capital and reserves					
Called up share capital	18	97.8	97.0	97.8	97.0
Share premium account	20	924.3	898.3	924.3	898.3
Other reserves	20	39.6	39.6	–	–
Profit and loss account	20	1,691.2	1,412.1	513.0	502.9
		2,752.9	2,447.0	1,535.1	1,498.2

14 ▷ Partnerships: Introduction

Objectives

After you have completed this chapter, you should be able to:
- write up the accounting records of a business owned by a partnership
- prepare the financial statements of a partnership

Introduction

The type of partnership that we find today evolved from business practices that started to become popular during the eighteenth century. As the industrial revolution gathered momentum, the size of business units began to increase and partnerships were seen as a logical way of extending the operations of a sole trader. But in 1855 it became legal to register limited liability companies, and because these offered entrepreneurs a type of organization that was more suitable for large-scale operations, partnerships became less common. Today, partnerships are found in various small-scale enterprises, farming, merchant banking, and in professions such as law, accountancy, dentistry and medical practice.

It is quite likely that the development of partnerships gave an impetus to the art of double-entry book-keeping and accounting. The need to determine each partner's share of the profits, and share of the equity, at regular intervals required the firm to set up a reliable system for recording its transactions.

As was mentioned in Chapter 10, the majority of accounting procedures are the same for all entities, irrespective of ownership. In many respects the accounts of a partnership are similar to those of a sole trader; there are no statutory regulations affecting their form and content. The main difference relates to the division of profit after it has been determined, and the need to keep a record of each partner's interest in the equity of the firm.

14.1 Legal background

You can get some idea of how often the legal system has thought it necessary to regulate the affairs of partnerships by looking at the date of the current Partnership Act; it was enacted more than 100 years ago and is known as the Partnership Act 1890.

Individual partners will be sharing in the fortunes (and disasters) of a jointly owned firm, but legislation offers them very little protection in terms of their individual interests. In the case of companies, volumes of legislation exist to protect the interests of shareholders. Think about why legislation has played such a small part in regulating the affairs of a partnership and make a note here of any ideas that occur to you.

There are some provisions in the Partnership Act 1890 regarding the rights of individual partners but these are 'fall-back' provisions and can only be invoked where the partners have not made their own private regulations on the points concerned.

The Partnership Act 1890 defines a partnership as: 'the relationship which subsists between persons carrying on business in common with a view of profit'. In practice it is sometimes difficult to establish whether or not there is a partnership. For example, in the case of a small business run by husband and wife it is not always easy to determine whether one is an employee of the other, or whether there is a partnership. The principal tests of whether a partnership exists are as follows:

- there must be a business (or profession) which is carried on with a view of profit
- the business (or profession) must be carried on for the mutual benefit of all partners
- each partner has authority to enter into contracts on behalf of the firm and therefore bind the other partners in respect of these contracts
- there is an arrangement to share the profits and losses.

Under English law the partnership is not a separate legal entity (although it is in Scotland). All partners are liable for the firm's debts, and all property of the firm is owned jointly by the partners. If the partnership assets are insufficient to meet its debts, the creditors are entitled to seek payment out of the private assets of individual partners.

The taxation of the firm's profits is different from either a sole trader or a company. Tax is assessed on the firm but the total amount of tax takes account of each partner's share of profits, personal reliefs, and any income from sources external to the partnership. The tax assessment shows how the total liability is divided among the partners. If this tax is paid by the firm (rather than by the individual partners) the firm is acting as a collecting agent for the Inland Revenue. Consequently, each partner's share of the liability paid by the firm is treated as drawings. Provisions for taxation are not normally made in partnership accounts.

14.2 Partnership agreements

It is not legally necessary for a partnership to have any written agreement setting out the rights of individual partners. A partnership can exist with any of the following:

- an express agreement (usually in a written document called a partnership agreement)
- an implied agreement (implied from conduct)
- no agreement, either express or implied.

It is advisable for a partnership to have a written agreement in order to avoid some of the acrimony that might otherwise arise. Partners are not likely to have contributed to the capital in equal shares, and they will not all have equal responsibilities in the day-to-day affairs of the business. Some kind of formula has to be agreed upon whereby these differences of contribution to the firm's fortunes can be compensated.

Activity 2

See if you can think of ways in which differences in contribution of capital, and differences in contribution of services, can be compensated. This is not such a difficult problem when you think about the way people are normally rewarded for investing money in an entity, or for providing their services.

1. Differences in contribution of capital:

2. Differences in contribution of services:

There are some provisions in Section 24 of the Partnership Act 1890 that must be applied if there is no written or implied agreement on certain matters. The most important provisions as far as accounting is concerned are as follows:

(a) profits and losses are to be shared equally
(b) capital must be contributed equally
(c) all partners may take part in the management of the firm but are not entitled to any salary for their services
(d) partners are not entitled to interest on their capital
(e) any partner who advances money to the partnership in excess of the amount of agreed capital is entitled to interest at the rate of 5% per annum on the excess.

Activity 3

A typical partnership agreement for a small firm will contain something like 20 to 25 clauses but they are not all related to accounting matters (some are concerned with partnership management). Think about the type of regulations you would expect to see in a partnership agreement, and make a note here of any that are likely to have an impact on the financial statements. If you think of six points you have done quite well.

Items 1 to 6 in the Key are the most important as far as this particular chapter is concerned.

14.3 Appropriation of profit

The net profit of a partnership is determined in exactly the same way as that of a sole trader. The first accounting problem that we have to address is the division of net profit among the partners, and the way in which each partner's share of profit is recorded in the books.

Some of the terms used earlier in this chapter to describe the way partners are compensated for their different contributions are a little misleading. A partnership salary is not a salary in the usual sense of the word, it is a device for dividing up (appropriating) profits. Partners do not pay PAYE on partnership salaries; any salary to which a partner is entitled will form a part of that partner's share of profits for tax purposes. It is quite likely that a partner will be entitled to both a salary and a share of any profits remaining after deducting the partnership salaries.

The same thing applies to interest on capital. This is not interest in the usual sense of the word; it is a way of appropriating some of the profit to partners before the balance of profits is divided.

We will see how it all works in terms of double-entry in a moment but it is important to recognize three things from the outset:

1. Partnership salaries and interest on capital are appropriations of profit, they are not expenses to be charged in arriving at net profit.
2. Any profits remaining after making appropriations for salaries and interest are divided according to the agreed profit sharing ratio.
3. Any actual payments made to the partners (however described) must be treated as drawings and are not dealt with as appropriations.

The first procedure is to draw up an appropriation account. This is simply a continuation of the profit and loss account after determining net profit. Try sorting this out by working through the following activity. It does not matter if you make a mess of this first attempt; you will soon become accustomed to the way these appropriation accounts are usually presented.

Activity 4

Bodgit and Leggit are partners running a small business in the building trade. The profit and loss account for year ending 31 December 1996 shows a net profit of £24,000. Bodgit has introduced capital of £10,000, and Leggit £4,000.

The partnership agreement provides for interest on capital at the rate of 10%. In order to recognize that Leggit does most of the professional work, the partnership agreement entitles him to a salary of £12,000 per annum; Bodgit's salary is nil. The balance of profits is to be shared equally. Bodgit has withdrawn £6,000 during the year and Leggit £13,000. Demonstrate how the net profit of £24,000 will be appropriated.

If the aggregate amount for partnership salaries and interest on capital is greater than the net profit, the balance is treated as a 'notional loss' which must be divided in the same ratio as for sharing profits.

Activity 5

All details are the same as Activity 4 except that the net profits for the year were £12,000. Set out the appropriation account.

In Activities 4 and 5, the figures have been presented in the form of a statement. In the books, the various amounts will have to be dealt with by double-entry. In order to keep a record of each partner's share in the equity of the firm, it is normal to keep two accounts for each partner, namely:

1. A partner's capital account, to record the amount(s) of capital introduced by each partner.
2. A partner's current account, to record the balance of retained profit attributable to each partner.

You will notice that this is similar to the way we have been dealing with a sole trader's equity interest, except that in the case of a partnership there is more than one proprietor. The idea of keeping retained profits separate from capital introduced is more firmly established in the case of partnerships, although you might sometimes come across an exam question where everything has been recorded on a single capital account for each partner.

The term **current account** is used to indicate that the account is used to record current dealings between the partner and the firm. In straightforward cases, the balance on the current account is simply the result of credits for a share of profits and debits for drawings. If the account is in credit, the balance could (subject to any restraints in the partnership agreement) be withdrawn by the partner concerned.

In the ledger there will be a separate current account for each partner. In exams you are usually dealing with small partnerships with only two or three partners. In these cases you are often expected to produce the current accounts in columnar form, as if there were only one ledger account but with separate columns (on both sides of the account) for each partner. You will be using this kind of account in the next activity.

The double-entry for each item of appropriation (salary, interest, and share of balance) is: debit profit and loss appropriation account; credit the respective partner's current account. Drawings will probably have been accumulated throughout the year on a separate drawings account for each partner. At the end of the year, the total drawings for each partner will be transferred to that partner's current account by a double-entry: credit drawings; debit current account.

Activity 6

Assume that the opening balances on the current accounts for Bodgit and Leggit were as follows:

Bodgit £1,500 (credit)
Leggit   200 (credit)

Write up their current accounts for the year, based on the details used in Activity 4. Use the proforma account set out below.

Partners' current accounts

	Bodgit	Leggit		Bodgit	Leggit

The way in which figures are presented to the partners in the financial statements will vary. The profit and loss appropriation account will be presented in a manner similar to that used for Activities 4 and 5. Sometimes the details for the current accounts are presented in a separate statement, in which case it is only necessary to show the final balance in the balance sheet. In other cases, details of the current account are set out on the face of the balance sheet. If the second of these two approaches is used, the equity side of Bodgit and Leggit's balance sheet will be as follows:

	Bodgit	Leggit	
Capital introduced	10,000	4,000	14,000
Current accounts:			
Balance brought forward	1,500	200	
Share of profits:			
Salary	–	12,000	
Interest on capital	1,000	400	
Share of balance	5,300	5,300	
	7,800	17,900	
Drawings	(6,000)	(13,000)	
Balance carried forward	1,800	4,900	6,700
			20,700

14.4 Interest on loans and interest on drawings

If a partner introduces cash in excess of the agreed capital contribution, the excess should be treated as a loan to the partnership. A rate of interest is normally agreed on these loans, although if no rate is agreed the partner will be entitled to interest at 5% under the Partnership Act 1890.

These advances are credited to a separate loan account in the partner's name. The interest paid must be treated as an expense in arriving at net profit; it is not an appropriation. If the interest has not been paid, it must be accrued and should either be shown as a creditor (in the same way as any other accrual) or added to the partner's current account.

Practices regarding presentation of a partner's loan account in the balance sheet vary. Most accountants would include it in the capital and reserves (equity) side of the balance sheet. Some accountants argue that because loans must be paid off in priority to capital, partners' loan accounts should be shown as deductions on the net asset side of the balance sheet. This is a dubious argument because if the firm became insolvent partners' loans would not be settled until all external creditors had been paid. In this respect, partners' loans are in the nature of equity. On balance it is preferable to include them on the capital side of the balance sheet since this will allow each partner to see their total interest in the firm.

Interest on drawings is a very old idea and was meant to give recognition to the fact that some partners might be making withdrawals at a higher rate than others. Partners are charged (through their current accounts) with an agreed rate of interest on their drawings, and the total amount of this interest is credited to the profit and loss appropriation account, thus augmenting the amount of profit available for appropriation.

The idea is sound enough in theory but it tends to have very little practical effect. The partners will be sharing in the augmented profits created by this interest, and consequently the net effect on their current accounts is usually so small that it is not worth all the effort of making the adjustment. A more modern approach is to limit the rate of drawings through the partnership agreement.

But interest on drawings does still crop up in examination questions. In these cases, the basis for the calculation will be given and it is only a matter of debiting current accounts and crediting the profit and loss appropriation account with the amount calculated. Where the appropriation account is presented as a statement, the total interest on drawings can be added to the net profit prior to making the appropriations.

14.5 Practice on a simple example

In order to conclude this study you should practise preparing a complete set of financial statements for a partnership. In partnership questions there will be all the usual information from which a detailed set of financial statements can be prepared. In the following activity, most of this detail has been abbreviated so as to allow you to concentrate on the partnership aspects. (In exams, you will also find that questions on partnerships are used to test your skills in other areas, such as error correction.)

Activity 7

Collins and Mitchell are in partnership as retailers. The following is the trial balance in their books after making most of the entries for year ended 31 December 1996.

	Debit	Credit
Sales		500,000
Cost of sales	350,000	
Operating expenses	100,000	
Capital accounts:		
Collins		10,000
Mitchell		6,000
Current accounts:		
Collins	500	
Mitchell		1,000
Loan account – Collins		4,000
Drawings:		
Collins	15,000	
Mitchell	12,000	
Fixed assets (at net book value)	38,000	
Stock at 31 December 1996	2,000	
Debtors and creditors	5,000	3,000
Bank balance	1,500	
	524,000	524,000

The partnership agreement provides for the following:

(a) interest on loans in excess of capital 12%
(b) interest on capital 10%
(c) partnership salaries – Collins £10,000, Mitchell £12,000
(d) balance of profits – Collins two-thirds Mitchell one-third.

The amounts for loan and capital shown in the trial balance have been brought forward from the previous year. No interest has been paid on the loan during the year, and no adjustment in respect of this interest has been made in the books.

Prepare financial statements for the partnership on your own paper. Include details of current accounts on the face of the balance sheet.

Summary

The main learning points in this chapter are as follows:

- the net profit of a partnership is determined in the same way as for a sole trader
- the net profit is divided among the partners in accordance with any agreement made
- if there is no partnership agreement (implied or written) or the agreement fails to deal with certain points, the provisions of the Partnership Act 1890 will apply
- appropriations of profit can consist of partnership salaries and interest on capital, with the balance being shared in some agreed ratio
- the appropriations are presented in a continuation statement following on from where the net profit has been determined
- permanent capitals are normally kept separate from current accounts
- current accounts keep a running account for each partner, the balance being derived from each partner's share of profits less drawings
- advances to the partnership in excess of agreed capitals carry interest (at 5% under the Partnership Act 1890), which is treated as an expense
- sometimes interest on drawings is charged to partners and credited to the appropriation account

Activity 1
Partners will be running the business as well as owning it, and their individual rights can easily be determined by private agreement among themselves.

Activity 2
1. Differences in capital; by crediting partners with interest on capital.
2. Differences in services; by providing partnership salaries.

Activity 3
You may have thought of: 1. Profit sharing basis. 2. Partners' salaries. 3. Amount of capital. 4. Rate of interest (if any) on capital. 5. Rate of interest on advances in excess of agreed capital. 6. Rate of drawings. 7. Limitations on partners' authority to enter into obligations for the firm. 8. Audit of the accounts (there is no statutory requirement to have the accounts audited). 9. Provisions regarding the admission of new partners, and arrangements on death or retirement of a partner.

Activity 4
The appropriation account can be presented as follows:

Net profit			24,000
Partnership salaries:	Bodgit	Nil	
	Leggit	12,000	
Interest on capital:	Bodgit	1,000	
	Leggit	400	
			13,400
Balance of profits			10,600
Share of balance:	Bodgit (one-half)	5,300	
	Leggit (one-half)	5,300	
			10,600

Activity 5

Net profit			12,000
Partnership salaries:	Bodgit	Nil	
	Leggit	12,000	
Interest on capital:	Bodgit	1,000	
	Leggit	400	
			13,400
Notional loss			(1,400)
Share of loss:	Bodgit (one-half)	(700)	
	Leggit (one-half)	(700)	
			(1,400)

Activity 6

Partners' current accounts

	Bodgit	Leggit		Bodgit	Leggit
Drawings	6,000	13,000	Balances b/d	1,500	200
Balances c/d	1,800	4,900	P & L appropriation a/c:		
			Interest on capital	1,000	400
			Salary	–	12,000
			Share of balance	5,300	5,300
	7,800	17,900		7,800	17,900
			Balances b/d	1,800	4,900

Activity 7

Profit and loss account, year ended 31 December 1996

Sales		500,000
Cost of sales		350,000
Gross profit		150,000
Operating expenses	100,000	
Interest on loan	480	
		100,480
Net profit		49,520
Partnership salaries:		
Collins	10,000	
Mitchell	12,000	
Interest on capital:		
Collins	1,000	
Mitchell	600	
		23,600
Balance of profits		25,920
Shared:		
Collins (two-thirds)	17,280	
Mitchell (one-third)	8,640	
		25,920

Balance sheet 31 December 1996

Fixed assets		38,000
Current assets:		
Stock	2,000	
Debtors	5,000	
Bank	1,500	
	8,500	
Creditors due within one year:		
Creditors and accruals (3,000 + 480)	3,480	
		5,020
		43,020

Capital and reserves:

	Collins	Mitchell	
Loan account	4,000		4,000
Capital accounts	10,000	6,000	16,000
Current accounts:			
Balance b/f	(500)	1,000	
Salaries	10,000	12,000	
Interest on capital	1,000	600	
Share of profits	17,280	8,640	
	27,780	22,240	
Drawings	(15,000)	(12,000)	
Balance c/f	12,780	10,240	23,020
			43,020

As with most types of ownership, examiners will use partnership questions to test your ability in other areas such as error correction.

Question for self-assessment

The answer to this self-assessment question is given at the end of the book.

The following question was set in the AEB A level examination. The description of the error under note 3, item (ii) is ambiguous. You will have to assume that the correct postings have been made to debtors and creditors (or the relevant control accounts) and that the description of these two errors relates solely to the accounts for sales and purchases. On this basis, the trial balance totals would not agree and so the correction will be completed through the suspense account. As regards item (i) under note 3, you will find it easier to do several journal entries to correct the error and make the necessary adjustments.

14.1 Splendor and Grass are trading in partnership. Their partnership agreement provides for interest on fixed capitals at 9% per annum and the balance of profits and losses to be shared in the ratio 3:2, respectively.

The following draft summarized revenue statement has been drawn up by an inexperienced book-keeper who, after failing to agree a trial balance, opened a suspense account.

Summarized Revenue Statement for the year ended 31 December 19X8

	£000	£000
Sales		2,000
Less cost of goods sold		1,350
Gross profit		650
Administration expenses	245	
Selling and distribution expenses	135	
Financial charges	80	460
Net profit		190

Additional information.
1. Partnership account balances as at 1 January 19X8:

	Capital Accounts £000	Current Accounts £000
Splendor	100	25 Cr
Grass	60	19 Cr

2. Monthly drawings during the year were:

Splendor	£5,000
Grass	£3,500

3. Subsequently the following errors were discovered.
   (i) The sales figure in the revenue statement includes the proceeds of the sale of a motor van, £3,500. The van, which cost £10,000 and had a net book value on 1 January 1988 of £5,000, was sold on 1 August 19X8.
   A year's depreciation charge of 10% of the cost of the van has been included in the selling and distribution expenses, contrary to the firm's normal policy of no depreciation in the year of sale.
   (ii) Goods returned inwards, worth £54,000, had been incorrectly deducted from

purchases. Goods returned outwards, worth £69,000, had been incorrectly deducted from sales.

(iii) The closing stock has been inadvertently included in the revenue statement valued at selling price. The cost price of the stock was £150,000 and the mark-up on cost was 25%. The net realizable value of the closing stock is £165,000.

(iv) Splendor has a private loan from his bank and the interest charge for the year of £1,500 was incorrectly included in the financial charges.

(v) On 1 January 19X8 rent of £2,500 was paid covering the five consecutive quarters until 31 March 19X9. On 1 April 19X8, a further £2,500 was incorrectly paid due to a filing error in the business. All the rent payments are included in the administration expenses and no action has been taken to recover the rent paid in error.

Required:
(a) Journal entries to correct the errors that have been made. (Narratives are required.)
(b) A corrected revenue statement and an appropriation account for the year ended 31 December 19X8.
(c) The partners' current accounts for the year ended 31 December 19X8 as they would appear in the ledger.

(AEB A Level)

Question without answer

The answer to this question is published separately in the *Teacher's Manual*.

14.2 Owen and Steel are in partnership, sharing profits equally after Owen has been allowed a salary of £5,000 per year. No interest is charged on drawings or allowed on current accounts, but interest of 10% p.a. is allowed on the opening capital account balances for each year. Their book-keeper has been having trouble balancing the books and has eventually produced the following list of balances as at 31 December.

	£
Capital account: Owen	9,000
Capital account: Steel	10,000
10% loan account: Steel	5,000
10% loan account: Williams	6,000
Current account balance 1 January: Owen	1,000
Current account balance 1 January: Steel	2,000
Drawings: Owen	6,500
Drawings: Steel	5,500
Sales	113,100
Sales returns	3,000
Closing stock	17,000
Cost of goods sold	70,000
Sales ledger control account	30,000
Purchase ledger control account	25,000
Operating expenses	26,100
Fixed assets at cost	37,000
Provision for depreciation	18,000
Bank overdraft	3,000
Suspense account	

You ascertain the following information:

(i) The sales ledger control account does not agree with the list of balances from the ledger. The following errors when corrected will remove the difference:
  (a) the sales returns day book has been undercast by £100;
  (b) a contra entry with the creditors ledger for £200 has been omitted from the control accounts;
  (c) an invoice for £2,000 was incorrectly entered in the sales day book as £200.

(ii) A fully depreciated fixed asset, original cost £5,000, was sold during the year. The proceeds of £1,000 were entered in the bank account only, and no other entries in connection with the disposal were made.

(iii) It is agreed that hotel bills for £500 paid by Steel from his personal bank account are proper business expenses. Owen has taken goods out of the business for his own use, costing £1,000. No entry has been made for either of these items.

(iv) No interest of any kind has yet been paid or recorded.

(v) Any remaining balance on the suspense account cannot be traced, and is to be treated in the most suitable manner.

Required:
(a) Prepare a trial balance and establish the balance on the suspense account.
(b) Incorporate the necessary adjustments, showing your workings clearly in any way you feel appropriate.
(c) Prepare final accounts for presentation to the partners.

(ACCA 1.1)

15 > Partnerships: Changes in ownership

Objectives

After you have completed this chapter, you should be able to:
- explain why it is necessary to adjust existing capital accounts to reflect the market value of the firm on a change of ownership
- calculate profits and losses arising on a change of ownership and account for these in the firm's books
- estimate the value of a business, and explain the nature of goodwill
- deal with any kind of accounting problem resulting from a change in ownership of a business owned by a sole trader or partnership

Introduction

When a new partner is admitted into a partnership, or when one of the partners leaves, there is a formal cessation of one firm and the commencement of another. Technically speaking, the same thing applies where there is no change in the number of partners but there is a change in the way profits are shared amongst existing partners.

This might suggest that we should close down the books of the old firm (as if it had been sold) and then open up a new set of books for the new firm on the basis that it had acquired the old firm's business. This does not seem very logical when you consider that the only change is in the composition of the firm's ownership; for all practical purposes the same business is continuing to operate.

But a change in ownership does alter the way in which any future capital gains or losses are shared, and part of these gains or losses could be related to an earlier period when the firm was under a different ownership with a different profit sharing basis. Consequently, the normal practice is to continue using the same set of books and to make an adjustment to the capital accounts of the former partners in order to recognize any capital gains or losses that are attributable to their period of ownership. The effect of these adjustments is to revise the capital accounts to what they would have been if the business of the old firm had been sold to the new firm at its market value.

Even when changes in ownership are more apparent, such as where the business of a sole trader progresses to a partnership, followed by a conversion of that partnership into a limited company, it is quite feasible to continue using the same accounting records both before and after the changes in ownership. The adjustments needed to recognize these transfers are not very extensive and relate mainly to the equity side of the balance sheet.

15.1 The central accounting problem

The various types of change in ownership of a partnership can create an almost endless permutation of circumstances. But there is only the one central problem and it is solved in exactly the same way for each situation. It is vital that you understand how to deal with this problem, otherwise you will find yourself having to study changes under several headings such as:

- sole trader takes on a partner
- admitting a new partner into the partnership
- a partner leaves or retires
- two partnership are amalgamated (or a sole trader's business is amalgamated with a partnership)
- a partnership is converted into a limited company

The central problem relates to the value of 'the business' at the time of change in ownership. The value of the business (built up by the former owners) is not revealed by balance sheets prepared on a going concern basis. We will study the central problem in the context of admitting a new partner, and then consider some of the variations.

Admitting a new partner

You will be able to discover the problem by working a series of activities based on the following abbreviated balance sheet of the A and B partnership.

A and B have owned a business for several years and have always shared profits and losses equally. Their balance sheet at 31 December was a follows:

Tangible fixed assets			100,000
Cash at bank			50,000
Other net current assets			150,000
			300,000
	A	B	
Capital accounts	140,000	160,000	300,000

Activity 1

Answer this question: how much is the business worth as a going concern?

Answer:

Now assume that A and B have decided to admit Miss C into the partnership as an equal (one-third) partner on the 1 January (the day following that for the above balance sheet). Miss C has agreed to introduce cash of £130,000 into the partnership. The firm's book-keeper has never been properly trained on partnership accounting and assumes that since the £130,000 was introduced by Miss C, the entire amount should be credited to an account in her name.

Activity 2

Draw up the balance sheet immediately following the introduction of Miss C.

Tangible fixed assets
Bank
Other net current assets

	A	B	C
Capital accounts			

Now imagine that on the very next day (2 January) someone offers the partnership £295,000 for the business. The purchaser has agreed to acquire all the assets, excluding the bank balance, and to take over all liabilities. In arriving at the price of £295,000, the purchaser places the following values on the various assets and liabilities:

Tangible fixed assets	124,000
Other net current assets	150,000

Activity 3

This is a short diversion. The purchaser is offering £295,000 for the business and yet has valued the net assets to be acquired at £274,000. Identify what the nature of this difference is likely to be and make a note of it here.

In the case of companies, goodwill is defined in both the Companies Act 1985 and in FRS 6. The following is an extract from paragraph 20 of FRS 6: 'The difference between the fair value of the net identifiable assets acquired and the fair value of the purchase consideration is goodwill, positive or negative.'

New let us see what would happen if the partnership is sold. When working the next activity you will need to keep in mind that capital profits are shared in exactly the same way as trading profits and so Miss C must be credited with a one-third share of the gain on disposal. The gain on disposal is (£295,000 – (£100,000 + £150,000)) £45,000.

Activity 4

Assume that the partners agree to sell the business for £295,000 and the cash is received on 2 January. Draw up the balance sheet immediately after receipt of the cash.

Bank ‗‗‗‗

	A	B	C
Capital accounts			
Balance at 1 January			
Profit on realization			
	‗‗	‗‗	‗‗

Activity 5

Now identify what is wrong with the above set of figures and make a note of it here.

We have got into this muddle because we have failed to recognize that the old partnership of A and B was transferred to a new partnership of A, B and C, on 1 January. If we had treated the old firm as having been sold to the new firm at its market value, the gain on realization would have been credited to A and B in their old profit sharing ratio. The new firm would have started off with a balance sheet showing the market value of the assets (including goodwill) at 1 January. If the business had then been sold on 2 January, there would be no gain accruing to Miss C and she would simply get back the £130,000 she had contributed.

Every time there is a change in the constitution of a partnership it is necessary to make adjustments to the capital account in order to reflect that one firm has been transferred to another at its market value at the time of transfer.

There are (roughly speaking) three ways of making these adjustments on the admission of a new partner. Two of them ensure that the assets which are subject to a revaluation (including goodwill) are carried in the new firm's balance sheet at their book values prior to the change.

- **Method 1.** Revalue the assets (including goodwill) and write these valuations into the books by crediting the former partners in their agreed profit sharing ratio. Cash introduced by a new partner can then be credited in total to the new partner's capital account. The revalued assets (and goodwill) are carried in the balance sheet at their revised value.
- **Method 2.** Ignore the asset revaluations in the books but treat some of the cash introduced by the new partner as being for the purchase of a share of the unrecorded capital gains from the former partners. The amount thus established is not credited to the new partner's capital account but is credited to the former partners in their old profit sharing ratios.

- **Method 3.** Write up the asset revaluations (including goodwill) and credit the former partners in their old profit sharing ratio. Then write off those revaluations by debiting partners in the new partnership in the new profit sharing ratio. This has the effect of debiting the incoming partner's capital account with the amount needed to purchase a share of the unrecorded gains from the former partners. Consequently, the total amount of cash introduced by the new partner can be credited to that partner's capital account.

Each method achieves exactly the same end result. You will see this by preparing three balance sheets adopting each method. These balance sheets are to show the position that would have been reached if the business were sold for £295,000 immediately after admitting Miss C. At this point, the cash held by the partnership will not have been distributed to the partners.

Activity 6

Assume that Method 1 (revaluation of assets on admission of Miss C) was applied. Complete the following balance sheet.

Bank (£50,000 + £130,000 + £295,000)				£475,000
	A	B	C	
Capital accounts				
Balance at 1 January				
Revaluation surplus				
Cash introduced (Miss C)				
	___	___	___	
	═══	═══	═══	═══

Now we will try Method 2 where there are no asset revaluations but some of the cash introduced by Miss C is to be credited to A and B in their old profit sharing ratio. The undisclosed gains which are attributed to A and B are £45,000. If Miss C is to purchase one-third interest in these gains then £15,000 of the cash which she introduces will be credited to A and B.

Activity 7

Assume Method 2 is applied. In this case assets are not revalued but some of the cash introduced by Miss C is treated as being for the purchase of a one-third share of unrecorded gains of the former partnership. Complete the following balance sheet.

Bank (as before)				£475,000
	A	B	C	
Capital accounts				
Balance at 1 January				
Cash introduced (Miss C)				
Gain on realization				
	___	___	___	
	═══	═══	═══	═══

Finally, we will use Method 3. This invloves writing up the asset revaluations and crediting A and B with their respective shares of the gain based on their old profit sharing ratio. The revaluations are then written off and debited to A, B and C in the new profit sharing ratio. The whole of the cash introduced by Miss C is credited to her own capital account.

Activity 8

Assume Method 3 (writing up and writing off revaluations) is applied. Complete the following balance sheet.

Bank as before   £475,000

	A	B	C
Capital accounts			
Balance at 1 January			
Revaluation written up			
Revaluation written off			
Cash introduced (Miss C)			
Gain on realization			

Note how Method 3 debits the new partner, and credits the old partners, with the share of unrecorded asset values relinquished by the old partners to the new partner at the time of admission. The amount could have been found directly by applying the following logic.

	A	B	C
Old profit sharing ratio	1/2	1/2	–
New profit sharing ratio	1/3	1/3	1/3
Share (relinquished)/acquired	(1/6)	(1/6)	(2/6)

These fractions (or percentages) could then have been used to make a single adjustment between the partners, as follows:

	Debit	Credit
A's capital account (1/6 × £45,000)		£7,500
B's capital account (1/6 × £45,000)		£7,500
C's capital account (2/6 × £45,000)	£15,000	

Providing this adjustment is made, the whole amount of cash introduced by the new partner can be credited to that partner's capital account and there is no need to write the revaluations into the books at all.

Most examination questions that include this topic require you to make the adjustment on the basis that the revised asset values (usually goodwill) are not to remain in the books. This suggests that although Method 1 is an option that the partnership could adopt, you are not likely to be using it in the examination. The most common approach is to write up the revaluation in the old books and then write if off in the new.

15.2 Variations on the central theme

The basic principle established in section 15.1 will have to be applied whenever there is a change in the partnership. It must also be applied when there is no change in the number of partners but there is a change in the profit sharing ratio. In some cases further adjustments will be needed depending on the circumstances. We will look at two situations: a partner leaves the firm, and a partnership is wound up.

A partner leaves the firm

The retirement (or death) of a partner does not necessarily occur at the accounting date. It is unlikely to do so in the case of a death. There could, therefore, be three accounting issues to deal with when a partner leaves the firm, namely:

1. the treatment of unrecorded asset values, including goodwill.
2. the outgoing partner's drawings and share of profits since the last accounting date.
3. the balance due to the outgoing partner (or partner's personal representatives).

The unrecorded asset values can be dealt with in much the same way as they were for the admission of a new partner. The assets (including goodwill) are revalued and the surplus credited to the capital accounts of the former partners (including the outgoing partner) in the old profit sharing ratio. If the surviving partners do not wish to retain the revised asset values, the revaluation can be reversed by debiting the surviving partners in their new profit sharing ratio.

It might be necessary to draw up a set of financial statements since the last accounting date so that the outgoing partner's drawings and share of profits can be determined. These will result in further adjustments to that partner's current account. The revised balance on the current account can then be transferred to that partner's capital account since there is no longer any purpose in keeping the two accounts.

After completing these accounting adjustments there will be a balance due to the outgoing partner (or that partner's estate in the case of a death) represented by the balance on the outgoing partner's capital account. If the balance is paid off, the matter is concluded. In some cases, however, the partnership is not in a position to repay the full amount immediately and so the amount due (or part of it) is retained in the partnership for a while. Any amount due to the outgoing partner that is not repaid immediately must be transferred to a loan account. It cannot be treated as partner's capital since the person concerned is no longer a partner in the firm. If there is an agreement to pay interest on the loan, the interest must be treated as an expense and not as an appropriation of profit.

Winding up a partnership

In the exercises concerning the partnership of A, B and C, we simply worked out the final effect on the balance sheet, particularly the partners' capital accounts. We did not carry out any book-keeping in the ledger.

Sometimes a 'Capital Adjustment account' is used as a clearing house for the adjustments on revaluation of assets following the admission of a new partner. This account is not likely to be necessary in exams because the adjustments can simply be made between the assets and the partners' capital accounts.

When dissolving a partnership, you will probably have to use an account called a 'Realization Account'. This account collects all the debits for the assets sold, and is credited with any liabilities taken over by the purchaser. The agreed sale price is credited to this account (the purchaser's account is debited) and the balance on the realization account represents the profit or loss on realization which is transferred to the partners' capital accounts in their profit sharing ratio.

When the purchaser pays the amount due, bank is debited and the purchaser's account credited. The cash at bank at this point should be equal to the amounts due to any creditors not taken over by the purchaser, plus the partners' capital accounts. The final payments by the partnership are simply a credit to bank and a debit to those to whom the money is paid.

The way that the realization account works is quite logical. The mechanics can be seen by listing the double-entry for each type of transaction:

1. The book value of assets sold to the purchaser:
   Debit: Realization account
   Credit: The respective asset accounts.
2. The liabilities taken over by the purchaser:
   Debit: The respective liability accounts
   Credit: Realization account.
3. The agreed purchase price:
   Debit: An account for the purchaser
   Credit   Realization account.
4. Agreed valuation of any assets taken over by a partner:
   Debit: The relevant partners' capital account
   Credit: The realization account.
5. Balance on the realization account (assuming a profit on realization):
   Debit: Realization account
   Credit: Partners' capital accounts in the agreed profit sharing ratio.
6. Receipt of cash from the purchaser:
   Debit: Bank
   Credit: The purchasers' account.
7. Paying off the liabilities not taken over by the purchaser:
   Debit: The relevant liability accounts
   Credit: Bank.
8. Paying out the balances due to partners:
   Debit: The capital account of each partner
   Credit: Bank.

You can practise using the realization account by writing it up for A, B and C on the assumption that Method 3 was used for dealing with the admission of Miss C. The balance sheet immediately after Miss C was admitted (and prior to sale of the firm) would be as follows:

Tangible fixed assets				100,000
Cash at bank (£50,000 + £130,000)				180,000
Other net current assets				150,000
				£430,000

	A	B	C	
Partners' capital accounts:	147,500	167,500	115,000	£430,000

The amount paid for the disposal of the business was £295,000. The purchaser acquired all assets and liabilities other than the bank balance.

Activity 9

Write up the realization account set out below this box.

Realization account

When the cash is received from the purchaser, the bank balance for the firm of A, B and C will be (£180,000 + £295,000) £475,000 and this will be equal to the total of the capital accounts. Each partner will be paid the amount due and the books are closed.

15.3 Conversion of a partnership to a limited company

There is a distinction between:

- conversion of a partnership into a limited company, and
- sale of a partnership business to an existing company.

Conversion to a limited company

The former partners will become shareholders in the new company and the same set of books can be transferred to the company. Even so, it is best to think of this problem as having two distinct stages: (1) closing down the books of the partnership, and (2) opening up a new set of books for the company.

If a partnership is converted into a limited company, the partners' capital accounts (as adjusted for any asset revaluations) will be paid off by an issue of shares by the company to the partners. The company will acquire the business (or businesses) at the agreed valuation, including any amount for goodwill. If the amount paid by the company for this business is settled entirely by an issue of shares, the double-entry in the company's books will be:

- Debit: the individual assets (and credit the liabilities) acquired from the partnership, at the agreed valuations. This will include the asset of goodwill in most cases.
- Credit: share capital and share premium account based on information regarding the share valuations.

If you are not given any information from which to determine the fair value of the shares issued by the company, you should assume they have been issued at their nominal value.

In some cases the company might raise additional cash by a separate issue of shares. In these cases the partnership could receive shares and cash from the company in settlement of the purchase price. The basis for dividing the shares among the partners will have to be agreed, but if no such agreement is stipulated, the most equitable basis is to allocate them among the partners in their old profit sharing ratio. This will give the former partners an interest in the equity of the company that equates to their former interests in the profits of the partnership. Any balance on capital accounts after debiting the shares received will be settled by cash.

Where the same set of books is transferred to the company, the basic procedure is to revalue the assets, including goodwill, by making adjustments to the partners' capital accounts. To the extent that these capital accounts are then settled by the receipt of shares from the company, the amounts involved can be transferred from the capital accounts to share capital (i.e. debit capital accounts, credit share capital). Any remaining balances will be the subject of a cash settlement.

Sale of business to an existing company

In this case, the agreed price for the business is likely to be settled by a mixture of cash and shares in the existing company. To the extent that the consideration paid includes an issue of shares, these will have to be treated as having a value equal to their market value. Any excess of market value over nominal value will be treated as a share premium in the issuing company's books.

Examination questions in this area can include two types of data, namely:

- **Type 1.** The fair values are given for the various assets (including goodwill) to be acquired, and for any liabilities taken over. In this case, the total fair value of net assets acquired will determine the fair value of any shares issued as consideration. Any difference between the fair value of the shares issued and their nominal value must be credited to a share premium account.
- **Type 2.** The value of shares in the consideration is given, together with the fair values of the separable assets and liabilities acquired. Goodwill is the difference between the fair value of the consideration and the total fair value of the separable net assets acquired.

Illustration

The balance sheet of a partnership includes the following:

	£	£
Tangible fixed assets		120,000
Current assets	60,000	
Creditors due within one year	(40,000)	
Net current assets		20,000
		140,000

Activity 10

Practise with a Type 1 problem. A company is formed to take over the entire business. The company values the tangible fixed assets at £130,000, goodwill at £50,000, and the net current asset at their book value of £20,000. The purchase consideration is to be settled by issuing 160,000 £1 ordinary shares. Set out the opening balance sheet of the company. Treat goodwill as an intangible fixed asset for the time being.

Activity 11

Practise with a Type 2 problem. The details for this activity are completely independent of those for Activity 10. Another company offers to acquire the entire business of the partnership. The company will satisfy the purchase consideration by the issue of 160,000 £1 ordinary shares which have an agreed value of £1.35 per share. The company values the tangible fixed assets at £138,000 and the net current assets at their book value of £20,000. Assuming that the offer is accepted by the partnership, set out in the figures that will appear in the balance sheet of the company for this acquisition. Show the figures for both sides of the company's balance sheet and treat goodwill as an intangible fixed asset for the time being.

There are many variations on the above but they are not too difficult to sort out if you use a logical approach based on the through process developed in this chapter. Any debentures, or preference shares, included in the consideration will usually be a nominal value. The value of cash is clearly the face value of the cash. If you are required to value goodwill (for use in a Type 1 problem) the basis of the valuation will be given.

15.4 Piecemeal realizations

If the partnership business is not sold as a going concern, the assets will be sold piecemeal and the cash distributed as and when received. The creditors must be paid first, followed by distributions to the partners. A problem then arises as to how the cash available for distribution to the partners should be shared between them. Before considering this problem, we must first consider the situation that arises when one of the partners is insolvent. The situation that can arise in this case applies to realizations generally, it is not restricted to piecemeal realizations.

Insolvent partner

When a partnership is being dissolved, the capital and current accounts for each partner are combined. The reason for keeping the two separate accounts no longer applies. Adjustments are then made to the capital accounts for any profit or loss on realization. If, at this point, any of the capital accounts show a deficiency (a debit balance) the partners concerned must pay cash into the firm in order to clear the deficit.

If a partner with a deficit capital account is insolvent, that partner will be unable to contribute any cash and so the firm suffers a loss which must be borne by the remaining partners. The problem then arises as to how the loss should be apportioned to the remaining partners. The partnership agreement might state how this is to be done but if it is silent on this point then a rule in a case known as *Garner v. Murray* (1904) will have to be applied.

The *Garner v. Murray* rule is that the loss should not be shared according to the profit sharing ratio but according to the capital sharing ratio. In other words, the deficit on the insolvent partner's capital account must be apportioned to the remaining partners according to the ratio of those partners' capital accounts. The capital accounts used for this purpose are those that were agreed at last accounting date of the firm.

The application of this rule is not restricted to piecemeal realizations but it is often used when calculating the amounts that can be distributed to partners during a piecemeal realization. If you have to apply the rule in the context of a full realization, you will be able to see the principle from the way the process is discussed here.

Distribution to partners

On a piecemeal realization it will be necessary to devise some scheme for distributing the cash to the partners as it is received. Sometimes a distribution basis is agreed by the partners but if this is not the case you should use a basis which is sometimes called the 'maximum possible loss' method. This assumes that after the sale of each asset the remaining assets will not realize any cash and the assumed loss is apportioned to the partners in their profit sharing ratio.

The following description of this method assumes that a point has been reached where the creditors have been paid off, and the task is to prepare a schedule of how the cash available from each sale should be distributed to the partners. You should keep in mind that this is mainly a calculation process, it does not describe book-keeping entries. The only book-keeping involved is to record the cash when it is received and to record the cash payments made to the partners.

- As each asset is sold, assume that the remaining assets will realize zero and calculate the loss on realization based on this assumption.
- Calculate what the balance would be on each partner's capital account if this loss is shared according to the profit sharing ratio.
- If this results in any partner's capital account going into deficit, apportion this to the other partners in the ratio of the credit balances on their capital accounts at the beginning of the accounting period (this assumes that the partnership agreement does not exclude the rule in *Garner v. Murray*).
- The total of the credit balances on the capital accounts following this calculation will be equal to the cash available for distribution to the partners.
- Distribute the cash according to the respective credit balances.
- The whole procedure is repeated for each sale.

- Distributions for the second and subsequent receipts must take account of how earlier distributions have changed the partners' capital accounts.

As stated earlier, the calculations are memorandum. For example, a deficit balance on one of the partner's capital accounts following a particular disposal is not actually transferred to the other partners. The full deficit (if any) will not be known until the last asset is sold and, even then, this partner must first be asked to clear the deficit by paying cash into the partnership.

Illustration

Partners D, E and F were sharing profits in the ratio of 3:1:1. They have decided to close down operations and since they have been unable to find a buyer for the business as a going concern, the assets will be sold on a piecemeal basis. The last agreed balance sheet at the date of closing the business was as follows:

	£	£
Assets other than bank		14,000
Bank balance	1,000	
Creditors	(2,000)	
		(1,000)
		13,000
Capital accounts:		
D		8,000
E		4,000
F		1,000
		13,000

The first two asset disposals realized the following amounts of cash:

Disposal 1 £3,000
Disposal 2 £3,000

Activity 12

Make a note here of the amount of cash available for distribution to the partners following the first receipt:

Activity 13

Now make a note of the assumed loss on realization following:

Disposal 1

Disposal 2

We can now set up the working schedules to show the amount of cash distributed to each partner following each realization. These will be as follows:

First realization	D	E	F
Capital account balances	8,000	4,000	1,000
Maximum possible loss (£11,000)			
divided in profit sharing ratio (3:1:1)	6,600	2,200	2,200
	1,400	1,800	1,200
Deficit divided in capital ratio (8:4)	(800)	(400)	1,200
First distribution (£2,000)	600	1,400	–

Second realization	D	E	F
Revised capital account balances (after first distribution)	7,400	2,600	1,000
Maximum possible loss (£8,000)			
divided in profit sharing ratio (3:1:1)	4,800	1,600	1,600
	2,600	1,000	(600)
Deficit divided in capital ratio at beginning of the year (8:4)	(400)	(200)	600
Second distribution (£3,000)	2,200	800	–

Notice how the assumed deficit on F's capital account following the second disposal is apportioned to D and E on the basis of their capital accounts in the last agreed balance sheet at the start of the liquidation. This follows from the rule of *Garner v. Murray* where the capital accounts used for the apportionment were defined as those agreed at the last accounting date prior to the liquidation. The capital accounts will change during a piecemeal realization but the revised balances should not be used to apportion the capital deficits

Summary

The variety of situations involving a change of ownership is almost endless but there is one common accounting problem. Your approach to solving any examination question on a change of ownership involves using this central problem as a focal point. The key learning points in this chapter are as follows:

- all changes in ownership must be seen as the transfer of a business to a new owner (or owners) at its market value
- in some cases there is a complete change of owners, in others there could be one (or more) of the former owners retaining an ownership interest following transfer of the business

- an owner's interest in the capital of the firm is represented by that owner's capital account, but this is based on the book value of the underlying net assets, not the market value
- on a complete change of owners, the assets have been sold and the capital accounts are adjusted to show each owners' interest in the market value of the firm by sharing the gain or loss found by preparing a realization account
- on a partial change of owners, the difference between the market value of the firm and the underlying net assets in the books will represent an unrealized gain (or loss) attributable to the former owners
- these gains (or losses) might be realized in a subsequent period and will then be shared among the new owners on a different basis to that of the former ownership
- this is corrected by treating the old firm as having been transferred to the new at its market value; any unrealized gains (and losses) at the time of transfer are recorded in the books by crediting (or debiting) the former owners' capital accounts according to the old profit sharing ratio
- since there is no actual sale of the business, its market value must be estimated by considering the fair value of all the assets transferred including goodwill
- goodwill is defined (by SSAP 22) as the difference between the value of the business as a whole, and the aggregate of the fair values of its separable net assets
- if the partnership does not wish to retain the figure for goodwill in its books, it can be written off by debiting all owners in the new firm according to the new profit sharing ratio
- in cases where a new partner introduces cash, goodwill can be kept out of the books altogether by treating part of the cash introduced as being for the purchase of a share of goodwill from the former owners; this part of the cash introduced is credited to the former owners' capital accounts
- the book-keeping on liquidation of a partnership centres around a realization account
- partners with deficits on their capital accounts following a liquidation must clear the deficit by paying cash to the firm
- if a partner with a deficit capital account is insolvent and unable to contribute cash, the loss is borne by the remaining partners in their capital sharing ratio
- piecemeal realizations involve devising a scheme for distributing cash to the partners as it is received

Activity 1
We do not know. It depends on how much someone is prepared to pay for the business.

Activity 2

Tangible fixed assets		100,000
Bank (£50,000 + £130,000)		180,000
Other net current assets		150,000
		£430,000

	A	B	C	
Capital accounts	140,000	160,000	130,000	£430,000

Activity 3
Most people would call it goodwill.

Activity 4

Bank (£180,000 + £295,000)		£475,000

Capital accounts	A	B	C	
Balance at 1 Jan	140,000	160,000	130,000	
Profit on realization	15,000	15,000	15,000	
	155,000	175,000	145,000	£475,000

Activity 5
Miss C has made a gain of £15,000 simply by being a partner for one day.

Activity 6

Bank		£475,000

Capital accounts	A	B	C	
Balance at 1 Jan	140,000	160,000		
Revaluation surplus	22,500	22,500		
Cash introduced			130,000	
	162,500	182,500	130,000	£475,000

Activity 7

Bank		£475,000

Capital accounts	A	B	C	
Balance at 1 Jan	140,000	160,000		
Cash introduced	7,500	7,500	115,000	
Gain on realization	15,000	15,000	15,000	
	162,500	182,500	130,000	£475,000

Activity 8

Bank   £475,000

Capital accounts	A	B	C	
Balance at 1 Jan	140,000	160,000		
Revaluation				
Written up	22,500	22,500		
Written off	(15,000)	(15,000)	(15,000)	
Cash introduced			130,000	
Gain on realization	15,000	15,000	15,000	
	162,500	182,500	130,000	£475,000

Activity 9

Realization account

Tangible fixed assets	100,000	Purchaser's account	295,000
Other net current assets	150,000		
Gain on realization:			
Capital account A	15,000		
Capital account B	15,000		
Capital account C	15,000		
	45,000		
	295,000		295,000

Activity 10

Tangible fixed assets (at cost)		130,000
Intangible fixed assets (goodwill)		50,000
Current assets	60,000	
Creditors due in one year	40,000	
		20,000
		£200,000
Capital and reserves		
Called up share capital		
160,000 × £1 ordinary shares		160,000
Share premium account		40,000
		£200,000

You should note that although the tangible fixed assets were valued at £130,000 by the company for the take-over, this amount represents the *cost* of those assets to the company.

Activity 11

Tangible fixed assets (at cost)		138,000
Intangible fixed assets (goodwill)		58,000
Current assets	60,000	
Creditors due in one year	40,000	
		20,000
		£216,000
Capital and reserves		
Called up share capital		
160,000 × £1 ordinary shares		160,000
Share premium account		56,000
		£216,000

In this case, goodwill of £58,000 is the difference between the fair value of the consideration given of £216,000, and the fair value of the separable net assets acquired of £158,000.

Activity 12
£2,000. There was £1,000 in the bank and the receipt will make this £4,000. After paying the creditors £2,000 there will be £2,000 remaining for distribution to the partners.

Activity 13
Maximum assumed losses:
After Disposal 1 (£14,000 − £3,000) £11,000.
After Disposal 2 (£11,000 − £3,000) £8,000.

Questions for self-assessment

Answers to self-assessment questions are given at the end of the book.

15.1 **Alpha, Beta and Gamma.** Tutorial note on point (iv) of the question: Goods sold to customers on a 'sale or return' basis must be treated as stock (and not as sales to a debtor) until they are formally accepted by the customer.

Alpha and Beta are in partnership. They share profits equally after Alpha has been allowed a salary of £4,000 p.a. No interest is charged on drawings or allowed on current accounts or capital accounts. The trial balance of the partnership at 31 December 1989, before adjusting for any of the items below, is as follows:

	Dr £000	Cr £000
Capital: Alpha		30
Capital: Beta		25
Current: Alpha		3
Current: Beta		4
Drawings: Alpha	4	
Drawings: Beta	5	
Sales		200
Stock 1 Jan 1989	30	
Purchases	103	
Operating expenses	64	
Loan: Beta (10%)		10
Loan: Gamma (10%)		20
Land and buildings	60	
Plant and machinery: cost	70	
Plant and machinery: depreciation to 31 December 1989		40
Debtors and creditors	40	33
Bank		11
	376	376

(i) Closing stock on hand at 31 December was £24,000.
(ii) On 31 December Alpha and Beta agree to take their manager, Gamma, into partnership. Gamma's loan account balance is to be transferred to a capital account as at 31 December. It is agreed that in future Alpha, Beta and Gamma will all share profits equally. Alpha will be allowed a salary of £4,000 as before, and Gamma will be allowed a salary of £5,000 p.a. (half of what he received in 1989 as manager, included in operating expenses).
The three partners agree that the goodwill of the business at 31 December should be valued at £12,000, but it is not to be recorded in the books. It is also agreed that land and buildings are to be revalued to a figure of £84,000 and that this revalued figure is to be retained and recorded in the accounts.
(iii) Interest on the loan has not been paid.
(iv) Included in sales are two items sold on 'sale or return' for £3,000 each. Each item had cost the business £1,000. One of these items was in fact returned on 4 January 1990 and the other one was formally accepted by the customer on 6 January 1990.

Required:
(a) Submit with appropriately labelled headings and subheadings:
    (i) partners' capital accounts in columnar form;
    (ii) partners' current accounts in columnar form;

(iii) trading, profit and loss and appropriation account for 1989;

(iv) balance sheet as at 31 December 1989.

(b) Write a brief note to Gamma, who cannot understand why his capital account balance seems so much less than those of Alpha and Beta. Explain to him the adjustments you have made.

(ACCA 1.1, Dec 89)

15.2 ABC

(a) The book-keeper of the ABC partnership needs your help with the following problems. You may assume that the trial balance already includes a suspense account.

(i) Partner A has taken from the partnership for his own use a motor car at an agreed value of £600. The car had originally cost £5,000 and had been depreciated down to a net book value of £1,000. The book-keeper had made no entries relating to this transfer.

(ii) Purchase ledger control balance had been understated by £2,000.

(iii) Sales day book had been understated by £300.

(iv) Purchase returns day book had been understated by £50.

(v) The balance on customer P in the sales ledger had been understated by £100.

(vi) An invoice for motor repairs of £123 had been paid twice by mistake. The first time it was posted correctly but the second time it was accidentally credited to the motor vans account as an amount of £231 (as well as being quite correctly entered in the cash book a second time).

(vii) Carriage inwards of £200 and carriage outwards of £225 have both been put on the wrong side of the trial balance.

Required:

Prepare journal entries necessary to correct the above. You may omit narratives, provided that each entry clearly states the name of the account to be entered, and is referenced to the note numbers above.

(b) A new partner has joined the business during the year and has paid in £10,000 'for goodwill'. This £10,000 has been credited by the book-keeper to the account of the new partner. The senior partner had objected to this, but the book-keeper had replied, 'Why not credit the £10,000 to the account of the new partner? It is his money after all.'

Required:

Give your advice as to the proper treatment of this £10,000. Explain your reasons fully.

(ACCA 1.1, Dec 90)

15.3 Stonehouse Ltd and Keir Don. The following A Level question requires you to apply the concept of treating goodwill as the difference between the fair value of the consideration given less the fair value of the 'separable' net assets acquired. In this case, the fair value of the consideration given includes shares that have a fair value equal to their market value. When it comes to answering part (d) you will find it best to work out the balances on share capital, share premium, and bank balance, prior to setting out the balance sheet.

The question included here has been printed in exactly the same way as the original. When you come to look at the balance sheet of Stonehouse Ltd you will find a small error in one of the descriptions. It will not interfere with the production of your answer. You can give yourself a bonus point if you spot it.

The balance sheet of Stonehouse Ltd as at 31 August 1989 was:

	£	£	£
Fixed assets			
Freehold premises, at cost		100,000	
Fixtures and fittings, at net book value		35,000	
11% Debenture loan stock in Brickland Ltd		12,000	147,000
Current assets		48,300	
Stocks		8,700	
Debtors		57,000	
Less Current liabilities			
Creditors	39,500		
Balance at bank	2,500	42,000	15,000
Net current assets			162,000
Long term liabilities			(15,000)
			£147,000
Capital and reserves			
75 000 Ordinary shares of £1 each		75,000	
Reserves		72,000	147,000
			£147,000

Additional information.
1. The authorized share capital of Stonehouse Ltd is 150,000 ordinary shares of £1 each.
2. The directors of Stonehouse Ltd have been considering the acquisition of the business of Keir Don, whose latest balance sheet showed:

	£		£	£
Capital	84,000	Goodwill	6,000	
Long-term liabilities	5,000	Fixtures and		
Creditors	17,000	fittings	79,000	85,000
		Stock		20,000
		Balance at bank		1,000
	£106,000			£ 106,000

3. The directors of Stonehouse Ltd have made an offer to acquire the business of Keir Don on the following terms:
   (i) 25,000 Ordinary shares of £1 each in Stonehouse Ltd, at a valuation of £3.20 per share.
   (ii) £5,000 in 12% Debentures 1999, at par.
   (iii) £8,000 in cash.
   (iv) Keir Don would retain the cash balance and Stonehouse Ltd would take over the assets at the following valuations:

	£000
Fixtures and fittings	89
Stock	20

4. Stonehouse Ltd would take over responsibility for the settlement of Keir Don's creditors.
5. In order to finance the acquisition and plans for future expansion, a rights issue of 1 ordinary share for every 3 shares held, at a price of £2.75 per share, has been made to the shareholders of Stonehouse Ltd. This issue has been fully underwritten and issue expenses will be £3,300.

Required:

(a) Prepare a statement showing the value of the consideration offered to Keir Don.

(b) Prepare a statement showing a calculation of the difference between the consideration offered by Stonehouse Ltd and the net assets acquired by the company.

(c) Explain the reason for the difference calculated in (b) and also how it would be dealt with in the accounts of Stonehouse Ltd.

(d) Prepare the balance sheet of Stonehouse Ltd as it would appear if the take-over and rights issue take place.

(e) Explain what is meant by a rights issue and how such an issue differs from a bonus issue.

(AEB, Nov 89)

Questions without answers

Answers to these questions are published separately in the *Teacher's Manual*.

15.4 **Chip & Co and Shave & Co.** The following A Level question involves an amalgamation of two partnerships. There are no inherent difficulties in the question, although you will have to use a carefully stepped approach in order to avoid becoming muddled.

The first step is to deal with the normal entries on the capital accounts for profits and drawings. Treat the car taken over as drawings. Then deal with the revaluation adjustments in each partnership prior to the amalgamation. The cash adjustments needed to bring each capital account to £12,500 (one-quarter of £50,000) will then be revealed.

You will notice that you are required to produce a balance sheet of the new firm for part (b), but the net asset side of each firm's balance sheet has not been given. You could put net assets in as a balancing figure but this is always a little bit risky since you have no way of checking the accuracy of your entries in the capital accounts. A far safer approach is to determine the net assets (in as much detail as the question allows) for each firm prior to amalgamation.

You can then determine the figures for the combined firm by making adjustments to these opening amounts. This approach was used in the answer to Question 14.1 at the end of Chapter 14.

Two partnerships, Chip & Co. and Shave & Co., decide to combine as 'Joiners & Co.' as from 1 June 1989.

The profit and loss appropriation accounts of the two partnerships for the year to 31 May 1989 were as follows:

	Chip & Co. £	Shave & Co. £
Net profit	26,000	24,000
Interest on drawings:		
John Chip	2,000	
Janet Chip	1,000	
	29,000	24,000
Salary: John Chip	10,000	
	19,000	24,000
Interest on capital:		
Phil Shave		(2,000)
Alice Shave		(2,000)
	19,000	20,000
Profit divided:		
John Chip (3/5)	11,400	
Janet Chip (2/5)	7,600	
Phil Shave (1/2)		10,000
Alice Shave (1/2)		10,000

Neither partnership operates current accounts, and the balances at 1 June 1988 on the capital accounts of the partners were as follows:

	£
John Chip	9,800
Janet Chip	7,680
Phil Shave	16,089
Alice Shave	2,000

Drawings during the year were:

	£
John Chip	11,000
Janet Chip	6,000
Phil Shave	12,000
Alice Shave	12,000

The terms of the merger were as follows.
1. John Chip was to acquire a car shown in the Chip & Co. balance sheet at its book value of £2,000.
2. As a result of a revaluation of assets, other than goodwill, the net asset total of Chip & Co. increased by £4,000, and that of Shave & Co. increased by £6,000.
3. The goodwill of Chip & Co. was agreed at £6,000, and that for Shave & Co. was agreed at £9,000. Goodwill accounts had not been opened in either partnership's ledgers.
4. The capital of the new partnership is to be £50,000, to be provided equally by the four partners. Assume that all partners have adequate private funds if transfers between partners are needed.

Required:
(a) For each of the two partnerships, prepare the partners' capital accounts for the year ended 31 May 1989, including any entries required to close the accounts.
(b) Prepare the opening balance sheet of Joiners & Co., as at 1 June 1989.
(c) Explain two advantages and one disadvantage of partnerships when compared with limited liability companies. *(ULSEB, Jun 89)*

15.5 A and B are in partnership, sharing profits equally after taking account of interest on opening balances on capital accounts at 10% p.a., and allowing A a management salary of £5,000 p.a. No interest is allowed or charged on current accounts or on drawings.
You are presented with the following trial balances as at 31 December 1991.

	£000	£000
Capital account A		50
Capital account B		30
Current account A		12
Current account B		3
Drawings A	7	
Drawings B	6	
Property	90	
Fixtures and fittings, cost and depreciation	40	14
Motor vehicles, cost and depreciation	40	24
Sales		250
Cost of sales	120	
Stocks	20	
Debtors and creditors	40	30
Operating expenses	40	
Goodwill	40	
Bank overdraft		10
Loan from A at 12% p.a.		15
Loan from D at 12% p.a.		5
	443	443

The following information is to be taken into account.

(i) Depreciation on motor vehicles has already been provided for the year 1991 at 20% p.a. by the reducing balance method. It is now decided to change this for the year 1991 to 25% p.a. by the reducing balance method.

(ii) It is agreed that a desk included in fixtures and fittings above, at a cost of £3,000, depreciation to date £1,000, is to be transferred to A personally at a valuation of £2,500.

(iii) Interest on the loans from A and D has been neither paid nor provided.

(iv) From the bank statement for December you discover that:
  (a) Bank charges of £500 have not been taken account of.
  (b) A standing order receipt for £1,000 from a customer has been omitted.
  (c) A cheque for £2,000 from a customer deposited on 29 December has been returned by the bank marked 'refer to drawer'.
  (d) A cheque for £3,000 sent to a supplier on 25 November is still outstanding.

(v) C is to join the partnership with effect from the close of business on 31 December 1991. It is agreed that for the purposes of this admission the property of the partnership is revalued at £120,000, and goodwill at £50,000. However, the property is to remain recorded in the books at the original figure, and goodwill is to be eliminated entirely from the balance sheet. A, B and C are in future to share profits in the ratio of 2:2:1, after taking account of interest on capital accounts at 10%, and allowing both A and C management salaries of £5,000 each. On 31 December C paid £20,000 into a special bank account in the name of the partnership as a capital contribution. This transaction was not accounted for on that date.

Required:
(a) Prepare journal entries to take account of item (i) to item (iv) above.
(b) Prepare capital and current accounts for A, B and C in columnar form.
(c) Prepare profit and loss account, appropriation account, and balance sheet for the partnership in relation to the year 1991.

(ACCA 1.1, Dec 91)

15.6 Combine and Company, converted to Unity Ltd. The following A Level question involves the transfer of a partnership business to a limited company. As with all questions on changes of ownership, the solution will gradually emerge from a series of logical steps. These usually start with the revaluation adjustments. Your approach to preparing the balance sheet for part (b) should be the same as for Question 15.4, i.e. find the net assets prior to the transfer in as much detail as the question permits, and use this to produce a figure for the company's first balance sheet.

At the close of business on 31 December 1989, the partners of Combine and Company had the following balances on their capital and current accounts:

Capital Accounts	£
Arthur	13,000
Barbara	12,000
Carl	10,000

Current Accounts	£
Arthur	6,000
Barbara	5,000
Carl	2,000 (Debit)

At 31 December 1989, the goodwill of the partnership was agreed at £38,000, but the goodwill account in the partnership's books had stood at a valuation of £2,000 for many years. Arthur, Barbara and Carl shared partnership profits and losses in the ration 5:3:2, respectively.

On 1 January 1990, the partners decided to convert their partnership into a limited company, Unity Limited, and the following decisions were taken.

1. That the company should have an issued and fully paid up share capital of 60,000 ordinary shares of £1 each, to be issued amongst the partners in equal proportions.

2. That Arthur should acquire a vehicle owned by the partnership at a valuation of

£1,500, which was £600 less than its book value. All other assets and liabilities will be transferred to the company.

3. Any balances remaining on partners' current accounts after the above decisions have been implemented should be transferred to partners' capital accounts. The balances on the capital accounts should then be settled by the partners paying in cash to or drawing out cash from the partnership bank account.

    Assume that sufficient cash is available for this purpose.

    (a) Show the entries in the partners' capital and current accounts required to close off the partnership books.

    (b) Show the opening balance sheet of Unity Limited as at 1 January 1990.

    (c) Advise Unity Limited regarding the permissible ways in which the asset of goodwill might be treated in the company balance sheet at 31 December 1990.

    (ULSEB, Jan 90)

15.7 A, B and C have been in partnership for many years, sharing profits equally. Their trial balance at 1 January 1994 is as follows:

		£000	£000
A Capital			30
Current			2
B Capital			28
Current			4
C Capital			32
Current		4	
Land and buildings:	cost	70	
Plant and machinery:	cost	100	
	depreciation		66
Stock		40	
Trade debtors		30	
Bank		3	
Creditors:	trade		40
	operating expenses		5
Loan from D, at 10% per annum			40
		247	247

With effect from 1 January 1994, the partnership agreement is changed. Profits are to be shared A:B:C – 3:2:1

At 1 January 1994, the partnership godwill is agreed at £60,000 but a ledger account for goodwill is not to be maintained in the accounting records. The land and buildings are agreed to be worth £100,000 and this figure is to be recorded in the accounting records.

At the end of each year each partner is to be allowed interest of 10% on the opening net balance on captial and current accounts (i.e. on the given balances before any adjustments). The following information relating to 1994 should be taken into account as necessary:

(a) The cash book summary for 1994 is as follows:

	£000		£000
Opening balance	3	To trade suppliers	110
Received from customers	172	For operating expenses	30
From sale of old plant	10	For new plant	50
Balance c/d	38	Drawings A	10
		B	11
		C	12
	223		223

(b) At 31 December 1994 £10,000 is prepaid for rent, and £2,000 is to be accrued for electricity. Rent and electricity are both included in operating expenses.

(c) All plant and machinery is depreciated at 10% p.a. straight line basis, assuming no scrap value, and with a full year's depreciation in the year of purchase and none in the year of sale. The old plant sold in 1994 had been bought in June 1986 at a cost of £60,000.

(d) At 31 December 1994 trade creditors were £35,000. Trade debtors, after deducting £4,000 of bad debts, were £40,000. Gross profit is consistently 50% of cost of sales.

Required:
Prepare trading, profit and loss and appropriation accounts for 1994 for the partnership, and a summary balance sheet at 31 December 1994. Submit all workings, which must be clear and legible. Ignore taxation.

(ACCA, Dec 94)

15.8 (a) A and B are in partnership sharing profits equally. The summarized balance sheet of AB and Co. at the close of business on 30 June 1995 is as follows.

	£000		£000
Land	30	Capital A	50
Buildings	100	Capital B	70
Other assets	70	Creditors	80
	200		200

The partners have agreed between themselves as follows.
(i) With effect from July 1 1995 profits are to be shared in the ratio A three-fifths, B two-fifths.
(ii) As at 30 June 1995 the land is valued at £55,000. The new valuation is to be recorded in the asset account.
(iii) As at 30 June 1995 the buildings are valued at £65,000. This new valuation is to be recorded in the asset account.
(iv) As at 30 June 1995 the business, i.e. the net assets, is valued at £170,000 (the 'other assets' and 'creditors' figures are valued as shown in the above balance sheet). The assets side of the balance sheet at commencement of business on 1 July 1995 is not to be altered from the figures at close of business on 30 June 1995 except for the figure for buildings, which is to be reduced to the newly agreed value.

Required:
Prepare a summarized balance sheet at the commencement of business on 1 July 1995, taking account of the above agreement between the partners. Show workings clearly.

(b) Partner A, on receipt of the balance sheet you have prepared in part (a), is not pleased. He is particularly concerned because the balance on his capital account, as compared with B's, has changed in both absolute and relative terms.

Required:
Draft a memorandum to A clarifying the whole situation. Your memorandum is required to contain five sections. The first four, referenced (i), (ii), (iii) and (iv), should explain the implications of the corresponding point in the four-part agreement between the partners given in the question. The final section, referenced (v), should summarize the reasons for the change in the balance on A's capital account and should include a comparison with the change in the balance on B's capital account.

(c) It is often said that the function of a balance sheet is to show the financial position of a business at a point in time.

Required:
To what extent do you believe that the balance sheets for AB and Co. one give in the question and one prepared in your answer to part (a), satisfy that function? Explain your answer briefly.

(ACCA, Dec 95)

16 ▷ Organizations not trading for profit

Objectives

After you have completed this chapter, you should be able to:
- prepare the financial statements for any organization not trading for profit
- examine and critically comment on the financial statements of any club or association

Introduction

This subject will seem like a refreshing holiday by comparison to those covered in some of the previous chapters. The skills involved are simply an adaptation of incomplete record techniques that you have already learned in the context of a trading organization. In fact, most accounting examiners see this subject as another opportunity of testing students on their basic accountancy skills.

The title **organizations not trading for profit** is used to refer to various associations of members (such as social and sports clubs) whose objective is not to bring a financial gain to the members, but to further the interests and objects of the group and to provide various facilities for their members to enjoy.

The financial statements of these associations are based on the same concepts as those developed for a commercial entity. Some of the terminology has to be changed in order to reflect the fact that the association is not trading for profit.

16.1 Legal status and constitution

The legal status of a members' association need not concern you as a student preparing for an accounting exam, but it is something in which you should take a general interest and which will help to broaden your perception of the subject.

Non-trading organizations can range from small informal (often unincorporated) sports and social clubs to large professional bodies such as the Association of Chartered Certified Accountants, or trade unions such as the National Union of Journalists.

In cases where an association is formed for purposes that can be established as being exclusively charitable, an application can be made to the Charity Commissioners for recognition as a charity. If the registration is accepted, the association will enjoy various taxation advantages.

Charitable purposes were classified by Lord MacNaghten (in the 1891 case of 'Pemsel') into four divisions, namely those for: (1) the relief of poverty; (2) the advancement of education; (3) the advancement of religion; and (4) other purposes beneficial to the community. The words 'religion' and 'community' are interpreted quite liberally; a religion does not have to be Christian, and a community can include the residents of a specified local area.

But registration as a charity is a separate issue to the way in which associations are legally constituted in the first place. In general terms, associations are either incorporated or unincorporated.

Most small members' clubs are unincorporated (not registered under any Act) and their constitution consists of a number of rules which its members have agreed to follow as a condition of membership. These rules are often written out on a membership card and sometimes include regulations regarding the financial statements. Unfortunately, most members tend to take very little interest in the financial affairs of their association, until something goes wrong, such as one of the officers absconding with most of the cash!

An unincorporated association is not a separate legal person, and although this does not usually discourage suppliers (e.g. suppliers of refreshments) from dealing with the association, there is a danger that members could be held responsible for payment of their association's debts.

There are various ways in which an association can be legally constituted as a separate person and the subject is quite complex. Briefly, associations can be incorporated either under the Companies Act 1985 as companies limited by guarantee, or under some general Act of Parliament (e.g. Acts relating to friendly and industrial and provident societies). In exceptional cases, they may be incorporated by special Act of Parliament (e.g. the National Trust) or by Royal Charter (e.g. certain universities and colleges).

You might be interested to learn that the Association of Certified Accountants was originally constituted as a company limited by guarantee. It was granted a Royal Charter in 1974. It then became known as the Chartered Association of Certified Accountants and later changed this to the Association of Chartered Certified Accountants. Companies limited by guarantee do not have a share capital; its members guarantee to contribute a specified sum in the event that their company should become insolvent.

The financial statements of incorporated associations have to comply with the requirements of its legal constitution. You do not have to worry about this for the accounting exam; you will be dealing only with small informal associations. In any event, the financial statements of any non-trading organization (incorporated or not) are prepared on similar lines.

16.2 Sources of funds

Organizations not trading for profit do not have a capital in the same way as a trading concern. They raise and accumulate funds by various means, including some activities that are akin to trading.

Activity 1

Think about any typical sports or social club, and make a note here of the various means by which it could raise money in order to provide (or improve) facilities for its members. Aim at listing about four different sources.

Some of the larger sports clubs (particularly tennis and golf clubs) issue debentures in order to raise money for new land, buildings, and equipment. These debentures are similar to those issued by a trading company and will be classified as a liability in the balance sheet. Apart from carrying the right to receive interest, these debentures quite often provide the holders with certain privileges (such as special seating facilities) at sporting events organized by the club.

16.3 Purpose of the financial statements

A trading concern exists in order to make profits for the owners. This profit is determined by preparing a profit and loss account under the accruals convention. The success (or otherwise) of the entity's performance is often assessed by reference to this profit.

In the case of a non-trading concern, the revenue statement that is analogous to the profit and loss account is called an **income and expenditure account**. This is also prepared under the accruals convention.

But sports and social clubs do not exist in order to generate profits; they exist to meet an identified objective. Consequently, performance in financial terms is not measured by the surplus of income over expenditure but rather by the way in which the income has been spent. The primary purpose of the financial statements of a non-trading association is to account for the stewardship of the funds entrusted to it by its members. If money is raised for specific purposes, this is reflected in the financial statements by an income and expenditure account for each specified purpose.

In the case of a small sports or social club, there is usually one general purpose, i.e. the provision of facilities for its members. Consequently, there is usually one income and expenditure account where the excess of income over expenditure each year is determined and then accumulated on a 'general fund'. This general fund is usually called the **accumulated fund** and is analogous to the capital account of a sole trader. It represents the sum total of all the various assets and liabilities of the association. The balance sheet is similar in appearance to that of a sole trader but with the accumulated fund taking the place of the proprietor's capital account.

Notice how the word 'fund' is used (as it often is in accounting) to refer to an aggregate of various assets and liabilities. The balance on the accumulated fund might represent the amount of cash that has been raised over the years but this cash will be invested in various assets (e.g. pavilions and sports equipment) provided for the benefit of members.

In some cases the association will raise funds for a specified (rather than general) purpose. A separate income and expenditure account is then prepared to determine the net amount raised each year for that purpose. These amounts are accumulated on a separate (named) fund which is then included on the 'capital' side of the balance sheet in addition to the general fund. Sometimes the assets representing these funds are specifically earmarked on the net assets side of the balance sheet, e.g. by being placed in a separate deposit account at the bank. But more often than not (due to poor financial control) the cash is used for general purposes and loses its separate identity.

16.4 Format of the financial statements

Some small associations are quite content to account for their activities by presenting members with a receipts and payments account. This account is nothing more than a summary of entries in the cash book. In the exams you are usually asked to prepare a full set of financial statements from information that includes the receipts and payments account. The financial statements required will consist of an income and expenditure account (prepared under the accruals and matching conventions) and a balance sheet.

The 'income' in the income and expenditure account is not likely to be the same as cash received in the cash book, and 'expenditure' is not likely to be the same as cash paid.

Activity 2

Make a note of as many points as you can that explain why income might differ from receipts, and why expenditure might differ from payments. List them under the following headings:

income/receipts   **expenditure/payments**

The difference between total income and total expenditure is not referred to as a profit (or a loss) but as the 'excess of income over expenditure' (or the excess of expenditure over income). We could determine this excess by simply listing all the different items of income and all the different items of expenditure. But this is not likely to be very helpful to the members.

The club might have generated funds from various functions, such as the summer fair, the autumn bring and buy sale, and the Christmas raffle. Each one of these will have generated its own surplus or loss. There is no need to prepare a separate income and expenditure account for each function since they are all contributing to the accumulated fund, but it is quite helpful to the membership if the income and expenses of each function are matched within the format of a single income and expenditure account. This is normally done before adding on any general items of income (such as subscriptions) and deducting general expenses such as repairs to premises.

The remaining activities in this chapter are based on the financial information provided for the Barnwood Orchard Club. The details for these activities are as follows:

The Barnwood Orchard Club is a club that provides social and keep-fit facilities for its members. The receipts and payments account for year ending 31 December 1996 was as follows:

Receipts		Payments	
Opening balance	305	Bar purchases	7,590
Bar sales	13,500	Barman's salary	2,600
Subscriptions	3,500	New bar furniture	1,095
Keep-fit course fees	4,580	New keep-fit equipment	800
		Loan repayment	200
		Loan interest	50
		General expenses	3,230
		Keep-fit tutor's salary	4,500
		Donations to charities	1,480
		Repairs to premises	110
		Closing balance	230
	21,885		21,885

The assets and liabilities of the club were as follows:

	1 Jan 1996 £	31 Dec 1996 £
Bar stock	290	410
Subscriptions in arrears	160	230
Subscriptions received in advance	35	20
Bar furniture at book value	675	(to be calculated)
Keep-fit equipment at book value	200	(to be calculated)
Creditors for bar stock	340	460
Loan payable	500	300
Premises	15,000	14,500

Bar furniture and keep-fit equipment is to be depreciated at the rate of 10% on book value. A full year's depreciation is provided in the year of purchase.

Activity 3

Review the information given for Barnwood Orchard Club to see if you find any separate activities where it should be possible to match the income and expenditure in order to determine the surplus (or deficit) arising from that activity. Make a note here of the ones you notice.

The surplus arising on bar sales is determined in a separate statement and only the net income is brought into the income and expenditure account. This separate statement is drawn up on similar lines to a trading and profit and loss account. It should include a calculation of the gross profit before any expenses are deducted.

Despite the fact that the organization is not trading for profit, it is quite common practice to refer to **gross profit** from activities that are akin to trading (such as bar sales). The gross profit figure is quite important; keeping an eye on the gross profit percentage is one of the financial controls that a small association can adopt. It should be possible to estimate the percentage expected, and any marked variation between this and the actual percentage achieved should be investigated.

Activity 4

Make a note of the types of expense (not the amount) that will be deducted from gross profit in order to determine the net income (or loss) from bar sales in the case of Barnwood Orchard Club.

The gain or loss on 'keep-fit courses' can be determined on the face of the income and expenditure account itself. This is done by an inset tabulation of the income and related expenses; the net result being extended into the main income column.

Activity 5

Make a note of the types of expense that will be deducted from the keep-fit course fees in the case of Barnwood Orchard Club.

16.5 Finding the missing figures

In order to calculate figures for the financial statements you must approach the problem in the same way as you did for a trading organization. In order to encourage you to develop a methodical approach (and deal with any problems peculiar to clubs) you should work through the following activities and check each one with the Key before proceeding to the next.

Activity 6

The opening balance on the accumulated fund will be the aggregate of the club's assets and liabilities at the beginning of the year. Calculate this figure now and make a note of it here. Take care over this; it is quite easy to miss one of the figures.

There are two other workings that are worth doing before you start to draft out the statements.

Activity 7

Calculate the amount to be included in the bar trading account for purchases.

Subscriptions are dealt with on an accruals basis, as with any other item. The subscriptions to be included in the 1996 accounts are those which relate to 1996.

Activity 8

Calculate the amount to be included in the income and expenditure account for subscriptions. Take care with this one, subscriptions is an income item not an expense. If you find it difficult to calculate, set out a 'T' account in the normal way.

Activity 9

Subscriptions for the year is another figure over which the members can keep a watchful eye. It is usually possible to predict what the amount for subscriptions should be in the financial statements. Make a note of how this could be done.

There is a further discussion of subscriptions in section 16.6, but the points covered are not relevant to the activities based on Barnwood Orchard Club.

Activity 10

The remaining calculations can be done at the same time as the financial statements are drafted. You should do these now on your own paper. Deal with the separate income statement for the bar first. This is given various names – perhaps the most appropriate is income from bar sales. This avoids having to use the word 'trading' as part of the title. The figure akin to net profit on bar sales should be called **net income from bar sales** in order to avoid using the term 'net profit'. The net asset side of the balance sheet takes the same form as with any other organization. The capital side is similar to that of a sole trader except that the capital account is called an accumulated fund.

16.6 Annual subscriptions and life subscriptions

Annual subscriptions and exam questions

The way in which examiners give information on annual subscriptions varies from question to question. In some cases you might have to work out the accruals and prepayments based on details of the numbers of members and an analysis of the cash received. There are no hard and fast rules on how to cope with all these variations other than to keep in mind that your calculations are aimed at finding the annual subscriptions applicable to the year. In some cases you might find it necessary to write off overdue subscriptions from previous years.

Life subscriptions

Another problem is that some clubs and associations allow members to pay what is known as a life subscription, in lieu of an annual subscription. This is a single payment which entitles the subscriber to enjoy the benefits of membership over a number of years.

Activity 11

Life subscriptions pose a particular accounting problem under the accruals convention. Make a note here of what you consider this problem to be.

A Statement of Recommended Practice (SORP) issued by the Charity Commission in October 1995 requires life subscriptions to be included as income on a consistent basis. An example given states that if the life subscription is twenty times the annual subscription, one-twentieth of it might be recognised as income each year.

In examinations, the question will state the basis by which life subscriptions are to be allocated to accounting periods. The problems remaining are as follows:

- dealing with the book-keeping entries and presentation of balances
- calculating the amount to be treated as income for the year in question

When cash is received for a life subscription it should be credited to a deferred income account. This account will probably be named simply as 'life subscriptions'. To the extent that this account (a credit balance) has not been transferred to the profit and loss account, it will be carried forward in the balance sheet. Although it is a credit balance, it is not a liability, it represents deferred income which will be allocated to future accounting periods.

You are familiar with the idea of deferring costs to future periods (as with fixed assets) but this is the first time deferred income has been mentioned in this book. You will come across the problem again in Chapter 19 when dealing with government grants under SSAP 4. The amount of deferred income (i.e. the amount to be allocated to future periods) can either be presented as a deduction from net assets, or included on the equity side of the balance sheet. Providing the credit balance is adequately described, there should be no misunderstanding over its true nature.

When it comes to calculating the amount to be treated as income for the year, examiners occasionally have a habit of contriving the detail. As with annual subscriptions, it is not possible to develop any rules for coping with these situations because examiners constantly change the way in which the details are presented. It is simply a matter of interpreting the information, and making the calculations based on a firm understanding of the concepts involved.

Summary

The main learning points in this chapter are as follows:

- the financial statements of a non-trading organization are based on the same principles as those of a trading concern
- the purpose of the financial statements is to show the income received and the way this income has been spent
- income is raised by various means and the excess of income over expenditure (or vice versa) for each year is accumulated on a general fund
- the accumulated fund is similar to a sole trader's capital account
- if the association raises funds for a specific purpose, a separate income and expenditure account is prepared and the net income is accumulated on a separate fund account
- most clubs raise funds by various activities and the net gain or loss on each activity is presented in the income and expenditure account by matching income from that activity with its related expenditure
- in cases where funds are raised by activities that are akin to trading (such as running a bar or a dining room) the net income from such activities should be calculated on a separate statement; the net income is then shown as a single figure in the income and expenditure account
- some members might pay life subscriptions instead of annual subscriptions
- life subscriptions should be allocated (as income) to the periods for which it is anticipated that the subscriptions will apply
- to the extent that life subscriptions have not been allocated as income they are carried forward as deferred income and suitably described in the balance sheet

Activity 1
The most common sources include: (1) members' subscriptions; (2) profits from (say) bar sales; (3) surpluses from activities such as fairs, gate entrance fees, and raffles; (4) donations from various sources; (5) legacies.

Activity 2
The learning point from this activity will have been made if you came up with lists similar to the following:

income/receipts	expenditure/payments
Subscriptions owing or prepaid	Expenditure will recognize creditors, accruals, prepayments, and stocks
Receipts include sale of fixed assets	Payments include purchase of fixed assets
Receipts include loans received	Expenditure includes depreciation
	Payments include loan repayments

Activity 3
There are only two: (1) bar sales and (2) keep-fit courses.

Activity 4
There are two: (1) barman's salary and (2) depreciation on bar furniture.

Activity 5
There are two: (1) the keep-fit tutor's salary and (2) depreciation on keep-fit equipment.

Activity 6
The answer is £15,755. If you did not come up with this figure you may have forgotten the opening bank balance (this is quite easy to miss because it is not in the list of balances). You must also recognize that subscriptions in arrears are debtors and subscriptions in advance are creditors.

Activity 7
The amount is £7,710 (i.e. 7,590 + 460 − 340).

Activity 8
The amount is £3,585. Subscriptions very nearly always involve making adjustments for income due and income prepaid. If you find this awkward to handle, set out a 'T' account as follows:

Subscriptions account

Subs in arrears b/d	160	Subs in advance b/d	35
Subs in advance c/d	20	Subs in arrears c/d	230
Income from subscriptions (balancing figure)	3,585	Bank	3,500
	3,765		3,765

Activity 9
From the number of members times the annual subscription. You will have to think on these lines in one of the self-assessment questions at the end of this chapter.

Activity 10

Income from bar sales for year ended 31 December 1996

Sales		13,500
Less cost of sales:		
Opening bar stock	290	
Purchases	7,710	
	8,000	
Closing bar stock	410	
		7,590
Gross income		5,910
Bar expenses:		
Barman's salary	2,600	
Depreciation of furniture	177	
		2,777
Net income		3,133

Income and expenditure account for year ended 31 December 1996

Net income from bar sales		3,133
Income from subscriptions		3,585
		6,718
Loss on keep-fit courses:		
Fees received	4,580	
Tutor's salary	(4,500)	
Depreciation of equipment	(100)	
		20
Total income		6,698
Expenditure:		
Loan interest	50	
General expenses	3,230	
Donations to charities	1,480	
Repairs to premises	110	
Depreciation of premises	500	
		5,370
Excess of income over expenditure		1,328

Balance sheet at 31 December 1996

Fixed assets:			
Premises at net book value			14,500
Bar furniture at net book value			1,593
Keep-fit equipment at net book value			900
			16,993
Current assets:			
Bar stock		410	
Subscriptions in arrears		230	
Bank balance		230	
		870	
Current liabilities:			
Creditors for bar stock	460		
Subscriptions in advance	20		
		480	
			390
Total assets less current liabilities			17,383

Long-term liabilities: Loan payable	300
	17,083

Accumulated general fund:

Accumulated balance at 1 January 1996	15,755
Excess of income over expenditure for 1996	1,328
Accumulated balance at 31 December 1996	17,083

Tutorial note: It was easy to miss the depreciation of £500 on the premises (see schedule of opening and closing balances). Don't be too cross with yourself if you missed it.

Activity 11

Allocating the income from life subscriptions over the years during which the subscriber will be receiving benefits from membership. This involves carrying some of the income forward to future years.

Questions for self-assessment

Answers to self-assessment questions are given at the end of the book.

16.1 Viewpoint Chamber Orchestra. The following A Level question will require you to use your own initiative regarding presentation (a fairly common feature of questions on this topic). You will also need to spend a little time trying to make sense of the subscription information.

The treasurer of the Viewpoint Chamber Orchestra has prepared the following receipts and payments account for the year ended 31 July 1988:

Receipts	£	Payments	£
Opening balance	1,130	Fees to conductor and	
Concert ticket sales	1,980	soloists for concerts	780
Concert programme sales	320	Secretary's honorarium	550
Donations received	550	Hire of music for concerts	970
Fund raising	970	Hire of halls for concerts	1,100
Investments income	300	Administration expenses	1,100
Members' subscriptions	1,375	Purchase of music scores	850
		Closing balance	1,175
	6,625		6,625

Additional information.
1. There were 47 orchestral members for the year ended 31 July 1988 and the annual subscription for the year was £25 for each member.
2. The subscriptions received above were analysed as follows:

	£
Subscriptions relating to year ended 31 July 1987	100
Subscriptions relating to year ended 31 July 1988	1,125

The balance on the subscriptions account relates to monies received from members for the year ending 31 July 1989.
3. The hire of music for concerts and hire of halls figures above did not include £170 and £140, respectively, relating to the last concert of the year on 10 June 1988.
4. The orchestra's assets were valued as follows:

	at 31 July 1987 £	at 31 July 1988 £
Music stands	235	200
Music scores	1,700	2,250
Investments	3,200	3,200

5. Donations are treated as revenue receipts.

Required:
(a) A statement to show the profit or loss on concert performances for the year ended 31 July 1988.
(b) The Viewpoint Chamber Orchestra's income and expenditure account for the year ended 31 July 1988 and a balance sheet as at that date.

(AEB, Nov 88)

16.2 The accounting records of the Happy Tickers Sports and Social Club are in a mess. You manage to find the following information to help you prepare the accounts for the year to 31 December:

Summarized balance sheet 31 December 1989

	£		£
Half-share in motorized		Insurance (3 months)	150
roller	600	Subscriptions 1990	120
New sports equipment, unsold	1,000	Life subscriptions	1,400
Used sports equipment at			1,670
valuation	700	Accumulated fund	2,900
Rent (2 months)	200		
Subscriptions 1989	60		
Cafe stocks	800		
Cash and bank	1,210		
	4,570		4,570

Receipts in the year to 31 December 1990:	£
Subscriptions – 1989	40
– 1990	1,100
– 1991	80
– life	200
From sales of new sports equipment	900
From sales of used sports equipment	14
Cafe takings	4,660
	6,994

Payments in the year to 31 December 1990:	
Rent (for 12 months)	1,200
Insurance (for 18 months)	900
To suppliers of sports equipment	1,000
To cafe suppliers	1,900
Wages of cafe manager	2,000
Total cost of repairing motorized roller	450
	7,450

Notes:

(i) Ownership and all expenses of the motorized roller are agreed to be shared equally with the Carefree Conveyancers Sports and Social Club, which occupies a nearby site. The roller cost a total of £2,000 on 1 January 1986 and had an estimated life of 10 years.

(ii) Life subscriptions are brought into income equally over 10 years, in a scheme begun in 1985. Since the scheme began the cost of £200 per person has been constant. Prior to 31 December 1989 10 life subscriptions had been received.

(iii) Four more annual subscriptions of £20 each had been promised relating to 1990, but not yet received. Annual subscriptions promised but unpaid are carried forward for a maximum of 12 months.

(iv) New sports equipment is sold to members at cost plus 50%. Used equipment is sold off to members at book valuation. Half the sports equipment bought in the year (all from a cash and carry supplier) has been used within the club, and half made available for sale, new, to members. The 'used equipment at valuation' figure in the 31 December 1990 balance sheet is to remain at £700.

(v) Closing cafe stocks are £850, and £80 is owed to suppliers at 31 December 1990.

Required:

(a) Calculate profit on cafe operations and profit on sale of sports equipment.

(b) Prepare a statement of subscription income for 1990.

(c) Prepare income and expenditure statement for the year to 31 December 1990, and balance sheet as at 31 December 1990.

(d) Why do life subscriptions appear as a liability?

(ACCA 1.1, Dec 90)

Questions without answers

Answers to these questions are published separately in the *Teacher's Manual*.

16.3 Scout troop. A scout troop collects subscriptions from its members, and also has to pay 60% of them to central scouting funds. In the year to 31 December 1988 the troop receives:

For 1987	£20
For 1988	£60
For 1989	£10

It pays to central funds in that year:

For 1987	£12
For 1988	£30
For 1989	nil

Required:
(a) Produce a summary of the subscription position for the troop for the year 1988, on:
    (i) a receipts and payments basis,
    (ii) a revenue and expenses basis.
(b) Outline the advantages and disadvantages of each basis with reference to appropriate accounting conventions. Give the scout troop leader your recommended method, with reasons. Discuss also any difficult decisions you have to make in deciding your answer to (a) above.

(ACCA 1.1, Jun 89)

16.4 You have been appointed the book-keeper of a tennis club called Rackets Unlimited. The club began on 1 July 1989, and no accounts have yet been prepared. The club has three ways of receiving subscriptions:
(i) £10 per year.
(ii) If two years' subscriptions are paid at once £1 may be deducted from the second year. If three years' subscriptions are paid at once, £2 may also be deducted from the third year.
(iii) If 10 years' subscriptions are paid at once no deductions are allowed, but members are regarded as members for life.
You have completed the following table of subscriptions receipts:

Member	relevant to membership year ended 30.6.90		relevant to membership year ended 30.6.91		relevant to membership year ended 30.6.92	
	date received	amount £	date received	amount £	date received	amount £
A	July 89	10				
B	July 89	10	July 90	10		
C	July 89	10	June 90	10	July 91	10
D	Sept 89	10	Sept 90	27		
E	Oct 89	27				
F	Oct 89	10	July 90	10	June 91	27
G	Oct 89	100				
H	Oct 89	10	June 90	10	June 91	100
I	Oct 89	10	June 90	19		
J	July 91	10	July 91	10		
K	July 90	27	July 90	27		
L	Dec 89	10			June 91	10
M	July 90	19				
N			July 91	100		

The club does not intend to accrue for any income not received by the date of preparation of financial statements.

Required:

(a) To assist in the preparation of some accounts, complete a table with the following headings:

Member	Income year to 30.6.90	Income year to 30.6.91	Balance c/f at 30.6.91	
			Dr.	Cr.

(b) State two comments about your table which you think might be helpful to the club committee.

(ACCA 1.1, Jun 92)

16.5 You have agreed to take over the role of book-keeper for the AB sports and social club. The summarized balance sheet on 31 December 1994 as prepared by the previous book-keeper contained the following items (all figures are in £s).

Assets

Heating oil for clubhouse		1,000
Bar and cafe stocks		7,000
New sportsware, for sale, at cost		3,000
Used sportsware, for hire, at valuation		750
Equipment for groundsperson – cost	5,000	
– depreciation	3,500	1,500
Subscriptions due		200
Bank – current account		1,000
– deposit account		10,000

Claims

Accumulated fund	23,150
Creditors – bar and cafe stocks	1,000
– sportsware	300

The bank account summary for the year to 31 December 1995 contained the following items:

Receipts

Subscriptions	11,000
Bankings – bar and cafe	20,000
– sale of sportsware	5,000
– hire of sportsware	3,000
Interest on deposit account	800

Payments

Rent and repairs of clubhouse	6,000
Heating oil	4,000
Sportsware	4,500
Groundsperson	10,000
Bar and cafe purchases	9,000
Transfer to deposit account	6,000

You discover that the subscriptions due figure as at 31 December 1994 was arrived at as follows:

Subscriptions unpaid for 1993	10
Subscriptions unpaid for 1994	230
Subscriptions paid for 1995	40

Corresponding figures at 31 December 1995 are:

Subscriptions unpaid for 1993	10
Subscriptions unpaid for 1994	20
Subscriptions unpaid for 1995	90
Subscriptions paid for 1996	200

Subscriptions due for more than 12 months should be written off with effect from 1 January 1995.

Asset balances at 31 December 1995 include:

Heating oil for clubhouse	700
Bar and cafe stocks	5,000
New sportsware, for sale, at cost	4,000
Used sportsware, for hire, at valuation	1,000

Closing creditors at 31 December 1995 are:

For bar and cafe stocks	800
For sportsware	450
For heating oil for clubhouse	200

Two-thirds of the sportsware purchases made in 1995 had been added to stock of new sportsware in the figures given in the list of assets above, and one-third had been added directly to the stock of used sportsware for hire.

Half of the resulting 'new sportsware for sale at cost' at 31 December 1995 is actually over two years old. You decide, with effect from 31 December 1995, to transfer these older items in the stock of used sportsware, at a valuation of 25% of their original cost.

No cash balances are held at 31 December 1994 or 31 December 1995. The equipment for the groundsperson is to be depreciated at 10% per annum, on cost.

Required:

Prepare income and expenditure account and balance sheet for the AB sports club for 1995, in a form suitable for circulation to members. The information given should be as complete and informative as possible within the limits of the information given to you. All workings must be submitted.

(ACCA, Jun 96)

Introduction

Foundation studies in accounting tend to concentrate on the way the financial statements are affected by different kinds of ownership rather than on the effect of specialized business activity. You might have noticed how many of the previous chapters in this book have been concerned with the influences of ownership rather than activity, one exception being Chapter 8, on manufacturing. This approach to learning accounting is quite sound; it is neither possible nor desirable to study the special problems associated with every kind of activity. This is clearly reflected in the various examinations at a foundation level.

It is quite useful to isolate three important aspects of accounting that have to be considered when dealing with specialized activity, namely:

- the special records and accounting reports required
- the control techniques to be incorporated in the accounting system
- the policy to be adopted for measuring profit, and any related assets or liabilities resulting from the activity

To a large extent, the question of accounting measurements has been resolved by requiring companies to comply with the accounting standards developed for particular types of activity. There are SSAPs to regulate how profits and balance sheet items should be measured for activities such as: hire-purchase trading, leasing, and long-term contracts in the civil engineering and construction industries. You will be studying certain aspects of these accounting standards in Chapter 19.

In this chapter you will be learning how 'sectional activity' creates its own peculiar brand of accounting problem. The term **sectional activity** is used to identify a situation where the total profit of an entity is derived from different segments of the business, such as departments or branches. Departmental and branch trading does not entail any specific problem of profit recognition for the business as a whole; profits are determined under the generally accepted principles of accounting (promulgated through SSAPs and FRSs). The problem faced by the accountant in these cases is mainly one of classifying the transactions so that the results of each sectional activity can be determined, in addition to setting up central accounting controls over activities that are carried on in separate locations.

Although financial accounting is used as a basis for the study, the accounting reports produced by the system are mainly for internal management purposes rather than for reporting to external users. The subject is, therefore, closely associated with management accounting in the sense that the information is used for control and decision making.

17.1 Types of sectional activity

Many large-scale enterprises (and some of the smaller ones) derive their total profit from sectional activity. The way in which an enterprise is divided into sections will vary, and the following table gives an indication of the most common bases adopted:

Basis of division	Examples
By activities or products	(a) retail store with several departments (b) manufacturing and merchandising (c) manufacture or sale of different products
By geographical location	(a) supermarkets and chain stores with several branches (b) coal mining from different pits
By legal separation	separate companies are formed for each division, each company being part of a 'group' under the control of a holding company

The accounting problems associated with 'groups' are dealt with in Chapter 18. The division of an entity into manufacturing and selling divisions was covered by Chapter 8. This leaves departmental and branch trading to be considered in this chapter.

17.2 Departmental trading

Any large departmental store with which you are familiar will provide a useful mental image on which to base this study, but you should keep in mind that the same set of principles can be applied to any kind of business (manufacturing or selling) where total profit is derived from sectional activity.

The problem is one of determining the profit contributed by each department. When you were working on the income and expenditure account for the Barnwood Orchard Club in Chapter 16, you produced a miniature version of a departmental profit report. The two sectional activities akin to trading were (1) bar sales and (2) keep-fit courses, and you produced a separate report for each of these in order to show the net amounts contributed by each activity to the total surplus of the club. The same concept applies to trading departments.

Activity 1

Give some thought as to why management might wish to know the results of each department. Aim at finding two reasons and make a note of them here:

1.

2.

Departmental profit reports are mainly for internal management purposes; the detailed figures are not submitted to shareholders. Since these reports are part of a management information system, you will find that some of the concepts involved are dealt with again in the study of management accounting. The last accounting standard promulgated by the old Accounting Standards Committee (SSAP 25) and adopted by the ASB does require listed companies to publish an additional report giving an analysis of results by business segment, but this is beyond the scope of accounting studies at a foundation level.

The problem faced by the accountant is mainly one of classification (and coding) of departmental costs and departmental income in order to prepare the profit reports for each department. Up to a point there will be little difficulty in identifying the costs incurred by a particular selling department.

Activity 2

Make a note of the types of cost that can easily be identified as directly attributable to a particular selling department in a departmental store. Aim at finding three but be satisfied with two before you turn to the Key for help if needed.

1.

2.

3.

A cost accountant refers to these items as 'direct costs' because there is no doubt that they are directly related to a particular department. These direct costs would not have been incurred if the department did not exist. The process of charging direct costs to departments is called cost allocation.

The term 'allocation' is used in order to differentiate between the accounting treatment of direct costs, and the treatment of certain costs that relate to the business as a whole and have to be 'apportioned' to the different departments. The process of cost apportionment is used when departments are sharing the benefits derived from certain types of expenditure that cannot be allocated to any one department. These non-specific costs are shared out and charged to all departments on a pro rata basis.

Activity 3

There will be many costs that are not specific to any one department, but where each department receives a benefit from that expenditure. Make a note of some of the costs that you consider might fall under this heading.

These costs are called the 'indirect costs' of the department. Notice that direct costs are **allocated** to departments, and indirect costs are **apportioned**. The basis used for apportionment of indirect costs should bear some relationship to the benefits received by each department from the costs concerned. It is not difficult to find an appropriate basis for estimating the benefits received; see how you get on with the next activity.

Activity 4

See if you can think of a reasonable basis for apportioning each of the following types of indirect cost to different departments:

Apportionment basis

1. Occupancy costs such as rent, rates, light and heat.

2. Insurance of total trading stock.

3. A floor supervisor overseeing several departments.

4. Advertising costs.

Although these apportionments appear to be based on some kind of logic, they are purely accounting apportionments based on a policy decision. The practice of cost apportionment can sometimes produce information that is misleading to management and it might be preferable to leave them out of the departmental report. We will look at that in a moment, but for now we need to think about the remaining costs, which are neither allocated nor apportioned.

Activity 5

There will be many costs that relate to the business as a whole that cannot logically be attributed to sales departments. Make a note of a few types of cost that would fall into this category.

In this chapter, we will refer to these costs as general overheads. The profit (or loss) of each department should be determined without reference to general overheads. Departmental profits can then be aggregated in a separate statement and general overheads deducted in order to arrive at a total net profit for the whole business.

You might find some examination questions require you to apportion the general overheads over all departments on an arbitrary basis. This can exacerbate the problem referred to earlier regarding apportionment of indirect costs, but you might find you have been asked to discuss this aspect as part of your answer.

You will get some idea of how cost apportionment can distort accounting information by working on a simple (imaginary) example. The details for the example are as follows:

A departmental store has three sales departments: jewellery sales, ladies clothes, and a restaurant for customers. The following data are available:

Departmental accounting data	Jewellery £	Ladies clothes £	Restaurant £
Sales	60,000	250,000	120,000
Cost of sales	36,000	130,000	70,000
Departmental salaries	12,000	40,000	30,000
Direct expenses	1,000	4,000	10,000
Statistical data			
Floor area in square metres	40	260	100

Other costs

Occupancy costs (rent, rates, insurance, etc.) of the whole building were £60,000, and general overheads were £12,000.

Activity 6

Prepare the departmental profit statements on the assumption that occupancy costs are apportioned to departments on the basis of floor area. General overheads are not apportioned. You can work this activity by completing the table below.

Departmental profit statements

	Jewellery		Ladies clothes		Restaurant	
Sales		60,000		250,000		120,000
Cost of sales		36,000		130,000		70,000
Gross profit		24,000		120,000		50,000
Departmental salaries	12,000		40,000		30,000	
Direct expenses	1,000		4,000		10,000	
Occupancy costs						
Profit (or loss)						

Check your figures with the Key before going on to the next activity.

Activity 7

A manager reviewing the departmental figures concludes that the restaurant should be closed because it is causing the company to lose money. Consider whether or not the restaurant is losing money and make a note of your observations.

One of the problems inherent in cost apportionment is that most of the costs are 'fixed'. In other words, the cost would be incurred whether a particular department existed or not. A part of these costs might be saved if the department is closed, but most of them (rent, rates, heating, etc.) would continue at the same level as before the closure. Closing down a department would simply load these costs on to the remaining departments.

Costs that can be saved by closing down a segment are often called avoidable costs since such costs will not be incurred if the department does not exist. Costs that will continue even though the department is closed down are then referred to as unavoidable costs. It is a pity that this concept is not understood more widely, particularly by politicians, who often talk about product costs in industries such as coal mining as if the 'cost' of a product is something known with certainty.

The 1984/85 miners' strike was precipitated by the proposed closure of the Cortonwood pit in Yorkshire. The National Coal Board (NCB) claimed that the pit was uneconomic and produced figures (based on the 1981/82 profit and loss account) to show that the operating costs of producing a tonne of coal were greater than the net sale proceeds. These figures revealed a loss of £6.20 per tonne. Yet on a subsequent analysis (November 1984) it was shown that some of the operating costs included in the calculation of this loss were unavoidable costs, such as an apportionment of the NCB's overheads and management services. These costs would continue to be incurred even after closure of the pit. When the unavoidable costs were taken out of the equation, each tonne of coal from the pit was shown to be contributing £5.75 to the NCB's profits.

Activity 8

In the case of our simple example of a departmental store, assume that none of the occupancy costs can be saved if the restaurant is closed. Assume also that by closing down the restaurant it is not going to be possible to increase the sales revenue of either of the other two departments and that future results would be the same as the current year. On the basis of these two assumptions, review the figures and calculate:

1. The total profit from departments (before general overheads) when the restaurant is included.

2. The total profit from departments (before general overheads) if the restaurant is closed down.

Any accounting information that includes apportioned fixed costs can easily be misunderstood by management. The quality of information on sectional activity can be improved by making use of a concept known as 'contribution'. The idea of contribution is that the difference between sales income and direct costs is contributing to the firm's total profits. Notice how the profits (in Activity 8) drop by £10,000 if the restaurant is closed. If you look at the figures more closely you will see that the restaurant is making a contribution of £10,000 to the firm's total profits. This contribution will be lost if the department is closed.

The contribution from each department can be calculated as follows:

	Jewellery		Ladies clothes		Restaurant	
Sales income		60,000		250,000		120,000
Cost of sales	36,000		130,000		70,000	
Salaries	12,000		40,000		30,000	
Direct expenses	1,000		4,000		10,000	
	49,000		174,000		110,000	
Contribution		11,000		76,000		10,000

The total contribution is £97,000. Fixed occupancy costs are £60,000, leaving a profit of £37,000 before deducting general overheads. This is the same as when the occupancy costs were apportioned, but at least we are showing that there is a contribution of £10,000 from the restaurant and so we are less likely to mislead management into making the wrong decision.

In our analysis of the departmental store we have simply considered the figures. These figures are referred to as the quantitative factors. Decision making will involve management in considering factors that are not revealed by the figures. These are known as qualitative factors, and require management to consider all related aspects (such as customer loyalty and customer behaviour) of making a particular decision.

Qualitative factors are just as important as the numbers, and you are quite often asked to comment on these qualitative factors when answering examination questions. It is only necessary to apply a little bit of imagination in order to come up with a few ideas, but you will have to drag your head out of the figures and think about the actual situation.

Activity 9

Assume we produced figures to show that the restaurant in our departmental store is actually causing the firm to lose money. Assume also that it is not considered possible to improve the profitability of the restaurant. Make a note of some factors that management should consider when deciding whether or not to close down the restaurant.

In matters of national interest (such as closing down a coal mine) there might be other factors such as 'green issues' or social problems to consider under this heading. Sometimes an attempt is made to quantify these factors in a 'cost/benefit' analysis but the figures are usually viewed with suspicion since they tend to be highly subjective.

17.3 Branch trading

Up to a point, the accounting problems of branch trading are the same as for departmental trading. In order to exercise control over the branches, central management will require the accounting system to provide profit reports of each branch. Branch managers might receive part of their remuneration (bonuses and commissions) based on branch profits. If head office provides support services to the branches there will probably be some method of apportioning the costs of these services to the branches.

These aspects of branch accounting are the same as for departmental trading. To this extent, the fact that each trading outlet is located in a different geographical area rather than being in the same building does not place any additional burden on the accounting system.

In exams, you are often asked to prepare figures to help management with the same kind of decision as for departments, e.g. whether or not to close down an unprofitable branch. Your approach to solving these problems should be exactly the same as for departments, i.e. determining the lost contribution if the branch is closed down. You might find that the branch incurs local fixed costs, and such costs would clearly cease if the branch is closed. But the amount of head office costs apportioned to the branch is not likely to be avoided simply by closing down a branch. There may be some saving in head office costs but it is more likely that they will continue at the same level as without the closure.

The way in which branch accounting systems differ from those for departmental accounting is related to the fact that management will need to exercise some kind of accounting control over operations carried on at a distant location.

There are wide variations in the degree of control exercised by a head office and, because the system of branch accounting is often related to this degree of control, there are wide variations in the accounting systems used.

It is helpful to draw a distinction between two extremes in the relationships that might exist between a head office and its branches. These two extremes can be identified as follows:

1. **Centrally controlled branches:** all major decisions made by head office. Stocks purchased centrally and distributed to branches.
2. **Autonomous branches:** the branch operates with a high degree of independence. Stocks are purchased locally.

In most cases, the relationship between head office and branch will be somewhere in between these two extremes. For example, a branch with a high degree of managerial autonomy might receive most of its supplies from a central warehouse but will also make some local purchases.

The distinction does, however, help us to understand something about the different forms of book-keeping systems that are found in practice. The kind of records kept for the branch, and the location of these records, is often linked to the degree of head office control.

A centrally controlled branch will have few (if any) accounting staff. Its local accounting records will consist of little more than a record of daily takings, local petty cash disbursements, and daily bankings. All double-entry accounting records concerning the branch's trading operations will be kept at head office and written up from the periodic (e.g. weekly) details submitted by the branch. The details submitted by the branch are usually called 'branch returns' (not to be confused with goods returned). The trading results of the branch are prepared from information recorded in the head office ledger.

An autonomous branch will maintain its own double-entry accounting system, have its own bank account, and be responsible for paying most of the costs incurred in running the branch. It will be possible to extract a trial balance from the branch books, and prepare the financial statements of the branch from this trial balance. Transactions between head office and branch (e.g. goods received by the branch from a central warehouse, and cash remitted to head office by the branch) are recorded on what are known as 'current accounts'. In the head office ledger there is a branch current account, and in the branch ledger there is a head office current account.

Activity 10

An autonomous branch maintains its own bank account and its own double-entry accounting records. On 31 January it sends a remittance (by cheque) of £80,000 to head office. Describe the double-entry for this transaction.

Debit:

Credit:

The branch current account in the head office ledger is a mirror image of the head office current account in the branch ledger. Consequently, when the remittance of £80,000 is received by head office it will be debited to bank and credited to the branch current account.

In the balance sheet of the branch, the head office current account will normally be a credit balance. This credit balance serves the same function as the capital account of a sole trader; it represents the sum of net assets at the branch which are (in a legal sense) owned by the head office organization.

In order to prepare the financial statements of the whole firm, it will be necessary to 'consolidate' the figures for the branch with those for the head office. But this consolidation procedure is outside the scope of foundation studies in accounting.

With regard to branches that are dominated by head office management, most of the internal accounting controls are concerned with exercising control over branch stocks and the cash received from sales. The head office will need some kind of accounting record to show how much stock has been sent to the branch, and how much of this has been accounted for by sales. Any difference between these two amounts will indicate how much stock there should still be at the branch, and this can be checked by a physical count.

Very many different systems have been devised to deal with this problem. Some of the methods described in financial accounting text books were developed in the days long before cost accounting methods (and computers) were being used to any great extent. Consequently, the systems described rely on the use of financial accounting information in order to write up a control account for stock.

One of the difficulties in using financial accounting information for keeping a control account over stock is that the two main movements of stock (stock received and stock sold) are recorded in the books at different prices; stock received is at cost price and sales are at selling price. Where financial accounting is used for keeping a control account over branch stock, the method has to rely on recording the selling price of goods sent to the branch.

If we assume (for purposes of explanation) that there were no opening stocks at the branch, then the difference between the sales value of goods sent to the branch and the actual sales money received should be represented by stock at the branch at sales value. This can then be checked and any major differences investigated. It is, however, necessary to make an adjustment to reduce the stock value to cost price for the purposes of preparing the annual financial statements.

The problem for students in trying to learn the book-keeping entries for these systems is that there are so many variations. In some methods, the control account for stock (at sales value) is a memorandum exercise, in others it is incorporated into a double-entry system. Some methods determine the transfer price by adding a fixed percentage to the cost, and then account for the cost and the fixed mark-up on separate ledger accounts.

It is not necessary to learn the details of all these different methods since accountancy students at a foundation level are usually working on the end results of the book-keeping rather than making entries in the ledger. The best approach to this subject is to ignore the underlying book-keeping system and use general principles of accounting in order to solve any problems given to you by the examiner.

For example, you may have to deal with a situation where the transfer price of goods sent to an autonomous branch from a central warehouse is in excess of cost. The head office will often charge the branch for these goods at cost plus a small percentage. The idea of this mark-up is to cover the head office costs of handling the goods. The head office will account for the transaction as a sale to the branch, and the branch will simply treat it as a purchase at the price charged. The problem which this creates is similar to the one that you came across in Chapter 8, where manufactured goods were transferred to the selling division at a price in excess of cost.

Consider the following details:

A business trades from a head office and one branch. All external purchases are made by head office and all goods are kept in a central warehouse under head office control. The branch receives all of its trading stock from the central warehouse. Goods sent to the branch are charged to the branch at cost price plus 10% to cover head office handling costs. The trading results for a period are set out in the following table.

	Head office		Branch
Sales to customers		560,000	240,000
Goods sent to branch		165,000	
		725,000	
Opening stock	60,000		11,000
Purchases	510,000		–
Goods from head office	–		165,000
	570,000		176,000
Closing stock	40,000		22,000
		530,000	154,000
Gross profit		195,000	86,000

Review the figures and then work through the following activity.

Activity 11

The figures set out above show the gross profit earned by each individual trading division, but the total gross profit of the firm is not (£195,000 + £86,000) £281,000. In order to calculate the total gross profit of the whole firm, it will be necessary to make one small adjustment to the figures. See if you can work out what this adjustment is and make a note of the effect this will have on the total gross profit of the firm. The principle is exactly the same as when you dealt with a manufacturing division transferring goods to the selling division at a price in excess of cost.

Now think about the balance sheet figures and do the following activity.

Activity 12

Calculate the total amount to be included as stock in the balance sheet of this firm.

If you find it difficult to see whether the increase in the provision does actually reduce the total gross profit to its true amount, the figures can be checked as follows:

		Whole firm £
Sales to external customers (560,000 + 240,000)		800,000
Cost of sales:		
Opening stock at cost (60,000 + 10,000)	70,000	
External purchases	510,000	
	580,000	
Closing stock at cost (40,000 + 20,000)	60,000	
		520,000
Gross profit		280,000

This is the same as taking the total of £281,000 from the two trading accounts and deducting the increase in the provision for unrealized profit on stocks of £1,000.

17.4 Stock losses

A fairly common feature of accounting questions based on sectional trading (departments or branches) is that you are expected to recognize stock losses in the operating reports. Stock losses can arise from a variety of causes, including theft and pilferage.

In the case of a small business operating from a single outlet (such as a sole trader's shop) the value of stock losses will not normally be known because there is not likely to be any accounting control over stock. In these cases, if stock has been lost its cost will simply be reflected in a lower gross profit than would have been made if the stock had not been lost. Any stock lost must have been purchased at a cost, but since the stock does not exist (and cannot be included in closing stock) its cost will be reflected in the figure for cost of sales. A significant fall in the gross profit percentage of such a trader is likely to be the only indication that stock might have been lost.

With sectional trading there is usually some kind of accounting control over stock; any losses can then be determined. The fact that we can determine the cost of stock losses will not alter the profit earned by the department or branch but at least it can be reflected as an item in the operating report. The usual procedure is to show the cost of stock lost as a credit in the trading account and as a debit (expense) in the profit and loss account. The credit in the trading account can be presented as a deduction from cost of sales. (Note that the loss is represented by the cost of the stock lost, not the selling price.)

The actual profit earned will be the same as it would be if the cost of stock losses had been ignored in the operating report. You will discover this for yourself by doing the next activity.

Activity 13

The operating figures for a branch show the following: sales £100,000; opening stock at cost £10,000; purchases £60,000; closing stock at cost £12,000. The figures for stocks are based on actual quantities of stock on hand. A check between the accounting records for stock and the actual stock at the branch at the end of the period reveals that stock losses of £1,000 (at cost price) have occurred. Prepare two profit reports for the branch as follows:

1. a profit report that ignores stock losses
2. a profit report that incorporates stock losses.

Ignore all other operating expenses in these reports. You can do this activity by completing the tables set out below.

Ignoring stock losses		Incorporating stock losses	
Sales	100,000	Sales	100,000
Less cost of sales:		Cost of sales	
Opening stock		Opening stock	
Purchases		Purchases	
Closing stock		Closing stock	
Gross profit actually earned		Less stock losses	
		Gross profit on goods sold	
		Less stock losses	
		Gross profit actually earned	

17.5 Cash in transit and stock in transit

Cash in transit and stock in transit will normally arise only where a branch operates on an autonomous basis and maintains a current account with head office in its own ledger. In order to consolidate the branch results at each accounting date, it will be necessary to ensure that the credit balance on the head office current account in the branch books is for the same amount as the debit balance on the branch current account in the head office books.

Differences between the two accounts can occur as a result of transactions that take place immediately prior to the balancing date. The branch might send a remittance to head office that is not received at head office until after the accounting date; or head office might despatch goods to the branch that are not received at the branch until after the accounting date.

These items will not have any effect on the financial statements for each individual office. For example, the trading account of a branch will include an amount for stocks actually received. The fact that there are some more stocks on the way is of no consequence. The same thing applies to cash. The balance sheet of a branch will show the bank balance as it stands in the branch books; the fact that some of the cheque payments might not have reached their destination does not have be taken into account.

The point at which cash in transit and goods in transit create an added complication is when the branch results are consolidated with those of head office in order to produce financial statements for the whole entity. In this respect it is outside the scope of this text book (see section 17.3) but examiners sometimes expect you to understand the nature of cash and goods in transit in certain types of question. It is quite easy to learn how these two items are dealt with by studying how differences on the inter-office current accounts are reconciled.

Read the following details and then work through the activities that follow.

Details for the activities

A business has two trading divisions, a head office and a branch. The branch operates on an autonomous basis and keeps its own double-entry ledger. Goods are transferred from head office to the branch at cost price. The following figures have been extracted from the head office and branch ledgers at 31 December 1996:

Head office books:
Branch current account £110,000 debit balance
Cash at bank £1,400
Stock at cost £80,000

Branch books:
Head office current account £98,000 credit balance
Cash at bank £2,300
Stock at cost £50,000

Activity 14

If differences on the inter-office current accounts are overlooked, how much would be included in the combined balance sheet of the whole business for:

1. Cash at bank

2. Stock

When it comes to preparing the combined balance sheet (for the whole entity) the inter-office current accounts will not be included. If you think about the balance sheet of the total entity you will realize that the balances on these two accounts do not represent amounts receivable from, or payable to, anyone outside of the firm. They arise as a result of internal transactions and are not debtors or creditors of the total entity.

The elimination of these two accounts for the combined balance sheet is quite straightforward when the balances are for the same amount, the debit balance on one account is simply cancelled by the credit balance on the other. But differences will occur due to timing differences on internal cash and stock transfers.

You will notice in our example that the debit balance on the branch current account in the head office is £12,000 greater than the corresponding credit balance in the branch ledger. This difference has to be investigated and adjustments made in order to ensure that the two balances are for the same amount.

Assume that on investigation of this difference we find the following:

1. a remittance of £2,000 sent to head office by the branch on 30 December 1996 was received at head office on 2 January 1997
2. a consignment of goods costing £10,000 sent by head office to the branch on 30 December 1996 was received at the branch on 3 January 1997.

If you now think about the whole business (rather than individual offices) you can see that cash of £2,000 has come out of the branch bank account but has not gone into the head office bank account by the end of the year; and that goods costing £10,000 have gone out of the head office stocks but have not been included in the branch stocks by the end of the year.

It is normal practice to make adjustments for both of these items in the head office books. Cash remitted by the branch but not received at head office by the end of the year is debited to an account called cash in transit, and stock sent to the branch but not received at the branch by the end of the year is debited to an account called goods in transit. In both cases the opposite entry is made to the branch current account.

Activity 15

Describe the double-entries that will be made in the head office books for:

1. Cash in transit: Debit:

                       Credit:

2. Goods in transit: Debit:

                       Credit:

The total credit to the branch current account is (£2,000 + £10,000) £12,000 and the debit balance is reduced to £98,000. This agrees with the head office current account in the branch books, and the two accounts cancel out for the combined balance sheet. When preparing the combined balance sheet, cash in transit is aggregated with the two cash balances shown in the trial balance, and stock in transit is aggregated with closing stock of the two branches.

Activity 16

Calculate the total cash at bank, and total stocks, for the combined balance sheet:

Cash at bank: Stock at cost:

The two adjustments for items in transit have to be reversed on the first day of the new accounting period. The adjustment was purely for consolidation purposes. The normal book-keeping entries will be made when the cash is received and the stock is received in the early part of the next period.

You should note that although these assets have been described as cash in transit and stock in transit in the above explanation, they are essentially a part of the firm's cash, and a part of its stock. The words 'in transit' do not convey anything useful to an external user. In fact they might seem quite mysterious because they conjure up an image of stock being half-way down the M1. The words 'in transit' are not usually included in the description of cash and stock in any published version of the combined balance sheet.

17.6 Manager's commission

There is nothing quite like sectional activity to bring out some of the foibles that examiners have picked up over the years. One of their favourites is to require you to calculate a commission (or bonus) for a departmental manager, or branch manager. These commissions might be based on turnover or on profit.

In many cases the basis given by the examiner for calculating the commission is quite easy to follow and will not cause any difficulty. There is, however, one basis that examiners persist in using from time to time that might seem slightly puzzling the first time you come across it. It is where the manager's commission is a percentage of the amount of profit after deducting the commission.

The profit and loss account will give the amount of profit before deducting the commission, but the profit after deducting commission will depend on the amount of the commission that you are being asked to calculate. The problem is quite easy to solve by a logical use of the fractions involved. See how you get on with the following activity.

Activity 17

The net profits of a branch before charging the manager's commission are £10,500. The branch manager is entitled to a commission of 5% of the branch profits after charging the commission. Calculate the amount of commission due to the manager.

You might recall having to think this way when calculating the unrealized profit on stock at the branch.

Activity 18

Head office adds 5% to cost in order to determine transfer prices. The branch stock includes stock received from head office which was charged to the branch at a transfer price of £10,500. Calculate the unrealized profit on this stock.

Which goes to show that the thought processes developed in one situation are often used in others.

Summary

The important learning points in this chapter can be summarized as follows:

- the total operations of an entity might be divided into sections according to the type of activity, the type of product, departments, or branches
- sectional activity requires the accountant to prepare operating statements for each section, and to set up internal accounting controls over the activities carried on in separate locations
- the operating statements for sectional activity will take account of the direct costs allocated to each section, and indirect costs apportioned to each section
- indirect costs are apportioned to sections using some kind of proxy (such as floor space) as a means of estimating the benefits received
- most indirect costs are fixed and will continue to be incurred at the same rate irrespective of sectional activity
- better decisions regarding closure of a section will be made by making a distinction between avoidable and unavoidable costs
- sectional operating reports are less misleading to management if prepared on the basis of each section's contribution to total profit
- contribution is determined by deducting direct costs from sales income
- some branches are centrally controlled and have few accounting records, others are autonomous and have a complete double-entry system
- most branch accounting problems can be solved by the application of general principles of accounting
- cash in transit and goods in transit can arise at the balancing date when consolidating the results of an autonomous branch with those of head office; they are not relevant to the individual operating statements of each office
- adjustments for cash in transit and goods in transit are usually made in the head office books

Activity 1

You might have thought of: 1. for control purposes, e.g. the profitability of each department; 2. departmental bonuses, e.g. the manager's bonus.

Activity 2

Your list should encompass the following: 1. cost of goods purchased; 2. salaries of the sales assistants in that department; 3. depreciation of any fixtures used in that department (recall how depreciation was dealt with in Barnwood Orchard Club).

Activity 3

You might have included: occupancy charges such as rent, rates, light and heat, depreciation of buildings, repairs to premises; insurance charges; advertising; welfare facilities such as a staff canteen; and some central accounting services such as stock control.

Activity 4

The most frequently used bases are as follows: 1. relative floor area occupied by each department; 2. value of stock in each department; 3. number of employees in each department; 4. total sales for each department.

Activity 5

The following list should give you an idea as to whether you were thinking on the right lines: most administration expenses, bank charges, interest payments, legal fees, accountancy charges.

Activity 6

Departmental profit statements						
	Jewellery		Ladies clothes		Restaurant	
Sales		60,000		250,000		120,000
Cost of sales		36,000		130,000		70,000
Gross profit		24,000		120,000		50,000
Departmental salaries	12,000		40,000		30,000	
Direct expenses	1,000		4,000		10,000	
Occupancy costs	6,000		39,000		15,000	
		19,000		83,000		55,000
Profit (or loss)		5,000		37,000		(5,000)

Activity 7

Probably not. It is quite likely that the £15,000 occupancy costs apportioned to the restaurant would have to be paid whether the restaurant existed or not.

Activity 8

1. Departmental profits are £37,000 (as per Activity 6).
2. The profits will drop to £27,000 (i.e. £42,000 from jewellery and ladies clothes, less the £15,000 occupancy costs that cannot now be apportioned to the restaurant).

Activity 9

Points such as: does the restaurant trade encourage people to come into the store and purchase goods from other departments (a loss leader)? What could be done with the space occupied by the restaurant if it were closed down? Will we lose existing customers if the restaurant is closed?

Activity 10

Debit head office current account £80,000 and credit bank £80,000.

Activity 11

The adjustment is for the unrealized profit on stock at the branch. We will have to deduct the increase in this provision from the total of the two profits.

Provision brought forward on opening stock (1/11 × 11,000)	1,000
Provision to be carried forward on closing stock (1/11 × 22,000)	2,000
Increase	1,000

Total gross profit is therefore £281,000 − £1,000 = £280,000.

Activity 12

The stock will be £60,000, i.e. £40,000 + £22,000 − £2,000.

Activity 13

Ignoring stock losses			Incorporating stock losses		
Sales		100,000	Sales		100,000
Less cost of sales:			Cost of sales		
Opening stock	10,000		Opening stock	10,000	
Purchases	60,000		Purchases	60,000	
	70,000			70,000	
Closing stock	12,000		Closing stock	12,000	
		58,000		58,000	
Gross profit actually earned		42,000	Less stock losses	1,000	
					57,000
			Gross profit on goods sold		43,000
			Less stock losses		1,000
			Gross profit actually earned		42,000

Activity 14

1. Bank is (1,400 + 2,300) £3,700.
2. Stock is (80,000 + 50,000) £130,000.

Activity 15

1. Debit cash in transit £2,000; credit branch current account £2,000.
2. Debit stock in transit £10,000; credit branch current account £10,000.

Activity 16

	Cash at bank	Stock at cost
Head office	1,400	80,000
Branch	2,300	50,000
In transit	2,000	10,000
Total	5,700	140,000

Activity 17

If the commission is 5/100 of the profit after commission, it must be 5/105 of the profits before charging the commission. The answer is, therefore, 5/105 of £10,500, i.e. £500. As can be seen, this leaves a net profit of £10,000; and 5% of £10,000 is £500.

Activity 18

The unrealized profit is 5/105 of £10,500, i.e. £500.

Some examination questions on this topic (particularly departmental accounts in the Certified Level 1 exam) contain a large volume of data. You should not let this deter you from attempting these questions; there is often an inverse ratio between the volume of data and the ease with which an answer can be prepared. They often carry a high proportion of the marks. Some of the niceties of format have to be abandoned when trying to squeeze figures into columns for departmental accounts.

Questions for self-assessment

Answers to self-assessment questions are given at the end of the book.

17.1 Keith Maltby

Tutorial note: The 'Enterprise Grant' of £5,000 mentioned in note 11 should be treated as deferred income in the same way as 'life subscriptions' for a club were dealt with in Chapter 16. In the case of a company, accounting for these grants is regulated by SSAP 4. In 1983, Keith Maltby had bought a café which he re-opened under the name 'Keith's Kaff'. In February 1985 he rented a grocery shop which he renamed 'Keith's Larder'.

Notes on the operations of the businesses:
1. The annual rental of the grocery shop is £3,200 payable quarterly in advance on the last day of March, June, September and December.
2. The shop buys food in bulk both for resale to the public and for supply to the café. Food is transferred to the café at cost.
3. Each establishment is under the control of a manageress who is paid a basic salary plus a commission of 10% (calculated to the nearest £1) of the net profit of her establishment *before* charging the commission (see note (9)) but after crediting the Enterprise Grant instalment (see note (11)).
4. The office work for both establishments is carried out by the shop manageress who receives an annual payment of £600 for the extra responsibility. Two-thirds of this sum is charged to the café (see note (9)).
5. Maltby's accounting year runs from 1 April to 31 March and he accounts for the café and the shop as separate departments.
6. The shop manageress lives above the shop in self-contained accommodation for which she pays an inclusive rental of £60 per month, payable one month in arrears (see note (9)).
7. Depreciation of fixed assets is provided on the reducing balance method at the following rates:

Premises	2%
Fixtures, etc.	10%
Vehicles	20%

8. Closing stocks at 31 March 1987, at cost:

		£
Food:	café	3,513
	shop	1,774
Cleaning materials:	café	30
	shop	24
Wrapping materials:	café	10
	shop	12

9. At 31 March 1987

		£
Electricity accrued:	café	131
	shop	78

General expenses accrued:	café		46
	shop		68
Shop manageress's office allowance due			600
Shop manageress's accommodation rent receivable			60
Commission:	café manageress		to be calculated
	shop manageress		to be calculated
Rent payable prepaid	shop		800

10. On 31 March 1986, Maltby had obtained a Business Development Loan for the café, to be repaid in one lump sum in 1991, at a concessionary rate of interest (10% per annum), payable half yearly on 30 August and 31 March.

11. Maltby has also been awarded an Enterprise Grant of £5,000 for the café, with effect from 1 April 1986. He has decided to hold this sum in suspense and to credit it to the café profit and loss account in five equal instalments in the years ended 31 March 1987 to 1991 inclusive. However, at 31 March 1987 the £5,000 had not yet been received.

12. The sales of both the shop and the café are for cash, except that the café has a contract to supply meals to a local factory which is then invoiced with the cost, for which seven days' credit is allowed.

13. The overdraft finances Maltby's operations in general but is accounted for as a liability of the shop.

At 31 March 1987, the following balances were extracted from the ledger.

	Café £	Shop £
Premises (at cost)	25,000	–
Fixtures, fittings (at cost)	7,500	–
Vehicles (at cost)	–	6,000
Provisions for depreciation at 1 April 1986:		
Premises	6,000	–
Fixtures, fittings	1,600	–
Vehicles	–	1,000
Rent paid (see note 1)	–	4,000
Manageresses' salaries and related charges (see notes 3 and 9)	4,200	3,900
Assistants' wages and related charges	2,100	900
Electricity charges	1,874	851
Telephone charges	209	411
Stationery (see note 4)	–	126
Turnover	36,791	27,430
Food transferred from shop to café (see note 2)	19,427 (debit)	19,427 (credit)
Stocks at 1 April 1986:		
Food	1,272	303
Cleaning materials	44	32
Wrapping materials	27	28
Purchases:		
Food (see note 2)	–	30,432
Cleaning materials	71	68
Wrapping materials	45	53
Loan interest paid (see note 10)	700	–
Business development loan (see note 10)	7,000	–
Bank overdraft (see note 13)	–	2,209
Bank overdraft interest (see note 13)	–	37

Creditors:		
Food	–	4,582
Other items	15	6
Rates (general and water)	2,943	1,864
General expenses	605	756
Cash	109	155
Rent receivable (see note 6)	–	660
Debtors:		
Trade (see note 12)	1,312	–

The only other balances are the personal accounts of the proprietor and are not allocated to departments:

	£
K. Maltby:	
Capital	9,000
Current account	1,634 (credit)

Required:
Prepare a departmental trading and profit and loss account for year ended 31 March 1987 and a departmental balance sheet at that date, in each case using separate columns for the café, the shop and the total business.

(ACCA 1.1, Jun 87)

17.2 Geotrad Ltd

Tutorial note: There are no inherent difficulties in the following A level question; most of the figures can be produced as you work through the requirements step by step. It is a little irritating to be given some figures in £000s and some in £s but you will have to try to do the best you can in this situation. Try not to be caught out by irrelevant information.

Geotrad Ltd operates as a retail organization trading at the Head Office in Newcastle and at a branch in Hexham.

The following summarized information was available for the year ended 31 May 1989.

	Head Office Newcastle £000	Branch Hexham £000
Sales	1,800	300
Cost of goods sold	1,050	190
Variable expenses	300	35
Fixed expenses	150	5

In addition to the branch's own fixed and variable expenses listed above, £90,000 of the Head Office expense costs are to be transferred from Head Office and charged against the branch.

Note: The above summarized year end figures do not include adjustments in respect of the additional information items 1, 3 and 4 below.

Additional information.

1.

	Head Office £	Branch £
Variable expenses in arrears	4,500	1,900
Fixed expenses in advance	2,800	1,000

2. Stocks of goods held at 31 May 1989 (excluding goods in transit) were:

	Head Office £	Branch £
Cost price	50,000	8,000
Market price	52,000	8,000

Goods sent to the branch are currently invoiced at cost price.

3. Geotrad pays all its salesmen commission on sales, but only after the relevant year's sales targets have been met.
   In the financial year ended 31 May 1989 the respective sales targets were:

	£
Head Office	1,400,000
Hexham Branch	290,000

   Commission is only paid on those sales that exceed the target and at the following rates:

	%
Head Office	2
Hexham Branch	3

   The commission is paid in the year following the year of the sale.

4. Goods, which cost £11,000, had been packed ready to send to the branch, but they were still in the Head Office warehouse. No documentation had been received by the branch, but appropriate entries had been made in the Head Office books.
   The goods had not been included in the Head Office end-of-year stock taking.

5. The management of Geotrad Ltd has been concerned about the recent poor trading performance of the branch, and is anticipating a branch loss for the first time. One director suggested that the branch should be closed down if any significant loss is recorded.

Required:
(a) For the year ended 31 May 1989, separate trading and profit and loss accounts for the branch and Head Office. Use columnar form.
(b) (i) Calculate the contribution made by the branch to the profits of the business as a whole.
    (ii) Write a brief report as to whether the branch should be closed.
(c) (i) State the normally accepted accounting basis for the valuation of the business closing stock.
    (ii) Determine the value of the closing stock for the whole business as at 31 May 1989.

(AEB A Level, Jun 89)

Questions without answers

Answers to these questions are published separately in the *Teacher's Manual*.

17.3 **TV AM.** The television company TV AM suffered a strike which lasted for two weeks. During that time, no programmes were produced. The company issued a press statement declaring the cost of the strike to be £1,000,000. This figure was arrived at by the managing director, who estimated that each day of programming could have been sold for £100,000. (Total cost of strike = 10 days at £100,000.)
The company's cost accountant felt that the managing director was overstating the cost of the strike and provided the following statement to support his view:

		£000
Loss of sales revenue		1,000
Expenses avoided:		
Materials (£10,000 per programme)	100	
Production staff (£30,000 per programme)	300	
Depreciation of studio equipment	100	
Overheads	300	
		800
Cost of strike		200

The following additional information became available:
1. Depreciation of studio equipment is based on the conventional straight line method. The programme producer estimates that the equipment will fall in value by £15,000 each week regardless of whether programmes are being produced or not. In addition to this, the use of equipment for programmes causes an increase in the rate of wear and tear to the extent of an additional £5,000 for each day of live programming.
2. Overhead expenses are an apportionment of general overheads, based on 100% of production staff costs. Most of these overheads are fixed (e.g. rent and rates) and are unaffected by the level of production. However, there are some variable overheads (such as power and lighting), which vary with the level of production. The producer estimates that variable overheads amount to £5,000 per day of live programming.
3. During the period of the strike the maintenance staff, whose wages are included in the fixed overhead expense, carried out a major overhaul of the sound equipment using materials costing £20,000. This overhaul would normally have been performed by an outside contractor at a price, including materials, of £40,000.

Required:
(a) A statement showing the cost to the company of the strike. State any assumptions made and explain any differences between your figures and those of the cost accountant.
(b) Discuss any other factors that might be of concern to management.

17.4 On 1 January Mr Bends starts a business buying and selling motor cars. He gives you a summary of the business receipts and payments account as follows, for the year to 31 December (all figures are in £000):

Receipts	£000
Capital introduced (1 January)	100
From customers (after deducting worthless cheque, see note (iii) below)	400
10% loan from his mother (1 January)	50
	550

Payments	
To suppliers of new cars	320
To suppliers of second-hand cars	93
Wages	36
Rent	15
Purchase of furniture	5
Purchase of showroom display equipment	5
Insurance, electricity and stationery	7
Bank charges	1
Transfers to private bank account	26
	508

You are informed that:
(i)   Rent payable is £3,000 for each 3-month period.
(ii)   Mr Bends has bought a total of 37 new cars at a cost of £10,000 each. One of these was destroyed by fire the day before Mr Bends signed his insurance policy, two were taken into use by Mr Bends and his senior salesman, and 27 have been sold at a mark up of 20% on cost (one of which has not yet been paid for).
(iii) Mr Bends had a problem with the very first second-hand car which he sold. He accepted a cheque for £5,000 which proved worthless, and he has been unable to trace the customer. Since then all sales of second-hand cars have been for cash. All purchases of second-hand cars have also been for cash.
(iv)   Four second-hand cars remain in stock at 31 December. The cost of these to Mr Bends was £6,000, £6,000, £7,000 and £8,000, respectively.
(v)   All fixed assets are to be depreciated at the rate of 20% for the year.

Required:

Prepare in good order:

- Trading account for new cars.
- Trading account for second-hand cars.
- Profit and loss account for the business for the year.
- Balance sheet as at 31 December.
- Indicate clearly the calculation of all figures in your solution.

(ACCA 1.1, Jun 90)

17.5 The trial balance of Principles plc at 31 December 19X6 was as follows:

	Dr £000	Cr £000
Ordinary shares of £0.50 each fully paid		5,000
Retained profit at 1 January 19X6		13,980
Fixed assets at cost	20,000	
Depreciation provision at 1 January 19X6		3,000
Stocks at 1 January 19X6:		
Materials	1,531	
Work-in-progress:		
Product X	25	
Product Y	60	
Finished products:		
Product X	875	
Product Y	3,900	
Debtors	5,000	
Bad debts provision		255
Cash at bank and in hand	150	
Creditors		1,320
Sales:		
Product X		24,000
Product Y		16,000
Purchases of materials	11,400	
Manufacturing wages:		
Product X	3,141	
Product Y	1,564	
Production overhead expenses	7,674	
Distribution costs	3,715	
Administration expenses	4,520	
	63,555	63,555

You are given the following information:
1.   Materials issued from stores during 19X6 were:

	£000
Direct:	
Product X	6,410
Product Y	4,785
Indirect: Manufacturing	105

A physical stocktaking at 31 December 19X6 valued materials stock at £1,600,000. Any difference with book stocks is to be regarded as a production overhead expense.

2.   Movements in respect of Products X and Y during 19X6 were:

	Product X units	Product Y units
Stock at 1 January 19X6	35,000	65,000
Manufactured during 19X6	640,000	160,000
	675,000	225,000
Sold during 19X6	600,000	200,000
Stock at 31 December 19X6	75,000	25,000

3.   Work-in-progress at 31 December 19X6 was valued at:

	£000
Product X	50
Product Y	30

4.   Finished product stocks at 31 December 19X6 were valued at:

	£000
Product X	1,875
Product Y	1,500

5.   Depreciation for 19X6 was £2,000,000, and is to be apportioned as follows:

	£000
Production	1,600
Distribution	200
Administration	200

6.   The bad debts provision is to be adjusted to 5% of debtors. Any increase or decrease is to be regarded as a distribution cost.

7.   Prepayments and accruals at 31 December 19X6 were:

	Prepayments £000	Accruals £000
Manufacturing wages:		
Product X		64
Product Y		31
Production overhead expenses	10	200
Distribution costs	5	95
Administrative expenses	30	110

8.   Production overhead expenses (including the proportion of depreciation) are to be divided between the product in proportion to manufacturing wages.

9.   Distribution costs (including the proportion of depreciation and any adjustment of the bad debts provision) are to be divided between the products in proportion to the quantities sold during 19X6.

10. Administrative expenses (including the proportion of depreciation) are to be divided between the products in proportion to the quantities of fully completed products manufactured during 19X6.

11. Provision is to be made for corporation tax at the rate of 40% of the net profit, and for a proposed dividend of 15p per share.

Required:

(a) Prepare for internal use only, in tabular and columnar form, a profit and loss account for the year ended 31 December 19X6, showing the amount of profit or loss before tax for each product and the amount of retained profit for the year.

(b) The profit for the year has been calculated according to the historic cost principle. Describe *two* other principles which may be used to calculate profit.

(CIMA, May 87)

18 Groups of companies: An introduction

Objectives

After you have completed this chapter, you should be able to:
- describe the nature of a group, and comment on matters relating to group accounting
- identify the investments that create a holding company and subsidiary relationship
- identify investments that are known as **participating interests** and describe the 'equity method' of accounting
- explain some of the concepts underlying a consolidated balance sheet

Introduction

The rapid growth of many companies from small local organizations to large multinational corporations, with assets running into hundreds of millions of pounds, has been amongst the most spectacular of all economic events during the second half of the twentieth century. In most cases this has not been entirely the result of organic growth of an original business; it has arisen through a series of business combinations whereby one company acquires control of an existing entity as a going concern. The enlarged organization emerging from the combination is able to exercise a much stronger influence over the market.

Business combinations can take one of several forms. In terms of the way business interests are integrated, we talk about vertical integration and horizontal integration. If a manufacturer acquires control of a supplier of raw materials, or of its main customer, the combination is referred to as vertical integration. When a retail outlet acquires control of other retail outlets, the combination is referred to as horizontal integration.

But this chapter is not so much concerned with the strategy of integration as with the financial device used to obtain control of an existing business. There are essentially two ways in which a company can acquire control of an existing business:

- it can purchase the net assets, including goodwill, from the owner
- if the business being acquired is owned by a company, the acquiring company can purchase the shares from the shareholders; the purchase negotiations are with the shareholders instead of the company.

You have already dealt with the accounting for the first of these two methods in Chapter 15. It must be used where the business being acquired is owned by a sole trader or partnership, although it can also be used when the business is owned by a company. The double-entry on purchase is to debit the acquired assets to their relevant class in the purchasing company's books, and credit cash (or credit share capital if paid for by an issue of shares). As far as the former owners are concerned, their business has been liquidated.

The second method (acquiring shares) forms the subject of this chapter. The double entry on acquisition of the shares is to debit an investment account and credit cash (or credit share capital if paid by an issue of shares). Each company remains as a separate legal entity but with the investing company able to control the other through its shareholding in that other company. It results in a relationship whereby the investing company is known as the parent company, and the other is called a subsidiary.

At a foundation level, students are not required to prepare the financial statements for a group but there are various syllabuses that require students to be able to explain features in group accounts. Since the principles involved are quite straightforward, the best way of dealing with the subject at this level is to learn the basis on which group accounts are prepared. In any event, this makes the subject much more interesting and complete.

18.1 What is a group?

The relationship mentioned in the introduction, where one company is able to control another through the ownership of shares in that other company, creates a group. The investing company is known as the parent company, and the company controlled through the investment is known as the subsidiary. The two companies, although continuing to retain their separate legal status and preparing their own separate financial statements, are members of a single (albeit artificial) economic entity known as a group.

The concept of treating a group as a single entity is purely artificial and was originally conceived (in 1948) for accounting purposes. It was recognized that because the results of the parent company are so inextricably linked to its subsidiary's operations, the shareholders of the parent company should be presented with an additional financial statement to show the combined results of all companies in the group. The individual financial statements of each company do not, unless they are combined in some way, give an overall view of the group.

The following diagram (using outline balance sheets to depict each company) gives an indication of a simple group comprising a parent company and one subsidiary. For the time being, assume that the parent company owns the entire share capital of the subsidiary.

The Group

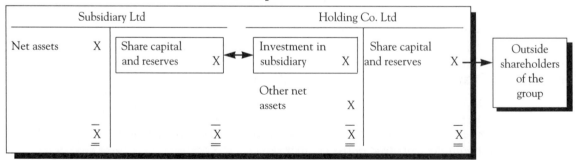

Notice that the owners of 'the group' are the shareholders of the parent company; it is for these shareholders that the group accounts are prepared.

The great majority of the public companies whose names have become household words are parent companies of extensive and complex groups. The parent company of a group is required to publish two sets of financial statements: its own, and a set of financial statements that combines the results of every company in the group. The combined financial statements are called 'consolidated accounts'.

Activity 1

You have already seen examples of consolidated balance sheets in this book; they were the balance sheets for ICI and Tesco in Chapter 13. Look at them again to see if there is anything on them to indicate whether the figures in the balance sheet are those for the parent company or for the group. Make a note here of what you find.

If you ever get a chance to look at the full set of published annual reports of these two companies, you will find the names of all the subsidiaries are listed in the section called 'notes to financial statements'.

Activity 2

Look at the balance sheet for the ICI group (Appendix 2 in Chapter 13) again and examine the items listed under fixed assets in the 'group' accounts. Make a note here of what you notice about the balance sheet figure for 'investments in subsidiaries'.

You cannot make the same observation on Tesco because the analysis of investments (showing the distinction between investments in subsidiaries and other investments) is given in the notes (note 9) rather than on the face of the balance sheet. If you were able to look at note 9 for the annual report of Tesco you would find that the group has no investments in subsidiaries.

This might (initially) seem a little puzzling; we have two large groups, each of them comprising a parent company and many subsidiaries, but where the group balance sheet shows there is no investment in subsidiaries. In fact, if you look at the consolidated balance sheet of any group you will find that the amount shown for investments in subsidiaries is nil.

There is a perfectly logical explanation as to why this is so; in fact the reason might have occurred to you already. If it has not, then try thinking about it now. You have to raise your viewpoint and look down on the whole group rather than at the individual companies. You might be able to use the diagram on page 460 to help with this.

Activity 3

Make a note of why you think that the group balance sheets of ICI and Tesco show investments in subsidiaries as nil.

The parent company is required to publish its own balance sheet in addition to the balance sheet of the group. The normal practice is to include the figures for the parent company on the same page as the group balance sheet by making use of additional columns next to the group figures. You will notice this has been done in the balance sheet of ICI and Tesco in the appendices for Chapter 13. Although the balance sheet for Tesco (Appendix 3) does not disclose the amount invested by the parent company in subsidiaries, it is possible to determine the amount without reference to note 9.

Activity 4

Refer to Appendix 3 in Chapter 13 and calculate the amount invested by the parent company in its subsidiaries.

The mechanics of eliminating investments in subsidiaries in order to produce a group balance sheet are quite easy to understand and are dealt with later in this chapter.

The main objective of Activities 1 to 4 was to assist you in the proper use of the terminology for discussing matters relating to groups. There is a tendency for those who have not studied accounting to use some of the terms rather loosely. You can see if you are thinking on the right lines by answering the following activity.

Activity 5

The expression 'parent company's accounts' is not the same thing as 'group accounts'. Make a note of why this is so.

Prior to the Companies Act 1989, group accounts could be presented in one of several forms. The 1989 Act requires group accounts to be presented as consolidated financial statements, and so the terms **group accounts** and **consolidated accounts** can be treated as synonymous.

Until fairly recently, it was more usual to refer to the parent company in the group as the holding company. The term 'parent company' has become more fashionable since the EC Seventh Directive on company law was adopted in 1983. This directive was incorporated into UK company law in 1989 and has altered some of the definitions relating to groups.

18.2 Definitions and accounting regulations

Before considering the legal definitions, you need to think about the relationship between a parent and subsidiary in more general terms. The text so far might have given you the impression that a parent company owns the entire share capital of its subsidiary. This is not necessarily the case.

The main criterion that has to be considered in determining the existence of a parent and subsidiary relationship is related to 'control'. If one company is in a position to exercise control over another company, then the company with this power is the parent company and the other is the subsidiary.

Control of the day-to-day operations of a company rests with the board of directors. Anyone (including a company) who owns a simple majority of the voting rights in a company is in a position to pass resolutions for removing and appointing that company's directors. Consequently, the ability to control another company can be obtained by purchasing more than 50% of the voting capital. The voting rights are usually attached to the ordinary shares and so any holding of more than 50% of the ordinary shares in another company will give the investor control of that company.

The acquisition of more than 50% of the voting shares will give the acquiring company control and create a parent and subsidiary relationship.

Your ability to identify parent company and subsidiary relationships is often tested by examiners. As far as groups are concerned, your examiners do not expect a great deal more from you than a demonstration of this ability. The next example and activity will give you some practice on this kind of problem. The following are the abbreviated balance sheets of three companies:

	Superbe Ltd	Grande Ltd	Moyenne Ltd
Investments at cost:			
12,000 Ordinary shares in Grande Ltd	18,000		
1,000 Ordinary shares in Moyenne Ltd	4,000		
400 Ordinary shares in Petite Ltd		1,000	
Other net assets	58,000	29,000	20,000
	80,000	30,000	20,000
Capital and reserves:			
Ordinary shares of £1 each	50,000	20,000	4,000
Reserves	30,000	10,000	16,000
	80,000	30,000	20,000

The called up share capital of Petite Ltd amounts to £1,250 and consists of ordinary shares of 25 pence each.

Activity 6

Refer to the above balance sheets and determine whether there are any relationships that fall to be treated as that of a parent company and subsidiary. If so, set out a full description of that relationship (including the percentage holding) here.

Note that although the shareholders of Superbe Ltd (the parent company) have no direct claim on the profits of Grande Ltd (the subsidiary), the directors of

Superbe Ltd are able to control the amount of dividends paid by Grande Ltd, some of which will be received by Superbe Ltd. This ability arises from the fact that Superbe Ltd can control Grande Ltd's board of directors, and it is the directors who decide on the amount to be paid as dividends.

Activity 7

If the directors of Grande Ltd decide to pay a dividend of 10 pence per share, calculate how much dividend would be received by Superbe Ltd.

When this dividend is received it will be credited to Superbe Ltd's profit and loss account in exactly the same way as any other type of investment income, although it must be described in an appropriate manner.

Activity 8

Refer to Chapter 12 and find the extract from the Companies Act formats as set out in Appendix 2. Make a note of how this format requires investment income from a subsidiary to be described.

Examiners might also expect you to be able to define terms such as parent company (or holding company) and subsidiary. As stated previously, the legal definitions have recently been changed as a result of incorporating the EC Seventh Directive into UK company law through the 1989 Companies Act.

Activity 9

State how you would define a 'parent company' based on the text in this chapter up to now.

There was originally a substantial inconsistency between accounting standards and the 1989 legislation. The accounting standards on groups promulgated by the former Accounting Standards Committee (ASC) were spread over SSAP 1, SSAP 14, SSAP 22, and SSAP 23. These standards (particularly SSAP 14) were based on the law prior to 1989. To some extent this has now been rectified by the Accounting Standards Board (ASB) and a new standard (FRS 2) was issued in July 1992. This standard does not deal with all of the matters covered by the former SSAPs and is mainly a substitution of SSAP 14. It brings the various definitions and practices into line with current legislation, and introduces regulations on certain matters that were not dealt with in the former SSAPs, such as the treatment of unrealized profits in inter-company transactions.

You should note that SSAP 22 (on goodwill) does not apply specifically to group accounts although business acquisitions occur more frequently in a group than in any other case. You have already encountered this particular SSAP when dealing with goodwill for a partnership. You will be looking at it again later in this chapter.

As regards definitions, the main criterion in determining the existence of a parent company and subsidiary relationship is whether one company is in a position to exercise control over another company. As stated previously, such control can be obtained by acquiring more than 50% of a company's voting capital.

But over the years, companies have devised various ways of being able to exercise control over another company which fall outside of the legal requirement to treat that company as a subsidiary. In most cases, these devices were used to enable the group to exclude financing liabilities from the group balance sheet. The companies concerned became known by the term 'controlled non-subsidiaries'. A further device was to set up (usually through a bank) something known as a 'quasi-subsidiary'.

You do not need to know the details of these schemes, but you should take an interest in the fact that accounting tends to suffer from a conflict between those who try to find ways of avoiding a truthful disclosure of information to their shareholders, and those who try to legislate in the best interests of shareholders. The practice of hiding the truth through various devious means has become known by the buzzword 'creative accounting' and such practices were quite prevalent during the 1980s.

For group accounting purposes, the 1989 Companies Act refers to 'undertakings' rather than 'companies' when defining parents and subsidiaries. This allows the legislation to be harmonized with practices in other European countries where a parent can be an unincorporated entity. In UK business practice, a parent undertaking will be a company and there is no requirement in the 1989 Act for parent undertakings other than companies to prepare consolidated accounts. The more important definitions can, therefore, be paraphrased as follows.

A company is a parent company in relation to another company, a subsidiary, in any of the following cases:

1. If it holds a majority of the voting rights in the other company
2. If it is a member of the other company and has the right to appoint or remove a majority of its board of directors
3. If it has the right to exercise a 'dominant influence' over the other company, either by:
   (a) provisions in that company's memorandum or articles, or
   (b) a control contract
4. If it is a member of the other company and can control alone, or through an agreement with other shareholders, a majority of the voting rights in that company.

There are many supporting definitions to assist with interpretation of the above, but these need not concern you for the accounting exam.

In 1994 the ASB issued an accounting standard known as FRS 5: Reporting the substance of transactions. This includes a definition of a quasi-subsidiary and requires the results of such a subsidiary to be consolidated in the group accounts.

18.3 The consolidated balance sheet

The most common method of preparing group accounts is known as 'acquisition accounting' and you will see why this term is used in a moment. There is another method called 'merger accounting' but it can be used only in certain circumstances that are very strictly defined by accounting standards and legislation. The remaining text in this chapter is concerned with acquisition accounting.

You will discover the basic mechanics of acquisition accounting by working through a series of activities based on the abbreviated balance sheets of the two companies set out below. At the time of preparing these balance sheets the two companies were not connected in any way.

	Company A		Company B	
Tangible fixed assets		30,000		9,000
Current assets	25,000		3,000	
Current liabilities	11,000		2,000	
		14,000		1,000
		44,000		10,000
Share capital		35,000		7,000
Reserves		9,000		3,000
		44,000		10,000

Company A wishes to acquire control of the business owned by Company B.

Activity 10

Assume that Company A acquires control of Company B's business by paying cash of £10,000 to Company B for its net assets. There are no group accounts in this case (there is no group) and Company A has simply paid out £10,000 in exchange for assets and liabilities acquired from Company B. Prepare Company A's balance sheet immediately after the acquisition. Use the outline balance sheet set out below.

Balance sheet of Company A

Tangible fixed assets

Current assets

Current liabilities

Share capital

Reserves

Following the acquisition, Company B has no operating assets. Its only asset is £10,000 cash and this will be paid out to Company B's shareholders if the company is liquidated (it could use the £10,000 to carry on a different business). You will notice that Company A did not acquire the capital and reserves of Company B. This might seem like an odd comment to make but you will see the significance of it in a moment.

Activity 11

Now assume that instead of paying £10,000 cash to Company B, the money is paid to the shareholders of Company B. By so doing Company A acquires 100% of the shares in Company B. Write up the new balance sheet of Company A following the payment. Don't forget, Company A has not acquired net assets through the payment of £10,000, it has acquired an investment.

Balance sheet of Company A

Tangible fixed assets

Investment in Company B

Current assets

Current liabilities

Share capital

Reserves

In this case, the only thing that needs to be done in Company B's books is to change the name of the shareholders in the share register. The entire share capital is now owned by Company A. Company B continues to exist and operate as a separate legal entity.

We have reached a point where there are two companies in existence, and whose balance sheets are as follows:

	Company A		Company B	
Tangible fixed assets		30,000		9,000
Investment in Company B		10,000		
Current assets	15,000		3,000	
Current liabilities	11,000		2,000	
		4,000		1,000
		44,000		10,000
Share capital		35,000		7,000
Reserves		9,000		3,000
		44,000		10,000

Company A now has a subsidiary and must prepare a consolidated balance sheet of the group for the benefit of its own shareholders. A consolidated balance sheet looks at the group through the eyes of the shareholders who own the parent company; we think of the shareholders of the parent company as being the shareholders of the group.

Consequently we use Company A's balance sheet as a starting point. We then pretend that instead of Company A owning an investment in Company B, it owns the individual assets and liabilities of Company B, which it controls through that investment. We simply eliminate the investment in Company B and replace it by the individual assets and liabilities of Company B. These are combined with the corresponding class of asset and liabilities in Company A.

Activity 12

See if you have managed to make sense of this explanation by preparing the first consolidated balance sheet of the group. Use the outline below.

Consolidated balance sheet of Company A and its subsidiary Company B

Tangible fixed assets

Current assets

Current liabilities _____

_____
_____

Share capital _____

Reserves

_____
_____

Check your balance sheet with the Key before going on to the next activity.

Activity 13

Compare the consolidated balance sheet in Activity 12 with the one you prepared for Activity 10 and make a note of your observations.

This is why the method is called acquisition accounting. We are making out that instead of the parent company having acquired an investment in the subsidiary, it has acquired the net assets controlled through that investment. Notice how the capital and reserves of Company B are not included in the consolidated balance sheet; this is in keeping with the situation that would have applied if Company A had acquired the net assets of Company B. Any profits earned by the subsidiary after acquisition will be brought into the group accounts, but we will not be considering post-acquisition profits in this chapter.

In the above example, the amount paid for the investment was exactly equal to the balance sheet value of net assets in Company B. It is unlikely that this would happen in practice. As you know from your study in Chapter 15, a business is likely to be worth more (or less) than the book value of net assets in the balance sheet. Consequently, the price paid for a business is likely to be different from the balance sheet value.

Lets us see what would happen if Company A paid £12,000 to the shareholders of Company B. We will assume that all of Company B's shareholders accept the offer and so Company A acquires 100% control.

Activity 14

First of all, draft out the revised balance sheet of Company A (not the consolidated balance sheet) immediately after paying £12,000 for the shares. Use the outline provided below.

Balance sheet of Company A

Tangible fixed assets

Investment in Company B

Current assets

Current liabilities

Share capital

Reserves

It is easier to understand how the consolidated balance sheet (in these new circumstances) is prepared by considering what would have happened if Company A had purchased the various assets and liabilities from Company B by paying £12,000 to the Company, instead of to the shareholders. In order to keep the explanation simple, we will assume that the assets and liabilities in Company B's balance sheet have a fair value equal to their book value.

Activity 15

Set out a schedule (in the space below) of the various assets and liabilities that would have been acquired from Company B, if the £12,000 had been paid to the company rather than to the shareholders. (You need to recall a similar situation in Chapter 15.)

Schedule of assets acquired:

The same principle is applied when we come to prepare a consolidated balance sheet by replacing the investment of £12,000 with the underlying net assets controlled through this investment. We again pretend that instead of Company A owning an investment of £12,000 it owns the various assets and liabilities of Company B that are controlled through this investment. In this new situation there is the additional asset called goodwill. This asset is classified as an intangible fixed asset.

Activity 16

Prepare the consolidated balance sheet (below) taking account of the new situation.

Consolidated balance sheet of Company A and its subsidiary Company B

Intangible fixed asset

Tangible fixed assets

Current assets

Current liabilities	_____	
	_____	
	_____	
Share capital	=========	
Reserves		
	_____	
	=========	

Notice from the Key how the additional asset is described as 'goodwill arising on consolidation'. There are regulations in SSAP 22 that prescribe how this asset must be dealt with in the case of companies (including groups) and we will study these in a moment. In the meanwhile, the goodwill arising on consolidation should be carried forward as an intangible fixed asset.

There is one further aspect to consider in relation to the basic mechanics of consolidation: what happens if the parent company acquires less than 100% of the subsidiary's shares? As mentioned earlier, it is not necessary to acquire 100% of the equity shares in another company in order to establish control, any holding in excess of 50% is sufficient. At this point of the explanation we will have to abandon the idea of making a comparison between acquiring an investment and acquiring the net assets; it would be impossible to control a business by acquiring a percentage of its net assets.

Let us see what happens in our example by assuming that Company A acquired 80% of the shares in Company B. We will assume that since Company A would have paid £12,000 for a 100% interest, it manages to obtain the 80% interest at a cost of £9,600.

Activity 17

Draft out the revised balance sheet of Company A (not the consolidated balance sheet) immediately after paying £9,600 for the shares. Use the outline below.

Balance sheet of Company A

Tangible fixed assets
Investment in Company B
Current assets
Current liabilities

$\qquad$ _____

Share capital $\qquad$ =========
Reserves

_____
=========

Activity 18

There are now two distinct classes of shareholders who have an interest in the net assets of the group. Describe the two classes, using your own terminology.

The external shareholders in Company B (the 20% not acquired by Company A) are referred to as 'minority interests'. They are a minority in the sense that the majority shareholder of their company is Company A.

The minority shareholders' interest in the net assets of the group is (in our example) valued at 20% of the net assets in their own company. In UK practice, we do not attribute any of the unrecorded goodwill of the subsidiary to the minority interests and so the amount attributable to minority interests for their share of the group's net assets will be based on 20% of the net assets in the balance sheet of Company B.

Activity 19

Calculate the amount of net assets of the group that are attributable to the minority interests in Company B, and make a note of it here.

This amount is simply described as minority interests in the group balance sheet. The prescribed formats in the Companies Act permit this item to be presented in either of two places. It can be shown either in the capital and reserves section of the group balance sheet, or as a deduction from net assets. If it is presented in the capital and reserves section it should be included as the last item, immediately following a sub-total of the capital and reserves attributable to the members of the holding company.

It might help if we now had an overview of the group on which we have been working. The group can again be depicted by using the idea of outline balance sheets as used at the beginning of the chapter. On this basis, the group can be illustrated as follows:

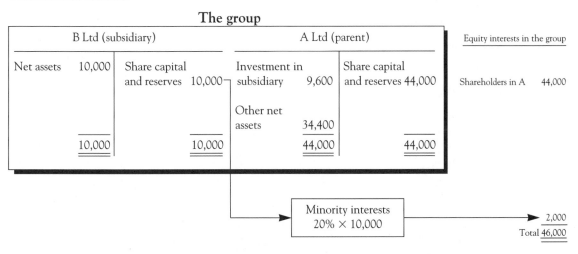

You can see from the above illustration that the total equity of the group is £46,000. If you add up the net assets in the group (excluding the investment in the subsidiary which is not an asset of the group) you will find that they amount to (£10,000 + £34,400) £44,400. Consequently, there must be another asset somewhere in the group which is not in either balance sheet.

Activity 20

The amount of this asset is obviously (£46,000 – £44,400) £1,600. Describe the nature of this asset, and see if you can determine how it might have been calculated (other than as the simple balancing figure derived here). If you do manage to sort this out, you are doing quite well; if you find it difficult, refer to the Key after giving it some thought.

You should now be able to prepare the consolidated balance sheet for the new group. The thought processes are the same as those developed in previous activities.

Activity 21

Using the outline format below this box, complete the consolidated balance sheet. You will notice that the format adopted is to present minority interests as the last item in the capital and reserves side of the balance sheet. When this form of presentation is adopted, the parent company's capital and reserves is normally sub-totalled before adding on the minority interests.

Consolidated balance sheet of Company A and its subsidiary Company B

Goodwill arising on consolidation

Tangible fixed assets

Current assets

Current liabilities

Share capital

Reserves

Minority interests

You should note that the preparation of a consolidated balance sheet is merely a memorandum exercise. There is no such thing as a set of double-entry records for the group; each individual company in the group keeps its own double-entry records and prepares its own financial statements. Consolidation is done on a piece of paper, not in anyone's books.

That is as far as we will be taking the lesson on preparation of consolidated balance sheets. I hope you found it interesting. As you can imagine, there is quite a lot more to learn on this subject but that is something you can look forward to on a more advanced course.

18.4 Accounting treatment of goodwill

The definition of goodwill in the Companies Act and FRS 6 was discussed in Chapter 15 on partnerships. Goodwill arising on consolidation is an example of purchased goodwill and is subject to the same accounting regulations as any other form of purchased goodwill (such as where a business is acquired through the purchase of assets).

The provisions on accounting for goodwill are contained in SSAP 22 and can be summarized as follows:

- non-purchased goodwill should not be shown in a company's balance sheet
- purchased goodwill should never be increased in value
- purchased goodwill should not be shown as a permanent asset, it must either be:
  - written off immediately by debiting reserves, or
  - amortized by writing it off against ordinary profits over its estimated useful economic life.

This is the first time the word **amortize** has been used in this book. It is often used in relation to intangible assets and is simply another way of describing the procedure of treating the cost of an asset as an expense by annual instalments. The concept is the same as depreciation. The word has been derived from the French verb 'amortir', which can mean various things, although we seem to use it in the context of extinguishing something by instalments (or absorbing something over a period of years).

Notice how there is an important difference between the immediate write off and the amortization basis. When the asset is written off immediately, the debit does not go to the profit and loss account for the year; it must be written off against one of the reserves that are legally available for the purpose (such as the balance of accumulated profits).

When the asset is amortized, the annual charge must be debited to the profit and loss account for the year and included as one of the expenses in arriving at profits on ordinary activities.

Activity 22

The question of identifying reserves against which the charge for an immediate write off may be made is quite complicated, and is not free from doubt. But there are some certainties in the subject. Consider whether or not goodwill could be written off against the following reserves; indicate your answer by deleting either yes or no as appropriate:

1. Capital redemption reserve	yes/no
2. Share premium account	yes/no
3. General reserve	yes/no
4. Balance of retained profits	yes/no

18.5 Associated companies

An investment in a company that does not fall to be treated as a subsidiary (usually because less than 50% of the equity capital is owned) might have to be accounted for as an associated company if the investment is in 20% or more of the equity capital.

At the time of writing this edition, the accounting standard for associated companies is covered by SSAP 1. The ASB have made amendments to SSAP 1 but these are mainly to bring the terminology into line with current legislation. SSAP 1 requires associated companies to be consolidated on a basis known as 'equity accounting'. This is a form of partial consolidation.

The definition of an associated company in SSAP 1 is a little complex but essentially it is an investment in a company over which the investor is able to exercise 'significant influence', usually through representation on the board of directors. The SSAP goes on to state that where the investment amounts to 20% or more of the equity capital, it should be presumed that the investor is able to exercise significant interest unless it can be demonstrated otherwise.

Although accountants frequently refer to these companies as associated companies, the term has become out of date following the introduction of the Companies Act 1989. The key term now is participating interests. The 1989 Act defines participating interests (in Section 260) in terms that resemble the definition of associated companies in SSAP 1. The presumption that a participating interest exists if the holding is 20% or more of the shares in another company is included in the legal definition.

Activity 23

Refer to Appendix 2 of Chapter 12 (formats for published accounts) and you will see that the term 'participating interests' is used in both the balance sheet and the profit and loss account. Make a note here of where they appear in:

1. The balance sheet

2. The profit and loss account

Notice how these items are reported separately to investments in subsidiaries, and investment income from subsidiaries (the term group undertakings relates to subsidiaries).

Activity 24

Refer to the balance sheets for Superbe Ltd, Grande Ltd, and Moyenne Ltd on page 463 and see if you can find any investments that will have to be dealt with as participating interests (associated companies). Make a note of your observations here.

As with the consolidation of a subsidiary, the equity method of accounting for an associated company is a memorandum exercise and no entries are made in the double-entry records of the investing company. For example, if Moyenne Ltd pays a dividend of 10 pence per share, then Superbe Ltd will simply report dividends received of £100 in its own profit and loss account, in much the same way as for any other type of investment. But when Superbe Ltd prepares the accounts for the group it will have to deal with the investment in Moyenne Ltd under the equity accounting method.

At a foundation level you will not be required to carry out any equity accounting adjustments in the examination, it is sufficient for you to be able to recognize associated companies. This is quite sensible because the equity method applies only to the consolidated accounts of a group and you are not required to prepare such accounts. If you are required to prepare the balance sheet of the investing company (which is not the same thing as a consolidated balance sheet) you should describe any associated companies as 'participating interests'.

An investment in an associated company does not warrant the full consolidation procedure because it represents a minority interest rather than a controlling interest. The idea of the equity method is to show the investment in the group balance sheet at an amount that represents the investor's share of the net assets (or equity) of the associated company instead of showing the investment at cost.

Since the associated company's net assets will increase if it earns and retains a profit, the carrying value of the investment will also have to be increased. This is dealt with in the group accounts by including a share of the associated company's profits (based on the proportion of shares held) in the consolidated profit and loss account. The existence of this profit in the group is then reflected by an increase in the carrying value of the investment in the associated company.

18.6 Summary of three types of investment

In this chapter you have encountered the three types of investment that you are most likely to find in the examination. The accounting requirements affecting each can be summarized as follows:

Shareholding %	Category	Accounting requirements
More than 50%	Subsidiary	Full consolidation
20% to 50%	Associated company	Equity accounting in the group accounts; describe as participating interests in the investor's accounts
Under 20%	Ordinary investment	Investment at cost in the balance sheet; dividends received in profit and loss account

Further reading:

Dodge, R. (1996) *Group Financial Statements*, International Thomson Business Press.

Summary

The important learning points in this chapter can be summarized as follows:
- a group consists of a parent company and its subsidiaries
- a parent company is one that is able to control another (the subsidiary), usually by owning more than 50% of that other company's voting capital
- each company in the group retains its separate identity and produces its own financial statements

- the parent company must produce consolidated accounts in addition to its own financial statements
- the consolidated financial statements are produced for the benefit of the shareholders in the parent company
- there are two methods of preparing consolidated accounts; they are known as acquisition accounting and merger accounting
- acquisition accounting results in a consolidated balance sheet that shows what the position would be if the parent company had acquired the assets and liabilities of a subsidiary instead of owning the investment
- where the holding in a subsidiary is less than 100%, part of the group is owned by shareholders other than shareholders in the parent company – these shareholders are called minority interests
- in a consolidated balance sheet, the minority interests are credited with their percentage of the net assets in their own company
- where the amount paid for an investment in a subsidiary exceeds the parent company's share of the fair value of the net assets in that subsidiary at the time of acquisition, the difference is called goodwill arising on consolidation
- goodwill arising on consolidation is an example of purchased goodwill and must either be written off immediately against group reserves, or amortized against ordinary profits over its estimated useful life
- an investment representing 20% or more (but not greater than 50%) of the voting capital of another company might have to be treated as an associated company
- an investment in an associated company must be described in the balance sheet as a **participating interest**, and consolidated by using the equity method of accounting
- the equity method requires the investment to be carried in the group balance sheet at an amount that equals the investor's share of the net assets in the associated company

Activity 1

You might have noticed the heading 'Group' above the column of figures. There are other clues in the balance sheet itself but you are not expected to understand their significance at the moment.

Activity 2

The amount is nil in the figures for the group.

Activity 3

It is the parent company that owns investments in the subsidiaries. The subsidiaries are part of the group and the group cannot own investments in itself.

Activity 4

£20.4m less £5.5m = £14.9m.

Activity 5

The parent company's accounts are those of the parent company itself; group accounts are the combined financial statements of the parent company and all of its subsidiaries.

Activity 6

Grande Ltd is a subsidiary of Superbe Ltd because Superbe Ltd owns 60% of Grande Ltd's ordinary shares. (Note: when looking for these relationships you have to ignore the amount paid for the investment; the clue is in the number of shares owned in a company compared to the number of shares issued by that company.)

Activity 7

£1,200.

Activity 8

Income from shares in group undertakings.

Activity 9

Perhaps you thought of something like: a company that is able to control another company, usually by owning more than 50% of the voting capital in that company.

Activity 10

Balance sheet of Company A

Tangible fixed assets (30,000 + 9,000)		39,000
Current assets (25,000 − 10,000 + 3,000)	18,000	
Current liabilities (11,000 + 2,000)	13,000	
		5,000
		44,000
Share capital		35,000
Reserves		9,000
		44,000

Activity 11

Balance sheet of Company A

Tangible fixed assets		30,000
Investment in subsidiary		10,000
Current assets (25,000 − 10,000)	15,000	
Current liabilities	11,000	
		4,000
		44,000
Share capital		35,000
Reserves		9,000
		44,000

Activity 12

Consolidated balance sheet of Company A and its subsidiary Company B

Tangible fixed assets (30,000 + 9,000)		39,000
Current assets (15,000 + 3,000)	18,000	
Current liabilities (11,000 + 2,000)	13,000	
		5,000
		44,000
Share capital		35,000
Reserves		9,000
		44,000

Activity 13

The workings are slightly different but the end result is the same.

Activity 14

Balance sheet of Company A

Tangible fixed assets		30,000
Investment in subsidiary		12,000
Current assets (25,000 − 12,000)	13,000	
Current liabilities	11,000	
		2,000
		44,000
Share capital		35,000
Reserves		9,000
		44,000

Activity 15

Schedule of assets acquired:

Goodwill		2,000
Tangible fixed assets		9,000
Current assets	3,000	
Current liabilities	2,000	
		1,000
		12,000

Activity 16

Consolidated balance sheet of Company A and its subsidiary Company B

Intangible fixed asset: Goodwill arising on consolidation		2,000
Tangible fixed assets (30,000 + 9,000)		39,000
Current assets (13,000 + 3,000)	16,000	
Current liabilities (11,000 + 2,000)	13,000	
		3,000
		44,000
Share capital		35,000
Reserves		9,000
		44,000

Activity 17

Balance sheet of Company A

Tangible fixed assets		30,000
Investment in subsidiary		9,600
Current assets (25,000 – 9,600)	15,400	
Current liabilities	11,000	
		4,400
		44,000
Share capital		35,000
Reserves		9,000
		44,000

Activity 18
The two groups are: (1) the shareholders of the parent company (Company A), and (2) 20% of the shareholders in the subsidiary (Company B).

Activity 19
20% of £10,000 = £2,000.

Activity 20
You probably realized that the asset was 'goodwill arising on consolidation'. It would have been calculated as follows:

Amount paid for the investment	9,600
Holding company's share of net assets controlled through this investment (80% × £10,000)	8,000
	1,600

Or you might have reasoned that since 100% of the goodwill is £2,000, then 80% of goodwill is (80% × 2,000) £1,600 (an acceptable approach).

Activity 21

Consolidated balance sheet of Company A and its subsidiary Company B

Goodwill arising on consolidation		1,600
Tangible fixed assets (30,000 + 9,000)		39,000
Current assets (15,400 + 3,000)	18,400	
Current liabilities (11,000 + 2,000)	13,000	
		5,400
		46,000
Share capital		35,000
Reserves		9,000
		44,000
Minority interests (Activity 19)		2,000
		46,000

Activity 22

The answers to 1 and 2 are no. The restrictive use of these two reserves has been covered on many occasions in previous chapters. The answers to 3 and 4 are yes. Note that there is a substantial difference between writing something off against the balance of retained profits and writing it off against profits for the year; the latter treatment would reduce reported profit, whereas the former is shown as a movement on reserves.

Activity 23

1. In the balance sheet under investments as item B, III, 3.
2. In the profit and loss account as item 8.

Activity 24

The investment of 1,000 shares in Moyenne Ltd by Superbe Ltd is an investment in an associated company since it represents 25% of Moyenne's ordinary share capital. Note that the number of ordinary shares issued by Petite Ltd is (£1,250 ÷ 0.25) 5,000 and so Grande Ltd's investment of 400 shares in that company represents a holding of 8%. This does not create any special relationship (subsidiary or associate) and will be treated as an ordinary investment.

Questions for self-assessment

Answers to self-assessment questions are given at the end of the book.

The following question was set by the AEB in their A Level examination for June 1990. It is fairly typical of examination questions requiring students to identify group relationships.

The way in which some of the detail for retained earnings has been presented seems unreasonable, to say the least. When you first look at this section of the balance sheet, you are likely to have difficulty in recognizing some of the information given. In a real exam this could set up a kind of panic, which would make it even more difficult for you to feel in control. You will have to try and convince yourself of two things in these circumstances:

1. the difficulty you are experiencing does not stem from your lack of knowledge (have some faith in yourself), and
2. the examiner has not set the question incorrectly; the chances are that the information has not been presented very clearly.

If you approach this question in this frame of mind you might eventually see that the difficulty stems from the fact that there are three separate balance sheets (in columns) but only one set of descriptions. This often necessitates having some descriptions that are applicable to one particular column but not to others (like the investment in subsidiaries in ICI's group balance sheet).

Unfortunately in this question, the examiner has used dashes to mean 'not applicable' whereas we are accustomed to thinking of the dash symbol as meaning nil. If you think of the dash symbol as nil in this case, the question does not make sense; for example, how can Atom's net profit for 1989 be nil? Or, how can Proton's retained earnings be nil when the retained earnings at 1 January 1989 were £20,000?

The answer at the back of the book for part (e) of the question has been expanded for tutorial purposes. It goes well beyond what would be expected from a student at this level. Some of the details given in the question have been converted into data that can be used in the analysis of share prices.

18.1 Atom/Neutron/Proton Ltd

The following financial information was available on three limited companies:

Balance sheets as at 31 December 1989

	Atom Ltd £000	Neutron Ltd £000	Proton Ltd £000
Fixed assets less depreciation	360	140	220
Investments in 15,000 shares in Neutron Ltd at cost	20	–	–
35,000 shares in Proton Ltd at cost	60	–	–
Current assets	250	70	160
	690	210	380
Called-up capital £1 Ordinary shares fully paid	–	90	75
50p Ordinary shares fully paid	150	–	–
Share premium	100	–	75
Retained earnings	150	20	–
Retained earnings as at 1 January 1989	–	–	20
Net profit for 1989	–	–	90
General reserve	120	40	60
Current liabilities	170	60	60
	690	210	380

Additional information.
1. Proton Ltd have not prepared a profit and loss appropriation account for the financial year ended 31 December 1989.
   The directors made the following recommendations:
   (i) An ordinary dividend for the year of 10% was declared, to be paid on 20 January 1990.
   (ii) A transfer of £50,000 is to be made to general reserve.
2. Subsequent to the preparation of a revised balance sheet in good format, Atom Ltd decided that stock of £15,000 (valued at cost) was obsolete. It was sold as scrap on 10 January 1990 for £2,500.
3. Atom Ltd decided to purchase further shares in the open market as follows:
   10,000 £1 Ordinary shares in Neutron Ltd at £2 per share.
   10,000 £1 Ordinary shares in Proton Ltd at £4.50 per share.
   The transactions were effected and paid for on 31 January 1990.
4. In order to finance the additional share purchases Atom Ltd sold surplus land and buildings for £200,000. The net book value of the land and buildings on 31 December 1989 was £50,000. The transaction was completed and cash received by 31 January 1990.
5. There were no other transactions in the month of January 1990.
6. Ignore taxation.

Required:
(a) A profit and loss appropriation account for the year ended 31 December 1989 for Proton Ltd.
(b) A revised balance sheet for Atom Ltd as at 31 January 1990.
(c) Define what is meant by the term 'subsidiary company'.
(d) Using suitable calculations determine whether or not Neutron Ltd and/or Proton Ltd are subsidiary companies of Atom Ltd as at 31 January 1990.
(e) What investment significance does the following information have for Atom Ltd?

	Neutron Ltd	Proton Ltd
1989 return on capital employed	5%	25%

Note: Capital employed is defined as total assets.

(AEB A Level, Jun 90)

18.2 Apple and Blackbury. Apple Ltd acquired a controlling interest in the shares of Blackbury Ltd on 1 January 1993. Immediately after the shares were acquired the balance sheets of the two companies were as follows:

	Apple Ltd	Blackbury Ltd
Fixed assets at net book value	164,300	130,000
Investment in Blackbury Ltd		
(48,000 ordinary shares)	90,000	
Investment in Raspbury Ltd		4,000
Net current assets	8,400	42,000
	262,700	176,000
Called up share capital (£1 ordinary shares)	200,000	80,000
Profit and loss account	62,700	66,000
10% Debenture 2010		30,000
	262,700	176,000

Blackbury Ltd's investment in Raspbury Ltd represents 8% of that company's ordinary shares. The fair value of Blackbury Ltd's net assets are considered to be the same as book value. Apple Ltd's accounting policy on goodwill is to write it off immediately against reserves.

Required:
Prepare a consolidated balance sheet at the date of acquisition.

19 ▷ Specialized accounting standards

Objectives

After you have completed this chapter, you should be able to:
- apply the specialized principles of SSAPs not covered in previous chapters, including SSAPs 3, 4, 5, 13, 17 and 18 (and parts of SSAP 21)
- apply the principles in SSAP 12 regarding the revision of asset lives, and describe the effect of depreciation of a revalued asset on realized profits
- calculate depreciation using methods other than straight line and reducing balance
- discuss how FRS 3 has changed the practice of calculating earnings per share

---

Introduction

The important accounting standards that are likely to apply to all companies have been dealt with at strategic points throughout the book. The objective of this chapter is to deal with particular SSAPs that have not been mentioned in earlier chapters, mainly because the SSAPs concerned relate to special types of business activity. The coverage of certain SSAPs dealt with in previous chapters will also be extended.

In producing the text for this chapter, a judgement had to be made on the depth of knowledge that examiners might expect at a foundation level. This judgement takes account of the guidance provided in various syllabuses (present and proposed) and a review of past examination questions.

19.1 Accounting standard profile

During the twenty years that the Accounting Standards Committee (ASC) was responsible for developing accounting standards, it issued twenty-five SSAPs. Three of these (SSAPs 7, 11 and 16) were withdrawn, leaving twenty-two SSAPs that were adopted by the Accounting Standards Board (ASB) when it took over the standard setting process in 1990.

The significance of this adoption by the ASB is that each SSAP has now become an accounting standard under provisions in the 1989 Companies Act. The 1989 Act introduced a requirement for directors to make a written declaration in the published financial statements on whether the accounts have been prepared in accordance with 'accounting standards' and, where not, to state reasons for not complying with any particular standard.

Prior to the 1989 Act, there were no specific provisions in company law requiring directors to adhere to accounting standards. Compliance relied upon persuasion by members of the accounting profession, whose only weapon was the threat of a qualified audit report if directors refused to observe SSAPs without justification.

Since the formation of the ASB, four of the twenty-two adopted SSAPs have been withdrawn (SSAPs 6, 10, 14 and 23) and replaced by accounting standards (FRSs 1, 2, 3 and 7) issued by the ASB. A complete list of the SSAPs and FRSs that were operative at the time of writing this edition is given in Appendix 1 to this chapter.

19.2 Accounting standards: Study index

Out of the 26 accounting standards listed in Appendix 1, the following have been adequately covered at a foundation level in previous chapters:

SSAP 1	Associated companies	Chapter 18
SSAP 2	Accounting policies and fundamental concepts	Chapter 4
SSAP 8	Taxation in company accounts	Chapters 10 and 12
SSAP 9	Stocks (excluding long-term contracts)	Chapter 4
SSAP 12	Depreciation (excluding revised asset lives)	Chapter 6
SSAP 22	Goodwill	Chapters 15 and 18
FRS 1	Cash flow statements (including 1996 revision)	Chapter 11
FRS 3	Reporting financial performance (including the provisions on exceptional, extraordinary items and prior year adjustments)	Chapter 12
FRS 4	Capital instruments	Chapter 10

There are seven SSAPs and four FRSs that can safely be excluded from foundation level studies in financial accounting. Some of these (such as SSAP 25, FRSs 2 and 5) have been mentioned in earlier chapters but there was no detailed discussion of them. This leaves the following accounting standards to be introduced by this chapter:

SSAP 3 and FRS 3	Earnings per share
SSAP 4	Government grants
SSAP 5	Accounting for VAT
SSAP 13	Research and development costs
SSAP 17	Post-balance sheet events
SSAP 18	Accounting for contingencies

In addition to these, the earlier coverage of SSAPs 9, 12 and FRS 3 will be extended, and some of the provisions in SSAP 21 on hire-purchase trading are to be introduced. We will also be examining further aspects of the ASB's Statement of Principles for Financial Reporting.

19.3 Earnings per share, SSAP 3 and FRS 3

SSAP 3 and FRS 3 requires all 'listed' companies to disclose their earnings per share (EPS) on the face of the profit and loss account. A 'listed company' is one whose shares are dealt with on a recognized stock exchange. EPS is one of the factors in the price earnings (P/E) ratio which, in the case of listed companies, is published alongside the daily share prices in various publications such as the *Financial Times* stock exchange listing.

The calculation of EPS is relevant only to ordinary shares (not preference shares) and so the basic calculation is to divide net profit by the number of ordinary shares in issue.

Activity 1

A company's net profit is £10,000 and its share capital consists of 50,000 ordinary shares of £1 each. Calculate earnings per share. EPS is normally stated in terms of pence per share.

That was relatively straightforward because there was no choice over the two figures needed for the calculation. In fact, the information was quite naive because there is no such thing as net profit in a company's profit and loss account (except in exam questions). There are several kinds of profit. Furthermore, there may be preference shareholders who are entitled to a prior claim to some of the profit (in the form of a dividend), which will reduce the amount of earnings attributable to ordinary shareholders.

We clearly need a definition of earnings for the EPS calculation. Consider the following situation:

Profit on ordinary activities before tax		50,000
Taxation on ordinary profit		10,000
Profit on ordinary activities after tax		40,000
Dividends: ordinary shares	10,000	
preference shares	7,000	
		17,000
Profit for year retained		23,000

The number of ordinary shares in issue is 100,000

The original definition of earnings in SSAP 3 was based on 'ordinary profit' available for the ordinary shareholders. Extraordinary profits and losses, if any, were ignored and so earnings were defined as: ordinary profit after tax, less any preference dividend.

Activity 2

Calculate EPS for the company referred to above based on the original definition in SSAP 3.

The standard also prescribes how the number of shares should be determined if the number in issue throughout the year has been changed by events such as a bonus issue or a rights issue. Some of these provisions are quite complex and are well beyond the requirements of examinations at a foundation level.

One of the problems with the original SSAP 3 was its relationship to the old SSAP 6, which allowed certain items to be treated as extraordinary. In order to keep EPS as high as possible, there was a tendency for directors to put forward arguments for treating abnormal losses as extraordinary and abnormal gains as exceptional. This had the effect of leaving abnormal losses out of the EPS calculation, whereas abnormal gains were included.

This led to a great deal of inconsistency between companies over the classification of extraordinary items. These practices have been stopped following the withdrawal of SSAP 6 and the introduction of FRS 3. The new accounting standard does two things in this connection, namely:

- items previously classed as extraordinary must now be treated as exceptional
- the definition of EPS in SSAP 3 has been revised so that extraordinary items (if any do occur) must be taken into account.

FRS 3 requires that any profit or loss on termination of a business segment should be treated as an exceptional item to be included with results from discontinued activities. The former SSAP 6 classified these events as extraordinary.

Volatile EPS and the IIMR basis

The revised definitions of ordinary activities and exceptional items (see Chapter 12 of this book) mean that it is unlikely that any event can be classed as extraordinary. Perhaps things like losses through an earthquake or events of that nature might be treated as extraordinary but these events are so rare in UK practice that we can almost say that extraordinary items will not arise. In any event, FRS 3 requires EPS to be calculated on profit after extraordinary items, if any, are reported.

The reclassification of items that were previously treated as extraordinary (such as losses on the closure of a business segment) as exceptional items arising from ordinary activities, means that the EPS of some companies could be quite volatile. EPS will fall dramatically if there is an exceptional loss in one year and will rise if there is an exceptional profit.

As a result, the investing community has chosen to ignore the EPS figures based on FRS 3 as quoted in the published annual reports of companies. The Institute of Investment Management and Research (IIMR) has devised a measure known as the 'headline earnings per share'. This measure is used by the various reporting services when quoting P/E ratios. If you look at the bottom right-hand corner of the last page of the share listings in the *Financial Times* (as mentioned in Chapter 1) you will see that the P/E ratios quoted are based on the IIMR headline EPS. The main difference between the IIMR EPS and the FRS 3 EPS relates to exceptional items such as the profits or losses on closure of a business segment. The IIMR basis excludes these items and so it has brought its EPS calculation back to the basis that was being used before the introduction of FRS 3.

It seems that the investing community does not know how to respond to volatile earnings, it can only make sense of steady changes in EPS. This is despite the fact that the ASB has been trying to warn investors not to pay too much attention to a single indicator such as EPS. This kind of discord is unlikely to cease until we stop thinking in terms of earnings per share and start thinking in terms of free cash flow per share (as discussed in Chapter 11).

19.4 Government grants, SSAP 4

The range of government assistance in the form of grants paid to business enterprises, particularly in development areas, is now quite vast. There are basically two classes of grant: revenue based grants, to assist with running expenses; and capital based grants, to assist with the cost of fixed assets.

There is no significant accounting problem with revenue based grants. The grant received is simply treated as reducing the relevant expense. SSAP 4 is mainly concerned with the accounting treatment of capital based grants.

The original SSAP 4 permitted companies to deal with these grants in one of two ways, namely:

- credit the grant to the asset account, thus reducing the asset's cost; depreciation is then based on the reduced cost, or
- credit the grant to a 'deferred credit' account, leaving the asset to be recorded at its original purchase price and depreciated in the normal way; the deferred credit is then transferred to the profit and loss account by annual instalments over the expected life of the asset.

The effect of these two methods on reported profits is the same. In one case there is a reduced depreciation charge because the asset cost has been reduced by the grant; in the other there is a higher depreciation charge (based on original purchase price) but this is effectively reduced through the annual transfer of deferred credit to the profit and loss account.

There was no conflict between the original SSAP (issued in 1974) and company law as it stood at that time. However, the first method (crediting grant to the asset) eventually fell into conflict with the 1985 Companies Act, which required fixed assets to be shown at their purchase price. Consequently, the SSAP has been revised so that the 'deferred credit' basis must now be adopted by all companies.

If the asset is written off on a straight line basis over a specified number of years, the deferred credit must also be written off by equal instalments over the same number of years. The amount of deferred credit not written off is carried forward in the balance sheet (described as a deferred credit, or deferred income) and can either be included in the capital and reserves section of the balance sheet, or deducted from net assets. You will recall dealing with life subscriptions as deferred income in Chapter 16; the same concept applies to government grants.

Activity 3

Refer to the balance sheet for ICI in Appendix 2 of Chapter 13 and make a note of the deferred income for government grants at the date of that balance sheet.

Activity 4

A company purchased a fixed asset at a cost of £200,000 at the beginning of its financial year and receives a government grant of £10,000 towards its cost. It is estimated that the asset will have a useful economic life of 20 years and a scrap value of nil. Depreciation is to be on a straight line basis. Determine the following figures for this company for the first year of ownership of this asset:

Depreciation charge in the profit and loss account:

Deferred credit written off to profit and loss account:

Balance on deferred credit at the end of the first year:

19.5 Accounting for value added tax (VAT), SSAP 5

The book-keeping for VAT was covered in Chapter 7 but has been virtually ignored in all subsequent chapters. This is perfectly reasonable because VAT has very little impact on the figures in the financial statements. If you look back through past examination questions in this book you will find that VAT has not been mentioned in any of them, except those at the basic book-keeping level.

The SSAP is not concerned with the book-keeping (book-keeping is a practical problem, not a matter of principle) and simply deals with presentation in the financial statements. Three matters of presentation are dealt with, namely: turnover, the VAT creditor, and any irrecoverable VAT on inputs.

The figure for turnover in the financial statements must be presented net of VAT. This is achieved automatically by the book-keeping because the VAT added to the sales price is credited to Customs and Excise, not to sales. You might recall from Chapter 2 that the 1985 Companies Act defines turnover as being **net of value added tax**. The SSAP permitted companies to present their turnover at the gross figure providing the output VAT is then shown as a deduction, but this now seems to conflict with the term **turnover** as defined in the Companies Act.

Any amount owing to Customs and Excise must be included in the appropriate category of creditors in the balance sheet but does not have to be disclosed as a separate item.

Activity 5

Refer to Appendix 2 (formats for published accounts) in Chapter 12 and see if you can find an appropriate heading for the VAT creditor.

If the account with Customs and Excise is a debit balance (refund due) it could be included with 'other debtors' (item C, II, 4).

For certain types of expenditure, the input VAT cannot be debited to Customs and Excise. This is so in the case of entertainment expenditure, and on the purchase of private motor cars. The SSAP requires the irrecoverable VAT in these cases to be treated as a part of the expenditure concerned.

19.6 Long-term contracts, SSAP 9

The text in previous chapters (particularly Chapter 4) on the provisions in SSAP 9 for stocks and work-in-progress was more than adequate for the examination in so far as it concerned trading stocks and manufactured products. In this chapter we are dealing with the specialized application of SSAP 9 to long-term contracts.

In some businesses, particularly in the civil engineering and construction industries, the work undertaken for a customer can take several years to complete. Strictly speaking, SSAP 9 defines a long-term contract as one that is started in one accounting period and completed in another. On this basis, a long-term contract can be one that takes less than 12 months, but we usually think of this subject in terms of contracts spanning a number of years.

During the construction phase, the contractor will be incurring costs on the contract, and will also be receiving what are known as stage payments (or progress payments) from the customer as the work progresses. These payments are payments on account of the agreed contract price, which are paid to the contractor in stages on the basis of a valuation of the work done to date. These valuations (based on a proportion of total contract price) are carried out by a professional consultant acting for the customer. We often refer to this value as the 'certified value' of work to date because the consultant issues a certificate to enable a stage payment to be made.

In the contractor's books, the costs incurred on the contract are debited to an account for each contract. The balance on this account represents the cost of work-in-progress for that contract. Similarly, the payments received from the customer at various stages of the contract are credited to a separate account, usually called 'progress payments', for each contract.

Prior to the introduction of the original SSAP 9 (in May 1975) companies could adopt one of two accounting policies on long-term contracts: the completed contracts method, and the percentage of completion method. A general explanation of these two methods is as follows:

1. **Completed contracts method:** the accumulated cost of work-in-progress and the accumulated progress payments received are carried forward (in the balance sheet) until the contract is completed. On completion of the contract, the balances on these two accounts are transferred to the profit and loss account.

   The effect of this method is to credit the profit and loss account with the total sales value of the contract, and to debit the total cost of the contract, in the year of completion. Consequently, recognition of the profit is delayed until the year when the contract is completed.

2. **Percentage of completion method:** under this method, the profit is recognized in stages each year as the contract progresses. Each year a proportion of the ultimate profit is estimated to have been earned on the basis of the work done to date and is recognized as such in the profit and loss account. Profit recognized prior to completion is called 'attributable profit'.

SSAP 9 prescribed that all long-term contracts should be accounted for on the percentage of completion method. SSAP 9 was revised in September 1988, and this revision altered the way in which 'attributable profit' was dealt with in the financial statements. This was necessary as a result of changes in company law, but the principle of recognizing attributable profit on the percentage of completion method remains the same.

Attributable profit is an estimated figure calculated on a memorandum basis; it is not a figure generated by the double-entry book-keeping system. Having calculated attributable profit, the company must then decide how this should be recognized in terms of turnover and cost of sales. There are, therefore, two levels at which an accounting policy must be adopted, namely:

- calculation of attributable profit
- a basis for recognizing turnover and cost of sales in order to report this attributable profit

SSAP 9 defines attributable profit as that part of the currently estimated total profit that fairly reflects the profit attributable to work performed at the accounting date. This clearly involves making an estimate of total profit, which should be relatively straightforward since estimates of costs would have been made when the contract price was quoted. But the SSAP is silent regarding bases for calculating the proportion of total estimated profit earned at the accounting date.

An international survey carried out in 1968 revealed that most companies used the proportion of total cost completed as a basis for determining the proportion of estimated profit earned. Consider the following example:

Agreed contract price	1,000,000
Estimated total costs	800,000
Estimated total profit	200,000

At the accounting date the following facts applied:

Contract costs incurred to date	600,000
Progress payments received	700,000
Certified value of work to date	740,000

In the contractor's books, the contract costs of £600,000 will be a debit balance on the contract account; the progress payments received of £700,000 will be a credit balance on a progress payments account. Certified value of work to date is simply an item of information (but see later regarding the use of this information for invoicing the customer).

The company must now decide on a policy for recording this profit in the profit and loss account in terms of turnover and cost of sales. At the moment, the company is carrying two balances in its books:

Contract costs   600,000 Debit balance
Progress payments   700,000 Credit balance

The figures for turnover and cost of sales will have to come out of these two accounts in some way. In our example, we will assume that the company is going to base the turnover recognized to date on the certified value of work to date. In this case the company will make the following double-entry:

Debit: Progress payments account   740,000
Credit: Profit and loss account (as turnover) 740,000

Activity 8

The figure for turnover (£740,000) is now in the profit and loss account. In order to recognize the attributable profit of £150,000 the company will also have to transfer some of the contract costs into the profit and loss account (as cost of sales). See if you can calculate and describe the double-entry needed for this.

Debit:

Credit:

You will notice that this procedure has left the two ledger accounts with the following balances:

Contract costs (600,000 – 590,000)   10,000 debit
Progress payments (700,000 – 740,000)   40,000 debit

SSAP 9 requires these to be presented in the balance sheet as follows:

- **Contract costs** of £10,000 (debit) to be included under stocks and described as 'long-term contract balances'
- **Progress payments** of £40,000 (debit) to be included under debtors and described as 'amounts recoverable on contracts'

You should note that there is no one universal method for calculating attributable profit, nor for recognizing turnover and cost of sales to date. The above explanation was based on one of many methods adopted in practice. Any numerical examination questions on this topic should either describe the accounting policy to be used, or recognize that there are several variations to the answer.

Notice that in the above explanation progress payments were dealt with on a cash basis. In other words, progress payments were only accounted for as they were received. A variation to this is that some contracting firms invoice the customer each time a valuation report is received. This is in keeping with the accruals concept. When a valuation certificate is received, the double-entry will be:

Debit: the customer
Credit: progress payments received and receivable

When the customer pays, the amount received is credited to the customer's account. At any one accounting date, there could be a debit balance on the customer's account. This will be presented as an ordinary debtor in the balance sheet; it has not arisen from any peculiarities in SSAP 9, it simply arises from adopting the accruals concept. Notice that the account formerly called 'progress payments' is now 'progress payments received and receivable'.

If this basis had been used in the above example, the progress payments (received and receivable) account would have been a credit balance (prior to transfer to the profit and loss account) of £740,000, and there would have been an ordinary debtor of £40,000. When the £740,000 was transferred to the profit and loss account as turnover, there would be a zero balance on the progress payments account.

19.7 Depreciation, SSAP 12

The mainstream requirements of SSAP 12 have been adequately covered in previous chapters, particularly Chapter 6. In this chapter, you will learn about some of the special situations that can arise, such as a revision of asset lives, which are subject to special provisions in the SSAP.

There is also a mention of some of the more unusual methods of depreciation. These have nothing to do with the SSAP but examiners do occasionally confront you with them, and they can come as a bit of a nasty shock if you have grown accustomed to thinking of depreciation methods as being either straight line or reducing balance.

As regards a revision of asset lives, the first problem to consider is whether or not a prior year adjustment should be allowed. If a company had initially decided to write off an asset over 20 years, and during the fifth year realized that the estimated life should have been 5 years, the directors might argue that the charges for depreciation in the previous four years had been understated.

The reverse of this situation (an extension of asset lives) creates a similar problem, although the directors are less likely to argue for a prior year adjustment in this case because future depreciation charges will be reduced.

SSAP 12, combined with FRS 3, does not allow a prior year adjustment in either case. A revision of an asset's life is regarded as a revision of an accounting estimate. You might be able to recall that FRS 3 (Chapter 12) specifically prevents a prior year adjustment from being made where it results from the revision of an accounting estimate. Prior year adjustments are permitted only when they result from a fundamental error or a change of accounting policy.

Activity 9

An asset that had cost £30,000 was originally estimated to have a useful life of 20 years and a scrap value of nil. After depreciating the asset (on a straight line basis) over 5 years, it was estimated that its remaining useful life was only 10 years. Deal with the following questions:

1. What is the net book value of the asset at the end of the fifth year?

2. What amount will be charged as annual depreciation in the future if this NBV is written off on a straight line basis over the remaining 10 years?

3. What amount will be charged as annual depreciation in the future if past provisions are adjusted so as to recognize that 5 out of 15 years should have been provided?

4. Is the difference between the annual charges in 2 and 3 sufficiently material to justify making an adjustment to past provisions?

The provisions in SSAP 12 on this subject state that if asset lives are reviewed regularly, and revised when necessary, there is not likely to be any material distortion to future results if the net book value is written off over the remaining estimated life. If material distortions are likely, an adjustment should be made to the accumulated depreciation by charging (or crediting) profits on ordinary activities for the year. In some cases this might have to be disclosed as an exceptional item. You will understand the principles better by working through the Activities 9 and 10.

Activity 10

An asset that had cost £150,000 was originally estimated to have a useful life of 50 years and a scrap value of nil. After depreciating the asset (on a straight line basis) over 5 years, it was estimated that its remaining useful life was only 5 years.

1. What is the net book value (NBV) of the asset at the end of the fifth year?

2. What amount will be charged as annual depreciation in the future if this NBV is written off on a straight line basis over the remaining 5 years?

3. What amount will be charged as annual depreciation if past provisions are adjusted so as to recognize that 5 out of 10 years should have been provided?

4. Assume that the difference between the annual charges in 2 and 3 is sufficiently material to justify making an adjustment to accumulated depreciation at the end of the fifth year. Describe the double-entry that will be made in order to recognize the depreciation under-provided in the previous 5 years:

Debit:

Credit:

Change of asset lives in practice

There is nothing in accounting regulations to prevent a company from changing an accounting estimate. In fact, SSAP 12 on depreciation positively encourages directors to review their estimates of asset lives on a regular basis, and to make adjustments to the accounts where appropriate. This guidance might have been more concerned with those assets where the remaining life is less than the original estimate but it works both ways.

The most famous case of where substantial increases to the estimate of asset lives were made is that of British Airports Authority (BAA). In two successive years, BAA made significant changes in its estimate of asset lives for two types of asset: airport terminals and airport runways. The asset lives were changed in 1989 and again in 1990. A summary of the asset lives used to calculate depreciation is as follows:

Year to 31 March	1988 (years)	1989 (years)	1990 (years)
Terminals	16	30	50
Runways	23.5	40	100

The effect on the profits for 1990 of revising the asset lives of terminals was stated in the annual report to be a reduction in depreciation charges of £8.6m (some

3.4% of the pre-tax profit for 1990). The benefit of these longer estimates of asset lives will also be felt in the future as more terminals are constructed.

Terry Smith (in *Accounting for Growth*) raises an interesting point on the choice of 100 years for airport runways. As you know, the estimated life used for calculating depreciation is meant to be the estimated number of years that the business intends to use the asset (not the estimated life of the asset itself). Bearing in mind that there were no aeroplanes in 1896 (100 years ago), he questions whether we will still be using aeroplanes 100 years from now. It's an interesting thought.

Asset revaluations

The other specialized area in SSAP 12 deals with asset revaluations. The practice of asset revaluations was dealt with in Chapter 10 (section 10.6). As was mentioned there, the annual depreciation charges following revaluation should be based on the carrying value of the asset.

There is a connection between depreciation of revalued assets and the subject of **distributable profit**. The total depreciation charge on a revalued asset can be identified as being partly on the original cost and partly on the revalued amount. The part that relates to original cost is considered to be a realized loss, whereas the part that relates to the increase in value is considered to be an unrealized loss. Since distributable profits are based on realized profits less realized losses, it might be necessary for a company to keep a record of the amount of unrealized losses charged to the profit and loss account. But this has no bearing on the amount charged as depreciation – it must be based on the revalued amount.

The 1985 Companies Act prescribes how the revaluation surplus or deficit should be dealt with. In those cases where the valuation exceeds the **net book value**, the difference must be credited to a revaluation reserve. Where the valuation is less than the net book value, there is (in accounting jargon) a 'diminution' in the value of the asset, which must be charged to the profit and loss account. If the amount is material it might have to be disclosed as an exceptional item.

Notice how the adjustment is made by comparing the value to the **net book value**. This is quite important because some companies (before the law was changed) compared the valuation to original cost and based the revaluation surplus on the difference between these two figures. The accumulated depreciation was then written back to the credit of the profit and loss account as 'provisions no longer required'. This practice is now illegal.

Disposal of revalued asset: FRS 3

Prior to FRS 3 there was some inconsistency in the way that profits (or losses) on the disposal of a revalued asset were treated in the accounts. Some companies were calculating the profit or loss on disposal by comparing the sale proceeds to the depreciated historical cost. This had the effect of transferring the past revaluation surplus (which was an unrealized gain at the time of the valuation) to the profit and loss account. The argument for this practice was that the gain which had been treated as unrealized in previous years was now realized and should form part of the profit for the year.

FRS 3 has prevented this practice by requiring the profit or loss on disposal to be calculated by comparing the sale proceeds to the carrying value of the asset in the books. The fact that the revaluation surplus is now realized can be reflected in the accounts by a transfer between reserves. The amount concerned can be transferred from the revaluation reserve to the balance on the profit and loss reserve but it should not be included in the calculation of profit for the year. The amount concerned will be treated as a realized profit for the purposes of calculating distributable profit.

19.8 Depreciation methods

The choice of method for calculating depreciation is a practical problem rather than a matter of principle. It is not, therefore, dealt with in SSAP 12 other than to require management to chose a method that is most appropriate to the asset and its use.

Throughout this book, you have been using the most widely applied methods: straight line and reducing balance. Other methods have been devised and on rare occasions they do crop up in exams. In some cases you might be able to work out what to do by a simple application of logic even if you have never encountered the method previously. For example, there was a question in an A Level exam requiring depreciation calculations for a particular machine using four different methods: reducing balance, straight line, usage, and sinking fund.

The information given for the 'usage' method was as follows: original cost of machine £28,000; estimated useful life 3 years; scrap value at end of third year £4,000. Anticipated usage was as follows:

Year	Hours used
1	800
2	2,100
3	1,100

Activity 11

See if you can calculate the depreciation charge for each of the years 1, 2 and 3 using the usage method. There is nothing complicated in this, you simply need to find an hourly rate rather than a rate for the accounting period.

Year 1

Year 2

Year 3

There is also nothing complicated in the sinking fund method providing the appropriate figures are given in the question (as they were in this case). As you know, there is no connection between the provision for depreciation and the provision of funds for replacing the asset at the end of its life. Depreciation merely ensures that an amount equal to the provision is retained in the business. The idea of a sinking fund is that an amount equal to the annual depreciation charge should be invested outside the business. This then provides a fund for replacement of the asset at the end of its life.

The amount to be invested each year will take account of the interest that the investments will earn. By the end of the asset's life, the total annual amount of cash invested, together with accumulated interest, should be equal to the estimated replacement cost.

The double-entry on each cash investment is simply:

Debit: investment
Credit: bank.

The double-entry for interest is:

Debit: investment (because the interest is re-invested)
Credit: profit and loss account (as investment income).

The double-entry for the depreciation provision is the same as under any other method, although the annual charge is based on the annual cash investment plus any interest re-invested during that year. For the sake of simplicity, it is usually assumed that the interest earned is re-invested at the end of the year.

In the exam question referred to earlier, the information for the sinking fund method was given as follows:

In order to secure sufficient funds for the replacement of the machine, the company will have to invest £7,250 at the end of each of the three years. Interest received on the investment will be 10% per annum.

Activity 12

See if you can work out the annual depreciation charges using the sinking fund method. Take care over year 1: there would be no re-investment of interest in that year because the investments are made at the end of the year.

Year 1

Year 2

Year 3

If you care to work out the total fund by the end of the third year, you will find that it approximates to £24,000. This reconciles to the information given for the machine (see Activity 11) of cost £28,000 less scrap value £4,000.

There is another method of depreciation called 'sum of digits', which we can look at briefly after dealing with hire-purchase sales in a moment.

19.9 Research and development costs, SSAP 13

This is another SSAP for which examination syllabuses tend to have an 'awareness' requirement. Quite often there is no guidance as to whether this 'awareness' will be tested numerically or by description. However, the subject is mainly knowledge based, and the numerical aspects are quite simple once you have understood the contents of the standard.

In certain industries, such as electronics, aircraft, and drug manufacturing, some companies expend substantial sums of money on research and development. For many years these companies argued that the expenditure on research and development created an intangible asset which would produce future benefits in the form of sales income as soon as the product being developed became marketable.

The accounting policy adopted by these companies was to carry forward research and development costs as an asset until the product started to produce sales income. The expenditure could then be matched with this income by amortizing the deferred costs on some systematic basis. The difficulty with this policy is that there is a conflict between prudence and accruals. In some cases, a great deal of the expenditure on research may prove to be fruitless and nothing marketable is ever developed from the cost. SSAP 13, which seeks to regulate the practice in this area, has been subject to a number of revisions but the latest position is as follows:

- A distinction must be made between research expenditure and development expenditure.
- All research costs must be written off to profit and loss account as they are incurred.
- Development costs may be deferred to future periods if all of the following criteria are satisfied:

  1. there is a clearly defined project
  2. expenditure on the project is separately identifiable
  3. the outcome of the project has been assessed with reasonable certainty as to its technical feasibility and commercial viability
  4. revenues (roughly the gross profit) to be earned by the product are reasonably expected to cover the development costs
  5. adequate resources exist (or are reasonably expected to be available) to complete the project.

As you can see, there is quite a lot to remember. You might find the mnemonic DIARCO will help; it stands for **D**efined, **I**dentifiable, **A**ssessed, **R**evenues, **CO**mplete.

Activity 13

A company has been experimenting with some new microelectronics and has incurred costs (wages, etc.) amounting to £20,000 on the project. It has solved most of the basic problems but is still working on how to apply the knowledge gained so that a marketable product can be developed. Comment on whether or not the expenditure of £20,000 should be deferred.

Sundry provisions in SSAP 13

Fixed assets that provide facilities for research and development should be capitalized and depreciated in accordance with SSAP 12. The depreciation expense should be included as part of research and development costs charged to the profit and loss account; it should not be included in the amount being deferred. Deferred development costs should be amortized on a systematic basis as soon as production commences. If the circumstances that justified deferral are no longer applicable, the balance of development expenditure should be written off immediately.

19.10 Accounting for post-balance sheet events

Financial statements are produced for a specified period up to a particular date. The financial position shown in the balance sheet is based upon the conditions that existed at the balance sheet date, even though some of the amounts are not known with certainty.

Generally speaking, events that take place after the balance sheet date are not recognized in the previous year's financial statements, they are dealt with in the financial statements for the following year. But occasionally something happens between the balance sheet date and the date when the accounts are approved for publication that should be reflected in those financial statements, even though the event did not occur during the year.

SSAP 17 refers to these events as post-balance sheet events, and identifies two types:

- adjusting events
- non-adjusting events.

Adjusting events, as the name implies, are events that require the figures to be altered. They are defined as events that provide additional evidence of conditions existing at the balance sheet date.

Non-adjusting events are events occurring after the balance sheet date that are concerned with conditions that did not exist at the balance sheet date. These events might require disclosure by way of a note to ensure that the financial statements are not misleading.

You will get an idea of the distinction between these two types of event by considering the following case:

A company prepared its accounts for year ending 30 June 1997. In the period between 30 June 1997 and the date when the accounts were approved by the directors, the following events occurred:

- **Event 1:** received a notification that a debtor, thought to be a good debt at 30 June, had gone into liquidation; the amount outstanding in the balance sheet was £300,000.
- **Event 2:** a fire occurred in one of the company's factories and the uninsured loss is estimated at £500,000.

Activity 14

Identify whether these events are adjusting events or non-adjusting events and justify your choice.

Event 1:

Event 2:

19.11 Accounting for contingencies, SSAP 18

SSAP 18 also requires a consideration of conditions existing at the balance sheet date that might not be reflected in the figures. A contingency is a condition existing at the balance sheet date where the outcome will be confirmed by the occurrence, or non-occurrence, of one or more uncertain future events (a bit of a mouthful, but it will make sense in a moment).

The future event, when it occurs, might result in a gain to the company or a loss. Consequently, we refer to these items as being contingent gains or contingent losses. For example, if a company has guaranteed a bank loan granted to another company, there is a contingent loss. The loss is contingent upon the other company defaulting on the loan and the guarantor company having to repay the loan under the terms of the guarantee. When the guarantee was offered in the first place, no figures were entered in the books of the guarantor, it was simply an arrangement between the three parties.

SSAP 18 addresses the problem of whether contingent gains and losses should be reflected in the figures, or whether they require disclosure in the notes. The approach taken is as follows:

- A contingent loss should be accrued (treated as a liability) where it is probable that the future event will confirm the loss, and the amount can be determined with reasonable accuracy. Where the loss is not accrued under this requirement it should be disclosed in the notes.
- A contingent gain should never be accrued, and should only be disclosed by way of a note if it is probable that the gain will be realized. In cases where it is reasonably certain that a gain will be realized, the gain does not fall to be treated as a contingent gain and should be accrued as a realized gain.

You will get a clearer understanding of SSAP 18 by considering the following details and working through the activity.

The following three unrelated situations apply to year ending 30 June 1997:

1. A holding company has guaranteed a bank loan of £500,000 granted to an associated company. The associated company is trading profitably and is financially solvent.
2. A company has been defending a court case for an alleged act of negligence. During the post-balance sheet period, judgement was given against the company and the court has awarded £500,000 damages to the claimant. The company is considering an appeal, but no decision had been made by the time the accounts were approved.
3. During the year, a company started a legal case against a competitor for an alleged breach of copyright. During the post-balance sheet period, the court found in favour of the company and awarded £500,000 damages. The defendant company has indicated that it has no intention of making an appeal against the award.

Activity 15

Review the three situations and decide how SSAP 18 would require each of them to be dealt with in the financial statements for year ending 30 June 1997. Make a note of your decisions here.

Situation 1:

Situation 2:

Situation 3:

Some companies, particularly those in the construction industry, often have substantial contingent liabilities which do not need to be accrued under the provisions of SSAP 18. The details are given in 'the notes' but these tend to be buried in a mass of detail. An unexpected crystallization of these liabilities has occasionally resulted in large public companies becoming insolvent – much to the surprise of the investors, who had not previously been aware of the note on contingent liabilities.

19.12 Leases and hire-purchase, SSAP 21

The following text deals with hire-purchase trading. SSAP 21 deals with several types of transaction that have a financing element to them; hire-purchase is only one of these.

It is a very long SSAP and was issued together with a separate guidance booklet. Most of the provisions are well outside the scope of any foundation syllabus, and some examination syllabuses do not mention SSAP 21 as an examinable document. The main reason for including part of it here is that occasionally questions on hire-purchase trading do appear in the various examinations for which this book is intended. It is doubtful whether these questions were intended to be answered in accordance with SSAP 21, but there is no harm in learning the subject according to codified practice.

Goods sold under hire-purchase arrangements contain two elements of profit, trading profit and interest. The trading profit is based on the difference between the normal cash selling price and the cost; interest is the difference between the cash sales price and the total amount to be received under the contract. In SSAP 21, the interest element is referred to as **gross earnings** in the seller's books, and as a **finance charge** in the buyer's books. Consider the following details:

> The normal cash selling price of an article is £2,250. The cost price of this article is £1,350. The article is also sold under hire-purchase arrangements for an immediate deposit of £200 plus three annual instalments (paid at the end of each year) of £825 each. The total cash received under a hire-purchase sale is therefore ((200 + (3 × 825)) £2,675. Since the cost price is £1,350, the total profit if sold under hire-purchase is (2,675 – 1,350) £1,325.

Activity 16

Split the total profit of £1,325 earned under a hire-purchase sale between the two elements of profit according to SSAP 21.

1. Trading profit:

2. Gross earnings:

In strict legal terms, the article has not been sold but has been hired to the user. Under most hire-purchase agreements, the user does not obtain title to the goods until the last instalment has been paid and (as is usual) a small option fee has been paid.

But SSAP 21 requires the trader to deal with the transaction as if the article had been sold. This is an application of a convention known as 'substance over form', meaning that we should account for the substance (or economic reality) of the transaction rather than its strict legal form. In the case of hire-purchase trading, the substance of the transaction is that the article has been sold and is to be paid for by instalments. Since the seller is effectively providing finance to the purchaser, the additional earnings (by comparison to a cash sale) are finance earnings.

SSAP 21 requires the normal trading profit to be recognized as soon as the contract is signed. The gross earnings (the interest element) should be recognized over the period of the contract. Using the transaction in Activity 16 as an example, the way in which this is set up through the double-entry can be explained as follows:

1. On signing the contract, the trader will:

Debit hire-purchase debtor (with total due)	2,675	
Credit sales (with normal selling price)		2,250
Credit gross earnings suspense		425

Note that at this point the trading profit of £900 will be reflected in the trading account, since the cost of £1,350 will form part of the cost of sales. The balance on 'interest suspense' is carried forward in the balance sheet; you will see what happens to it in a moment.

2. On the receipt of the deposit of £200, the trader will:

Debit bank	200	
Credit hire-purchase debtor		200

If the balance sheet were to be prepared immediately after payment of this deposit, the hire-purchase debtor would be shown as follows:

Balance due (2,675 – 200)	2,475
Less gross earnings allocated to future periods	(425)
	2,050

Notice that the £2,050 is (in effect) the cash sales price of £2,250 less the deposit of £200. In SSAP 21 this is referred to as the 'net investment in the contract'.

The gross earnings will be transferred to the profit and loss account over the period of the contract. There are two common methods for doing this, namely the 'actuarial' (or effective rate of interest) method, and the 'sum of digits' method. The results of these two methods are more or less identical.

In order to work out figures for the actuarial method, you need to be told the effective rate of interest in the contract. There is no simple way in which you can work this out yourself from the above data. In the above contract, the effective rate is 10% per annum. Given the rate of interest, we can then work out how the total interest of £425 should be spread over the 3 years.

The computation would run as follows:

At start of Year 1	Cash sales price	2,250	
	Deposit received	(200)	
	Balance	2,050	
At end of Year 1	Interest earned (10%)	205	205
	Instalment received	(825)	
	Balance	1,430	
At end of Year 2	Interest earned (10%)	143	143
	Instalment received	(825)	
	Balance	748	
At end of Year 3	Interest earned (see note)	77	77
	Instalment	(825)	
	Balance	nil	
	Total interest		425

Note: The interest had to be rounded up by £2 at the end of Year 3 in order to balance off the computation. This was because the effective interest rate is slightly in excess of 10%.

Immediately after signing the contract, the gross earnings suspense account was a credit balance of £425. At the end of the first year, this is reduced to £220 by transferring £205 to the profit and loss account. At the end of the second year it is reduced to £77 (by transferring £143 to the profit and loss account) and the remaining £77 is recognized in year 3. Any balance on the gross earnings suspense during the life of the contract is, therefore, in the nature of deferred income. SSAP 21 requires this credit to be deducted from hire-purchase debtors.

Practices vary as to where the gross earnings recognized in any year are presented in the published profit and loss account. A common practice is to show the amount as a set-off against interest paid in that section of the profit and loss account which follows on from where operating profit is determined.

The sum of digits method for allocating gross earnings to accounting periods is sometimes called the 'rule of 78'. This is quite an interesting name and will help you to remember how it works. It is derived from the fact that the sum of a progression of the digits 1 to 12 is 78. If instalments are spread over 12 months, as is often the case in hire-purchase, the interest could be spread on the following basis:

    month 1:   12/78ths of the amount
    month 2:   11/78ths of the amount
    month 3:   10/78ths of the amount

and so on until

    month 12:   1/78th of the amount.

Note how the numerator starts with 12 and gradually reduces to 1. Where the number of repayments is three (as in our former example) the sum of the digits is (1 + 2 + 3) 6. See if you can use this to show how the amount of £425 would be spread over the three years in the previous example.

Activity 17

Calculate how the £425 would be allocated to each of the three years using the sum of digits method. When you have done this, compare your result to the actuarial method.

| Year 1 | Year 2 | Year 3 |

In the buyer's books, the standard practice is to capitalize the asset at its normal cash purchase price by crediting the HP creditor. When the instalments are paid they are split; part of the instalment is treated as reduction of the creditor, and part as the finance charge to be debited to the profit and loss account as an expense. Methods for allocating the total finance charge to accounting periods can be the same as those mentioned for the seller, although in practice the allocation is often done on a straight line basis.

The sum of digits methods is sometimes used for depreciation calculations. The principle of spreading an asset cost over a number of years is the same as spreading an interest charge.

In cases where a large number of instalments are involved, the sum of the digits can be found more quickly by using the formula: $n \times (n + 1)/2$, where n is the number of instalments. You could check this formula by seeing how it works for 12 instalments and 3 instalments where you already know the answer.

19.13 Statement of principles

The ASB published a revised draft of its Statement of Principles for Financial Reporting in 1996. It is a lengthy document and has seven chapters, as follows:

Chapter 1:   The objective of financial statements
Chapter 2:   The qualitative characteristics of financial information
Chapter 3:   The elements of financial statements
Chapter 4:   Recognition in financial statements
Chapter 5:   Measurement in financial statements
Chapter 6:   Presentation of financial information
Chapter 7:   The reporting entity

It also has an Introduction which provides a clear and concise overview of the contents of each chapter. We have reproduced some extracts from the Introduction in Appendix 2 to this chapter. These extracts give an overview of the contents of Chapters 2, 3 and 4 and you will be asked to read them for the activities.

The extent to which foundation students will be expected to have a detailed knowledge of the Statement of Principles will vary from syllabus to syllabus. A great deal of the content in the earlier chapters of the document is not controversial and the principles have been discussed in text books on accounting for some time. The Statement of Principles now provides an authoritative document to which reference can be made and no doubt most examiners will refer to this when setting theoretical questions.

It seems reasonable to expect foundation students to have some knowledge of the contents of Chapters 1 to 4. You have already studied extracts from Chapter 1 (in Chapter 1 of this book) and so we will consider some of the issues that arise from Chapters 2 to 4.

Assets: definition

One of the most interesting aspects for students will be the definition of assets. Up to now we have been thinking of assets as being things that were owned by the entity. The thing owned might have been a tangible asset such as a delivery van, or an intangible asset such as goodwill. But tangible or intangible, we still thought of ownership as being central to the definition of an asset. Yet this is not how assets are discussed in the Statement of Principles.

Activity 18

Read through the extracts in Appendix 2. Find the definition of assets which forms a part of Chapter 2 in the Statement of Principles.
Do you see the word ownership being mentioned at all?

The definition provided becomes quite useful in circumstances where the business entity does not own the asset in a legal sense but has possession of the risks and rewards associated with ownership.

Activity 19

In the previous section (19.12) we considered the accounting for items sold on hire-purchase terms. Now consider the position of the hirer, the person using the asset and paying for it by hire-purchase instalments. If it is being used by a business entity, the asset is not legally owned by that entity. Will the Statement of Principles require this asset to be treated as an asset of that entity?

As it happens there are provisions in SSAP 21 that require the hirer to treat the item as an asset equal to its normal cash purchase price. This was the normal practice prior to SSAP 21 in any event. It was justified on the grounds of a concept known as 'substance over form'. This meant that a reporting entity should account for an item based on the commercial substance of a transaction rather than on its strict legal form.

The definition of assets and liabilities, together with supporting definitions and principles, has helped to settle a number of controversial issues and the ASB has used the Statement of Principles in various accounting standards such as FRS 5: Reporting the substance of transactions. It is, however, unreasonable to expect definitions and principles to solve every conceivable aspect of financial reporting. There will always be some problems that will have to be dealt with by requiring companies to comply with specific accounting standards.

Summary

The topics covered by this chapter are too vast and varied for any meaningful list of learning points to be made. The various subjects dealt with tend to be on the fringe of foundation examinations; they are not mainstream topics, so do not despair if there seems to be a lot to remember. The self-assessment questions at the end of the chapter will give an indication of examination standards. As is usual, these questions include topics that were dealt with in earlier chapters.

Activity 1
EPS: £10,000 ÷ 50,000 = 20 pence.

Activity 2
EPS: (£40,000 – £7,000) ÷ 100,000 = 33 pence.

Activity 3
£49m.

Activity 4
Depreciation charge £10,000; deferred credit written off £500; balance on deferred credit £9,500. (Note that if the grant had been credited to the cost of the asset, the depreciation charge would have been £9,500, which is the same cost as depreciation of £10,000 less deferred credit written off £500.)

Activity 5
Item E, 8, 'Other creditors including taxation and social security'.

Activity 6
Reported results would be erratic if profit recognition is deferred until the contract is completed. In years when few contracts were finished there would be low profits or a loss; in years when many were finished there would be very high profits. Recall that UK investors do not like to see erratic profits.

Activity 7
600,000/800,000 × £200,000 = £150,000.

Activity 8
Debit profit and loss account (cost of sales) £590,000; credit contract costs account £590,000.

Activity 9
1. £22,500 (£30,000 – (5 × £1,500)).
2. £2,250 per annum.
3. £2,000 per annum.
4. The difference is not material and no adjustment to past provisions is necessary.

Activity 10
1. £135,000 (£150,000 – (5 × £3,000)).
2. £27,000.
3. £15,000.
4. The amount underprovided is 5 × (£15,000 – £3,000) = £60,000.
   The double-entry is:
   Debit: Profit and loss account (ordinary activities) £60,000.
   Credit: Provision for depreciation   £60,000.

Activity 11
Total depreciation is (£28,000 – £4,000) £24,000; total hours in use is 4,000; depreciation rate is (£24,000 ÷ 4,000) £6 per hour used.

Depreciation charges:
Year 1 (800 × £6)   4,800
Year 2 (2,100 × £6)   12,600
Year 3 (1,100 × £6)   6,600
                       24,000

Activity 12

Year 1 (no interest)   7,250
Year 2 (£7,250 + (10% × £7,250))   7,975
Year 3 (£7,250 + (10% × £15,225))   8,773
                        Total   23,998

Activity 13

This would appear to be research costs and should be written off.

Activity 14

Event 1 is an adjusting event. It provides additional information regarding conditions existing at the balance sheet date (i.e. the amount recoverable from a debtor).

Event 2 is a non-adjusting event. The condition (loss through fire) arose subsequent to the accounting date. If the amount is considered material, it should be disclosed in the notes to the financial statements.

Activity 15

Situation 1: there is a contingent loss but it does not have to be accrued since there seems to be no likelihood of the loss arising in the near future. It should be disclosed in the notes.

Situation 2: this loss should be accrued. It could be argued that this is not a contingent loss but an actual loss which should be treated as an adjusting event under SSAP 17. (It would be a contingent loss if the case had been taken to the Court of Appeal because the loss would then be contingent upon losing the case, but it should still be accrued even under those circumstances.)

Situation 3: this is not a contingent gain, but a realized gain. It should be treated as an adjusting event under the provisions of SSAP 17.

Activity 16

1. Trading profit (£2,250 – £1,350)   900
2. Gross earnings (derived as a balance):   425

Activity 17

Year 1 (3/6 × £425) £212
Year 2 (2/6 × £425) £142
Year 3 (1/6 × £425) £71

Notice how this simple method gives a close approximation to the more sophisticated actuarial method.

Activity 18

No, it does not mention ownership.

Activity 19

Yes, it represents rights to future economic benefits controlled by the entity.

Questions for self-assessment

Answers to self-assessment questions are given at the end of the book.

19.1 The directors of Morrison Hill plc have been sent a letter by their auditors concerning a number of items which are relevant to the published accounts of the company for the financial year ended 30 April 1990, which are in the course of preparation. The following paragraphs are extracted from the directors' reply.

(a) You asked for details of the development expenditure of £45,000 shown as a deferred asset (not depreciated) in the balance sheet. It represents the cost of laboratory buildings and equipment for the development of our new wonder drug 'Aspracetamol', which will definitely be on sale in four years' time.

(b) The fire in the stock warehouse which destroyed the entire month's production of the soft toys division (£35,000) occurred on 2 May 1990. It is irrelevant to the year being dealt with.

(c) The buildings bought on 1 May 1987 are being depreciated for the first time this year, so we have charged P&L account with three years' depreciation (£15,000).

(d) The earnings per share figure (17p) is irrelevant; nobody is interested in it, so we haven't bothered to show it.

(e) The asset replacement reserve (£5,000) shown in the balance sheet is based on the difference between the current cost of the fixed assets and the historic cost.

For each of the five items listed above, explain whether the auditors are likely to accept or reject the accounting treatment adopted by the directors.

(ULSEB A Level, Jun 1990)

19.2 George and Margaret decide that they wish to start building bridges. They enter into an agreement to work in partnership.

On 11 December 1989 they begin to build bridge A. The agreed fixed contract price is £4 million. The bridge is expected to take 18 months to complete. On 10 December 1990 costs incurred by the venture were £2.8 million of which £2.5 million had been paid for. The bridge was agreed to be 80% complete, and payments on account of £3 million had been received.

You discover, however, that £0.1 million of the costs incurred by the venture related to a detailed survey of the site for an intended bridge B. Additional costs necessary to complete bridge A are now (at 10 December 1990) estimated at £0.8 million.

Required:
Calculate and discuss the profit which should be reported on bridge A for the 12 month period to 10 December 1990. Show workings clearly, state assumptions clearly, and explain and justify the assumptions you have made.

(ACCA 1.1, Dec 1990)

19.3 The accounting statements of Gershwin plc have been prepared for the year ended 30 April 1989, but have not yet been approved by the directors. During the year, the sales totalled £58 million, net profit was £5 million, and the total assets at the year end exceeded £400 million. The directors called a meeting on 26 June 1989 to consider the following events which have arisen since the date of the balance sheet.

1. A strike by employees began on 2 May 1989, and finished on 26 May 1989. The loss to the company is estimated at £10 million.

2. Stock at 30 April 1989 had been overvalued by £2 million.

3. On 23 May 1989 the company bought all the shares of Berlin plc at a cost of £34 million.

4. A rights issue to shareholders was announced on 24 May 1989, with the intention of raising £40 million.

5. Porter Ltd, a company which owed Gershwin plc £5,000 at 30 April 1989, went into liquidation on 2 May 1989. The debt is considered to be irrecoverable.

Advise the directors of Gershwin plc how each of the five events should be treated in the accounting statements for the year ended 30 April 1989. Reasons for the advice should be provided, and reference made to any relevant Statements of Standard Accounting Practice.

(ULSEB A Level, Jun 1989)

Questions without answers

Answers to these questions are published separately in the *Teacher's Manual*.

19.4 With regard to SSAP 12 Accounting for Depreciation:

(a) How is the useful economic life of an asset defined?

(b) Ahab started in business on 1 January 1988 taking fare paying passengers on river trips. He bought a 10 seater boat for £20,000 but his business plan projects that by 1 January 1990 he will need one 20 seater boat. The boat has an expected life of 10 years. Ahab estimates that the residual value of the boat, based on prices prevailing at the date of acquisition, is £15,000 at 31 December 1989 and £3,000 at 31 December 1997. However, if future inflation is taken into account the projected residual values would be £18,000 and £5,000, respectively. Realization costs are estimated at 10% of residual value.

(i) Using the straight line method of charging depreciation, calculate the depreciation charges for the years ended 31 December 1988 and 1989 and explain the basis of your calculation.

(ii) Calculate any profit or loss on disposal of the boat at 31 December 1989 assuming that the above estimates prove accurate and comment upon the nature of the profit or loss in the context of historical cost accounts.

(c) Nemo bought an asset in January 1980 for £4,200. At that time, the estimated residual value was nil and the estimated useful life 10 years. In January 1984 the remaining useful life of the asset is estimated at only 3 years.

(i) Using the straight line method of calculating depreciation, calculate the depreciation charge for the years ended 31 December 1984, 1985 and 1986 if:
the revised charge will not materially affect the results of future years;
the results will materially affect the results of future years.

(ii) In relation to (c)(i) above, do you consider that where the results of future years are materially affected, the necessary adjustment should be presented as:
an ordinary item
an exceptional item
an extraordinary item
or a prior year item?
State your reasons.

(ACCA 2.8)

19.5 The directors of Kern plc have prepared the following statements of accounting policies which they believe have been followed in the preparation of the draft accounts of the company for the year ended 31 December 1989.

1. Basis of accounting
The accounts have been prepared under the historical cost convention, as modified by the revaluation of certain fixed assets.

2. Depreciation
No depreciation has been charged on land and buildings, but all other assets have been depreciated on the straight line basis over their expected useful lives.

3. Stocks
Stocks are valued at the higher of cost and net realizable value. Cost comprises purchase cost of goods, direct labour and manufacturing, distribution and administrative overheads.

4. Research and development
   All research and development costs are carried forward as a deferred asset in the balance sheet.
5. Prior year adjustments
   There was an underprovision for corporation tax in last year's accounts. This amount has been shown as a 'prior year adjustment' deducted from the recorded profit for the current year.

The directors have asked your advice as to the extent to which the above policies comply with the requirements of standard accounting practice. They are also confused because SSAP 2, Disclosure of Accounting Policies, refers not only to accounting policies, but also to accounting concepts and accounting bases.

(a) Explain how accounting policies differ from accounting concepts and accounting bases.

(b) Explain the extent to which each of the five accounting policies listed is in accordance with standard accounting practice.

(ULSEB, Jan 1990)

19.6 (a)   The United Kingdom Accounting Standards Board (ASB) has for some years been issuing draft parts of what it eventually intends as a substantive 'Statement of Principles'.

Required:
What is the purpose of the Statement of Principles?

(b)   Brief extracts from issued drafts from the Statement of Principles are given in Appendix 1 at the end of the paper and you should study them carefully.
   You are given four brief situations, as follows:
   (i) Firm A has paid £10,000 to buy a patent right, giving it the right to sole use, for 5 years, of a manufacturing method which saves costs.
   (ii) Firm B is the freehold legal owner of a waste disposal site. It has charged customers for the right to dispose of their waste for many years. The tip is now full, and heavily polluted with chemicals. If cleaned up, which would cost £5 million, the site could be sold for housing purposes for £3 million.
   (iii) Firm C has paid £1 million towards the cost of a new hospital in the nearby town, on condition that the hospital agrees to give priority treatment to its employees if they are injured at work.
   (iv) Firm D has signed a contract to pay its managing director £100,000 per year for the next three years. He has agreed to work full time for the firm over that period.

Required:
For each of the situations 1 to 4 above you are required to state, with reasons and explanation, whether the situation creates an asset or a liability within the definitions given in Appendix 1.

(c)   It is clear from Appendix 1 that items meeting the definitions of asset and liability are not automatically to be recognized in financial statements.

Required:
Give an example of
(i) an asset item,
(ii) a liability item
which meets the given definition but would not normally be recognized in financial statements. Explain your illustrations briefly.

(ACCA, Jun 96)

Authors note: The appendix mentioned in the quesiton gave extracts from the Statement of Principles. You can use Appendix 2 to this chapter.

Appendix 1

List of Accounting Standards

SSAP 1	Accounting for associated companies
	Extract from ASB Interim Statement
SSAP 2	Disclosure of accounting policies
SSAP 3	Earnings per share
SSAP 4	Accounting for government grants
SSAP 5	Accounting for value added tax
SSAP 8	The treatment of taxation under the imputation system in the accounts of companies
SSAP 9	Stocks and long-term contracts
SSAP 12	Accounting for depreciation
SSAP 13	Accounting for research and development
SSAP 15	Accounting for deferred tax
SSAP 17	Accounting for post balance sheet events
SSAP 18	Accounting for contingencies
SSAP 19	Accounting for investment properties
SSAP 20	Foreign currency translation
SSAP 21	Accounting for leases and hire purchase contracts
	Guidance Notes on SSAP 21
SSAP 22	Accounting for goodwill
SSAP 24	Accounting for pension costs
SSAP 25	Segmental reporting
FRS 1	Cash Flow Statements
FRS 2	Accounting for Subsidiary Undertakings
FRS 3	Reporting Financial Performance
FRS 4	Capital Instruments
FRS 5	Reporting the Substance of Transactions
FRS 6	Acquisitions and Mergers
FRS 7	Fair Values in Acquisition Accounting
FRS 8	Related Party Disclosures

Extracts from the ASB's Statement of Principles for Financial Reporting

The draft document includes an Introduction giving an overview of the contents for each chapter. The following text is an edited version of extracts from that Introduction relating to Chapters 2, 3 and 4. The numbers in the main headings refer to the chapter numbers in which the various matters are discussed.

2 The qualitative characteristics of financial information

Qualitative characteristics
Qualitative characteristics are the characteristics that make the information provided in financial statements useful to users for assessing the financial position, performance and financial adaptability of an enterprise.

Some qualitative characteristics relate to the content of the information contained in financial statements: others relate to how that information is presented.

The primary qualitative characteristics relating to content are relevance and reliability. The primary qualitative characteristics relating to presentation are comparability and understandability.

Threshold quality: materiality
Materiality is a threshold quality. If any information is not material, it does not need to be considered further. Information is material if it could influence users' decisions taken on the basis of the financial statements. If that information is misstated or if certain information is omitted the materiality of the misstatement or omission depends on the size and nature of the item in question judged in the particular circumstances of the case.

Characteristics relating to content
Relevance
To be useful, information must be relevant to the decision-making needs of users. Information has the quality of relevance when it has the ability to influence the decisions of users by helping them evaluate past, present or future events or confirming, or correcting, their past evaluations.

Choice of attribute
The choice of the attribute to be reported in financial statements should be based on its relevance to the economic decisions of users.

Reliability
To be useful, information must also be reliable. Information has the quality of reliability when it is free from material error and bias and can be depended upon by users to represent faithfully what it either purports to represent or could reasonably be expected to represent.

Faithful representation
Information must represent faithfully the effect of the transactions and other events it either purports to represent or could reasonably be expected to represent.

Substance
If information is to represent faithfully the transactions and other events that it purports to represent, it is necessary that they are accounted for and presented in accordance with their substance and commercial effect and not merely their legal form.

Neutrality
The information contained in financial statements must be neutral, i.e. free from bias.

Prudence
Uncertainties are recognised by the disclosure of their nature and extent and by the exercise of prudence in the preparation of the financial statements. Prudence is the inclusion of a degree of caution in the exercise of the judgements needed in making the estimates required under conditions of uncertainty, such that income or assets are not overstated and expenses or liabilities are not understated.

Completeness
The information in financial statements must be complete within the bounds of materiality and cost.

Characteristics relating to presentation
Comparability
Users must be able to compare the financial statements of an enterprise over time to identify trends in its financial position and performance. Users must also be able to compare the financial statements of different enterprises to evaluate their relative financial position, performance and financial adaptability. It is therefore necessary for similar events and states of affairs to be represented in a similar manner.

Consistency
Comparability requires the measurement and display of the financial effect of like transactions and other events to be carried out in a consistent way within each accounting period and from one period to the next, and also in a consistent way by different entities. Although consistency is necessary to attain comparability, it is not in itself always sufficient.

Disclosures
A prerequisite of comparability is disclosure of the accounting policies employed in the preparation of the financial statements, and also any changes in those policies and the effects of such changes.

Because users wish to compare the financial position, performance and changes in financial position of an enterprise over time, it is important that the financial statements show corresponding information for one or more preceding periods.

Understandability
An essential quality of the information provided in financial statements is that it should be readily understandable by users.

Aggregation and classification
An important factor in the understandability of financial information is the manner in which the information is presented. An understandable presentation requires that items are aggregated and classified in an appropriate way.

Users' abilities
Financial information is generally prepared on the assumption that users have a reasonable knowledge of business and economic activities and accounting and a willingness to study the information with reasonable diligence. Information about complex matters that should be included in the financial statements because of its relevance to the economic decision-making needs of users should not be excluded merely on the grounds that it may be too difficult for some users to understand.

3 The elements of financial statements

The elements of financial statements are:
- assets
- liabilities
- ownership interest

- gains
- losses
- contributions from owners
- distributions to owners.

Any item that does not fall within one of the definitions of elements should not be included in financial statements.

Assets and liabilities

Assets are rights or other access to future economic benefits controlled by an entity as a result of past transactions or events.

Liabilities are obligations of an entity to transfer economic benefits as a result of past transactions or events.

Ownership interest

Ownership interest is the residual amount found by deducting all of the entity's liabilities from all of the entity's assets.

Gains and losses

Gains are increases in ownership interest, other than those relating to contributions from owners.

Losses are decreases in ownership interest, other than those relating to distributions to owners.

Contributions from owners and distributions to owners

Contributions from owners are increases in ownership interest resulting from investments made by owners in their capacity as owners.

Distributions to owners are decreases in ownership interest resulting from transfers made to owners in their capacity as owners.

4 Recognition in financial statements

Recognition

Recognition involves depiction of the element both in words and by a monetary amount, and the inclusion of that amount in the statement totals.

The stages of recognition

The recognition of assets and liabilities falls into three stages:

(a)　initial recognition;
(b)　subsequent remeasurement; and
(c)　derecognition.

Recognition criteria

Initial recognition

An element should be recognised if:

(a)　there is sufficient evidence that the change in assets or liabilities inherent in the element has occurred (including, where appropriate, evidence that a future inflow or outflow of benefit will occur); and
(b)　it can be measured at a monetary amount with sufficient reliability.

Subsequent remeasurement

A change in the amount at which an asset or liability is recorded should be recognised if:

(a)　there is sufficient evidence that the amount of an asset or liability has changed; and
(b)　the new amount of the asset or liability can be measured with sufficient reliability.

Derecognition

An asset or liability should cease to be recognised if there is no longer sufficient evidence that the entity has access to future economic benefits or an obligation to transfer economic benefits (including, where appropriate, evidence that a future inflow or outflow of benefit will occur).

Recognition of gains and losses

At any stage in the recognition process, where a change in total assets is not offset by an equal change in total liabilities or a transaction with owners, a gain or a loss will arise.

The recognition process

Past events

Recognition is triggered where a past event gives rise to a measurable change in the assets or liabilities of the entity.

The event that triggers recognition must have occurred before the balance sheet date.

To the extent that a past event has resulted in access to future economic benefits (or obligations to transfer economic benefits), assets (or liabilities) are recognised; to the extent that it has resulted in previously recognised access to future economic benefits (or obligations to transfer economic benefits) being transferred or ceasing to exist, assets (or liabilities) are derecognised; and to the extent that it has resulted in a flow of economic benefits in the current period (other than one relating to a transaction with owners), a gain or loss is recognised.

Transactions

Transactions are arrangements under which services or interests in property are acquired by one entity from another. Where a transaction takes place it is necessary to recognise the assets and liabilities acquired. If the transaction is negotiated at arm's length and the consideration is monetary, transactions provide strong evidence of the amount of assets acquired.

Where initial recognition is triggered by a transaction, any asset acquired or liability assumed will be measured at the amount inherent in the transaction (i.e. the amount of assets or liabilities given or received as consideration).

Events other than transactions

Initial recognition of assets and liabilities and subsequent remeasurement may also be triggered by events other than transactions.

Some of the events that trigger subsequent remeasurement involve the revaluation of the flow of benefits associated with an asset or liability.

Derecognition

Derecognition is appropriate where a transaction or other past event has eliminated a previously recognised asset or liability or where the expectation of a future benefit flow on which recognition was originally based is no longer sufficiently strong to support continued recognition.

The recognition of gains and losses

The recognition of gains

The recognition of gains involves consideration of whether there is sufficient evidence that an increase in net assets (i.e. in ownership interest) had occurred before the end of the reporting period.

The recognition of losses

The recognition of losses involves consideration of whether there is sufficient evidence that a decrease in ownership interest had occurred before the end of the reporting period. Prudence has the effect that less evidence of occurrence and reliability of measurement is required for the recognition of a loss than for a gain.

Where expenditure cannot justifiably be assumed to be associated with the generation of specific gains in the future, it should be recognised as a loss in the period in which it is incurred.

Ethics and creative accounting

Objectives

The main purpose of this chapter is to explore the evolution of accounting standards and professional ethics, and to suggest some possible developments for the future.

After you have completed this chapter, you should be able to:

- discuss why the standard setting regime was changed in 1990
- describe the constitution and authority of the present regulatory authorities
- contribute to the debate on the need for ethical training in the future

---

Introduction

When the late and notorious tycoon Robert Maxwell was negotiating for the sale of Pergamon Press Ltd to an American corporation called Leasco in the late 1960s, the audited accounts for the year on which the share price was to be based showed a profit of £2m. Accountants acting for Leasco prepared accounts based on the same data; these showed a loss of £0.5m. During the enquiries which followed, the late Robert Maxwell is quoted as saying 'it seems that accounting is not the exact science we all believed it to be'.

In September 1990 Polly Peck International published its interim results for the six months ended 30 June 1990, revealing a profit before tax of £110.5m. The total market value of the shares at that point was £1.05bn. One month later the company was in the hands of administrators, who announced that an immediate liquidation would result in the shareholders receiving nothing; prior claims on the assets would leave a deficiency of £384m.

The 1991 published financial statements of Trafalgar House (the engineering, property and construction group) revealed that profits before tax were £122.4m. In October 1992, the company succumbed to pressure from a new regulatory body (set up in 1990) and agreed to amend its 1991 results. These amendments required the profit before tax to be reduced by £102.7m, and for £20m to be added to the tax charge.

All three cases are examples of where public companies have used **creative**

accounting techniques. They also focus on the three stages in the evolution of setting and enforcing accounting standards. The Pergamon Press affair was one example among several that gave an impetus to the formation of the Accounting Standards Committee (ASC) in 1970. The Polly Peck case was not instrumental in bringing about changes to the standard setting regime in 1990, but it is a good example of why these changes were needed.

The Trafalgar House case is an example of what the new regulatory process has been able to achieve. Apart from strengthening the role of those who are trying to improve the quality of financial reporting, this case might herald a new era in professional ethics. There was nothing illegal in the way Trafalgar House had treated certain items; if the accounts had been produced in the 1980s they would have remained as published. Some accountants might even have had a sneaking admiration for what seemed like a 'clever wheeze' in order to massage the figures. A climate developed during the 1980s of thinking it was clever to find ways of exploiting the rules; ethics were neglected without thought being given to the consequences.

But the consequences could be people out of work, people who have lost their savings, and people who have lost their pensions. The climate has now changed; ethical training now has its place alongside the more traditional technical training. Creativity should be directed towards keeping people informed, not hiding the truth.

20.1 Evolution in perspective

The original standard setting process was established by the accountancy profession in 1970. Until then, no regulations on accounting principles existed and companies could choose from a wide range of acceptable practices when reporting the results of certain transactions. The case of Pergamon Press, mentioned in the introduction, is one example where this freedom was abused in order to influence those relying on financial reports.

As you know from earlier chapters (particularly Chapters 1 and 19) the development of accounting standards in the United Kingdom was originally the responsibility of the Accounting Standards Committee (ASC). The main aim of the ASC was to reduce the number of acceptable practices by developing Statements of Standard Accounting Practice (SSAPs).

The constitution of the ASC varied over the years; for most of its life it was a joint committee of the six major accountancy bodies, who act collectively through a body known as the Consultative Committee of Accountancy Bodies (CCAB). Despite a number of reforms in the ASC's procedures, the following two criticisms of the way standards were produced and enforced were never successfully resolved:

- The ASC was not autonomous in the sense that it could issue SSAPs on its own authority. The ASC developed and prepared accounting standards, which were then issued and enforced by the six major accountancy bodies. In seeking approval of a proposed standard from these bodies it was sometimes necessary for the ASC to reach a compromise before the final SSAP could be drafted.
- Enforcement of SSAPs relied upon the six accountancy bodies requiring members to observe accounting standards. If directors were not members of these accountancy bodies, there was nothing to force them to comply with SSAPs apart from the sanction of a qualified audit report.

Further, as was mentioned in the introduction, a climate of avoidance had developed during the 1980s. It became quite difficult for accountants and auditors to take a stand against some of these abuses. It was a period of economic growth, the stock market was booming, and companies were under pressure from the market to perform. If directors found ways of massaging the figures that lawyers had confirmed were legal, an auditor trying to insist that the accounts were misleading had little chance of persuading the directors to alter the accounts. If one company had used the device and been given a clean audit report, competitor companies insisted on being allowed to do the same thing. This whole period was characterized by the question 'where does it say that we can't do that?'

In 1987 the CCAB appointed a Review Committee under the chairmanship of Sir Ronald Dearing. The task of this committee was to consider various matters, including:

- what the composition and powers of the standard setting body should be
- what the status of accounting standards should be in relation to company law
- how compliance with standards should be monitored and enforced.

The Dearing Committee reported in November 1988 and eventually the CCAB accepted its findings. In late 1989 the Secretary of State for Trade and Industry invited Sir Ron Dearing to bring the new arrangements into being and (in parallel) the government introduced related provisions into the Companies Act 1989. These provisions were designed to give legal support for the proposed regime and were put into effect following formation of the new regulatory bodies.

20.2 The new regulatory process

The Companies Act 1989 made several important changes to accounting regulations contained in the Companies Act 1985. Changes relating to accounting standards included:

- A requirement that directors should state in 'Notes to the Accounts' whether the accounts have been prepared in accordance with applicable accounting standards and give particulars of any material departure from those standards. Legal advice taken by the Financial Reporting Review Panel (see below) confirmed that this requirement was in addition to (and not a substitute for) an earlier provision requiring companies to disclose details of all accounting policies chosen.
- Defining 'accounting standards' as meaning 'statements of standard accounting practice issued by such body or bodies as may be prescribed by regulations'. The Accounting Standards Board Limited (see below) was prescribed for this purpose by Statutory Instrument in August 1990.
- Making provisions for the compulsory revision of accounts where the court is satisfied that the original accounts do not show a true and fair view. Applications to the court in respect of defective accounts may be made by the Secretary of State, or by a person authorized by the Secretary of State for the purpose. The Financial Reporting Review Panel Limited was authorized for this purpose by Statutory Instrument in January 1991.

The new regulatory bodies which came into existence as a result of the Dearing Report are:

- the Financial Reporting Council Ltd (FRC) – the parent body
- the Accounting Standards Board Ltd (ASB) – a subsidiary of FRC
- the Financial Reporting Review Panel Ltd (FRRP) – a subsidiary of FRC
- the Urgent Issues Task Force (UITF) – a sub-committee of the ASB.

The three main bodies (FRC, ASB, and FRRP) are constituted as companies limited by guarantee. The FRC acts as the sole director of both of its operational subsidiaries, the ASB and the FRRP. The organizational structure of these bodies can be illustrated as follows:

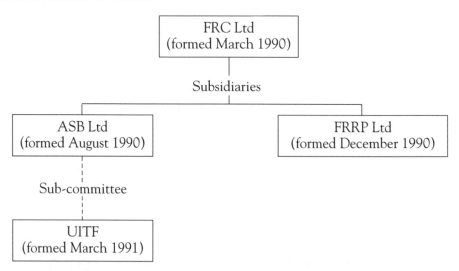

Although these new bodies receive strong government backing by way of funding and supporting legislation, they are not government controlled. They continue to operate as a part of the private sector process of self-regulation. Funding is approximately one-third from government sources, one-third from the six major accountancy bodies, and one-third from the London Stock Exchange and the banking community. The label most frequently used to identify the status of these bodies is 'semi-quango' (in the UK, the acronym QUANGO stands for **qu**asi **a**utonomous **n**ational **g**overnment **o**rganization; in the USA, **qu**asi **a**utonomous **n**on-governmental organization).

The principle aim of the FRC is to promote good financial reporting, an objective which it seeks to achieve through the operations of its two companion bodies, the ASB and the FRRP.

The main role of the ASB is to make, amend and withdraw accounting standards. Its membership is much wider than that of the former ASC and includes an academic advisor, a legal advisor, and two observers. At its first meeting (in August 1990) the Board unanimously agreed to adopt the 22 extant SSAPs developed by the former ASC. The powers of the ASB differ significantly from those of the former ASC. It is autonomous in the sense that it produces accounting standards on its own authority; it does not require outside approval (nor approval from the FRC) before it can issue an accounting standard.

At the time of writing this edition, the ASB has issued eight accounting standards, as detailed in Chapter 19.

The function of the UITF is to assist the ASB in areas where an accounting standard or legislation exists, but where conflicting or unsatisfactory interpretations have developed or seem likely to develop. It also advises the Board on significant developments in areas of financial reporting where no standard or legislation exists.

Pronouncements by the UITF are called 'Abstracts', and are issued following the achievement of a 'consensus' among its members. These statements do not have the same legal force as accounting standards, although the ASB considers them to be accepted practice for the area in question and, therefore, part of the corpus of practices which form the basis of a true and fair view. The requirement that published financial statements should show a true and fair view is an overriding requirement in the Companies Act. In some cases it might be necessary for companies to depart from the rules in accounting standards in order to show a true and fair view. The UITF Abstracts are an official interpretation of how rules should be applied to specific transactions in order to show a true and fair view.

At the time of writing this edition, the UITF had issued 16 Abstracts. Some of these have since been superseded by later FRSs.

The role of the FRRP is to examine instances where a company's financial statements depart from accounting requirements of the Companies Act 1985, particularly the requirement to show a true and fair view. It is empowered by the Act to seek an order from the court to have the defective accounts revised. Since its inception it has examined the accounts of several companies, the most notable case being that of Trafalgar House, mentioned in the introduction. If the directors of Trafalgar House had not agreed to revise their 1991 accounts voluntarily, the FRRP could have used its powers to enforce a revision through the court.

Exemptions and exceptions

Legal authority for the new accounting standards rests in Part VII of the Companies Act 1985, which requires that a company's individual accounts should comply with Schedule 4 of the Act. This Schedule contains the operative paragraph (paragraph 36A) requiring directors to declare compliance with applicable accounting standards. But exemptions from the requirements of paragraph 36A are provided for companies which qualify as small or medium-sized. These companies are also exempt from the requirement to file full accounts with the Registrar of Companies.

Companies are classified as small or medium-sized if they meet two of the following three criteria:

	Small	Medium
Turnover not exceeding	£2.8m	£11.2m
Balance sheet total	£1.4m	£5.6m
Number of employees not more than	50	250

The term 'balance sheet total' means the aggregate of amounts shown under headings corresponding to A to D in Format 1 (i.e. the total of all assets). The thresholds are changing form time to time. The above were those that applied at the time of writing this edition.

The modification of accounts for companies classified as small or medium-sized relates to the accounts filed with the Registrar; shareholders are entitled to all information prescribed by the Act. At a foundation level you do not need to learn the rules for preparing modified accounts, although you should be aware that the provisions exist. You also need to be aware that direct legal support for the new regime of accounting standards is limited in its application to large companies (i.e. those not qualifying as small or medium-sized) and to any small or medium-sized companies who do not qualify for these exemptions, such as:

- public companies
- banking, insurance and shipping companies.

In general terms, however, it will be necessary for small and medium-sized companies to comply with accouting standards in order for their financial statements to show a true and fair view. The foreword to accounting standards issued by the ASB in June 1993 includes the following key paragraph:

> Accounting standards are authoritive statements of how particular types of transaction and other events should be reflected in financial statements and accordingly compliance with accounting standards will normally be necessary for financial statements to give a true and fair view.

Some accounting standards are restricted in their application. For example, SSAP 3 (Earnings per share) applies only to companies listed on a recognized stock exchange. Small companies (as defined in the Companies Act) are exempt from the requirements to produce a cash flow statement under FRS 1.

20.3 Rules versus principles

One of the problems in devising a set of rules for any particular group to follow is that someone will find a way of exploiting them to their own advantage. This is considered fair play in the case of taxation, where a whole industry has been set up to find legitimate ways of avoiding taxes. Taxation law is based mainly on statutes (although there are legal cases which provide precedents for interpretation of the law) and if a transaction is conducted in such a way that it avoids being caught by the wording of the statute, it cannot be taxed – despite all the intentions of those who drafted the law. This kind of activity leads to even more rules, such as anti-avoidance provisions in subsequent legislation.

Since accountants are usually in the forefront of the tax avoidance industry, there has been a tendency for accountants to adopt the same kind of approach with accounting standards. There is an inclination to account according to the rules rather than the facts. This can result in practices which violate the spirit of a standard in either of two ways, namely:

- the rules are followed when (in order to show a true and fair view) they should be broken
- if a transaction can be contrived in such a way as to fall outside the wording in the rule, it escapes being dealt with according to the standard.

This kind of abuse has been taking place despite the fact that the 'Explanatory Foreword' to accounting standards required members of the accountancy bodies to 'have regard to the spirit and the reasoning behind the relevant accounting standard, and to the overriding aim of giving a true and fair view'. However, as mentioned earlier in this chapter, an atmosphere developed during the 1980s which made it quite difficult for the profession to take a stand. The Trafalgar House case is likely to reverse this trend.

During the earlier meetings of the ASB, a policy of attempting to keep standards general rather than prescriptive was announced. This policy is made apparent by the work of the ASB on its draft 'Statement of Principles'.

It will be quite interesting to see how the conflict between the freedom to apply general principles and the need to maintain some kind of order in financial reporting is eventually resolved. It could well be that training in professional ethics holds the key to future developments.

20.4 A return to ethics

Ethical conduct in the medical profession is assumed without question and forms part of a doctor's training. If a doctor behaves in an unethical way it is likely to make headline news. The misdeeds of a wayward doctor might affect the life of one person, albeit causing distress for everyone involved with that person in some way. The misdeeds of a wayward accountant can affect the lives of thousands of individuals. The repercussions might be felt by people far outside of those directly affected (such as shareholders and employees) because the greatest proportion of shares in public companies are held by institutional investors such as those who manage pension funds.

The stewardship of a public company is the responsibility of the directors. Some directors might be members of the accounting profession, but even where this is not the case the company's accountant is usually in a key position to advise directors on important financial transactions. The dilemma faced by accountants working in industry is what action to take when it becomes clear that directors are involved in some kind of practice that is clearly wrong.

The key phrase used by the accountancy bodies in relation to compliance with accounting standards is that members should 'use their best endeavours' to ensure that the standards are observed. Up to now there has been very little backing for an accountant who wanted to take a firm stand against unscrupulous directors; resignation was the only option. But the threat of directors being called to appear before the Review Committee of the FRRP in serious cases should provide the accountant with greater powers of persuasion.

Further changes in our profession are needed if we wish to convince the public that accountants can be trusted to behave in an ethical way. These changes are likely to take place on two fronts:

- a more stringent regime of disciplinary action by the professional bodies
- ethical training.

Ethical training was unheard of a few years ago. Some aspects of particular statements on professional ethics might have been studied when preparing for auditing exams but no attempt was made to alter the way we thought and behaved. We simply learned the rules so that we could write about them in the exam; moral behaviour was something learned as a child.

Historically, medical students were required to take the 'Hippocratic Oath' as a part of their ethical (as opposed to technical) training. The nearest parallel to this in the accountancy profession is the 'fundamental principles of professional conduct', which we all agree to accept when we become members of our professional body.

This procedure fails on two counts at least; the rules are given to us when our student training is finished and, since there is no solemnity in their acceptance, we are not made to think about them seriously. Further, the general public is not aware that we operate under rules of ethics; as far as the public is concerned we work in the murky world of money where anything goes.

This state of affairs is likely to change. Training in professional ethics has been taken seriously by the Institute of Chartered Accountants in Scotland for quite some time, and now forms part of its case study designed to test professional competence. It is starting to take root in the United States.

The problem of ethical training was recognized by the Association of Chartered Certified Accountants when it published its consultative document on the new examination structure (effective from June 1994). This document includes the following paragraph:

> In order to equip individuals with all the necessary attributes the new scheme must develop technical competence alongside professional and managerial attributes, such as judgement, professional ethics, communication skills, imagination and problem solving ability.

These attributes are usually referred to by academics as 'soft skills' and, while no one would doubt their importance, the problem we face is how they can be taught and assessed. Ethical behaviour is largely concerned with an attitude of mind. It would be a pity if the subject is simply left to learning some of the rules (such as those on 'independence') in order to recite them in an exam.

Attitudes can be changed by one being made to think about the long-term effects of what one is doing now, and it should be possible to build this into a student's practical training if this takes place in one of the large professional firms. But not all accountants receive their practical training in professional firms. It will require some leap of imagination to find a way of testing the state of a person's integrity in a written examination. It might even be impossible and some other way will have to be found of testing the professional competence of those entering the profession.

David Tweedie (chairman of the ASB), speaking on various issues in an interview that was reported in the *Certified Accountant* journal (February 1992), suggested that without our reputation we have nothing; he concluded: 'if we're not teaching professional ethics, we ought to shut up shop.' I cannot think of anything more appropriate with which to end this book and start the debate. Good luck in your foundation exams and subsequent studies.

20.5 Further reading

Students wishing to take their reading further on the subject of professional ethics should realize that the fundamental principles of professional conduct mentioned above are supported (at the moment) by twenty-six detailed statements on various matters, including:

- integrity, objectivity and independence
- confidentiality
- advertising
- changes in professional appointments
- fees
- clients' monies.

The most appropriate document for a learner at the foundation stage to read is the statement on 'Integrity, objectivity and independence'. A copy of this document can be found in any of the 'Rule Books' of the major professional accountancy bodies. This document might not necessarily be appropriate to your syllabus. The Association of Chartered Certified Accountants did originally include ethics and independance in its foundation accounting exam (Paper 1) but it has been deleted from the syllabus for that paper with effect from December 1997.

Foundation students should also read the report of the committee on *The Financial Aspects of Corporate Governance* (known colloquially as the 'Cadbury Report'). The implementation of 'The Code of Best Practice' included in this report has had a profound impact on the ethos that surrounds financial reporting.

Finally, for some light (and interesting) reading on the subject of creative accounting, you should obtain a copy of *Accounting for Growth – Stripping the Camouflage from Company Accounts* by Terry Smith (2nd edition, 1996, Century Business). You must make sure that you obtain a copy of the second edition. Many of the creative accounting devices mentioned in the first edition have been eliminated by subsequent accounting regulations.

Summary

The main learning points in this chapter can be summarized as follows:

- accounting standards were originally established by the ASC as a means of reducing the number of acceptable practices where there was a choice
- the ASC established 22 accounting standards before the process was transferred to the new ASB
- the former regime of developing accounting standards through the offices of the ASC had certain weaknesses, particularly in respect of the way SSAPs were developed and enforced
- the process of developing and issuing standards was transferred to a new autonomous body (the ASB) in 1990
- the new process is supported by legislation which requires directors to declare compliance with accounting standards, and empowers the FRRP to seek a revision of previously published accounts where the Review Panel considers that these accounts do not show a true and fair view
- the new regulatory process is likely to bring the more serious cases of 'creative accounting' to an end
- ethical training has been neglected in the past but is likely to be far more dominant in the future

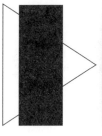

Suggested answers to self-assessment questions

Chapter 1

1.1 Some figures in financial statements are derived from facts, such as the cost of an asset. These figures are said to be 'objective'. Other figures are derived from estimates, such as the number of years over which the cost of a fixed asset should be spread when calculating the amount to be treated as annual expense. These figures are said to be 'subjective'.

The imposition of subjective figures can detract from the usefulness of the information. The judgements made by one business can be completely different from another. For example, one business might consider that a particular fixed asset will be used up over 20 years, whereas another might consider the same type of asset will be used up over 10 years. The reported results of these two businesses will differ, making comparisons between them difficult.

The problem of comparability can be ameliorated by the disclosure (in supplementary notes) of the accounting policy used by each business for the item concerned.

1.2 Three deliberate mistakes:

1. The report is addressed to the directors, when it should have been addressed to the shareholders. The intervention of the auditor is to protect the interests of shareholders. The company's financial statements are prepared by the directors and represent a record of the directors' stewardship of the shareholders' funds. Without an audit by an independent accountant, unscrupulous directors could mislead the shareholders.

2. It is does not make sense to describe financial statements as being 'correct'. Many of the figures in these statements are estimated. Further, some figures result from the adoption of a particular accounting policy; these figures would differ if a different policy had been applied. The law requires directors to produce financial statements that show a 'true and fair view'. These words recognize that estimates have been made and judgement applied in selecting the appropriate accounting policy.

3. The word 'certify' has been used, which implies some kind of guarantee. But in most companies there will be millions of accounting transactions throughout the

year and in these circumstances it is unreasonable to expect the auditor to inspect every one. The auditor is, therefore, required to give an opinion.

1.3 Three regulatory influences:

- Companies Act 1985
- Accounting standards
- Stock Exchange regulations

The role of the Companies Act 1985 is to regulate on various matters, including those on:

- the publication of the accounts
- the accounting principles to be applied
- the format to be used
- the information that the accounts must contain

Accounting standards are developed by the accounting profession, in conjunction with other interested parties from outside of the profession. The role of accounting standards is to prescribe standard practices in those areas of accounting where different practices could be used, and where a different result would arise depending on the practice adopted. Their main aim is to improve comparability by restricting the choice of practices that companies may adopt. They also contain provisions regarding presentation and disclosure of information.

Some accounting standards issued in the 1970s were subsequently incorporated into law but, generally speaking, they are seen as rules that augment those in the Companies Act 1985.

Stock Exchange regulations are those that companies agree to comply with in order to secure the benefit of a listing on the Stock Exchange. Most of these regulations are additional to those in the Companies Act 1985 and in accounting standards. In some cases, compliance with an accounting standard ensures compliance with a relevant Stock Exchange regulation.

1.4 Historic (strictly speaking this should be 'historical') cost accounting records the purchase of assets at their original monetary cost. When prices are rising, distortions in the financial statements can arise, as follows:

Balance sheet:

- most fixed assets (particularly freehold property) will have a current value that differs significantly from their original cost.
- comparing the financial position of one company with another is misleading. Two companies may own exactly the same physical assets, but the monetary values of these assets will differ if the assets were bought at different times.

Profit and loss account:

- profits are calculated by deducting the original cost of the stock sold. It will cost more than original cost to replace the stock sold but no allowance is made for the extra cost when calculating profit.
- the original cost of fixed assets is treated as an expense for the years during which the asset is used. It will cost more than original cost to replace the asset at the end of this time, but no allowance is made for the extra cost when calculating profit.

Chapter 2

2.1 Monetary effect on net assets:

(a) Net assets reduced by £50 (same as drawings).

(b) No effect (assets increase and liabilities increase by the same amount).

(c) Net assets reduced by £500 (an asset of £4,000 is replaced by an asset of £3,500).

(d) Net assets reduced by £600 (there is nothing to take the place of the money spent).

(e) No effect (reduction of cash is replaced by another asset of the same value. Loans payable to the business are usually called a 'loan receivable').

(f) Net assets reduced by £200 (an asset of £5,000 is replaced by an asset of £4,800).

(g) No effect (cash is reduced and liabilities are reduced by the same amount).

(h) No effect (debtors are an asset. In this case the increase in cash is equal to the reduction of debtors).

(i) No effect (in this case the increase in fixed assets of £65,000 is equal to a reduction in cash of £60,000 and an increase in liabilities of £5,000).

(j) Net assets reduced by £1,000 (cash has gone out and nothing of value remains).

2.2 Transaction 1. Purchased stock for £5,000 on credit (stock and creditors have increased by £5,000).

Transaction 2. Sold stock which had cost £7,000 for cash of £10,000, making a profit of £3,000 (stock reduced by £7,000, cash increased by £10,000, and retained profits increased by £3,000).

Transaction 3. Purchased plant for cash at a cost of £20,000, partly financed by a loan of £10,000 (plant increased by £20,000, loan increased by £10,000, cash reduced by £10,000).

2.3 Mrs Thakrar

Balance sheet at 1 January 1996

	£	£
Fixed assets		
Delivery van	4,000	
Office equipment	1,000	
		5,000
Current assets		
Stock	600	
Debtors	100	
Bank	2,000	
	2,700	
Creditors due within one year		
Trade creditors	500	
Net current assets		2,200
Total assets less current liabilities		7,200
Creditors due after one year:		
Loan – Miss Laxmi		800
Total net assets		6,400
Capital and reserves		
Contributed capital (cash introduced)		5,000
Retained profits (see note)		1,400
Total ownership interest		6,400

Note: The amount for retained profits had to be derived as a balancing figure.

2.4 Mrs Thakrar's profit and loss account, statement of retained profits, and balance sheet

Profit and loss account week ending 7 January 1996

Sales	300
Cost of sales	200
Gross profit	100
Expenses:	
Motor repairs	10
Net profit	90

Statement of retained profits:

Retained profits at 1 January 1993	1,400
Add net profit for the week	90
	1,490
Less drawings	50
Retained profits at 7 January 1993	1,440

Balance sheet at 7 January 1996

	£	£
Fixed assets		
Delivery van	4,000	
Office equipment	1,000	
		5,000
Current assets		
Stock	500	
Debtors	100	
Bank	2,140	
	2,740	
Creditors due within one year		
Trade creditors	600	
Net current assets		2,140
Total assets less current liabilities		7,140
Creditors due after one year:		
Loan – Miss Laxmi		700
Total net assets		6,440
Capital and reserves		
Contributed capital (cash introduced)		5,000
Retained profits (see note)		1,440
Total ownership interest		6,440

Workings: Bank balance: 2,000 + 300 − 10 − 100 − 50 = £2,140. Stock: 600 − 200 + 100 = £500

Chapter 3

3.1 (a) and (b) After bringing down the opening balances, posting transactions for the period, and determining closing balances where needed, the ledger accounts should be as follows:

Bank account

8.1.96	Balance b/d	2,140	9.1.96	Creditors	400
8.1.96	Debtors	50	10.1.96	Office equipment	100
10.1.96	Sales	700	14.1.96	Wages	80
			14.1.96	Drawings	100
			14.1.96	Balance c/d	2,210
		2,890			2,890
15.1.96	Balance b/d	2,210			

Stock account

8.1.96	Balance b/d	500	10.1.96	Cost of sales	400
			14.1.96	Balance c/d	100
		500			500
15.1.96	Balance b/d	100			

Debtors

8.1.96	Balance b/d	100	8.1.96	Bank	50
			14.1.96	Balance c/d	50
		100			100
15.1.96	Balance b/d	50			

Creditors

9.1.96	Bank	400	8.1.96	Balance b/d	600
14.1.96	Balance c/d	200			
		600			600
			15.1.96	Balance b/d	200

Motor vehicles

8.1.96	Balance b/d	4,000			

Office equipment

8.1.96	Balance b/d	1,000	14.1.96	Balance c/d	1,100
10.1.96	Bank	100			
		1,100			1,100
15.1.96	Balance b/d	1,100			

Loan payable – Miss Laxmi

		8.1.96 Balance b/d	700

Wages

14.1.96 Bank	80		

Drawings

14.1.96 Bank	100		

Cost of sales

14.1.96 Stock	400		

Sales

		10.1.96 Bank	700

Capital – cash introduced

		8.1.96 Balance b/d	5,000

Capital – retained profits

		8.1.96 Balance b/d	1,440

(c) Trial balance

	Debit	Credit
Bank	2,210	
Stock	100	
Debtors	50	
Creditors		200
Motor vehicles	4,000	
Office equipment	1,100	
Loan		700
Wages	80	
Drawings	100	
Cost of sales	400	
Sales		700
Capital – cash introduced		5,000
Capital – retained profits		1,440
	8,040	8,040

(d) Profit and loss account, week ending 14 January 1996

Sales		700
Cost of sales		400
Gross profit		300
Expenses:		
Wages		80
Net profit		220

Statement of retained profits

Retained profits brought forward	1,440
Add: Net profit for the period	220
	1,660
Less: Drawings during the period	100
Retained profits carried forward	1,560

Balance sheet at 14 January 1996

Fixed assets:

Delivery van		4,000
Office equipment		1,100
		5,100
Current assets:		
Stocks	100	
Debtors	50	
Cash	2,210	
	2,360	
Creditors due within one year		
Trade creditors	200	
Net current assets		2,160
Total assets less current liabilities		7,260
Long-term liabilities:		
Loan		700
		6,560
Capital and reserves		
Cash introduced by proprietor		5,000
Retained profits		1,560
		6,560

You should note that it would be very unusual to produce weekly accounts. Generally speaking, the financial statements for a small business are produced annually. In some cases, monthly financial statements are produced for management purposes.

3.2 Trial balance for T. Zatopec

	Debits	Credits
Drawings	13,600	
Commission earned		34,384
Staff salaries	14,430	
Rent and business rates	2,800	
Telephone, postage and stationery	1,200	
Travelling and entertaining expenses	800	
Loan payable		1,000
Office equipment	5,000	
Debtors	6,000	
Creditors		4,000
Cash at bank	5,000	
Investments	3,000	
Interest received on investments		200
Interest paid	100	
Capital account:		
cash introduced		10,000
retained profits b/f (balancing figure)		2,346
	51,930	51,930

3.3 Errors in Miss L. Gifford's ledger

No.	Type	Effect on agreement of trial balance totals	Notes to answer
1.	error of omission	no effect	
2.	error of principle	no effect	1
3	transposition error	credits will exceed debits by £270	
4.	error of principle	credits will exceed debits by £200	2
5.	error of commission	credits will exceed debits by £360	
6.	compensating error	combined effect is nil; one error causes credits to be overstated by £10, the other causes debits to be overstated by £10	
7.	error of commission	no effect	3

Notes to answer:

1. Error number 2 has been classified as an error of principle because the title 'office equipment' usually applies to a fixed asset account for items such as furniture and computers. By applying the concept of 'materiality', the cost of a stapling machine should be treated as an expense.

2. This can be classified as an error of principle under two headings. First, the amount has been credited to an account instead of being debited. Second, the entry has been made in the wrong class of account (it has been treated as income instead of an expense).

3. If fixed assets are thought of as a 'class' of accounts, this amount has been debited to the wrong account in the right class. Both 'land and buildings' and 'motor vehicles' are classed as fixed assets.

Chapter 4

4.1 Ann Ford
Profit and loss account, year ended 30 June 1993

Sales		100,000
Less cost of sales:		
Opening stock	10,000	
Purchases	70,000	
	80,000	
Less closing stock	13,000	
		67,000
Gross profit		33,000
Less expenses:		
Delivery expenses	2,000	
Salaries and wages	20,000	
Electricity	1,000	
		23,000
Net profit		10,000
Statement of retained profit		
Retained profits brought forward		21,000
Add net profit for the year		10,000
		31,000
Less drawings		5,000
Retained profits carried forward		26,000

Balance sheet at 30 June 1996

Fixed assets:

Freehold property		50,000
Motor vehicles		10,000
		60,000

Current assets:

Stock	13,000	
Debtors	4,000	
Bank	1,000	
	18,000	
Creditors due within one year		
Creditors	2,000	
Net current assets		16,000
Total assets less current liabilities		76,000
Long-term loan		10,000
		66,000
Capital and reserves		
Cash introduced		40,000
Retained profits		26,000
		66,000

4.2 Brian Fuzzy

(a) The trial balance includes several errors.

The opening stock should be a debit item, and the closing stock should not be there at all. Closing stock appears in the trial balance when cost of sales has already been determined, in which case the opening stock would not appear; clearly not the case here.

Normally the trial balance would not have agreed as a result of the errors on stock. By pure chance, the trial balance does agree but only because the debtors, creditors and loan payable are all listed on the wrong side.

The corrected trial balance is as follows:

	Debit	Credit
Sales		130,690
Stock at 1 January 1993	10,700	
Purchases	92,150	
Selling and distribution expenses	6,000	
Administration expenses	10,600	
Drawings	9,000	
Debtors	5,000	
Creditors		5,800
Bank	7,100	
Long-term loan payable		6,000
Freehold property	50,000	
Motor vehicles	10,000	
Capital – cash introduced		40,000
Capital – retained profits		18,060
	200,550	200,550

(b) The effect of each adjustment required is as follows:

(i) reduce the closing stock (which has not yet been written into the books) by £500.

(ii) reduce sales by £300 and reduce debtors by £300.

(iii) reduce purchases by £600 and reduce creditors by £600.

Profit and loss account, year ended 31 December 1996

Sales		130,390
Less cost of sales:		
Opening stock	10,700	
Purchases	91,550	
	102,250	
Less closing stock	7,300	
		94,950
Gross profit		35,440
Less expenses:		
Selling and distribution	6,000	
Administration	10,600	
		16,600
Net profit		18,840

Statement of retained profit

Retained profits brought forward	18,060
Add net profit for the year	18,840
	36,900
Less drawings	9,000
Retained profits carried forward	27,900

Balance sheet at 30 June 1993

Fixed assets:

Freehold property		50,000
Motor vehicles		10,000
		60,000
Current assets:		
Stock	7,300	
Debtors	4,700	
Bank	7,100	
	19,100	
Creditors due within one year		
Creditors	5,200	
Net current assets		13,900
Total assets less current liabilities		73,900
Long-term loan		6,000
		67,900
Capital and reserves		
Cash introduced		40,000
Retained profits		27,900
		67,900

4.3 The narrative sections of the following give a basic outline of the points that should have been covered in your answer. (Note that certain parts of this answer differ from the answer published by ACCA. These differences result from a different interpretation of the data.)

(a) Application of the accruals and prudence concepts. Revenue recognized as soon as its ultimate receipt is reasonably certain. On a credit sale this will be in advance of cash receipt and is usually determined at the point when the sale is accepted by the customer. Sales to a bad credit risk would not normally be made on credit terms, and so if a sale on credit has been made, it is reasonable to assume the amount due will eventually be received.

(b) Legally, the sale had actually taken place at stage F. However, there may still be uncertainties in the transaction at this stage. Accountants would normally consider stage G to be the point at which the revenue should be recognized.

(c) *Author's note:* You need to be careful with your answer here, and make reasonable assumptions from the data given. The following points should have been discussed:

Gross profit is the difference between sales revenue and the cost of sales. Sales revenue is not the same as net realizable value because selling and distribution costs are deducted in arriving at the latter. There appear to be £10 delivery costs in the question (the difference between costs at stage F and stage G). Assuming these were estimated in the calculation of net realizable value, the selling price must be (300 + 10) £310. The gross profit must therefore be (310 – 170) £140.

Author's note: It is a little difficult to interpret the examiner's information as far as net realizable value is concerned. If you try to see how net realizable values may have been calculated at points B and C, there seems to have been no attempt to base them on ultimate selling price less cost of completion and selling (unless the estimates were very poor). It is also a bit strange to talk about net realizable value of stock of £300 at the time delivered and the time cash is paid. However, you will often find ambiguities in exam questions. You should not let these put you off. If you make an intelligent argument to support your answer, you are bound to be given good marks.

(d) Delaying recognition of the revenue until stage H would mean that the accounts are being prepared on a cash basis instead of on an accruals basis. The only argument in favour of this is that it does remove all the uncertainties. It would, however, be in complete violation of the long-standing and fundamental concept of accruals.

Author's note: If the sale is recognized at point G, and the cash is not eventually paid, accountants will treat the loss (the amount not received) as an expense, called 'bad debts', in the period during which it becomes apparent that the debtor is not going to pay. You will learn more about this in a later chapter.

(e) Recognizing revenue at points B, C and D would be a violation of the going concern concept since assets would have to be carried in the books at their net realizable value.

The arguments in its favour are that the net realizable value of assets could be quite useful information to those who use accounting information. Profits could be determined on the basis of an increase in the realizable net worth of the business over the year. However, net realizable value is a highly subjective figure, and could be abused in practice. The information in financial statements is far more reliable when objective amounts, such as the actual historic cost of assets, is used.

Chapter 5

5.1 P. Muhone

Trial Balance:	Debit	Credit
Capital		10,000
Motor vehicles	5,000	
Purchases	5,500	
Stationery	50	
Sales		7,850
Motor expenses	500	
Drawings	1,000	
Bank	7,400	
Debtors	2,550	
Creditors		4,150
	22,000	22,000

Profit and loss account for the month of January

Sales		7,850
Less cost of sales:		
Purchases	5,500	
Less closing stock	500	
		5,000
Gross profit		2,850
Less expenses:		
Stationery	50	
Motor expenses	500	
		550
Net profit		2,300

Statement of retained profits

Net profit for the month	2,300
Less drawings	1,000
Retained profits at the end of the month	1,300

Balance Sheet at 31 January:

Fixed assets:		
Motor vehicle		5,000
Current assets:		
Stock	500	
Debtors	2,550	
Bank	7,400	
	10,450	

Creditors due within one year

Creditors	4,150	
		6,300
		11,300

Capital and reserves

Cash introduced	10,000
Retained profits	1,300
	11,300

5.2 Mary McGregor

Purchase ledger control account

Dec 31	Bank	262,318	Jan 1	Balance b/d	15,892
	Returns	1,456	Dec 31	Purchases	278,560
	Balance c/d	30,678			
		294,452			294,452
			Jan 1	Balance b/d	30,678

Sales ledger control account

Jan 1	Balance b/d	34,975	Dec 31	Bank	398,764
	Sales	418,930	Dec 31	Returns	682
				Balance c/d	54,459
		453,905			453,905
Jan 1	Balance b/d	54,459			

5.3 Sellabrick
(a)

Purchase ledger control account

Purchase invoice for Green		Balance as per question	25,450
overstated by (600 – 350)	250	Purchase day book undercast	2,220
Returns omitted	800		
Revised balance c/d	26,620		
	27,670		27,670

(b) Errors affecting both the control account and the total of creditors have to be ignored in this type of calculation.

Prior to the corrections, the total of the list of creditors would have been:

Original balance on the control account	25,450
Plus the day book undercasting (which affects the control account only)	2,220
Revised balance (prior to correcting the errors that affect list and control)	27,670
Less creditor understated in the list (1,550 – 1,500)	50
	27,620

If you are not convinced on this, it can be checked by working as if the opening balance on the uncorrected creditors list had been given by the examiner as £27,620, and you had been asked to do a reconciliation. For example:

	Creditors listing	Control account
Original balance (above)	27,620	(per question) 25,450
Errors affecting both listing and control:		
Invoice overstated	(250)	(250)
Returns omitted	(800)	(800)
Error affecting control a/c only		Day book undercast 2,220
Error affecting creditors list only		
Creditor understated	50	
Corrected balances	26,620	26,620

5.4 Wholesalers plc
(a)

Sales ledger control account

1 Jan 91	Balance b/d	50,000	31 Dec 91	Sales returns	5,000
31 Dec 91	Sales (see note)	107,000		Bank	114,000
				Balance c/d	38,000
		157,000			157,000

Note: There was an error in the casting of the sales day book (hence the cryptic clue 'unaudited' in the question). The correct total has been posted to the above control account.

Summary memorandum ledger accounts. All figures are in £000s, and credit items are shown in brackets:

	A	B	C	D	E	F	G	Total
Balance b/d	10	20	8	9	6	(2)	(1)	50
Sales		30	35	18	9	8	7	107
Sales returns	(2)					(3)		(5)
Cash receipts	(37)	(30)	(5)	(20)	(12)	(6)	(4)	(114)
Balance c/d	1	25	3	7	3	(3)	2	38

(b) Answers could include the following:

(i) As a check on the accuracy of processing in the personal ledgers.
(ii) Control against fraud by separation of duties.
(iii) Isolation of book-keeping errors.
(iv) Draft financial statements can be produced more quickly (control account totals can be used without having to balance all the individual accounts).

Chapter 6

6.1 Amy

(a) The amount to be capitalized and depreciated should be based on all the costs of bringing the asset into use – excluding any costs incurred through actually using it. Since the additional components increase the productive capacity they should be treated as part of the asset's capital cost (some accountants refer to such expenditure as 'improvements').

Maintenance costs and replacement parts are clearly costs of using the asset and should be treated as expenses charged to the profit and loss account. The cost used as a basis for depreciation should therefore be based on the purchase price of £11,000, plus delivery, erection, and the additional component.

The total capital expenditure is (11,000 + 100 + 200 + 400) £11,700.

(b) Depreciation allocates the cost (less residual value) to the accounting periods over which the asset is used (useful economic life). It is necessary in order to comply with the matching principle whereby sales revenue should be matched with all costs of earning that revenue.

(c) Straight line charges a constant amount each year, based on the original cost (less estimated residual value if any) divided by the estimated number of years over which the trader intends to use the asset. The reducing balance method charges a fixed percentage of the net book value at the beginning of the year – the annual amounts will therefore decrease as the net book value reduces.

(d) Objectivity refers to the determination of accounting figures in a way that is not affected by human bias. Such figures are usually based on facts, e.g. the cost of paying wages for the year was the amount expended – all accountants would measure this figure in exactly the same way. Depreciation is not objective; in fact it is highly subjective. Judgement is necessary to determine factors such as the estimated useful life and the manner in which the benefit is consumed.

(e) This practice appears to violate the fundamental concept of consistency as established in UK practice and codified in SSAP 2. The only argument in its favour is that of prudence, since the expense will always be the higher of the two alternatives. However, it makes no attempt to match the cost of the asset consumed against the benefits produced in the form of sales income.

6.2 Vale & Co.

Workings:

Amount paid for new van	Full price	6,800	
	Less 10% discount	680	
	Purchase price	6,120	
	Part exchange	1,650	
	Cash paid	4,470	

Depreciation previously provided on van sold as part exchange

Cost in year ended 28 February 1995	6,000	
Depreciation for year ended 28 Feb 1995 (40%)	2,400	2,400
	3,600	
Depreciation for year ended 28 Feb 1996	1,440	1,440
Total provided by 1 March 1996		3,840

Depreciation on vans for year ended 28 February 1997

Cost of vans:

At 1 March 1996	13,050
Less cost of van sold 1996/97	6,000
	7,050
Addition during 1996/97	6,120
	13,170

Depreciation provision:

At 1 March 1996	8,975
Less depreciation on van sold	3,840
	5,135

Depreciation for year ended 28 February 1997 40% of $(13,170 - 5,135) = 3,214$.

Vans – cost

1 Mar 96	Balance b/d	13,050	28 Feb 97	Sale of fixed assets	6,000
1 Dec 96	Bank	4,470	28 Feb 97	Balance c/d	13,170
28 Feb 97	Sale of fixed assets	1,650			
		19,170			19,170
1 Mar 97	Balance b/d	13,170			

Depreciation provision – vans

28 Feb 97	Sale of fixed assets	3,840	1 Mar 96	Balance b/d	8,975
28 Feb 97	Balance c/d	8,349	28 Feb 97	Depreciation expense	3,214
		12,189			12,189
			1 Mar 97	Balance b/d	8,349

Sale of fixed assets account

28 Feb 97	Vans – cost	6,000	28 Feb 97	Vans – cost	1,650
			28 Feb 97	Depreciation provision	3,840
			28 Feb 97	Profit and loss a/c (loss on sale)	510
		6,000			6,000

6.3 Tipsy Turvey Traders

Workings:

Provision required at 31 March 1997

Debtors per trial balance	12,360
Less debts to be written off (210 + 50)	260
Revised debtors	12,100

provision should be: $2\% \times 12,100 = 242$

(a)

Provision for doubtful debts

31 Mar 97	Balance c/d	242	1 Apr 96	Balance b/d	410
31 Mar 97	Profit and loss a/c	168			
		410			410
			1 Apr 97	Balance b/d	242

(b) The profit and loss account will include the following items:

	Expenses	Credits
Bad debts written off	260	
Bad debts recovered		970
Reduction in provision for doubtful debts		168

Author's notes:

1. These may be shown as three separate items in the profit and loss account, or they may be amalgamated into one net credit of £878 – which can still be described as bad and doubtful debts even though it is a credit.

2. For presentation purposes, any 'negative' expense items (such as bad debts recovered) are normally included in the list of expenses (in the profit and loss account) in brackets. For example, if the three items are to be shown separately they could be presented as follows:

Expenses:	
Bad debts written off	260
Bad debts recovered	(970)
Reduction in provision for doubtful debts	(168)

3. Presentation in the balance sheet will be in one of two ways, i.e. either:

Debtors (less provision doubtful debts)	£11,858

or (in detail) as:

Debtors	£12,100	
Less provision for doubtful debts	242	
		£11,858

Current practices favour the first presentation. This gives adequate information to the user but does not clutter the balance sheet with too much detail.

Chapter 7

7.1 Leslie
Opening balance for cash book:

Balance per bank statement	85
Less unpresented cheque (C. Lord)	142
Overdrawn balance	57

Cash book

May	Bankings		May		
			May	Balance b/d	57
Cash		210	Cheques		
Johnson		45	J. Green		150
Cash		350	R. Black		220
Cash		410	F. Jones		415
Jackson		76	G. Smith		324
Lawton		186	T. Pryce		81
Arnold		210	A. Wright		47
Credit transfer			Standing order (Insurance)		10
Mills		25	Bank interest		24
			Balance c/d		184
		1,512			1,512
Jun	Balance b/d	184			

Reconciliation statement:

Balance per bank statement		250
Less unpresented cheques:		
A. Wright	47	
F. Jones	415	
	462	
		(212)
Uncleared lodgements:		
Lawton	186	
Arnold	210	
		396
Balance per cash book		184

7.2 Whenever you see expressions similar to 'inexperienced book-keeper' in a question you can usually assume that a number of errors exist in the information presented. In this case, a preliminary examination of the summary cash book reveals the following:

- An overdrawn balance has been brought down on the debit side instead of the credit side
- Discounts have been added to the cash banked
- The first block of receipts for December add up to £331.26 (not £329.26)
- Cheque 7655 has been entered in the cash book as £192.79 whereas it appears on the bank statement as £129.79 (assumed to be correct – as per question)

These can be incorporated in the corrected cash book summary requested for (a). You also had to establish that the balance on the bank statement is overdrawn.

(a) Corrected cash book summary:

Cash book summary – draft

Jan–Nov receipts		39,500.54	Jan 1 overdraft b/d	7,000.12
Dec receipts	178.19		Jan – Nov cheques	35,000.34
	121.27		Dec cheques	
	14.92		7654	37.14
	16.88		7655 (as statement)	129.79
	3,100.00		7656	5,000.00
	171.23		7657	123.45
	1,198.17		7658	678.90
		4,800.66	7659	1.47
Dec receipt (per			7660	19.84
statement)		117.98	7661	10.66
			Standing order	50.00
Jan overdraft c/d		3,712.53	Bank charges	80.00
		48,131.71		48,131.71
			Jan overdraft b/d	3,712.53

Bank reconciliation statement:

Balance per statement			3,472.34 (overdrawn)
Add unpresented cheques	7657	123.45	
	7660	19.84	
			143.29
			3,615.63
Balance per cash book			3,712.53
Unexplained difference			96.90

(b) The reconciliation shows that the overdraft per the bank statement is less than the overdraft stated in the cash book. There are several explanations; the most likely is that there is a further unpresented cheque written prior to December (probably November) – notice that cheque 7652 does not appear in the sequence of numbers on the bank statement.

7.3
(a)

Sales ledger control account

Balance b/d	12,087	Bank	90,019
		Discounts allowed	3,000
Sales	117,635	Sales returns	4,200
		Bad debts expense	1,550
		Balance c/d	
		(prior to corrections)	30,953
	129,722		129,722
Uncorrected balance b/d	30,953		
Corrections:			
Sales (omitted)	3,400		
Cash sales (credited in error)	600		
Purchase ledger	400	Revised balance c/d	
	35,353		35,353
Revised balance b/d	35,353		35,353

(b) Reconciliation of sales ledger listing:

Balance per question (35,588 – 185)		35,403
Add: sales omitted		3,400
		38,803
Less: discounts allowed (omitted)	350	
correction of error on bad debts (2 × 1,550)	3,100	
		3,450
		35,353

(c) The credit balances should be included in with trade creditors.

Chapter 8

8.1 Carter

(a) Manufacturing account:

Raw materials consumed (280,000 – 4,000 + 2,000 – 40,000)		238,000
Direct labour		125,000
Direct expense (royalties)		12,000
Prime cost		375,000
Manufacturing overheads:		
Rent (two-thirds of 12/15 × 15,000)	8,000	
Indirect factory labour	24,000	
General factory expenses	15,000	
Depreciation of plant and machinery (140,000 × 0.2)	28,000	
		75,000
Total production costs		450,000

(b) Trading and profit and loss accounts:

	Marginal cost		Absorbed cost	
Sales (540,000 – 1,000)		539,000		539,000
Less cost of sales:				
Cost of goods manufactured	450,000		450,000	
Less closing stock	45,000		54,000	
		405,000		396,000
Gross profit		134,000		143,000
Expenses:				
Selling and distribution costs	31,000		31,000	
Administrative costs	39,000		39,000	
		70,000		70,000
Net profit		64,000		73,000

Workings:
1. Closing stock: Marginal cost = 375,000/25,000 = £15.00 per unit. Absorbed cost = 450,000/25,000 = £18.00 per unit.
2. Selling and distribution costs = £20,000 (per TB) + accrual of £8,000 + the depreciation of delivery vans amounting to £3,000.
3. Administrative costs = £35,000 (per TB) + the apportionment of rent £4,000.

(c) In order to determine the cost of sales for each of the three products it would be necessary to set up a detailed cost accounting system. The figures produced above are based on averages. Unless each product has identical characteristics, the average cost per unit when three different types are produced is a fiction. From the information produced by the financial accounting system there is no way of determining the material, labour and overhead content of each product for the closing stock valuation. Some products will use more materials than others, some will take longer to make.

The overhead content per unit has been calculated at a uniform amount for each type of product. Most overheads accrue on a time basis and the overhead cost per unit should bear some relationship to the amount of time it takes to produce that unit. Where products pass through several production departments it would be necessary to determine the overhead cost of each department and the amount of time it takes for each type of product to be processed by that department.

Chapter 9

(Most of the workings are shown in brackets between the description and the amount.)

9.1 Jean Black
(a)

Trading and profit and loss account for year ended 31 October 1990

Sales (390 + 110 + 920 + 37,500 + 3,900 – 3,100)		48,000
Cost of sales:		
Opening stock	1,900	
Purchases (24,300 + 5,400 – 2,100 – 800)	26,800	
	28,700	
Less closing stock	2,500	
		26,200
Gross profit		21,800
Expenses:		
Wages (7,400 + 810)	8,210	
General expenses (240 + 6,510 + 390 – 82 + 36)	7,094	
Depreciation of motor vehicle (9,872 – 7,404)	2,468	
Profit on sale of motor vehicle (500 – 300)	(200)	
Bank charges	40	
		17,612
Net profit		4,188

(Goods taken for own use could be presented as a deduction from cost of sales on the face of the trading account.)

(b)

Balance sheet at 31 October 1990

Fixed assets	Cost	Depn	Net
Motor vehicle	9,872	2,468	7,404

Current assets:		
Stock		2,500
Debtors		3,900
Cash in hand		250
		6,650

Creditors due within one year

Creditors and accruals (5,400 + 36 + 810)	6,246	
Bank overdraft (1,400 + 40)	1,440	
	7,686	
		(1,036)
		6,368

Capital

Opening capital (142 + 2,830 + 300 + 1,900 + 3,100 + 390 – 82 – 2,100)	6,480
Add: cash introduced	8,000
net profit	4,188
Less: drawings (900 + 10,600 + 800)	(12,300)
	6,368

9.2 Jim Hastings

(a)

Bank account

Cash introduced	6,500	Lease payments (rent)	4,800
Loan	5,300	Wages	7,050
Cash takings banked (balance)	124,450	Repairs and renewals	1,235
		General expenses	1,375
		Purchases	105,950
		Lighting and heating	965
		Fixtures and fittings	4,895
		Interest	425
		Accountancy	355
		Car expenses	1,050
		Balance c/d	8,150
	136,250		136,250

Cash account

Cash takings (balance)	133,545	Wages	3,200
		General expenses	320
		Lighting and heating	95
		Car expenses	155
		Bank	124,450
		Drawings (52 × £100)	5,200
		Balance c/d	125
	133,545		133,545

(b)

Trading and profit and loss account for year ended 30 April 19X8

Sales		133,545
Cost of sales:		
Purchases (105,950 + 10,940 − 335)	116,555	
Less closing stock	14,500	
		102,055
Gross profit		31,490
Lease payments (rent) (960 × 4)	3,840	
Wages (3,200 + 7,050)	10,250	
Repairs and renewals	1,235	
General expenses (1,375 + 320 − 215)	1,480	
Lighting and heating (965 + 95)	1,060	
Interest (9/12 × 16% × 5,300)	636	
Accountancy	355	
Car expenses ((4/5ths × (1,050 + 155))	964	
Depreciation:		
Fixtures and fittings (4,895 − 4,200)	695	
Car (4/5ths × (4,100 − 3,150))	760	
		21,275
Net profit		10,215

Statement of retained profits:

Net profit for the year	10,215	
Drawings (5,200 + 215 + 335 + (1/5 × 1,205) + (1/5 × 950))	6,181	
Retained profit carried forward	4,034	

Balance sheet at 30 April 19X8

Fixed assets:	Cost	Depn	Net
Car	4,100	950	3,150
Fixtures and fittings	4,895	695	4,200
	8,995	1,645	7,350

Current assets:		
Stock	14,500	
Rent prepaid (4,800 − 3,840)	960	
Cash	125	
Bank	8,150	
	23,735	
Creditors due within one year:		
Creditors	10,940	
Interest accrued (636 − 425)	211	
	11,151	
Net current assets		12,584
Total assets less current liabilities		19,934
Long-term loan		5,300
		14,634
Capital and reserves		
Capital introduced (6,500 + 4,100)		10,600
Retained profit		4,034
		14,634

Note: One-fifth of the car expenses, and one-fifth of the car depreciation, has been charged to drawings.

Chapter 10

10.1 Queue plc
Profit and loss account year ending 31 December 19X9

			working note
Turnover		100,000	
Cost of sales		72,000	1
Gross profit		28,000	
Selling and distribution costs	2,875		2
Administration expenses	9,000		
		11,875	
Operating profit		16,125	
Interest payable and similar charges		1,375	3
Profit before tax		14,750	
Corporation tax		5,000	
Profit after tax		9,750	
Dividends:			
Interim paid	1,500		
Final proposed	1,800		4
		3,300	
Retained profit for the financial year		6,450	
Retained profit at 1 January 19X9		5,500	
Retained profit at 31 December 19X9		11,950	

Balance sheet at 31 December 19X9

	Cost	Depn	Net	working note
Fixed assets:				
Freehold properties	40,000	–	40,000	
Motor vehicles	9,500	3,125	6,375	5
	49,500	3,125	46,375	
Current assets:				
Stock		10,000		
Debtors		25,000		
Bank		11,500		7
		46,500		

Creditors: amounts falling due within one year				
Trade creditors and accruals	16,625			6
Proposed dividends	1,800			
Corporation tax	5,000			
		23,425		

Net current assets	23,075	
Total assets less current liabilities	69,450	
Creditors: amounts falling due after more than one year:		
10% Debentures	15,000	
	54,450	
Capital and reserves:		
Called up share capital	40,000	7
Share premium account	2,500	7
Profit and loss account	11,950	
	54,450	

Working notes
1. Stock valuation:
   (a) Stock at cost (10,200 – 600)   9,600
   (b) Stock at net realizable value:

ultimate selling price	500	
less future repair costs	100	
		400
		10,000

2. Selling and distribution costs

per question	2,000
depreciation of vehicles (see 5)	2,500
profit on sale of motor vehicle (see 5)	(1,625)
	2,875

3. Interest paid and similar charges
   Debenture interest

Full charge for period (9/12 × 10% × 15,000)	1,125
Bank interest	250
	1,375

Note:

Debenture interest accrued (1,125 – 750)	375

4. Proposed dividend: 30,000 × 6p = 1,800
5. Motor vehicles:

Cost:		
	Brought forward	10,000
	Cost of vehicle sold	(4,500)
	Cost of addition	4,000
	Carried forward	9,500

Depreciation:		
provision	Brought forward	4,000
	Charge for the year (see note)	
	25% × 10,000	2,500
		6,500
	Less depreciation on vehicle	
	sold (3 × 1,125)	3,375
		3,125

Note: A full year's depreciation has been provided on the vehicle sold since it was sold on the last day of the year. This is included in the £3,375 adjustment to the depreciation provision. No depreciation has been provided on the new van.

Profit on sale of vehicle
Net book value at time of sale:

Cost	4,500
Depreciation provided	3,375
	1,125
Sale proceeds	2,750
Profit	1,625

An alternative would be to provide no depreciation in the year of sale and thereby reduce the profit on sale. This would make no difference to the net charge in the profit and loss account; the depreciation charge would be reduced by 1,125 and the profit on sale would be reduced by 1,125. Either method is acceptable

6.   Trade creditors and accruals

Creditors per question	15,000
Debenture interest accrued	375
	15,375

7. Share issue:

Share capital increased by (10,000 × £1)	10,000
Share premium account (10,000 × £0.25)	2,500
Cash received	12,500
Bank balance is (12,500 – 1,000)	11,500

10.2 Equity Ltd

It is assumed that the share premium (90p per share) was due on the date of issue (allotment).

(a)

Ordinary share capital account

31 Dec 92 Balance c/d	280,000	1 Jan 92 Appln & allot a/c	10,000
		(100,000 × 10p)	
		28 Feb 92 First call a/c	40,000
		(100,000 × 40p)	
		31 Mar 92 Second call a/c	50,000
		(100,000 × 50p)	
		30 Jun 92 Appln & allot a/c	40,000
		(40,000 × £1)	
		30 Nov 92 Share premium a/c	140,000
	280,000		280,000
		1 Jan 93 Balance b/d	280,000

Share premium account

30 Nov 92 Ordinary share capital	140,000	1 Jan 92 Appln & allot a/c	90,000
(bonus issue)		(100,000 × 90p)	
		20 Jun 92 Appln & allot a/c	
		(40,000 × £1.25)	50,000
	140,000		140,000

(b)

	Number	Price	Paid
Original application	1,400	£1.90	£2,660
Rights issue (1 for 2)	700	2.25	1,575
Bonus issue (1 for 1)	2,100	nil	nil
	4,200		4,235

The terms of the bonus issue (1 for 1) are derived from the amount of nominal value transferred from the share premium account.

(c) Reasons for bonus issue:

In theory, the shareholders receive nothing of value in a bonus issue although they may not see it this way. They do seem to be receiving a benefit in the form of extra shares. But the effect of the bonus issue is to divide the equity of the company (whether looked at from the point of view of balance sheet figures, or the total market value of equity) into a larger number of units.

Sometimes the division into a larger number of units does increase market activity in the shares and this can result in a slight gain in their total market value. This often happens when the market value per share, prior to the bonus issue, is substantially in excess of the nominal value.

The directors may have been motivated to make the bonus issue by several factors. There is a 'keeping the shareholders happy' syndrome, and making a bonus issue does appear to be giving the shareholders something without having to pay out any cash. In any case, as stated above, this may result in a real gain to shareholders and this possibility might have been considered by the directors.

Sometimes a bonus issue is made when a company has built up reserves that it has no intention of ever distributing. By turning this into share capital, such reserves are prevented from being available for distribution and the permanent capital is more in line with reality. Furthermore, the company may be carrying reserves that cannot legally be applied for a cash distribution (such as the share premium account) but can be applied for a bonus issue of shares.

10.3 Thingummy Ltd

Trial balance at 31 December 19X9	Debit £000	Credit £000
Share capital (200 + 50)		250
Share premium (75 – 50)		25
Profit and loss account – balance at 1 Jan 19X9		80
Debtors (100 + 500 – 440 – 20 – 5 – 15)	120	
Bad debt provision (10% × 120)		12
Creditors (90 + 300 – 310 – 5 – 10)		65
Land and buildings (110 + 40)	150	
Plant and machinery: cost (Working 1)	182	
depreciation (50 – 9)		41
Stock at 1 January 19X9	100	
Bank account (Working 2)	45	
Sales		500
Bad debt expense	20	
Increase in provision for bad debts (12 – 4)	8	
Purchases	300	
Discounts allowed	15	
Discounts received		10
Operating expenses (95 + 4 – 10)	89	
Profit on disposal of plant and machinery		6
Revaluation reserve		40
	1,029	1,029

Workings:
1. Plant and machinery at cost:

Written down value of plant at time of sale (15 – 6)		9
Written down value was half original cost. Cost = 2 × 9		18
Depreciation previously provided on plant sold		9
Cost brought forward	140	
Less cost of plant sold (above)	18	
	122	
Cost of additions	60	
Cost carried forward	182	

2. Bank balance

Overdraft brought forward	20
Receipts (440 + 75 + 15)	530
	510
Payments (310 + 95 + 60)	465
Closing balance (cash at bank)	45

Chapter 11

11.1
Cash flow statement for the period:

Net cash inflow from operating activities	43,000
Returns on investments and servicing of finance	nil
Taxation	
Corporation tax paid	(8,000)
Capital expenditure	
Payments to acquired fixed assets	(60,000)
	(25,000)
Equity dividends paid	(6,000)
Net cash outflow before financing	(31,000)
Financing	
Cash received on new issue of shares	25,000
Decrease in cash	(6,000)

Notes to the cash flow statement:
Reconciliation of operating profit to net cash inflow from operating activities:

Operating profit	30,000
Depreciation	20,000
Increase in stock	(10,000)
Increase in debtors	(2,000)
Increase in creditors	5,000
	43,000

Working notes:

1. Fixed assets purchased could have been reasoned as: opening balance £200,000 less depreciation of £20,000 = £180,000 compared to the closing balance of £240,000, hence purchases (since there were no sales) of £60,000.

2. Out of the dividends paid and proposed for the year, there is £4,000 owing in the closing balance sheet, leaving £4,000 paid for the year. The proposed dividend of £2,000 for the previous year would also have been paid during the current year, hence total payments during the year were £6,000. These must be equity dividends since the company's share capital consists of ordinary shares only.

11.2 (a)
Cash flow statement, year ending 31 December 1989

Net cash inflow from operating activities		152,000
Returns on investments and servicing of finance		
Interest paid		(5,000)
Taxation		
Corporation tax paid		(14,000)
Capital expenditure		
Payments to acquire fixed assets	(172,000)	
Cash received on sale of fixed assets	8,500	
		(163,500)
		(30,500)
Equity dividends paid		(19,000)
Net cash outflow before financing		(49,500)
Financing		
Cash received on new issue of shares	7,000	
Cash received on issue of debentures	110,000	
		117,000
Increase in cash		67,500

Notes to cash flow statement:

Reconciliation of operating profit to net cash inflow from operating activities:

Operating profit (68,500 + 5,000)	73,500
Depreciation	61,000
Profit on sale of fixed assets	(4,500)
Decrease in stock	26,000
Increase in debtors	(3,000)
Decrease in creditors	(1,000)
Net cash inflow from operating activities	152,000

(b) The asset revaluation reserve is an unrealized profit and as such it does not represent a reserve which can be used for the payment of dividends.

Author's working and guidance notes:
The main difficulty was sorting out the fixed assets. You were given the account for cost; it was a matter of using this to determine figures for the depreciation provision. The asset sold had clearly been written down to (8,500 – 4,500) £4,000. The depreciation provision can then be built up as follows:

Depreciation on asset sold (17 – 4)	13,000	Provision b/d (270 – 190)	80,000
Provision c/d (465 – 337)	128,000	Charge for year (balance)	61,000
	141,000		141,000

Chapter 12

12.1 Greco Ltd Profit and loss account for year ended 31 May 19X9

	£	£
Turnover		657,462
Cost of sales (50,580 + 378,474 – 94,400)		334,654
Gross profit		322,808
Selling and distribution costs (37,406 + 14,375)	51,781	
Administrative expenses (Working 1)	168,884	
		220,665
Operating profit		102,143
Loss on disposal of discontinued operations		8,578
Profit on ordinary activities before interest		93,565
Interest paid and similar charges (5,060 + 3,420 + 3,420)		11,900
Profit on ordinary activities before tax		81,665
Taxation on odinary shares		23,500
Profit on ordinary activities after tax		58,165
Dividends:		
Ordinary Shares (20,000 + 12,000)	32,000	
Preference shares	5,400	
		37,400
Retained profit for the year		20,765

Balance sheet at 31 May 19X9

	Note	£	£
Fixed assets:			
Tangible assets (Working 2)	1		548,005
Current assets:			
Stock		94,400	
Debtors (406,840 + 500)		407,340	
		501,740	
Creditors: due within one year			
Creditors (464,565 + 4,500 + 3,420)		472,485	
Corporation tax		23,500	
Proposed dividends		17,400	
Bank overdraft		64,450	
		577,835	

Net current liabilities		(76,095)
Total assets less current liabilities		471,910
Creditors: due after one year		
12% debenture 1996/2001		57,000
		414,910
Capital and reserves		
Share capital	2	245,000
Share premium account		45,550
Profit and loss account (103,595 + 20,765)		124,360
		414,910

Workings:
1. Admin expenses:

Figures from trial balance:	
Audit fee	2,500
Bad debts	8,584
Directors' salaries	46,700
Rent	40,285
Wages and salaries	44,745
Depreciation (calculated)	
Leasehold	11,600
Fixtures and fittings	10,470
Accruals/prepayments – per notes	
Wages and salaries	4,500
Rent	(500)
	168,884

2. Tangible assets

Per trial balance:	
Fixtures and fittings	34,900
Leasehold premises	525,000
Motor vehicles	24,550
Depreciation for year:	
Fixtures	(10,470)
Leasehold	(11,600)
Motor vehicles	(14,375)
	548,005

12.2 Dennis plc

(a) Regulations in the Companies Act specifically prohibit the share premium account and the capital redemption reserve from being applied for the payment of dividends. The asset revaluation reserve represents an unrealized profit and is therefore not available for distribution. It is assumed that both the general reserve and the profit and loss account do represent realized profits and are, therefore, available for payment of dividends.

(b) The total amount available for payment of dividends is (50,000 + 100,000) £150,000. The issued share capital is (2,000,000 × 25p) £500,000. Therefore, the maximum percentage dividend which could be paid is (150/500 × 100/1) 30%.

(c) The mere transfer of profits to a reserve does not, by itself, ensure that cash will be available for the asset replacement. The profits transferred to the reserve are represented by various types of funds within the company. The transfer will reduce the amount that the directors consider to be available for a dividend and thus help to conserve funds within the business.

Legally, the amounts transferred to the asset replacement reserve will (subject to the company's articles) be available for a dividend. The company is simply dividing profits between those considered to be available for distribution now, and those which will be available later. If the company wishes to provide cash out of current operations for the asset replacement, it should set the actual cash aside each year (e.g. by external investment) so that a sufficient amount is accumulated over the next four years.

Chapter 13

Case study for self-assessment

Overload Ltd

Name
Address

Dear Mrs Firty

re: Overload Ltd

Thank you for consulting me in respect of the above, and I hope that you found our initial meeting helpful. I have now carried out an analysis of the financial statements for year ending 31 December 1996 and my report on these is set out hereunder. The ratios to which I refer are summarized in a separate schedule attached to this report.

1. Value of the business

I realize you have not asked me to advise you on the price you should pay for the shares, but since the information in my report is directed towards helping you in this respect, I feel obliged to include some comment. I am mainly concerned to clarify your friend's comments regarding the value of the business, and have two initial points to make:

(a) Balance sheets are not drawn up in order to show what a business is worth. For example, the amount shown for fixed assets is based on what the company originally paid for these assets several years ago, less amounts that have been written off against profit. This procedure is used in order to measure the profit, not to value the assets.

(b) Your friend has referred to the wrong figure when saying the balance sheet shows a value of £145,000. This figure is before deducting the loan of £58,350, which the company has regarded as part of its capital. This loan is repayable in 1994 and the balance sheet value of net assets (total assets less all liabilities) is £86,650.

In negotiating a price for the business, you really need to think of the total amount paid as an investment which earns a return in the form of profits. If you use this idea as a basis you need to determine the rate of return you are looking for on your investment, and also estimate the amount of profit that the company is likely to generate in the near future.

If you use the latest profit as a starting point you will see that after interest payments this amounts to £29,000. If you are looking for a 32% return (the industry average) on your investment, this profit represents 32% of £90,625. I merely put this to you as an example of how you might be able to value the business; you will have to take account of my later comments regarding maintainable future profits. It might also be preferable to base your valuation on projected future cash flows rather than profits.

2. Growth

The company enjoyed substantial growth during 1996, having increased its turnover on the previous year by 45%. Even with inflation rates in the industry running at 6% there appears to be an increase in the volume of trade of 39%. The increase in turnover should, however, be viewed in the light of my comments below on the possibility that the company has stimulated sales by reducing prices and offering credit terms that are more generous than those offered by its competitors.

3. Return on capital

As mentioned earlier, this is a key factor in determining the price that you might wish to pay for the company. It is also a good indicator of the company's profitability. I have set out, on the attached schedule, the return on total capital for Overload Ltd but it is difficult to make a comparison with the industry average. I cannot be sure from the information provided whether the return shown for the industry has been calculated on the same basis as my figures.

Capital employed is quite often viewed from two different angles. Looked at from inside the business, capital is usually considered to be the total capital as represented by the proprietor's capital plus long-term debt. But a proprietor of the business would view the long-term debt as a liability rather than as a part of capital.

The proprietor's view of return on capital is usually referred to as the return on equity rather than the return on capital. I have included the return on equity in my schedule, but I suspect the industry average refers to the return on total capital. You should check with your cousin on this in order to be sure.

Your friend was quite right to point out that Overload Ltd was less profitable during 1996 but it is not the reduction in the bank balance (to which I shall refer later) that gives an indication of this, it is the fall in return on capital. You will see from my schedule that the company suffered a serious reduction in its return on capital during 1996 when compared with the previous year. This reduction is almost entirely due to the trading factors to which I refer in Section 4 of my report.

You must, however, be cautious over how you interpret the return on capital in the case of a private company. The directors can obviously determine the amount of their remuneration and quite often this reflects a withdrawal of profit in addition to a payment for services. I have no information on the directors' remuneration and cannot tell whether the amount charged is reasonable for the services they provide.

4. Trading profitability

My analysis of the fall in return on capital for 1996 shows that it is almost entirely due to trading factors rather than arising from a less efficient use of the company's assets. You may be interested to learn how this kind of conclusion can be reached.

You will notice that the schedule produced by your cousin includes a ratio called 'asset turnover'. This reflects the relationship between net assets and turnover. This ratio tells us the value of sales produced by each £1 of net assets. For example, if you look at the industry average you can determine that each £1 of net assets produced £4 in sales. You will also see that the percentage of profit on sales is 8% and so the amount of profit earned on sales of £4 would be 32 pence. This 32 pence has arisen from an investment of £1 in net assets; hence the return on capital being stated at 32%.

When the return on capital falls, this could arise from either a fall in the amount of sales produced by each £1 of net assets (a less efficient use of assets) or a fall in the amount of profit earned on each £1 of sales. In the case of Overload Ltd, you will see that there is a slight improvement in the asset to turnover ratio; in 1996 each £1 of net assets produced £4 in sales, whereas this was only £3.57 in 1995.

The fall in the company's net profit as a percentage of its turnover (from 8.25% to 6%) raises two serious questions that you should investigate further: a fall in the gross profit margin, and the ratio of expenses to sales.

As regards the fall in gross profit margin, there could be several explanations for this but I suspect that it results from a deliberate policy of price cutting in order to stimulate sales. This might explain the considerable growth in trade during 1996.

Unfortunately, the additional gross profit earned by the increased turnover has not resulted in very much by way of increased profits (from £28,000 in 1995 to £29,000 in 1996), mainly because the running costs have risen in step with the increased turnover. This seems rather strange since a fair proportion of these costs (staff salaries, office expenses, etc.) would not normally increase with an increase in the turnover.

This could be explained by the fact that these costs include a high proportion of costs that do vary with turnover, such as sales commissions and delivery expenses. It might also be explained by an increase in directors' remuneration, which, as suggested earlier, may have been increased in order to obtain a tax advantage. The expenses will also include a higher depreciation charge than in the previous year due to the additional fixed assets purchased.

When it comes to considering the price you will offer to acquire the company, you will have to estimate how much profit it is likely to generate in the future. I have set out a few pointers on this in Section 6 of this report.

5. Financial management

The company seems to have managed its affairs reasonably well during 1996. The current ratio is slightly less than the industry average. This is mainly a reflection of the longer period being taken by Overload Ltd to pay its creditors.

The trend in the debt collection period is not a good sign and requires further investigation. It could (as suggested earlier) be part of a deliberate policy to encourage trade, or may be an indication that the company is starting to accumulate bad debts. You really need to examine the debtors in more detail because if some have to be written off as bad, this will clearly affect any estimates of future profits and, therefore, the price you would pay for the company.

As regards the stock turnover ratio, I have converted the figure that your cousin provided into one that shows how many days (on average) stock is held before being sold. Unfortunately, the stock used for this ratio might be different to those in my calculations. The ratio is sometimes calculated on average stock (average of opening and closing stock) and sometimes on closing stock. I have set out both calculations on the schedule. You will notice that the company is holding its stock for a much shorter period than the average within the industry. This suggests that stocks have not been acquired too far in advance of anticipated demand.

You might be concerned with the increase in this ratio between 1995 and 1996 (from 30 days to 45 days) but this quite often happens during a period of rapid expansion. It is a point that needs watching, but since the company seems to be operating well within the industry average, it should not be the cause of too much alarm.

The expansion of trade during 1996 has involved the company in making additional investment in fixed assets and working capital. The effect that this has had on the company's cash resources is shown on the cash flow statement included with this report. With regard to the purchase of additional fixed assets, the cash flow statement shows that something like 44% was financed through an additional loan; the remaining 56% came from internal sources (cash from profits and a reduction in cash holding levels).

The increase in net working capital by the end of 1996 is very much in line with the increase in trade for that year. At the end of 1995 the net amount invested in stocks, debtors and creditors was 10 pence for each £1 of sales; at the end of 1996 the amount was 11.6 pence. This increase is related to the extension of debt collection and stock holding periods.

There is no need to be too concerned with the fall in the bank balance (you will notice I have excluded it from my working capital analysis in the previous paragraph). Most businesses try to keep their cash balance as low as possible because it is uneconomical to hold large amounts of uninvested cash. In any case, the balance sheet only shows the balance of cash at a particular date, and cash balances are subject to many peaks and troughs resulting from factors that fall outside of the day-to-day trading transactions. You will see some examples of these in the cash flow statement.

The gearing ratio supplied by the association does not state how it has been calculated. There are different interpretations of the gearing ratio. I suspect the ratio given is the ratio of long-term loans to total capital. If you compare the gearing ratio of Overload Ltd with the industry average you will notice that a higher proportion of its total capital is in the form of loans. However, interest payments are adequately covered by profits and there seems to be ample security for the loan.

6. Profit forecasts and general points

In assessing future profits, you will need to consider the role played in the business by the two brothers. If they are going to retire following your acquisition of their shares, you should try to assess the likely impact this will have on the company's profits. There are at least two factors to think about in this respect: (1) customer loyalty, and (2) management salaries.

It could be that the reputation of the firm rests largely on the skills and personality of the two directors, and there might be a loss of trade should they depart. On the other hand, it is quite likely that the cost of employing a manager to take their place will be less than the amount currently being charged for directors' remuneration.

I trust you will find this report helpful in your negotiations. Should you require any further assistance, or should any points in my report not be clear to you, please do not hesitate to get in touch.

Yours faithfully,

Schedule of ratios attached to the report

Overload Ltd	1995	1996	Industry
Return on total capital employed	29.5%	24%	32% (see Section 3)
Return on equity	45%	33.5%	? (see Section 3)
Asset turnover	3.57	4	4
Gross profit margin	25%	22%	24%
Expense to sales ratio	16.75%	16%	not given
Net profit to sales margin	8.25%	6%	8%
Stock turnover cycle:			
using average stock	29 days	33 days	50 days (see Section 5)
using closing stock	30 days	45 days	
Debt collection period	34 days	42 days	36 days
Creditor payment period	26 days	42 days	30 days
Current ratio	2.67:1	2.05:1	2.8:1
Net working capital (stocks, debtors and creditors) for each £1 sales	10 pence	11.6 pence?	(not given)
Gearing ratio			
debt to total capital	45%	40%	35% (see Section 5)
debt to equity	80%	67%	

Guidance notes: The net working capital for each £1 of sales was calculated as follows: 1991 39,090/400,000; 1992 67,515/580,000. Conversion of the stock turnover ratio into days was simply 365/7.3.

Cash flow statement for year ending 31 December 1996

Net cash inflow from operating activities		15,210
Servicing of finance:		
Interest paid	5,835	
		(5,835)
Taxation		
Corporation tax paid		(4,200)
Capital expenditure		
Payment for the purchase of fixed assets		(19,025)
Net cash outflow before financing		(13,850)
Financing:		
Additional loan obtained		8,350
Decrease in cash and cash equivalents		(5,500)

13.1 Jane Winters

(a) Selected ratios

Description	Formula	A Ltd	B Ltd
1. Return on capital	$\dfrac{\text{Profit before interest}}{\text{Total assets less current liabilities}}$	10.91%	7.71%
2. Gross profit margin	$\dfrac{\text{Gross profit}}{\text{Sales}}$	25%	25%
3. Expense to sales ratio	$\dfrac{\text{Total expenses less interest}}{\text{Sales}}$	17.5%	17.3%
4. Net profit to sales	$\dfrac{\text{Profit before interest}}{\text{Sales}}$ *(Notice how Ratio 4 reconciles to Ratio 2 less Ratio 3.)*	7.5%	7.7%
5. Asset utilization (sales from £1 of assets)	$\dfrac{\text{Sales}}{\text{Total assets less current liabilities}}$	£1.45	£1.00
6. Stock turnover	$\dfrac{\text{Cost of sales}}{\text{Average stock}}$	6 times	3 times
7. Debtor collection period	$\dfrac{\text{Debtors} \times 365}{\text{Sales}}$	14 days	30 days
8. Creditor payment period	$\dfrac{\text{Creditors} \times 365}{\text{Purchases}}$	26 days	46 days
9. Capital gearing	$\dfrac{\text{Long-term debt}}{\text{Long-term debt plus equity}}$	27.27%	2.08%
10. Interest cover	$\dfrac{\text{Profit before interest}}{\text{Interest}}$	4	37

The above schedule gives ten ratios but only eight were requested. Others could include the current ratio (4:1 in both companies) and liquidity ratio (1:1 in A Ltd, 1.5:1 in B Ltd). DOG could be calculated by assuming that establishment expenses and administrative expenses are fixed expenses. On this basis the DOG for A Ltd is 2.83, and for B Ltd it is 2.73.

(b) The report to Jane Winters

The following points should be brought out in the report:

Context:
Discuss that an acquisition of 100% of the equity gives total control, whereas an acquisition of 40% would be classed as a minority interest. A 40% interest might give Jane effective control if the remaining shares are widely dispersed, but can only guarantee giving her the ability to exercise significant influence over the company.

Profitability:

The return on capital is quite low in both companies. In A Ltd it is barely more than the 10% being paid on the loan capital, in B Ltd it is substantially less than the rate of interest. On the face of it, Jane could probably earn as much (if not more) from her inheritance by investing it in long-term debenture stocks. Such an investment would carry less risk than either of the two proposals.

As it stands, if Jane is looking for a return of say 20% on her investment, the business of A Ltd is worth only (£12,000/0.2) £60,000 compared to a book value of £110,000. On the same basis the total worth of B Ltd is (£18,500/0.2) £92,500 compared to a book value of £240,000 (a 40% interest would be valued at around £37,000).

Although Jane might have some knowledge that leads her to think that profits can be improved, both proposals should be rejected if the asking price does not give her the return required.

Comparisons:

The lower profitability in B Ltd is mainly due to a less efficient use of assets (£1 of sales from each £1 of assets, compared to A Ltd's £1.45 of sales from each £1 of assets).

The debt collection period in A Ltd is considerably less than in B Ltd, suggesting that A Ltd has a higher proportion cash sales than B Ltd.

A Ltd carries a higher degree of financial risk than B Ltd due to its higher gearing level, but interest cover in A Ltd is adequate.

Caution:

Conclusions should not be drawn from the results of a single year.

Chapter 14

14.1 Splendor and Grass

(a) Journal entries
(i) Working in stages, the journal entries could be as follows:

	Debit	Credit
Sales	3,500	
Disposal of fixed assets		3,500

Being adjustment for sales proceeds of van credited to sales in error.

	Debit	Credit
Provision for depreciation on vans	1,000	
Selling and distribution expenses		1,000

Being the elimination of depreciation charged in the year on van sold.

	Debit	Credit
Provision for depreciation on vans	5,000	
Disposal of fixed assets		5,000

Being elimination of depreciation provision (as adjusted) on van sold.

	Debit	Credit
Sale of fixed assets	10,000	
Motor vans – cost		10,000

Being the elimination of the cost of van sold.

	Debit	Credit
Selling and distribution expenses	1,500	
Disposal of fixed assets		1,500

Being loss on sale now transferred to the expense account.

(ii) In the following answer, the net effect of both errors has been adjusted.

Suspense account	30,000	
Sales		15,000
Purchases		15,000

Being correction to incorrect netting off for goods returned, as follows:

Deduction from purchases for goods returned	54,000
Actual cost of goods returned to suppliers	69,000
Amount under-deducted	15,000
Deducted from sales for goods returned	69,000
Actual sales price of goods returned	54,000
Amount over-deducted	15,000

(iii) Net realizable value is greater than cost and so the cost price should be used. The 25% mark up amounts to £37,500 and must be eliminated. It is assumed that closing stock in the balance sheet was also shown at selling price (if this assumption is wrong, and it was shown at cost, the credit entry would be to the suspense account and not to closing stock.

Cost of sales	37,500	
Closing stock		37,500

Being reduction of closing stock to cost.

(iv) This item should be treated as drawings

Drawings – Splendor	1,500	
Finance charges		1,500

Being correction of a private expense of Splendor which was treated as an expense.

(v) Two corrections are required, one for the prepayment and one for the debtor in respect of the overpayment:

Sundry debtors (landlord)	2,500	
Prepayments	500	
Administration expenses		3,000

Being correction for overpayment to landlord, and prepayment in respect of rent charges for year ended 31 December 1988.

(b) Corrected revenue statement for year ended 31 December 19X8

Sales (2,000,000 – 3,500 + 15,000)		2,011,500
Cost of goods sold (1,350,000 – 15,000 + 37,500)		1,372,500
Gross profit		639,000
Administration expenses (245,000 – 3,000)	242,000	
Selling and distribution expenses		
(135,000 – 1,000 + 1,500)	135,500	
Finance charges (80,000 – 1,500)	78,500	
		456,000
Net profit		183,000
Appropriated as follows:		
Interest on capital:		
Splendor	9,000	
Grass	5,400	
		14,400

Balance		168,600
Shared as follows:		
Splendor (3/5ths)	101,160	
Grass (2/5ths)	67,440	
		168,600

(c) Partners' current accounts:

Splendor's current account

Drawings	60,000	Balance b/d	25,000
Finance charges	1,500	P & L appropriation a/c:	
Balance c/d	73,660	interest on capital	9,000
		share of balance	101,160
	135,160		135,160

Grass's account

Drawings	42,000	Balance b/d	19,000
Balance c/d	49,840	P & L appropriation a/c:	
		interest on capital	5,400
		share of balance	67,440
	91,840		91,840

Tutorial note: The absence of balance sheet details makes it difficult to prove the accuracy of your work. A rough reconciliation can be done as follows:

The net assets prior to error correction would have equalled the profit for the year plus capital accounts and current accounts, less drawings.

Profit	190,000
Capital accounts	160,000
Current accounts	44,000
Drawings accounts	(102,000)
	292,000

But these will have included a suspense account that showed a credit balance of £30,000, and so the actual net assets would be (292 + 30) £322,000. Following the correction of errors, the net assets would be:

Original net assets	322,000
Elimination of van (in books at 5,000 – 1,000)	(4,000)
Reduction of stock	(37,500)
Debtor and prepayments added	3,000
Revised net assets after corrections	283,500

At the end of the period, the partners' equity is as follows:

Capital accounts		160,000
Current accounts (as in (c) above)		
Splendor	73,660	
Grass	49,840	
		123,500
		283,500

Chapter 15

15.1 Alpha, Beta and Gamma
(a) (i) Capital accounts

	Alpha	Beta	Gamma
Balances brought forward	30,000	25,000	–
Loan account transferred			20,000
Land and buildings revaluation	12,000	12,000	
Goodwill adjustment (see below)	2,000	2,000	(4,000)
Balances carried forward	44,000	39,000	16,000
Goodwill adjustment:			
Old profit sharing ratio	3/6	3/6	nil
New profit sharing ratio	2/6	2/6	2/6
Goodwill relinquished/(acquired)	1/6	1/6	(2/6)

(ii) Current accounts (completed after preparing appropriation account)

Balances brought forward	3,000	4,000
Salary	4,000	
Share of profits	8,000	8,000
Drawings	(4,000)	(5,000)
Balances carried forward	11,000	7,000

(Gamma was not a partner during 1989)

(iii) Profit and loss account, year ending 31 December 1989

Sales (200 – 6)		194,000
Cost of sales (see below)		107,000
Gross profit		87,000
Expenses:		
Operating expenses	64,000	
Loan interest (0.1 × 30)	3,000	
		67,000
Net profit		20,000
Appropriations:		
Salary Alpha		4,000
		16,000
Balance Alpha	8,000	
Beta	8,000	
		16,000

Cost of sales: closing stock should be increased by (2 × £1,000) £2,000, giving a closing stock of £26,000. Cost of sales is then 30,000 + 103,000 – 26,000 = £107,000.

(iv) Balance sheet at 31 December 1989

	Cost	Dep	NBV
Fixed assets:			
Land and buildings at valuation			84,000
Plant and machinery	70,000	40,000	30,000
			114,000

Current assets:

Stock (as adjusted)	26,000	
Debtors (40 – 6)	34,000	
	60,000	

Current liabilities:

Creditors and accruals (33 + 3)	36,000	
Bank overdraft	11,000	
		47,000
		13,000
		127,000

Partners' equity and loan capital	Alpha	Beta	Gamma	
Capital accounts	44,000	39,000	16,000	99,000
Current accounts	11,000	7,000	–	18,000
Loan account		10,000		10,000
	65,000	46,000	16,000	127,000

(b) The note to Gamma should include the following points: The two adjustments relate to the capital gains that accrued prior to his admission into the partnership. The increase in value of freehold property that has been credited to the former partners arose prior to 31 December 1989 and is attributable to the period when the business was owned by the former partners. The goodwill adjustment reflects the fact that this asset is valued (at 31 December 1989) at £12,000 but is being carried in the balance sheet at a value of zero. If the asset were realized subsequent to Gamma's admission, Gamma would be credited with one-third of the sale proceeds since the whole proceeds would represent a capital gain. Yet £12,000 of these proceeds should really be shared by Alpha and Beta since it represents the goodwill built up during their period of ownership. The adjustment recognizes that Gamma must pay for the right to share in this £12,000.

15.2 ABC partnership
(a) Journal entries

	Debit	Credit
(i) Drawings – Partner A	600	
Provision for depreciation (MV)	4,000	
Profit and loss (loss on transfer)	400	
Cost of motor vehicles (MV)		5,000
(ii) Suspense account	2,000	
Purchase ledger control		2,000
(iii) Sales ledger control	300	
Sales		300
(iv) Purchase ledger control	50	
Purchase returns		50

(v) No entry required (correct the memorandum record)

	Debit	Credit
(vi) Motor vans	231	
Prepayments	123	
Suspense		354

(vii) No journal entry required. If the balances are listed on the correct side, the suspense account will require an adjustment of £850 credit. This will reduce or increase the suspense account depending on whether it was originally a credit or debit balance.

(b) Advice regarding payment for goodwill

The senior partner was correct to object to the treatment, providing the asset for goodwill had not been written into the books at its value when the new partner was admitted. Since the payment by the new partner is described as being 'for goodwill' it would seem that the goodwill account has not been written up.

The reason for requiring the new partner to make a payment of £10,000 is that he (or she) is now a part-owner of the business and will share in all of its future gains, including capital gains. The £10,000 represents the new partner's share of the capital gain attributable to the period when the business was owned by the former partners. Since the new partner will be credited with this should the asset be realized, it must be purchased from the former owners.

The £10,000 should be credited to the former partners, according to the shares which they have relinquished as a result of taking the new partner into the firm. This can be demonstrated by assuming the following facts.

Value of goodwill in the books = zero.

New partner's share = 1/2. Value of goodwill on admission is, therefore, £20,000.

Former partners shared profits equally and will be on an equal profit sharing basis following the admission of C.

	A	B	C
Old profit sharing ratio	2/4	2/4	
New profit sharing ratio	1/4	1/4	2/4
Share relinquished	1/4	1/4	
Share acquired			2/4

Since both A and B are giving up equal shares, the payment of £10,000 should be credited to them in equal shares. Partner C should notice that if the goodwill were sold for £20,000, there would be a capital gain of £20,000 and he (or she) would be credited with one-half of this, i.e. £10,000. A and B would only be credited with £5,000 each for an asset valued at £20,000 which they created. But since they have already been credited with £5,000 each following C's payment, they are not at a disadvantage.

15.3 Stonehouse Ltd acquiring the business of Keir Don
(a) Valuation of consideration offered

25,000 Ordinary £1 shares with a fair value of £3.20 each	80,000
£5,000 12% Debentures 1999 at par	5,000
Cash	8,000
	93,000

(b) Difference between fair value of consideration offered and fair value of net assets acquired:

Fair value of 'separable' net assets acquired

Fixtures and fittings	89,000
Stock	20,000
	109,000
Less creditors	17,000
Net assets	92,000
Fair value of consideration	93,000
Difference	1,000

It is assumed that creditors taken over by Stonehouse Ltd are the trade creditors only, and do not include the long-term liabilities.

(c) The difference relates to goodwill. Stonehouse Ltd would have agreed a price for the business based on its earning potential. This price would have taken account of the fact that the business of Keir Don should, because of its established reputation and position, be able to maintain a certain level of profits. Since the price offered exceeds the fair value of the separable net assets acquired, an amount is being paid for the goodwill of the business.

It will be treated as an asset in the books of Stonehouse Ltd until it is dealt with according to SSAP 22.

(d) Balance sheet of Stonehouse Ltd, following take-over and rights issue

Workings:

Share capital:	Number	Nominal value	Share premium
Opening balance	75,000	75,000	nil
Rights issue	25,000	25,000	43,750
Issue to Keir Don	25,000	25,000	55,000
Revised balance	125,000	125,000	98,750
Less share issue expenses written off			3,300
			95,450

Bank balance:	
Opening balance	(2,500)
Received on rights issue	68,750
Share issue expenses	(3,300)
Paid to Keir Don	(8,000)
Closing balance	54,950

Balance sheet:

Fixed assets

Goodwill	1,000
Freehold premises at cost	100,000
Fixtures and fittings (35,000 + 89,000)	124,000
11% Debenture loan stock in Brickland Ltd	12,000
	237,000

Current assets

Stock (48,300 + 20,000)	68,300
Debtors	8,700
Bank	54,950
	131,950

Creditors: falling due within one year

Creditors (39,500 + 17,000)	56,500	
		75,450
Total assets less current liabilities		312,450

Creditors: falling due after more than one year

Long-term liabilities	15,000	
12% Debentures 1999	5,000	
		20,000
		292,450

Capital and reserves

125,000 Ordinary shares of £1 each	125,000
Share premium account (working)	95,450
Reserves	72,000
	292,450

(The mistake in the question as set was to describe 'total assets less current liabilities' as 'net current assets'.)

(e) In a rights issue, existing shareholders are invited to subscribe for shares at a price which is less than the current market price of the shares. It is therefore a means of raising additional cash. A bonus issue is the capitalization of existing reserves. The shares are issued as fully paid and no cash is received by the company.

Chapter 16

16.1 Viewpoint Chamber Orchestra

(a) Income statement for concert performances, year ended 31 July 1988

Concert income:

Ticket sales			1,980
Programme sales			320
			2,300

Concert expenses:

Conductors' and soloists' fees		780	
Hire of music (970 + 170)		1,140	
Hire of halls (1,200 + 140)		1,340	
Cost of music scores:			
Opening stock	1,700		
Purchases	850		
	2,550		
Closing stock	2,250		
		300	
Depreciation of music stands		35	
			3,595
Loss on concert performances			1,295

(b) Income and expenditure account for year ended 31 July 1988

Income:

Donations received	550
Subscriptions	1,175
Investment income	300
Fund raising	970
	2,995
Less loss on concert performances	1,295
	1,700

Expenditure:

Secretary's honorarium	550	
Administration expenses	1,100	
		1,650
Excess of income over expenditure		50

Workings for the balance sheet:

1. The opening general fund is represented by

Bank balance	1,130
Subscriptions in arrears (Working 2)	100
Music stands	235
Music scores	1,700
Investments	3,200
	6,365

2. The position regarding subscriptions is as follows:

Subscriptions received were		1,375
Less relating to the previous year	100	
relating to current year	1,125	
		1,225
Received in advance for year ending 31 July 1989		150
Subscriptions due for current year (47 × £25)		1,175
Less received per bank account		1,125
Subscriptions in arrears for current year		50

Balance sheet at 31 July 1988

Long-term assets:

Investments	3,200	
Music scores	2,250	
Music stands	200	
		5,650

Current assets:

Bank balance	1,175	
Subscriptions in arrears	50	
	1,225	

Cretitors due within one year

Creditors (170 + 140)	310	
Subscriptions in advance	150	
		460
		765
		6,415

Accumulated general fund:

Balance at 1 August 1987	6,365
Excess of income over expenditure	50
Balance at 31 July 1988	6,415

16.2 Happy Tickers Sports and Social Club

(a) Profit on café operations

Café takings		4,660
Opening stock	800	
Purchases (1,900 + 80)	1,980	
	2,780	
Closing stock	850	
		1,930
Gross surplus		2,730
Café manager's wages		2,000
Profit		730

Profit on sales of sports equipment

Sales of new equipment	900
Cost of equipment sold (100/150 × 900)	600
Profit	300

Additional workings:

1. Closing stock of new equipment for the balance sheet:

Opening stock (new equipment)	1,000
One-half of purchases	500
	1,500
Deduct cost of sales (as above)	600
Closing stock	900

2. Cost of sports equipment consumed:

Opening stock of used equipment	700
Purchases of new equipment for club use (1/2 of 1,000)	500
	1,200
Closing stock of used equipment at valuation	700
	500
Less cash received from sales	14
	486

(b) Subscription income for 1990

Annual subscriptions (120 + 1,100 + (4 × 20))	1,300
Life subscriptions (10 + 1) × £20	220
	1,520

Additional workings:

1. Subscriptions to be written off:

Owing at 31 December 1989	60
1989 subscriptions received during 1990	40
To be written off (owing for more than 12 months)	20

2. Deferred income for the balance sheet:
Life subscriptions (1,400 + 200 – 220)   1,380

(c) Income and expenditure statement, year ending 31 December 1990

Income:

Subscription income	1,520	
Profit on sale of new sports equipment	300	
Profit from café operations	730	
	2,550	

Expenses:

Rent (1,200 – 200 + 200)	1,200		
Insurance (900 – 150 – 150)	600		
Subscription arrears written off	20		
Sports equipment consumed	486		
Roller repairs (450 – 225)	225		
Depreciation of roller (1,000 × 0.1)	100		
		2,631	
Excess of expenses over income		81	

Balance sheet at 31 December 1990

Long-term assets:

Half interest in roller at net book value (600 – 100)	500	

Current assets:

Cafe stocks	850	
Stock of used sports equipment	700	
Stock of new sports equipment	90	
Subscriptions due for 1990	80	
Due from Carefree Conveyancers	225	
Rent prepaid	200	
Insurance prepaid	150	
Bank balance (1,210 + 6,994 – 7,450)	754	
	3,859	

Creditors due within one year:

Cafe suppliers	80	
Subscriptions prepaid	80	
		160
		3,699
		4,199

Deferred income:

Life subscriptions carried forward to future years	1,380
	2,819

Accumulated fund:

Balance at 1 January 1990	2,900
Less excess of expenses over income for the year	81
	2,819

(d) Life subscriptions do not appear as a **liability** in the balance sheet; they are presented as deferred income. They only look like a liability in the question because the balance sheet there has been badly prepared. The credit balance represents income which is being carried forward to be treated as income in future years.

Chapter 17

17.1 Keith Maltby

Tutorial note: In this kind of question some time can be saved by including only key totals in the 'Total' column. You will not earn full marks by doing this, but you will pass the exam with good marks. This approach has been adopted in the following answer.

Profit and loss account for year ended 31 March 1987

	Cafe		Shop		Total
Turnover		36,791		27,430	64,221
Cost of sales:					
Opening stock	1,272		303		
Purchases			30,432		
Transfer	19,427		(19,427)		
Closing stock	(3,513)		(1,774)		
		17,186		9,534	26,720
Gross profit		19,605		17,896	37,501
Enterprise grant		1,000			1,000
Rent received			(660 +60)	720	720
		20,605		18,616	39,221
Expenses:					
Rent (note 1)			3,200		
Employment costs:					
Manageresses	4,200		3,900		
Assistants	2,100		900		
Electricity	2,005		929		
Telephone	209		411		
Stationery			126		
Cleaning materials	85		76		
Wrapping materials	62		69		
Loan interest	700				
Overdraft interest			37		
Rates	2,943		1,864		
General expenses	651		824		
Office allowance	400 (2/3)		200 (1/3)		
Depreciation:					
Premises	380				
Fixtures	590				
Vehicles			1,000		
		14,325		13,536	27,861
Profit		6,280		5,080	11,360
Commission (10%)		628		508	1,136
Net profit		5,652		4,572	10,224

Workings have not been presented. Most of the figures are taken from the list of balances and adjustments made for opening and closing balances (accruals, prepayments, stocks).

Balance sheet at 31 March 1987

	Café	Shop	Total
Fixed assets:			
Premises at cost	25,000		
Depreciation	6,380		
	18,620		
Fixtures at cost	7,500		
Depreciation	2,190		
	5,310		
Vehicles at cost		6,000	
Depreciation		2,000	
		4,000	
Total NBV	23,930	4,000	27,930
Current assets:			
Stocks:			
Food	3,513	1,774	
Cleaning materials	30	24	
Wrapping materials	10	12	
	3,553	1,810	
Debtors:			
Trade	1,312		
Rent receivable		60	
Grant due	5,000		
Rent prepaid		800	
Cash	109	155	
	9,974	2,825	12,799
Creditors due within one year:			
Creditors:			
Food		4,582	
Others	15	6	
Office allowance		600	
Commission	628	508	
Accruals	177	146	
Bank overdraft		2,209	
	820	8,051	8,871
Net assets (liabilities)	33,084	(1,226)	31,858
Long-term loan			(7,000)
Deferred income			(4,000)
			20,858
Capital account			9,000
Current account	(1,634 + 10,224)		11,858
			20,858

17.2 Geotrad Ltd

(a) Trading and profit and loss account for year ended 31 May 1989

	Head office	Branch
Sales	1,800,000	300,000
Cost of goods sold	1,050,000	190,000
Gross profit	750,000	110,000
Variable expenses:		
As given (300 + 4.5) 304,500	(35 + 1.9) 36,900	
Sales commission (wkng) 8,000	300	
Fixed expenses:		
As given (150 – 2.8) 147,200	(5 – 1) 4,000	
Apportioned to branch (90,000)	90,000	
	369,700	131,200
Operating profit or (loss)	380,300	(21,200)

Workings:

Sales commissions: Head office 2% of (£1,800,000 – £1,400,000) = £8,000; Branch 3% of (£300,000 – £290,000) = £300. Note that stock in transit has no effect on the reported results of either head office or branch. The information is only required for part (c) of the question. If it were to be brought in as a purchase by the branch, it would also be included as stock at the branch and so the net effect on cost of sales would be nil.

(b)(i) Contribution from the branch:

Gross profit (as above)		110,000
Variable expenses (36,900 + 300)	37,200	
Fixed expenses at the branch	4,000	
		41,200
Contribution		68,800

(ii) Brief report

On the basis of the current figures, the branch is contributing £68,800 to the fixed costs incurred by Geotrad Ltd's head office. The net loss of the branch is shown as £21,200 because £90,000 of head office costs have been apportioned to the branch. The branch should be closed down only if by doing so the head office fixed costs will be reduced by more than £68,800.

(c) (i) Stocks should be valued at the total of the lower of cost and net realizable value for the different categories of stock.

(ii) At 31 May 1989, the total value of stock for the whole firm is:

Cost of stock at head office	50,000
Cost of stock at branch	8,000
Cost of stock in transit	11,000
Total	69,000

Chapter 18

18.1 Atom/Neutron/Proton Ltd

(a) Proton Ltd. Profit and loss appropriation account, year ended 31 December 1989

Net profit		90,000
Transfer to general reserve	50,000	
Proposed dividends	7,500	
		57,500
Profit for the year retained		32,500
Retained earnings at 1 January 1989		20,000
Retained earnings at 31 December 1989		52,500

(b) Revised balance sheet for Atom Ltd at 31 January 1990

Fixed assets less depreciation (360,000 – 50,000)		310,000
Investments:		
25,000 shares in Neutron Ltd at cost (20,000 + 20,000)		40,000
45,000 shares in Proton Ltd at cost (60,000 + 45,000)		105,000
Current assets (Working 1)	372,500	
Creditors due within one year	170,000	
		202,500
		657,500
Capital and reserves		
Share capital: 50p ordinary shares fully paid		150,000
Share premium		100,000
General reserve		120,000
Retained earnings (Working 2)		287,500
		657,500

Workings:

1. Current assets:

at 31 December 1989 – per question	250,000	
less cost of stock sold	15,000	
	235,000	
add: sale proceeds of stock	2,500	
sale proceeds of land and buildings	200,000	
	437,500	
less cost of investments (20,000 + 45,000)	65,000	
	372,500	

2. Retained earnings:

at 31 December 1989 – per question	150,000	
loss on sale of stock (15,000 – 2,500)	12,500	
	137,500	
profit on sale of land (200,000 – 50,000)	150,000	
	287,500	

(c) Definition of a subsidiary:

A subsidiary is a company whose operational and financial policies are controlled by another company, its parent company. This control by the parent company is derived from powers that enable it to control the decisions made by the board of directors of the subsidiary, usually through holding more than 50% of the voting capital. The meaning of a subsidiary has been extended by the 1989 Companies Act so as to include companies which, hitherto, would have been classed as controlled non-subsidiaries.

(d) The only relevant information available in the question is the number of shares owned by Atom in each of the other two companies. On this basis, the two investments represent the following interests at 31 January 1990:

> in Neutron Ltd (25,000/90,000) 28% (approx.)
> in Proton Ltd (45,000/75,000) 60%

Based on these calculations, Neutron will be classified as an associated company (requiring disclosure as a participating interest), and Proton is a subsidiary.

(e) Comment:

The information given for Proton's return on capital does not reconcile to the facts in the question. If the return on Proton's total assets is 25%, the profit for 1989 should be (25% of £380,000) £95,000 and yet the net profit is given as £90,000 (i.e. 25% of £360,000).

Tutorial notes:

The return on capital employed is the primary indicator of a company's operating performance and is clearly of interest to an investor, particularly in a private company. However, investment decisions quite frequently centre around the relationship between share prices and the earnings of the company concerned. Investors usually watch two indicators, both of which are based on the company's earnings, namely: the earnings yield, and the price/earnings ratio.

The earnings yield simply expresses a company's total earnings as a percentage of the total market value of the shares. The price/earnings ratio is found by dividing the price per share by the earnings per share (see Chapter 13).

The utility of these two ratios is related to the observed fact that there is usually a very strong correlation between a company's earnings and the share price. Any increase in earnings is usually followed by a relative increase in the share price so that the relationship between price and earnings remains relatively static. Where share prices change as a result of some influence other than earnings (such as rumours of a take-over bid) there will be a noticeable change in these two ratios. This attracts the interest of investors and leads to increased market activity for the share concerned.

Consequently, these two ratios (as with most ratios) will provide useful information only when they are compared to the same ratio at an earlier time in the same company, or compared to the same ratio in another company operating in the same line of business.

In the case of this examination question, there is insufficient data to make a comparison with earlier periods in the same company. But on the assumption that Neutron and Proton are operating in the same line of business, we can approach the question in the following manner:

Answer:

Neutron Ltd:
The profits earned by this company during 1989 amount to (5% × £210,000) £10,500. If the profit of £10,500 is expressed as a percentage of the total market value of the shares at 31 January 1990 (90,000 × £2) the earnings yield is 5.8%. This is clearly very low (by comparison with Proton) and raises questions as to why the share market is able to demand a price of £2 per share. There must be something other than earnings that is having an influence on the share price; for example, is there an impending take-over bid?

The earnings per share for 1989 are (£10,500/90,000) 11.67 pence. The price/earnings ratio (P/E ratio) at 31 January 1990 is then (200/11.67) = 17 to 1. An investor would compare this to the P/E ratio in similar companies and with earlier P/E ratios for the same company in order to judge whether the share is over-priced or under-priced in relation to the company's earnings. The only company we can compare it to is Proton Ltd (see below), where the P/E ratio is 3.75 to 1. This raises the same question: what factors other than earnings are having an influence on the price which can be demanded for these shares?

It is just possible that the price of £2.00 per share was struck on the basis of false hopes regarding the 1989 profits, but this seems unlikely since draft accounts for 1989 would have been available by 30 January 1990. Atom Ltd would have made a fairly careful investigation of Neutron's profits before entering into a transaction to purchase a further 10,000 shares at £2 each. (I doubt if the examiner was expecting us to assume the directors of Atom were stupid!)

Proton Ltd:
If the market is valuing Proton's shares at £4.50 per share, the total market value is £337,500. The earnings yield is therefore (£90,000/£337,500 × 100/1) 26.66%.

The earnings per share are (£90,000/75,000) 120 pence per share. The P/E ratio is therefore (450/120) 3.75 to 1.

In the situation presented by the question, the only significance that these indicators have is that they provide a yardstick against which it is possible to compare the same indicators for Neutron.

Further tutorial notes: In the case of take-overs, and the ownership of a controlling interest in another company, it is necessary to take account of the unusual circumstances when trying to interpret information given in the form of accounting ratios. For example:

1. Market prices are somewhat volatile during a take-over bid and the price of £4.50 might have been influenced by the impending bid by Atom to acquire the controlling interest.
2. Where one company controls another, the return on capital employed in the controlled company can be misleading. For example, if a manufacturer is able to control the operations of a supplier of raw materials, it can dictate the price at which these materials are purchased. This power could be used to enhance the profits earned by the parent company at the expense of the subsidiary's profits. In the case of groups, it is more useful to base the calculation for return on capital on the group accounts, not on the accounts of individual companies within the group.

18.2 Apple and Blackbury

Consolidated balance sheet at 1 January 1993

Fixed assets at net book value	294,300
Investments	4,000
Net current assets	50,400
	348,700
10% Debenture 2010	30,000
	318,700
Called up share capital	200,000
Profit and loss account (workings)	60,300
	260,300
Minority interests (workings)	58,400
	318,700

Workings:
Goodwill arising on consolidation:

Blackbury Ltd's net assets at date of acquisition (176,000 – 30,000)	146,000
Less minority interests share (32,000 shares = 40%)	58,400
Apple Ltd's share of net assets at date of acquisition	87,600
Amount paid for the investment	90,000
Goodwill	2,400
Profit and loss account – Apple Ltd	62,700
Less goodwill (above) written off	2,400
Balance	60,300

Chapter 19

19.1 Morrison Hill plc

(a) This treatment would not be acceptable to the auditors because it contravenes the provisions in SSAP 13. Expenditure on fixed assets that provide facilities for research and/or development must be capitalized (treated as fixed assets) and written off over the useful lives of the assets concerned, in the same way as any fixed asset which has a finite life.

In this particular case the expenditure on buildings will have to be separated from the expenditure on equipment, so that depreciation can be based on the useful life of each type of asset. The depreciation charge in the profit and loss account should be included as part of research and development costs written off during the year. The amount of this depreciation will also have to be included in the total of depreciation charges disclosed in the notes in order to comply with the disclosure requirements under the 1985 Companies Act.

(b) SSAP 17 describes post-balance sheet events as those events, both favourable and unfavourable, which occur between the balance sheet date and the date when the financial statements are approved by the directors. The destruction of stock by fire on 2 May 1990 is clearly such an event.

Financial statements are prepared on the basis of conditions that existed at the balance sheet date. Post-balance sheet events will fall to be treated as either adjusting events (requiring a change of the figures) or a non-adjusting event (requiring disclosure in the notes) depending on whether or not the event provides additional evidence of conditions existing at the balance sheet date.

In this case, the condition at the balance sheet date was that the company owned stock which had a cost of £35,000. The event on 2 May 1990 does not alter this condition, and so it should be treated as a non-adjusting event. If the amount is considered to be material, it should be disclosed by way of a note.

(c) This particular treatment might be acceptable to the auditors, although the company could treat the £15,000 as a prior year adjustment by restating the accumulated profits brought forward. The effects on previous years resulting from a change of accounting policy (clearly the case here) are permitted to be treated as prior year adjustments by FRS 3.

In this case the amount involved does not seem to be particularly material. Furthermore, by treating the £15,000 as a charge against the current year's profit the company is taking a prudent view, which might be persuasive in convincing the auditors to accept the treatment.

(d) The disclosure of earnings per share is regulated by SSAP 3 and FRS 3, which requires all listed companies to disclose earnings per share on the face of the profit and loss account. In this case, the company is a public company (plc) but there is no information as to whether its ordinary shares are dealt on a recognized stock exchange. There are many public companies that are not listed on any stock exchange. However, since the auditors must have queried the non-disclosure in the first place, it can be assumed that it is a listed company and the treatment of refusing to disclose the amount will not be acceptable.

(e) There is nothing in SSAP 12 to preclude companies from appropriating retained profits to an asset replacement reserve. In fact it is a prudent policy to do so.

SSAP 12 does, however, state that supplementary depreciation, namely that in excess of the depreciation based on the carrying amount of the assets, should not be charged in the profit and loss account. Providing the reserve has been built up by appropriations of retained profits, rather than by a charge in the profit and loss account, the auditors will accept the policy.

19.2 George and Margaret

Total estimated profit:

Contract price		£4.0m
Total costs (less those relating to Bridge B)		
Costs to date (2.8 – 0.1)	£2.7m	
Future costs to complete	£0.8m	
		3.5m
Estimated profit when completed		£0.5m

Attributable profit

(a) based on proportion of cost completed (2.7/3.5 × £0.5m) = £285,700 (approximately).
(b) based on the bridge being 80% complete (£0.5m × 0.8) = £400,000.
(c) based on proportion of sales value received in cash (3/4 × £0.5m) £375,000.

Discussion points should include:
Cash outflows and cash inflows are not relevant to profit measurements under the accruals convention. SSAP 9 requires attributable profit to be a proportion of total estimated profit. Prudence should be applied. This can be done by taking a conservative view of the costs needed to complete the bridge. Attributable profit under method (c) above can be considered to be in conflict with the accruals convention since it uses cash received as a basis (but it is more prudent than using the 80% basis). If the bridge is 80% complete, presumably revenue earned to date (certified value of work) is (£4.0m × 0.8) £3.2m; if this is compared to the costs incurred to date there appears to be a profit to date of (3.2 − 2.7) £0.5m. This suggests that no further profit will be earned during the final stages of the contract. SSAP 9 requires the inequalities of profit at the various stages to be smoothed; this is done by reporting attributable profit as a portion of total estimated profit. Method (a) is used by most companies (according to empirical studies). Attributable profit will have to be presented in the profit and loss account as turnover and cost of sales.

19.3 Gershwin plc

All five items in the question are related to the question of post-balance sheet events. It is, therefore, appropriate to provide a general description of the provisions in SSAP 17 as an introduction to your answer. It will then be easier to deal with each item because your answers can be seen to be in the context of the provisions stated in the introduction.

Introduction:
SSAP 17 describes post-balance sheet events as those events, both favourable and unfavourable, that occur between the balance sheet date and the date when the financial statements are approved by the directors.
   Financial statements are prepared on the basis of conditions that existed at the balance sheet date. Post-balance sheet events will fall to be treated as either adjusting events (requiring a change of the figures) or a non-adjusting event (requiring disclosure in the notes) depending on whether or not the event provides additional evidence of conditions existing at the balance sheet date.
   Post-balance sheet events of the non-adjusting type must also be disclosed in the 'directors' report' under provisions in the 1985 Companies Act.

(1) The loss of £10 million is clearly a non-adjusting event since the condition (loss through a strike) did not exist at 30 April 1989. The amount is clearly material (being 200% of the previous year's profit) and the event should be disclosed by way of a note, together with an explanation of the tax implications. The event must also be disclosed in the directors' report in order to comply with the 1985 Companies Act.
   In exceptional circumstances (not explained in Chapter 19) an event that would

otherwise be classified as non-adjusting may require changes to the financial statements in addition to disclosure. One of these is where the impact of the event is of such magnitude as to negate the application of the going concern concept. In this case, the loss of £10 million should be seen against the fact that the company's net assets are £400 million, and although the loss will cause the company severe problems, it is not likely to cause it to fail as a going concern.

(2) The discovery of this error is clearly an adjusting event since it affects conditions (the value of the stock) at 30 April 1989. The closing stock must be reduced by £2 million, and profit reduced by £2 million. Adjusting events do not require disclosure, they merely provide evidence in support of measurements used in the financial statements.

(3) This 'acquisition' of a subsidiary does not affect conditions existing at the balance sheet date and must be dealt with as a non-adjusting event. Acquisitions of subsidiaries after the balance sheet date comprise one of the examples given in SSAP 17 as an event that should normally be classified as a non-adjusting event.

(4) This event relates to an issue of shares after the balance sheet date and should be dealt with as a non-adjusting event. The success of the issue may be influenced by knowledge of the substantial loss of £10 million caused by the strike, but a discussion of this is beyond the requirements of the question.

(5) The notification of Porter Ltd's liquidation on 2 May 1989 is an adjusting event. The debt of £5,000 must be written off against profit for the year. Unless the amount is considered material (which does not seem likely with profit of (5 – 2) £3 million), no disclosure is required.

Index

completed contracts method 489
computers
    book-keeping 12-13, 58, 79, 104, 121-4
    errors 120
    examinations xii, 123
    suspense accounts 187-8
conservatism, *see* prudence
consistency concept 99, 512
consolidated accounts 462
contingent gains and losses 498-9
contra balances 188
contributed capital 45-6
contribution 438
contribution from owners 513
control accounts 115-118
controlled non-subsidiaries 465
conversion to limited company 397-9
corporate report, the 11
cost accounting 203
cost of sales 80
cost of stock 85
creative accounting 465, 515-6
credit purchases 88, 108-9
credit sales 88, 107-8
creditor payment period 345-6
cumulative preference shares 247
current assets 38
current ratio 347

day books 107
Dearing Committee 517
debenture redemption 315-6
debentures and loans
    issue 255
    total borrowing costs (FRS 4) 256-7
debit and credit 57-9
debtor collection period 345
debtor management 180
deferred credit 487
deferred income 422
degree of operational gearing 351-2
degree of financial gearing 352-3
departmental accounts 434-9
depreciation
    book-keeping 149-50
    definition 144
    general nature 35, 143-4
    methods 145-7, 495-6
    purpose 154
    revision of asset lives 492-3
DFG, *see* Degree of financial gearing
direct costs 435
direct labour 204
direct materials 204
direct method 289-90
disciplinary committees 9

discontinued activities 308-9, 356
discounts 177-9
distributable profit 316, 494
dividend yield 354
dividends 6, 242, 259
divisional activity 211-13
DOG, *see* degree of operational gearing
double-entry principle 37
doubtful debts 155-7
drawings 34-5

earnings per share 485-7
EC Seventh Directive 462
elements of financial statements 512-3
entity concept 4
EPS, *see* earnings per share
equity accounting 474
equity shareholders 247-8
error correction 61, 118-20
    see also, computers
error types 62
ethics 521-2
exceptional items 309-10
expenditure, expenses and costs 32
extended trial balance 160
external users, *see* User groups
extraordinary items 309-10

FIFO/LIFO/AVCO 86-8
finance charge 500
Financial Reporting Council 518
Financial Reporting Review Panel 518-9
Financial Reporting Standards,
    see Statements of Standard Accounting
        Practice
financial risk, *see* degree of financial gearing
Financial Times
    annual report service 9
    price earnings ratio 486
fixed assets
    adjustments on sale 150-3
    capitalised expenditure 154-5
    definition 38
    register 153
    revised asset life 492-4
    sale of 150-53
fixed cost 205, 437
forfeiture 252-3
format 1 (Companies Act) 329-31
FRC, *see* Financial Reporting Council
free cash flow xii, 282-7
FRRP, *see* Financial Reporting Review Panel
FRS, *see* Statements of Standard Accounting
        Practice
fundamental accounting concepts 91

primary ratio 339-41
primary recording 103-4
primary statements 311
prime cost 205
prior year adjustments 310
private companies 5
profit and loss ledger account 62-3
progress payments 491
prudence 83-4, 91, 512
public companies 5
purchase and redemption of own shares 313-5
purchase returns 121
purchases
    day book 108-10
    description 31
    ledger 114-5

qualitative characteristics 12, 503, 511-12
quasi-subsidiaries 465

raw materials consumed 205
realization account 395-7
realization principle 76
realized profit 494
recognition 513
redemption of loans 315-6
redemption of shares,
    see purchase and redemption of own shares
reducing balance method 146-7
registrar of companies 7
relevance 12, 511
reliability 12, 511
research and development costs 496-7
retained profits 39, 45, 261
return on capital employed,
    see primary ratio
revaluation of fixed assets 263-4, 494
revaluation reserve 263-4, 494
revenue expenditure 32
revenue recognition 88-89
revenue 33
revision of asset lives 492-4
rights issue 262
risk 334-5, 349-53
ROCE/ROI/RONA, *see* primary ratio
Royal Charter 416

sales
    day book 107
    description 30
    ledger 114-5
    returns 120
secondary ratios 342-5
settlement by contra 188
share certificate 243

share premium account
    nature of 245
    restricted use 263
shareholders 243
significant influence 474
sinking fund depreciation 495-6
small and medium sized companies 519
sole traders 3
SORP, *see* Statement of Recommended Practice
SSAPs, *see* Statements of Standard Accounting
    Practice
Statement of Principles
    Chapter 1, extracts 26-7
    Chapters 2, 3 and 4, extracts 511-4
    Contents 503-4
    Introduction 11
Statement of Recommended Practice (Charity
    Commission) 422
Statements of Standard Accounting Practice
    and Financial Reporting Standards
    extant (listed) 510

FRS 1	282-96
FRS 2	464
FRS 3	308-11, 485-7, 494
FRS 4	248, 256-7,
FRS 5	465
FRS 6	391, 473
SSAP 1	474
SSAP 2	91-2
SSAP 3	485
SSAP 4	487
SSAP 5	488
SSAP 8	311-12
SSAP 9	84-86, 185, 489-92
SSAP 12	144-5, 492-4
SSAP 13	496-7
SSAP 14	464
SSAP 17	498
SSAP 18	498-9
SSAP 21	500-2
SSAP 22	473

statement of total recognized gains and
    losses 311, 325
stewardship accounting xi, 7
stock book-keeping 73-82
Stock Exchange 5-6
stock in transit 444-7
stock in the trial balance 82-3
stock losses 79-80, 443-4
stocks, pricing methods 86-8
stock turnover ratio 345
straight line depreciation 145
substance over form 500, 511
sum of digits 502
suspense accounts 186-8
    see also, computers

taxation 259, 311-312
timing differences (cash flow) 280
Trafalgar House 515
transfer prices 211-3, 441-2
trend analysis 338, 356
trial balance 60
turnover, definition 30

understandability 12, 512
underwriters commission 254
unrealized losses 84
unrealized profit 212-3, 442-3
Urgent Issues Task Force 518-9
usage depreciation 495
user groups 26-27
users' abilities 512

value added tax 181-4, 488

work-in-progress 202, 206-8
working capital analysis 345

year on year changes 356